P9-CLR-700

THE
AMERICAN
MARKETPLACE

WITHDRAWN

THE
AMERICAN
MARKETPLACE

Demographics and Spending Patterns

11th **EDITION**

BY THE EDITORS OF NEW STRATEGIST PRESS

New Strategist Press, LLC
Amityville, New York

Schaumburg Township District Library
130 South Roselle Road
Schaumburg, IL 60193

New Strategist Press, LLC
P.O. Box 635, Amityville, New York 11701
800/848-0842; 631/608-8795
www.newstrategist.com

Copyright 2014. NEW STRATEGIST PRESS, LLC

All rights reserved.

No part of this book may be reproduced, stored in a retrieval system, or transmitted in any form or by any means, electronic, mechanical, photocopying, microfilming, recording, or otherwise without written permission from the Publisher.

ISBN 978-1-940308-33-3 (hardcover)
ISBN 978-1-940308-34-0 (paper)

Printed in the United States of America

Table of Contents

Chapter 4. Housing

Chapter 5. Income

Chapter 6. Labor Force

Chapter 7. Living Arrangements

Chapter 8. Population

Chapter 9. Spending

Chapter 10. Time Use

Chapter 11. Wealth

List of Tables

Chapter 3. Health

Chapter 4. Housing

Chapter 5. Income

Chapter 6. Labor Force

Chapter 7. Living Arrangements

Chapter 8. Population

Chapter 9. Spending

Chapter 10. Time Use

List of Charts

Chapter 5. Income

Chapter 6. Labor Force

Chapter 7. Living Arrangements

Chapter 8. Population

Chapter 9. Spending

Chapter 10. Time Use

Chapter 11. Wealth

Introduction

For years the United States has been struggling to recover from the Great Recession, the most severe economic downturn since the Great Depression. Household incomes still are well below what they were before the Great Recession. Household spending, however, is growing again. Homeownership rates are down, but household formation is picking up. The wealth of the average household is less than it was, but educational attainment is at a record high. Americans may be struggling, but they are positioning themselves for a better future.

By tracking demographic trends, businesses and policymakers can position themselves to help Americans achieve a better future. In contrast to the volatility of economics, demographic change is slow and steady. By understanding the trends, businesses and policymakers can provide the products and services that will improve the lives of the American people. But if demographic insight is the goal, where do you start? Billions of statistics are only a mouse click away, creating a confusing cacophony of numbers. To find direction, start here, with the 11th edition of *The American Marketplace: Demographics and Spending Patterns*—a demographic reference tool that cuts through the statistical clutter and offers a roadmap into the future.

The American Marketplace reveals the latest demographic trends and tells the American story. It examines changing lifestyles in rich detail, from growing racial and ethnic diversity to declining homeownership, from disappearing nuclear families to recovery in household spending, from another baby bust to new attitudes toward gay marriage. With an understanding of these trends, businesses and government can adapt to a socioeconomic reality that was largely unexpected but is not without opportunity. *The American Marketplace* shows you where we stand today and where we will be tomorrow.

The Outsourcing of Trend Analysis

The first edition of *The American Marketplace* was published in 1992, before the Internet had a name. Today, the Internet is the repository of the government's massive demographic and socioeconomic databases. These are of great value to researchers with the time to search, download, and analyze information. For many, however, the job of understanding demographic trends has become increasingly difficult because the government no longer publishes much in the way of analysis. Essentially, the job of uncovering the trends has been outsourced to bloggers, market researchers, students, and library visitors, many of whom are overwhelmed by computer screens filled with numbers. In short, it has become more time consuming than ever to get no-nonsense answers to questions about demographic and socioeconomic trends.

In *The American Marketplace*, New Strategist has done the work for you. Our editors have spent hundreds of hours scouring government web sites, extracting numbers, creating tables that reveal trends, and producing indexes, percent distributions, and other calculations that provide context. *The American Marketplace* has the numbers and the stories behind them. Thumbing through its pages, you can gain more insight into the dynamics of the U.S. population than you could by spending all afternoon surfing databases on the Internet. By having *The American Marketplace* on your computer (with links to the Excel version of each table) or on your bookshelf, you can get the answers to your questions faster than you can online—no calculator required.

New to this edition of *The American Marketplace* are 2012 population estimates for the nation, states, and metropolitan areas, revealing new patterns of growth. The Attitudes chapter has data from the 2012 General Social Survey, broken down by age, race and Hispanic origin, region, and education. This edition of *The American Marketplace* has the latest data on the changing demographics of homeownership, based on the Census Bureau's 2012 Housing Vacancy Survey and the 2011 American Housing Survey. The Income chapter, with 2012 income statistics from the 2013 Current Population Survey, reveals the struggle to stay afloat. In the Labor Force chapter, 2012 data show significant recovery in labor force participation following the economic downturn. The Time Use chapter reveals how Americans spent their time in 2012, with data from the American Time Use Survey. In the Spending chapter, 2012 Consumer Expenditure Survey data reveal how households are adapting to the new economic reality. In the Wealth chapter, you will see what the Great Recession did to household wealth, with trends from 2005 to 2011.

How to Use This Book

The American Marketplace is designed for easy use. It is divided into 11 chapters, organized alphabetically: Attitudes, Education, Health, Housing, Income, Labor Force, Living Arrangements, Population, Spending, Time Use, and Wealth.

Most of the tables in *The American Marketplace* are based on data collected by the federal government, in particular the Census Bureau, the Bureau of Labor Statistics, the National Center for Education Statistics, and the National Center for Health Statistics. The federal government continues to be the best, if not the only, source of up-to-date, reliable information on the changing characteristics of Americans. Although the government collected most of the data presented here, each table in *The American Marketplace* was handcrafted by New Strategist's demographers, individually compiled and created with calculations that reveal the stories behind the statistics.

Each chapter of *The American Marketplace* includes the demographic and lifestyle data that are important for understanding unfolding events in the United States. A page of text accompanies most of the tables, analyzing the data and highlighting the trends. If you want more statistical detail than the tables provide, you can plumb the original source of the data, listed at the bottom of each table. The book contains a comprehensive table list to help you locate the information you need. For a more detailed search, use the index at the back of the book. Also at the back of the book is the glossary, which defines the terms commonly used in the tables and text.

The American Marketplace is a reference tool that will help you cut through the clutter and track the trends. Use it and prosper.

1

Attitudes

Trends

A growing share of the public thinks life is exciting.

Fifty-three percent of Americans aged 18 or older think life is exciting, up from 47 percent in 2000.

Few Americans believe others can be trusted.

Only 25 percent of 18-to-44-year-olds say most people can be trusted.

The largest share of Americans says their family income is average.

Forty-six percent call their income average, 33 percent say it's below average, and 22 percent believe their income is above average.

The American Dream has taken a hit recently.

Only 55 percent of Americans agree with the statement, "The way things are in America, people like me and my family have a good chance of improving our standard of living." The figure was a much higher 77 percent in 2000.

Belief in God is strong.

The 59 percent majority of Americans believe in God without a doubt.

Nearly half the public supports gay marriage.

Forty-nine percent support the right of gays and lesbians to marry, including 58 percent of adults under age 45.

Most support gun control.

Gun regulation is supported by the majority of men and women, older and younger Americans, blacks, Hispanics, non-Hispanic whites, people in every geographic region, college graduates, and those with less education.

Most People Are Pretty Happy

Among the married, most say their marriage is very happy.

When asked how happy they are, only 33 percent of Americans say they are "very happy," but the 54 percent majority is "pretty happy." A slightly higher share said they were "not too happy" in 2012 than in 2000 (13 versus 10 percent).

The share of Americans who say life is "exciting" (53 percent) substantially tops the percentage who say it is "pretty routine" (43 percent), a reversal from 2000. Younger adults are behind the growing feeling of excitement—52 to 55 percent of adults under age 65 say life is exciting compared with only 45 percent of older Americans.

Only 32 percent of the public agrees that most people can be trusted. The proportion ranges from a low of 25 percent among 18-to-44-year-olds to a high of 39 percent among people aged 65 or older. Blacks and Hispanics are far less trusting than non-Hispanic whites.

■ Blacks and Hispanics are less likely than non-Hispanic whites to report feeling very happy.

Only one in four younger adults trusts others

(percent of people aged 18 or older who think most people can be trusted, by age, 2012)

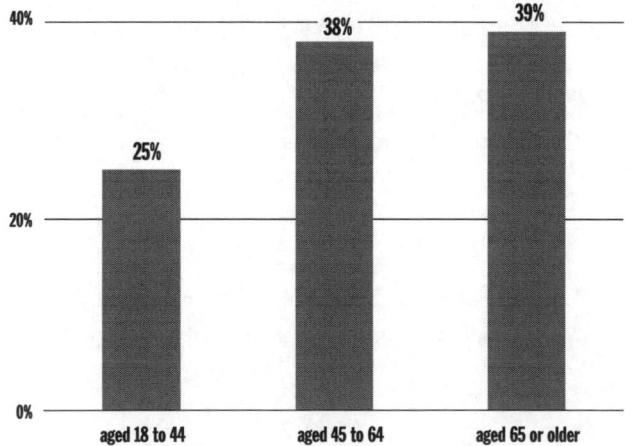

Table 1.1 General Happiness, 2000 and 2012

"Taken all together, how would you say things are these days—would you say
that you are very happy, pretty happy, or not too happy?"

(percent of people aged 18 or older responding, 2000 and 2012; and percent responding by selected characteristics, 2012)

	total	very happy	pretty happy	not too happy
TREND				
2012	100.0%	32.9%	54.2%	12.9%
2000	100.0	33.9	56.4	9.6
2012 PROFILE				
Total people	**100.0**	**32.9**	**54.2**	**12.9**
Men	100.0	31.4	55.7	12.9
Women	100.0	34.2	52.9	12.9
Aged 18 to 44	100.0	32.9	55.6	11.4
Aged 45 to 64	100.0	33.0	52.9	14.1
Aged 65 or older	100.0	33.1	53.1	13.8
Black	100.0	23.3	57.5	19.2
Hispanic	100.0	27.7	57.3	15.0
Non-Hispanic white	100.0	35.8	52.7	11.5
Northeast	100.0	28.8	57.7	13.5
Midwest	100.0	32.9	56.8	10.3
South	100.0	32.3	53.7	14.0
West	100.0	37.0	49.8	13.2
Not a college graduate	100.0	31.5	53.6	14.8
Bachelor's degree or more	100.0	36.5	55.5	7.9

Source: Survey Documentation and Analysis, Computer-assisted Survey Methods Program, University of California, Berkeley, General Social Survey, 1972–2012 Cumulative Data Files, Internet site http://sda.berkeley.edu/cgi-bin/hsda?harcsda+gss12; calculations by New Strategist

Table 1.2 Happiness of Marriage, 2000 and 2012

"Taking all things together, how would you describe your marriage?"

(percent of married people aged 18 or older responding, 2000 and 2012; and percent responding by selected characteristics, 2012)

	total	very happy	pretty happy	not too happy
TREND				
2012	100.0%	65.4%	32.2%	2.3%
2000	100.0	62.4	34.4	3.2
2012 PROFILE				
Total married people	**100.0**	**65.4**	**32.2**	**2.3**
Men	100.0	66.4	32.7	0.9
Women	100.0	64.6	31.8	3.6
Aged 18 to 44	100.0	71.7	26.8	1.5
Aged 45 to 64	100.0	59.8	36.1	4.1
Aged 65 or older	100.0	63.4	36.2	0.4
Black	100.0	49.0	44.6	6.4
Hispanic	100.0	60.7	36.2	3.1
Non-Hispanic white	100.0	67.6	30.6	1.8
Northeast	100.0	70.7	25.2	4.1
Midwest	100.0	66.5	32.8	0.7
South	100.0	60.6	35.9	3.4
West	100.0	69.2	29.8	1.0
Not a college graduate	100.0	65.0	32.7	2.3
Bachelor's degree or more	100.0	66.3	31.2	2.4

Source: Survey Documentation and Analysis, Computer-assisted Survey Methods Program, University of California, Berkeley, General Social Survey, 1972–2012 Cumulative Data Files, Internet site http://sda.berkeley.edu/cgi-bin/hsda?harcsda+gss12; calculations by New Strategist

Table 1.3 Is Life Exciting, 2000 and 2012

"In general, do you find life exciting, pretty routine, or dull?"

(percent of people aged 18 or older responding, 2000 and 2012; and percent responding by selected characteristics, 2012)

	total	exciting	pretty routine	dull
TREND				
2012	100.0%	52.7%	42.6%	4.7%
2000	100.0	46.6	49.1	4.3
2012 PROFILE				
Total people	**100.0**	**52.7**	**42.6**	**4.7**
Men	100.0	55.9	39.4	4.7
Women	100.0	50.0	45.3	4.7
Aged 18 to 44	100.0	55.1	40.1	4.8
Aged 45 to 64	100.0	52.5	42.1	5.4
Aged 65 or older	100.0	45.1	52.0	2.9
Black	100.0	47.6	45.7	6.7
Hispanic	100.0	61.5	35.2	3.3
Non-Hispanic white	100.0	51.3	43.6	5.0
Northeast	100.0	57.0	40.5	2.5
Midwest	100.0	54.2	42.1	3.7
South	100.0	48.4	44.9	6.7
West	100.0	55.2	40.8	4.0
Not a college graduate	100.0	50.1	43.8	6.1
Bachelor's degree or more	100.0	59.4	39.6	1.1

Source: Survey Documentation and Analysis, Computer-assisted Survey Methods Program, University of California, Berkeley, General Social Survey, 1972–2012 Cumulative Data Files, Internet site http://sda.berkeley.edu/cgi-bin/hsda?harcsda+gss12; calculations by New Strategist

Table 1.4 Trust in People, 2000 and 2012

"Generally speaking, would you say that most people can be trusted
or that you can't be too careful in life?"

(percent of people aged 18 or older responding, 2000 and 2012; and percent responding by selected characteristics, 2012)

	total	can trust	cannot trust	depends
TREND				
2012	100.0%	32.2%	64.2%	3.7%
2000	100.0	35.2	58.5	6.3
2012 PROFILE				
Total people	**100.0**	**32.2**	**64.2**	**3.7**
Men	100.0	34.5	62.5	3.0
Women	100.0	30.2	65.6	4.3
Aged 18 to 44	100.0	25.0	71.5	3.5
Aged 45 to 64	100.0	38.5	58.7	2.8
Aged 65 or older	100.0	38.9	55.2	5.8
Black	100.0	17.6	78.8	3.6
Hispanic	100.0	15.8	82.4	1.8
Non-Hispanic white	100.0	39.0	56.8	4.2
Northeast	100.0	33.5	62.7	3.8
Midwest	100.0	36.2	61.2	2.6
South	100.0	28.2	66.9	4.8
West	100.0	33.5	63.7	2.8
Not a college graduate	100.0	23.9	72.5	3.5
Bachelor's degree or more	100.0	52.3	43.7	4.0

Source: Survey Documentation and Analysis, Computer-assisted Survey Methods Program, University of California, Berkeley, General Social Survey, 1972–2012 Cumulative Data Files, Internet site http://sda.berkeley.edu/cgi-bin/hsda?harcsda+gss12; calculations by New Strategist

Middle Class Identity Is Strong among Older Americans

Most young adults identify as working rather than middle class.

How do people get ahead? Nearly 70 percent of Americans say it is by hard work, and another 20 percent cite a combination of hard work and luck. Only 10 percent believe luck alone is the reason people get ahead.

The public is evenly split on whether they are working or middle class, at 44 percent each. Another 8 percent identify themselves as lower class, up from less than 5 percent in 2000. Only among older Americans does the majority identify with the middle class (59 percent). Most young adults, blacks, and Hispanics identify with the working class.

Forty-six percent of Americans believe their family income is average, a percentage that varies little by demographic characteristic. Non-Hispanic whites (26 percent), the middle aged (25 percent), and college graduates (43 percent) are most likely to say their family income is above average. Hispanics are most likely to say their income is below average (44 percent).

The percentage of people who are "satisfied" with their financial situation is about the same as the percentage who say they are "not at all satisfied"—27 and 28 percent, respectively. Satisfaction has declined slightly since 2000, and dissatisfaction has increased. In 2012, older Americans and college graduates were most satisfied (41 and 40 percent, respectively) and Hispanics were least likely to be satisfied (18 percent).

■ Americans with a bachelor's degree are much more likely than those with less education to live in a different state from the one they resided in at age 16 (47 versus 33 percent).

Hispanics are least likely to be satisfied with their financial situation

(percent of people aged 18 or older who are "satisfied" with their present financial situation, by race and Hispanic origin, 2012)

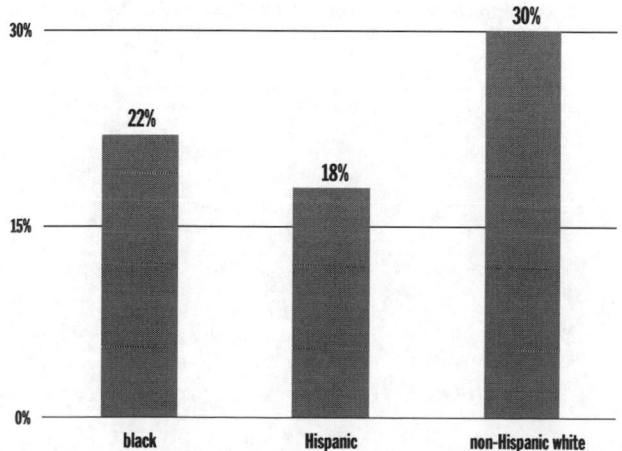

	black	Hispanic	non-Hispanic white
	22%	18%	30%

Table 1.5 How People Get Ahead, 2000 and 2012

"Some people say that people get ahead by their own hard work; others say that lucky breaks or help from other people are more important. Which do you think is most important?"

(percent of people aged 18 or older responding, 2000 and 2012; and percent responding by selected characteristics, 2012)

	total	hard work	both equally	luck or help
TREND				
2012	100.0%	69.9%	20.1%	10.0%
2000	100.0	65.8	23.9	10.2
2012 PROFILE				
Total people	**100.0**	**69.9**	**20.1**	**10.0**
Men	100.0	66.0	20.5	13.5
Women	100.0	73.1	19.8	7.1
Aged 18 to 44	100.0	72.6	17.4	9.9
Aged 45 to 64	100.0	65.9	23.8	10.3
Aged 65 or older	100.0	70.8	19.3	9.9
Black	100.0	70.3	19.5	10.2
Hispanic	100.0	76.4	11.3	12.4
Non-Hispanic white	100.0	68.9	21.7	9.4
Northeast	100.0	61.3	26.0	12.6
Midwest	100.0	75.6	13.9	10.5
South	100.0	70.4	21.0	8.5
West	100.0	70.0	20.0	10.0
Not a college graduate	100.0	72.7	16.7	10.6
Bachelor's degree or more	100.0	62.5	29.0	8.5

Source: Survey Documentation and Analysis, Computer-assisted Survey Methods Program, University of California, Berkeley, General Social Survey, 1972–2012 Cumulative Data Files, Internet site http://sda.berkeley.edu/cgi-bin/hsda?harcsda+gss12; calculations by New Strategist

Table 1.6 Class Identification, 2000 and 2012

"If you were asked to use one of four names for your social class,
which would you say you belong in: the lower class, the
working class, the middle class, or the upper class?"

(percent of people aged 18 or older responding, 2000 and 2012; and percent responding by selected characteristics, 2012)

	total	lower class	working class	middle class	upper class
TREND					
2012	100.0%	8.4%	44.3%	43.7%	3.6%
2000	100.0	4.5	45.6	46.0	3.9
2012 PROFILE					
Total people	**100.0**	**8.4**	**44.3**	**43.7**	**3.6**
Men	100.0	8.3	43.1	44.1	4.5
Women	100.0	8.5	45.3	43.3	2.8
Aged 18 to 44	100.0	8.1	51.5	37.3	3.0
Aged 45 to 64	100.0	8.3	41.7	45.7	4.4
Aged 65 or older	100.0	9.7	28.3	58.6	3.3
Black	100.0	12.4	51.0	33.7	3.0
Hispanic	100.0	7.7	64.3	26.1	1.9
Non-Hispanic white	100.0	7.9	38.2	49.5	4.4
Northeast	100.0	7.7	38.8	48.0	5.4
Midwest	100.0	7.4	47.8	41.4	3.4
South	100.0	8.6	45.5	43.3	2.6
West	100.0	9.7	43.0	43.3	4.0
Not a college graduate	100.0	10.9	52.5	34.6	2.0
Bachelor's degree or more	100.0	2.1	23.1	67.1	7.7

Source: Survey Documentation and Analysis, Computer-assisted Survey Methods Program, University of California, Berkeley, General Social Survey, 1972–2012 Cumulative Data Files, Internet site http://sda.berkeley.edu/cgi-bin/hsda?harcsda+gss12; calculations by New Strategist

Table 1.7 Family Income Relative to Others, 2000 and 2012

"Compared with American families in general, would you say
your family income is far below average, below average,
average, above average, or far above average?"

(percent of people aged 18 or older responding, 2000 and 2012; and percent responding by selected characteristics, 2012)

	total	far below average	below average	average	above average	far above average
TREND						
2012	100.0%	6.8%	25.9%	45.5%	19.0%	2.7%
2000	100.0	5.3	20.9	49.3	21.4	3.1
2012 PROFILE						
Total people	**100.0**	**6.8**	**25.9**	**45.5**	**19.0**	**2.7**
Men	100.0	6.2	25.7	43.7	21.5	2.9
Women	100.0	7.4	26.1	47.1	16.8	2.6
Aged 18 to 44	100.0	6.7	26.2	46.9	17.8	2.4
Aged 45 to 64	100.0	8.2	24.1	42.6	21.6	3.5
Aged 65 or older	100.0	4.3	29.0	48.1	16.4	2.2
Black	100.0	9.0	29.9	45.5	12.5	3.1
Hispanic	100.0	8.6	35.6	43.3	10.9	1.7
Non-Hispanic white	100.0	6.1	23.6	44.4	23.0	3.0
Northeast	100.0	5.5	21.4	48.8	22.2	2.1
Midwest	100.0	4.6	27.4	48.0	16.8	3.3
South	100.0	7.9	26.7	43.1	19.2	3.0
West	100.0	8.2	26.6	44.6	18.3	2.3
Not a college graduate	100.0	8.1	31.6	46.9	11.8	1.6
Bachelor's degree or more	100.0	3.4	11.4	42.0	37.4	5.8

Source: Survey Documentation and Analysis, Computer-assisted Survey Methods Program, University of California, Berkeley, General Social Survey, 1972–2012 Cumulative Data Files, Internet site http://sda.berkeley.edu/cgi-bin/hsda?harcsda+gss12; calculations by New Strategist

Table 1.8 Satisfaction with Financial Situation, 2000 and 2012

"We are interested in how people are getting along financially these days.
So far as you and your family are concerned, would you say that you
are pretty well satisfied with your present financial situation,
more or less satisfied, or not satisfied at all?"

(percent of people aged 18 or older responding, 2000 and 2012; and percent responding by selected characteristics, 2012)

	total	satisfied	more or less satisfied	not at all satisfied
TREND				
2012	100.0%	27.0%	45.0%	28.0%
2000	100.0	30.6	45.4	24.0
2012 PROFILE				
Total people	**100.0**	**27.0**	**45.0**	**28.0**
Men	100.0	27.8	45.8	26.4
Women	100.0	26.2	44.3	29.5
Aged 18 to 44	100.0	22.5	48.4	29.1
Aged 45 to 64	100.0	26.8	42.7	30.5
Aged 65 or older	100.0	40.6	39.7	19.7
Black	100.0	22.0	39.0	39.0
Hispanic	100.0	18.3	52.2	29.5
Non-Hispanic white	100.0	30.3	43.5	26.2
Northeast	100.0	30.3	41.3	28.4
Midwest	100.0	29.5	42.9	27.5
South	100.0	26.5	45.4	28.1
West	100.0	22.7	49.3	28.0
Not a college graduate	100.0	21.8	46.3	32.0
Bachelor's degree or more	100.0	40.4	41.9	17.8

Source: Survey Documentation and Analysis, Computer-assisted Survey Methods Program, University of California, Berkeley, General Social Survey, 1972–2012 Cumulative Data Files, Internet site http://sda.berkeley.edu/cgi-bin/hsda?harcsda+gss12; calculations by New Strategist

Table 1.9 Geographic Mobility since Age 16, 2000 and 2012

"When you were 16 years old, were you living
in this same (city/town/county)?"

(percent of people aged 18 or older responding, 2000 and 2012; and percent responding by selected characteristics, 2012)

	total	same city, town, or county	same state, different city, town, or county	different state
TREND				
2012	100.0%	39.5%	23.8%	36.6%
2000	100.0	39.9	26.0	34.1
2012 PROFILE				
Total people	**100.0**	**39.5**	**23.8**	**36.6**
Men	100.0	40.9	22.1	37.0
Women	100.0	38.3	25.3	36.4
Aged 18 to 44	100.0	43.7	24.5	31.8
Aged 45 to 64	100.0	36.4	23.5	40.2
Aged 65 or older	100.0	34.1	22.2	43.8
Black	100.0	51.4	18.2	30.4
Hispanic	100.0	34.0	17.0	48.9
Non-Hispanic white	100.0	38.5	28.2	33.4
Northeast	100.0	43.3	24.7	32.0
Midwest	100.0	44.8	29.1	26.1
South	100.0	39.8	21.0	39.1
West	100.0	31.1	22.6	46.3
Not a college graduate	100.0	45.0	22.4	32.5
Bachelor's degree or more	100.0	25.4	27.4	47.2

Source: Survey Documentation and Analysis, Computer-assisted Survey Methods Program, University of California, Berkeley, General Social Survey, 1972–2012 Cumulative Data Files, Internet site http://sda.berkeley.edu/cgi-bin/hsda?harcsda+gss12; calculations by New Strategist

Many Think Their Standard of Living Is Falling

But most still believe they are better off than their parents.

When comparing their own standard of living now with that of their parents when they were the same age, 62 percent of respondents say they are better off—a figure that has fallen slightly from the 67 percent of 2000. The oldest Americans are most likely to think they are better off than their parents were at the same age. Hispanics and blacks are more likely than non-Hispanic whites to feel better off.

When asked whether they think they have a good chance of improving their present standard of living, only 55 percent of Americans agree. In 2000, fully 77 percent felt their standard of living could improve. Young adults are most likely to believe things will get better (63 percent) and older Americans are least likely (43 percent). By race and Hispanic origin, non-Hispanic whites are least likely to feel that they will be able to get ahead. Just 46 percent of non-Hispanic whites think they have a good chance of improving their standard of living.

Only 51 percent of the public believes children will have a better standard of living when they reach their age. The share was a larger 61 percent in 2000. Hispanics and blacks are far more optimistic than non-Hispanic whites. By region, the percentage who think children will be better off ranges from a low of 43 percent in the Northeast to a high of 54 percent in the West.

■ Americans who have the least are most likely to believe that things will be better in the future.

Blacks and Hispanics think their children will be better off

(percent of people aged 18 or older who think their children's standard of living will be "somewhat better" or "much better" than theirs is today, by race and Hispanic origin, 2012)

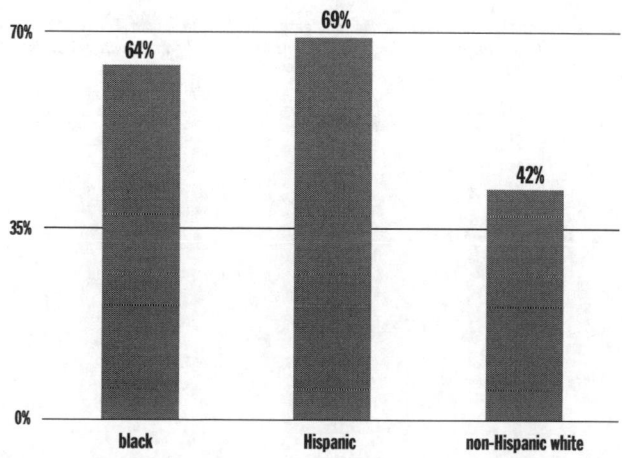

Table 1.10 Parents' Standard of Living, 2000 and 2012

"Compared to your parents when they were the age you are now, do you think
your own standard of living now is much better, somewhat better, about
the same, somewhat worse, or much worse than theirs was?"

(percent of people aged 18 or older responding, 2000 and 2012; and percent responding by selected characteristics, 2012)

	total	much better	somewhat better	about the same	somewhat worse	much worse
TREND						
2012	100.0%	33.5%	28.6%	21.2%	12.0%	4.6%
2000	100.0	35.7	31.3	21.0	8.9	3.2
2012 PROFILE						
Total people	**100.0**	**33.5**	**28.6**	**21.2**	**12.0**	**4.6**
Men	100.0	34.9	30.5	20.8	10.3	3.7
Women	100.0	32.3	27.0	21.6	13.6	5.5
Aged 18 to 44	100.0	32.7	29.6	21.3	11.3	5.2
Aged 45 to 64	100.0	32.0	27.0	21.6	13.8	5.5
Aged 65 or older	100.0	38.8	29.1	20.4	10.3	1.5
Black	100.0	35.7	33.2	19.0	8.9	3.3
Hispanic	100.0	45.1	27.0	14.3	10.9	2.8
Non-Hispanic white	100.0	28.9	27.8	24.5	13.7	5.1
Northeast	100.0	36.0	25.1	22.5	11.6	4.8
Midwest	100.0	26.5	34.0	22.1	13.3	4.1
South	100.0	35.2	29.1	20.0	11.4	4.4
West	100.0	35.5	25.3	21.4	12.3	5.5
Not a college graduate	100.0	33.3	29.6	18.9	12.7	5.4
Bachelor's degree or more	100.0	33.9	26.1	26.8	10.4	2.7

Source: Survey Documentation and Analysis, Computer-assisted Survey Methods Program, University of California, Berkeley, General Social Survey, 1972–2012 Cumulative Data Files, Internet site http://sda.berkeley.edu/cgi-bin/hsda?harcsda+gss12; calculations by New Strategist

Table 1.11 Standard of Living Will Improve, 2000 and 2012

"The way things are in America, people like me and my family have a good chance of improving our standard of living. Do you agree or disagree?"

(percent of people aged 18 or older responding, 2000 and 2012; and percent responding by selected characteristics, 2012)

	total	strongly agree	agree	neither	disagree	strongly disagree
TREND						
2012	100.0%	14.1%	40.7%	17.9%	23.4%	4.0%
2000	100.0	23.7	53.7	9.4	11.1	2.2
2012 PROFILE						
Total people	**100.0**	**14.1**	**40.7**	**17.9**	**23.4**	**4.0**
Men	100.0	15.2	43.1	17.5	21.6	2.5
Women	100.0	13.1	38.6	18.2	24.9	5.2
Aged 18 to 44	100.0	19.9	42.7	18.2	16.4	2.9
Aged 45 to 64	100.0	9.0	41.5	18.0	26.1	5.4
Aged 65 or older	100.0	8.5	34.2	17.0	36.3	4.0
Black	100.0	19.1	52.1	9.7	17.1	2.0
Hispanic	100.0	25.6	47.5	17.7	5.7	3.4
Non-Hispanic white	100.0	9.2	36.5	19.9	29.6	4.8
Northeast	100.0	13.6	38.9	21.5	22.6	3.4
Midwest	100.0	10.1	37.6	20.0	29.5	2.8
South	100.0	14.2	42.8	14.9	23.8	4.2
West	100.0	18.1	41.7	17.9	17.3	5.0
Not a college graduate	100.0	15.7	40.3	17.8	22.5	3.8
Bachelor's degree or more	100.0	10.1	41.8	18.2	25.5	4.4

Source: Survey Documentation and Analysis, Computer-assisted Survey Methods Program, University of California, Berkeley, General Social Survey, 1972–2012 Cumulative Data Files, Internet site http://sda.berkeley.edu/cgi-bin/hsda?harcsda+gss12; calculations by New Strategist

Table 1.12 Children's Standard of Living, 2000 and 2012

"When your children are at the age you are now, do you think their standard
of living will be much better, somewhat better, about the same,
somewhat worse, or much worse than yours is now?"

(percent of people aged 18 or older responding, 2000 and 2012; and percent responding by selected characteristics, 2012)

	total	much better	somewhat better	about the same	somewhat worse	much worse	no children
TREND							
2012	100.0%	27.9%	22.7%	18.2%	14.5%	5.5%	11.2%
2000	100.0	29.1	31.5	17.0	7.6	3.2	11.5
2012 PROFILE							
Total people	**100.0**	**27.9**	**22.7**	**18.2**	**14.5**	**5.5**	**11.2**
Men	100.0	26.4	19.2	17.6	17.0	6.0	13.8
Women	100.0	29.1	25.7	18.7	12.4	5.1	9.0
Aged 18 to 44	100.0	20.3	20.1	19.6	22.9	9.0	8.1
Aged 45 to 64	100.0	21.6	21.8	19.8	18.5	5.9	12.3
Aged 65 or older	100.0	20.3	20.1	19.6	22.9	9.0	8.1
Black	100.0	44.3	20.1	7.8	9.4	6.0	12.4
Hispanic	100.0	45.0	24.1	14.1	9.0	2.9	5.0
Non-Hispanic white	100.0	19.0	22.8	22.6	17.6	6.0	12.0
Northeast	100.0	23.0	20.1	23.3	11.9	6.4	15.3
Midwest	100.0	21.8	27.9	17.8	18.5	4.2	9.8
South	100.0	33.8	18.7	15.4	15.1	6.6	10.4
West	100.0	28.2	26.2	19.2	11.5	4.2	10.7
Not a college graduate	100.0	32.3	23.4	15.5	13.8	6.4	8.7
Bachelor's degree or more	100.0	17.2	21.2	24.9	16.3	3.1	17.4

Source: Survey Documentation and Analysis, Computer-assisted Survey Methods Program, University of California, Berkeley, General Social Survey, 1972–2012 Cumulative Data Files, Internet site http://sda.berkeley.edu/cgi-bin/hsda?harcsda+gss12; calculations by New Strategist

The Two-Child Family Is Most Popular

But larger families have grown in popularity.

In nearly every demographic segment, the plurality of Americans thinks two is the ideal number of children. The two-child ideal has weakened, however, falling from the preference of 52 percent of the public in 2000 to 47 percent in 2012. The 51 percent majority of non-Hispanic whites consider two children to be ideal, as do 54 percent of college graduates. Among Hispanics, however, 43 percent consider three children to be best and a smaller 36 percent consider two ideal.

The great majority of the public believes it is sometimes necessary to discipline a child with a "good, hard spanking." In every demographic segment, more than 60 percent feel this way.

Only 32 percent of Americans believe it is better for the husband to be the breadwinner and the wife to care for the home (traditional sex roles). Only 27 percent of adults under age 45 prefer traditional sex roles compared with 45 percent of those aged 65 or older. Regardless of sex, age, race, region of residence, or education, most people agree that a working mother can have as warm a relationship with her children as a mother who does not work.

■ Only 3 percent of Americans consider the one-child family ideal.

Even among the oldest Americans, a minority believes traditional sex roles are best

(percent of people aged 18 or older who think traditional sex roles are best, by age, 2012)

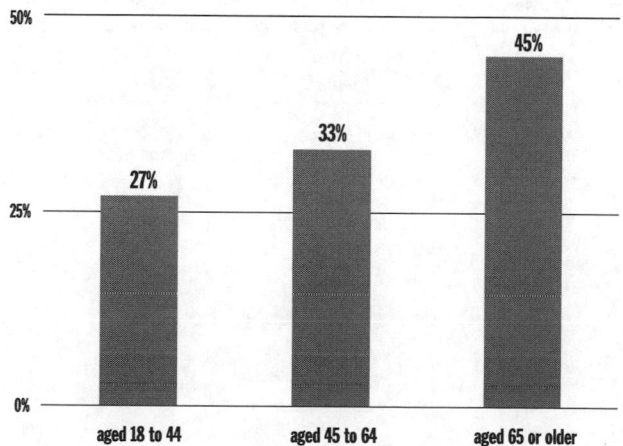

Table 1.13 Ideal Number of Children, 2000 and 2012

"What do you think is the ideal number of children for a family to have?"

(percent of people aged 18 or older responding, 2000 and 2012; and percent responding by selected characteristics, 2012)

	total	none	one	two	three	four or more	as many as want
TREND							
2012	100.0%	0.8%	2.6%	46.8%	27.8%	11.3%	10.7%
2000	100.0	1.2	3.5	52.3	25.8	10.0	7.2
2012 PROFILE							
Total people	**100.0**	**0.8**	**2.6**	**46.8**	**27.8**	**11.3**	**10.7**
Men	100.0	1.0	3.4	45.5	29.3	12.5	8.3
Women	100.0	0.6	1.9	47.9	26.5	10.3	12.8
Aged 18 to 44	100.0	0.6	3.3	45.1	32.6	9.8	8.6
Aged 45 to 64	100.0	1.3	2.2	49.8	23.7	9.1	13.9
Aged 65 or older	100.0	0.4	1.3	45.6	20.5	20.7	11.4
Black	100.0	1.1	0.7	35.7	34.3	20.9	7.3
Hispanic	100.0	0.0	5.0	35.7	43.2	11.5	4.6
Non-Hispanic white	100.0	0.9	2.6	50.6	24.6	8.7	12.6
Northeast	100.0	1.2	4.6	48.5	23.2	9.2	13.3
Midwest	100.0	1.1	1.8	45.3	30.2	11.2	10.4
South	100.0	0.4	1.8	45.1	28.3	13.5	10.9
West	100.0	0.6	3.4	49.6	27.9	9.6	8.9
Not a college graduate	100.0	0.6	2.3	44.3	30.0	13.9	8.9
Bachelor's degree or more	100.0	1.1	3.5	53.6	21.9	4.1	15.8

Source: Survey Documentation and Analysis, Computer-assisted Survey Methods Program, University of California, Berkeley, General Social Survey, 1972–2012 Cumulative Data Files, Internet site http://sda.berkeley.edu/cgi-bin/hsda?harcsda+gss12; calculations by New Strategist

Table 1.14 Favor Spanking to Discipline Child, 2000 and 2012

"Do you strongly agree, agree, disagree, or strongly disagree that it is sometimes necessary to discipline a child with a good, hard spanking?"

(percent of people aged 18 or older responding, 2000 and 2012; and percent responding by selected characteristics, 2012)

	total	strongly agree	agree	disagree	strongly disagree
TREND					
2012	100.0%	23.4%	47.4%	21.0%	8.1%
2000	100.0	31.9	42.5	18.1	7.6
2012 PROFILE					
Total people	**100.0**	**23.4**	**47.4**	**21.0**	**8.1**
Men	100.0	26.6	50.6	17.3	5.4
Women	100.0	20.7	44.6	24.3	10.5
Aged 18 to 44	100.0	23.3	49.0	19.8	8.0
Aged 45 to 64	100.0	23.9	46.2	21.0	8.9
Aged 65 or older	100.0	23.3	45.3	24.3	7.1
Black	100.0	34.7	46.1	13.7	5.5
Hispanic	100.0	21.4	51.6	18.2	8.8
Non-Hispanic white	100.0	21.5	48.9	22.1	7.5
Northeast	100.0	16.9	46.0	25.3	11.7
Midwest	100.0	24.7	47.6	22.4	5.2
South	100.0	30.3	47.5	15.3	7.0
West	100.0	15.8	48.1	25.8	10.4
Not a college graduate	100.0	24.6	47.8	19.6	8.0
Bachelor's degree or more	100.0	20.2	46.3	25.1	8.4

Source: Survey Documentation and Analysis, Computer-assisted Survey Methods Program, University of California, Berkeley, General Social Survey, 1972–2012 Cumulative Data Files, Internet site http://sda.berkeley.edu/cgi-bin/hsda?harcsda+gss12; calculations by New Strategist

Table 1.15 Better for Man to Work and Woman to Stay Home, 2000 and 2012

"It is much better for everyone involved if the man is the achiever
outside the home and the woman takes care of the home
and family. Do you agree or disagree?"

(percent of people aged 18 or older responding, 2000 and 2012; and percent responding by selected characteristics, 2012)

	total	strongly agree	agree	disagree	strongly disagree
TREND					
2012	100.0%	6.5%	25.2%	48.3%	20.0%
2000	100.0	11.1	28.9	40.7	19.3
2012 PROFILE					
Total people	**100.0**	**6.5**	**25.2**	**48.3**	**20.0**
Men	100.0	9.0	28.7	48.3	13.9
Women	100.0	4.2	22.1	48.2	25.4
Aged 18 to 44	100.0	6.9	20.0	50.9	22.2
Aged 45 to 64	100.0	5.8	27.6	46.8	19.8
Aged 65 or older	100.0	6.6	38.1	41.7	13.6
Black	100.0	5.2	24.7	46.9	23.2
Hispanic	100.0	7.3	31.4	47.7	13.5
Non-Hispanic white	100.0	5.8	23.8	48.5	21.8
Northeast	100.0	7.0	15.5	51.7	25.9
Midwest	100.0	6.8	20.9	47.5	24.8
South	100.0	6.7	30.8	46.1	16.4
West	100.0	5.5	27.3	50.0	17.2
Not a college graduate	100.0	7.1	29.3	47.2	16.5
Bachelor's degree or more	100.0	4.9	14.2	51.3	29.6

Source: Survey Documentation and Analysis, Computer-assisted Survey Methods Program, University of California, Berkeley, General Social Survey, 1972–2012 Cumulative Data Files, Internet site http://sda.berkeley.edu/cgi-bin/hsda?harcsda+gss12; calculations by New Strategist

Table 1.16 A Working Mother's Relationship with Children, 2000 and 2012

"A working mother can establish just as warm and secure a relationship with her children as a mother who does not work. Do you agree or disagree?"

(percent of people aged 18 or older responding, 2000 and 2012; and percent responding by selected characteristics, 2012)

	total	strongly agree	agree	disagree	strongly disagree
TREND					
2012	100.0%	25.0%	46.7%	23.1%	5.2%
2000	100.0	20.3	41.4	29.4	8.9
2012 PROFILE					
Total people	**100.0**	**25.0**	**46.7**	**23.1**	**5.2**
Men	100.0	17.7	47.0	29.0	6.3
Women	100.0	31.5	46.4	17.9	4.2
Aged 18 to 44	100.0	20.3	49.1	25.2	5.4
Aged 45 to 64	100.0	24.5	45.6	24.8	5.0
Aged 65 or older	100.0	20.3	49.1	25.2	5.4
Black	100.0	30.8	42.0	23.1	4.1
Hispanic	100.0	14.0	42.5	34.8	8.8
Non-Hispanic white	100.0	27.0	49.2	19.8	4.0
Northeast	100.0	29.4	49.9	19.7	1.0
Midwest	100.0	30.0	45.4	18.7	5.9
South	100.0	22.2	44.9	27.7	5.2
West	100.0	21.7	48.5	22.5	7.2
Not a college graduate	100.0	22.9	47.3	24.4	5.4
Bachelor's degree or more	100.0	30.8	45.3	19.4	4.5

Source: Survey Documentation and Analysis, Computer-assisted Survey Methods Program, University of California, Berkeley, General Social Survey, 1972–2012 Cumulative Data Files, Internet site http://sda.berkeley.edu/cgi-bin/hsda?harcsda+gss12; calculations by New Strategist

Religion Is Important to Americans

Most consider themselves at least moderately religious.

Asked whether "science makes our way of life change too fast," the 56 percent majority of Americans disagree. Not surprisingly, the college-educated are most likely to disagree (66 percent). (Note: This question was not asked in 2000.)

Most Americans believe in evolution. But there are still skeptics out there. The majority of women, older Americans, blacks, and people who live in the South do not believe in evolution. (Note: This question was not asked in 2000.)

Americans are a religious people, with 58 percent identifying themselves as at least moderately religious. Interestingly, however, the share who says they are "not religious" slightly surpasses the share who says they are "very religious," especially among adults under age 45. Religiosity is especially high among women, the elderly, blacks, and people who live in the South. (Note: This question was not asked in 2000.) The same groups are also most likely to see the Bible as the "word of God."

■ Only 44 percent of Americans describe themselves as Protestant, down from the 53 percent majority in 2000.

One in five Americans has no religious preference

(percent distribution of people aged 18 or older by religious preference, 2012)

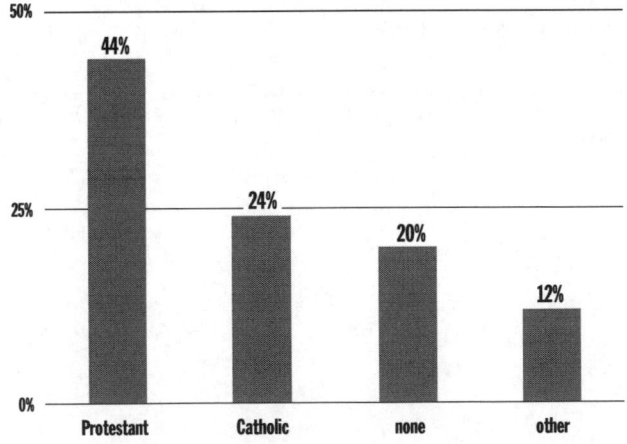

Table 1.17 Science Makes Our Way of Life Change Too Fast, 2012

"Science makes our way of life change too fast."

(percent of people aged 18 or older responding by selected characteristics, 2012)

	total	strongly agree	agree	disagree	strongly disagree
Total people	**100.0%**	**9.8%**	**33.7%**	**52.5%**	**4.0%**
Men	100.0	9.8	34.7	51.0	4.5
Women	100.0	9.7	32.9	53.8	3.6
Aged 18 to 44	100.0	8.1	32.6	54.2	5.1
Aged 45 to 64	100.0	11.7	34.4	50.4	3.4
Aged 65 or older	100.0	9.2	35.5	52.6	2.6
Black	100.0	15.8	28.6	50.1	5.5
Hispanic	100.0	17.8	48.7	30.5	3.0
Non-Hispanic white	100.0	6.3	30.2	59.3	4.3
Northeast	100.0	11.5	39.4	44.2	4.9
Midwest	100.0	10.5	25.1	59.6	4.9
South	100.0	8.2	36.4	52.4	3.0
West	100.0	10.2	33.5	52.3	4.0
Not a college graduate	100.0	10.6	36.8	49.0	3.7
Bachelor's degree or more	100.0	7.7	26.2	61.3	4.7

Source: Survey Documentation and Analysis, Computer-assisted Survey Methods Program, University of California, Berkeley, General Social Survey, 1972–2012 Cumulative Data Files, Internet site http://sda.berkeley.edu/cgi-bin/hsda?harcsda+gss12; calculations by New Strategist

Table 1.18 Scientific Knowledge: Human Beings Developed from Animals, 2012

"Human beings, as we know them today, developed from earlier species of animals. Is that true or false?"

(percent of people aged 18 or older responding by selected characteristics, 2012)

	total	true	false
Total people	**100.0%**	**55.8%**	**44.2%**
Men	100.0	63.6	36.4
Women	100.0	48.7	51.3
Aged 18 to 44	100.0	61.2	38.8
Aged 45 to 64	100.0	55.7	44.3
Aged 65 or older	100.0	41.4	58.6
Black	100.0	46.9	53.1
Hispanic	100.0	53.3	46.7
Non-Hispanic white	100.0	57.4	42.6
Northeast	100.0	72.6	27.4
Midwest	100.0	57.2	42.8
South	100.0	47.4	52.6
West	100.0	51.1	48.9
Not a college graduate	100.0	53.0	47.0
Bachelor's degree or more	100.0	63.1	36.9

Source: Survey Documentation and Analysis, Computer-assisted Survey Methods Program, University of California, Berkeley, General Social Survey, 1972–2012 Cumulative Data Files, Internet site http://sda.berkeley.edu/cgi-bin/hsda?harcsda+gss12; calculations by New Strategist

Table 1.19 Religious Preference, 2000 and 2012

"What is your religious preference?"

(percent of people aged 18 or older responding, 2000 and 2012; and percent responding by selected characteristics, 2012)

	total	Protestant	Catholic	none	Jewish	Moslem/ Islam	Hinduism	Buddhism	other
TREND									
2012	100.0%	44.3%	24.2%	19.7%	1.5%	1.1%	0.5%	0.4%	8.3%
2000	100.0	52.7	25.4	14.1	2.2	0.6	0.4	0.6	3.9
2012 PROFILE									
Total people	**100.0**	**44.3**	**24.2**	**19.7**	**1.5**	**1.1**	**0.5**	**0.4**	**8.3**
Men	100.0	39.4	24.9	23.6	1.3	2.0	0.5	0.6	7.7
Women	100.0	48.5	23.7	16.4	1.6	0.2	0.6	0.2	8.8
Aged 18 to 44	100.0	35.0	24.9	25.8	1.3	1.0	0.9	0.7	10.4
Aged 45 to 64	100.0	49.5	24.0	15.9	1.2	1.6	0.3	0.1	7.4
Aged 65 or older	100.0	61.9	22.1	9.9	2.4	0.3	0.0	0.0	3.4
Black	100.0	65.9	6.8	17.1	0.6	2.0	0.0	0.1	7.5
Hispanic	100.0	21.0	56.9	15.7	0.0	0.0	0.0	0.0	6.4
Non-Hispanic white	100.0	47.3	20.9	21.2	2.0	0.5	0.0	0.2	7.9
Northeast	100.0	29.5	33.3	23.9	3.6	2.9	0.9	0.4	5.5
Midwest	100.0	48.2	23.8	18.7	0.3	0.5	0.2	0.3	8.0
South	100.0	58.1	16.8	14.6	1.2	1.0	0.6	0.1	7.6
West	100.0	29.3	29.9	25.8	1.5	0.4	0.4	1.0	11.7
Not a college graduate	100.0	44.4	25.8	18.3	0.8	0.9	0.2	0.3	9.3
Bachelor's degree or more	100.0	44.1	20.1	23.4	3.1	1.5	1.4	0.4	6.0

Source: Survey Documentation and Analysis, Computer-assisted Survey Methods Program, University of California, Berkeley, General Social Survey, 1972–2012 Cumulative Data Files, Internet site http://sda.berkeley.edu/cgi-bin/hsda?harcsda+gss12; calculations by New Strategist

Table 1.20 Degree of Religiosity, 2012

"To what extent do you consider yourself a religious person?"

(percent of people aged 18 or older responding by selected characteristics, 2012)

	total	very religious	moderately religious	slightly religious	not religious
Total people	**100.0%**	**18.8%**	**39.5%**	**21.6%**	**20.1%**
Men	100.0	16.1	37.1	24.1	22.7
Women	100.0	21.2	41.5	19.5	17.8
Aged 18 to 44	100.0	13.7	35.8	24.5	26.0
Aged 45 to 64	100.0	24.3	40.7	18.3	16.7
Aged 65 or older	100.0	22.2	47.7	20.3	9.8
Black	100.0	30.1	47.4	13.7	8.8
Hispanic	100.0	12.6	42.4	30.8	14.2
Non-Hispanic white	100.0	17.0	38.1	21.2	23.8
Northeast	100.0	14.1	34.9	22.5	28.5
Midwest	100.0	13.8	44.7	25.0	16.6
South	100.0	27.1	41.9	17.0	14.0
West	100.0	14.1	33.8	25.1	27.0
Not a college graduate	100.0	18.5	39.8	23.6	18.1
Bachelor's degree or more	100.0	19.6	38.6	16.6	25.2

Source: Survey Documentation and Analysis, Computer-assisted Survey Methods Program, University of California, Berkeley, General Social Survey, 1972–2012 Cumulative Data Files, Internet site http://sda.berkeley.edu/cgi-bin/hsda?harcsda+gss12; calculations by New Strategist

Table 1.21 Belief in God, 2000 and 2012

"Which statement comes closest to expressing what you believe about God?
1) I don't believe in God; 2) I don't know whether there is a God and I don't
believe there is any way to find out; 3) I don't believe in a personal God, but I do
believe in a Higher Power of some kind; 4) I find myself believing in God some
of the time, but not at others; 5) While I have doubts, I feel that I do believe in
God; 6) I know God really exists and I have no doubts about it."

(percent of people aged 18 or older responding, 2000 and 2012; and percent responding by selected characteristics, 2012)

	total	1 don't believe	2 no way to find out	3 higher power	4 believe sometimes	5 believe but have doubts	6 know God exists
TREND							
2012	100.0%	3.1%	5.6%	11.6%	4.2%	16.5%	59.1%
2000	100.0	2.9	4.3	7.5	3.9	16.6	64.8
2012 PROFILE							
Total people	**100.0**	**3.1**	**5.6**	**11.6**	**4.2**	**16.5**	**59.1**
Men	100.0	4.8	7.3	11.9	4.4	18.0	53.6
Women	100.0	1.6	4.2	11.4	4.0	15.2	63.7
Aged 18 to 44	100.0	3.6	6.8	14.8	4.8	17.3	52.7
Aged 45 to 64	100.0	2.9	4.8	9.2	3.5	16.1	63.6
Aged 65 or older	100.0	2.0	3.8	7.0	3.8	14.9	68.5
Black	100.0	0.7	2.2	3.2	1.2	10.8	81.8
Hispanic	100.0	2.2	5.3	7.8	2.1	15.6	67.0
Non-Hispanic white	100.0	3.8	6.4	14.0	5.1	18.3	52.4
Northeast	100.0	5.5	7.0	15.4	4.4	19.8	47.9
Midwest	100.0	3.1	4.5	12.6	4.7	20.7	54.4
South	100.0	1.6	4.2	7.8	2.4	11.8	72.2
West	100.0	3.6	7.9	14.1	6.4	17.5	50.5
Not a college graduate	100.0	2.7	4.4	10.8	4.2	16.0	62.0
Bachelor's degree or more	100.0	4.1	8.7	13.8	4.1	17.7	51.6

Source: Survey Documentation and Analysis, Computer-assisted Survey Methods Program, University of California, Berkeley, General Social Survey, 1972–2012 Cumulative Data Files, Internet site http://sda.berkeley.edu/cgi-bin/hsda?harcsda+gss12; calculations by New Strategist

Table 1.22 Belief in the Bible, 2000 and 2012

"Which of these statements comes closest to describing your feelings about the Bible? a) The Bible is the actual word of God and is to be taken literally, word for word; b) The Bible is the inspired word of God but not everything in it should be taken literally, word for word; c) The Bible is an ancient book of fables, legends, history, and moral precepts recorded by men."

(percent of people aged 18 or older responding, 2000 and 2012; and percent responding by selected characteristics, 2012)

	total	word of God	inspired word	book of fables	other
TREND					
2012	100.0%	32.1%	44.6%	21.8%	1.5%
2000	100.0	33.8	49.4	15.9	0.9
2012 PROFILE					
Total people	**100.0**	**32.1**	**44.6**	**21.8**	**1.5**
Men	100.0	28.3	44.1	25.5	2.0
Women	100.0	35.3	45.1	18.6	1.0
Aged 18 to 44	100.0	28.3	44.9	25.8	1.0
Aged 45 to 64	100.0	34.0	45.9	18.4	1.8
Aged 65 or older	100.0	40.0	40.3	17.3	2.4
Black	100.0	55.8	35.1	8.6	0.5
Hispanic	100.0	34.5	45.5	18.6	1.4
Non-Hispanic white	100.0	26.4	47.3	24.7	1.5
Northeast	100.0	23.8	43.2	31.0	2.0
Midwest	100.0	27.9	48.2	23.0	0.9
South	100.0	42.3	42.9	13.0	1.8
West	100.0	25.8	45.0	27.9	1.3
Not a college graduate	100.0	37.0	42.5	19.3	1.2
Bachelor's degree or more	100.0	19.6	50.2	28.0	2.2

Source: Survey Documentation and Analysis, Computer-assisted Survey Methods Program, University of California, Berkeley, General Social Survey, 1972–2012 Cumulative Data Files, Internet site http://sda.berkeley.edu/cgi-bin/hsda?harcsda+gss12; calculations by New Strategist

Growing Acceptance of Same-Sex Relationships

Most Americans say premarital sex is OK.

The share of Americans who believe premarital sex is "not wrong at all" grew from 42 percent in 2000 to 58 percent in 2012. Among Americans aged 65 or older, however, only 36 percent think premarital sex is "not wrong at all."

When it comes to sexual relations between adults of the same sex, the trend of growing tolerance is there as well, but in 2012 acceptance was still below the 50-percent mark. Overall 44 percent say homosexuality is "not wrong at all," up from 29 percent in 2000. Women are more accepting of same-sex relations than men (51 percent of women versus 35 percent of men say it is not wrong at all), and young adults are more accepting than the elderly (51 versus 26 percent).

On the issue of whether gays and lesbians should have the right to marry, 49 percent of the public agrees. Support is greatest among women (54 percent), young adults (58 percent), people in the Northeast (58 percent), and college graduates (60 percent). (Note: This question was not asked in 2000.)

■ As younger, more tolerant adults replace older, less tolerant generations, American attitudes toward sexuality will continue to change.

Nearly half the public thinks same-sex couples should have the right to marry

*(percent distribution of people aged 18 or older by response to the statement,
"Homosexual couples should have the right to marry one another," 2012)*

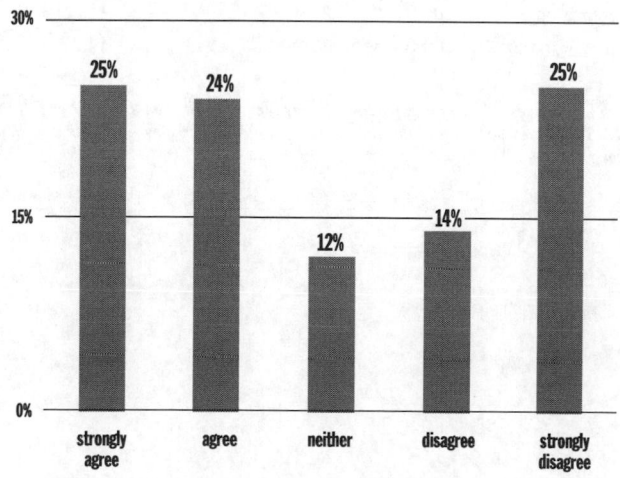

Table 1.23 Premarital Sex, 2000 and 2012

"There's been a lot of discussion about the way morals and attitudes about sex are changing in this country. If a man and woman have sex relations before marriage, do you think it is always wrong, almost always wrong, wrong only sometimes, or not wrong at all?"

(percent of people aged 18 or older responding, 2000 and 2012; and percent responding by selected characteristics, 2012)

	total	always wrong	almost always wrong	sometimes wrong	not wrong at all
TREND					
2012	100.0%	21.9%	5.1%	15.5%	57.5%
2000	100.0	27.7	8.6	21.4	42.2
2012 PROFILE					
Total people	**100.0**	**21.9**	**5.1**	**15.5**	**57.5**
Men	100.0	20.1	4.1	15.7	60.1
Women	100.0	23.5	6.0	15.3	55.2
Aged 18 to 44	100.0	17.8	4.2	15.3	62.7
Aged 45 to 64	100.0	21.3	5.2	14.0	59.5
Aged 65 or older	100.0	36.3	7.8	19.4	36.4
Black	100.0	26.5	5.5	14.1	53.9
Hispanic	100.0	25.0	6.2	14.0	54.8
Non-Hispanic white	100.0	21.1	4.7	15.3	58.9
Northeast	100.0	13.1	0.6	15.5	70.8
Midwest	100.0	21.1	6.5	15.5	56.9
South	100.0	30.4	5.6	15.5	48.6
West	100.0	15.8	6.2	15.4	62.6
Not a college graduate	100.0	21.6	5.5	15.8	57.2
Bachelor's degree or more	100.0	22.7	4.1	14.7	58.5

Source: Survey Documentation and Analysis, Computer-assisted Survey Methods Program, University of California, Berkeley, General Social Survey, 1972–2012 Cumulative Data Files, Internet site http://sda.berkeley.edu/cgi-bin/hsda?harcsda+gss12; calculations by New Strategist

Table 1.24 Same-Sex Relations, 2000 and 2012

"What about sexual relations between two adults of the same sex—
do you think it is always wrong, almost always wrong,
wrong only sometimes, or not wrong at all?"

(percent of people aged 18 or older responding, 2000 and 2012; and percent responding by selected characteristics, 2012)

	total	always wrong	almost always wrong	sometimes wrong	not wrong at all
TREND					
2012	100.0%	45.7%	2.9%	7.7%	43.8%
2000	100.0	58.7	4.4	8.1	28.8
2012 PROFILE					
Total people	**100.0**	**45.7**	**2.9**	**7.7**	**43.8**
Men	100.0	50.9	3.5	10.4	35.3
Women	100.0	41.2	2.4	5.4	51.0
Aged 18 to 44	100.0	37.0	3.1	8.9	51.0
Aged 45 to 64	100.0	48.7	2.8	7.5	41.0
Aged 65 or older	100.0	66.9	2.2	4.5	26.3
Black	100.0	61.4	1.8	7.3	29.5
Hispanic	100.0	45.6	6.0	7.0	41.3
Non-Hispanic white	100.0	42.1	2.3	7.3	48.4
Northeast	100.0	33.5	2.0	10.1	54.4
Midwest	100.0	45.1	4.0	6.0	44.9
South	100.0	57.6	2.7	7.5	32.2
West	100.0	34.9	2.7	7.9	54.5
Not a college graduate	100.0	50.5	3.4	7.7	38.3
Bachelor's degree or more	100.0	33.4	1.4	7.7	57.5

Source: Survey Documentation and Analysis, Computer-assisted Survey Methods Program, University of California, Berkeley, General Social Survey, 1972–2012 Cumulative Data Files, Internet site http://sda.berkeley.edu/cgi-bin/hsda?harcsda+gss12; calculations by New Strategist

Table 1.25 Gay Marriage, 2012

"Do you agree or disagree: Homosexual couples should
have the right to marry one another?"

(percent of people aged 18 or older responding by selected characteristics, 2012)

	total	strongly agree	agree	neither agree nor disagree	disagree	strongly disagree
Total people	**100.0%**	**25.2%**	**23.7%**	**12.0%**	**14.2%**	**24.9%**
Men	100.0	20.7	22.3	12.2	15.7	29.2
Women	100.0	29.0	24.9	11.8	12.9	21.3
Aged 18 to 44	100.0	31.8	26.2	11.9	9.7	20.5
Aged 45 to 64	100.0	23.3	19.7	13.9	16.3	26.9
Aged 65 or older	100.0	10.0	25.2	8.1	22.9	33.8
Black	100.0	21.1	22.3	13.0	15.7	27.9
Hispanic	100.0	26.9	25.0	16.0	12.8	19.4
Non-Hispanic white	100.0	26.4	23.7	9.5	15.2	25.2
Northeast	100.0	37.3	20.5	10.7	8.8	22.7
Midwest	100.0	25.8	26.8	11.1	16.1	20.3
South	100.0	16.5	22.3	11.2	17.9	32.2
West	100.0	29.8	25.8	15.3	10.2	18.9
Not a college graduate	100.0	21.4	23.2	12.9	14.7	27.8
Bachelor's degree or more	100.0	35.0	25.1	9.6	12.8	17.5

Source: Survey Documentation and Analysis, Computer-assisted Survey Methods Program, University of California, Berkeley, General Social Survey, 1972–2012 Cumulative Data Files, Internet site http://sda.berkeley.edu/cgi-bin/hsda?harcsda+gss12; calculations by New Strategist

Television News Is Most Important

The Internet is number two.

Nearly half of Americans get most of their news from television, 30 percent from the Internet, and 12 percent from the newspaper. But there are big differences in primary news sources by demographic segment. Nearly half (46 percent) of younger adults depend on the Internet as their main source of news versus a smaller 39 percent who get their news from television. Sixty percent of blacks identify television as their main news source compared with only 44 percent of non-Hispanic whites. (Note: This question was not asked in 2000.)

When asked about their political leanings, the largest share of the public calls itself moderate (38 percent). Thirty-five percent say they are slightly to extremely conservative, and 27 percent say they are slightly to extremely liberal. These figures have changed surprisingly little since 2000. Democrats far outnumber Republicans in political party identification. Forty-six percent of adults say they are Democrats or lean Democrat, up from 43 percent in 2000. A smaller 32 percent say they are Republicans or lean Republican, down from 35 percent in 2000. Among non-Hispanic whites, the split is nearly even. Among blacks and Hispanics, Democrats vastly outnumber Republicans.

■ The political leanings of Americans have changed surprisingly little over the years, despite the seeming polarization of the public.

Newspapers are in third place as a source of news

(percent distribution of people aged 18 or older by response to the question "Where do you get most of your information about current news events?" 2012)

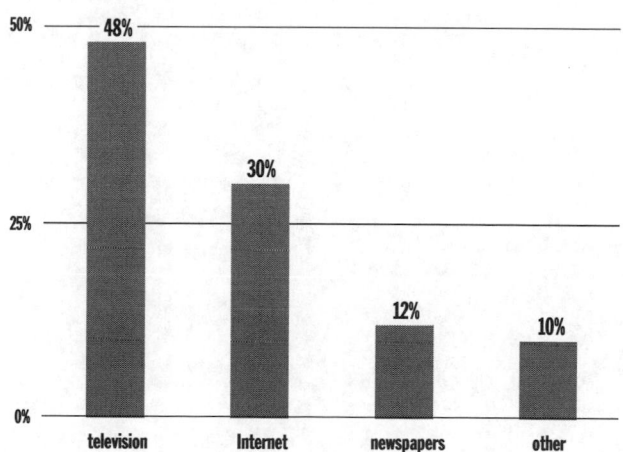

Table 1.26 Main Source of Information about Events in the News, 2012

"We are interested in how people get information about events in the news.
Where do you get most of your information about current news events?"

(percent of people aged 18 or older responding by selected characteristics, 2012)

	total	television	Internet	newspapers	radio	family, friends, or colleagues	magazines, books, other
Total people	**100.0%**	**47.9%**	**30.0%**	**12.4%**	**4.7%**	**3.6%**	**1.4%**
Men	100.0	45.3	29.5	14.3	6.7	3.4	0.8
Women	100.0	50.3	30.5	10.7	2.8	3.9	1.8
Aged 18 to 44	100.0	38.6	45.7	6.5	3.7	4.9	0.6
Aged 45 to 64	100.0	52.8	22.7	14.3	5.3	3.3	1.6
Aged 65 or older	100.0	59.1	8.9	22.6	5.8	1.2	2.6
Black	100.0	60.0	15.8	20.5	1.8	0.6	1.3
Hispanic	100.0	59.3	24.7	7.2	2.6	5.6	0.6
Non-Hispanic white	100.0	44.4	31.7	12.1	6.0	4.2	1.6
Northeast	100.0	50.0	23.6	15.7	5.6	3.6	1.5
Midwest	100.0	49.3	30.2	12.0	5.2	2.3	1.0
South	100.0	50.9	27.5	13.3	3.0	3.5	1.9
West	100.0	40.4	39.0	8.7	6.0	5.3	0.6
Not a college graduate	100.0	56.7	24.0	10.8	4.1	4.3	0.1
Bachelor's degree or more	100.0	25.5	45.7	16.6	6.2	2.0	4.0

Source: Survey Documentation and Analysis, Computer-assisted Survey Methods Program, University of California, Berkeley, General Social Survey, 1972–2012 Cumulative Data Files, Internet site http://sda.berkeley.edu/cgi-bin/hsda?harcsda+gss12; calculations by New Strategist

Table 1.27 Political Leanings, 2000 and 2012

"We hear a lot of talk these days about liberals and conservatives.
On a seven-point scale from extremely liberal (1) to extremely
conservative (7), where would you place yourself?"

(percent of people aged 18 or older responding, 2000 and 2012; and percent responding by selected characteristics, 2012)

	total	1 extremely liberal	2 liberal	3 slightly liberal	4 moderate	5 slightly conservative	6 conservative	7 extremely conservative
TREND								
2012	100.0%	4.0%	11.8%	11.2%	38.5%	15.4%	15.5%	3.7%
2000	100.0	3.9	11.5	10.8	39.9	14.5	15.9	3.6
2012 PROFILE								
Total people	**100.0**	**4.0**	**11.8**	**11.2**	**38.5**	**15.4**	**15.5**	**3.7**
Men	100.0	3.9	11.0	10.0	38.2	17.9	15.7	3.4
Women	100.0	4.2	12.4	12.2	38.7	13.2	15.3	4.0
Aged 18 to 44	100.0	4.0	12.1	12.4	41.0	15.5	12.1	2.9
Aged 45 to 64	100.0	4.7	11.8	10.7	36.1	14.5	18.4	3.8
Aged 65 or older	100.0	2.8	10.0	8.7	36.6	17.2	18.7	6.0
Black	100.0	6.1	10.1	13.6	46.2	10.7	10.2	3.1
Hispanic	100.0	4.6	11.8	10.8	41.0	12.7	12.5	6.7
Non-Hispanic white	100.0	3.2	12.0	11.1	35.5	16.7	18.0	3.5
Northeast	100.0	3.6	20.1	11.4	34.0	16.9	11.5	2.5
Midwest	100.0	3.0	9.7	12.6	41.7	15.5	14.2	3.4
South	100.0	4.4	7.7	9.6	39.6	14.9	19.2	4.5
West	100.0	5.0	14.2	12.0	36.8	14.8	13.7	3.6
Not a college graduate	100.0	3.8	9.9	10.8	41.3	14.4	15.4	4.4
Bachelor's degree or more	100.0	4.6	16.4	12.0	31.5	17.7	15.6	2.0

Source: Survey Documentation and Analysis, Computer-assisted Survey Methods Program, University of California, Berkeley, General Social Survey, 1972–2012 Cumulative Data Files, Internet site http://sda.berkeley.edu/cgi-bin/hsda?harcsda+gss12; calculations by New Strategist

Table 1.28 Political Party Affiliation, 2000 and 2012

"Generally speaking, do you usually think of yourself as a
Republican, Democrat, Independent, or what?"

(percent of people aged 18 or older responding, 2000 and 2012; and percent responding by selected characteristics, 2012)

	total	strong Democrat	not strong Democrat	independent, near Democrat	independent	independent, near Republican	not strong Republican	strong Republican	other party
TREND									
2012	100.0%	16.7%	17.0%	12.4%	19.8%	8.2%	13.7%	9.8%	2.3%
2000	100.0	13.8	17.9	11.5	20.4	9.3	14.9	10.6	1.7
2012 PROFILE									
Total people	**100.0**	**16.7**	**17.0**	**12.4**	**19.8**	**8.2**	**13.7**	**9.8**	**2.3**
Men	100.0	15.1	14.3	15.6	17.6	10.2	14.5	9.5	3.3
Women	100.0	18.0	19.3	9.7	21.8	6.6	13.1	10.1	1.5
Aged 18 to 44	100.0	13.1	18.3	13.6	24.4	8.2	14.5	5.8	2.1
Aged 45 to 64	100.0	19.4	14.4	12.7	17.4	7.8	13.0	12.4	2.9
Aged 65 or older	100.0	21.6	18.3	8.5	10.9	9.4	12.9	16.4	1.9
Black	100.0	45.1	22.5	13.1	13.7	2.2	0.7	1.2	1.4
Hispanic	100.0	10.8	22.5	12.3	31.5	7.0	10.1	5.3	0.6
Non-Hispanic white	100.0	11.7	14.6	12.3	17.5	10.0	18.0	12.9	3.1
Northeast	100.0	18.5	19.1	13.9	24.0	6.0	9.4	5.8	3.3
Midwest	100.0	17.4	17.8	13.3	18.1	7.6	13.5	10.3	2.1
South	100.0	17.5	14.3	11.3	17.5	9.8	15.2	12.5	1.8
West	100.0	13.3	18.8	12.4	22.2	8.0	14.7	7.9	2.7
Not a college graduate	100.0	15.9	16.5	11.9	22.9	8.2	12.6	9.8	2.1
Bachelor's degree or more	100.0	18.5	18.2	13.8	11.9	8.3	16.6	9.7	3.0

Source: Survey Documentation and Analysis, Computer-assisted Survey Methods Program, University of California, Berkeley, General Social Survey, 1972–2012 Cumulative Data Files, Internet site http://sda.berkeley.edu/cgi-bin/hsda?harcsda+gss12; calculations by New Strategist

Most Support Gun Laws

More than two-thirds of the public supports capital punishment.

Most Americans favor requiring a police permit for gun ownership. In 2012, 74 percent supported this type of gun regulation, down from 81 percent in 2000. Those most opposed are men (33 percent) and people who live in the South (30 percent).

Americans have long supported the death penalty for convicted murderers, with 65 percent of the public favoring it in 2012. This share is slightly below the 70 percent of 2000. Blacks are the only demographic segment in which the majority opposes the death penalty. The strongest support for the death penalty is found among men (71 percent) and non-Hispanic whites (71 percent).

Support for legal abortion under certain circumstances is overwhelming and has changed little since 2000. Eighty-seven percent of Americans support abortion if a women's health is in serious danger, and about three-quarters do if the pregnancy is the result of rape or there is a chance of serious defect in the baby. Other reasons garner substantially lower approval ratings (41 to 45 percent).

More than two-thirds of Americans support the right of the terminally ill to die with a doctor's assistance. The biggest differences are by race and Hispanic origin. Seventy-four percent of non-Hispanic whites favor the right to die compared with 61 percent of Hispanics and only 49 percent of blacks.

■ Although some states are outlawing the death penalty, the public continues to support it.

There is growing support for the legalization of marijuana

(percent of people aged 18 or older who think marijuana should be made legal, 2000 and 2012)

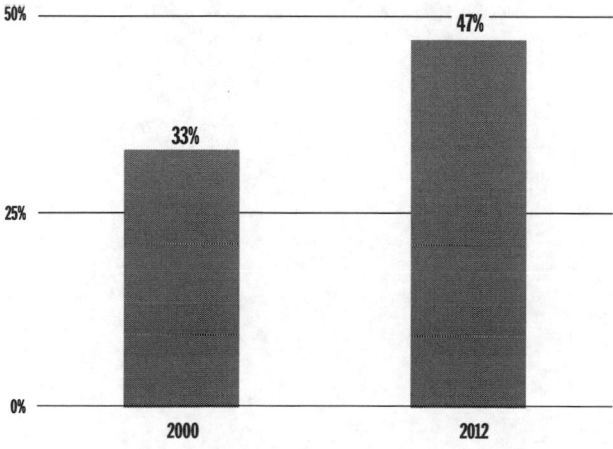

Table 1.29 Should Marijuana Be Made Legal, 2000 and 2012

"Do you think the use of marijuana should be made legal or not?"

(percent of people aged 18 or older responding, 2000 and 2012; and percent responding by selected characteristics, 2012)

	total	legal	not legal
TREND			
2012	100.0%	46.9%	53.1%
2000	100.0	32.9	67.1
2012 PROFILE			
Total people	**100.0**	**46.9**	**53.1**
Men	100.0	52.5	47.5
Women	100.0	42.3	57.7
Aged 18 to 44	100.0	50.3	49.7
Aged 45 to 64	100.0	49.7	50.3
Aged 65 or older	100.0	32.6	67.4
Black	100.0	40.8	59.2
Hispanic	100.0	32.9	67.1
Non-Hispanic white	100.0	52.5	47.5
Northeast	100.0	49.1	50.9
Midwest	100.0	48.2	51.8
South	100.0	44.3	55.7
West	100.0	48.5	51.5
Not a college graduate	100.0	45.7	54.3
Bachelor's degree or more	100.0	50.1	49.9

Source: Survey Documentation and Analysis, Computer-assisted Survey Methods Program, University of California, Berkeley, General Social Survey, 1972–2012 Cumulative Data Files, Internet site http://sda.berkeley.edu/cgi-bin/hsda?harcsda+gss12; calculations by New Strategist

Table 1.30 Favor or Oppose Gun Permits, 2000 and 2012

"Would you favor or oppose a law which would require a person
to obtain a police permit before he or she could buy a gun?"

(percent of people aged 18 or older responding, 2000 and 2012; and percent responding by selected characteristics, 2012)

	total	favor	oppose
TREND			
2012	100.0%	73.7%	26.3%
2000	100.0	81.0	19.0
2012 PROFILE			
Total people	**100.0**	**73.7**	**26.3**
Men	100.0	66.9	33.1
Women	100.0	79.5	20.5
Aged 18 to 44	100.0	71.2	28.8
Aged 45 to 64	100.0	75.4	24.6
Aged 65 or older	100.0	77.5	22.5
Black	100.0	82.9	17.1
Hispanic	100.0	72.2	27.8
Non-Hispanic white	100.0	72.2	27.8
Northeast	100.0	82.5	17.5
Midwest	100.0	75.6	24.4
South	100.0	69.6	30.4
West	100.0	72.0	28.0
Not a college graduate	100.0	74.2	25.8
Bachelor's degree or more	100.0	72.5	27.5

Source: Survey Documentation and Analysis, Computer-assisted Survey Methods Program, University of California, Berkeley, General Social Survey, 1972–2012 Cumulative Data Files, Internet site http://sda.berkeley.edu/cgi-bin/hsda?harcsda+gss12; calculations by New Strategist

Table 1.31 Favor or Oppose Death Penalty for Murder, 2000 and 2012

"Do you favor or oppose the death penalty for persons convicted of murder?"

(percent of people aged 18 or older responding, 2000 and 2012; and percent responding by selected characteristics, 2012)

	total	favor	oppose
TREND			
2012	100.0%	65.1%	34.9%
2000	100.0	69.6	30.4
2012 PROFILE			
Total people	**100.0**	**65.1**	**34.9**
Men	100.0	70.6	29.4
Women	100.0	60.3	39.7
Aged 18 to 44	100.0	64.6	35.4
Aged 45 to 64	100.0	66.7	33.3
Aged 65 or older	100.0	63.6	36.4
Black	100.0	47.9	52.1
Hispanic	100.0	55.8	44.2
Non-Hispanic white	100.0	71.1	28.9
Northeast	100.0	60.0	40.0
Midwest	100.0	69.9	30.1
South	100.0	64.5	35.5
West	100.0	64.8	35.2
Not a college graduate	100.0	67.1	32.9
Bachelor's degree or more	100.0	59.8	40.2

Source: Survey Documentation and Analysis, Computer-assisted Survey Methods Program, University of California, Berkeley, General Social Survey, 1972–2012 Cumulative Data Files, Internet site http://sda.berkeley.edu/cgi-bin/hsda?harcsda+gss12; calculations by New Strategist

Table 1.32 Support for Legal Abortion by Reason, 2000 and 2012

"Do you think it should be possible for a pregnant woman to obtain a legal abortion if the woman wants it?"

(percent of people aged 18 or older responding "yes," 2000 and 2012; and percent responding "yes" by selected demographic characteristic, 2012)

	her health is seriously endangered	pregnancy is the result of rape	there is a serious defect in the baby	she is married, but does not want more children	she cannot afford more children	she is single and does not want to marry the man	for any reason
TREND							
2012	86.7%	75.8%	73.3%	44.9%	42.4%	41.1%	42.7%
2000	88.5	79.8	77.9	39.9	41.0	38.0	38.9
2012 PROFILE							
Total people	**86.7**	**75.8**	**73.3**	**44.9**	**42.4**	**41.1**	**42.7**
Men	85.5	75.5	74.8	45.0	42.4	40.9	40.9
Women	87.7	76.0	72.1	44.7	42.5	41.3	44.3
Aged 18 to 44	85.1	76.5	71.3	44.2	43.4	40.7	43.9
Aged 45 to 64	89.3	75.4	75.5	49.8	44.3	43.9	45.1
Aged 65 or older	86.5	74.8	75.5	36.0	35.5	36.6	34.1
Black	87.1	74.1	68.9	45.9	44.4	40.3	43.1
Hispanic	81.2	65.8	69.0	35.7	31.0	28.3	31.5
Non-Hispanic white	88.5	79.6	75.4	46.6	44.5	43.9	45.6
Northeast	86.5	76.0	76.3	52.3	52.0	49.8	53.7
Midwest	91.7	80.3	75.3	44.2	42.2	41.4	42.0
South	84.2	72.1	69.4	37.9	34.7	33.3	35.7
West	86.2	77.6	75.8	52.0	48.5	47.9	46.9
Not a college graduate	85.0	72.8	71.3	38.4	36.9	32.3	36.8
Bachelor's degree or more	91.0	83.1	78.2	61.6	56.8	56.5	58.1

Source: Survey Documentation and Analysis, Computer-assisted Survey Methods Program, University of California, Berkeley, General Social Survey, 1972–2012 Cumulative Data Files, Internet site http://sda.berkeley.edu/cgi-bin/hsda?harcsda+gss12; calculations by New Strategist

Table 1.33 Allow Patients with Incurable Disease to Die, 2000 and 2012

"When a person has a disease that cannot be cured, do you think doctors should be allowed by law to end the patient's life by some painless means if the patient and his family request it?"

(percent of people aged 18 or older responding, 2000 and 2012; and percent responding by selected characteristics, 2012)

	total	yes	no
TREND			
2012	100.0%	68.3%	31.7%
2000	100.0	68.0	32.0
2012 PROFILE			
Total people	**100.0**	**68.3**	**31.7**
Men	100.0	74.1	25.9
Women	100.0	63.1	36.9
Aged 18 to 44	100.0	71.0	29.0
Aged 45 to 64	100.0	66.9	33.1
Aged 65 or older	100.0	61.7	38.3
Black	100.0	48.7	51.3
Hispanic	100.0	60.6	39.4
Non-Hispanic white	100.0	73.7	26.3
Northeast	100.0	78.6	21.4
Midwest	100.0	70.9	29.1
South	100.0	59.6	40.4
West	100.0	72.3	27.7
Not a college graduate	100.0	67.8	32.2
Bachelor's degree or more	100.0	69.7	30.3

Source: Survey Documentation and Analysis, Computer-assisted Survey Methods Program, University of California, Berkeley, General Social Survey, 1972–2012 Cumulative Data Files, Internet site http://sda.berkeley.edu/cgi-bin/hsda?harcsda+gss12; calculations by New Strategist

2

Education

Trends

Middle-aged and younger adults are well educated.

Most under age 65 have college experience, and more than one-third of those under age 45 have a bachelor's degree.

Asians are much better educated than others.

Most Asians have a bachelor's degree. Among Hispanics, only 15 percent have graduated from college.

Parents are satisfied with their child's school.

A substantial 59 percent of parents with children in kindergarten through 12th grade say they are "very satisfied" with their child's school.

College costs and debt have grown.

The cost of a year of college increased 37 percent between 2000–01 and 2011–12, after adjusting for inflation. Most students go into debt to pay the cost.

College enrollment fell between 2011 and 2012.

The biggest decline occurred at four-year public institutions, their enrollment falling by 5.6 percent.

College campuses are becoming more diverse.

Non-Hispanic whites account for only 58 percent of the nation's college students, down from 69 percent in 2000.

Women earn most degrees.

Fifty-seven percent of bachelor's degrees were awarded to women in 2010–11.

Many Americans Are Well Educated

More than half the adult population has some college experience.

The educational attainment of Americans has increased dramatically over the past few decades. A half-century ago, most adults had not even graduated from high school. Today, most adults have at least some college education, and 32 percent have at least a bachelor's degree.

Among men, educational attainment does not vary much by age, with 31 to 33 percent of every age group having a bachelor's degree. Among women, educational attainment varies greatly by age. Nearly 38 percent of women aged 25 to 44 have a bachelor's degree compared with just 20 percent of women aged 65 or older. Women under age 55, in fact, are better educated than their male counterparts.

■ Because the educational attainment of younger women is higher than that of younger men, women's incomes should continue to gain on men's.

Among Americans under age 55, women are better educated than men

(percent of people with a bachelor's degree by age and sex, 2013)

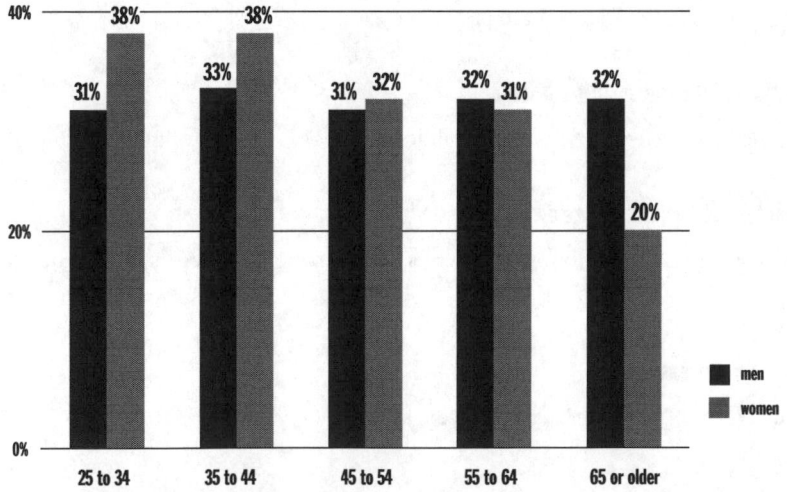

Table 2.1 Educational Attainment by Age, 2013

(number and percent distribution of people aged 25 or older by educational attainment and age, 2013; numbers in thousands)

	total	25 to 34	35 to 44	45 to 54	55 to 64	65 or older
Total people	**206,899**	**41,797**	**39,877**	**43,446**	**38,491**	**43,287**
Not a high school graduate	24,517	4,411	4,226	4,600	3,732	7,547
High school graduate only	61,704	10,950	10,454	13,254	11,926	15,120
Some college, no degree	34,805	7,719	6,769	6,990	6,738	6,590
Associate's degree	20,367	4,236	4,272	4,801	3,974	3,085
Bachelor's degree	41,575	10,353	8,852	8,938	7,218	6,214
Master's degree	17,395	3,157	3,948	3,532	3,504	3,254
Professional degree	3,066	473	668	660	658	607
Doctoral degree	3,470	497	689	673	741	871
High school graduate or more	182,382	37,386	35,651	38,847	34,759	35,740
Some college or more	120,678	26,435	25,197	25,593	22,832	20,621
Associate's degree or more	85,873	18,716	18,428	18,603	16,094	14,030
Bachelor's degree or more	65,506	14,481	14,157	13,803	12,120	10,945

PERCENT DISTRIBUTION

	total	25 to 34	35 to 44	45 to 54	55 to 64	65 or older
Total people	**100.0%**	**100.0%**	**100.0%**	**100.0%**	**100.0%**	**100.0%**
Not a high school graduate	11.8	10.6	10.6	10.6	9.7	17.4
High school graduate only	29.8	26.2	26.2	30.5	31.0	34.9
Some college, no degree	16.8	18.5	17.0	16.1	17.5	15.2
Associate's degree	9.8	10.1	10.7	11.0	10.3	7.1
Bachelor's degree	20.1	24.8	22.2	20.6	18.8	14.4
Master's degree	8.4	7.6	9.9	8.1	9.1	7.5
Professional degree	1.5	1.1	1.7	1.5	1.7	1.4
Doctoral degree	1.7	1.2	1.7	1.5	1.9	2.0
High school graduate or more	88.2	89.4	89.4	89.4	90.3	82.6
Some college or more	58.3	63.2	63.2	58.9	59.3	47.6
Associate's degree or more	41.5	44.8	46.2	42.8	41.8	32.4
Bachelor's degree or more	31.7	34.6	35.5	31.8	31.5	25.3

Source: Bureau of the Census, 2013 Current Population Survey, Internet site http://www.census.gov/hhes/www/income/data/ incpovhlth/2012/dtables.html; calculations by New Strategist

Table 2.2 Educational Attainment of Men by Age, 2013

(number and percent distribution of men aged 25 or older by educational attainment and age, 2013; numbers in thousands)

	total	25 to 34	35 to 44	45 to 54	55 to 64	65 or older
Total men	**99,305**	**20,816**	**19,623**	**21,244**	**18,323**	**19,298**
Not a high school graduate	12,277	2,490	2,313	2,522	1,778	3,174
High school graduate only	30,014	6,058	5,623	6,794	5,711	5,828
Some college, no degree	16,508	3,885	3,346	3,241	3,162	2,873
Associate's degree	8,775	1,865	1,838	2,048	1,720	1,305
Bachelor's degree	19,860	4,859	4,042	4,202	3,457	3,299
Master's degree	7,804	1,155	1,696	1,667	1,602	1,684
Professional degree	1,876	262	365	363	414	472
Doctoral degree	2,192	243	400	407	480	662
High school graduate or more	87,028	18,327	17,310	18,723	16,545	16,124
Some college or more	57,014	12,268	11,687	11,928	10,834	10,296
Associate's degree or more	40,506	8,384	8,341	8,687	7,672	7,422
Bachelor's degree or more	31,731	6,519	6,503	6,640	5,952	6,118

PERCENT DISTRIBUTION

	total	25 to 34	35 to 44	45 to 54	55 to 64	65 or older
Total men	**100.0%**	**100.0%**	**100.0%**	**100.0%**	**100.0%**	**100.0%**
Not a high school graduate	12.4	12.0	11.8	11.9	9.7	16.4
High school graduate only	30.2	29.1	28.7	32.0	31.2	30.2
Some college, no degree	16.6	18.7	17.1	15.3	17.3	14.9
Associate's degree	8.8	9.0	9.4	9.6	9.4	6.8
Bachelor's degree	20.0	23.3	20.6	19.8	18.9	17.1
Master's degree	7.9	5.5	8.6	7.8	8.7	8.7
Professional degree	1.9	1.3	1.9	1.7	2.3	2.4
Doctoral degree	2.2	1.2	2.0	1.9	2.6	3.4
High school graduate or more	87.6	88.0	88.2	88.1	90.3	83.6
Some college or more	57.4	58.9	59.6	56.1	59.1	53.4
Associate's degree or more	40.8	40.3	42.5	40.9	41.9	38.5
Bachelor's degree or more	32.0	31.3	33.1	31.3	32.5	31.7

Source: Bureau of the Census, 2013 Current Population Survey, Internet site http://www.census.gov/hhes/www/income/data/ incpovhlth/2012/dtables.html; calculations by New Strategist

Table 2.3 Educational Attainment of Women by Age, 2013

(number and percent distribution of women aged 25 or older by educational attainment and age, 2013; numbers in thousands)

	total	25 to 34	35 to 44	45 to 54	55 to 64	65 or older
Total women	**107,594**	**20,981**	**20,254**	**22,202**	**20,168**	**23,990**
Not a high school graduate	12,240	1,921	1,913	2,078	1,954	4,373
High school graduate only	31,690	4,892	4,831	6,459	6,215	9,292
Some college, no degree	18,298	3,834	3,423	3,748	3,576	3,717
Associate's degree	11,592	2,371	2,434	2,753	2,255	1,780
Bachelor's degree	21,715	5,494	4,810	4,736	3,761	2,914
Master's degree	9,591	2,002	2,251	1,865	1,902	1,570
Professional degree	1,191	212	303	296	244	135
Doctoral degree	1,278	254	289	265	261	209
High school graduate or more	95,354	19,059	18,341	20,124	18,213	19,617
Some college or more	63,665	14,167	13,510	13,664	11,998	10,325
Associate's degree or more	45,367	10,333	10,088	9,916	8,422	6,608
Bachelor's degree or more	33,775	7,962	7,654	7,163	6,168	4,828
PERCENT DISTRIBUTION						
Total women	**100.0%**	**100.0%**	**100.0%**	**100.0%**	**100.0%**	**100.0%**
Not a high school graduate	11.4	9.2	9.4	9.4	9.7	18.2
High school graduate only	29.5	23.3	23.9	29.1	30.8	38.7
Some college, no degree	17.0	18.3	16.9	16.9	17.7	15.5
Associate's degree	10.8	11.3	12.0	12.4	11.2	7.4
Bachelor's degree	20.2	26.2	23.8	21.3	18.6	12.1
Master's degree	8.9	9.5	11.1	8.4	9.4	6.5
Professional degree	1.1	1.0	1.5	1.3	1.2	0.6
Doctoral degree	1.2	1.2	1.4	1.2	1.3	0.9
High school graduate or more	88.6	90.8	90.6	90.6	90.3	81.8
Some college or more	59.2	67.5	66.7	61.5	59.5	43.0
Associate's degree or more	42.2	49.3	49.8	44.7	41.8	27.5
Bachelor's degree or more	31.4	37.9	37.8	32.3	30.6	20.1

Source: Bureau of the Census, 2013 Current Population Survey, Internet site http://www.census.gov/hhes/www/income/data/ incpovhlth/2012/dtables.html; calculations by New Strategist

Most Asian Men Have a College Degree

Only 14 percent of Hispanic men are college graduates.

Among both men and women, Asians are far better educated than non-Hispanic whites, blacks, or Hispanics. The 55 percent majority of Asian men have a bachelor's degree versus a much smaller 36 percent of non-Hispanic white men, 20 percent of black men, and just 14 percent of Hispanic men. The story is similar for Asian women. Fifty percent are college graduates versus 34 percent of non-Hispanic white women, 24 percent of black women, and 16 percent of Hispanic women.

Many Hispanics have not graduated from high school. Among Hispanic men, only 65 percent are high school graduates. The figure is a slightly higher 68 percent among Hispanic women. In contrast, 84 to 93 percent of Asians, blacks, and non-Hispanic whites have a high school diploma.

■ The educational attainment of Hispanics is well below that of the rest of the population because many are immigrants from countries with little formal schooling.

Blacks are much better educated than Hispanics

(percent of people aged 25 or older with a bachelor's degree, by sex, race, and Hispanic origin, 2013)

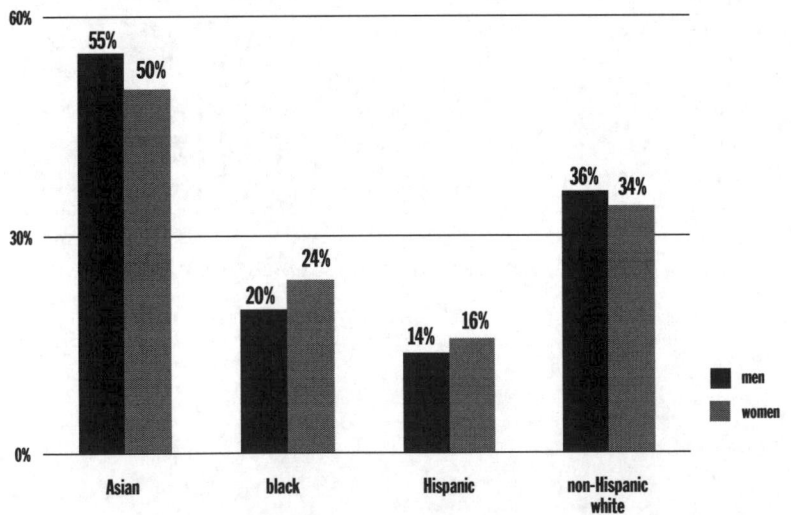

Table 2.4 Educational Attainment by Race and Hispanic Origin, 2013

(number and percent distribution of people aged 25 or older by educational attainment, race, and Hispanic origin, 2013; numbers in thousands)

	total	Asian	black	Hispanic	non-Hispanic white
Total people	**206,899**	**11,735**	**25,416**	**29,130**	**139,685**
Not a high school graduate	24,517	1,136	3,793	9,838	9,894
High school graduate	61,704	2,302	8,432	8,869	41,667
Some college, no degree	34,805	1,241	5,153	3,960	24,154
Associate's degree	20,367	862	2,447	2,079	14,818
Bachelor's degree	41,575	3,586	3,629	3,121	31,105
Master's degree	17,395	1,694	1,577	978	13,111
Professional degree	3,066	403	186	144	2,331
Doctorate degree	3,470	513	199	141	2,605
High school graduate or more	182,382	10,599	21,623	19,292	129,791
Some college or more	120,678	8,297	13,190	10,423	88,123
Associate's degree or more	85,873	7,056	8,037	6,463	63,970
Bachelor's degree or more	65,506	6,195	5,590	4,384	49,152

PERCENT DISTRIBUTION

	total	Asian	black	Hispanic	non-Hispanic white
Total people	**100.0%**	**100.0%**	**100.0%**	**100.0%**	**100.0%**
Not a high school graduate	11.8	9.7	14.9	33.8	7.1
High school graduate	29.8	19.6	33.2	30.4	29.8
Some college, no degree	16.8	10.6	20.3	13.6	17.3
Associate's degree	9.8	7.3	9.6	7.1	10.6
Bachelor's degree	20.1	30.6	14.3	10.7	22.3
Master's degree	8.4	14.4	6.2	3.4	9.4
Professional degree	1.5	3.4	0.7	0.5	1.7
Doctorate degree	1.7	4.4	0.8	0.5	1.9
High school graduate or more	88.2	90.3	85.1	66.2	92.9
Some college or more	58.3	70.7	51.9	35.8	63.1
Associate's degree or more	41.5	60.1	31.6	22.2	45.8
Bachelor's degree or more	31.7	52.8	22.0	15.1	35.2

Note: Asians and blacks are those who identify themselves as being of the race alone and those who identify themselves as being of the race in combination with other races. Hispanics may be of any race. Non-Hispanic whites are those who identify themselves as being white alone and not Hispanic.
Source: Bureau of the Census, 2013 Current Population Survey, Internet site http://www.census.gov/hhes/www/income/data/ incpovhlth/2012/dtables.html; calculations by New Strategist

Table 2.5 Educational Attainment of Men by Race and Hispanic Origin, 2013

(number and percent distribution of men aged 25 or older by educational attainment, race, and Hispanic origin, 2013; numbers in thousands)

	total men	Asian	black	Hispanic	non-Hispanic white
Total men	**99,305**	**5,419**	**11,323**	**14,499**	**67,570**
Not a high school graduate	12,277	453	1,799	5,139	4,957
High school graduate	30,014	991	4,043	4,599	20,171
Some college, no degree	16,508	590	2,232	1,900	11,657
Associate's degree	8,775	380	983	850	6,453
Bachelor's degree	19,860	1,586	1,496	1,421	15,273
Master's degree	7,804	872	588	438	5,880
Professional degree	1,876	222	80	65	1,502
Doctorate degree	2,192	324	101	86	1,677
High school graduate or more	87,028	4,966	9,524	9,360	62,612
Some college or more	57,014	3,975	5,481	4,761	42,442
Associate's degree or more	40,506	3,385	3,248	2,860	30,785
Bachelor's degree or more	31,731	3,006	2,265	2,010	24,332
PERCENT DISTRIBUTION					
Total men	**100.0%**	**100.0%**	**100.0%**	**100.0%**	**100.0%**
Not a high school graduate	12.4	8.4	15.9	35.4	7.3
High school graduate	30.2	18.3	35.7	31.7	29.9
Some college, no degree	16.6	10.9	19.7	13.1	17.3
Associate's degree	8.8	7.0	8.7	5.9	9.6
Bachelor's degree	20.0	29.3	13.2	9.8	22.6
Master's degree	7.9	16.1	5.2	3.0	8.7
Professional degree	1.9	4.1	0.7	0.4	2.2
Doctorate degree	2.2	6.0	0.9	0.6	2.5
High school graduate or more	87.6	91.6	84.1	64.6	92.7
Some college or more	57.4	73.3	48.4	32.8	62.8
Associate's degree or more	40.8	62.5	28.7	19.7	45.6
Bachelor's degree or more	32.0	55.5	20.0	13.9	36.0

Note: Asians and blacks are those who identify themselves as being of the race alone and those who identify themselves as being of the race in combination with other races. Hispanics may be of any race. Non-Hispanic whites are those who identify themselves as being white alone and not Hispanic.
Source: Bureau of the Census, 2013 Current Population Survey, Internet site http://www.census.gov/hhes/www/income/data/incpovhlth/2012/dtables.html; calculations by New Strategist

Table 2.6 Educational Attainment of Women by Race and Hispanic Origin, 2013

(number and percent distribution of women aged 25 or older by educational attainment, race, and Hispanic origin, 2013; numbers in thousands)

	total women	Asian	black	Hispanic	non-Hispanic white
Total women	**107,594**	**6,316**	**14,093**	**14,631**	**72,115**
Not a high school graduate	12,240	683	1,994	4,699	4,937
High school graduate	31,690	1,310	4,389	4,269	21,496
Some college, no degree	18,298	651	2,921	2,060	12,497
Associate's degree	11,592	482	1,464	1,229	8,365
Bachelor's degree	21,715	1,999	2,133	1,700	15,832
Master's degree	9,591	821	989	540	7,232
Professional degree	1,191	180	105	79	829
Doctorate degree	1,278	188	98	55	927
High school graduate or more	95,354	5,633	12,099	9,932	67,178
Some college or more	63,665	4,323	7,709	5,663	45,682
Associate's degree or more	45,367	3,671	4,788	3,603	33,185
Bachelor's degree or more	33,775	3,189	3,325	2,374	24,820
PERCENT DISTRIBUTION					
Total women	**100.0%**	**100.0%**	**100.0%**	**100.0%**	**100.0%**
Not a high school graduate	11.4	10.8	14.1	32.1	6.8
High school graduate	29.5	20.7	31.1	29.2	29.8
Some college, no degree	17.0	10.3	20.7	14.1	17.3
Associate's degree	10.8	7.6	10.4	8.4	11.6
Bachelor's degree	20.2	31.7	15.1	11.6	22.0
Master's degree	8.9	13.0	7.0	3.7	10.0
Professional degree	1.1	2.9	0.7	0.5	1.1
Doctorate degree	1.2	3.0	0.7	0.4	1.3
High school graduate or more	88.6	89.2	85.9	67.9	93.2
Some college or more	59.2	68.4	54.7	38.7	63.3
Associate's degree or more	42.2	58.1	34.0	24.6	46.0
Bachelor's degree or more	31.4	50.5	23.6	16.2	34.4

Note: Asians and blacks are those who identify themselves as being of the race alone and those who identify themselves as being of the race in combination with other races. Hispanics may be of any race. Non-Hispanic whites are those who identify themselves as being white alone and not Hispanic.
Source: Bureau of the Census, 2013 Current Population Survey, Internet site http://www.census.gov/hhes/www/income/data/ incpovhlth/2012/dtables.html; calculations by New Strategist

Educational Attainment Varies Widely by State

Massachusetts has the largest share of college graduates.

Among regions, the Northeast has the highest level of education. Thirty-three percent of people aged 25 or older in the Northeast have a bachelor's degree. This compares with a low of 27 percent in the South.

Educational attainment varies more by state than by region. The proportion of state populations that have a high school diploma ranges from a low of 81 percent in Texas to a high of 93 percent in Montana. The figures vary for college graduates as well. In West Virginia, only 19 percent of people aged 25 or older have a bachelor's degree, the smallest share among the 50 states. In contrast, at least 35 percent of adults are college graduates in Massachusetts, Colorado, Connecticut, Maryland, New Jersey, Vermont, Virginia, and the District of Columbia. Since income rises with education, it is no surprise that the states with the least-educated populations—such as Arkansas, Mississippi, and West Virginia—are also some of the poorest.

■ Better-educated populations attract business investment, increasing economic diversity and employment opportunities.

West Virginia's population is least likely to be college educated

(percentage of people aged 25 or older with a bachelor's degree in the states with the largest and smallest percentage of college-educated residents, 2012)

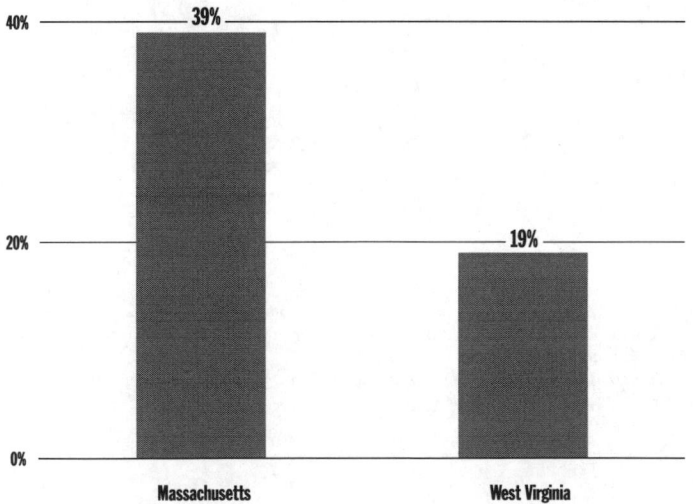

Table 2.7 Educational Attainment by Region, 2012

(number and percent of people aged 25 or older who are high school or college graduates, by region, 2012; numbers in thousands)

	number	percent
Total with a high school diploma or more	**180,249**	**86.4%**
Northeast	33,500	87.8
Midwest	39,968	89.2
South	65,809	84.8
West	40,973	85.1
Total with a bachelor's degree or more	**60,743**	**29.1**
Northeast	12,734	33.4
Midwest	12,421	27.7
South	20,952	27.0
West	14,635	30.4

Source: Bureau of the Census, 2012 American Community Survey, American Factfinder, Internet site http://factfinder2.census .gov/faces/nav/jsf/pages/index.xhtml

Table 2.8 Educational Attainment by State, 2012

(percent of people aged 25 or older who are high school or college graduates, by state, 2012)

	high school diploma or more	bachelor's degree or more
United States	**86.4%**	**29.1%**
Alabama	84.0	23.3
Alaska	92.0	28.0
Arizona	85.7	27.3
Arkansas	84.8	21.0
California	81.5	30.9
Colorado	90.6	37.5
Connecticut	89.9	37.1
Delaware	88.5	29.5
District of Columbia	88.6	53.0
Florida	86.5	26.8
Georgia	85.0	28.2
Hawaii	90.4	30.1
Idaho	89.8	25.5
Illinois	87.6	31.6
Indiana	87.6	23.4
Iowa	91.6	26.3
Kansas	90.2	30.4
Kentucky	83.8	21.8
Louisiana	83.0	22.0
Maine	91.6	28.0
Maryland	89.1	36.9
Massachusetts	89.7	39.3
Michigan	89.2	26.0
Minnesota	92.5	33.2
Mississippi	82.3	20.7
Missouri	88.0	26.4
Montana	92.8	29.4
Nebraska	90.5	29.0
Nevada	84.9	22.4
New Hampshire	91.8	34.6
New Jersey	88.3	36.2
New Mexico	84.4	26.1
New York	85.3	33.4
North Carolina	85.2	27.4
North Dakota	91.7	27.9
Ohio	88.8	25.2
Oklahoma	86.7	23.8
Oregon	89.9	29.9
Pennsylvania	88.9	27.8

	high school diploma or more	bachelor's degree or more
Rhode Island	86.1%	31.4%
South Carolina	84.9	25.1
South Dakota	90.5	26.3
Tennessee	85.1	24.3
Texas	81.4	26.7
Utah	91.0	30.7
Vermont	91.7	35.8
Virginia	87.9	35.5
Washington	90.4	31.7
West Virginia	84.5	18.6
Wisconsin	90.7	27.1
Wyoming	91.7	24.7

Source: Bureau of the Census, 2012 American Community Survey, American Factfinder, Internet site http://factfinder2.census
.gov/faces/nav/jsf/pages/index.xhtml

More than One in Four Americans Are in School

School enrollment exceeded 78 million in 2012.

Americans start school at a tender age, and many stay in school—or go back to school—well into middle age. In 2012, 26 percent of people aged 3 or older were in school, including most of the nation's 3-to-4-year-olds.

The nation's elementary schools enrolled 20 million students in 2012, while middle schools enrolled 12 million and high schools 17 million. Among students in 1st through 12th grade, fewer than 10 percent are in private schools. Among public school students, a substantial 48 percent are minorities. In 12 states and the District of Columbia, minorities account for more than half the student body.

■ Fewer than 2 million children are homeschooled, which is just 3 percent of children aged 5 to 17.

Number of students in college surpasses number in high school

(number of people enrolled in school by level, 2012)

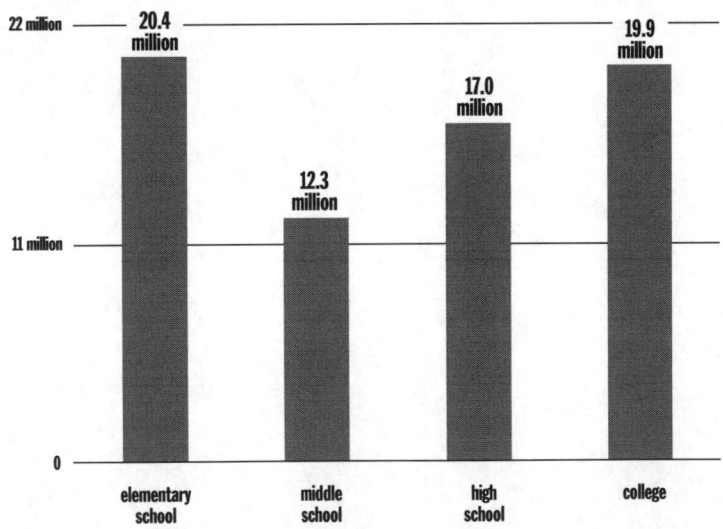

Table 2.9 School Enrollment by Age, 2012

(total number of people aged 3 or older, and number and percent enrolled in school by age, fall 2012; numbers in thousands)

		enrolled in school	
	total	number	percent
Total population	**297,229**	**78,426**	**26.4%**
Aged 3 to 4	8,014	4,289	53.5
Aged 5 to 6	8,290	7,728	93.2
Aged 7 to 9	12,190	11,951	98.0
Aged 10 to 13	16,520	16,196	98.0
Aged 14 to 15	8,232	8,085	98.2
Aged 16 to 17	8,423	8,070	95.8
Aged 18 to 19	8,484	5,855	69.0
Aged 20 to 21	8,870	4,789	54.0
Aged 22 to 24	13,023	4,004	30.7
Aged 25 to 29	20,674	2,888	14.0
Aged 30 to 34	20,437	1,532	7.5
Aged 35 to 44	39,629	1,642	4.1
Aged 45 to 54	43,558	1,008	2.3
Aged 55 or older	80,885	388	0.5

Source: Bureau of the Census, School Enrollment, CPS October 2012—Detailed Tables, Internet site http://www.census.gov/ hhes/school/data/cps/2012/tables.html; calculations by New Strategist

Table 2.10 School Enrollment by Grade and Year of College, 2012

(number and percent distribution of students enrolled in school by grade and year of college, fall 2012; numbers in thousands)

	number	percent distribution
Total students	**78,426**	**100.0%**
Nursery school	4,628	5.9
Kindergarten	4,138	5.3
ELEMENTARY	**20,411**	**26.0**
1st grade	4,042	5.2
2nd grade	4,139	5.3
3rd grade	4,095	5.2
4th grade	3,879	4.9
5th grade	4,256	5.4
MIDDLE SCHOOL	**12,272**	**15.6**
6th grade	4,098	5.2
7th grade	4,212	5.4
8th grade	3,962	5.1
HIGH SCHOOL	**17,048**	**21.7**
9th grade	4,249	5.4
10th grade	4,096	5.2
11th grade	4,248	5.4
12th grade	4,455	5.7
COLLEGE	**19,930**	**25.4**
Undergraduate	16,170	20.6
First year	4,887	6.2
Second year	4,744	6.0
Third year	3,756	4.8
Fourth or higher year	2,783	3.5
Graduate	3,760	4.8
First year	1,328	1.7
Second or higher year	2,432	3.1

Source: Bureau of the Census, School Enrollment, CPS October 2012—Detailed Tables, Internet site http://www.census.gov/ hhes/school/data/cps/2012/tables.html; calculations by New Strategist

Table 2.11 School Enrollment by Control of School, 2012

(number and percent distribution of students enrolled in school by control of school, fall 2012; numbers in thousands)

	total	public	private
Total students	**78,426**	**67,763**	**10,663**
Nursery school	4,628	2,732	1,896
Kindergarten	4,138	3,684	454
1st through 8th grade	32,683	29,865	2,818
9th through 12th grade	17,047	15,704	1,343
College	19,930	15,778	4,152

PERCENT DISTRIBUTION BY CONTROL OF SCHOOL

Total students	**100.0%**	**86.4%**	**13.6%**
Nursery school	100.0	59.0	41.0
Kindergarten	100.0	89.0	11.0
1st through 8th grade	100.0	91.4	8.6
9th through 12th grade	100.0	92.1	7.9
College	100.0	79.2	20.8

Source: Bureau of the Census, School Enrollment, CPS October 2012—Detailed Tables, Internet site http://www.census.gov/ hhes/school/data/cps/2012/tables.html; calculations by New Strategist

Table 2.12 Enrollment in Public Elementary and Secondary School by State, Race, and Hispanic Origin, 2010

(percent distribution of students enrolled in public elementary and secondary school by state, race, and Hispanic origin, 2010)

	total	minority students						non-Hispanic white
		total	American Indian	Asian or Pacific Islander	black	two or more races	Hispanic	
Total public school children	**100.0%**	**47.6%**	**1.1%**	**5.0%**	**16.0%**	**2.4%**	**23.1%**	**52.4%**
Alabama	100.0	41.7	0.8	1.3	34.6	0.3	4.7	58.3
Alaska	100.0	47.8	23.0	8.0	3.6	7.2	5.9	52.2
Arizona	100.0	57.1	5.2	3.0	5.6	1.2	42.2	42.9
Arkansas	100.0	35.2	0.7	1.9	21.5	1.3	9.8	64.8
California	100.0	73.4	0.7	11.7	6.7	2.9	51.4	26.6
Colorado	100.0	43.2	0.9	3.1	4.8	2.8	31.6	56.8
Connecticut	100.0	38.0	0.4	4.3	13.2	1.4	18.6	62.0
Delaware	100.0	49.9	0.5	3.4	32.3	1.4	12.4	50.1
District of Columbia	100.0	92.9	0.1	1.4	77.8	1.0	12.6	7.1
Florida	100.0	57.0	0.4	2.6	23.0	3.0	28.0	43.0
Georgia	100.0	55.6	0.2	3.4	37.0	3.0	11.9	44.4
Hawaii	100.0	85.5	0.6	69.6	2.5	8.4	4.5	14.5
Idaho	100.0	21.5	1.4	1.7	1.0	1.5	15.9	78.5
Illinois	100.0	48.7	0.3	4.2	18.4	2.9	22.9	51.3
Indiana	100.0	26.9	0.3	1.6	12.1	4.4	8.4	73.1
Iowa	100.0	18.5	0.5	2.1	5.1	2.2	8.5	81.5
Kansas	100.0	32.0	1.3	2.6	7.4	4.3	16.4	68.0
Kentucky	100.0	18.1	0.1	1.4	10.8	1.8	3.9	81.9
Louisiana	100.0	51.5	0.9	1.5	45.4	1.0	2.6	48.5
Maine	100.0	7.5	0.7	1.1	1.8	2.5	1.5	92.5
Maryland	100.0	57.1	0.4	5.9	35.8	3.5	11.5	42.9
Massachusetts	100.0	32.0	0.2	5.6	8.2	2.4	15.4	68.0
Michigan	100.0	30.2	0.8	2.7	19.0	1.9	5.8	69.8
Minnesota	100.0	26.2	1.9	6.1	9.2	1.8	7.2	73.8
Mississippi	100.0	54.0	0.2	0.9	49.9	0.5	2.5	46.0
Missouri	100.0	25.3	0.5	2.0	17.1	1.3	4.5	74.7
Montana	100.0	18.3	11.1	1.1	1.0	1.6	3.5	81.7
Nebraska	100.0	29.2	1.5	2.1	6.7	2.9	16.0	70.8
Nevada	100.0	61.3	1.3	7.1	9.9	4.2	38.7	38.7
New Hampshire	100.0	10.2	0.3	2.8	2.0	1.5	3.7	89.8
New Jersey	100.0	48.5	0.1	8.9	16.7	0.7	22.1	51.5
New Mexico	100.0	74.0	10.2	1.3	2.1	1.0	59.4	26.0
New York	100.0	50.8	0.5	8.3	19.0	0.6	22.4	49.2
North Carolina	100.0	46.8	1.5	2.5	26.5	3.7	12.6	53.2
North Dakota	100.0	16.3	9.1	1.3	2.4	3.3	0.1	83.7
Ohio	100.0	25.8	0.1	1.7	16.3	4.2	3.4	74.2
Oklahoma	100.0	45.4	17.7	2.1	10.2	3.2	12.3	54.6
Oregon	100.0	33.7	1.9	4.5	2.6	4.2	20.5	66.3
Pennsylvania	100.0	28.8	0.2	3.2	15.7	1.5	8.3	71.2
Rhode Island	100.0	34.8	0.7	3.0	8.0	2.4	20.8	65.2

		minority students						
	total	total	American Indian	Asian or Pacific Islander	black	two or more races	Hispanic	non-Hispanic white
South Carolina	100.0%	46.6%	0.3%	1.4%	36.2%	2.3%	6.4%	53.4%
South Dakota	100.0	20.2	11.6	1.5	2.5	1.1	3.5	79.8
Tennessee	100.0	32.7	0.2	1.7	23.9	0.7	6.1	67.3
Texas	100.0	68.8	0.5	3.6	12.9	1.6	50.3	31.2
Utah	100.0	22.0	1.3	3.4	1.4	0.8	15.1	78.0
Vermont	100.0	7.2	0.3	1.6	1.8	2.1	1.3	92.8
Virginia	100.0	45.9	0.3	6.0	24.1	4.1	11.4	54.1
Washington	100.0	37.2	1.7	8.1	4.8	4.6	18.0	62.8
West Virginia	100.0	8.0	0.1	0.7	5.2	0.8	1.1	92.0
Wisconsin	100.0	25.6	1.3	3.6	9.9	1.5	9.3	74.4
Wyoming	100.0	19.0	3.3	0.9	1.1	1.4	12.3	81.0

Note: American Indians, Asians, and blacks are those who identify themselves as being of the race alone. Numbers do not sum to total because Hispanics may be of any race.
Source: National Center for Education Statistics, Digest of Education Statistics: 2012, Internet site http://nces.ed.gov/programs/ digest/2012menu_tables.asp; calculations by New Strategist

Table 2.13 Homeschooled Children by Selected Characteristics, 2011–12

(number and percent of children aged 5 to 17 who are homeschooled by selected characteristics, 2011–12)

	number (in 000s)	homeschooling rate
Total homeschooled children	**1,770**	**3.2%**
Race and Hispanic origin of child		
Asian	73	2.6
Black	139	1.9
Hispanic	267	2.3
Two or more races	90	3.2
Non-Hispanic white	1,201	4.5
Location of student's household		
City	489	3.2
Suburb	601	3.1
Town	132	2.7
Rural	548	4.5
Student's grade equivalent		
Kindergarten through 2nd grade	415	3.1
3rd through 5th grade	416	3.4
6th through 8th grade	425	3.5
9th through 12th grade	514	3.7
Educational attainment of parent		
Not a high school graduate	203	3.4
High school graduate	355	3.4
Vocational/technical or some college	525	3.4
Bachelor's degree	436	3.7
Graduate degree	252	3.3

Note: The homeschooling rate is the percentage of the demographic segment that is homeschooled. Asians and blacks are those who identify themselves as being of the race alone and not Hispanic. The multiracial are not Hispanic.
Source: National Center for Education Statistics, Parent and Family Involvement in Education, from the National Household Education Surveys Program of 2012, Internet site http://nces.ed.gov/pubsearch/pubsinfo.asp?pubid=2013028

Parents Are Involved in Their Children's Education

In the past year, most parents have attended a school meeting, a parent–teacher conference, or a school event.

Most parents are actively involved in their children's education. The parents of 87 percent of the nation's elementary and secondary students say they attended a PTA or general school meeting during the past year, according to a survey by the National Center for Education Statistics. Seventy-six percent attended a parent–teacher conference, 74 percent attended a class event, and 42 percent volunteered.

Participation in a child's education typically rises with the educational attainment of the parent. The percentage of children whose parents attended a class event, for example, climbs from 48 percent among parents who did not graduate from high school to more than 80 percent among parents with at least a bachelor's degree.

■ Parents in poverty are slightly more likely than those above poverty level to check and make sure their child has done his homework.

Educated parents are more likely to take their children to plays, concerts, and other live shows

(percent of children in kindergarten through 12th grade whose parents took them to a play, concert or other live show, by educational attainment of parent, 2011–12)

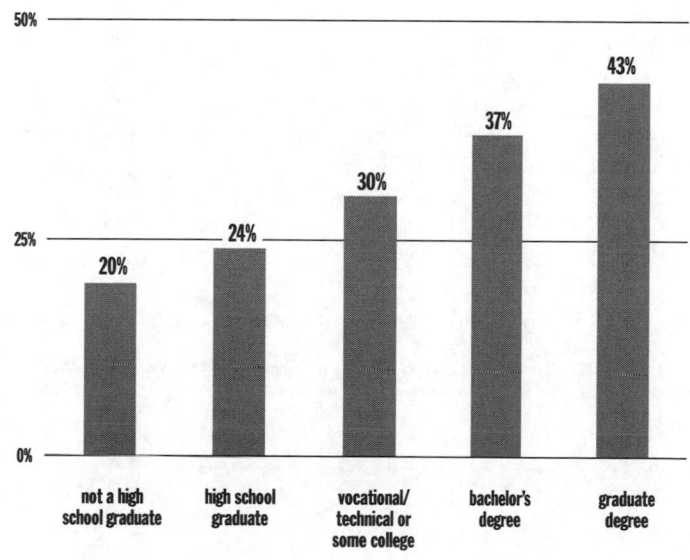

Table 2.14 Parental Involvement in School Functions, 2011–12

(total number and percent of children in kindergarten through 12th grade whose parents reported participation in school functions, by selected characteristics of child and parent, 2011–12)

	total number (in 000s)	percent	parent attended a PTA or general school meeting	parent attended a parent–teacher conference	parent attended a school or class event	parent volunteered at school	parent participated in school fundraising
Total children	**52,211**	**100%**	**87%**	**76%**	**74%**	**42%**	**58%**
Race and Hispanic origin of child							
Asian	2,871	100	84	72	65	37	47
Black	7,466	100	85	76	68	31	52
Hispanic	12,110	100	86	73	64	32	46
Two or more races	2,827	100	88	78	76	44	58
Non-Hispanic white	26,938	100	89	77	82	50	67
Educational attainment of parent							
Not a high school graduate	6,335	100	77	64	48	19	31
High school graduate	10,571	100	82	72	62	28	46
Vocational/technical or some college	15,810	100	88	77	77	41	61
Bachelor's degree	11,839	100	92	80	85	55	71
Graduate degree	7,656	100	95	82	89	61	75
School type							
Public, assigned	40,097	100	86	74	73	38	56
Public, chosen	7,448	100	89	76	75	44	57
Private, religious	3,271	100	96	85	88	69	84
Private, nonreligious	788	100	95	89	91	66	78
Student's grade level							
Kindergarten through 2nd grade	13,610	100	93	89	79	56	67
3rd through 5th grade	12,243	100	92	89	82	51	69
6th through 8th grade	11,717	100	87	71	70	32	53
9th through 12th grade	14,642	100	79	57	66	28	47
Poverty status							
Poor	10,333	100	82	71	60	27	41
Not poor	41,878	100	89	77	78	45	63

Note: Asians and blacks are those who identify themselves as being of the race alone and not Hispanic. The multiracial are not Hispanic.
Source: National Center for Education Statistics, Parent and Family Involvement in Education, from the National Household Education Surveys Program of 2012, Internet site http://nces.ed.gov/pubsearch/pubsinfo.asp?pubid=2013028; calculations by New Strategist

Table 2.15 Parental Involvement in Activities with Children, 2011–12

(total number and percent of children in kindergarten through 12th grade whose parents reported engaging in activity with children, by selected characteristics of child and parent, 2011–12)

	total		visited library	visited bookstore	attended play, concert, or other live show	visited art gallery, museum, or historical site	visited zoo or aquarium	attended community religious or ethnic event	attended sporting event
	number (in 000s)	percent							
Total children	52,211	100%	39%	38%	31%	21%	19%	54%	42%
Race and Hispanic origin of child									
Asian	2,871	100	53	42	33	22	25	52	30
Black	7,466	100	47	37	32	21	21	65	43
Hispanic	12,110	100	38	36	26	20	24	52	39
Two or more races	2,827	100	40	37	29	23	17	55	41
Non-Hispanic white	26,938	100	36	38	33	22	15	53	44
Educational attainment of parent									
Not a high school graduate	6,335	100	37	30	20	17	25	46	33
High school graduate	10,571	100	38	26	24	15	17	48	36
Vocational/technical or some college	15,810	100	35	36	30	20	18	54	41
Bachelor's degree	11,839	100	41	46	37	25	18	60	47
Graduate degree	7,656	100	48	50	43	30	18	65	49
School type									
Public, assigned	40,097	100	38	36	30	20	18	53	41
Public, chosen	7,448	100	44	41	33	25	19	55	42
Private, religious	3,271	100	44	47	39	25	17	72	50
Private, nonreligious	788	100	40	48	46	41	23	49	46
Student's grade level									
Kindergarten through 2nd grade	13,610	100	48	38	31	28	29	56	38
3rd through 5th grade	12,243	100	46	41	33	24	21	59	45
6th through 8th grade	11,717	100	38	39	32	19	15	55	44
9th through 12th grade	14,642	100	27	33	29	15	10	48	40
Poverty status									
Poor	10,333	100	42	28	23	17	22	51	35
Not poor	41,878	100	39	40	33	22	18	55	43

Note: Asians and blacks are those who identify themselves as being of the race alone and not Hispanic. The multiracial are not Hispanic.
Source: National Center for Education Statistics, Parent and Family Involvement in Education, from the National Household Education Surveys Program of 2012, Internet site http://nces.ed.gov/pubsearch/pubsinfo.asp?pubid=2013028; calculations by New Strategist

Table 2.16 Parental Involvement in Child's Homework, 2011–12

(total number and percent of children in kindergarten through 12th grade whose parents reported involvement with child's homework, by selected characteristics of child and parent, 2011–12)

| | total | | student does homework outside of school | | |
	number (in 000s)	percent	total	place in home set aside for homework	adult in household checks that homework is done
Total children	**52,211**	**100%**	**96%**	**86%**	**67%**
Race and Hispanic origin of child					
Asian	2,871	100	98	91	65
Black	7,466	100	96	89	71
Hispanic	12,110	100	97	84	69
Two or more races	2,827	100	96	87	70
Non-Hispanic white	26,938	100	95	85	65
Educational attainment of parent					
Not a high school graduate	6,335	100	94	83	67
High school graduate	10,571	100	95	86	65
Vocational/technical or some college	15,810	100	96	87	69
Bachelor's degree	11,839	100	97	85	67
Graduate degree	7,656	100	97	86	66
School type					
Public, assigned	40,097	100	97	86	67
Public, chosen	7,448	100	94	88	69
Private, religious	3,271	100	87	85	65
Private, nonreligious	788	100	95	83	64
Student's grade level					
Kindergarten through 2nd grade	13,610	100	94	87	94
3rd through 5th grade	12,243	100	98	89	85
6th through 8th grade	11,717	100	97	86	58
9th through 12th grade	14,642	100	95	82	34
Poverty status					
Poor	10,333	100	94	84	72
Not poor	41,878	100	96	86	66

Note: Asians and blacks are those who identify themselves as being of the race alone and not Hispanic. The multiracial are not Hispanic.
Source: National Center for Education Statistics, Parent and Family Involvement in Education, from the National Household Education Surveys Program of 2012, Internet site http://nces.ed.gov/pubsearch/pubsinfo.asp?pubid=2013028; calculations by New Strategist

Most Parents Are Satisfied with Their Child's School

Most are also satisfied with their child's teachers and the amount of homework.

Complaints about the nation's schools are commonplace, but in fact the parents of most children in kindergarten through 12th grade are "very satisfied" with various aspects of their child's school. The parents of 59 percent of students say they are very satisfied with their child's school. Sixty percent are very satisfied with their child's teachers. Similar proportions are very satisfied with the school's academic standards and discipline. Seventy-seven percent say the amount of homework assigned to their child is "about right."

The biggest difference in satisfaction levels is by type of school and grade level. Typically, private school parents are happier than public school parents, and the parents of younger children are happier than the parents of children in middle or high school. Nevertheless, at least 50 percent of parents, regardless of type of school or grade level, say they are very satisfied with their child's school.

■ By race and Hispanic origin, non-Hispanic whites are most satisfied with their child's school.

Blacks are least likely to be "very satisfied" with their child's school

(percent of children in kindergarten through 12th grade whose parents are "very satisfied" with their child's school, by race and Hispanic origin, 2011–12)

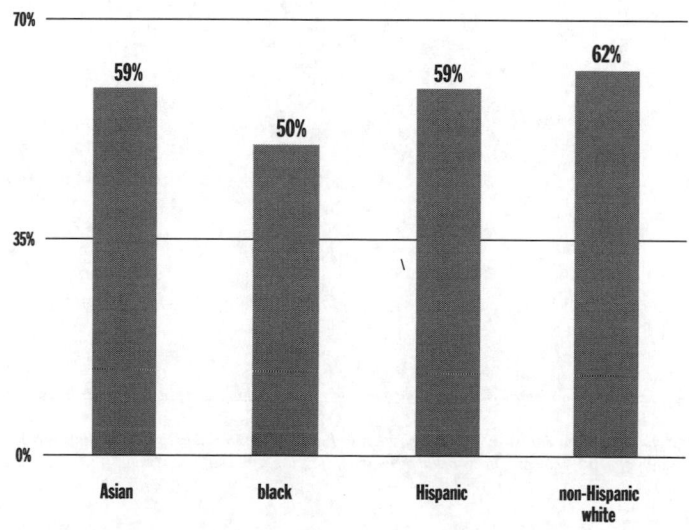

Table 2.17 Parental Satisfaction with School, 2011–12

(total number and percent of children in kindergarten through 12th grade whose parents reported being "very satisfied" with school characteristics and amount of homework, by selected characteristics of child and parent, 2011–12)

	total		parent reports being "very satisfied"					
	number (in 000s)	percent	with the school	with teachers student had this year	with academic standards of the school	with order and discipline at the school	with the way school staff interacts with parents	amount of homework assigned is "about right"
Total children	**52,211**	**100%**	**59%**	**60%**	**59%**	**60%**	**52%**	**77%**
Race and Hispanic origin of child								
Asian	2,871	100	59	57	58	60	51	75
Black	7,466	100	50	53	51	54	47	77
Hispanic	12,110	100	59	60	58	61	52	80
Two or more races	2,827	100	57	57	59	59	53	75
Non-Hispanic white	26,938	100	62	61	62	61	54	77
Educational attainment of parent								
Not a high school graduate	6,335	100	60	61	58	60	55	81
High school graduate	10,571	100	55	57	57	56	48	78
Vocational/technical or some college	15,810	100	54	55	55	55	48	76
Bachelor's degree	11,839	100	64	64	64	64	57	77
Graduate degree	7,656	100	66	64	65	66	57	75
School type								
Public, assigned	40,097	100	56	58	56	56	49	77
Public, chosen	7,448	100	62	59	64	63	56	76
Private, religious	3,271	100	80	76	80	82	72	85
Private, nonreligious	788	100	82	82	84	81	78	81
Student's grade level								
Kindergarten through 2nd grade	13,610	100	70	75	68	71	66	85
3rd through 5th grade	12,243	100	63	67	62	66	60	78
6th through 8th grade	11,717	100	53	52	53	54	45	73
9th through 12th grade	14,642	100	50	44	52	49	39	73
Poverty status								
Poor	10,333	100	55	59	55	56	51	78
Not poor	41,878	100	60	60	60	60	53	77

Note: Asians and blacks are those who identify themselves as being of the race alone and not Hispanic. The multiracial are not Hispanic.
Source: National Center for Education Statistics, Parent and Family Involvement in Education, from the National Household Education Surveys Program of 2012, Internet site http://nces.ed.gov/pubsearch/pubsinfo.asp?pubid=2013028; calculations by New Strategist

School Enrollment Is Projected to Rise

Non-Hispanic whites will become a minority of public school students.

Between 2012 and 2021, enrollment in the nation's schools is projected to rise by 6 percent, according to projections by the National Center for Education Statistics. Overall, schools will gain more than 3 million additional students in pre-K through 12th grade during those years.

High school enrollment is projected to grow by less than 4 percent between 2012 and 2021, while enrollment in pre-K through 8th grade is expected to rise by a larger 7 percent. Private school enrollment should increase more slowly than public school enrollment overall, and the number of students in private high schools is projected to decline by a substantial 13 percent.

The number of non-Hispanic whites in public school is projected to decline slightly between 2012 and 2021. The non-Hispanic white share of public school students will fall from 51 to 48 percent during those years, and the Hispanic share will rise from 24 to 27 percent.

■ The black share of public school students will remain fairly stable between 2012 and 2021 at about 16 percent.

Minorities will account for the majority of public school students by 2021

(percent distribution of public school students by race and Hispanic origin, 2012 and 2021)

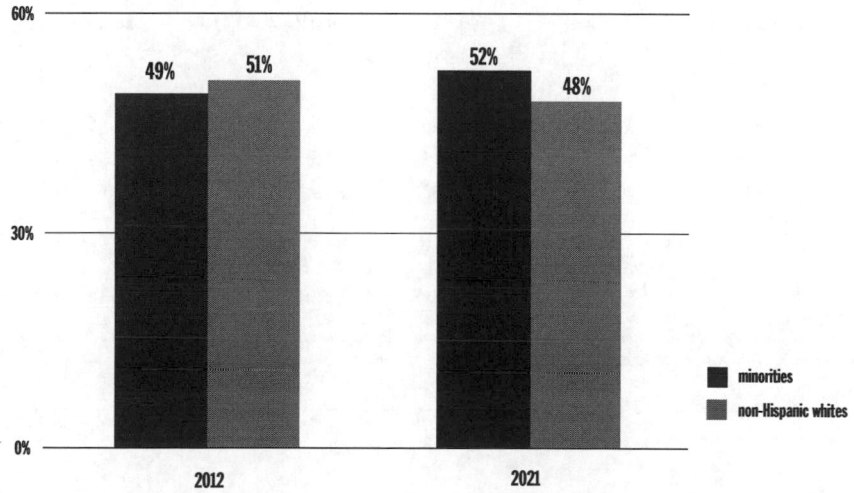

Table 2.18 School Enrollment Projections by Control of School, 2012 and 2021

(number of students enrolled in prekindergarten through 12th grade by control of institution, fall 2012 and fall 2021; percent change, 2012–21; numbers in thousands)

	2012	2021	percent change
TOTAL ENROLLMENT	**55,091**	**58,444**	**6.1%**
Pre-K through 8th grade	39,115	41,861	7.0
9th through 12th grade	15,976	16,583	3.8
PUBLIC SCHOOLS	**49,828**	**53,113**	**6.6**
Pre-K through 8th grade	35,076	37,598	7.2
9th through 12th grade	14,752	15,515	5.2
PRIVATE SCHOOLS	**5,263**	**5,331**	**1.3**
Pre-K through 8th grade	4,039	4,263	5.5
9th through 12th grade	1,224	1,068	−12.7

Source: National Center for Education Statistics, Projections of Education Statistics to 2021, Internet site http://nces.ed.gov/ programs/projections/projections2021/; calculations by New Strategist

Table 2.19 School Enrollment Projections by Race and Hispanic Origin, 2012 to 2021

(number of students enrolled in prekindergarten through 12th grade in public schools, by race and Hispanic origin, fall 2012 and fall 2021; percent change, 2012–21; numbers in thousands)

	2012		2021		percent change
	number	percent distribution	number	percent distribution	
Total enrolled in public school	**49,828**	**100.0%**	**53,113**	**100.0%**	**6.6%**
American Indian	576	1.2	657	1.2	14.1
Asian	2,595	5.2	3,117	5.9	20.1
Black	7,876	15.8	8,273	15.6	5.0
Two or more races	1,234	2.5	1,558	2.9	26.3
Hispanic	11,920	23.9	14,169	26.7	18.9
Non-Hispanic white	25,627	51.4	25,339	47.7	−1.1

Note: Asians and blacks are those who identify themselves as being of the race alone and not Hispanic. The multiracial are not Hispanic.
Source: National Center for Education Statistics, Projections of Education Statistics to 2021, Internet site http://nces.ed.gov/ programs/projections/projections2021/; calculations by New Strategist

Fewer Students Are Dropping Out of High School

The dropout rate is still high among Hispanics, however.

Among people aged 16 to 24 in 2011, only 7.1 percent were neither high school graduates nor currently enrolled in school, down from 10.9 percent in 2000. Since 2000, the dropout rate has fallen for both men and women and for every racial and ethnic group.

The dropout rate remains high for Hispanics. While just 5.0 percent of whites and 7.3 percent of blacks aged 16 to 24 have dropped out of high school, a much larger 13.6 percent of Hispanics are high school dropouts. Among Hispanic men, the dropout rate was 14.6 percent in 2011, down sharply from 31.8 in 2000. Among Hispanic women aged 16 to 24, a smaller 12.4 percent were high school dropouts in 2011, down from 23.5 percent in 2000.

■ The arrival of millions of poorly educated immigrants to the United States during the past decade explains the high dropout rate among Hispanics. Some did not, in fact, "drop out" of an American high school, but arrived in the United States without a high school diploma.

Non-Hispanic whites have the lowest dropout rate

(percent of people aged 16 to 24 who were neither enrolled in school nor high school graduates, by race and Hispanic origin, 2011)

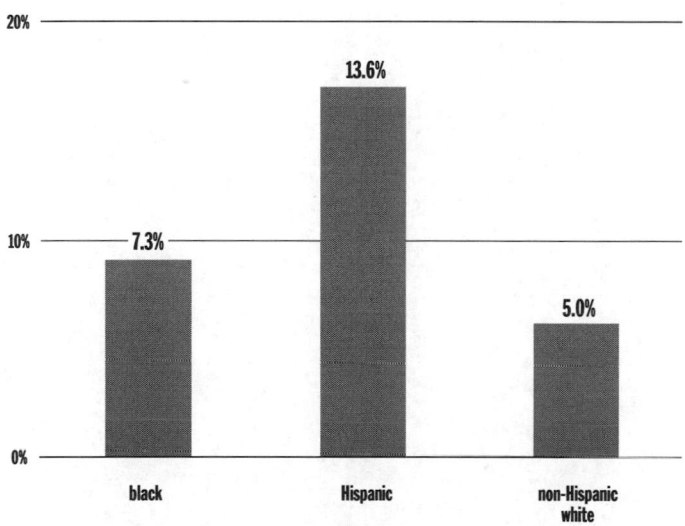

Table 2.20 High School Dropouts by Sex, Race, and Hispanic Origin, 2000 and 2011

(percentage of people aged 16 to 24 who were not enrolled in school and were not high school graduates by sex, race, and Hispanic origin, 2000 and 2011; percentage point change, 2000–11)

	2011	2000	percentage point change
Total people	**7.1%**	**10.9%**	**–3.8**
Black	7.3	13.1	–5.8
Hispanic	13.6	27.8	–14.2
Non-Hispanic white	5.0	6.9	–1.9
Total men	**7.7**	**12.0**	**–4.3**
Black	8.3	15.3	–7.0
Hispanic	14.6	31.8	–17.2
Non-Hispanic white	5.4	7.0	–1.6
Total women	**6.5**	**9.9**	**–3.4**
Black	6.4	11.1	–4.7
Hispanic	12.4	23.5	–11.1
Non-Hispanic white	4.6	6.9	–2.3

Note: Blacks are those who identify themselves as being of the race alone.
Source: National Center for Education Statistics, Digest of Education Statistics: 2012, Internet site http://nces.ed.gov/programs/digest/2012menu_tables.asp; calculations by New Strategist

Stability in High School Graduates

The number of people graduating from high school will barely change between 2011–12 and 2021–22.

The number of high school graduates is projected to remain stable at about 3.3 to 3.4 million a year between 2011–12 and 2021–22. The number of public high school graduates will increase by 3 percent during those years, however, while the number of private high school graduates is projected to fall by a substantial 20 percent.

Among public high school graduates, the number of non-Hispanic whites is projected to fall by 5 percent between 2011–12 and 2021–22. The non-Hispanic white share of public high school graduates will shrink from 59 to 54 percent. Hispanics will account for nearly one in four public high school graduates in 2021–22.

■ Fewer than 9 percent of the nation's high school graduates attend private school, a figure that is projected to decline to 7 percent by 2021–22.

Little change is forecast in the total number of high school graduates

(number of high school graduates, 2011–12 and 2021–22)

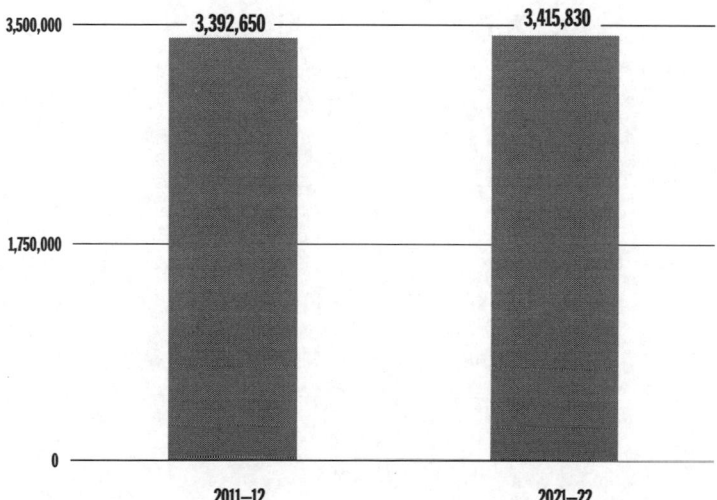

	2011–12	2021–22
	3,392,650	3,415,830

Table 2.21 Projections of High School Graduates by Control of School, 2011–12 to 2021–22

(number of students graduating from high school by control of institution, and percent graduating from private high schools, 2011–12 to 2021–22; percent change and percentage point change, 2011–12 to 2021–22)

| | | | private | |
	total	public	number	percent
2011–12	3,392,650	3,100,510	292,140	8.6%
2012–13	3,375,660	3,092,290	283,370	8.4
2013–14	3,314,600	3,037,040	277,560	8.4
2014–15	3,307,080	3,043,290	263,790	8.0
2015–16	3,325,230	3,066,000	259,230	7.8
2016–17	3,347,990	3,096,730	251,260	7.5
2017–18	3,396,230	3,148,670	247,560	7.3
2018–19	3,396,260	3,155,320	240,940	7.1
2019–20	3,368,740	3,136,780	231,960	6.9
2020–21	3,392,510	3,163,350	229,160	6.8
2021–22	3,415,830	3,183,360	232,470	6.8

| | | | | percentage point change |
PERCENT CHANGE				
2011–12 to 2021–22	0.7%	2.7%	–20.4%	–1.8

Source: National Center for Education Statistics, Projections of Education Statistics to 2021, Internet site http://nces.ed.gov/ programs/projections/projections2021/; calculations by New Strategist

Table 2.22 Projections of Public High School Graduates by Race and Hispanic Origin, 2011–12 to 2021–22

(number of people graduating from public high school by race and Hispanic origin, and percent distribution by race and Hispanic origin, 2011–12 to 2021–22; percent change 2011–12 to 2021–22)

	total	American Indians	Asians	blacks	Hispanics	non-Hispanic whites
2011–12	3,100,510	33,080	174,840	505,250	564,160	1,823,190
2012–13	3,092,290	31,920	179,630	490,850	585,520	1,804,370
2013–14	3,037,040	30,010	179,900	463,570	582,940	1,780,630
2014–15	3,043,290	30,060	184,100	468,630	604,550	1,755,950
2015–16	3,066,000	31,220	182,960	467,850	622,060	1,761,910
2016–17	3,096,730	31,420	188,610	471,260	642,440	1,763,000
2017–18	3,148,670	31,570	201,290	478,830	667,990	1,768,990
2018–19	3,155,320	31,730	201,780	474,540	692,820	1,754,460
2019–20	3,136,780	31,840	206,420	466,060	703,310	1,729,150
2020–21	3,163,350	32,140	216,380	456,850	722,570	1,735,420
2021–22	3,183,360	32,190	222,420	456,020	741,310	1,731,420

PERCENT CHANGE

2011–12 to 2021–22	2.7%	–2.7%	27.2%	–9.7%	31.4%	–5.0%

PERCENT DISTRIBUTION BY RACE AND HISPANIC ORIGIN

2011–12	100.0	1.1	5.6	16.3	18.2	58.8
2012–13	100.0	1.0	5.8	15.9	18.9	58.4
2013–14	100.0	1.0	5.9	15.3	19.2	58.6
2014–15	100.0	1.0	6.0	15.4	19.9	57.7
2015–16	100.0	1.0	6.0	15.3	20.3	57.5
2016–17	100.0	1.0	6.1	15.2	20.7	56.9
2017–18	100.0	1.0	6.4	15.2	21.2	56.2
2018–19	100.0	1.0	6.4	15.0	22.0	55.6
2019–20	100.0	1.0	6.6	14.9	22.4	55.1
2020–21	100.0	1.0	6.8	14.4	22.8	54.9
2021–22	100.0	1.0	7.0	14.3	23.3	54.4

Note: Asians and blacks are those who identify themselves as being of the race alone and not Hispanic.
Source: National Center for Education Statistics, Projections of Education Statistics to 2021, Internet site http://nces.ed.gov/programs/projections/projections2021/; calculations by New Strategist

SAT Scores Vary by Income and Parent's Education

The more educated the parent, the higher the child's score.

It is well known that SAT scores vary by race and Hispanic origin. Asians and whites get higher scores than blacks or Hispanics. It is also no surprise that students with the best grades get the biggest scores. Students with an A+ GPA (97 to 100) averaged a 620 out of 800 on the math section of the SAT in 2011–12, for example. Students with a B GPA (80 to 89) scored a much lower 478 on the math section of the test.

SAT scores also vary by family income and parental education. Students with family incomes below $20,000 scored a 461 on the math portion of the SAT in 2011–12 compared with a score of 589 among students with family incomes of $200,000 or more. Parental education also has a big impact on test scores. Among students with a parent who did not graduate from high school, the average SAT math score was 450. Among those whose parent had a graduate degree, the average math score was 577.

■ Affluent, educated parents can afford SAT prep courses for their children, which can boost test scores.

Parent's education influences child's test score

(average SAT mathematics score by highest level of parental education, 2011–12)

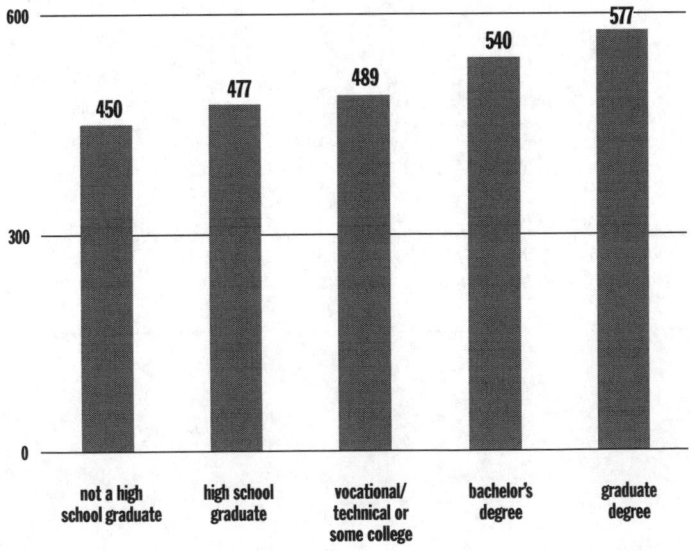

Table 2.23 SAT Scores by Selected Characteristics, 2011–12

(SAT scores of college-bound seniors by selected student and parent characteristics, 2011–12)

	critical reading	mathematics	writing
Total students	**496**	**514**	**488**
Sex			
Men	498	532	481
Women	493	499	494
Race and Hispanic origin			
American Indian or Alaska Native	482	489	462
Asian or Pacific Islander	518	595	528
Black	428	428	417
Mexican American	448	465	443
Puerto Rican	452	452	442
Other Hispanic	447	461	442
White	527	536	515
High school grade point average			
A+ (97 to 100)	593	620	593
A (93 to 96)	557	581	554
A– (90 to 92)	524	545	518
B (80 to 89)	466	478	455
C (70 to 79)	414	421	400
D or F (below 70)	411	429	399
Family income			
Less than $20,000	433	461	428
$20,000 to $39,999	463	481	453
$40,000 o $59,999	485	500	473
$60,000 to $79,999	499	512	486
$80,000 to $99,999	511	525	499
$100,000 to $119,999	523	539	512
$120,000 to $139,999	527	543	517
$140,000 by $159,999	534	551	525
$160,000 to $199,999	540	557	534
$200,000 or more	567	589	566
Highest level of parental education			
Not a high school graduate	420	450	418
High school graduate	463	477	452
Associate's degree	479	489	465
Bachelor's degree	522	540	513
Graduate degree	560	577	555

Source: National Center for Education Statistics, Digest of Education Statistics: 2012, Internet site http://nces.ed.gov/programs/digest/2012menu_tables.asp; calculations by New Strategist

College Enrollment Rates Are below Their Peak

Among Hispanics, however, the rate has never been higher.

The rate at which high school graduates enroll in college peaked in 2009 and was slightly below that level in 2011. Among men and women aged 16 to 24 who graduated from high school in 2011, 68 percent enrolled in college (either two-year or four-year schools) within 12 months. Women's 2011 enrollment rate of 72.2 percent was higher than in 2000, but below the all-time high of 74.0 percent in 2010. Men's college enrollment rate grew over the decade, but the 64.7 percent rate of 2011 was slightly below the peak rate of 66.5 in 2005.

The 2011 college enrollment rate of blacks (67.1 percent) was below the 2009 peak of 69.5 percent. Among non-Hispanic whites, the 68.3 percent enrollment rate was well below the 73.2 percent high reached in 2005, and the Asian rate of 86.1 percent was also down from its 2009 peak of 92.1 percent. In contrast, the Hispanic enrollment rate of 66.6 percent in 2011 was at a record high.

■ The economic downturn spurred more young adults to go to college in an attempt to boost their credentials for the job market. With the economy improving, slightly fewer are enrolling in school.

Enrollment rate was lower in 2011 than in 2009

(percent of people aged 16 to 24 who graduated from high school in the previous 12 months and were enrolled in college as of October, 2000 to 2011)

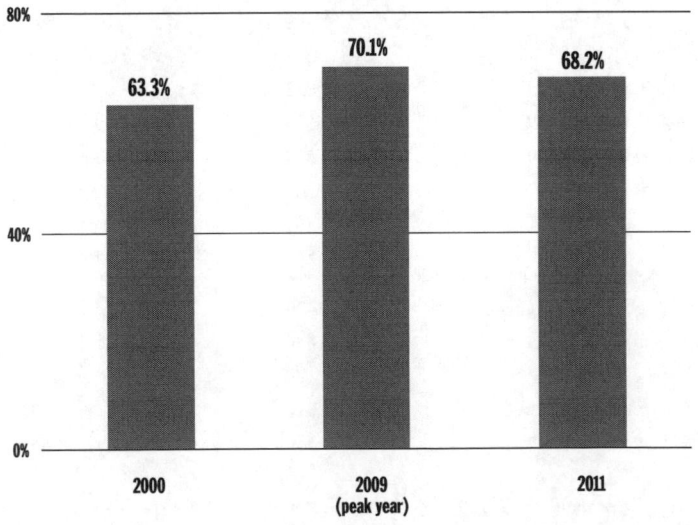

Table 2.24 College Enrollment Rate by Sex, 2000 to 2011

(percentage of people aged 16 to 24 who graduated from high school in the previous 12 months and were enrolled in college as of October, by sex, 2000 to 2011; percentage point change in enrollment rate, 2000–11)

	total	men	women
2011	68.2%	64.7%	72.2%
2010	68.1	62.8	74.0
2009	70.1	66.0	73.8
2008	68.6	65.9	71.6
2007	67.2	66.1	68.3
2006	66.0	65.8	66.1
2005	68.6	66.5	70.4
2004	66.7	61.4	71.5
2003	63.9	61.2	66.5
2002	65.2	62.1	68.3
2001	61.7	59.7	63.6
2000	63.3	59.9	66.2

PERCENTAGE POINT CHANGE

2000 to 2011	4.9	4.8	6.0

Source: National Center for Education Statistics, Digest of Education Statistics 2012, Internet site http://nces.ed.gov/programs/ digest/2012menu_tables.asp; calculations by New Strategist

Table 2.25 College Enrollment Rate by Race and Hispanic Origin, 2000 to 2011

(percentage of people aged 16 to 24 who graduated from high school in the previous 12 months and were enrolled in college as of October, by race and Hispanic origin, 2000 to 2011; percentage point change in enrollment rate, 2000–11)

	total	Asian	black	Hispanic	non-Hispanic white
2011	68.2%	86.1%	67.1%	66.6%	68.3%
2010	68.1	84.7	62.0	59.7	70.5
2009	70.1	92.1	69.5	59.3	71.3
2008	68.6	88.4	55.7	63.9	71.7
2007	67.2	88.8	55.7	64.0	69.5
2006	66.0	82.3	55.5	57.9	68.5
2005	68.6	86.7	55.7	54.0	73.2
2004	66.7	75.6	62.5	61.8	68.8
2003	63.9	84.1	57.5	58.6	66.2
2002	65.2	–	59.4	53.6	69.1
2001	61.7	–	55.0	51.7	64.3
2000	63.3	–	54.9	52.9	65.7

PERCENTAGE POINT CHANGE

	total	Asian	black	Hispanic	non-Hispanic white
2000 to 2011	4.9	–	12.2	13.7	2.6

Note: "–" means data are not available.
Source: National Center for Education Statistics, Digest of Education Statistics 2012, Internet site http://nces.ed.gov/programs/digest/2012menu_tables.asp; calculations by New Strategist

College Costs Have Grown by More than One-Third

The increasing cost of college makes it harder for students to avoid debt.

Between 2000–01 and 2011–12, the average annual cost of attending a four-year college (including tuition, fees, room, and board) grew by 37 percent, after adjusting for inflation. In 2000–01, the cost of one year of college was $16,795. By 2011–12, the price had escalated to $23,066.

The cost of attending a public college grew 49 percent between 2000–01 and 2011–12 (to $16,789), after adjusting for inflation. Private nonprofit college costs rose by a smaller 32 percent (to $37,906) during those years. The cost of attending a private nonprofit four-year school fell slightly over the past decade.

Half of first-time, full-time undergraduates take out student loans to pay for their education, the proportion rising from 40 to 50 percent between 2000–01 and 2011–12. At private for-profit four-year schools, the figure reaches as high as 83 percent. It is 64 percent for their counterparts at private nonprofit schools and 51 percent at public four-year schools.

■ The burden of student loans is hurting the automotive and housing industries, preventing young adults from buying cars and homes until their loans are paid off.

Cost of one year of college exceeds $23,000

(average annual tuition, fees, room, and board for undergraduate programs at four-year institutions, 2000–01 and 2011–12; in 2011–12 dollars)

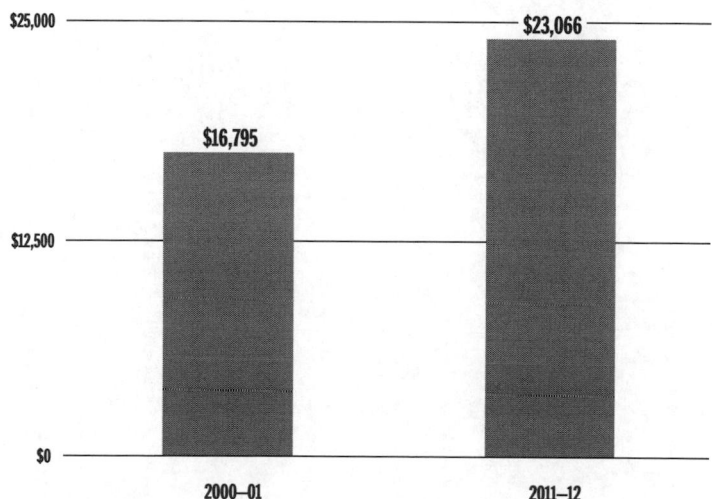

Table 2.26 College Costs, 2000–01 to 2011–12

(average annual tuition, fees, room, and board for undergraduate programs at four-year institutions, by control of school, 2000–01 to 2011–12, percent change in cost, 2000–01 to 2011–12; in 2011–12 dollars)

	total institutions	public institutions	private nonprofit	private for-profit
2011–12	$23,066	$16,789	$37,906	$23,364
2010–11	22,740	16,384	37,430	23,993
2009–10	22,147	15,764	36,813	24,733
2008–09	21,636	15,119	35,837	25,917
2007–08	20,813	14,435	34,452	26,963
2006–07	20,591	14,266	33,800	27,545
2005–06	19,957	13,847	32,812	26,560
2004–05	19,599	13,564	32,355	27,797
2003–04	18,961	13,053	31,615	26,760
2002–03	18,043	12,230	30,548	25,041
2001–02	17,418	11,744	29,701	25,251
2000–01	16,795	11,247	28,814	23,681

PERCENT CHANGE

2000–01 to 2011–12	37.3%	49.3%	31.6%	–1.3%

Source: National Center for Education Statistics, Digest of Education Statistics: 2012, Internet site http://nces.ed.gov/programs/digest/2012menu_tables.asp; calculations by New Strategist

Table 2.27 Student Borrowing, 2000–01 to 2010–11

(percent of full-time, first-time degree/certificate-seeking undergraduate students enrolled in degree-granting institutions who received student loans, by type and control of institution, 2000–01 to 2010–11)

	all institutions	public		private nonprofit		private for-profit	
		four-year	two-year	four-year	two-year	four-year	two-year
2010–11	50.1%	51.5%	24.8%	64.3%	65.2%	82.8%	81.5%
2009–10	51.1	50.0	23.7	63.0	58.6	86.1	77.5
2008–09	48.6	46.9	21.1	60.6	58.1	81.4	77.5
2007–08	45.6	45.2	19.4	60.3	54.1	68.7	77.9
2006–07	43.5	43.8	19.6	59.4	53.5	52.0	76.4
2005–06	44.6	44.4	19.0	59.8	55.9	67.2	73.4
2000–01	40.1	40.7	15.3	58.1	49.5	57.7	67.3

Note: Student loans include only loans made directly to students, not loans to parents.
Source: National Center for Education Statistics, Digest of Education Statistics: 2012, Internet site http://nces.ed.gov/programs/digest/2012menu_tables.asp; calculations by New Strategist

College Enrollment Is Declining

Enrollment in four-year colleges fell 5 percent between 2011 and 2012.

Between 2000 and 2012, the number of students enrolled in college—from two-year schools through graduate school—climbed 30 percent, peaking at 20.4 million in 2011. Between 2011 and 2012, enrollment fell 2 percent. Four-year schools accounted for most of the decline, their enrollment falling by 5 percent. Enrollment at two-year schools increased by 2 percent between 2011 and 2012, and enrollment in graduate school fell by a small 0.3 percent.

On the nation's college campuses, women outnumber men by a wide margin. In 2012, women accounted for 57 percent of college students. Full-time students are in the majority at every level of college from two-year schools through graduate school. Part-timers are least likely to be found at four-year schools, where only 17 percent of students attend part-time.

■ With the economy in recovery from the Great Recession, it is no surprise that college enrollment is declining. Many young adults were in school because they could not find a job.

Most students at four-year schools are in the 20-to-24 age group

(percent distribution of students attending four-year institutions, by age, 2012)

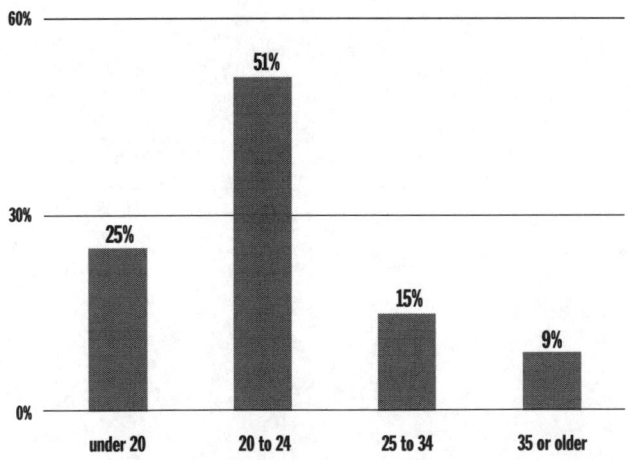

Table 2.28 College Enrollment by Type of School, 2000 to 2012

(number of students aged 14 or older enrolled in college by type of school, 2000 to 2012; percent change in enrollment for selected years; numbers in thousands)

	total students	two-year colleges	four-year colleges	graduate schools
2012	19,930	5,830	10,340	3,760
2011	20,398	5,705	10,920	3,773
2010	20,275	5,904	10,450	3,921
2009	19,764	5,551	10,461	3,752
2008	18,631	5,345	9,610	3,676
2007	17,955	4,814	9,550	3,591
2006	17,232	4,294	9,560	3,378
2005	17,473	4,327	9,842	3,304
2004	17,382	4,340	9,664	3,378
2003	16,638	4,384	8,986	3,268
2002	16,498	4,378	9,048	3,072
2001	15,873	4,159	8,393	3,321
2000	15,314	3,881	8,520	2,913

PERCENT CHANGE

2011 to 2012	−2.3%	2.2%	−5.3%	−0.3%
2000 to 2012	30.1	50.2	21.4	29.1

Source: Bureau of the Census, School Enrollment, Historical Tables, Internet site http://www.census.gov/hhes/school/data/cps/ historical/index.html; calculations by New Strategist

Table 2.29 Enrollment in Four-Year Colleges by Control of School, 2000 to 2012

(number of students aged 14 or older enrolled in four-year colleges by control of school, 2000 to 2012; percent change in enrollment for selected years; numbers in thousands)

	total students	public colleges	private colleges
2012	10,340	8,074	2,266
2011	10,920	8,551	2,369
2010	10,450	8,251	2,199
2009	10,461	8,261	2,200
2008	9,610	7,334	2,277
2007	9,550	7,393	2,158
2006	9,560	7,391	2,169
2005	9,842	7,402	2,439
2004	9,664	7,445	2,219
2003	8,986	6,981	2,004
2002	9,048	6,882	2,164
2001	8,393	6,439	1,954
2000	8,520	6,454	2,066
PERCENT CHANGE			
2011 to 2012	−5.3%	−5.6%	−4.3%
2000 to 2012	21.4	25.1	9.7

Source: Bureau of the Census, School Enrollment, Historical Tables, Internet site http://www.census.gov/hhes/school/data/cps/ historical/index.html; calculations by New Strategist

Table 2.30 College Students by Age and Sex, 2012

(number and percent distribution of people aged 15 or older enrolled in institutions of higher education, by age and sex, 2012; numbers in thousands)

	total	male	female
Total college students	**19,930**	**8,602**	**11,327**
Under age 20	4,284	1,933	2,351
Aged 20 to 21	4,562	2,049	2,513
Aged 22 to 24	3,879	1,878	2,001
Aged 25 to 29	2,817	1,194	1,623
Aged 30 to 34	1,516	576	940
Aged 35 or older	2,871	971	1,899
PERCENT DISTRIBUTION BY SEX			
Total college students	**100.0%**	**43.2%**	**56.8%**
Under age 20	100.0	45.1	54.9
Aged 20 to 21	100.0	44.9	55.1
Aged 22 to 24	100.0	48.4	51.6
Aged 25 to 29	100.0	42.4	57.6
Aged 30 to 34	100.0	38.0	62.0
Aged 35 or older	100.0	33.8	66.1
PERCENT DISTRIBUTION BY AGE			
Total college students	**100.0**	**100.0**	**100.0**
Under age 20	21.5	22.5	20.8
Aged 20 to 21	22.9	23.8	22.2
Aged 22 to 24	19.5	21.8	17.7
Aged 25 to 29	14.1	13.9	14.3
Aged 30 to 34	7.6	6.7	8.3
Aged 35 or older	14.4	11.3	16.8

Source: Bureau of the Census, School Enrollment, Historical Tables, Internet site http://www.census.gov/hhes/school/data/cps/ historical/index.html; calculations by New Strategist

Table 2.31 College Students by Age and Type of School, 2012

(number and percent distribution of people aged 15 or older enrolled in institutions of higher education, by age and type of school, 2012; numbers in thousands)

	total	two-year	four-year	graduate school
Total college students	**19,930**	**5,830**	**10,340**	**3,760**
Under age 20	4,284	1,624	2,612	49
Aged 20 to 24	8,441	2,199	5,246	997
Aged 25 to 34	4,333	1,205	1,578	1,550
Aged 35 or older	2,872	802	904	1,165
PERCENT DISTRIBUTION BY TYPE OF SCHOOL				
Total college students	**100.0%**	**29.3%**	**51.9%**	**18.9%**
Under age 20	100.0	37.9	61.0	1.1
Aged 20 to 24	100.0	26.1	62.1	11.8
Aged 25 to 34	100.0	27.8	36.4	35.8
Aged 35 or older	100.0	27.9	31.5	40.6
PERCENT DISTRIBUTION BY AGE				
Total college students	**100.0**	**100.0**	**100.0**	**100.0**
Under age 20	21.5	27.9	25.3	1.3
Aged 20 to 24	42.4	37.7	50.7	26.5
Aged 25 to 34	21.7	20.7	15.3	41.2
Aged 35 or older	14.4	13.8	8.7	31.0

Source: Bureau of the Census, School Enrollment, CPS October 2012—Detailed Tables, Internet site http://www.census.gov/ hhes/school/data/cps/2012/tables.html; calculations by New Strategist

Table 2.32 College Students by Attendance Status and Type of School, 2012

(number and percent distribution of people aged 15 or older enrolled in institutions of higher education, by type of school and attendance status, 2012; numbers in thousands)

	total	two-year	four-year	graduate school
Total college students	**19,930**	**5,830**	**10,340**	**3,760**
Full-time students	14,602	3,784	8,607	2,211
Part-time students	5,328	2,046	1,734	1,549
PERCENT DISTRIBUTION BY TYPE OF SCHOOL				
Total college students	**100.0%**	**29.3%**	**51.9%**	**18.9%**
Full-time students	100.0	25.9	58.9	15.1
Part-time students	100.0	38.4	32.5	29.1
PERCENT DISTRIBUTION BY ATTENDANCE STATUS				
Total college students	**100.0**	**100.0**	**100.0**	**100.0**
Full-time students	73.3	64.9	83.2	58.8
Part-time students	26.7	35.1	16.8	41.2

Source: Bureau of the Census, School Enrollment, CPS October 2012—Detailed Tables, Internet site http://www.census.gov/hhes/school/data/cps/2012/tables.html; calculations by New Strategist

More than 40 Percent of College Students Are Minorities

Among the nation's 20 million college students, 8 million are Asian, black, Hispanic, or another minority.

College campuses are becoming more diverse. Non-Hispanic whites accounted for only 58 percent of college students in 2012, down from 69 percent in 2000. Among students at two-year schools, 49 percent are minorities. At four-year schools, the minority share is a smaller 39 percent.

Non-Hispanic whites received about two-thirds of college degrees awarded in 2010–11. Blacks receive a larger share of associate's, bachelor's, or master's degrees than Hispanics or Asians. In 2010–11, blacks received 14 percent of associate's degrees, 10 percent of bachelor's degrees, and 11 percent of master's degrees. At the doctoral and first-professional level, Asians earn a larger share of degrees (10 percent) than blacks (7 percent).

■ Blacks account for more than one in five college students aged 30 or older.

Blacks, Hispanics, and Asians account for a substantial share of college students

(percent distribution of college students by race and Hispanic origin, 2012)

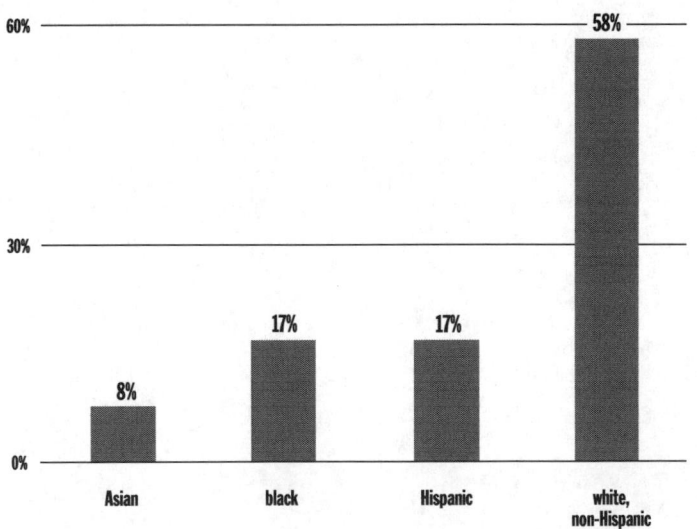

Table 2.33 College Enrollment by Race and Hispanic Origin, 2000 to 2012

(number and percent distribution of students aged 14 or older enrolled in college by race and Hispanic origin, 2000 to 2012; percent change, 2000–12; numbers in thousands)

	total students	non-Hispanic white	minority
2012	19,930	11,650	8,280
2011	20,398	12,703	7,695
2010	20,275	12,613	7,662
2009	19,764	12,825	6,939
2008	18,631	12,325	6,306
2007	17,955	11,867	6,088
2006	17,232	11,485	5,747
2005	17,473	11,715	5,758
2004	17,382	11,571	5,811
2003	16,638	11,295	5,343
2002	16,498	11,236	5,262
2001	15,873	10,602	5,271
2000	15,314	10,636	4,678

PERCENT CHANGE

2000 to 2012	30.1%	9.5%	77.0%

PERCENT DISTRIBUTION BY RACE AND HISPANIC ORIGIN

2012	100.0	58.5	41.5
2011	100.0	62.3	37.7
2010	100.0	62.2	37.8
2009	100.0	64.9	35.1
2008	100.0	66.2	33.8
2007	100.0	66.1	33.9
2006	100.0	66.6	33.4
2005	100.0	67.0	33.0
2004	100.0	66.6	33.4
2003	100.0	67.9	32.1
2002	100.0	68.1	31.9
2001	100.0	66.8	33.2
2000	100.0	69.5	30.5

Note: Minority students are American Indians, Asians, blacks, people of other race, and Hispanics.
Source: Bureau of the Census, School Enrollment, Historical Tables, Internet site http://www.census.gov/hhes/school/data/cps/historical/index.html; calculations by New Strategist

Table 2.34 College Students by Age, Race, and Hispanic Origin, 2012

(number and percent distribution of people aged 15 or older enrolled in institutions of higher education, by age, race, and Hispanic origin, 2012; numbers in thousands)

	total	Asian	black	Hispanic	non-Hispanic white
Total college students	**19,930**	**1,617**	**3,335**	**3,400**	**11,650**
Under age 20	4,284	307	612	888	2,513
Aged 20 to 21	4,562	348	721	912	2,620
Aged 22 to 24	3,879	421	592	664	2,207
Aged 25 to 29	2,817	266	465	365	1,734
Aged 30 to 34	1,516	124	348	257	778
Aged 35 or older	2,871	151	598	313	1,799

PERCENT DISTRIBUTION BY RACE AND HISPANIC ORIGIN

Total college students	**100.0%**	**8.1%**	**16.7%**	**17.1%**	**58.5%**
Under age 20	100.0	7.2	14.3	20.7	58.7
Aged 20 to 21	100.0	7.6	15.8	20.0	57.4
Aged 22 to 24	100.0	10.9	15.3	17.1	56.9
Aged 25 to 29	100.0	9.4	16.5	13.0	61.6
Aged 30 to 34	100.0	8.2	23.0	17.0	51.3
Aged 35 or older	100.0	5.3	20.8	10.9	62.7

PERCENT DISTRIBUTION BY AGE

Total college students	**100.0**	**100.0**	**100.0**	**100.0**	**100.0**
Under age 20	21.5	19.0	18.4	26.1	21.6
Aged 20 to 21	22.9	21.5	21.6	26.8	22.5
Aged 22 to 24	19.5	26.0	17.8	19.5	18.9
Aged 25 to 29	14.1	16.5	13.9	10.7	14.9
Aged 30 to 34	7.6	7.7	10.4	7.6	6.7
Aged 35 or older	14.4	9.3	17.9	9.2	15.4

Note: Asians and blacks are those who identify themselves as being of the race alone and those who identify themselves as being of the race in combination with other races.
Source: Bureau of the Census, School Enrollment, Historical Tables, Internet site http://www.census.gov/hhes/school/data/cps/historical/index.html; calculations by New Strategist

Table 2.35 College Students by Type of School, Race, and Hispanic Origin, 2012

(number and percent distribution of people aged 15 or older enrolled in institutions of higher education, by type of school, race, and Hispanic origin, 2012; numbers in thousands)

	total	Asian	black	Hispanic	non-Hispanic white
Total college students	**19,930**	**1,617**	**3,335**	**3,400**	**11,650**
Two-year schools	5,830	321	1,076	1,381	2,951
Four-year schools	10,340	676	1,425	1,652	6,358
Graduate schools	3,760	451	537	367	2,340

PERCENT DISTRIBUTION BY RACE AND HISPANIC ORIGIN

Total college students	**100.0%**	**8.1%**	**16.7%**	**17.1%**	**58.5%**
Two-year schools	100.0	5.5	18.5	23.7	50.6
Four-year schools	100.0	6.5	13.8	16.0	61.5
Graduate schools	100.0	12.0	14.3	9.8	62.2

PERCENT DISTRIBUTION BY A TYPE OF SCHOOL

Total college students	**100.0**	**100.0**	**100.0**	**100.0**	**100.0**
Two-year schools	29.3	22.2	35.4	40.6	25.3
Four-year schools	51.9	46.7	46.9	48.6	54.6
Graduate schools	18.9	31.2	17.7	10.8	20.1

Note: Asians and blacks are those who identify themselves as being of the race alone.
Source: Bureau of the Census, School Enrollment, Historical Tables, Internet site http://www.census.gov/hhes/school/data/cps/ historical/index.html; calculations by New Strategist

Table 2.36 Degrees Conferred by Race and Hispanic Origin, 2010–11

(number and percent distribution of degrees conferred by institutions of higher education by level of degree, race, and Hispanic origin of degree holder, 2010–11)

	total	Asian	black	Hispanic	non-Hispanic white
Total degrees	**3,552,640**	**227,748**	**393,351**	**335,116**	**2,355,350**
Associate's degrees	942,327	45,876	128,703	125,616	604,110
Bachelor's degrees	1,715,913	121,066	173,017	154,063	1,182,405
Master's degrees	730,635	43,728	80,706	46,787	462,903
Doctoral and first-professional degrees	163,765	17,078	10,925	8,650	105,932

PERCENT DISTRIBUTION BY RACE AND HISPANIC ORIGIN

Total degrees	**100.0%**	**6.4%**	**11.1%**	**9.4%**	**66.3%**
Associate's degrees	100.0	4.9	13.7	13.3	64.1
Bachelor's degrees	100.0	7.1	10.1	9.0	68.9
Master's degrees	100.0	6.0	11.0	6.4	63.4
Doctoral and first-professional degrees	100.0	10.4	6.7	5.3	64.7

Note: Numbers do not add to total because not all races are shown, nor are degrees awarded to nonresident aliens.
Source: National Center for Education Statistics, Digest of Education Statistics 2012, Internet site http://nces.ed.gov/programs/digest/2012menu_tables.asp; calculations by New Strategist

Earning a Bachelor's Degree Often Takes More than Five Years

Women earned more than half of all bachelor's degrees awarded in 2010–11.

Many students spend more than four years getting a bachelor's degree, according to data from the Census Bureau's Survey of Income and Program Participation. In fact, many students spend more than four years earning an associate's degree. Americans aged 18 or older who have a bachelor's degree report having spent an average of 5.6 years working on their degree from start to finish. Those with an associate's degree spent an average of 4.6 years getting their degree from start to finish.

Women now earn most college degrees regardless of degree level, but in many programs men are still in the majority. Women earned only 18 percent of bachelor's degrees in computer and information science and only 19 percent of bachelor's degrees in engineering in 2010–11. But they accounted for 49 percent of bachelor's degrees in business and 80 percent of those in education.

■ Now that the educational attainment of women exceeds that of men in the younger age groups, the earnings gap between women and men should narrow.

Men earn less than half of college degrees

(men's share of degrees awarded, by level of degree, 2010–11)

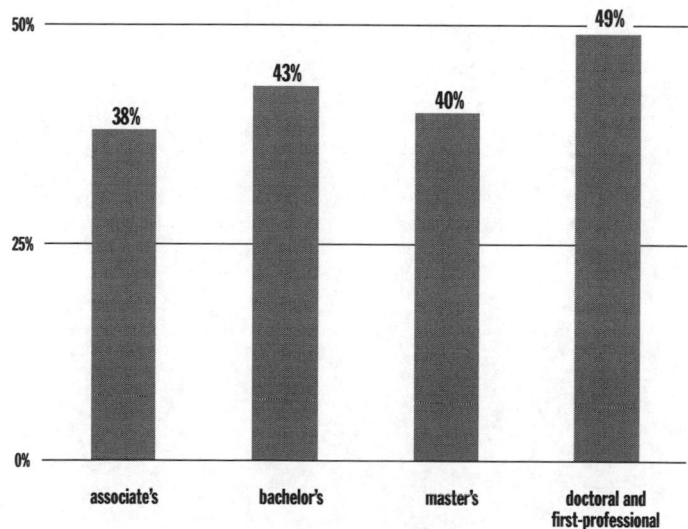

Table 2.37 Average Years to Complete a College Degree, 2009

(average number of years from start of postsecondary education to completion of vocational, associate's, and bachelor's degrees, and average number of years from bachelor's to completion of master's and doctoral degrees, 2009)

	average years
Vocational certificate	1.9 yrs.
Associate's degree	4.6
Bachelor's degree	5.6
Master's degree	7.2
Professional degree	5.7
Doctoral degree	9.3

Source: Bureau of the Census, What's It Worth: Field of Training and Economic Status in 2009, Detailed Tables, Internet site http://www.census.gov/hhes/socdemo/education/data/sipp/2009/tables.html

Table 2.38 Associate's Degrees Earned by Field of Study and Sex, 2010–11

(number of associate's degrees conferred by sex, and percent earned by women, by field of study, 2010–11)

	total	men	women number	women percent of total
Total associate's degrees	**942,327**	**361,309**	**581,018**	**61.7%**
Agriculture and natural resources	6,425	4,089	2,336	36.4
Architecture and related programs	569	310	259	45.5
Area, ethnic, and cultural studies	209	60	149	71.3
Biological and biomedical sciences	3,245	1,116	2,129	65.6
Business	139,986	51,171	88,815	63.4
Communication, journalism, and related programs	3,051	1,411	1,640	53.8
Communications technologies	4,209	2,774	1,435	34.1
Computer and information sciences	37,677	29,060	8,617	22.9
Construction trades	5,402	5,105	297	5.5
Education	20,459	2,733	17,726	86.6
Engineering	2,825	2,426	399	14.1
Engineering technologies	35,521	31,094	4,427	12.5
English language and literature/letters	2,019	647	1,372	68.0
Family and consumer sciences	8,532	358	8,174	95.8
Foreign languages and literatures	1,876	377	1,499	79.9
Health professions and related sciences	201,831	30,073	171,758	85.1
Homeland security, law enforcement, and firefighting	44,923	23,931	20,992	46.7
Legal professions and studies	11,620	1,835	9,785	84.2
Liberal arts and sciences, general studies, and humanities	306,670	118,556	188,114	61.3
Library science	160	21	139	86.9
Mathematics and statistics	1,644	1,024	620	37.7
Mechanic and repair technologies	19,969	18,998	971	4.9
Military technologies	856	693	163	19.0
Multi-/interdisciplinary studies	23,729	8,905	14,824	62.5
Parks, recreation, leisure, and fitness	2,366	1,432	934	39.5
Philosophy and religion	283	177	106	37.5
Physical sciences	5,078	2,958	2,120	41.7
Precision production trades	3,254	3,024	230	7.1
Psychology	3,866	896	2,970	76.8
Public administration and social services	7,472	1,025	6,447	86.3
Social sciences and history	12,767	4,511	8,256	64.7
Theology and religious vocations	758	395	363	47.9
Transportation and material moving	1,697	1,418	279	16.4
Visual and performing arts	21,379	8,706	12,673	59.3

Source: National Center for Education Statistics, Digest of Education Statistics 2012, Internet site http://nces.ed.gov/programs/digest/2012menu_tables.asp; calculations by New Strategist

Table 2.39 Bachelor's Degrees Earned by Field of Study and Sex, 2010–11

(number of bachelor's degrees conferred by sex, and percent earned by women, by field of study, 2010–11)

			women	
	total	men	number	percent of total
Total bachelor's degrees	**1,715,913**	**734,133**	**981,780**	**57.2%**
Agriculture and natural resources	28,623	14,675	13,948	48.7
Architecture and related programs	9,832	5,696	4,136	42.1
Area, ethnic, and cultural studies	9,100	2,801	6,299	69.2
Biological and biomedical sciences	90,003	36,892	53,111	59.0
Business	365,093	187,081	178,012	48.8
Communication, journalism, and related programs	83,274	29,515	53,759	64.6
Communications technologies	4,858	3,508	1,350	27.8
Computer and information sciences	43,072	35,478	7,594	17.6
Construction trades	328	303	25	7.6
Education	103,992	21,195	82,797	79.6
Engineering	76,376	62,119	14,257	18.7
Engineering technologies	16,187	14,469	1,718	10.6
English language and literature/letters	52,744	16,916	35,828	67.9
Family and consumer sciences	22,444	2,762	19,682	87.7
Foreign languages, literatures, and linguistics	21,706	6,720	14,986	69.0
Health professions and related sciences	143,430	21,536	121,894	85.0
Homeland security, law enforcement, and firefighting	47,602	24,361	23,241	48.8
Legal professions and studies	4,429	1,317	3,112	70.3
Liberal arts and sciences, general studies, and humanities	46,727	16,488	30,239	64.7
Library science	96	13	83	86.5
Mathematics and statistics	17,182	9,783	7,399	43.1
Mechanic and repair technologies	226	209	17	7.5
Military technologies	64	50	14	21.9
Multi-/interdisciplinary studies	42,228	13,602	28,626	67.8
Parks, recreation, leisure, and fitness	35,924	18,936	16,988	47.3
Philosophy and religion	12,836	8,149	4,687	36.5
Physical sciences	24,712	14,782	9,930	40.2
Precision production trades	43	22	21	48.8
Psychology	100,893	23,229	77,664	77.0
Public administration and social services	26,774	4,908	21,866	81.7
Social sciences and history	177,144	89,814	87,330	49.3
Theology and religious vocations	9,074	6,118	2,956	32.6
Transportation and material moving	4,941	4,345	596	12.1
Visual and performing arts	93,956	36,341	57,615	61.3

Source: National Center for Education Statistics, Digest of Education Statistics 2012, Internet site http://nces.ed.gov/programs/digest/2012menu_tables.asp; calculations by New Strategist

Table 2.40 Master's Degrees Earned by Field of Study and Sex, 2010–11

(number of master's degrees conferred by sex, and percent earned by women, by field of study, 2010–11)

			women	
	total	men	number	percent of total
Total master's degrees	730,635	291,551	439,084	60.1%
Agriculture and natural resources	5,773	2,750	3,023	52.4
Architecture and related programs	7,788	4,265	3,523	45.2
Area, ethnic, and cultural studies	1,914	723	1,191	62.2
Biological and biomedical sciences	11,327	4,871	6,456	57.0
Business	187,213	101,450	85,763	45.8
Communication, journalism, and related programs	8,303	2,520	5,783	69.6
Communications technologies	502	300	202	40.2
Computer and information sciences	19,446	13,956	5,490	28.2
Education	185,009	42,022	142,987	77.3
Engineering	38,719	30,090	8,629	22.3
Engineering technologies	4,515	3,328	1,187	26.3
English language and literature/letters	9,476	3,137	6,339	66.9
Family and consumer sciences	2,918	395	2,523	86.5
Foreign languages, literatures, and linguistics	3,727	1,256	2,471	66.3
Health professions and related sciences	75,579	14,041	61,538	81.4
Homeland security, law enforcement, and firefighting	7,433	3,416	4,017	54.0
Legal professions and studies	6,300	3,054	3,246	51.5
Liberal arts and sciences, general studies, and humanities	3,971	1,619	2,352	59.2
Library science	7,727	1,483	6,244	80.8
Mathematics and statistics	5,843	3,453	2,390	40.9
Multi-/interdisciplinary studies	6,748	2,561	4,187	62.0
Parks, recreation, leisure, and fitness	6,553	3,585	2,968	45.3
Philosophy and religion	1,833	1,166	667	36.4
Physical sciences	6,386	3,907	2,479	38.8
Precision production trades	5	3	2	40.0
Psychology	25,051	5,118	19,933	79.6
Public administration and social services	38,634	9,793	28,841	74.7
Social sciences and history	21,084	10,578	10,506	49.8
Theology and religious vocations	13,191	8,668	4,523	34.3
Transportation and material moving	1,390	1,161	229	16.5
Visual and performing arts	16,277	6,882	9,395	57.7

Source: National Center for Education Statistics, Digest of Education Statistics 2012, Internet site http://nces.ed.gov/programs/digest/2012menu_tables.asp; calculations by New Strategist

Table 2.41 Doctoral and First-Professional Degrees Earned by Field of Study and Sex, 2010–11

(number of doctoral and first-professional degrees conferred by sex, and percent earned by women, by field of study, 2010–11)

	total	men	women number	women percent of total
Total doctoral and first-professional degrees	**163,765**	**79,654**	**84,111**	**51.4%**
Agriculture and natural resources	1,246	675	571	45.8
Architecture and related programs	205	110	95	46.3
Area, ethnic, and cultural studies	278	116	162	58.3
Biological and biomedical sciences	7,693	3,648	4,045	52.6
Business	2,286	1,357	929	40.6
Communication, journalism, and related programs	577	207	370	64.1
Communications technologies	1	0	1	100.0
Computer and information sciences	1,588	1,267	321	20.2
Education	9,623	3,064	6,559	68.2
Engineering	8,369	6,510	1,859	22.2
Engineering technologies	56	38	18	32.1
English language and literature/letters	1,344	529	815	60.6
Family and consumer sciences	320	59	261	81.6
Foreign languages, literatures, and linguistics	1,158	477	681	58.8
Health professions and related sciences	60,153	25,361	34,792	57.8
Homeland security, law enforcement, and firefighting	131	62	69	52.7
Legal professions and studies	44,877	23,720	21,157	47.1
Liberal arts and sciences, general studies, and humanities	95	40	55	57.9
Library science	50	18	32	64.0
Mathematics and statistics	1,586	1,132	454	28.6
Multi-/interdisciplinary studies	660	276	384	58.2
Parks, recreation, leisure, and fitness	257	140	117	45.5
Philosophy and religion	805	530	275	34.2
Physical sciences	5,295	3,608	1,687	31.9
Psychology	5,851	1,481	4,370	74.7
Public administration and social services	851	327	524	61.6
Social sciences and history	4,390	2,331	2,059	46.9
Theology and religious vocations	2,374	1,801	573	24.1
Visual and performing arts	1,646	770	876	53.2

Source: National Center for Education Statistics, Digest of Education Statistics 2012, Internet site http://nces.ed.gov/programs/digest/2012menu_tables.asp; calculations by New Strategist

3

Health

Trends

Most Americans say their health is very good or excellent.

The share is below 50 percent only among people aged 55 or older.

Weight problems affect the majority of Americans.

Sixty-three percent of the nation's adults are overweight, and 28 percent are obese.

The babies being born today promise great diversity tomorrow.

Of the nearly 4 million babies born in 2012, only 54 percent were born to non-Hispanic whites.

Fifteen percent of Americans do not have health insurance.

The number without health insurance climbed 31 percent between 2000 and 2012, to 48 million.

Many children have asthma.

Fourteen percent of children have been diagnosed with asthma. Seven percent have a learning disability.

Millions of Americans have physical difficulties.

More than one in five Americans aged 65 or older cannot walk a quarter of a mile.

Heart disease and cancer are the biggest killers.

Americans aged 65 or older account for 73 percent of deaths.

Most Americans Feel Very Good or Excellent

Just 17 percent say their health is only fair or poor.

Overall, 52 percent of adults say their health is "very good" or "excellent," ranging from a high of 63 percent among people aged 18 to 24 to a low of 41 percent among people aged 65 or older. Even among the oldest Americans, only 25 percent rate their health as only fair or poor.

Whites are much more likely than blacks or Hispanics to rate their health as very good or excellent. The 56 percent majority of whites say they are in very good or excellent health compared with 44 percent of blacks and only 40 percent of Hispanics. Conversely, Hispanics are most likely to say their health is only fair or poor (25 percent) and whites least likely (15 percent).

■ Men and women are about equally likely to report very good or excellent health.

Most people under age 55 say their health is very good or excellent

(percentage of people aged 18 or older who say their health is "very good" or "excellent," by age, 2012)

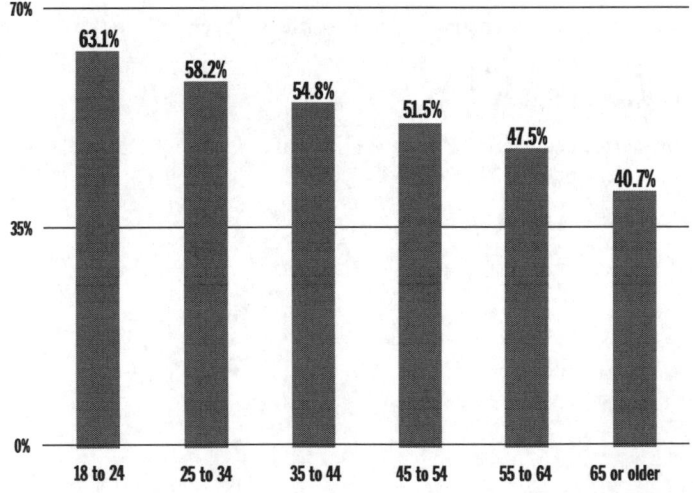

Table 3.1 Health Status by Selected Characteristics, 2012

"How is your general health?"

(percent distribution of people aged 18 or older by health status and selected characteristics, 2012)

| | total | excellent or very good | | | good | fair | poor |
		total	excellent	very good			
Total people	100.0%	52.2%	18.8%	33.4%	30.9%	12.5%	4.4%
Sex							
Men	100.0	51.9	19.3	32.6	30.8	12.0	4.6
Women	100.0	51.2	18.5	32.7	30.9	12.7	4.5
Age							
Aged 18 to 24	100.0	63.1	25.3	37.8	28.8	7.2	0.0
Aged 25 to 34	100.0	58.2	23.5	34.7	30.6	9.0	2.0
Aged 35 to 44	100.0	54.8	20.3	34.5	30.7	10.1	3.5
Aged 45 to 54	100.0	51.5	18.4	33.1	30.0	12.7	5.2
Aged 55 to 64	100.0	47.5	16.0	31.5	30.7	14.7	7.3
Aged 65 or older	100.0	40.7	12.3	28.4	34.1	17.7	7.4
Race and Hispanic origin							
Black	100.0	44.5	17.0	27.5	34.3	16.7	5.3
Hispanic	100.0	40.3	15.6	24.7	35.7	18.6	6.0
White	100.0	55.6	19.4	36.2	29.2	10.8	4.1

Note: Numbers do not add to total because some people did not report their health status.
Source: Centers for Disease Control and Prevention, Behavioral Risk Factor Surveillance System, Prevalence Data, Internet site http://apps.nccd.cdc.gov/brfss/; calculations by New Strategist

Weight Problems Are the Norm

Sixty-three percent of adults are overweight.

Americans have a weight problem. The average man weighed 195.5 pounds in 2007–10, according to a government survey that measures the height and weight of a nationally representative sample of the population. The average woman weighs 166.2 pounds. Weight peaks in the middle and older age groups at more than 200 pounds among men and more than 170 pounds among women.

Sixty-three percent of people aged 18 or older are overweight, according to another survey of self-reported heights and weights. When Americans self-report their weight, however, they often lowball it, so the 63 percent estimate is conservative. Twenty-eight percent of adults are obese, according to body mass index calculations based on self-reported heights and weights. Most men and women are overweight, as is the majority in every age group. By race and Hispanic origin, Asians are the only group in which the majority has a healthy weight. Only 39 percent of Asians are overweight.

■ Most Americans lack the willpower to eat less or exercise more—fueling a diet and weight loss industry that never lacks for customers.

The overweight dominate every age group

(percent of people aged 18 or older who are overweight, by age, 2011)

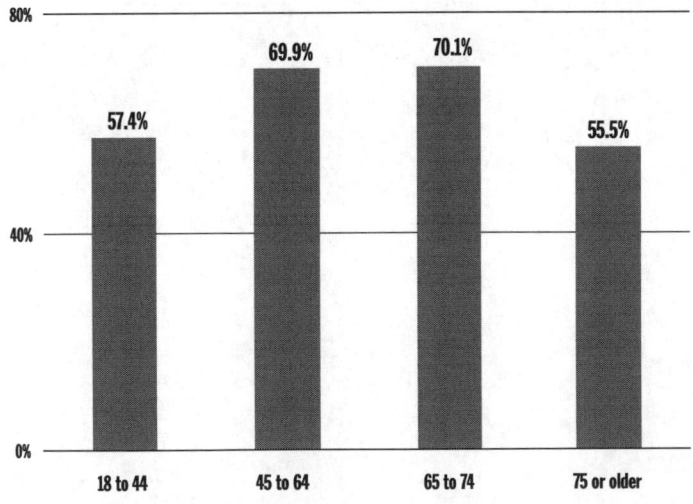

Table 3.2 Weight by Age and Sex, 2007–10

(average measured weight in pounds of people aged 20 or older by age and sex, 2007–10)

	men	women
Total aged 20 or older	**195.5 lbs.**	**166.2 lbs.**
Aged 20 to 29	183.9	161.9
Aged 30 to 39	199.5	169.1
Aged 40 to 49	200.6	168.0
Aged 50 to 59	201.3	170.0
Aged 60 to 69	199.4	170.5
Aged 70 to 79	190.6	164.9
Aged 80 or older	174.9	143.1

Note: Data are based on the measured weight of a representative sample of the civilian noninstitutionalized population.
Source: National Center for Health Statistics, National Health and Nutrition Examination Surveys, Internet site http://www.cdc.gov/nchs/nhanes.htm; calculations by New Strategist

Table 3.3 Weight Status by Selected Characteristics, 2011

(total number of people aged 18 or older and percent distribution by selected characteristics and weight status based on self-reported height and weight, 2011; numbers in thousands)

	total		underweight	healthy weight	overweight	
	number	percent			total	obese
Total people	**231,376**	**100.0%**	**1.6%**	**35.6%**	**62.8%**	**28.3%**
Sex						
Men	112,093	100.0	0.7	30.3	69.1	28.4
Women	119,283	100.0	2.5	42.1	55.4	27.5
Age						
Aged 18 to 44	110,815	100.0	1.8	40.8	57.4	26.2
Aged 45 to 64	80,849	100.0	1.0	29.1	69.9	32.2
Aged 65 to 74	21,902	100.0	1.4	28.5	70.1	31.6
Aged 75 or older	17,810	100.0	3.2	41.2	55.5	19.5
Race and Hispanic origin						
Asian	11,468	100.0	4.2	56.7	39.1	9.3
Black	27,666	100.0	1.0	26.4	72.6	38.9
Hispanic	32,762	100.0	0.9	29.2	69.8	31.8
Non-Hispanic white	156,482	100.0	1.7	38.2	60.1	26.2

Note: "Overweight" is defined as a body mass index of 25 or higher. "Obesity" is defined as a body mass index of 30 or higher. Body mass index is calculated by dividing weight in kilograms by height in meters squared. Data are based on self-reported height and weight of a representative sample of the civilian noninstitutionalized population. Asians and blacks are those who identify themselves as being of the race alone. Non-Hispanic whites are those who identify themselves as being white alone and not Hispanic.
Source: National Center for Health Statistics, Summary Health Statistics for U.S. Adults: National Health Interview Survey, 2011, Vital and Health Statistics, Series 10, No. 256, 2012, Internet site http://www.cdc.gov/nchs/nhis.htm; calculations by New Strategist

Most Americans Do Not Get Enough Exercise

Many do not meet federal guidelines.

One reason Americans are gaining weight is that many do not get enough exercise. Nearly half of adults do not meet federal guidelines for aerobic and muscle-strengthening activities.

The percentage of adults who do not meet federal guidelines for aerobic and muscle-strengthening activities rises with age. The 59 percent majority of 18-to-44-year-olds meet at least one guideline and 26 percent meet both guidelines. Among Americans aged 45 or older, however, fewer than half meet either guideline and less than 20 percent meet both guidelines. By race and Hispanic origin, non-Hispanic whites are the only group that meets at least one physical activity guideline.

■ Government efforts to get people to eat less and exercise more have so far failed to change people's lifestyles.

Young adults are most likely to meet federal physical activity guidelines

(percentage of people aged 18 or older who met one or both federal guidelines for aerobic and muscle-strengthening activities, by age, 2011)

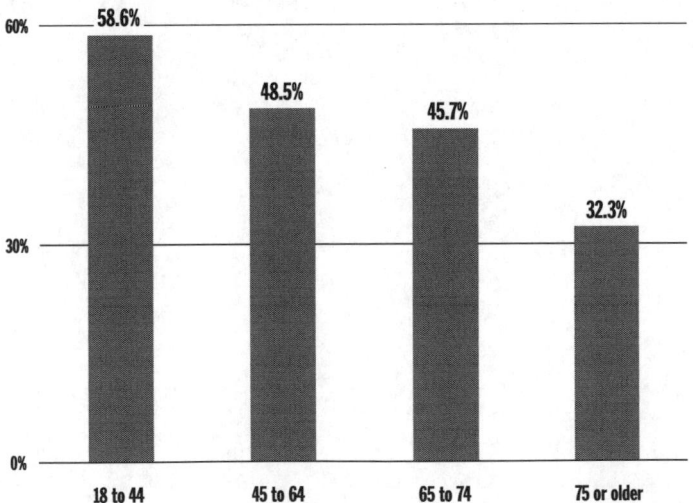

Table 3.4 Physical Activity Status by Selected Characteristics, 2011

(number of people aged 18 or older and percent distribution by muscle-strengthening and aerobic-activity federal guideline status, by age, 2011; numbers in thousands)

	total		met neither guideline	met at least one guideline			
	number	percent		total	met muscle-strengthening guideline only	met aerobic guideline only	met both guidelines
Total people	**231,376**	**100.0%**	**48.1%**	**51.9%**	**3.5%**	**27.8%**	**20.6%**
Sex							
Men	112,093	100.0	43.5	56.5	3.9	27.7	24.9
Women	119,283	100.0	51.6	48.4	3.1	28.3	17.1
Age							
Aged 18 to 44	110,815	100.0	41.4	58.6	2.9	29.7	26.0
Aged 45 to 64	80,849	100.0	51.5	48.5	3.7	27.3	17.5
Aged 65 to 74	21,902	100.0	54.3	45.7	4.9	26.5	14.3
Aged 75 or older	17,810	100.0	67.7	32.3	4.9	19.7	7.7
Race and Hispanic origin							
Asian	11,468	100.0	52.5	47.5	2.6	28.2	16.7
Black	27,666	100.0	55.1	44.9	3.5	23.6	17.8
Hispanic	32,762	100.0	56.3	43.7	3.6	24.7	15.4
Non-Hispanic white	156,482	100.0	44.1	55.9	3.4	29.4	23.0

Note: Federal aerobic guideline recommends that adults perform at least 150 minutes per week of moderate-intensity or 75 minutes per week of vigorous-intensity aerobic physical activity or equivalent combination. Federal muscle-strengthening guideline recommends muscle-strengthening activities of moderate or high intensity involving all major muscle groups on two or more days per week. Asians and blacks are those who identify themselves as being of the race alone. Non-Hispanic whites are those who identify themselves as being white alone and not Hispanic.
Source: National Center for Health Statistics, Summary Health Statistics for U.S. Adults: National Health Interview Survey, 2011, Vital and Health Statistics, Series 10, No. 256, 2012, Internet site http://www.cdc.gov/nchs/nhis.htm; calculations by New Strategist

Most Women of Childbearing Age Use Contraceptives

The pill and female sterilization are the most popular contraceptives.

Among the nation's women of childbearing age—15 to 44—the 62 percent majority uses contraceptives. The pill is most popular, with 17.1 percent of women using it, according to the federal government's National Survey of Family Growth. Female sterilization is the contraceptive choice of 16.5 percent of women, while condoms rank third at 10.2 percent. Use of the pill peaks at 27 percent among women aged 20 to 24, while women aged 30 or older are more likely to have been sterilized than to be on the pill.

Among women who are not using contraceptives, most are either not sexually active, pregnant, or post-partum. Only 8 percent of women aged 15 to 44 are not using contraceptives, able to become pregnant, and sexually active.

■ Contraception is a vital element of health care for American women.

The pill is popular among young women

(percent of women aged 15 to 44 who are using the contraceptive pill, 2006–10)

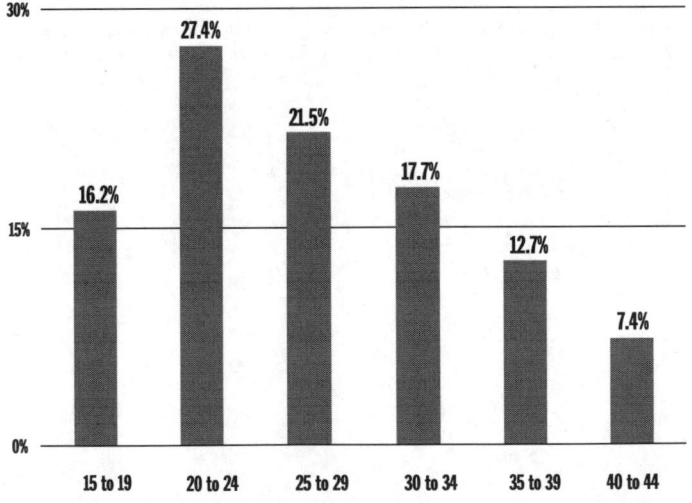

Table 3.5 Contraceptive Use by Age, 2006–10

(total number of women aged 15 to 44 and percent distribution by contraceptive status and age, 2006–10; numbers in thousands)

	total	15 to 19	20 to 24	25 to 29	30 to 34	35 to 39	40 to 44
Total women aged 15 to 44 (number)	61,755	10,478	10,365	10,535	9,188	10,538	10,652
Total women aged 15 to 44 (percent)	100.0%	100.0%	100.0%	100.0%	100.0%	100.0%	100.0%
USING CONTRACEPTION	**62.2%**	**30.5%**	**58.3%**	**65.3**	**69.7%**	**74.6%**	**75.3%**
Female sterilization	16.5	–	1.5	10.7	20.9	27.9	38.1
Male sterilization	6.2	–	0.5	2.7	6.6	12.4	15.1
Pill	17.1	16.2	27.4	21.5	17.7	12.7	7.4
Other hormonal methods	4.5	4.9	7.1	7.4	3.9	2.0	1.4
Implant, Lunelle, or Patch	0.9	0.7	1.1	1.5	0.9	0.5	–
Three-month injectable (Depo-Provera)	2.3	3.5	3.3	3.4	1.7	1.0	0.6
Contraceptive ring	1.3	0.7	2.7	2.4	1.4	0.5	0.4
Intrauterine device (IUD)	3.5	0.8	3.3	4.7	4.9	4.8	2.4
Condom	10.2	6.1	14.9	13.6	10.8	9.0	6.8
Periodic abstinence— calendar rhythm method	0.6	–	0.2	0.5	0.8	1.0	1.1
Periodic abstinence— natural family planning	0.1	0.0	0.0	0.0	0.4	–	–
Withdrawal	3.2	2.1	3.3	4.1	3.2	4.1	2.6
Other methods	0.3	0.2	–	0.3	0.5	0.6	0.4
NOT USING CONTRACEPTION	**37.8**	**69.5**	**41.7**	**34.7**	**30.3**	**25.4**	**24.7**
Surgically sterile-female (noncontraceptive)	0.4	–	–	0.2	–	0.4	1.5
Nonsurgically sterile, female or male	1.7	0.5	1.4	1.4	1.8	2.0	3.1
Pregnant or postpartum	5.0	3.2	8.1	8.4	7.2	2.3	1.4
Seeking pregnancy	4.0	0.6	4.0	6.3	6.0	4.8	2.4
Never had intercourse	11.8	51.4	11.6	3.1	1.9	1.1	0.6
No intercourse in past three months	7.3	7.1	7.9	7.0	6.6	6.5	8.6
Had intercourse during past three months	7.7	6.7	8.7	8.4	6.7	8.4	7.1

Note: "Other methods" includes diaphragm, emergency contraceptive, Today sponge, cervical cap, female condom, and other methods. "–" means sample is too small to make a reliable estimate.
Source: National Center for Health Statistics, Current Contraceptive Use in the United States, 2006–2010, and Changes in Patterns of Use since 1995, National Health Statistics Reports, No. 60, 2012, Internet site http://www.cdc.gov/nchs/nsfg.htm; calculations by New Strategist

Fertility Rate Is Falling

Decline has been especially pronounced among women under age 25.

The Great Recession has created a new baby bust. Between 2007 and 2012, the fertility rate (the number of live births per 1,000 women aged 15 to 44) fell from 69.3 to 63.0—a substantial 9 percent decline.

Among women aged 15 to 19, the fertility rate plunged by a stunning 29 percent between 2007 and 2012. Among women aged 20 to 24, the rate fell 21 percent during those years. The decline was smaller among women in their late twenties and thirties. Consequently, in an unprecedented turn of events, women aged 30 to 34 now have a higher fertility rate than women aged 20 to 24.

■ The fertility rate among women aged 35 or older is rising as those who postponed childbearing hurry to catch up.

The fertility rate of women aged 30 to 34 now exceeds that of women aged 20 to 24

(number of births per 1,000 women in selected age groups, 2007 and 2012)

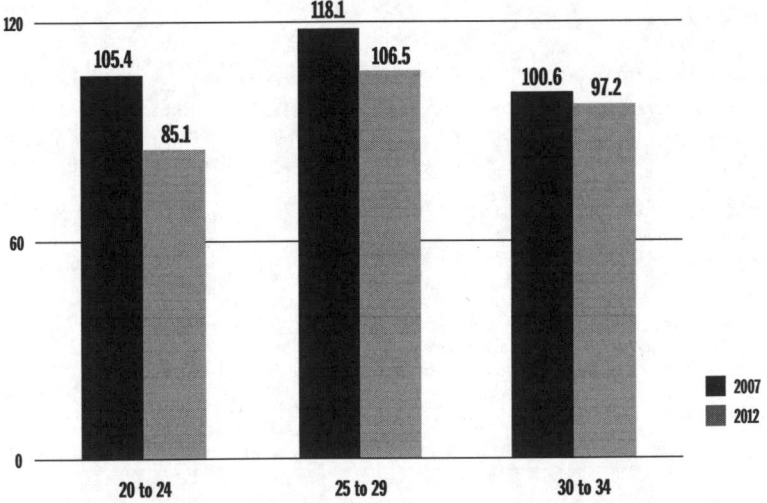

Table 3.6 Fertility Rate by Age, 2000 to 2012

(number of live births per 1,000 women aged 15 to 44 by age, 2000 to 2012; percent change in rate for selected years)

	total*	15 to 19	20 to 24	25 to 29	30 to 34	35 to 39	40 to 44	45 or older
2012	63.0	29.4	83.1	106.5	97.2	48.3	10.4	0.7
2011	63.2	31.3	85.3	107.2	96.5	47.2	10.3	0.7
2010	64.1	34.2	90.0	108.3	96.5	45.9	10.2	0.7
2009	66.2	37.9	96.2	111.5	97.5	46.1	10.0	0.7
2008	68.1	40.2	101.8	115.0	99.4	46.8	9.9	0.7
2007	69.3	41.5	105.4	118.1	100.6	47.6	9.6	0.6
2006	68.6	41.1	105.5	118.0	98.9	47.5	9.4	0.6
2005	66.7	39.7	101.8	116.5	96.7	46.4	9.1	0.6
2004	66.4	40.5	101.5	116.5	96.2	45.5	9.0	0.5
2003	66.1	41.1	102.3	116.7	95.7	43.9	8.7	0.5
2002	65.0	42.6	103.1	114.7	92.6	41.6	8.3	0.5
2001	65.1	45.0	105.6	113.8	91.8	40.5	8.1	0.5
2000	65.9	47.7	109.7	113.5	91.2	39.7	8.0	0.5
Percent change								
2007 to 2012	−9.1%	−29.2%	−21.2%	−9.8	−3.4	1.5%	8.3%	16.7%
2000 to 2012	−4.4	−38.4	−24.2	−6.2	6.6	21.7	30.0	40.0

* Total is the number of births per 1,000 women aged 15 to 44.
Source: National Center for Health Statistics, Birth Data, Internet site http://www.cdc.gov/nchs/births.htm; calculations by New Strategist

Forty-Six Percent of the Nation's Newborns Are Minorities

The babies being born today promise great diversity tomorrow.

Of the nearly 4 million babies born in 2012, fully 23 percent were born to Hispanic mothers and 15 percent to non-Hispanic black mothers. Only 54 percent were born to non-Hispanic whites. As today's children grow up, they will create an increasingly multicultural society with no single racial or ethnic group claiming the majority of the U.S. population.

In the future, many adults will have little experience with married parents. Forty-one percent of births in 2012 were to unwed mothers, up from just 11 percent in 1970. Among non-Hispanic blacks, 72 percent of births are out-of-wedlock compared with just 17 percent among Asians.

Among all women giving birth in 2012, the 40 percent plurality was having the first child, and another 31 percent were having the second child. Only 16 percent of women were having their third child and an even smaller 12 percent were having a fourth or higher-order birth.

■ With so many babies born to unmarried mothers, reducing poverty among children is an uphill task.

The nation's newborns are diverse

(percent distribution of births by race and Hispanic origin of mother, 2012)

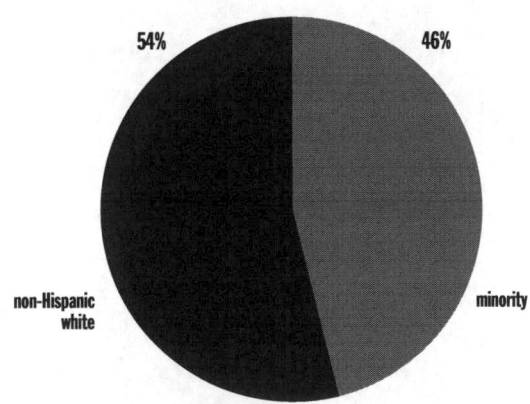

54%   46%

non-Hispanic
white

minority

Table 3.7 Births by Age, Race, and Hispanic Origin, 2012

(number and percent distribution of births by age, race, and Hispanic origin, 2012)

	total	American Indian	Asian	non-Hispanic black	Hispanic	non-Hispanic white
Total births	**3,952,937**	**46,093**	**272,949**	**583,080**	**907,405**	**2,133,115**
Under age 15	3,674	89	62	1,263	1,397	866
Aged 15 to 19	305,420	6,478	5,544	71,271	102,698	119,777
Aged 20 to 24	916,868	15,168	28,580	187,386	241,049	444,371
Aged 25 to 29	1,124,010	12,290	74,254	149,548	244,403	641,353
Aged 30 to 34	1,013,473	7,871	97,986	107,768	193,106	602,549
Aged 35 to 39	472,206	3,355	53,392	51,461	99,820	261,509
Aged 40 to 44	109,535	778	12,196	13,360	23,657	58,515
Aged 45 to 54	7,750	64	935	1,022	1,275	4,174

PERCENT DISTRIBUTION BY RACE AND HISPANIC ORIGIN

	total	American Indian	Asian	non-Hispanic black	Hispanic	non-Hispanic white
Total births	**100.0%**	**1.2%**	**6.9%**	**14.8%**	**23.0%**	**54.0%**
Under age 15	100.0	2.4	1.7	34.4	38.0	23.6
Aged 15 to 19	100.0	2.1	1.8	23.3	33.6	39.2
Aged 20 to 24	100.0	1.7	3.1	20.4	26.3	48.5
Aged 25 to 29	100.0	1.1	6.6	13.3	21.7	57.1
Aged 30 to 34	100.0	0.8	9.7	10.6	19.1	59.5
Aged 35 to 39	100.0	0.7	11.3	10.9	21.1	55.4
Aged 40 to 44	100.0	0.7	11.1	12.2	21.6	53.4
Aged 45 to 54	100.0	0.8	12.1	13.2	16.5	53.9

PERCENT DISTRIBUTION BY AGE

	total	American Indian	Asian	non-Hispanic black	Hispanic	non-Hispanic white
Total births	**100.0**	**100.0**	**100.0**	**100.0**	**100.0**	**100.0**
Under age 15	0.1	0.2	0.0	0.2	0.2	0.0
Aged 15 to 19	7.7	14.1	2.0	12.2	11.3	5.6
Aged 20 to 24	23.2	32.9	10.5	32.1	26.6	20.8
Aged 25 to 29	28.4	26.7	27.2	25.6	26.9	30.1
Aged 30 to 34	25.6	17.1	35.9	18.5	21.3	28.2
Aged 35 to 39	11.9	7.3	19.6	8.8	11.0	12.3
Aged 40 to 44	2.8	1.7	4.5	2.3	2.6	2.7
Aged 45 to 54	0.2	0.1	0.3	0.2	0.1	0.2

Note: Births by race and Hispanic origin do not add to total because Hispanics may be of any race and "not stated" is not shown.
Source: National Center for Health Statistics, Births: Preliminary Data for 2012, Internet site http://www.cdc.gov/nchs/births .htm; calculations by New Strategist

Table 3.8 Births to Unmarried Women by Age, 2012

(total number of births and number and percent to unmarried women, by age, 2012)

| | | unmarried women | | |
	total	number	percent distribution	percent of total
Total births	**3,952,937**	**1,609,912**	**100.0%**	**40.7%**
Under age 15	3,674	3,640	0.2	99.1
Aged 15 to 19	305,420	270,888	16.8	88.7
Aged 20 to 24	916,868	593,969	36.9	64.8
Aged 25 to 29	1,124,010	393,931	24.5	35.0
Aged 30 to 34	1,013,473	222,382	13.8	21.9
Aged 35 to 39	472,206	97,862	6.1	20.7
Aged 40 to 54	117,285	27,240	1.7	23.2

Source: National Center for Health Statistics, Births: Preliminary Data for 2012, Internet site http://www.cdc.gov/nchs/births .htm; calculations by New Strategist

Table 3.9 Characteristics of Births by Race and Hispanic Origin, 2012

(total number of births, fertility rate, births in lifetime, and percent of births to unmarried women, by race and Hispanic origin, 2012)

	total	fertility rate	births in lifetime	percent of births to unmarried women
Total births	**3,952,937**	**63.0**	**1.88**	**40.7%**
American Indian	46,093	47.0	1.35	66.9
Asian	272,949	62.2	1.77	17.1
Black, non-Hispanic	583,080	65.0	1.90	72.2
Hispanic	907,405	74.4	2.19	53.5
White, non-Hispanic	2,133,115	58.7	1.76	29.4

Note: The fertility rate is the number of births per 1,000 women aged 15 to 44. Births by race and Hispanic origin do not add to total because Hispanics may be of any race and "not stated" is not shown.
Source: National Center for Health Statistics, Births: Preliminary Data for 2012, Internet site http://www.cdc.gov/nchs/births .htm; calculations by New Strategist

Table 3.10 Births by Age and Birth Order, 2012

(number and percent distribution of births by age and birth order, 2012)

	total	first child	second child	third child	fourth or later child
Total births	**3,952,937**	**1,569,943**	**1,244,555**	**650,242**	**465,673**
Under age 15	3,674	3,580	60	8	8
Aged 15 to 19	305,420	250,985	45,522	6,380	865
Aged 20 to 24	916,868	461,445	298,047	111,071	41,077
Aged 25 to 29	1,124,010	421,522	369,862	202,018	124,590
Aged 30 to 34	1,013,473	299,379	346,482	201,814	160,074
Aged 35 to 39	472,206	106,715	151,769	105,269	105,457
Aged 40 to 44	109,535	24,208	30,851	22,471	31,219
Aged 45 to 54	7,750	2,109	1,960	1,211	2,383

PERCENT DISTRIBUTION BY BIRTH ORDER

Total births	**100.0%**	**39.7%**	**31.5%**	**16.4%**	**11.8%**
Under age 15	100.0	97.4	1.6	0.2	0.2
Aged 15 to 19	100.0	82.2	14.9	2.1	0.3
Aged 20 to 24	100.0	50.3	32.5	12.1	4.5
Aged 25 to 29	100.0	37.5	32.9	18.0	11.1
Aged 30 to 34	100.0	29.5	34.2	19.9	15.8
Aged 35 to 39	100.0	22.6	32.1	22.3	22.3
Aged 40 to 44	100.0	22.1	28.2	20.5	28.5
Aged 45 to 54	100.0	27.2	25.3	15.6	30.7

PERCENT DISTRIBUTION BY AGE

Total births	**100.0**	**100.0**	**100.0**	**100.0**	**100.0**
Under age 15	0.1	0.2	0.0	0.0	0.0
Aged 15 to 19	7.7	16.0	3.7	1.0	0.2
Aged 20 to 24	23.2	29.4	23.9	17.1	8.8
Aged 25 to 29	28.4	26.8	29.7	31.1	26.8
Aged 30 to 34	25.6	19.1	27.8	31.0	34.4
Aged 35 to 39	11.9	6.8	12.2	16.2	22.6
Aged 40 to 44	2.8	1.5	2.5	3.5	6.7
Aged 45 to 54	0.2	0.1	0.2	0.2	0.5

Note: Numbers do not add to total by age because "not stated" is not shown.
Source: National Center for Health Statistics, Births: Preliminary Data for 2012, Internet site http://www.cdc.gov/nchs/births .htm; calculations by New Strategist

Cigarette Smoking Is Becoming Uncommon

Drinking is more popular than smoking.

Only 19 percent of people aged 18 or older smoke cigarettes. Smoking declines with age, from 21 percent of 18-to-44-year-olds to just 4 percent of those aged 75 or older. Non-Hispanic whites are more likely to smoke than any other race or Hispanic origin group.

Drinking is far more common than smoking, with 51.5 percent of adults consuming alcohol regularly. Those most likely to drink regularly are men (60 percent), people aged 18 to 44 (57 percent), and non-Hispanic whites (57 percent).

Nearly half the Americans aged 12 or older have ever used an illicit drug, but only 9 percent have done so in the past month. The most commonly used illicit drug is marijuana, with 43 percent of people aged 12 or older having ever used it. The share exceeds 50 percent at most ages from 20 to 59.

■ Older Americans are far less likely to smoke than younger ones because many of the smokers among them died prematurely.

Men are more likely than women to drink

(percentage of people aged 18 or older who are regular drinkers, by sex, 2011)

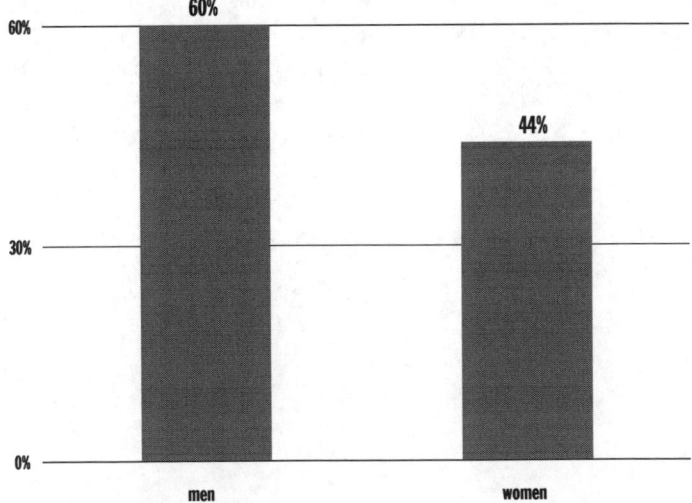

Table 3.11 Cigarette Smoking Status by Selected Characteristics, 2011

(total number of people aged 18 or older and percent distribution by cigarette smoking status and selected characteristics, 2011; numbers in thousands)

| | total | | all current smokers | | | former smokers | nonsmokers |
	number	percent	total	every-day smokers	some-day smokers		
Total people	**231,376**	**100.0%**	**19.0%**	**14.8%**	**4.2%**	**21.8%**	**59.2%**
Sex							
Men	112,093	100.0	21.3	16.0	5.2	24.8	54.0
Women	119,283	100.0	16.7	13.3	3.4	18.0	65.2
Age							
Aged 18 to 44	110,815	100.0	21.2	15.6	5.7	12.2	66.6
Aged 45 to 64	80,849	100.0	21.4	17.7	3.7	25.6	53.0
Aged 65 to 74	21,902	100.0	10.7	9.0	1.7	41.6	47.6
Aged 75 or older	17,810	100.0	4.4	3.6	0.8	40.6	55.0
Race and Hispanic origin							
Asian	11,468	100.0	9.6	7.2	2.4	13.7	76.7
Black	27,666	100.0	18.6	13.4	5.2	15.3	66.1
Hispanic	32,762	100.0	12.3	7.0	5.4	16.3	71.4
Non-Hispanic white	156,482	100.0	21.2	17.2	4.0	23.6	55.2

Note: "Current smokers" have smoked at least 100 cigarettes in lifetime and still smoke; "every-day smokers" are current smokers who smoke every day; "some-day smokers" are current smokers who smoke on some days; "former smokers" have smoked at least 100 cigarettes in lifetime but currently do not smoke; "nonsmokers" have smoked less than 100 cigarettes in lifetime. Numbers do not add to total because "unknown" is not shown. Asians and blacks are those who identify themselves as being of the race alone. Non-Hispanic whites are those who identify themselves as being white alone and not Hispanic.
Source: National Center for Health Statistics, Summary Health Statistics for U.S. Adults: National Health Interview Survey, 2011, Vital and Health Statistics, Series 10, No. 256, 2012, Internet site http://www.cdc.gov/nchs/nhis.htm; calculations by New Strategist

Table 3.12 Alcohol Drinking Status by Selected Characteristics, 2011

(total number of people aged 18 or older and percent distribution by alcohol drinking status and selected characteristics, 2011; numbers in thousands)

	total		current			lifetime
	number	percent	regular	infrequent	former	abstainer
Total people	**231,376**	**100.0%**	**51.5%**	**13.6%**	**14.7%**	**19.8%**
Sex						
Men	112,093	100.0	60.2	10.2	14.5	14.6
Women	119,283	100.0	43.8	16.7	14.1	25.2
Age						
Aged 18 to 44	110,815	100.0	56.8	13.3	8.7	20.8
Aged 45 to 64	80,849	100.0	51.8	14.7	17.8	15.5
Aged 65 to 74	21,902	100.0	41.1	13.3	23.9	21.5
Aged 75 or older	17,810	100.0	29.9	11.1	27.1	31.8
Race and Hispanic origin						
Asian	11,468	100.0	34.1	12.1	9.8	43.7
Black	27,666	100.0	39.3	14.4	16.5	29.5
Hispanic	32,762	100.0	42.1	12.7	14.6	30.2
Non-Hispanic white	156,482	100.0	57.3	13.6	14.0	14.9

Note: "Current drinker" had more than 12 drinks in lifetime and drinks in past year; "regular drinker" had more than 12 drinks in one year; "infrequent drinker" had fewer than 12 drinks in one year; "former drinker" had more than 12 drinks in lifetime, no drinks in past year; "lifetime abstainer" had fewer than 12 drinks in lifetime, no drinks in past year. Numbers do not add to total because "unknown" is not shown. Asians and blacks are those who identify themselves as being of the race alone. Non-Hispanic whites are those who identify themselves as being white alone and not Hispanic.
Source: National Center for Health Statistics, Summary Health Statistics for U.S. Adults: National Health Interview Survey, 2011, Vital and Health Statistics, Series 10, No. 256, 2012, Internet site http://www.cdc.gov/nchs/nhis.htm; calculations by New Strategist

Table 3.13 Illicit Drug Use by Age, 2012

(percent of people aged 12 or older who ever used any illicit drug, who used an illicit drug in the past year, and who used an illicit drug in the past month, by age, 2012)

	ever used any illicit drug	used in past year	used in past month
Total people	**48.0%**	**16.0%**	**9.2%**
Aged 12	8.1	5.0	2.5
Aged 13	12.9	8.8	4.6
Aged 14	19.1	13.3	6.8
Aged 15	27.1	19.3	9.5
Aged 16	34.8	27.5	14.7
Aged 17	42.1	32.4	18.4
Aged 18	49.3	38.4	22.5
Aged 19	52.2	38.2	24.3
Aged 20	58.3	42.4	25.0
Aged 21	58.8	37.7	21.4
Aged 22	60.9	37.6	22.6
Aged 23	61.0	32.2	18.1
Aged 24	61.3	32.8	19.2
Aged 25	61.2	30.2	17.1
Aged 26 to 29	61.7	26.4	14.6
Aged 30 to 34	60.0	21.5	13.2
Aged 35 to 39	55.5	15.7	8.8
Aged 40 to 44	54.5	13.8	7.3
Aged 45 to 49	59.0	13.4	7.7
Aged 50 to 54	60.7	12.1	7.2
Aged 55 to 59	56.8	10.8	6.6
Aged 60 to 64	47.6	6.0	3.6
Aged 65 or older	19.3	2.3	1.3

Note: Illicit drugs include marijuana, hashish, cocaine (including crack), heroin, hallucinogens, inhalants, and any prescription-type psychotherapeutic used nonmedically.
Source: SAMHSA, Office of Applied Studies, National Survey on Drug Use and Health, 2012, Internet site http://www.samhsa .gov/data/NSDUH/2012SummNatFindDetTables/Index.aspx

Table 3.14 Marijuana Use by Age, 2012

(percent of people aged 12 or older who ever used marijuana, who used marijuana in the past year, and who used marijuana in the past month, by age, 2012)

	ever used marijuana	used in past year	used in past month
Total people	**42.8%**	**12.1%**	**7.3%**
Aged 12	1.4	1.1	0.2
Aged 13	5.1	4.1	2.1
Aged 14	10.4	8.4	4.4
Aged 15	18.8	14.7	7.9
Aged 16	28.7	23.0	12.1
Aged 17	36.0	28.5	16.0
Aged 18	43.3	34.2	20.0
Aged 19	46.1	34.4	22.1
Aged 20	53.4	37.3	22.5
Aged 21	52.9	33.2	18.8
Aged 22	55.7	32.1	19.3
Aged 23	55.8	27.7	15.7
Aged 24	55.9	27.6	16.7
Aged 25	55.4	24.3	14.5
Aged 26 to 29	56.2	20.1	11.9
Aged 30 to 34	54.3	16.5	10.8
Aged 35 to 39	49.6	10.8	6.6
Aged 40 to 44	47.8	9.1	5.1
Aged 45 to 49	53.7	9.4	5.2
Aged 50 to 54	56.7	8.0	5.1
Aged 55 to 59	53.0	7.4	4.8
Aged 60 to 64	44.4	4.4	2.4
Aged 65 or older	14.8	1.2	0.9

Source: SAMHSA, Office of Applied Studies, National Survey on Drug Use and Health, 2012, Internet site http://www.samhsa .gov/data/NSDUH/2012SummNatFindDetTables/Index.aspx

Millions of Americans Do Not Have Health Insurance

The proportion is highest among young adults.

Eighty-five percent of Americans have health insurance, the 55 percent majority being covered by an employer's health plan. Medicare, the federal government's health insurance program for people aged 65 or older, covers 16 percent. Medicaid, the federal health insurance program for the poor, covers another 16 percent.

Fifteen percent of Americans (48 million) did not have health insurance in 2012, the number of uninsured growing by 31 percent between 2000 and 2012. The percentage without health insurance is highest among 25-to-34-year-olds (27 percent) and Hispanics (29 percent). Among those without health insurance in 2012, the 44 percent plurality say cost is the reason.

■ The Affordable Care Act has reduced the number of young adults without health insurance, allowing those up to the age of 26 to be covered under their parents' health plan.

More than one in four 25-to-34-year-olds is uninsured

(percent of people without health insurance coverage, by age, 2012)

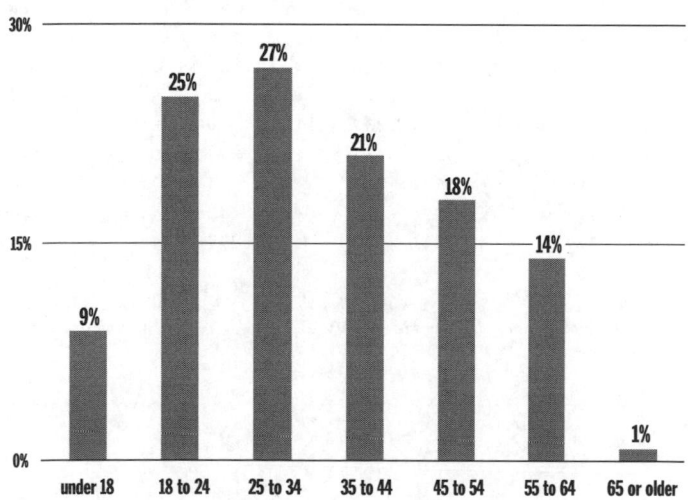

Table 3.15 Health Insurance Coverage by Age, 2012

(number and percent distribution of people by age and health insurance coverage status, 2012; numbers in thousands)

			covered by private and/or government health insurance							
			private health insurance			government health insurance				
	total	total with coverage	total with private	employment based	direct purchase	total with government	Medicaid	Medicare	military	not covered
Total people	311,116	263,165	198,812	170,877	30,622	101,493	50,903	48,884	13,702	47,951
Under age 65	267,828	220,517	174,637	156,493	19,434	61,163	47,279	8,817	9,939	47,311
Under age 18	74,187	67,601	44,586	41,095	4,325	29,055	26,610	764	2,595	6,586
Aged 18 to 24	30,030	22,425	18,170	13,713	1,879	5,820	4,706	371	1,025	7,605
Aged 25 to 34	41,797	30,362	25,833	23,378	2,464	6,098	4,514	713	1,322	11,435
Aged 35 to 44	39,877	31,449	27,586	25,718	2,621	5,406	3,790	1,005	1,143	8,428
Aged 45 to 54	43,446	35,559	30,906	28,247	3,822	6,497	3,966	2,108	1,555	7,887
Aged 55 to 64	38,491	33,121	27,556	24,342	4,323	8,287	3,693	3,856	2,299	5,370
Aged 65 or older	43,287	42,648	24,147	14,383	11,188	40,329	3,624	40,067	3,762	639

PERCENT DISTRIBUTION BY COVERAGE STATUS

Total people	100.0%	84.6%	63.9%	54.9%	9.8%	32.6%	16.4%	15.7%	4.4%	15.4%
Under age 65	100.0	82.3	65.2	58.4	7.3	22.8	17.7	3.3	3.7	17.7
Under age 18	100.0	91.1	60.1	55.4	5.8	39.2	35.9	1.0	3.5	8.9
Aged 18 to 24	100.0	74.7	60.5	45.7	6.3	19.4	15.7	1.2	3.4	25.3
Aged 25 to 34	100.0	72.6	61.8	55.9	5.9	14.6	10.8	1.7	3.2	27.4
Aged 35 to 44	100.0	78.9	69.2	64.5	6.6	13.6	9.5	2.5	2.9	21.1
Aged 45 to 54	100.0	81.8	71.1	65.0	8.8	15.0	9.1	4.9	3.6	18.2
Aged 55 to 64	100.0	86.0	71.6	63.2	11.2	21.5	9.6	10.0	6.0	14.0
Aged 65 or older	100.0	98.5	55.8	33.2	25.8	93.2	8.4	92.6	8.7	1.5

PERCENT DISTRIBUTION BY AGE

Total people	100.0	100.0	100.0	100.0	100.0	100.0	100.0	100.0	100.0	100.0
Under age 65	86.1	83.8	87.8	91.6	63.5	60.3	92.9	18.0	72.5	98.7
Under age 18	23.8	25.7	22.4	24.0	14.1	28.6	52.3	1.6	18.9	13.7
Aged 18 to 24	9.7	8.5	9.1	8.0	6.1	5.7	9.2	0.8	7.5	15.9
Aged 25 to 34	13.4	11.5	13.0	13.7	8.0	6.0	8.9	1.5	9.6	23.8
Aged 35 to 44	12.8	12.0	13.9	15.1	8.6	5.3	7.4	2.1	8.3	17.6
Aged 45 to 54	14.0	13.5	15.5	16.5	12.5	6.4	7.8	4.3	11.3	16.4
Aged 55 to 64	12.4	12.6	13.9	14.2	14.1	8.2	7.3	7.9	16.8	11.2
Aged 65 or older	13.9	16.2	12.1	8.4	36.5	39.7	7.1	82.0	27.5	1.3

Note: Numbers do not add to total because some people have more than one type of health insurance coverage.
Source: Bureau of the Census, Health Insurance, Internet site http://www.census.gov/hhes/www/hlthins/; calculations by New Strategist

Table 3.16 People without Health Insurance by Age, 2000 to 2012

(number and percent of people without health insurance coverage by age, 2000 to 2012; percent change in number and percentage point change in share for selected years; numbers in thousands)

	2012	2007	2000	percent change 2007–12	percent change 2000–12
Total without coverage	**47,951**	**44,088**	**36,586**	**8.8%**	**31.1%**
Under age 18	6,586	7,877	7,756	−16.4	−15.1
Aged 18 to 24	7,605	7,638	6,895	−0.4	10.3
Aged 25 to 34	11,435	9,987	7,985	14.5	43.2
Aged 35 to 44	8,428	7,513	6,466	12.2	30.3
Aged 45 to 54	7,887	6,545	4,290	20.5	83.8
Aged 55 to 64	5,370	3,853	2,860	39.4	87.8
Aged 65 or older	639	674	334	−5.2	91.3
				percentage point change	percentage point change
Total without coverage	**15.4%**	**14.7%**	**13.1%**	**0.7**	**2.3**
Under age 18	8.9	10.6	10.7	−1.7	−1.8
Aged 18 to 24	25.3	26.9	25.7	−1.6	−0.4
Aged 25 to 34	27.4	24.9	20.5	2.5	6.9
Aged 35 to 44	21.1	17.8	14.5	3.3	6.6
Aged 45 to 54	18.2	14.9	11.1	3.3	7.1
Aged 55 to 64	14.0	11.6	11.6	2.4	2.4
Aged 65 or older	1.5	1.8	1.0	−0.3	0.5

Source: Bureau of the Census, Health Insurance, Internet site http://www.census.gov/hhes/www/hlthins/; calculations by New Strategist

Table 3.17 People without Health Insurance by Race and Hispanic Origin, 2012

(total number of people, number and percent without health insurance coverage, and percent distribution of people without coverage by race and Hispanic Origin, 2012; numbers in thousands)

	total	without insurance number	without insurance percent of total	without insurance percent distribution
Total people	**311,116**	**47,951**	**15.4%**	**100.0%**
Asian	18,191	2,659	14.6	5.5
Black	43,692	8,099	18.5	16.9
Hispanic	53,230	15,500	29.1	32.3
Non-Hispanic white	195,330	21,585	11.1	45.0

Note: Asians and blacks are those who identify themselves as being of the race alone and those who identify themselves as being of the race in combination with other races. Non-Hispanic whites are those who identify themselves as being white alone and not Hispanic.
Source: Bureau of the Census, Health Insurance, Internet site http://www.census.gov/hhes/www/hlthins/; calculations by New Strategist

Table 3.18 Reason for Lack of Health Insurance Coverage by Selected Characteristics, 2011

(total number and percent distribution of people under age 65 without health insurance by reason for lack of insurance coverage, by selected characteristics, 2011; numbers in thousands)

	total number	total percent	lost job or change in employment	change in marital status or death of parent	ineligible due to age or left school	employer didn't offer or insurance company refused	cost	Medicaid stopped	other reason
Total without health insurance	45,376	100.0%	27.6%	2.7%	9.3%	11.9%	44.3%	11.7%	6.3%
Sex									
Female	20,605	100.0	26.0	3.6	6.3	9.3	40.5	20.4	6.6
Male	24,771	100.0	27.7	1.7	7.8	11.8	45.0	11.0	7.6
Age									
Under age 12	3,000	100.0	23.5	1.3	1.2	5.7	31.5	33.9	9.8
Aged 12 to 17	2,173	100.0	18.0	3.3	1.8	6.3	47.6	19.6	11.3
Aged 18 to 44	27,844	100.0	24.1	2.2	14.5	12.6	43.1	11.3	5.7
Aged 45 to 64	12,359	100.0	37.9	4.0	0.7	12.8	49.6	6.0	5.9
Race and Hispanic origin									
Asian	2,199	100.0	21.6	1.8	5.5	7.9	48.7	8.8	12.9
Black	6,617	100.0	25.9	2.4	9.4	9.6	35.3	22.4	5.6
Hispanic	14,574	100.0	17.1	1.4	4.9	12.5	51.0	16.6	9.1
Non-Hispanic white	21,242	100.0	34.3	3.4	8.1	10.0	39.0	13.1	5.7

Note: Numbers do not add to total because more than one reason may have been cited. "Other reason" includes moved, self-employed, never had coverage, does not want or need coverage. Asians and blacks are those who identify themselves as being of the race alone. Non-Hispanic whites are those who identify themselves as being white alone and not Hispanic.
Source: National Center for Health Statistics, Summary Health Statistics for the U.S. Population: National Health Interview Survey, 2011, Vital and Health Statistics, Series 10, No. 255, 2012, Internet site http://www.cdc.gov/nchs/nhis.htm; calculations by New Strategist

Asthma and Allergies Affect Many Children

Boys are more likely than girls to have learning disabilities.

Asthma is a growing problem among children. Fourteen percent of the nation's children have been diagnosed with asthma. Nine percent have had asthma in the past year. Black children are most likely to have ever had asthma (21 percent).

Nearly 5 million children aged 3 to 17 (7 percent) have been diagnosed with a learning disability, and about the same number have been diagnosed with attention deficit hyperactivity disorder. Boys are more likely than girls to have these conditions, accounting for 63 percent of those with learning disabilities and 73 percent of those with attention deficit hyperactivity disorder.

Many children use prescription medications. Ten million children have taken prescription medications regularly for at least three months during the past year. That's a substantial 13 percent of the nation's children. Among 12-to-17-year-olds, the figure is an even higher 18 percent.

■ Prescription drug use is growing, even among children.

Among black children, asthma is common

(percentage of people under age 18 who have been diagnosed with asthma, by race and Hispanic origin, 2011)

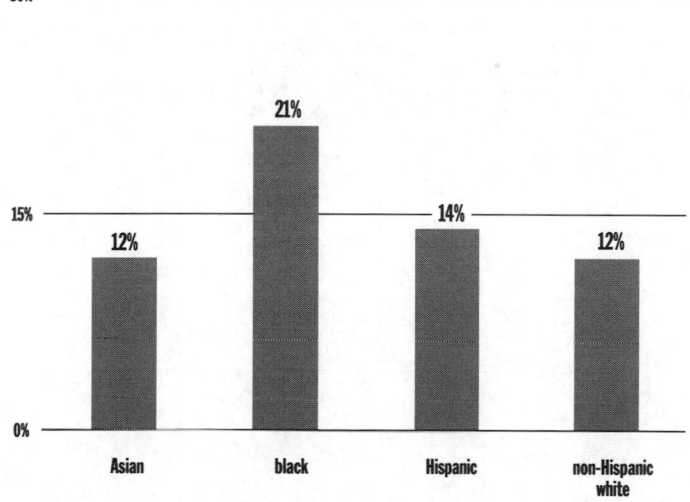

Table 3.19 Health Conditions among Children by Selected Characteristics, 2011: Number with Condition

(number of people under age 18 with health condition, by selected characteristics and type of condition, 2011; numbers in thousands)

	total children	asthma ever had	asthma still have	hay fever	respiratory allergies	food allergies	skin allergies	prescription medication taken regularly at least 3 months
					in last 12 months			
Total children	74,518	10,463	7,074	6,711	8,269	4,126	9,516	10,019
Sex								
Female	36,415	4,642	3,198	3,259	3,792	1,969	4,767	4,400
Male	38,103	5,821	3,876	3,452	4,476	2,157	4,749	5,620
Age								
Aged 0 to 4	21,210	1,753	1,452	1,012	1,838	994	3,174	1,853
Aged 5 to 11	28,845	4,139	2,849	2,611	3,342	1,637	3,580	3,761
Aged 12 to 17	24,463	4,571	2,773	3,088	3,089	1,495	2,762	4,405
Race and Hispanic Origin								
American Indian	873	134	69	86	63	52	84	106
Asian	3,455	419	240	347	228	244	463	230
Black	10,990	2,282	1,804	761	1,342	717	1,885	1,712
Hispanic	17,517	2,452	1,679	1,359	1,104	707	1,980	1,635
Non-Hispanic white	40,459	4,993	3,157	3,998	4,781	2,361	4,920	6,087
Family structure								
Mother and father	51,243	6,179	4,146	4,702	5,624	2,780	6,257	6,387
Mother, no father	18,388	3,559	2,465	1,570	2,099	1,129	2,784	2,909
Father, no mother	2,596	327	208	233	263	90	213	275
Neither mother nor father	2,292	398	255	206	284	128	261	448

Note: "Mother and father" can include biological, adoptive, step, in-law, or foster relationships. Legal guardians are classified as "neither mother nor father." Asians and blacks are those who identify themselves as being of the race alone. Non-Hispanic whites are those who identify themselves as being white alone and not Hispanic.
Source: National Center for Health Statistics, Summary Health Statistics for U.S. Children: National Health Interview Survey, 2011, Vital and Health Statistics, Series 10, No. 254, 2012, Internet site http://www.cdc.gov/nchs/nhis.htm

Table 3.20 Health Conditions among Children by Selected Characteristics, 2011: Percent with Condition

(percent of people under age 18 with selected health condition, by type of condition and selected characteristics, 2011)

	total children	asthma ever had	asthma still have	hay fever	respiratory allergies (in last 12 months)	food allergies (in last 12 months)	skin allergies (in last 12 months)	prescription medication taken regularly at least 3 months
Total children	100.0%	14.0%	9.5%	9.0%	11.1%	5.5%	12.8%	13.4%
Sex								
Female	100.0	12.7	8.8	8.9	10.4	5.4	13.1	12.1
Male	100.0	15.3	10.2	9.1	11.7	5.7	12.5	14.7
Age								
Aged 0 to 4	100.0	8.3	6.8	4.8	8.7	4.7	15.0	8.7
Aged 5 to 11	100.0	14.3	9.9	9.1	11.6	5.7	12.4	13.0
Aged 12 to 17	100.0	18.7	11.3	12.6	12.6	6.1	11.3	18.0
Race and Hispanic Origin								
American Indian	100.0	15.3	7.9	9.9	7.2	6.0	9.6	12.1
Asian	100.0	12.1	6.9	10.0	6.6	7.1	13.4	6.7
Black	100.0	20.8	16.4	6.9	12.2	6.5	17.2	15.6
Hispanic	100.0	14.0	9.6	7.8	6.3	4.0	11.3	9.3
Non-Hispanic white	100.0	12.3	7.8	9.9	11.8	5.8	12.2	15.0
Family structure								
Mother and father	100.0	12.1	8.1	9.2	11.0	5.4	12.2	12.5
Mother, no father	100.0	19.4	13.4	8.5	11.4	6.1	15.1	15.8
Father, no mother	100.0	12.6	8.0	9.0	10.1	3.5	8.2	10.6
Neither mother nor father	100.0	17.4	11.1	9.0	12.4	5.6	11.4	19.5

Note: "Mother and father" can include biological, adoptive, step, in-law, or foster relationships. Legal guardians are classified as "neither mother nor father." Asians and blacks are those who identify themselves as being of the race alone. Non-Hispanic whites are those who identify themselves as being white alone and not Hispanic.
Source: National Center for Health Statistics, Summary Health Statistics for U.S. Children: National Health Interview Survey, 2011, Vital and Health Statistics, Series 10, No. 254, 2012, Internet site http://www.cdc.gov/nchs/nhis.htm

Table 3.21 Health Conditions among Children by Selected Characteristics, 2011: Distribution by Condition

(percent distribution of people under age 18 with health condition by selected characteristics, 2011)

	total children	asthma ever had	asthma still have	hay fever	respiratory allergies	food allergies	skin allergies	prescription medication taken regularly at least 3 months
					in last 12 months			
Total children	100.0%	100.0%	100.0%	100.0%	100.0%	100.0%	100.0%	100.0%
Sex								
Female	48.9	44.4	45.2	48.6	45.9	47.7	50.1	43.9
Male	51.1	55.6	54.8	51.4	54.1	52.3	49.9	56.1
Age								
Aged 0 to 4	28.5	16.8	20.5	15.1	22.2	24.1	33.4	18.5
Aged 5 to 11	38.7	39.6	40.3	38.9	40.4	39.7	37.6	37.5
Aged 12 to 17	32.8	43.7	39.2	46.0	37.4	36.2	29.0	44.0
Race and Hispanic Origin								
American Indian	1.2	1.3	1.0	1.3	0.8	1.3	0.9	1.1
Asian	4.6	4.0	3.4	5.2	2.8	5.9	4.9	2.3
Black	14.7	21.8	25.5	11.3	16.2	17.4	19.8	17.1
Hispanic	23.5	23.4	23.7	20.3	13.4	17.1	20.8	16.3
Non-Hispanic white	54.3	47.7	44.6	59.6	57.8	57.2	51.7	60.8
Family structure								
Mother and father	68.8	59.1	58.6	70.1	68.0	67.4	65.8	63.7
Mother, no father	24.7	34.0	34.8	23.4	25.4	27.4	29.3	29.0
Father, no mother	3.5	3.1	2.9	3.5	3.2	2.2	2.2	2.7
Neither mother nor father	3.1	3.8	3.6	3.1	3.4	3.1	2.7	4.5

Note: "Mother and father" can include biological, adoptive, step, in-law, or foster relationships. Legal guardians are classified as "neither mother nor father." Asians and blacks are those who identify themselves as being of the race alone. Non-Hispanic whites are those who identify themselves as being white alone and not Hispanic.

Source: National Center for Health Statistics, Summary Health Statistics for U.S. Children: National Health Interview Survey, 2011, Vital and Health Statistics, Series 10, No. 254, 2012, Internet site http://www.cdc.gov/nchs/nhis.htm

Table 3.22 Children with Learning Disabilities or Attention Deficit Hyperactivity Disorder, 2011

(total number of children aged 3 to 17 and number and percent who have been told they have a learning disability or attention deficit hyperactivity disorder, by selected characteristics, 2011; numbers in thousands)

		learning disability		hyperactivity disorder	
	total	number	percent	number	percent
Total children	**62,166**	**4,660**	**7.5%**	**5,240**	**8.4%**
Sex					
Female	30,423	1,732	5.7	1,436	4.7
Male	31,742	2,928	9.2	3,803	12.0
Age					
Aged 3 to 4	8,858	233	2.6	158	1.8
Aged 5 to 11	28,845	2,029	7.0	2,174	7.5
Aged 12 to 17	24,463	2,398	9.8	2,907	11.9
Race and Hispanic Origin					
American Indian	711	61	8.6	71	10.0
Asian	2,938	147	5.0	81	2.8
Black	9,307	783	8.4	792	8.5
Hispanic	14,365	900	6.3	802	5.6
Non-Hispanic white	33,913	2,743	8.1	3,435	10.1
Family structure					
Mother and father	41,981	2,662	6.3	3,115	7.4
Mother, no father	15,666	1,543	9.8	1,601	10.2
Father, no mother	2,484	230	9.3	234	9.4
Neither mother nor father	2,035	225	11.1	289	14.2

Note: "Mother and father" can include biological, adoptive, step, in-law, or foster relationships. Legal guardians are classified as "neither mother nor father." Asians and blacks are those who identify themselves as being of the race alone. Non-Hispanic whites are those who identify themselves as being white alone and not Hispanic.
Source: National Center for Health Statistics, Summary Health Statistics for U.S. Children: National Health Interview Survey, 2011, Vital and Health Statistics, Series 10, No. 254, 2012, Internet site http://www.cdc.gov/nchs/nhis.htm

Health Problems Are Common among Older Americans

Lower back pain is one of the most frequently reported health conditions.

Thirty percent of Americans aged 18 or older have experienced chronic joint symptoms lasting at least three months, making this the most frequently reported health problem. Not far behind is lower back pain, reported by 29 percent of adults. One in four adults has hypertension, and 23 percent have arthritis.

Many ailments are more common among older than younger Americans. Fifty-three percent of people aged 75 or older have been diagnosed with arthritis, for example, compared with 8 percent of 18-to-44-year-olds. Forty-seven percent of the oldest Americans have hearing problems. But only 6 percent of people aged 75 or older get migraines or severe headaches compared with 19 percent of people aged 18 to 44.

■ More than 1 million Americans have been diagnosed with AIDS, the majority of them when they were aged 25 to 44.

Most people aged 75 or older have arthritis

(percent of people diagnosed with arthritis, by age, 2011)

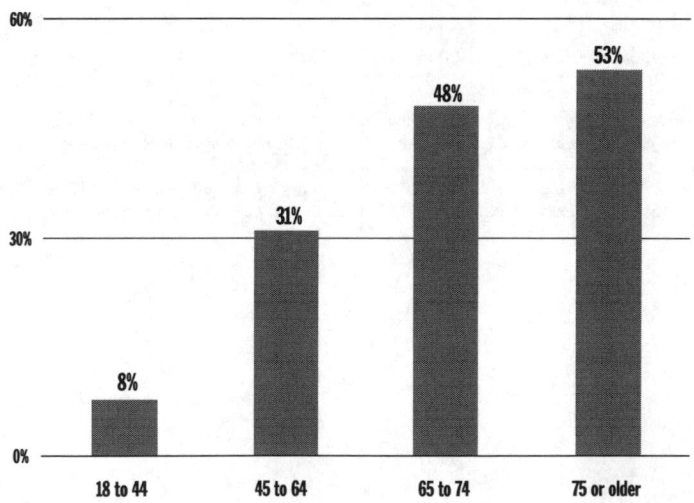

Table 3.23 Health Conditions among Adults by Age, 2011: Number with Condition

(number of people aged 18 or older with selected health conditions, by type of condition and age, 2011; numbers in thousands)

	total	18 to 44	45 to 64	65 or older total	65 to 74	75 or older
TOTAL PEOPLE	231,376	110,815	80,849	39,712	21,902	17,810
Selected circulatory diseases						
Heart disease, all types	26,485	3,952	10,323	12,209	5,843	6,366
Coronary	15,300	981	5,952	8,367	3,991	4,376
Hypertension	58,959	10,058	26,531	22,371	12,149	10,222
Stroke	6,171	577	2,296	3,298	1,428	1,870
Selected respiratory conditions						
Emphysema	4,680	365	2,146	2,170	1,275	895
Asthma, ever	29,041	15,090	9,840	4,111	2,458	1,653
Asthma, still	18,869	8,850	7,010	3,009	1,807	1,202
Hay fever	16,869	6,142	7,985	2,741	1,694	1,047
Sinusitis	29,611	10,890	12,820	5,901	3,594	2,307
Chronic bronchitis	10,071	3,170	4,356	2,545	1,487	1,058
Cancer						
Any cancer	19,025	2,044	7,140	9,842	4,955	4,887
Breast cancer	3,221	150	1,244	1,826	860	966
Cervical cancer	1,188	507	470	212	103	109
Prostate cancer	2,280	–	356	1,923	943	980
Other selected diseases and conditions						
Diabetes	20,589	2,708	9,702	8,179	4,860	3,319
Ulcers	15,502	4,556	6,541	4,406	2,492	1,914
Kidney disease	4,381	1,007	1,491	1,883	868	1,015
Liver disease	3,016	764	1,747	506	383	123
Arthritis	53,782	8,833	25,182	19,767	10,408	9,359
Chronic joint symptoms	68,749	18,753	30,948	19,048	10,151	8,897
Migraines or severe headaches	37,904	21,495	13,250	3,160	2,077	1,083
Pain in neck	35,798	13,686	15,700	6,411	3,866	2,545
Pain in lower back	66,917	27,079	26,874	12,964	7,270	5,694
Pain in face or jaw	11,436	5,346	4,494	1,596	929	667
Selected sensory problems						
Hearing	37,122	6,832	15,245	15,045	6,603	8,442
Vision	21,232	6,126	9,727	5,379	2,677	2,702
Absence of all natural teeth	18,038	2,754	6,183	9,101	4,071	5,030

Note: The conditions shown are those that have ever been diagnosed by a doctor, except as noted. Hay fever, sinusitis, and chronic bronchitis have been diagnosed in the past 12 months. Kidney and liver disease have been diagnosed in the past 12 months and exclude kidney stones, bladder infections, and incontinence. Chronic joint symptoms are shown if respondent had pain, aching, or stiffness in or around a joint (excluding back and neck) and the condition began more than three months ago. Migraines, pain in neck, lower back, face, or jaw are shown only if pain lasted a whole day or more. "–" means sample is too small to make a reliable estimate.
Source: National Center for Health Statistics, Summary Health Statistics for U.S. Adults: National Health Interview Survey, 2011, Vital and Health Statistics, Series 10, No. 256, 2012, Internet site http://www.cdc.gov/nchs/nhis.htm; calculations by New Strategist

Table 3.24 Health Conditions among Adults by Age, 2011: Percent with Condition

(percent of people aged 18 or older with selected health condition, by type of condition and age, 2011)

	total	18 to 44	45 to 64	65 or older total	65 to 74	75 or older
TOTAL PEOPLE	100.0%	100.0%	100.0%	100.0%	100.0%	100.0%
Selected circulatory diseases						
Heart disease, all types	11.4	3.6	12.8	30.7	26.7	35.7
Coronary	6.6	0.9	7.4	21.1	18.2	24.6
Hypertension	25.5	9.1	32.8	56.3	55.5	57.4
Stroke	2.7	0.5	2.8	8.3	6.5	10.5
Selected respiratory conditions						
Emphysema	2.0	0.3	2.7	5.5	5.8	5.0
Asthma, ever	12.6	13.6	12.2	10.4	11.2	9.3
Asthma, still	8.2	8.0	8.7	7.6	8.3	6.7
Hay fever	7.3	5.5	9.9	6.9	7.7	5.9
Sinusitis	12.8	9.8	15.9	14.9	16.4	13.0
Chronic bronchitis	4.4	2.9	5.4	6.4	6.8	5.9
Cancer						
Any cancer	8.2	1.8	8.8	24.8	22.6	27.4
Breast cancer	1.4	0.1	1.5	4.6	3.9	5.4
Cervical cancer	0.5	0.5	0.6	0.5	0.5	0.6
Prostate cancer	1.0	–	0.4	4.8	4.3	5.5
Other selected diseases and conditions						
Diabetes	8.9	2.4	12.0	20.6	22.2	18.6
Ulcers	6.7	4.1	8.1	11.1	11.4	10.7
Kidney disease	1.9	0.9	1.8	4.7	4.0	5.7
Liver disease	1.3	0.7	2.2	1.3	1.7	0.7
Arthritis	23.2	8.0	31.1	49.8	47.5	52.5
Chronic joint symptoms	29.7	16.9	38.3	48.0	46.3	50.0
Migraines or severe headaches	16.4	19.4	16.4	8.0	9.5	6.1
Pain in neck	15.5	12.4	19.4	16.1	17.7	14.3
Pain in lower back	28.9	24.4	33.2	32.6	33.2	32.0
Pain in face or jaw	4.9	4.8	5.6	4.0	4.2	3.7
Selected sensory problems						
Hearing	16.0	6.2	18.9	37.9	30.1	47.4
Vision	9.2	5.5	12.0	13.5	12.2	15.2
Absence of all natural teeth	7.8	2.5	7.6	22.9	18.6	28.2

Note: The conditions shown are those that have ever been diagnosed by a doctor, except as noted. Hay fever, sinusitis, and chronic bronchitis have been diagnosed in the past 12 months. Kidney and liver disease have been diagnosed in the past 12 months and exclude kidney stones, bladder infections, and incontinence. Chronic joint symptoms are shown if respondent had pain, aching, or stiffness in or around a joint (excluding back and neck) and the condition began more than three months ago. Migraines, pain in neck, lower back, face, or jaw are shown only if pain lasted a whole day or more. "–" means sample is too small to make a reliable estimate.
Source: National Center for Health Statistics, Summary Health Statistics for U.S. Adults: National Health Interview Survey, 2011, Vital and Health Statistics, Series 10, No. 256, 2012, Internet site http://www.cdc.gov/nchs/nhis.htm; calculations by New Strategist

Table 3.25 Health Conditions among Adults by Age, 2011: Distribution by Condition

(percent distribution of people aged 18 or older with selected health conditions, by type of condition and age, 2011)

	total	18 to 44	45 to 64	65 or older total	65 to 74	75 or older
TOTAL PEOPLE	100.0%	47.9%	34.9%	17.2%	9.5%	7.7%
Selected circulatory diseases						
Heart disease, all types	100.0	14.9	39.0	46.1	22.1	24.0
Coronary	100.0	6.4	38.9	54.7	26.1	28.6
Hypertension	100.0	17.1	45.0	37.9	20.6	17.3
Stroke	100.0	9.4	37.2	53.4	23.1	30.3
Selected respiratory conditions						
Emphysema	100.0	7.8	45.9	46.4	27.2	19.1
Asthma, ever	100.0	52.0	33.9	14.2	8.5	5.7
Asthma, still	100.0	46.9	37.2	15.9	9.6	6.4
Hay fever	100.0	36.4	47.3	16.2	10.0	6.2
Sinusitis	100.0	36.8	43.3	19.9	12.1	7.8
Chronic bronchitis	100.0	31.5	43.3	25.3	14.8	10.5
Cancer						
Any cancer	100.0	10.7	37.5	51.7	26.0	25.7
Breast cancer	100.0	4.7	38.6	56.7	26.7	30.0
Cervical cancer	100.0	42.7	39.6	17.8	8.7	9.2
Prostate cancer	100.0	–	15.6	84.3	41.4	43.0
Other selected diseases and conditions						
Diabetes	100.0	13.2	47.1	39.7	23.6	16.1
Ulcers	100.0	29.4	42.2	28.4	16.1	12.3
Kidney disease	100.0	23.0	34.0	43.0	19.8	23.2
Liver disease	100.0	25.3	57.9	16.8	12.7	4.1
Arthritis	100.0	16.4	46.8	36.8	19.4	17.4
Chronic joint symptoms	100.0	27.3	45.0	27.7	14.8	12.9
Migraines or severe headaches	100.0	56.7	35.0	8.3	5.5	2.9
Pain in neck	100.0	38.2	43.9	17.9	10.8	7.1
Pain in lower back	100.0	40.5	40.2	19.4	10.9	8.5
Pain in face or jaw	100.0	46.7	39.3	14.0	8.1	5.8
Selected sensory problems						
Hearing	100.0	18.4	41.1	40.5	17.8	22.7
Vision	100.0	28.9	45.8	25.3	12.6	12.7
Absence of all natural teeth	100.0	15.3	34.3	50.5	22.6	27.9

Note: The conditions shown are those that have ever been diagnosed by a doctor, except as noted. Hay fever, sinusitis, and chronic bronchitis have been diagnosed in the past 12 months. Kidney and liver disease have been diagnosed in the past 12 months and exclude kidney stones, bladder infections, and incontinence. Chronic joint symptoms are shown if respondent had pain, aching, or stiffness in or around a joint (excluding back and neck) and the condition began more than three months ago. Migraines, pain in neck, lower back, face, or jaw are shown only if pain lasted a whole day or more. "–" means sample is too small to make a reliable estimate.
Source: National Center for Health Statistics, Summary Health Statistics for U.S. Adults: National Health Interview Survey, 2011, Vital and Health Statistics, Series 10, No. 256, 2012, Internet site http://www.cdc.gov/nchs/nhis.htm; calculations by New Strategist

Table 3.26 Cumulative Number of AIDS Cases by Selected Characteristics, through 2010

(cumulative number and percent distribution of AIDS cases by sex, age at diagnosis, and race and Hispanic origin, through 2010)

	number	percent distribution
Total cases	1,129,127	100.0%
Sex		
Males aged 13 or older	893,058	79.1
Females aged 13 or older	226,593	20.1
Age		
Under age 13	9,475	0.8
Aged 13 to 14	1,398	0.1
Aged 15 to 24	52,531	4.7
Aged 25 to 34	348,275	30.8
Aged 35 to 44	432,124	38.3
Aged 45 to 54	204,740	18.1
Aged 55 to 64	62,152	5.5
Aged 65 or older	18,431	1.6
Race and Hispanic origin		
American Indian	3,690	0.3
Asian	8,710	0.8
Black	467,498	42.2
Hispanic	195,520	16.8
Non-Hispanic white	428,205	39.1

Note: American Indians, Asians, and blacks are those who identify themselves as being of the race alone. Non-Hispanic whites are those who identify themselves as being white alone and not Hispanic.
Source: National Center for Health Statistics, Health United States, 2012, Internet site http://www.cdc.gov/nchs/hus.htm; calculations by New Strategist

Many Older Americans Have Physical Difficulties

The biggest problem is inability to stand for long periods of time.

A 2011 survey by the National Center for Health Statistics estimated that 37 million Americans—16 percent of people aged 18 or older—have physical difficulties. The survey asks about difficulties with tasks ranging from walking a quarter mile to climbing stairs to stooping, standing, and grasping small objects. Not surprisingly, older Americans are much more likely than younger adults to have physical difficulties.

Just 6 percent of people aged 18 to 44 reported having any physical difficulty. The proportion rises to 19 percent among 45-to-64-year-olds and peaks at 48 percent among people aged 75 or older. The single most common problem is inability to stand for two hours, with 10 percent of people aged 18 or older saying standing would be "very difficult" or they could not do it at all. Almost the same proportion of adults say they would have difficulty stooping, bending, or kneeling. Eight percent say they could not walk a quarter of a mile, including more than one in five people aged 65 or older.

■ Although Americans aged 65 or older are most likely to report physical difficulties, younger adults account for the majority of those with physical difficulties.

Difficulty walking increases with age

(percent of people who cannot walk a quarter of a mile, by age, 2011)

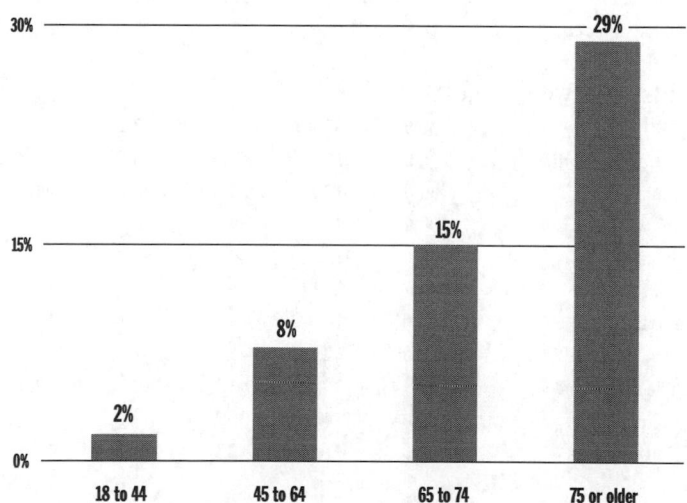

Table 3.27 Difficulties in Physical Functioning among Adults by Age, 2011

(number of people aged 18 or older with difficulties in physical functioning, by type of difficulty and age, 2011; numbers in thousands)

	total	18 to 44	45 to 64	65 or older total	65 to 74	75 or older
TOTAL PEOPLE	231,376	110,815	80,849	39,712	21,902	17,810
Total with any physical difficulty	37,368	6,598	15,492	15,279	6,733	8,546
Walk quarter of a mile	17,597	2,336	6,734	8,528	3,373	5,155
Climb 10 steps without resting	12,887	1,442	5,142	6,303	2,452	3,851
Stand for two hours	22,369	3,434	9,002	9,933	4,021	5,912
Sit for two hours	7,724	1,810	3,930	1,985	1,130	855
Stoop, bend, or kneel	21,677	3,090	9,355	9,232	3,913	5,319
Reach over head	6,550	833	2,979	2,738	1,163	1,575
Grasp or handle small objects	4,329	602	1,902	1,825	837	988
Lift or carry 10 pounds	10,677	1,528	4,177	4,972	1,803	3,169
Push or pull large objects	15,998	2,498	6,733	6,768	2,656	4,112
PERCENT WITH PHYSICAL DIFFICULTY						
TOTAL PEOPLE	100.0%	100.0%	100.0%	100.0%	100.0%	100.0%
Total with any physical difficulty	16.2	6.0	19.2	38.5	30.7	48.0
Walk quarter of a mile	7.6	2.1	8.3	21.5	15.4	28.9
Climb 10 steps without resting	5.6	1.3	6.4	15.9	11.2	21.6
Stand for two hours	9.7	3.1	11.1	25.0	18.4	33.2
Sit for two hours	3.3	1.6	4.9	5.0	5.2	4.8
Stoop, bend, or kneel	9.4	2.8	11.6	23.2	17.9	29.9
Reach over head	2.8	0.8	3.7	6.9	5.3	8.8
Grasp or handle small objects	1.9	0.5	2.4	4.6	3.8	5.5
Lift or carry 10 pounds	4.6	1.4	5.2	12.5	8.2	17.8
Push or pull large objects	6.9	2.3	8.3	17.0	12.1	23.1
PERCENT DISTRIBUTION BY AGE						
TOTAL PEOPLE	100.0	47.9	34.9	17.2	9.5	7.7
Total with any physical difficulty	100.0	17.7	41.5	40.9	18.0	22.9
Walk quarter of a mile	100.0	13.3	38.3	48.5	19.2	29.3
Climb 10 steps without resting	100.0	11.2	39.9	48.9	19.0	29.9
Stand for two hours	100.0	15.4	40.2	44.4	18.0	26.4
Sit for two hours	100.0	23.4	50.9	25.7	14.6	11.1
Stoop, bend, or kneel	100.0	14.3	43.2	42.6	18.1	24.5
Reach over head	100.0	12.7	45.5	41.8	17.8	24.0
Grasp or handle small objects	100.0	13.9	43.9	42.2	19.3	22.8
Lift or carry 10 pounds	100.0	14.3	39.1	46.6	16.9	29.7
Push or pull large objects	100.0	15.6	42.1	42.3	16.6	25.7

Note: Respondents were classified as having difficulties if they responded "very difficult" or "can't do at all."
Source: National Center for Health Statistics, Summary Health Statistics for U.S. Adults: National Health Interview Survey, 2011, Vital and Health Statistics, Series 10, No. 256, 2012, Internet site http://www.cdc.gov/nchs/nhis.htm; calculations by New Strategist

Most Americans See a Health Care Provider More than Once a Year

Older Americans are most likely to be hospitalized.

Among Americans aged 18 or older, 80 percent see a health care provider at least once a year. The figure rises above 90 percent among people aged 65 or older. A substantial 26 percent of 18-to-44-year-olds have not seen a health care provider in the past 12 months. Among Hispanics, the proportion is an even larger 32 percent.

In 2011, only 8 percent of the population experienced an overnight hospitalization. People aged 65 or older are most likely to experience a hospital stay, with 17 percent hospitalized in 2011.

■ Among people aged 45 to 64, nearly one in ten did not receive medical care and 13 percent delayed getting medical care due to cost.

Many do not go to the doctor

(percent of people who have not visited a doctor or other health care provider in the past year, by race and Hispanic origin, 2011)

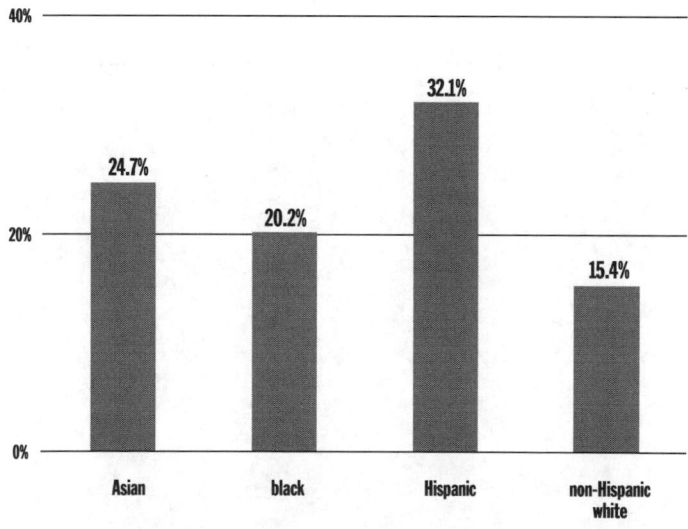

Table 3.28 Health Care Office Visits by Selected Characteristics, 2011

(number of people aged 18 or older and percent distribution by number of office visits to a health care provider in past 12 months, by selected characteristics, 2011; numbers in thousands)

	total			one or more visits				
	number	percent	no visits	total	one	two to three	four to nine	10 or more
Total people	231,376	100.0%	18.8%	80.1%	17.1%	25.6%	24.1%	13.3%
Sex								
Men	112,093	100.0	25.2	73.8	19.5	24.4	20.1	9.8
Women	119,283	100.0	12.9	86.0	14.8	26.8	27.8	16.6
Age								
Aged 18 to 44	110,815	100.0	25.8	73.4	19.8	25.0	18.3	10.4
Aged 45 to 64	80,849	100.0	15.6	83.4	16.7	27.0	25.8	14.0
Aged 65 to 74	21,902	100.0	6.5	91.7	10.7	25.4	35.8	19.8
Aged 75 or older	17,810	100.0	5.6	92.3	10.0	23.5	38.2	20.5
Race and Hispanic origin								
Asian	11,468	100.0	24.7	74.4	20.7	25.1	20.7	7.9
Black	27,666	100.0	20.2	78.4	17.0	26.4	22.4	12.7
Hispanic	32,762	100.0	32.1	66.9	17.6	21.6	18.5	9.2
Non-Hispanic white	156,482	100.0	15.4	83.6	16.8	26.3	25.8	14.6

Note: Health care visits exclude overnight hospitalizations, visits to emergency rooms, home visits, dental visits, and telephone calls. Numbers do not add to total because "unknown" is not shown. Asians and blacks are those who identify themselves as being of the race alone. Non-Hispanic whites are those who identify themselves as being white alone and not Hispanic.
Source: National Center for Health Statistics, Summary Health Statistics for U.S. Adults: National Health Interview Survey, 2011, Vital and Health Statistics, Series 10, No. 256, 2012, Internet site http://www.cdc.gov/nchs/nhis.htm; calculations by New Strategist

Table 3.29 Overnight Hospital Stays by Selected Characteristics, 2011

(total number of people and percent distribution by experience of an overnight hospital stay in past 12 months, by age, 2011; numbers in thousands)

	total		number of hospital stays	
	number	percent	none	one or more
Total people	**305,088**	**100.0%**	**92.1%**	**7.9%**
Sex				
Female	150,193	100.0	90.6	9.4
Male	155,695	100.0	93.8	6.2
Age				
Under age 12	50,267	100.0	93.2	6.8
Aged 12 to 17	24,249	100.0	97.7	2.3
Aged 18 to 44	110,813	100.0	93.6	6.4
Aged 45 to 64	80,852	100.0	91.8	8.2
Aged 65 or older	39,707	100.0	83.3	16.7
Race and Hispanic origin				
Asian	14,958	100.0	95.0	5.0
Black	38,774	100.0	91.1	8.9
Hispanic	50,277	100.0	93.0	7.0
Non-Hispanic white	197,065	100.0	92.0	8.0

Note: Asians and blacks are those who identify themselves as being of the race alone. Non-Hispanic whites are those who identify themselves as being white alone and not Hispanic.
Source: National Center for Health Statistics, Summary Health Statistics for the U.S. Population: National Health Interview Survey, 2011, Series 10, No. 255, 2012, Internet site http://www.cdc.gov/nchs/nhis.htm; calculations by New Strategist

Table 3.30 Problems Getting Medical Care by Selected Characteristics, 2011

(total number of people and percent who did not receive or delayed getting needed medical care in past year due to cost, by selected characteristics, 2011; numbers in thousands)

	total number	percent	did not receive care due to cost	delayed getting care due to cost
Total people	305,088	100.0%	6.5%	9.0%
Sex				
Female	150,193	100.0	6.9	9.5
Male	155,695	100.0	5.9	8.1
Age				
Under age 12	50,267	100.0	1.5	3.0
Aged 12 to 17	24,249	100.0	2.3	3.9
Aged 18 to 44	110,813	100.0	9.1	11.7
Aged 45 to 64	80,852	100.0	9.4	12.9
Aged 65 or older	39,707	100.0	2.6	4.0
Race and Hispanic origin				
Asian	14,958	100.0	3.9	5.6
Black	38,774	100.0	8.4	9.2
Hispanic	50,277	100.0	8.0	10.2
Non-Hispanic white	197,065	100.0	5.9	8.7

Note: Asians and blacks are those who identify themselves as being of the race alone. Non-Hispanic whites are those who identify themselves as being white alone and not Hispanic.
Source: National Center for Health Statistics, Summary Health Statistics for the U.S. Population: National Health Interview Survey, 2011, Series 10, No. 255, 2012, Internet site http://www.cdc.gov/nchs/nhis.htm; calculations by New Strategist

Heart Disease Is the Number-One Cause of Death

Cancer is number two.

Nearly half of the 2.5 million deaths that occurred in the United States in 2011 were caused by heart disease (24 percent) or cancer (23 percent). Among those who died of heart disease, people aged 65 or older accounted for the 80 percent majority. The 65-or-older age group accounted for 69 percent of deaths from cancer.

Overall, people aged 65 or older account for 73 percent of deaths—or 1.8 million of the 2.5 million deaths in 2011. Accidents and suicide are the only causes of death among the top 10 that are more likely to claim people under age 65.

■ More effective treatments for heart disease and cancer are extending the lives of Americans.

Most deaths occur to people aged 65 or older

(percent of deaths occurring to people aged 65 or older, by cause, 2011)

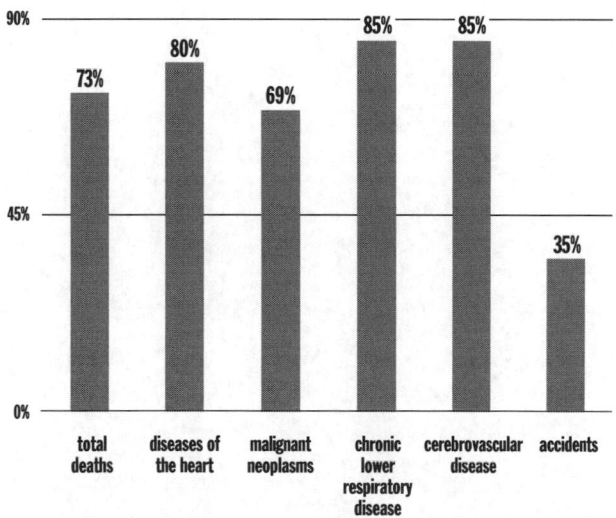

Table 3.31 Deaths from the 10 Leading Causes by Age, 2011

(total number of deaths and percent distribution by cause, and number and percent of deaths occurring to people aged 65 or older, for the 10 leading causes of death, 2011)

			aged 65 or older	
	number	percent distribution	number	percent of total
Total deaths	**2,512,873**	**100.0%**	**1,830,553**	**72.8%**
1. Diseases of the heart	596,339	23.7	476,220	79.9
2. Malignant neoplasms (cancer)	575,313	22.9	396,126	68.9
3. Chronic lower respiratory diseases	143,382	5.7	122,381	85.4
4. Cerebrovascular diseases	128,931	5.1	109,393	84.8
5. Accidents	122,777	4.9	42,635	34.7
6. Alzheimer's disease	84,691	3.4	83,746	98.9
7. Diabetes mellitus	73,282	2.9	52,068	71.1
8. Influenza and pneumonia	53,667	2.1	45,321	84.4
9. Nephritis, nephrotic syndrome, and nephrosis	45,731	1.8	37,927	82.9
10. Suicide	38,285	1.5	6,195	16.2
All other causes	650,475	25.9	458,541	70.5

Source: National Center for Health Statistics, Deaths: Preliminary Data for 2011, National Vital Statistics Report, Vol. 61, No. 6, 2012, Internet site http://www.cdc.gov/nchs/deaths.htm; calculations by New Strategist

Americans Are Living Longer

Medical advances have reduced death rate.

The longer people live, the longer they can expect to live, on average. Life expectancy increases as people get older because they have managed to live through life's dangers up to that point.

Women aged 20 in 2011 could expect to live to be 82 years old (61.8 years of life remaining), on average. But a 50-year-old woman could expect to live to be 83 (33.2 years remaining). A woman aged 80 could expect to reach the ripe old age of nearly 90 (9.7 years of life remaining). Men have shorter life expectancy than women, but the pattern is the same.

Despite the poorer self-reported health of Hispanics, their life expectancy is longer than any other racial or ethnic group. At birth, Hispanics have a life expectancy of 81.4 years versus 78.8 years for non-Hispanic whites and 75.3 years for blacks. The reason for the longer life expectancy of Hispanics is a medical mystery that has yet to be explained.

■ The dramatic increase in life expectancy since 1950 is the result of a decline in infant mortality and life-sustaining treatment of heart disease and cancer.

Life expectancy is highest among Hispanics

(number of years of life remaining at birth, by race and Hispanic origin, 2011)

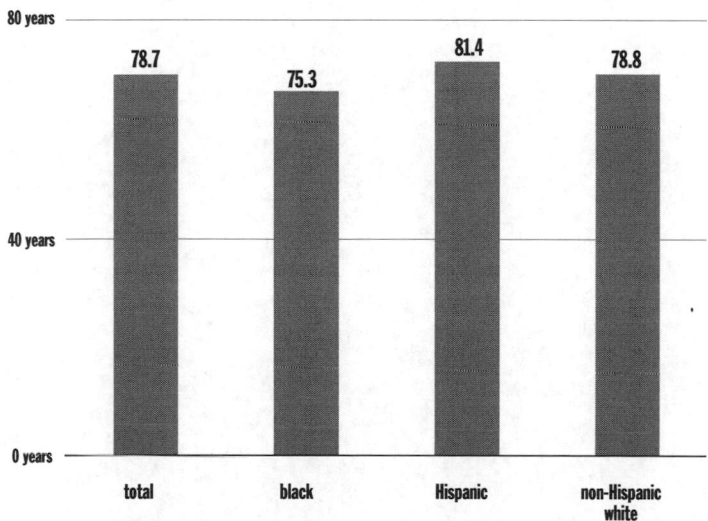

Table 3.32 Life Expectancy by Age, 1950 to 2011

(expected years of life remaining at birth and age 65, 1950 to 2011; change in years of life remaining for selected years)

	at birth	age 65
2011	78.7 yrs.	19.2 yrs.
2000	77.0	17.9
1990	75.4	17.2
1980	73.7	16.4
1970	70.8	15.2
1960	69.7	14.3
1950	68.2	13.9
CHANGE		
2000 to 2011	1.7	1.3
1950 to 2011	10.5	5.3

Source: National Center for Health Statistics, Deaths: Preliminary Data for 2011, National Vital Statistics Report, Vol. 61, No. 6, 2012, Internet site http://www.cdc.gov/nchs/deaths.htm; calculations by New Strategist

Table 3.33 Life Expectancy by Age and Sex, 2011

(expected years of life remaining at selected ages, by sex, 2011)

	total	females	males
At birth	78.7 yrs.	81.1 yrs.	76.3 yrs.
Aged 1	78.2	80.5	75.8
Aged 5	74.3	76.6	71.9
Aged 10	69.3	71.6	66.9
Aged 15	64.4	66.7	62.0
Aged 20	59.5	61.8	57.2
Aged 25	54.8	56.9	52.5
Aged 30	50.0	52.0	47.9
Aged 35	45.3	47.2	43.2
Aged 40	40.6	42.5	38.6
Aged 45	36.0	37.8	34.0
Aged 50	31.5	33.2	29.6
Aged 55	27.2	28.8	25.5
Aged 60	23.1	24.5	21.5
Aged 65	19.2	20.4	17.8
Aged 70	15.5	16.5	14.3
Aged 75	12.1	12.9	11.0
Aged 80	9.1	9.7	8.2
Aged 85	6.5	6.9	5.9
Aged 90	4.6	4.8	4.1
Aged 95	3.2	3.3	2.9
Aged 100	2.3	2.3	2.1

Source: National Center for Health Statistics, Deaths: Preliminary Data for 2011, National Vital Statistics Report, Vol. 61, No. 6, 2012, Internet site http://www.cdc.gov/nchs/deaths.htm

Table 3.34 Life Expectancy by Race and Hispanic Origin, 2011

(expected number of years of life remaining at birth by race, Hispanic origin, and sex, and difference in life expectancy by race and Hispanic origin to average for each sex, 2011)

	total	females	males
Total	**78.7 yrs.**	**81.1 yrs.**	**76.3 yrs.**
Black	75.3	78.2	72.1
Hispanic	81.4	83.7	78.9
Non-Hispanic white	78.8	81.1	76.4
Difference between race and Hispanic origin group and average			
Black	–3.4 yrs.	–2.9 yrs.	–4.2 yrs.
Hispanic	2.7	2.6	2.6
Non-Hispanic white	0.1	0.0	0.1

Source: National Center for Health Statistics, Deaths: Preliminary Data for 2011, National Vital Statistics Report, Vol. 61, No. 6, 2012, Internet site http://www.cdc.gov/nchs/deaths.htm; calculations by New Strategist

4

Housing

Trends

The homeownership rate is falling.

In 2012, 65.4 percent of households owned their home. This figure was 3.6 percentage points lower than the peak of 69.0 percent in 2004.

Householders aged 35 to 44 experienced the biggest decline in homeownership.

The homeownership rate among householders aged 35 to 44 fell 7.8 percentage points between 2004 and 2012.

The homeownership rate fell in all but six states between 2004 and 2012.

The biggest decline was in Nevada, where the rate fell 10 percentage points during those years.

American homes have a median of 1,800 square feet of living space.

Most homes have three or more bedrooms and two or more bathrooms.

Most householders are happy with their home.

When asked how they would rate their housing unit on a scale of 1 (worst) to 10 (best), nearly three out of four householders rate their home an 8 or higher.

The median value of owned homes fell to $160,000 in 2011.

Mortgage loans as a percentage of home values grew from 54 to 71 percent between 2007 and 2011 as housing prices fell.

Homeownership Rate Is Falling

Rate has decreased in most age groups since peaking in 2004.

In 2012, 65.4 percent of households owned their home—3.6 percentage points below the record high of 69.0 percent reached in 2004. The homeownership rate fell in every age group under age 65 between 2004 and 2012. Householders aged 35 to 44 experienced the biggest decline in homeownership, their rate falling to 61.4 percent—7.8 percentage points lower than in 2004.

The homeownership rate fell for every household type and every race and Hispanic origin group between 2004 and 2012. Among married couples, 80.8 percent owned their home in 2012—the highest rate of homeownership among all household types. Among non-Hispanic whites, the homeownership rate was 73.5 percent compared with 43.9 percent among blacks and 46.1 percent among Hispanics.

■ Despite the collapse of the housing bubble and the record number of foreclosures, nearly two-thirds of households are homeowners.

The homeownership rate is highest among older Americans

(percent of householders who own their home, by age, 2012)

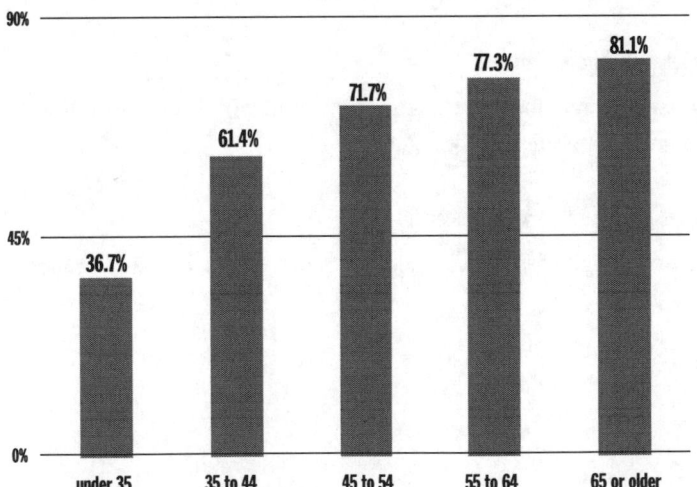

Table 4.1 Homeownership Rate by Age, Household Type, Race, and Hispanic Origin, 2000 to 2012

(percent of households that own their home by age of householder, household type, and race and Hispanic origin of householder, 2000 to 2012; percentage point change for selected years)

	2012	2004 (peak year)	2000	percentage point change 2004–12	percentage point change 2000–12
Total households	**65.4%**	**69.0%**	**67.5%**	**–3.6**	**–2.1**
Age of householder					
Under age 35	36.7	43.1	40.7	–6.4	–4.0
Aged 35 to 44	61.4	69.2	68.0	–7.8	–6.6
Aged 45 to 54	71.7	77.2	76.8	–5.5	–5.1
Aged 55 to 64	77.3	81.7	80.2	–4.4	–2.9
Aged 65 or older	81.1	81.1	80.5	0.0	0.6
Type of household					
Married couples	80.8	84.0	82.4	–3.2	–1.6
Female householders, no spouse present	46.7	50.9	48.9	–4.2	–2.2
Male householders, no spouse present	55.9	59.6	58.6	–3.7	–2.7
Women living alone	58.3	59.9	57.9	–1.6	0.4
Men living alone	49.8	50.5	47.8	–0.7	2.0
Race and Hispanic origin of householder					
American Indian	51.1	55.6	56.2	–4.5	–5.1
Asian	56.6	59.8	52.8	–3.2	3.8
Black	43.9	49.1	47.2	–5.2	–3.3
Hispanic	46.1	48.1	46.3	–2.0	–0.2
Non-Hispanic white	73.5	76.0	73.8	–2.5	–0.3

Note: American Indians, Asians, blacks, and whites are those who identified themselves as being of the race alone.
Source: Bureau of the Census, Housing Vacancy Survey, Internet site http://www.census.gov/housing/hvs/; calculations by New Strategist

Table 4.2 Homeownership Status by Age of Householder, 2012

(number and percent distribution of households by age of householder and homeownership status, 2012; numbers in thousands)

	total	owner	renter
Total households	**114,224**	**74,744**	**39,480**
Under age 35	24,756	9,074	15,682
Aged 35 to 44	20,182	12,401	7,781
Aged 45 to 54	22,755	16,316	6,439
Aged 55 to 64	21,184	16,386	4,798
Aged 65 or older	25,346	20,568	4,778
PERCENT DISTRIBUTION BY HOMEOWNERSHIP STATUS			
Total households	**100.0%**	**65.4%**	**34.6%**
Under age 35	100.0	36.7	63.3
Aged 35 to 44	100.0	61.4	38.6
Aged 45 to 54	100.0	71.7	28.3
Aged 55 to 64	100.0	77.4	22.6
Aged 65 or older	100.0	81.1	18.9
PERCENT DISTRIBUTION BY AGE			
Total households	**100.0**	**100.0**	**100.0**
Under age 35	21.7	12.1	39.7
Aged 35 to 44	17.7	16.6	19.7
Aged 45 to 54	19.9	21.8	16.3
Aged 55 to 64	18.5	21.9	12.2
Aged 65 or older	22.2	27.5	12.1

Source: Bureau of the Census, Housing Vacancy Survey, Internet site http://www.census.gov/housing/hvs/; calculations by New Strategist

Table 4.3 Homeownership Status by Type of Household, 2012

(number and percent distribution of households by household type and homeownership status, 2012; numbers in thousands)

	total	owner	renter
Total households	**114,224**	**74,744**	**39,480**
Married couples	55,433	44,790	10,643
Female householders, no spouse present	14,578	6,801	7,777
Male householders, no spouse present	5,835	3,261	2,574
Women living alone	17,180	10,021	7,159
Men living alone	14,062	6,997	7,065

PERCENT DISTRIBUTION BY HOMEOWNERSHIP STATUS

Total households	**100.0%**	**65.4%**	**34.6%**
Married couples	100.0	80.8	19.2
Female householders, no spouse present	100.0	46.7	53.3
Male householders, no spouse present	100.0	55.9	44.1
Women living alone	100.0	58.3	41.7
Men living alone	100.0	49.8	50.2

PERCENT DISTRIBUTION BY HOUSEHOLD TYPE

Total households	**100.0**	**100.0**	**100.0**
Married couples	48.5	59.9	27.0
Female householders, no spouse present	12.8	9.1	19.7
Male householders, no spouse present	5.1	4.4	6.5
Women living alone	15.0	13.4	18.1
Men living alone	12.3	9.4	17.9

Note: Numbers do not sum to total because not all household types are shown.
Source: Bureau of the Census, Housing Vacancy Survey, Internet site http://www.census.gov/housing/hvs/; calculations by New Strategist

Table 4.4 Homeownership Status by Race and Hispanic Origin of Householder, 2011

(number and percent distribution of households by race and Hispanic origin of householder and homeownership status, 2011; numbers in thousands)

	total	owner	renter
Total households	**114,907**	**76,091**	**38,816**
American Indian	965	409	556
Asian	4,620	2,714	1,907
Black	14,694	6,662	8,033
Hispanic	13,841	6,530	7,311
Non-Hispanic white	80,190	59,274	20,916
PERCENT DISTRIBUTION BY HOMEOWNERSHIP STATUS			
Total households	**100.0%**	**66.2%**	**33.8%**
American Indian	100.0	42.4	57.6
Asian	100.0	58.7	41.3
Black	100.0	45.3	54.7
Hispanic	100.0	47.2	52.8
Non-Hispanic white	100.0	73.9	26.1
PERCENT DISTRIBUTION BY RACE AND HISPANIC ORIGIN			
Total households	**100.0**	**100.0**	**100.0**
American Indian	0.8	0.5	1.4
Asian	4.0	3.6	4.9
Black	12.8	8.8	20.7
Hispanic	12.0	8.6	18.8
Non-Hispanic white	69.8	77.9	53.9

Note: American Indians, Asians, blacks, and whites are those who identify themselves as being of the race alone.
Source: Bureau of the Census, American Housing Survey for the United States: 2011, Internet site http://www.census.gov/housing/ahs/data/national.html; calculations by New Strategist

Homeownership Rises with Income

Because the educated are the most affluent, homeownership also rises with education.

Despite troubles in the housing market and the rise in foreclosures, most Americans are homeowners in all but the lowest income groups. In 2011, renters outnumbered homeowners only among households with incomes below $25,000. The higher the household income, the greater the homeownership rate. The rate peaks at 89.4 percent among households with incomes of $120,000 or more.

Homeownership also rises with education, although not as sharply. Among householders without a high school diploma, 53.4 percent are homeowners. Among those with a bachelor's degree the figure is 74.6 percent.

Not surprisingly, native-born Americans are more likely to be homeowners than residents of the United States who were born in another country. Nevertheless, the 51.8 percent majority of immigrants are homeowners.

■ Among immigrants who came to the United States before 1980, more than 73 percent are homeowners.

Nearly 90 percent of the most-affluent households own their home

(percent distribution of households with incomes of $100,000 or more by homeownership status, 2011)

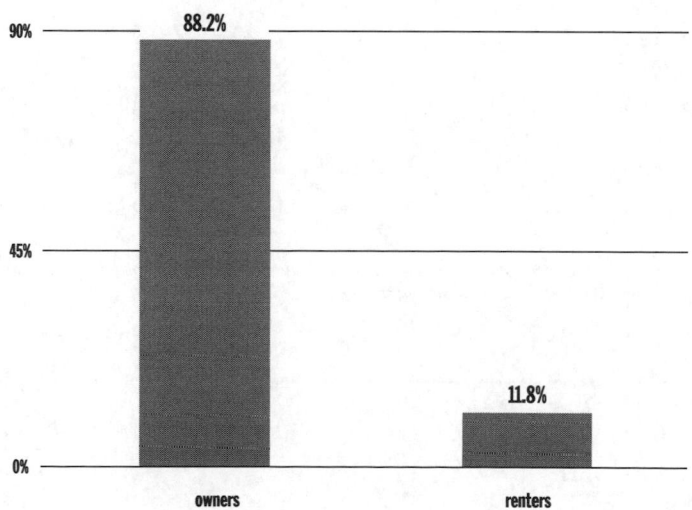

Table 4.5 Homeownership Status by Household Income, 2011

(number and percent distribution of households by household income and homeownership status, 2011; numbers in thousands)

	total	owner	renter
Total households	**114,907**	**76,091**	**38,816**
Less than $25,000	30,498	13,715	16,783
$25,000 to $50,000	30,104	18,664	11,441
$50,000 to $79,999	22,705	16,596	6,107
$80,000 to $99,999	9,830	7,922	1,908
$100,000 or more	21,771	19,194	2,577
$100,000 to $119,999	6,842	5,845	997
$120,000 or more	14,929	13,349	1,580
Median income	**$46,000**	**$58,919**	**$28,000**

PERCENT DISTRIBUTION BY HOMEOWNERSHIP STATUS

Total households	**100.0%**	**66.2%**	**33.8%**
Less than $25,000	100.0	45.0	55.0
$25,000 to $50,000	100.0	62.0	38.0
$50,000 to $79,999	100.0	73.1	26.9
$80,000 to $99,999	100.0	80.6	19.4
$100,000 or more	100.0	88.2	11.8
$100,000 to $119,999	100.0	85.4	14.6
$120,000 or more	100.0	89.4	10.6

PERCENT DISTRIBUTION BY HOUSEHOLD INCOME

Total households	**100.0**	**100.0**	**100.0**
Less than $25,000	26.5	18.0	43.2
$25,000 to $50,000	26.2	24.5	29.5
$50,000 to $79,999	19.8	21.8	15.7
$80,000 to $99,999	8.6	10.4	4.9
$100,000 or more	18.9	25.2	6.6
$100,000 to $119,999	6.0	7.7	2.6
$120,000 or more	13.0	17.5	4.1

Source: Bureau of the Census, American Housing Survey for the United States: 2011, Internet site http://www.census.gov/housing/ahs/data/national.html; calculations by New Strategist

Table 4.6 Homeownership Status by Educational Attainment of Householder, 2011

(number and percent distribution of households by educational attainment of householder and homeownership status, 2011; numbers in thousands)

	total	owner	renter
Total households	**114,907**	**76,091**	**38,816**
Not a high school graduate	15,137	8,084	7,053
High school graduate	33,934	22,177	11,757
Some college, no degree	20,582	12,601	7,981
Associate's degree	9,802	6,766	3,037
Bachelor's degree or more	35,452	26,463	8,990

PERCENT DISTRIBUTION BY HOMEOWNERSHIP STATUS

	total	owner	renter
Total households	**100.0%**	**66.2%**	**33.8%**
Not a high school graduate	100.0	53.4	46.6
High school graduate	100.0	65.4	34.6
Some college, no degree	100.0	61.2	38.8
Associate's degree	100.0	69.0	31.0
Bachelor's degree or more	100.0	74.6	25.4

PERCENT DISTRIBUTION BY EDUCATIONAL ATTAINMENT

	total	owner	renter
Total households	**100.0**	**100.0**	**100.0**
Not a high school graduate	13.2	10.6	18.2
High school graduate	29.5	29.1	30.3
Some college, no degree	17.9	16.6	20.6
Associate's degree	8.5	8.9	7.8
Bachelor's degree or more	30.9	34.8	23.2

Source: Bureau of the Census, American Housing Survey for the United States: 2011, Internet site http://www.census.gov/housing/ahs/data/national.html; calculations by New Strategist

Table 4.7 Homeownership Status by Nativity of Householder, 2011

(number and percent distribution of households headed by native- and foreign-born householders by year of immigration and homeownership status, 2011; numbers in thousands)

	total	owner	renter
Total households	**114,907**	**76,091**	**38,816**
Native-born	99,355	68,034	31,321
Foreign-born	15,552	8,057	7,495
YEAR OF IMMIGRATION			
Total immigrant householders	**15,552**	**8,057**	**7,495**
2010 or later	382	21	361
2005 to 2009	1,513	317	1,196
2000 to 2004	2,167	701	1,466
1990 to 1999	4,238	2,115	2,125
1980 to 1989	3,423	2,100	1,323
1979 or earlier	3,827	2,803	1,024
PERCENT DISTRIBUTION BY HOMEOWNERSHIP STATUS			
Total households	**100.0%**	**66.2%**	**33.8%**
Native-born	100.0	68.5	31.5
Foreign-born	100.0	51.8	48.2
YEAR OF IMMIGRATION			
Total immigrant householders	**100.0**	**51.8**	**48.2**
2010 or later	100.0	5.5	94.5
2005 to 2009	100.0	21.0	79.0
2000 to 2004	100.0	32.3	67.7
1990 to 1999	100.0	49.9	50.1
1980 to 1989	100.0	61.3	38.7
1979 or earlier	100.0	73.2	26.8

Source: Bureau of the Census, American Housing Survey for the United States: 2011, Internet site http://www.census.gov/ housing/ahs/data/national.html; calculations by New Strategist

Homeownership Is Highest in the Midwest

Central city households are least likely to own their home.

The Midwest has the highest homeownership rate in the nation—69.6 percent of households in the region owned their home in 2012. The homeownership rate is lowest in the West, at 59.8 percent. Half of the nation's homeowners live in the suburbs, where 72.1 percent of households own their home.

The homeownership rate fell in all but six states between 2004 (when the overall homeownership rate peaked) and 2012. The biggest decline was in Nevada, where the rate fell 10 percentage points between 2004 and 2012. Homeownership in 2012 was highest in West Virginia (75.8 percent) and lowest in the District of Columbia (45.0 percent) and New York (53.6 percent).

The homeownership rate fell in all but 13 of the nation's 75 largest metropolitan areas between 2005 (the earliest year available) and 2012. The biggest decline was in Columbia, South Carolina—a 10.7 percentage point drop. Among the 75 largest metropolitan areas, the homeownership rate is highest in Grand Rapids, Michigan (76.9 percent) and lowest in Los Angeles, California (49.9 percent).

■ Despite the downturn in the housing market, the homeownership rate is rising in some states and metropolitan areas.

The West has the lowest homeownership rate

(percent of households that own their home, by region, 2012)

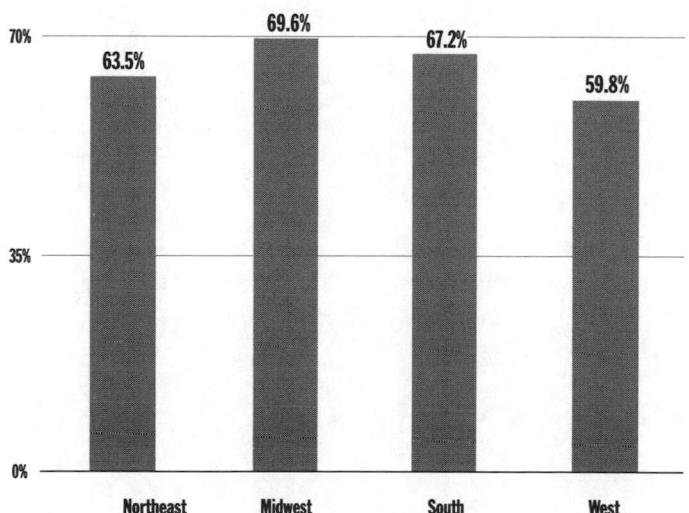

Table 4.8 Homeownership Status by Region of Residence, 2012

(number and percent distribution of households by region of residence and homeownership status, 2012; numbers in thousands)

	total	owner	renter
Total households	**114,224**	**74,744**	**39,480**
Northeast	20,689	13,140	7,550
Midwest	25,850	17,988	7,862
South	42,344	28,463	13,881
West	25,340	15,154	10,187
PERCENT DISTRIBUTION BY HOMEOWNERSHIP STATUS			
Total households	**100.0%**	**65.4%**	**34.6%**
Northeast	100.0	63.5	36.5
Midwest	100.0	69.6	30.4
South	100.0	67.2	32.8
West	100.0	59.8	40.2
PERCENT DISTRIBUTION BY REGION			
Total households	**100.0**	**100.0**	**100.0**
Northeast	18.1	17.6	19.1
Midwest	22.6	24.1	19.9
South	37.1	38.1	35.2
West	22.2	20.3	25.8

Source: Bureau of the Census, Housing Vacancy Survey, Internet site http://www.census.gov/housing/hvs/; calculations by New Strategist

Table 4.9 Homeownership Status by Metropolitan Residence, 2011

(number and percent distribution of households by metropolitan residence and homeownership status, 2011; numbers in thousands)

	total	owner	renter
Total households	**114,907**	**76,091**	**38,816**
In metropolitan areas	92,110	59,357	32,753
In central cities	33,892	17,390	16,502
In suburbs	58,218	41,967	16,251
Outside metropolitan areas	22,797	16,735	6,062
PERCENT DISTRIBUTION BY HOMEOWNERSHIP STATUS			
Total households	**100.0%**	**66.2%**	**33.8%**
In metropolitan areas	100.0	64.4	35.6
In central cities	100.0	51.3	48.7
In suburbs	100.0	72.1	27.9
Outside metropolitan areas	100.0	73.4	26.6
PERCENT DISTRIBUTION BY METROPOLITAN RESIDENCE			
Total households	**100.0**	**100.0**	**100.0**
In metropolitan areas	80.2	78.0	84.4
In central cities	29.5	22.9	42.5
In suburbs	50.7	55.2	41.9
Outside metropolitan areas	19.8	22.0	15.6

Source: Bureau of the Census, American Housing Survey for the United States: 2011, Internet site http://www.census.gov/ housing/ahs/data/national.html; calculations by New Strategist

Table 4.10 Homeownership Rate by State, 2000 to 2012

(percent of householders who own their home by state, 2000 to 2012; percentage point change for selected years)

	2012	2004 (peak year)	2000	percentage point change 2004–12	percentage point change 2000–12
Total households	**65.4%**	**69.0%**	**67.5%**	**–3.6**	**–2.1**
Alabama	71.9	78.0	73.2	–6.1	–1.3
Alaska	63.7	67.2	66.4	–3.5	–2.7
Arizona	65.3	68.7	68.0	–3.4	–2.7
Arkansas	66.0	69.1	68.9	–3.1	–2.9
California	54.5	59.7	57.1	–5.2	–2.6
Colorado	65.3	71.1	68.3	–5.8	–3.0
Connecticut	68.8	71.7	70.0	–2.9	–1.2
Delaware	73.4	77.3	72.0	–3.9	1.4
District of Columbia	45.0	45.6	41.9	–0.6	3.1
Florida	67.0	72.2	68.4	–5.2	–1.4
Georgia	64.3	70.9	69.8	–6.6	–5.5
Hawaii	57.2	60.6	55.2	–3.4	2.0
Idaho	73.0	73.7	70.5	–0.7	2.5
Illinois	66.8	72.7	67.9	–5.9	–1.1
Indiana	72.1	75.8	74.9	–3.7	–2.8
Iowa	70.2	73.2	75.2	–3.0	–5.0
Kansas	63.2	69.9	69.3	–6.7	–6.1
Kentucky	68.7	73.3	73.4	–4.6	–4.7
Louisiana	68.7	70.6	68.1	–1.9	0.6
Maine	74.1	74.7	76.5	–0.6	–2.4
Maryland	68.5	72.1	69.9	–3.6	–1.4
Massachusetts	65.8	63.8	59.9	2.0	5.9
Michigan	74.8	77.1	77.2	–2.3	–2.4
Minnesota	72.0	76.4	76.1	–4.4	–4.1
Mississippi	74.2	74.0	75.2	0.2	–1.0
Missouri	70.8	72.4	74.2	–1.6	–3.4
Montana	67.8	72.4	70.2	–4.6	–2.4
Nebraska	69.3	71.2	70.2	–1.9	–0.9
Nevada	55.7	65.7	64.0	–10.0	–8.3
New Hampshire	74.8	73.3	69.2	1.5	5.6
New Jersey	66.6	68.8	66.2	–2.2	0.4
New Mexico	66.8	71.5	73.7	–4.7	–6.9
New York	53.6	54.8	53.4	–1.2	0.2
North Carolina	67.2	69.8	71.1	–2.6	–3.9
North Dakota	66.2	70.0	70.7	–3.8	–4.5
Ohio	67.9	73.1	71.3	–5.2	–3.4
Oklahoma	68.8	71.1	72.7	–2.3	–3.9
Oregon	66.1	69.0	65.3	–2.9	0.8

	2012	2004 (peak year)	2000	percentage point change	
				2004–12	2000–12
Pennsylvania	71.0%	74.9%	74.7%	–3.9	–3.7
Rhode Island	62.1	61.5	61.5	0.6	0.6
South Carolina	71.5	76.2	76.5	–4.7	–5.0
South Dakota	69.2	68.5	71.2	0.7	–2.0
Tennessee	67.9	71.6	70.9	–3.7	–3.0
Texas	64.3	65.5	63.8	–1.2	0.5
Utah	71.1	74.9	72.7	–3.8	–1.6
Vermont	73.4	72.0	68.7	1.4	4.7
Virginia	67.8	73.4	73.9	–5.6	–6.1
Washington	63.5	66.0	63.6	–2.5	–0.1
West Virginia	75.8	80.3	75.9	–4.5	–0.1
Wisconsin	67.5	73.3	71.8	–5.8	–4.3
Wyoming	70.3	72.8	71.0	–2.5	–0.7

Source: Bureau of the Census, Housing Vacancy Survey, Internet site http://www.census.gov/housing/hvs/; calculations by New Strategist

Table 4.11 Homeownership Rate by Metropolitan Area, 2005 and 2012

(percent of householders who own their home in the 75 largest metropolitan areas, 2005 and 2012; percentage point change, 2005–12)

	2012	2005	percentage point change 2005–12
Total inside metropolitan areas	**63.9%**	**67.4%**	**–3.5**
Akron, OH	70.0	78.1	–8.1
Albany–Schenectady–Troy, NY	70.6	66.3	4.3
Alburquerque, NM	62.8	69.2	–6.4
Allentown–Bethlehem–Easton, PA–NJ	75.5	73.5	2.0
Atlanta–Sandy Springs–Marietta, GA	62.1	66.4	–4.3
Austin–Round Rock, TX	60.1	63.9	–3.8
Bakersfield, CA	53.1	60.5	–7.4
Baltimore–Towson, MD	66.1	70.6	–4.5
Baton Rouge, LA	71.4	71.0	0.4
Birmingham–Hoover, AL	73.2	75.1	–1.9
Boston–Cambridge–Quincy, MA–NH	66.0	63.0	3.0
Bridgeport–Stamford–Norwalk, CT	70.6	68.2	2.4
Buffalo–Cheektowaga–Tonawanda, NY	63.5	66.3	–2.8
Charlotte–Gastonia–Concord, NC–SC	58.3	65.8	–7.5
Chicago–Naperville–Joliet, IL	67.1	70.0	–2.9
Cincinnati–Middletown, OH–KY–IN	63.4	68.4	–5.0
Cleveland–Elyria–Mentor, OH	64.2	74.4	–10.2
Columbia, SC	65.6	76.3	–10.7
Columbus, OH	60.7	68.9	–8.2
Dallas–Ft. Worth–Arlington, TX	61.8	62.3	–0.5
Dayton, OH	67.1	66.1	1.0
Denver–Aurora, CO	61.8	70.7	–8.9
Detroit–Warren–Livonia, MI	73.4	75.1	–1.7
El Paso, TX	67.4	72.6	–5.2
Fresno, CA	53.1	51.8	1.3
Grand Rapids–Wyoming, MI	76.9	72.6	4.3
Greensboro–High Point, NC	64.9	66.3	–1.4
Hartford–West Hartford–East Hartford, CT	70.8	72.2	–1.4
Honolulu, HI	56.1	58.0	–1.9
Houston–Baytown–Sugar Land, TX	62.1	61.7	0.4
Indianapolis, IN	67.1	77.1	–10.0
Jacksonville, FL	66.6	67.9	–1.3
Kansas City, MO–KS	65.1	71.3	–6.2
Las Vegas–Paradise, NV	52.6	61.4	–8.8
Los Angeles–Long Beach–Santa Ana, CA	49.9	54.6	–4.7
Louisville, KY–IN	63.3	62.9	0.4
Memphis, TN–AR–MS	60.5	64.8	–4.3
Miami–Fort Lauderdale–Miami Beach, FL	61.8	69.2	–7.4

	2012	2005	percentage point change 2005–12
Milwaukee–Waukesha–West Allis, WI	61.9%	65.7%	−3.8
Minneapolis–St. Paul–Bloomington, MN–WI	70.8	74.9	−4.1
Nashville–Davidson–Murfreesboro, TN	64.9	73.0	−8.1
New Haven–Milford, CT	62.2	66.9	−4.7
New Orleans–Metairie–Kenner, LA	62.4	71.2	−8.8
New York–Northern New Jersey–Long Island, NY	51.5	54.6	−3.1
Oklahoma City, OK	67.3	72.9	−5.6
Omaha–Council Bluffs, NE–IA	72.4	69.7	2.7
Orlando, FL	68.0	70.5	−2.5
Oxnard–Thousand Oaks–Ventura, CA	66.1	73.4	−7.3
Philadelphia–Camden–Wilmington, PA	69.5	73.5	−4.0
Phoenix–Mesa–Scottsdale, AZ	63.1	71.2	−8.1
Pittsburgh, PA	67.9	73.1	−5.2
Portland–Vancouver–Beaverton, OR–WA	63.9	68.3	−4.4
Poughkeepsie–Newburgh–Middletown, NY	70.0	74.2	−4.2
Providence–New Bedford–Fall River, RI–MA	61.7	63.1	−1.4
Raleigh–Cary, NC	67.7	71.4	−3.7
Richmond, VA	67.0	69.7	−2.7
Riverside–San Bernardino–Ontario, CA	58.2	68.5	−10.3
Rochester, NY	68.2	74.9	−6.7
Sacramento–Arden-Arcade–Roseville, CA	58.6	64.1	−5.5
St. Louis, MO–IL	72.0	74.4	−2.4
Salt Lake City, UT	66.9	68.8	−1.9
San Antonio, TX	67.5	66.0	1.5
San Diego–Carlsbad–San Marcos, CA	55.4	60.5	−5.1
San Francisco–Oakland–Fremont, CA	53.2	57.8	−4.6
San Jose–Sunnyvale–Santa Clara, CA	58.6	59.2	−0.6
Seattle–Bellevue–Everett, WA	60.4	64.5	−4.1
Springfield, MA	69.1	64.5	4.6
Syracuse, NY	57.0	59.8	−2.8
Tampa–St. Petersburg–Clearwater, FL	67.0	71.7	−4.7
Toledo, OH	61.9	72.4	−10.5
Tucson, AZ	64.9	66.1	−1.2
Tulsa, OK	66.5	71.7	−5.2
Virginia Beach–Norfolk–Newport News, VA	62.0	68.0	−6.0
Washington–Arlington–Alexandria, DC–VA–MD–WV	66.9	68.4	−1.5
Worcester, MA	61.9	65.3	−3.4

Note: 2004 was the peak year for homeownership nationwide, but 2005 is the earliest year for which comparable metropolitan area data are available.
Source: Bureau of the Census, Housing Vacancy Survey, Internet site http://www.census.gov/housing/hvs/; calculations by New Strategist

Most Americans Live in a Single-Family Home

More than one in four homes have a room used for business.

Nearly two out of three households live in a single-family detached housing unit, a reflection of the low population density in the United States. Only 24 percent of households are in apartment buildings, 6 percent are in duplexes, and another 6 percent are in mobile homes. Not surprisingly, renters are far more likely than homeowners to live in apartment buildings—61 percent of renters versus just 5 percent of homeowners.

American homes have a median of 1,800 square feet of living space. Sixty-four percent have three or more bedrooms and most have two or more bathrooms. Thirty-two percent of homeowners have a room they use for business, as do 22 percent of renters. Half the nation's occupied housing units were built in 1974 or later.

Natural gas is the main heating fuel for the 50.4 percent majority of households. Another 35 percent depend on electricity as their main heating fuel.

■ The slump in the housing market has barely put a dent in the size of American homes.

Two bathrooms are a must for most homeowners

(percent distribution of homeowners by number of bathrooms in home, 2011)

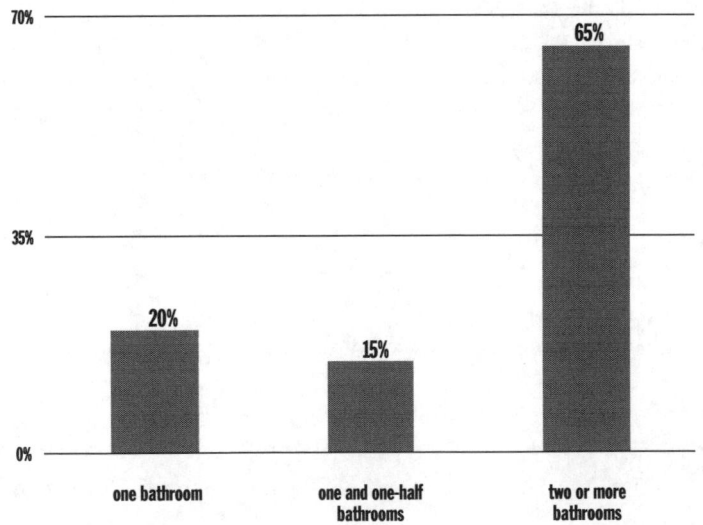

Table 4.12 Units in Structure by Homeownership Status, 2011

(number and percent distribution of households by number of units in structure and homeownership status, 2011; numbers in thousands)

	total	owner	renter
Total households	**114,907**	**76,091**	**38,816**
One, detached	73,761	62,662	11,099
One, attached	6,744	4,090	2,654
Two to four	8,956	1,419	7,537
Five to nine	5,410	583	4,827
10 to 19	5,032	518	4,514
20 to 49	3,665	408	3,257
50 or more	4,150	734	3,415
Mobile home	7,190	5,678	1,512

PERCENT DISTRIBUTION BY HOMEOWNERSHIP STATUS

	total	owner	renter
Total households	**100.0%**	**66.2%**	**33.8%**
One, detached	100.0	85.0	15.0
One, attached	100.0	60.6	39.4
Two to four	100.0	15.8	84.2
Five to nine	100.0	10.8	89.2
10 to 19	100.0	10.3	89.7
20 to 49	100.0	11.1	88.9
50 or more	100.0	17.7	82.3
Mobile home	100.0	79.0	21.0

PERCENT DISTRIBUTION BY NUMBER OF UNITS IN STRUCTURE

	total	owner	renter
Total households	**100.0**	**100.0**	**100.0**
One, detached	64.2	82.4	28.6
One, attached	5.9	5.4	6.8
Two to four	7.8	1.9	19.4
Five to nine	4.7	0.8	12.4
10 to 19	4.4	0.7	11.6
20 to 49	3.2	0.5	8.4
50 or more	3.6	1.0	8.8
Mobile home	6.3	7.5	3.9

Source: Bureau of the Census, American Housing Survey for the United States: 2011, Internet site http://www.census.gov/housing/ahs/data/national.html; calculations by New Strategist

Table 4.13 Size of Housing Unit by Homeownership Status, 2011

(number and percent distribution of households by size and characteristics of unit and homeownership status, 2011; numbers in thousands)

	number			percent distribution		
	total	owner	renter	total	owner	renter
Total households	**114,907**	**76,091**	**38,816**	**100.0%**	**100.0%**	**100.0%**
BEDROOMS						
None	912	72	840	0.8	0.1	2.2
One bedroom	12,067	1,731	10,336	10.5	2.3	26.6
Two bedrooms	28,656	13,197	15,459	24.9	17.3	39.8
Three bedrooms	48,565	39,306	9,259	42.3	51.7	23.9
Four or more bedrooms	24,707	21,785	2,921	21.5	28.6	7.5
BATHROOMS						
None	494	190	304	0.4	0.2	0.8
One bathroom	39,268	15,118	24,150	34.2	19.9	62.2
One-and-one-half bathrooms	15,066	11,232	3,834	13.1	14.8	9.9
Two or more bathrooms	60,079	49,551	10,528	52.3	65.1	27.1
ROOM(S) USED FOR BUSINESS	32,425	24,068	8,355	28.2	31.6	21.5
Median square footage of unit	**1,800**	**1,800**	**1,301**	–	–	–
Median size of lot (acres)	**0.26**	**0.30**	**0.19**	–	–	–

Note: Square footage of unit and size of lot for single-family detached and mobile homes only. "–" means not applicable.
Source: Bureau of the Census, American Housing Survey for the United States: 2011, Internet site http://www.census.gov/housing/ahs/data/national.html; calculations by New Strategist

Table 4.14 Year Unit Built by Homeownership Status, 2011

(number and percent distribution of occupied housing units by year structure was built and homeownership status, 2011; numbers in thousands)

	total	owners	renters
Total households	**114,907**	**76,091**	**38,816**
2010 or later	550	403	147
2005 to 2009	7,098	5,182	1,917
2000 to 2004	8,206	6,319	1,887
1990 to 1999	14,170	10,811	3,359
1980 to 1989	14,494	9,311	5,184
1970 to 1979	21,340	12,906	8,434
1960 to 1969	13,596	8,679	4,917
1950 to 1959	11,905	8,548	3,357
1940 to 1949	6,624	4,172	2,451
1930 to 1939	4,705	2,697	2,008
1920 to 1929	4,612	2,598	2,014
1919 or earlier	7,607	4,467	3,141
Median year built	**1974**	**1976**	**1972**
PERCENT DISTRIBUTION			
Total households	**100.0%**	**100.0%**	**100.0$**
2010 or later	0.5	0.5	0.4
2005 to 2009	6.2	6.8	4.9
2000 to 2004	7.1	8.3	4.9
1990 to 1999	12.3	14.2	8.7
1980 to 1989	12.6	12.2	13.4
1970 to 1979	18.6	17.0	21.7
1960 to 1969	11.8	11.4	12.7
1950 to 1959	10.4	11.2	8.6
1940 to 1949	5.8	5.5	6.3
1930 to 1939	4.1	3.5	5.2
1920 to 1929	4.0	3.4	5.2
1919 or earlier	6.6	5.9	8.1

Source: Bureau of the Census, American Housing Survey for the United States: 2011, Internet site http://www.census.gov/ housing/ahs/data/national.html; calculations by New Strategist

Table 4.15 Fuels Used by Homeownership Status, 2011

(number and percent of households by fuels used and homeownership status, 2011; numbers in thousands)

	total	owners	renters
Total households	**114,907**	**76,091**	**38,816**
Electricity	114,848	76,043	38,805
Piped gas	69,992	46,535	23,458
Bottled gas	9,517	8,148	1,369
Fuel oil	9,217	6,198	3,018
Kerosene or other liquid fuel	551	369	181
Coal or coke	82	68	14
Wood	1,977	1,699	278
Solar energy	156	134	22
Other	493	325	167
All-electric homes	**31,674**	**18,269**	**13,405**
PERCENT USING FUEL			
Total households	**100.0%**	**100.0%**	**100.0%**
Electricity	99.9	99.9	100.0
Piped gas	60.9	61.2	60.4
Fuel oil	8.3	10.7	3.5
Wood	8.0	8.1	7.8
Bottled gas	0.5	0.5	0.5
Kerosene or other liquid fuel	0.1	0.1	0.0
Coal or coke	1.7	2.2	0.7
Solar energy	0.1	0.2	0.1
Other	0.4	0.4	0.4
All-electric homes	**27.6**	**24.0**	**34.5**

Note: Numbers do not add to total because many householders use more than one fuel.
Source: Bureau of the Census, American Housing Survey for the United States: 2011, Internet site http://www.census.gov/housing/ahs/data/national.html; calculations by New Strategist

Table 4.16 Main Heating Fuel Used by Homeownership Status, 2011

(number and percent distribution of households by main heating fuel used and homeownership status, 2011; numbers in thousands)

	total	owners	renters
Households using heating fuel	**114,439**	**75,876**	**38,563**
Electricity	40,385	22,901	17,484
Piped gas	57,721	40,657	17,064
Bottled gas	5,415	4,540	875
Fuel oil	8,061	5,490	2,571
Kerosene or other liquid fuel	538	357	181
Coal or coke	79	65	14
Wood	1,971	1,694	278
Solar energy	14	10	5
Other	255	164	91

PERCENT DISTRIBUTION BY HOMEOWNERSHIP STATUS

Households using heating fuel	**100.0%**	**66.3%**	**33.7%**
Electricity	100.0	56.7	43.3
Piped gas	100.0	70.4	29.6
Bottled gas	100.0	83.8	16.2
Fuel oil	100.0	68.1	31.9
Kerosene or other liquid fuel	100.0	66.4	33.6
Coal or coke	100.0	82.3	17.7
Wood	100.0	85.9	14.1
Solar energy	100.0	71.4	35.7
Other	100.0	64.3	35.7

PERCENT DISTRIBUTION BY PRIMARY HEATING FUEL

Households using heating fuel	**100.0**	**100.0**	**100.0**
Electricity	35.3	30.2	45.3
Piped gas	50.4	53.6	44.2
Bottled gas	4.7	6.0	2.3
Fuel oil	7.0	7.2	6.7
Kerosene or other liquid fuel	0.5	0.5	0.5
Coal or coke	0.1	0.1	0.0
Wood	1.7	2.2	0.7
Solar energy	0.0	0.0	0.0
Other	0.2	0.2	0.2

Source: Bureau of the Census, American Housing Survey for the United States: 2011, Internet site http://www.census.gov/housing/ahs/data/national.html; calculations by New Strategist

American Households Are Well Equipped

Most have a dishwasher, clothes washer, and clothes dryer.

American households are well equipped with appliances and have a variety of other amenities. Eighty-five percent of households have a porch, deck, balcony, or patio. Sixty-six percent have a garage or carport. Thirty-five percent have a useable fireplace.

Not surprisingly, homeowners are more likely than renters to have various amenities. The 57 percent majority of homeowners have a separate dining room, while the figure is just 30 percent for renters. Seventy-two percent of homeowners have central air conditioning compared with 53 percent of renters. Nearly one in five renters do not have a vehicle compared with just 3 percent of homeowners.

■ Many Americans regard air conditioning as a necessity rather than a luxury.

Most American homes have central air conditioning

(percent of households with central air conditioning, by homeownership status, 2011)

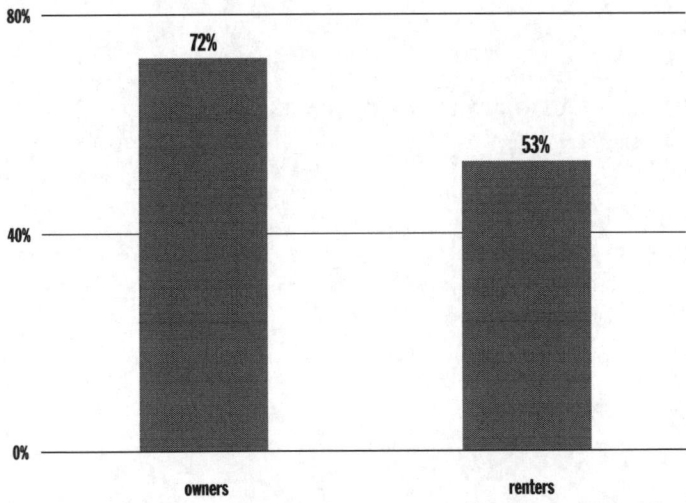

Table 4.17 Kitchen, Laundry, and Safety Equipment by Homeownership Status, 2011

(number and percent of households by presence of kitchen, laundry, and safety equipment and homeownership status, 2011; numbers in thousands)

	total	owners	renters
Total households	**114,907**	**76,091**	**38,816**
With complete kitchen equipment	112,898	75,642	37,256
Dishwasher	77,069	57,759	19,310
Disposal in kitchen sink	58,958	40,715	18,243
Washing machine	95,567	73,624	21,943
Clothes dryer	93,052	72,397	20,655
Working smoke detector	106,733	70,801	35,932
Working fire extinguisher	49,486	35,985	13,501
Working carbon monoxide detector	47,841	35,215	12,626
Sprinkler system	5,791	2,125	3,666
PERCENT WITH EQUIPMENT			
Total households	**100.0%**	**100.0%**	**100.0%**
With complete kitchen equipment	98.3	99.4	96.0
Dishwasher	67.1	75.9	49.7
Disposal in kitchen sink	51.3	53.5	47.0
Washing machine	83.2	96.8	56.5
Clothes dryer	81.0	95.1	53.2
Working smoke detector	92.9	93.0	92.6
Fire extinguisher	43.1	47.3	34.8
Working carbon monoxide detector	41.6	46.3	32.5
Sprinkler system	5.0	2.8	9.4

Note: Complete kitchen equipment includes a sink, refrigerator, and oven or burners.
Source: Bureau of the Census, American Housing Survey for the United States: 2011, Internet site http://www.census.gov/housing/ahs/data/national.html; calculations by New Strategist

Table 4.18 Amenities of Home by Homeownership Status, 2011

(number and percent of households with selected amenities by homeownership status, 2011; numbers in thousands)

	total	owners	renters
Total households	**114,907**	**76,091**	**38,816**
Telephone	112,073	74,729	37,344
Car, truck, or van	105,483	73,969	31,514
Porch, deck, balcony, or patio	97,550	69,885	27,665
Garage or carport	75,431	60,389	15,042
Separate dining room	54,923	43,300	11,623
Usable fireplace	40,371	34,700	5,672
Two or more living or recreation rooms	34,576	31,242	3,334
PERCENT WITH AMENITY			
Total households	**100.0%**	**100.0%**	**100.0%**
Telephone	97.5	98.2	96.2
Car, truck, or van	91.8	97.2	81.2
Porch, deck, balcony, or patio	84.9	91.8	71.3
Garage or carport	65.6	79.4	38.8
Separate dining room	47.8	56.9	29.9
Usable fireplace	35.1	45.6	14.6
Two or more living or recreation rooms	30.1	41.1	8.6

Source: Bureau of the Census, American Housing Survey for the United States: 2011, Internet site http://www.census.gov/ housing/ahs/data/national.html; calculations by New Strategist

Table 4.19 Air Conditioning by Homeownership Status, 2011

(number and percent of households with air conditioning by homeownership status, 2011; numbers in thousands)

	total	owners	renters
Total households	**114,907**	**76,091**	**38,816**
With any air conditioning	101,782	68,957	32,825
With central air conditioning	75,748	55,133	20,615
With room units	26,034	13,824	12,210
One room unit	11,923	5,101	6,822
Two room units	8,474	4,810	3,664
Three or more room units	5,637	3,913	1,724
PERCENT WITH EQUIPMENT			
Total households	**100.0%**	**100.0%**	**100.0%**
With any air conditioning	88.6	90.6	84.6
With central air conditioning	65.9	72.5	53.1
With room units	22.7	18.2	31.5
One room unit	10.4	6.7	17.6
Two room units	7.4	6.3	9.4
Three or more room units	4.9	5.1	4.4

Source: Bureau of the Census, American Housing Survey for the United States: 2011, Internet site http://www.census.gov/ housing/ahs/data/national.html; calculations by New Strategist

Most Are Satisfied with Home and Neighborhood

Homeowners are happier than renters, but few renters are dissatisfied.

When asked how they would rate their housing unit on a scale of 1 (worst) to 10 (best), 71 percent of householders rate their home an 8 or higher. Homeowners rate their home more highly than renters. While 76 percent of homeowners rate their home an 8 or higher, a smaller 60 percent of renters are that positive. Thirty-three percent of homeowners, but only 21 percent of renters, give their home a 10. Although few rate their home a 5 or less on the 10-point scale, those who do are primarily renters.

The patterns are the same when Americans are asked to rate their neighborhood. Sixty-seven percent of households rate their neighborhood an 8 or higher, including 71 percent of homeowners and 60 percent of renters. Among the few who rate their neighborhood a 5 or below, the majority are renters.

■ Americans rate their home and neighborhood highly because those who are unhappy are likely to move elsewhere.

Most households rate their home and neighborhood highly

(percent of householders who rate their home and neighborhood an 8 or higher on a scale of 1 (worst) to 10 (best), by homeownership status, 2011)

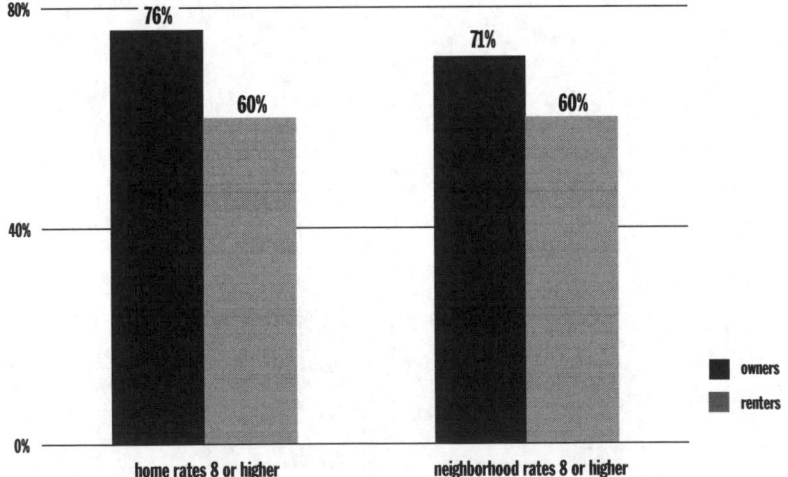

Table 4.20 Opinion of Housing Unit by Homeownership Status, 2011

(number and percent distribution of households by householder's opinion of housing unit and homeownership status, 2011; numbers in thousands)

	total	owners	renters
Total households	**114,907**	**76,091**	**38,816**
1 (worst)	611	213	398
2	357	101	256
3	736	270	467
4	1,081	415	666
5	5,207	2,402	2,805
6	5,534	2,651	2,883
7	15,337	8,726	6,611
8	29,890	19,479	10,411
9	17,629	12,881	4,748
10 (best)	33,671	25,452	8,220

PERCENT DISTRIBUTION BY HOMEOWNERSHIP STATUS

	total	owners	renters
Total households	**100.0%**	**66.2%**	**33.8%**
1 (worst)	100.0	34.9	65.1
2	100.0	28.3	71.7
3	100.0	36.7	63.5
4	100.0	38.4	61.6
5	100.0	46.1	53.9
6	100.0	47.9	52.1
7	100.0	56.9	43.1
8	100.0	65.2	34.8
9	100.0	73.1	26.9
10 (best)	100.0	75.6	24.4

PERCENT DISTRIBUTION BY OPINION OF HOUSING UNIT

	total	owners	renters
Total households	**100.0**	**100.0**	**100.0**
1 (worst)	0.5	0.3	1.0
2	0.3	0.1	0.7
3	0.6	0.4	1.2
4	0.9	0.5	1.7
5	4.5	3.2	7.2
6	4.8	3.5	7.4
7	13.3	11.5	17.0
8	26.0	25.6	26.8
9	15.3	16.9	12.2
10 (best)	29.3	33.4	21.2

Note: Numbers do not add to total because "not reported" is not shown.
Source: Bureau of the Census, American Housing Survey for the United States: 2011, Internet site http://www.census.gov/ housing/ahs/data/national.html; calculations by New Strategist

Table 4.21 Opinion of Neighborhood by Homeownership Status, 2011

(number and percent distribution of households by householder's opinion of neighborhood and homeownership status, 2011; numbers in thousands)

	total	owners	renters
Total households	**114,907**	**76,091**	**38,816**
1 (worst)	1,115	452	663
2	935	453	482
3	1,253	559	695
4	2,080	1,026	1,053
5	6,635	3,602	3,033
6	6,204	3,533	2,671
7	14,379	8,853	5,526
8	27,863	18,756	9,107
9	17,709	12,773	4,936
10 (best)	31,656	22,467	9,189

PERCENT DISTRIBUTION BY HOMEOWNERSHIP STATUS

Total households	**100.0%**	**66.2%**	**33.8%**
1 (worst)	100.0	40.5	59.5
2	100.0	48.4	51.6
3	100.0	44.6	55.5
4	100.0	49.3	50.6
5	100.0	54.3	45.7
6	100.0	56.9	43.1
7	100.0	61.6	38.4
8	100.0	67.3	32.7
9	100.0	72.1	27.9
10 (best)	100.0	71.0	29.0

PERCENT DISTRIBUTION BY OPINION OF NEIGHBORHOOD

Total households	**100.0**	**100.0**	**100.0**
1 (worst)	1.0	0.6	1.7
2	0.8	0.6	1.2
3	1.1	0.7	1.8
4	1.8	1.3	2.7
5	5.8	4.7	7.8
6	5.4	4.6	6.9
7	12.5	11.6	14.2
8	24.2	24.6	23.5
9	15.4	16.8	12.7
10 (best)	27.5	29.5	23.7

Note: Numbers do not add to total because "not reported" and "no neighborhood" are not shown.
Source: Bureau of the Census, American Housing Survey for the United States: 2011, Internet site http://www.census.gov/housing/ahs/data/national.html; calculations by New Strategist

Monthly Housing Costs Are Higher for Homeowners

But renters devote a much larger share of their income to housing.

Homeowners had median monthly housing costs of $1,008 in 2011, while the median for renters was a smaller $845. Because homeowners have higher incomes than renters, however, housing costs absorb only 21 percent of the monthly income of owners versus a larger 35 percent of renters' income.

Homeowners pay more than renters for utilities, in large part because their homes are bigger. Homeowners pay a median of $121 per month for electricity, for example, versus the $90 paid by renters. Homeowners pay a median of $42 per month for water versus the $30 paid by renters.

■ Homeowners who have paid off their mortgage have lower monthly housing costs than those with mortgages.

Nearly one in four homeowners pays less than $500 per month for housing

(percent distribution of homeowners by total monthly housing costs, 2011)

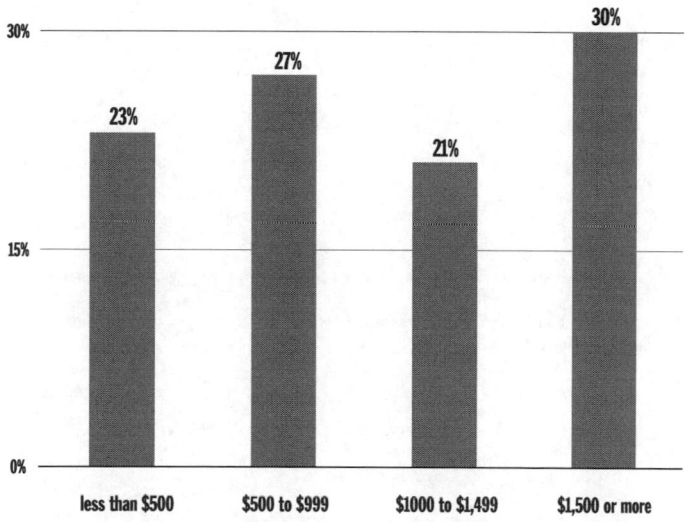

Table 4.22 Monthly Housing Costs by Homeownership Status, 2011

(number and percent distribution of households by monthly housing costs and homeownership status, 2011; households in thousands)

	total	owners	renters
Total households	**114,907**	**76,091**	**38,816**
Less than $300	8,755	6,342	2,413
$300 to $499	14,435	11,068	3,369
$500 to $799	23,767	12,931	10,837
$800 to $999	13,988	7,359	6,629
$1,000 to $1,249	13,963	8,520	5,443
$1,250 to $1,499	10,530	7,186	3,344
$1,500 to $1,999	12,315	9,441	2,873
$2,000 to $2,499	6,481	5,556	925
$2,500 or more	8,403	7,690	713
No cash rent	2,271	–	2,271
Median monthly costs	**$927**	**$1,008**	**$845**
PERCENT DISTRIBUTION			
Total households	**100.0%**	**100.0%**	**100.0%**
Less than $300	7.6	8.3	6.2
$300 to $499	12.6	14.5	8.7
$500 to $799	20.7	17.0	27.9
$800 to $999	12.2	9.7	17.1
$1,000 to $1,249	12.2	11.2	14.0
$1,250 to $1,499	9.2	9.4	8.6
$1,500 to $1,999	10.7	12.4	7.4
$2,000 to $2,499	5.6	7.3	2.4
$2,500 or more	7.3	10.1	1.8
No cash rent	2.0	–	5.9

Note: Housing costs include mortgages, rent, utilities, real estate taxes, property insurance, and regime fees. "–" means not applicable.
Source: Bureau of the Census, American Housing Survey for the United States: 2011, Internet site http://www.census.gov/housing/ahs/data/national.html; calculations by New Strategist

Table 4.23 Monthly Housing Costs as Percent of Income by Homeownership Status, 2011

(number and percent distribution of households by monthly housing costs as a percent of current income, by homeownership status, 2011; households in thousands)

	total	owners	renters
Total households	**114,907**	**76,091**	**38,816**
Less than 5 percent	2,532	2,349	183
5 to 9 percent	9,815	8,935	880
10 to 14 percent	12,935	10,829	2,106
15 to 19 percent	14,358	11,346	3,012
20 to 24 percent	13,657	9,955	3,701
25 to 29 percent	11,330	7,345	3,984
30 to 34 percent	8,543	5,286	3,257
35 to 39 percent	6,416	3,715	2,701
40 to 49 percent	8,341	4,606	3,735
50 to 59 percent	5,214	2,609	2,605
60 to 69 percent	3,392	1,711	1,681
70 to 99 percent	5,034	2,387	2,648
100 percent or more	8,676	4,066	4,610
Median percent of current income	**25%**	**21%**	**35%**
PERCENT DISTRIBUTION			
Total households	**100.0%**	**100.0%**	**100.0%**
Less than 5 percent	2.2	3.1	0.5
5 to 9 percent	8.5	11.7	2.3
10 to 14 percent	11.3	14.2	5.4
15 to 19 percent	12.5	14.9	7.8
20 to 24 percent	11.9	13.1	9.5
25 to 29 percent	9.9	9.7	10.3
30 to 34 percent	7.4	6.9	8.4
35 to 39 percent	5.6	4.9	7.0
40 to 49 percent	7.3	6.1	9.6
50 to 59 percent	4.5	3.4	6.7
60 to 69 percent	3.0	2.2	4.3
70 to 99 percent	4.4	3.1	6.8
100 percent or more	7.6	5.3	11.9

Note: Housing costs include mortgages, rent, utilities, real estate taxes, property insurance, and regime fees; monthly cost as a percent of income excludes no cash rent and zero income.
Source: Bureau of the Census, American Housing Survey for the United States: 2011, Internet site http://www.census.gov/housing/ahs/data/national.html; calculations by New Strategist

Table 4.24 Monthly Utility and Property Insurance Costs by Homeownership Status, 2011

(total number of households, number with utility or insurance expense, and median monthly cost of utility or insurance for households with expense, by homeownership status, 2011; numbers in thousands)

	total	owners	renters
Total households	**114,907**	**76,091**	**38,816**
Electricity			
Number with electricity	114,848	76,043	38,805
Median monthly cost of electricity	$111	$121	$90
Piped gas			
Number with piped gas	69,992	46,535	23,458
Median monthly cost of piped gas	$69	$75	$54
Fuel oil			
Number with fuel oil	9,217	6,198	3,018
Median monthly cost of fuel oil	$150	$159	$100
Water			
Number paying for water separately	63,269	52,907	10,362
Median monthly cost for water	$40	$42	$30
Trash			
Number paying for trash separately	53,150	44,630	8,520
Median monthly cost for trash removal	$22	$23	$20
Property insurance			
Number paying for property insurance	83,017	71,568	11,449
Median monthly cost for property insurance	$50	$58	$16

Source: Bureau of the Census, American Housing Survey for the United States: 2011, Internet sitehttp://www.census.gov/ housing/ahs/data/national.html; calculations by New Strategist

Home Values Have Fallen Sharply

Most homeowners with a mortgage owe less than their home is worth, however.

The median value of the homes owned by Americans stood at $160,000 in 2011, down from $191,471 in 2007 (not adjusted for inflation). Nine percent of homeowners said their home was worth more than $500,000 in 2011, substantially less than the 14 percent who reported such a high value in 2007.

Among the nation's 76 million homeowners in 2011, 63 percent had a mortgage on their home. Homeowners with a mortgage owed a median of 71 percent of the value of their home, up from a much smaller 54 percent in 2007. Fourteen percent owed more than the value of their home, much greater than the 5 percent who were underwater in 2007.

■ Although homeowners have seen their home's value decline, most still have considerable equity in their house.

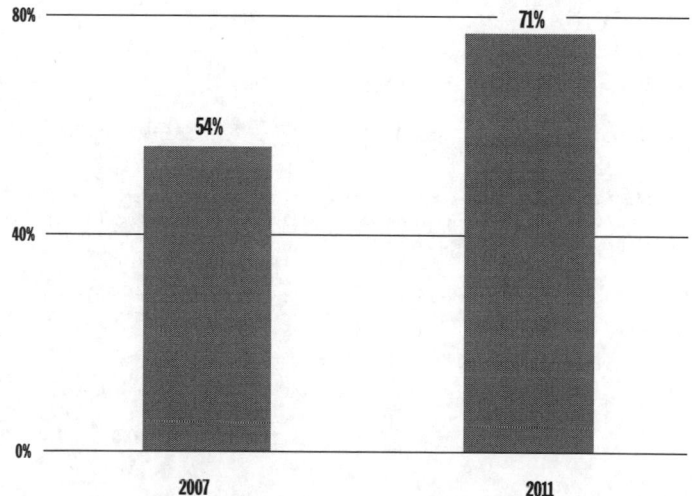

Owners have less equity in their home

(median current mortgage as a percent of home value, 2007 and 2011)

Table 4.25 Homeowners by Housing Value and Purchase Price, 2007 and 2011

(number and percent distribution of homeowners by value and purchase price of home, 2007 and 2011; households in thousands)

	2011 number	2011 percent distribution	2007 number	2007 percent distribution
VALUE OF HOME				
Total homeowners	**76,091**	**100.0%**	**75,647**	**100.0%**
Under $100,000	20,020	26.3	18,779	24.8
$100,000 to $119,999	5,367	7.1	4,313	5.7
$120,000 to $149,999	8,277	10.9	6,735	8.9
$150,000 to $199,999	11,677	15.3	9,643	12.7
$200,000 to $299,999	13,487	17.7	13,132	17.4
$300,000 to $399,999	7,063	9.3	8,060	10.7
$400,000 to $499,999	3,696	4.9	4,740	6.3
$500,000 to $749,999	3,964	5.2	6,234	8.2
$750,000 or more	2,541	3.3	4,013	5.3
Median value	**$160,000**	–	**$191,471**	–
PURCHASE PRICE OF HOME				
Total homes purchased or built	**71,608**	**100.0**	**70,334**	**100.0**
Under $50,000	16,476	23.0	17,976	25.6
$50,000 to $99,999	14,560	20.3	14,816	21.1
$100,000 to $119,999	4,390	6.1	4,216	6.0
$120,000 to $149,999	6,708	9.4	6,320	9.0
$150,000 to $199,999	8,306	11.6	7,581	10.8
$200,000 to $249,999	5,025	7.0	4,522	6.4
$250,000 to $299,999	3,205	4.5	2,820	4.0
$300,000 or more	8,639	12.1	7,483	10.6
Median purchase price	**$110,000**	–	**$100,539**	–

Note: Numbers do not add to total because "not reported" is not shown. "–" means not applicable.
Source: Bureau of the Census, American Housing Survey for the United States: 2011, Internet site http://www.census.gov/housing/ahs/data/national.html; calculations by New Strategist

Table 4.26 Homeowners by Source and Amount of Down Payment, 2007 and 2011

(number and percent distribution of homeowners by first-home status, major source and amount of down payment, 2007 and 2011; households in thousands)

	2011 number	2011 percent distribution	2007 number	2007 percent distribution
FIRST-HOME STATUS				
Total homeowners (reporting status)	**74,782**	**100.0%**	**73,090**	**100.0%**
First home	31,892	42.6	30,267	41.4
Not first home	42,890	57.4	42,823	58.6
MAJOR SOURCE OF DOWN PAYMENT				
Total homes purchased or built	**71,608**	**100.0**	**70,334**	**100.0**
Savings or cash on hand	32,528	45.4	31,005	44.1
Sale of previous home	21,096	29.5	22,897	32.6
Borrowing, other than mortgage on this property	2,312	3.2	2,444	3.5
Inheritance or gift	1,417	2.0	1,375	2.0
Sale of other investment	712	1.0	737	1.0
Land where building built used for financing	620	0.9	584	0.8
Other	3,424	4.8	3,060	4.4
No down payment	7,359	10.3	6,616	9.4
DOWN PAYMENT AS PERCENT OF PURCHASE PRICE				
Total homes purchased or built	**71,608**	**100.0**	**70,334**	**100.0**
No down payment	7,359	10.3	6,616	9.4
Less than 3 percent	5,090	7.1	4,700	6.7
3 to 5 percent	7,589	10.6	5,933	8.4
6 to 10 percent	9,831	13.7	8,545	12.1
11 to 15 percent	3,911	5.5	3,355	4.8
16 to 20 percent	8,651	12.1	6,881	9.8
21 to 40 percent	8,254	11.5	6,841	9.7
41 to 99 percent	4,693	6.6	3,904	5.6
Bought outright	6,743	9.4	5,668	8.1

Note: Numbers do not add to total because "not reported" is not shown.
Source: Bureau of the Census, American Housing Survey for the United States: 2011, Internet site http://www.census.gov/ housing/ahs/data/national.html; calculations by New Strategist

Table 4.27 Homeowners by Mortgage Characteristics, 2007 and 2011

(number of total homeowners, and number and percent distribution of homeowners with mortgages by selected mortgage characteristics, 2007 and 2011; numbers in thousands)

	2011 number	2011 percent distribution	2007 number	2007 percent distribution
Total homeowners	**76,091**	**100.0%**	**75,647**	**100.0%**
Homeowners with mortgages	48,294	63.5	46,461	61.4
REMAINING YEARS MORTGAGED				
Homeowners with mortgages	**48,294**	**100.0**	**46,461**	**100.0**
Less than 8 years	6,905	14.3	5,981	12.9
8 to 12 years	4,897	10.1	5,549	11.9
13 to 17 years	6,078	12.6	4,602	9.9
18 to 22 years	6,511	13.5	4,879	10.5
23 to 27 years	12,904	26.7	12,263	26.4
28 to 32 years	10,563	21.9	12,791	27.5
33 years or more	197	0.4	241	0.5
Variable	239	0.5	156	0.3
Median years remaining	**22**	–	**24**	–
TOTAL OUTSTANDING PRINCIPAL				
Homeowners with mortgages	**48,294**	**100.0**	**46,461**	**100.0**
Under $50,000	6,177	12.8	11,579	24.9
$50,000 to $99,999	8,341	17.3	11,480	24.7
$100,000 to $119,999	3,057	6.3	3,790	8.2
$120,000 to $149,999	4,265	8.8	4,751	10.2
$150,000 to $199,999	4,905	10.2	5,511	11.9
$200,000 to $249,999	3,098	6.4	3,081	6.6
$250,000 to $299,999	1,968	4.1	2,008	4.3
$300,000 or more	4,111	8.5	4,261	9.2
Median outstanding principal	**$120,000**	–	**$100,904**	–
CURRENT TOTAL LOAN AS PERCENT OF HOUSING VALUE				
Homeowners with mortgages	**48,294**	**100.0**	**46,461**	**100.0**
Less than 20 percent	3,237	6.7	7,204	15.5
20 to 39 percent	4,589	9.5	9,102	19.6
40 to 59 percent	5,691	11.8	9,626	20.7
60 to 79 percent	7,663	15.9	10,365	22.3
80 to 89 percent	3,878	8.0	4,489	9.7
90 to 99 percent	3,744	7.8	3,220	6.9
100 percent or more	6,823	14.1	2,456	5.3
Median percent of value	**71%**	–	**54%**	–

Note: Numbers do not add to total because "not reported" is not shown. "–" means not applicable.
Source: Bureau of the Census, American Housing Survey for the United States: 2007 and 2011, Internet site http://www.census .gov/housing/ahs/data/national.html; calculations by New Strategist

Income

Trends

Median household income was $51,017 in 2012.

The 2012 median was 8 percent below the $55,627 of 2007, after adjusting for inflation.

Householders under age 55 have experienced double-digit declines in median income since 2000.

Householders aged 65 or older saw their median income grow 10 percent between 2000 and 2012, after adjusting for inflation.

Four percent of households had an income of $200,000 or more in 2012.

More than one in five households had an income of $100,000 or more.

Among married couples, blacks have higher incomes than Hispanics.

The $64,954 median income of black couples is 27 percent above the all-household median. The $50,398 median income of Hispanic couples is slightly below the all-household median.

College-educated householders had a median income of $86,419 in 2012.

The median income of households headed by college graduates has fallen by 8 percent since 2007, after adjusting for inflation.

Women are no longer catching up to men.

Among full-time workers in 2012, women's earnings were 77 percent as high as men's, down from 78 percent in 2007.

Minorities account for most of the poor.

Among non-Hispanic whites, 9.7 percent are poor. The figure exceeds 25 percent among blacks and Hispanics.

Many Households Have Incomes of $100,000 or More

A larger share of households is at the lowest end of the income distribution.

Despite the Great Recession and its aftermath, the distribution of households by income has changed little over the past 12 years. Demographics explain the stability. The upper end of the income distribution is inflated by millions of dual-earner baby-boom couples in their peak earning years. The share of households with incomes of $100,000 or more is well above 20 percent, a proportion that fell only slightly during the Great Recession.

At the other extreme, the size of the lower end of the income distribution (household income below $25,000) has expanded somewhat because of the increasing share of households headed by retirees. Meanwhile, the share of households in the middle (household income between $25,000 and $100,000) has barely changed since 2000.

■ The proportion of households with incomes of $100,000 or more is likely to decline in the years ahead as boomers retire.

Little change in proportion of households with incomes of $100,000 or more, despite the Great Recession

(percent of households with incomes of $100,000 or more, 2000 to 2012; in 2012 dollars)

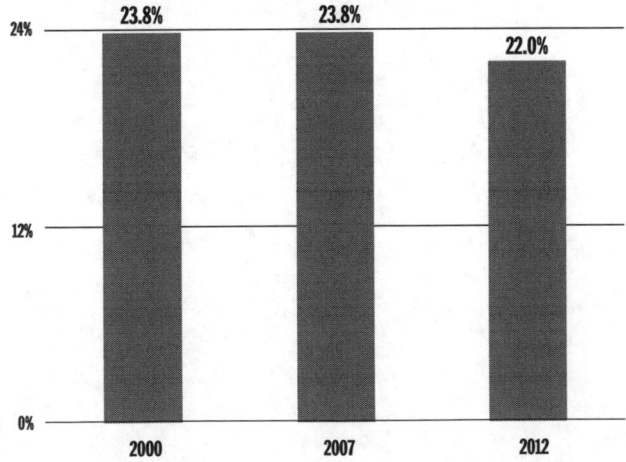

Table 5.1 Distribution of Households by Income, 2000 to 2012

(number of households and percent distribution by income, 2000 to 2012, in 2012 dollars; households in thousands as of the following year)

	total households number	total households percent	under $25,000	$25,000– $49,999	$50,000– $74,999	$75,000– $99,999	$100,000 or more total	$100,000 or more $100,000– $149,999	$100,000 or more $150,000– $199,999	$100,000 or more $200,000 or more
2012	122,459	100.0%	24.7%	24.3%	17.5%	11.7%	22.0%	12.5%	5.0%	4.5%
2011	121,084	100.0	24.6	24.6	17.7	11.4	21.7	12.2	5.1	4.4
2010	119,927	100.0	24.4	24.2	17.6	11.6	22.1	12.8	4.9	4.4
2009	117,538	100.0	23.2	24.5	17.8	11.9	22.5	12.9	5.1	4.5
2008	117,181	100.0	23.2	24.2	17.7	12.3	22.7	13.1	5.1	4.5
2007	116,783	100.0	22.3	23.9	17.5	12.5	23.8	13.8	5.3	4.7
2006	116,011	100.0	21.9	24.3	18.0	12.1	23.7	13.5	5.3	4.9
2005	114,384	100.0	22.9	23.7	17.9	12.6	22.8	13.1	5.0	4.7
2004	113,343	100.0	23.0	24.3	17.6	12.6	22.6	13.0	5.2	4.4
2003	112,000	100.0	23.1	23.8	17.6	12.4	23.1	13.5	5.1	4.5
2002	111,278	100.0	22.3	24.3	17.7	13.0	22.9	13.6	4.9	4.4
2001	109,297	100.0	21.9	24.0	18.0	13.0	23.1	13.5	4.9	4.7
2000	108,209	100.0	21.2	23.9	18.4	12.7	23.8	13.9	5.3	4.6

Source: Bureau of the Census, Historical Income Data, Internet site http://www.census.gov/hhes/www/income/; calculations by New Strategist

Income Inequality Has Grown

The richest 20 percent of households control more than half of household income.

If you add up all the money going to American households, including earnings, interest, dividends, Social Security benefits, and so on, the result is called "aggregate household income." Year-to-year changes in how this aggregate is divided among the nation's households can reveal trends in income inequality. The numbers on the next page show how much aggregate income each fifth of households receives, from poorest to richest. It also shows how much accrues to the 5 percent of households with the highest incomes.

For years, a growing share of income had been accruing to the most-affluent households. The percentage of aggregate income received by the richest 20 percent of households (with an income of $104,096 or more in 2012) rose from 49.8 percent in 2000 to 51.0 percent in 2012. Despite the recession, the richest 20 percent of households have maintained their hold on the majority of aggregate household income.

■ A rise or fall in the amount of income accruing to each fifth of households reveals trends in the distribution of income among households, not the economic well-being of individual households.

Wealthiest households control more than half the nation's income

(percent of aggregate household income accruing to the richest 20 percent of households, 2000 to 2012)

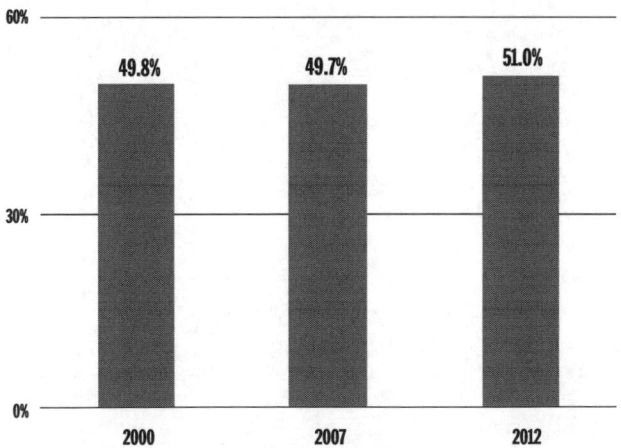

Table 5.2 Share of Aggregate Income Received by Each Fifth and Top 5 Percent of Households, 2000 to 2012

(total number of households, income limit and percent distribution of aggregate income by household income quintile and top 5 percent, 2000 to 2012; in 2012 dollars)

INCOME LIMITS	total households (in 000s)	upper limit of bottom fifth	upper limit of second fifth	upper limit of third fifth	upper limit of fourth fifth	lower limit of top 5 percent
2012	122,459	$20,599	$39,764	$64,582	$104,096	$191,156
2011	121,084	20,262	38,520	62,434	101,582	186,000
2010	119,927	20,000	38,000	61,500	100,029	180,485
2009	117,538	20,453	38,550	61,801	100,000	180,001
2008	117,181	20,712	39,000	62,725	100,240	180,000
2007	116,783	20,291	39,100	62,000	100,000	177,000
2006	116,011	20,035	37,774	60,000	97,032	174,012
2005	114,384	19,178	36,000	57,660	91,705	166,000
2004	113,343	18,486	34,675	55,230	88,002	157,152
2003	112,000	17,984	34,000	54,453	86,867	154,120
2002	111,278	17,916	33,377	53,162	84,016	150,002
2001	109,297	17,970	33,314	53,000	83,500	150,499
2000	108,209	17,920	33,000	52,174	81,766	145,220

SHARE OF AGGREGATE INCOME	total household income	bottom fifth	second fifth	third fifth	fourth fifth	top fifth	top 5 percent
2012	100.0%	3.2%	8.3%	14.4%	23.0%	51.0%	22.3%
2011	100.0	3.2	8.4	14.3	23.0	51.1	22.3
2010	100.0	3.3	8.5	14.6	23.4	50.3	21.3
2009	100.0	3.4	8.6	14.6	23.2	50.3	21.7
2008	100.0	3.4	8.6	14.7	23.3	50.0	21.5
2007	100.0	3.4	8.7	14.8	23.4	49.7	21.2
2006	100.0	3.4	8.6	14.5	22.9	50.5	22.3
2005	100.0	3.4	8.6	14.6	23.0	50.4	22.2
2004	100.0	3.4	8.7	14.7	23.2	50.1	21.8
2003	100.0	3.4	8.7	14.8	23.4	49.8	21.4
2002	100.0	3.5	8.8	14.8	23.3	49.7	21.7
2001	100.0	3.5	8.7	14.6	23.0	50.1	22.4
2000	100.0	3.6	8.9	14.8	23.0	49.8	22.1

Source: Bureau of the Census, Historical Income Data, Internet site http://www.census.gov/hhes/www/income/; calculations by New Strategist

Rich and Poor Have Unique Characteristics

High-income households have more earners than low-income households.

One common way to examine income differences among households is to divide the total number of households into five equally sized groups (called quintiles) based on income and compare household characteristics. The numbers on the next two pages show the distribution of households by income quintile and the characteristics of households within income quintile.

The demographics of the poorest and richest households are strikingly different and account in large part for their income differences. Among households with two or more earners, for example, only 2 percent are in the lowest income quintile (incomes below $20,599) and 38 percent are in the highest income quintile (incomes of $104,096 or more). To look at the numbers another way, three out of four households in the highest income quintile have two or more earners. Among households in the lowest income quintile, fewer than 5 percent have two or more earners. The 61 percent majority of households in the lowest income quintile have no earners.

■ Households in the highest income quintile are disproportionately headed by middle-aged married couples. The elderly and people who live alone head a disproportionate share of households in the lowest income quintile.

Married couples are typically found in the higher income quintiles because their households are likely to include two or more earners

(percent distribution of married couples by income quintile, 2012)

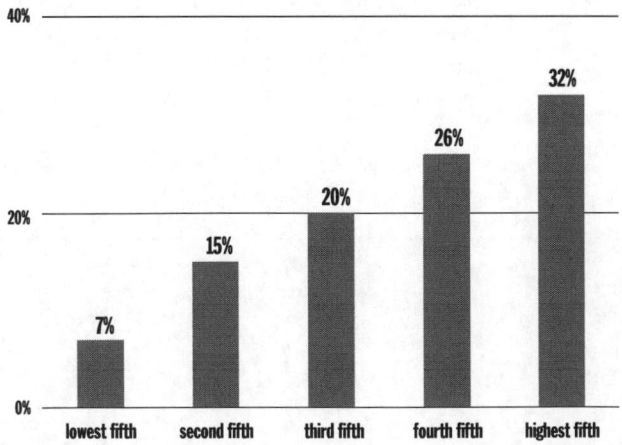

Table 5.3 Distribution of Household Characteristics by Income Quintile, 2012

(total number of households, lower income limit of each income quintile and top 5 percent, and percent distribution of selected household characteristics by quintile, 2012)

	total	bottom fifth	second fifth	third fifth	fourth fifth	top fifth	top 5 percent
Total households (in 000s)	122,459	24,492	24,492	24,492	24,492	24,492	6,126
Lower limit of income quintile	–	–	$20,599	$39,764	$64,582	$104,096	$191,156
AGE OF HOUSEHOLDER							
Total households	100.0%	20.0%	20.0%	20.0%	20.0%	20.0%	5.0%
Under age 25	100.0	34.9	25.9	19.4	13.1	6.6	0.9
Aged 25 to 34	100.0	17.8	20.5	22.9	22.8	16.1	2.7
Aged 35 to 44	100.0	13.7	16.9	20.1	23.8	25.5	6.6
Aged 45 to 54	100.0	14.9	14.6	19.3	22.1	29.1	7.8
Aged 55 to 64	100.0	18.1	16.7	19.7	21.7	23.8	6.9
Aged 65 or older	100.0	28.9	28.0	18.9	13.4	10.7	2.5
Aged 65 to 74	100.0	21.9	25.1	21.4	17.1	14.6	3.5
Aged 75 or older	100.0	37.6	31.6	15.9	9.0	6.0	1.2
TYPE OF HOUSEHOLD							
Total households	100.0	20.0	20.0	20.0	20.0	20.0	5.0
Family households	100.0	12.2	17.7	20.5	23.5	26.1	6.6
Married couple	100.0	7.0	14.8	19.9	26.3	32.1	8.4
Female householder, no spouse present	100.0	30.2	26.6	20.9	14.5	7.8	1.3
Male householder, no spouse present	100.0	16.9	23.3	25.8	19.6	14.4	2.7
Nonfamily households	100.0	35.2	24.5	19.0	13.1	8.2	1.9
Female householder	100.0	40.9	25.1	17.1	10.9	6.0	1.2
Living alone	100.0	45.7	26.0	16.5	8.5	3.4	0.7
Male householder	100.0	28.9	23.8	21.1	15.6	10.6	2.6
Living alone	100.0	34.3	26.0	20.6	12.4	6.8	1.7
RACE AND HISPANIC ORIGIN OF HOUSEHOLDER							
Total households	100.0	20.0	20.0	20.0	20.0	20.0	5.0
Asian	100.0	14.4	14.5	18.7	21.4	31.0	9.3
Black	100.0	33.1	23.0	19.3	14.7	9.9	1.7
Hispanic	100.0	25.7	25.1	21.6	16.6	11.0	2.1
Non-Hispanic white	100.0	16.7	18.9	19.9	21.6	22.9	5.9
NUMBER OF EARNERS							
Total households	100.0	20.0	20.0	20.0	20.0	20.0	5.0
No earners	100.0	52.2	27.2	12.3	5.6	2.6	0.3
One earner	100.0	18.2	26.8	25.4	18.0	11.7	3.0
Two earners or more	100.0	2.5	9.2	19.4	30.5	38.3	9.7
Two earners	100.0	2.9	10.3	20.8	30.9	35.0	8.8
Three earners	100.0	0.8	5.4	15.8	29.8	48.2	11.4
Four earners	100.0	0.4	1.9	7.6	25.9	64.2	19.5

Note: Asians and blacks are those who identify themselves as being of the race alone and those who identify themselves as being of the race in combination with other races. Non-Hispanic whites are those who identify themselves as being white alone and not Hispanic. Hispanics may be of any race. "–" means not applicable.
Source: Bureau of the Census, 2013 Current Population Survey, Internet site http://www.census.gov/hhes/www/income/data/incpovhlth/2012/dtables.html; calculations by New Strategist

Table 5.4 Distribution of Households within Income Quintile by Household Characteristics, 2012

(total number of households, lower income limit of each income quintile and top 5 percent, and percent distribution of households within quintile by selected characteristics, 2012)

	total	bottom fifth	second fifth	third fifth	fourth fifth	top fifth	top 5 percent
Total households (in 000s)	122,459	24,492	24,492	24,492	24,492	24,492	6,126
Lower limit of income quintile	–	–	$20,599	$39,764	$64,582	$104,096	$191,156
AGE OF HOUSEHOLDER							
Total households	100.0%	100.0%	100.0%	100.0%	100.0%	100.0%	100.0%
Under age 25	5.2	9.0	6.7	5.0	3.4	1.7	0.9
Aged 25 to 34	16.3	14.5	16.8	18.7	18.6	13.1	8.7
Aged 35 to 44	17.4	11.9	14.7	17.5	20.8	22.2	23.0
Aged 45 to 54	19.7	14.7	14.3	18.9	21.7	28.6	30.5
Aged 55 to 64	18.6	16.8	15.6	18.3	20.2	22.2	25.7
Aged 65 or older	22.8	33.0	31.9	21.6	15.3	12.2	11.2
Aged 65 to 74	12.5	13.7	15.7	13.4	10.7	9.1	8.8
Aged 75 or older	10.3	19.3	16.2	8.2	4.6	3.1	2.4
TYPE OF HOUSEHOLD							
Total households	100.0	100.0	100.0	100.0	100.0	100.0	100.0
Family households	66.1	40.3	58.5	67.8	77.7	86.1	87.4
Married couple	48.3	17.0	35.7	48.0	63.6	77.5	81.4
Female householder, no spouse present	12.6	19.1	16.8	13.2	9.1	4.9	3.3
Male householder, no spouse present	5.1	4.3	5.9	6.6	5.0	3.7	2.7
Nonfamily households	33.9	59.7	41.5	32.2	22.3	13.9	12.6
Female householder	17.8	36.4	22.3	15.3	9.7	5.4	4.2
Living alone	15.2	34.6	19.7	12.5	6.4	2.6	2.1
Male householder	16.1	23.3	19.2	17.0	12.6	8.6	8.3
Living alone	12.3	21.0	15.9	12.6	7.6	4.2	4.1
RACE AND HISPANIC ORIGIN OF HOUSEHOLDER							
Total households	100.0	100.0	100.0	100.0	100.0	100.0	100.0
Asian	4.8	3.5	3.5	4.5	5.1	7.4	8.9
Black	13.5	22.4	15.5	13.0	9.9	6.7	4.5
Hispanic	12.7	16.3	16.0	13.8	10.6	7.0	5.4
Non-Hispanic white	68.4	57.0	64.5	68.1	74.0	78.5	80.9
NUMBER OF EARNERS							
Total households	100.0	100.0	100.0	100.0	100.0	100.0	100.0
No earners	23.4	61.0	31.8	14.4	6.6	3.0	1.6
One earner	37.4	34.1	50.2	47.5	33.6	21.8	22.4
Two earners or more	39.2	4.9	18.1	38.1	59.8	75.2	76.0
Two earners	31.6	4.6	16.3	32.8	48.9	55.3	55.6
Three earners	5.8	0.2	1.6	4.6	8.6	13.9	13.1
Four earners	1.9	0.0	0.2	0.7	2.4	6.0	7.3

Note: Asians and blacks are those who identify themselves as being of the race alone and those who identify themselves as being of the race in combination with other races. Non-Hispanic whites are those who identify themselves as being white alone and not Hispanic. Hispanics may be of any race. "–" means not applicable.
Source: Bureau of the Census, 2013 Current Population Survey, Internet site http://www.census.gov/hhes/www/income/data/ incpovhlth/2012/dtables.html; calculations by New Strategist

Median Household Income Fell between 2000 and 2012

Householders under age 55 have experienced the biggest declines.

The $51,017 median household income of 2012 was a substantial 9 percent below the $55,987 of 2000, after adjusting for inflation. But trends in household income have varied significantly by age over the 12 years. Householders aged 65 or older saw their median household income rise 10 percent between 2000 and 2012. In contrast, householders under age 55 had a lower median household income in 2012 than their counterparts did in 2000.

Although many blame the Great Recession for the decline in household incomes, in fact incomes were already declining in the years prior to the start of the Great Recession in 2007. Householders under age 55 saw their median household income fall by 4 to 6 percent between 2000 and 2007, after adjusting for inflation. The Great Recession exacerbated the decline, but did not initiate it. In contrast, the Great Recession did trigger the income decline among householders aged 55 to 64. Meanwhile, householders aged 65 or older made gains throughout the decade.

■ The median income of households headed by people aged 65 or older is at a record high.

Oldest householders made gains between 2007 and 2012

(percent change in median household income by age of householder, 2007 to 2012)

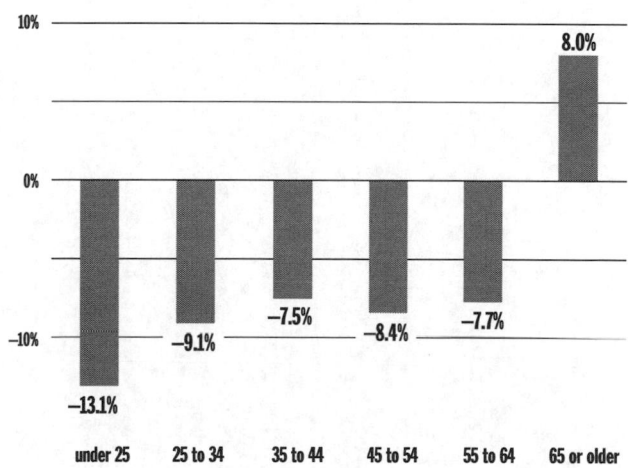

Table 5.5 Median Household Income by Age of Householder, 2000 to 2012

(median household income by age of householder, 2000 to 2012; percent change for selected years; in 2012 dollars)

	total households	under 25	25 to 34	35 to 44	45 to 54	55 to 64	65 or older total	65 to 74	75 or older
2012	$51,017	$30,604	$51,381	$63,629	$66,411	$58,626	$33,848	$42,343	$26,606
2011	51,100	31,096	51,835	63,209	65,195	57,106	33,810	42,467	26,826
2010	51,892	29,722	52,525	64,679	65,651	59,472	33,131	41,877	26,698
2009	53,285	32,899	53,737	65,388	68,762	60,988	33,564	41,636	27,504
2008	53,644	34,413	54,814	67,135	68,623	61,068	31,719	39,855	25,649
2007	55,627	35,204	56,495	68,795	72,507	63,549	31,345	39,901	25,725
2006	54,892	35,231	55,988	68,789	73,879	62,170	31,656	38,666	25,982
2005	54,486	33,838	55,724	68,315	73,420	61,465	30,622	37,248	25,689
2004	53,891	33,519	55,266	68,901	74,183	61,255	29,801	37,539	24,875
2003	54,079	33,774	55,903	68,718	75,208	61,441	29,696	37,003	24,307
2002	54,127	35,517	57,855	68,309	75,329	60,245	29,549	35,957	24,633
2001	54,766	36,568	58,465	69,152	75,280	59,482	29,982	36,537	24,867
2000	55,987	37,129	59,219	71,683	76,856	59,804	30,777	37,535	25,085

PERCENT CHANGE

	total households	under 25	25 to 34	35 to 44	45 to 54	55 to 64	65 or older total	65 to 74	75 or older
2007 to 2012	–8.3%	–13.1%	–9.1%	–7.5%	–8.4%	–7.7%	8.0%	6.1%	3.4%
2000 to 2007	–0.6	–5.2	–4.6	–4.0	–5.7	6.3	1.8	6.3	2.5
2000 to 2012	–8.9	–17.6	–13.2	–11.2	–13.6	–2.0	10.0	12.8	6.1

Source: Bureau of the Census, Historical Income Data, Internet site http://www.census.gov/hhes/www/income/; calculations by New Strategist

Every Household Type Lost Ground between 2000 and 2012

Most of the decline occurred during and after the Great Recession.

Every type of household saw its median income fall between 2007 and 2012, the biggest decline occurring among male-headed family households—a 12 percent loss, after adjusting for inflation. Women who live alone (most of them aged 55 or older) and married couples experienced the smallest loss in median household income between 2007 and 2012, with declines of 4.5 and 6.1 percent, respectively.

In the years leading up to the Great Recession, which began in 2007, median household income fell slightly for households overall (down 0.6 percent, after adjusting for inflation). Male- and female-headed families and men who live alone lost a larger 2 to 3 percent. Although many blame the Great Recession for the decline in American household incomes, in fact the losses for many households started well before the recession.

■ Married couples have the highest incomes because most are dual-earners.

Median income of married couples fell 6 percent between 2007 and 2012

(percent change in median household income by household type, 2007 to 2012; in 2012 dollars)

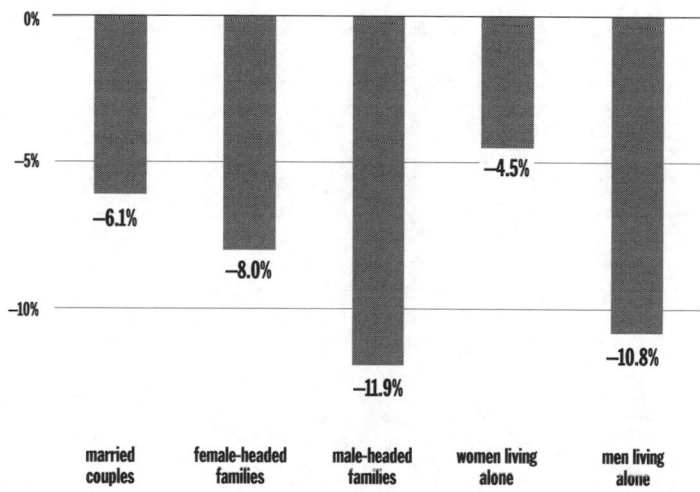

Table 5.6 Median Income of Households by Type of Household, 2000 to 2012

(median household income by type of household, 2000 to 2012; percent change for selected years; in 2012 dollars)

	total households	family households			nonfamily households	
		married couples	female householder, no spouse present	male householder, no spouse present	women living alone	men living alone
2012	$51,017	$75,694	$34,002	$48,634	$22,794	$31,212
2011	51,100	75,679	34,340	50,602	22,727	31,263
2010	51,892	76,344	33,667	52,458	23,305	31,833
2009	53,285	76,892	34,894	51,473	23,897	33,822
2008	53,644	77,859	35,269	52,453	23,480	32,767
2007	55,627	80,601	36,954	55,191	23,860	35,000
2006	54,892	79,393	36,234	53,613	24,309	35,608
2005	54,486	77,704	36,049	54,992	23,718	35,308
2004	53,891	77,568	36,256	54,725	23,719	33,323
2003	54,079	77,908	36,588	52,383	23,316	34,254
2002	54,127	78,179	37,014	53,236	22,831	34,215
2001	54,766	78,426	36,498	52,804	23,173	36,681
2000	55,987	79,029	37,685	56,207	23,769	36,203

PERCENT CHANGE

2007 to 2012	−8.3%	−6.1%	−8.0%	−11.9%	−4.5%	−10.8%
2000 to 2007	−0.6	2.0	−1.9	−1.8	0.4	−3.3
2000 to 2012	−8.9	−4.2	−9.8	−13.5	−4.1	−13.8

Source: Bureau of the Census, Historical Income Data, Internet site http://www.census.gov/hhes/www/income/; calculations by New Strategist

Every Racial and Ethnic Group Has Lost Ground

For most households, incomes were declining before the Great Recession.

Overall, median household income fell by a substantial 9 percent between 2000 and 2012, after adjusting for inflation. Asians, blacks, Hispanics, and non-Hispanic whites saw their median household income decline during those years.

The median household income of Asians, blacks, and Hispanics was in decline before the start of the Great Recession in 2007. The decline worsened once the Great Recession was underway. Median household income fell 8 percent overall between 2007 and 2012. By race and Hispanic origin, the decline ranged from 6 to 11 percent during those years.

■ Since 2000, blacks and Hispanics have lost more ground than Asians or non-Hispanic whites.

Median income of non-Hispanic whites fell 6 percent between 2007 and 2012

(percent change in median household income by race and Hispanic origin, 2007 to 2012; in 2012 dollars)

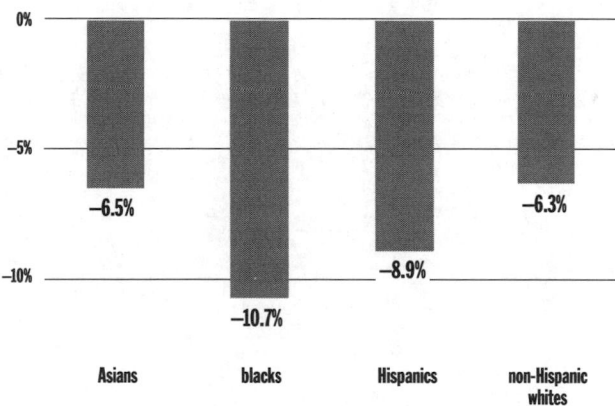

Table 5.7 Median Household Income by Race and Hispanic Origin of Householder, 2000 to 2012

(median household income by race and Hispanic origin of householder, 2000 to 2012; percent change in median for selected years; in 2012 dollars)

	total households	Asian households	black households	Hispanic households	non-Hispanic white households
2012	$51,017	$68,182	$33,718	$39,005	$57,009
2011	51,100	66,353	33,042	39,431	56,570
2010	51,892	66,900	33,863	39,629	57,351
2009	53,285	69,659	35,058	40,720	58,299
2008	53,644	69,922	36,626	40,431	59,218
2007	55,627	72,950	37,752	42,833	60,818
2006	54,892	72,770	36,592	43,025	59,700
2005	54,486	71,801	36,406	42,302	59,729
2004	53,891	69,833	36,753	41,659	59,454
2003	54,079	68,991	37,065	41,194	59,646
2002	54,127	66,732	37,239	42,250	59,859
2001	54,766	69,560	38,220	43,531	60,054
2000	55,987	74,343	39,556	44,224	60,831

PERCENT CHANGE

2007 to 2012	−8.3%	−6.5%	−10.7%	−8.9%	−6.3%
2000 to 2007	−0.6	−1.9	−4.6	−3.1	0.0
2000 to 2012	−8.9	−8.3	−14.8	−11.8	−6.3

Note: Beginning in 2002, Asians and blacks are those who identify themselves as being of the race alone and those who identify themselves as being of the race in combination with other races. Hispanics may be of any race. Beginning in 2002, non-Hispanic whites are those who identify themselves as being white alone and not Hispanic.
Source: Bureau of the Census, Historical Income Data, Internet site http://www.census.gov/hhes/www/income/; calculations by New Strategist

College Graduates Are Losing Ground

Households headed by college graduates had a lower median income in 2012 than they did in 2000.

Among households headed by people aged 25 or older, median income fell 10 percent between 2000 and 2012, after adjusting for inflation. Income declines have been steep for nearly every educational group, and they began well before the Great Recession.

Households headed by high school graduates saw their median income fall 18 percent between 2000 and 2012, after adjusting for inflation. Households headed by people with an associate's degree experienced a 15 percent decline. Households headed by college graduates saw their median household income fall 10 percent.

Between 2007 and 2012, the decline in median household income was in the double digits for many. Householders with a doctoral or professional degree made gains during those years.

■ A college education does not guarantee smooth sailing in today's slow-moving economy.

Median income of college graduates fell between 2007 and 2012

(median income of households headed by people aged 25 or older with a bachelor's degree or more education, 2007 to 2012; in 2012 dollars)

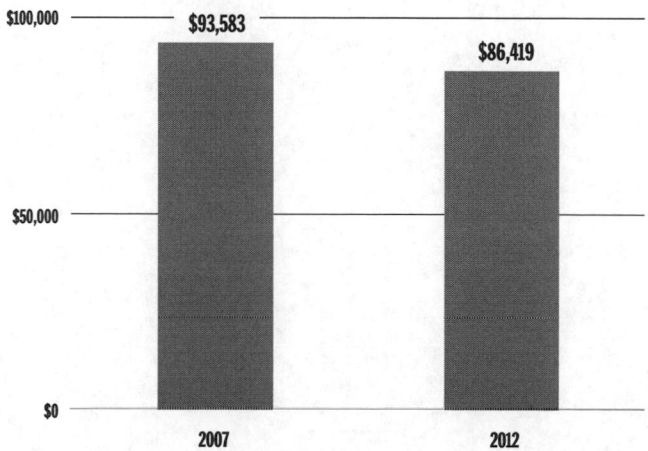

Table 5.8 Median Income of Households by Education of Householder, 2000 to 2012

(median income of households by educational attainment of householders aged 25 or older, 2000 to 2012; percent change for selected years; in 2012 dollars)

	total households	less than 9th grade	9th to 12th grade	high school graduate	some college	associate's degree	bachelor's degree or more total	bachelor's degree	master's degree	professional degree	doctoral degree
2012	$52,119	$22,496	$23,347	$39,845	$48,987	$57,460	$86,419	$80,549	$92,362	$129,588	$116,983
2011	52,314	22,279	25,211	40,243	48,476	57,096	85,739	79,886	92,847	123,099	109,282
2010	53,391	22,410	26,074	40,947	51,289	59,777	86,410	79,498	95,546	126,172	124,789
2009	54,563	23,160	27,408	42,441	51,825	60,791	88,552	80,840	98,120	132,508	129,392
2008	54,801	22,653	27,003	42,616	53,665	63,092	90,781	83,490	98,795	106,641	106,641
2007	56,950	23,039	27,122	44,801	55,833	66,590	93,583	85,939	100,396	110,739	110,739
2006	56,945	23,802	29,509	44,899	56,588	63,792	93,067	86,391	100,695	113,880	113,880
2005	56,121	23,786	29,021	44,918	56,789	64,346	90,773	85,181	95,295	117,614	117,614
2004	55,859	23,711	27,337	45,377	57,557	65,532	90,321	83,166	97,406	121,557	121,557
2003	56,199	23,454	28,362	45,986	57,245	64,881	91,692	85,802	98,053	124,843	120,885
2002	56,207	23,459	29,696	45,495	57,859	65,166	93,936	88,264	97,599	127,631	125,885
2001	56,535	23,500	30,155	46,761	59,412	66,353	93,747	87,108	102,330	129,692	120,362
2000	57,707	23,340	30,229	48,701	59,497	67,335	95,789	88,821	104,440	133,333	126,771

PERCENT CHANGE

	total households	less than 9th grade	9th to 12th grade	high school graduate	some college	associate's degree	bachelor's degree or more total	bachelor's degree	master's degree	professional degree	doctoral degree
2007 to 2012	−8.5%	−2.4%	−13.9%	−11.1%	−12.3%	−13.7%	−7.7%	−6.3%	−8.0%	17.0%	5.6%
2000 to 2007	−1.3	−1.3	−10.3	−8.0	−6.2	−1.1	−2.3	−3.2	−3.9	−16.9	−12.6
2000 to 2012	−9.7	−3.6	−22.8	−18.2	−17.7	−14.7	−9.8	−9.3	−11.6	−2.8	−7.7

Source: Bureau of the Census, Historical Income Data, Internet site http://www.census.gov/hhes/www/income/; calculations by New Strategist

Median Income of Middle-Aged Married Couples Tops $94,000

The median income of married couples aged 45 to 54 is 85 percent above average.

Median household income stood at $51,017 in 2012. Incomes vary considerably by age and household type. The most-affluent households are married couples with a householder in the 45-to-54 age group. Their median income stood at $94,191 in 2012. Not only are 45-to-54-year-olds in their peak earning years, but most couples are dual-earners, boosting incomes well above average.

Men under age 25 who live alone have the lowest median household income, just $17,126 in 2012—or 34 percent as high as the all-household median. Their female counterparts had a slightly higher median of $18,507. Many of these men and women are in college and likely to make more money in the future. Women aged 65 or older who live by themselves had a median income of just $18,663.

■ Married couples spanning the ages from 25 to 64 have median incomes well above average.

Incomes vary sharply by age and living arrangement

(median income of the richest and poorest households by household type and age of householder, 2012)

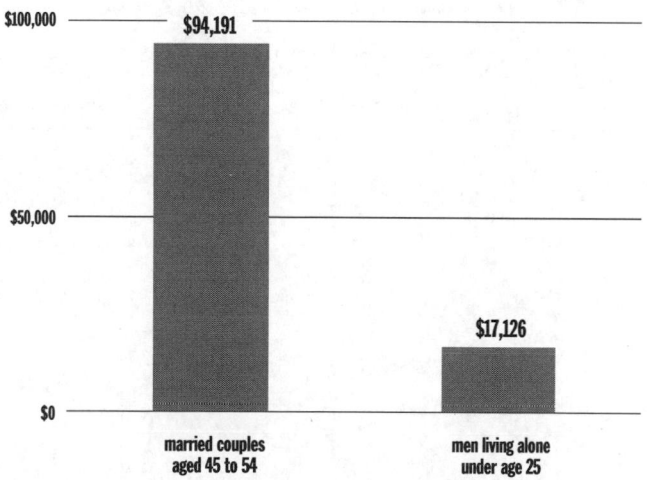

Table 5.9 Median Household Income by Household Type and Age of Householder, 2012

(median household income by type of household and age of householder; and index of age median to national median by household type, 2012)

	total	under 25	25 to 34	35 to 44	45 to 54	55 to 64	65 or older
Total households	$51,017	$30,604	$51,381	$63,629	$66,411	$58,626	$33,848
Family households	64,053	35,123	55,246	70,220	79,683	75,321	49,196
Married couples	75,694	39,127	69,727	85,448	94,191	82,959	51,416
Female householders, no spouse present	34,002	24,445	25,525	34,776	41,492	43,657	37,715
Male householders, no spouse present	48,634	45,184	50,660	48,828	48,389	51,458	44,566
Nonfamily households	30,880	26,078	46,465	44,940	38,652	32,360	20,856
Female householders	26,016	24,947	43,653	42,687	34,791	31,038	19,192
Living alone	22,794	18,507	35,477	37,517	30,782	27,990	18,663
Male householders	36,989	26,832	48,425	45,500	40,998	35,463	25,944
Living alone	31,212	17,126	37,730	39,579	35,860	31,192	24,084

INDEX

Total households	100	60	101	125	130	115	66
Family households	126	69	108	138	156	148	96
Married couples	148	77	137	167	185	163	101
Female householders, no spouse present	67	48	50	68	81	86	74
Male householders, no spouse present	95	89	99	96	95	101	87
Nonfamily households	61	51	91	88	76	63	41
Female householders	51	49	86	84	68	61	38
Living alone	45	36	70	74	60	55	37
Male householders	73	53	95	89	80	70	51
Living alone	61	34	74	78	70	61	47

Note: The index is calculated by dividing the median income of each age/household type group by the national median and multiplying by 100.
Source: Bureau of the Census, 2013 Current Population Survey, Internet site http://www.census.gov/hhes/www/income/data/incpovhlth/2012/dtables.html; calculations by New Strategist

Median Income of Black Married Couples Tops $64,000

The median income of black couples is well above the national median.

The $33,718 median income of the average black household is 34 percent below the national household median of $51,017 (with an index of 66). But the median income of black married couples is 27 percent above the all-household median (with an index of 127). In 2012, black couples had a median household income of $64,954. Asian couples had the highest median income, $87,675.

Interestingly, while the median income of the average Hispanic household is higher than that of the average black household ($39,005 versus $33,718), the median income of Hispanic couples is well below that of their black counterparts ($50,398 versus $64,954). Behind this pattern are differences in the living arrangements of Hispanics and blacks. The average Hispanic household has a higher income than the average black household because Hispanic households are more likely to be headed by married couples. Black couples have higher incomes than Hispanic couples because black couples are better educated and more likely to be employed in professional or managerial occupations.

■ Hispanic incomes are low regardless of household type because many Hispanics are recent immigrants with little education or earning power.

Incomes of married couples are lowest among Hispanics

(median income of households headed by married couples, by race and Hispanic origin, 2012)

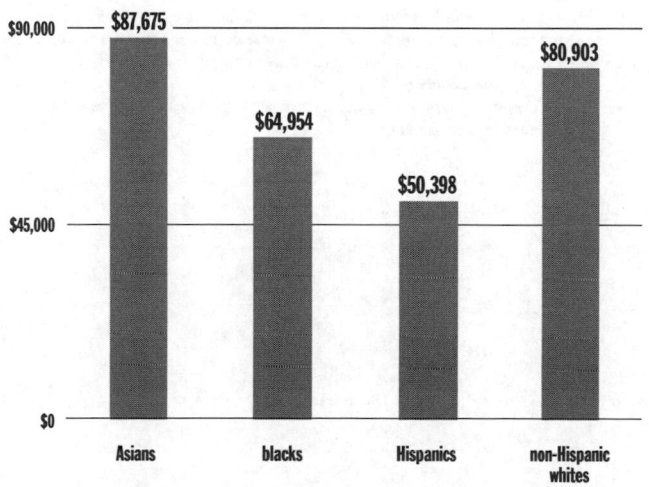

Table 5.10 Median Household Income by Household Type and Race and Hispanic Origin of Householder, 2012

(median household income by race and Hispanic origin of householder, 2000 to 2012; percent change in median for selected years; in 2012 dollars)

	total	Asian	black	Hispanic	non-Hispanic white
Total households	$51,017	$68,182	$33,718	$39,005	$57,009
Family households	64,053	79,405	42,611	42,578	72,587
Married couples	75,694	87,675	64,954	50,398	80,903
Female householders, no spouse present	34,002	49,010	27,064	28,075	41,206
Male householders, no spouse present	48,634	60,792	40,301	45,015	51,640
Nonfamily households	30,880	42,143	22,501	26,682	32,774
Female householders	26,016	32,409	20,733	20,041	27,414
Living alone	22,794	27,372	19,165	15,675	24,233
Male householders	36,989	49,928	25,820	31,895	40,457
Living alone	31,212	40,711	23,163	26,517	34,191
INDEX					
Total households	100	134	66	76	112
Family households	126	156	84	83	142
Married couples	148	172	127	99	159
Female householders, no spouse present	67	96	53	55	81
Male householders, no spouse present	95	119	79	88	101
Nonfamily households	61	83	44	52	64
Female householders	51	64	41	39	54
Living alone	45	54	38	31	47
Male householders	73	98	51	63	79
Living alone	61	80	45	52	67

Note: The index is calculated by dividing the median income of each race/Hispanic origin/household type group by the national median and multiplying by 100. Asians and blacks are those who identify themselves as being of the race alone and those who identify themselves as being of the race in combination with other races. Non-Hispanic whites are those who identify themselves as being white alone and not Hispanic. Hispanics may be of any race.
Source: Bureau of the Census, 2013 Current Population Survey, Internet site http://www.census.gov/hhes/www/income/data/ incpovhlth/2012/dtables.html; calculations by New Strategist

Householders Aged 45 to 54 Have the Highest Incomes

Median household income peaks at $66,411 in the 45-to-54 age group.

Nearly 27 million American households had an income of $100,000 or more in 2012—22 percent of total households. Among householders aged 45 to 54, a larger 32 percent had an income of $100,000 or more.

Households headed by people aged 75 or older have the lowest incomes, a median of just $26,606. Householders aged 65 to 74 have a much higher median income ($42,343) than those under age 25 ($30,604).

■ The household incomes of 55-to-64-year-olds should rise as early retirement becomes less common.

Household income peaks in middle age

(median income of households by age of householder, 2012)

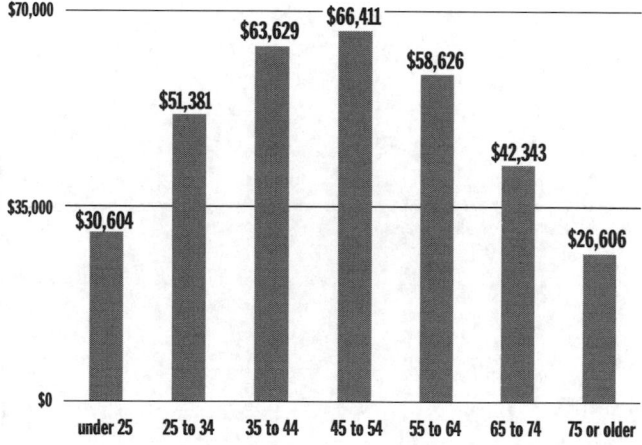

Table 5.11 Household Income by Age of Householder, 2012: Total Households

(number and percent distribution of households by household income and age of householder, 2012; households in thousands as of 2013)

	total households	under 25	25 to 34	35 to 44	45 to 54	55 to 64	65 or older total	65 to 74	75 or older
Total households	122,459	6,314	20,017	21,334	24,068	22,802	27,924	15,349	12,575
Under $25,000	30,204	2,648	4,410	3,634	4,311	5,064	10,138	4,277	5,861
$25,000 to $49,999	29,728	1,766	5,197	4,698	4,836	4,809	8,421	4,524	3,897
$50,000 to $74,999	21,418	982	4,051	4,035	4,217	4,123	4,010	2,666	1,344
$75,000 to $99,999	14,284	459	2,736	3,015	3,053	2,913	2,108	1,447	661
$100,000 or more	26,825	460	3,624	5,952	7,650	5,893	3,247	2,434	812
$100,000 to $124,999	9,490	219	1,581	2,112	2,474	1,883	1,221	868	352
$125,000 to $149,999	5,759	83	832	1,223	1,637	1,252	732	565	167
$150,000 to $174,999	3,870	62	483	874	1,166	846	440	317	124
$175,000 to $199,999	2,247	45	252	494	708	497	252	205	47
$200,000 or more	5,460	51	475	1,249	1,667	1,416	602	480	123
Median income	$51,017	$30,604	$51,381	$63,629	$66,411	$58,626	$33,848	$42,343	$26,606
Total households	100.0%	100.0%	100.0%	100.0%	100.0%	100.0%	100.0%	100.0%	100.0%
Under $25,000	24.7	41.9	22.0	17.0	17.9	22.2	36.3	27.9	46.6
$25,000 to $49,999	24.3	28.0	26.0	22.0	20.1	21.1	30.2	29.5	31.0
$50,000 to $74,999	17.5	15.6	20.2	18.9	17.5	18.1	14.4	17.4	10.7
$75,000 to $99,999	11.7	7.3	13.7	14.1	12.7	12.8	7.5	9.4	5.3
$100,000 or more	21.9	7.3	18.1	27.9	31.8	25.8	11.6	15.9	6.5
$100,000 to $124,999	7.7	3.5	7.9	9.9	10.3	8.3	4.4	5.7	2.8
$125,000 to $149,999	4.7	1.3	4.2	5.7	6.8	5.5	2.6	3.7	1.3
$150,000 to $174,999	3.2	1.0	2.4	4.1	4.8	3.7	1.6	2.1	1.0
$175,000 to $199,999	1.8	0.7	1.3	2.3	2.9	2.2	0.9	1.3	0.4
$200,000 or more	4.5	0.8	2.4	5.9	6.9	6.2	2.2	3.1	1.0

Source: Bureau of the Census, 2013 Current Population Survey, Internet site http://www.census.gov/hhes/www/income/data/incpovhlth/2012/dtables.html; calculations by New Strategist

Household Income Peaks in Middle Age in Every Racial and Ethnic Group

Median household income peaks between the ages of 35 and 54.

Among non-Hispanic whites, the median income of households headed by people aged 45 to 54 stood at $75,863 in 2012. Among Asians, median household income peaks at a much higher $88,727 in the same age group. More than one in ten Asian households headed by people ranging in age from 35 to 54 has an income of $200,000 or more. Household incomes are much lower among Hispanics, where the median peaks at $47,653 in the 45-to-54 age group. Among blacks, median household income peaks in the 35-to-44 age group at $41,918.

Householders aged 65 or older have the lowest median income among Asians ($38,109) and Hispanics ($24,122). In contrast, among non-Hispanic whites and blacks, householders under age 25 have the lowest median income ($33,656 and $20,786, respectively).

■ Black household income is below average because black households are less likely to be headed by married couples—the most-affluent household type. Hispanic household income is below average because many Hispanics are immigrants with little education or earning power.

More than one-third of Asian households has an income of $100,000 or more

(percent of households with incomes of $100,000 or more, by race and Hispanic origin, 2012)

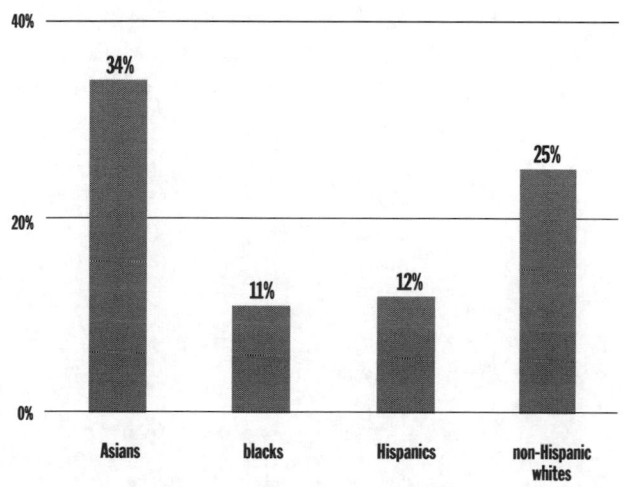

Table 5.12 Household Income by Age of Householder, 2012: Asian Households

(number and percent distribution of Asian households by household income and age of householder, 2012; households in thousands as of 2013)

	total	under 25	25 to 34	35 to 44	45 to 54	55 to 64	65 or older
Total Asian households	**5,872**	**363**	**1,289**	**1,439**	**1,133**	**840**	**809**
Under $25,000	1,037	133	182	146	158	138	279
$25,000 to $49,999	1,103	68	257	266	184	139	189
$50,000 to $74,999	1,041	87	252	273	147	162	119
$75,000 to $99,999	722	38	218	170	130	102	64
$100,000 or more	1,970	36	380	584	513	299	158
$100,000 to $124,999	591	17	143	144	145	86	56
$125,000 to $149,999	364	4	63	98	102	63	33
$150,000 to $174,999	329	5	61	113	87	42	21
$175,000 to $199,999	185	0	30	59	57	24	15
$200,000 or more	500	10	83	170	122	83	33
Median income	**$68,182**	**$41,288**	**$69,698**	**$77,381**	**$88,727**	**$71,485**	**$38,109**
Total Asian households	**100.0%**	**100.0%**	**100.0%**	**100.0%**	**100.0%**	**100.0%**	**100.0%**
Under $25,000	17.7	36.7	14.1	10.2	14.0	16.4	34.5
$25,000 to $49,999	18.8	18.7	19.9	18.5	16.3	16.6	23.3
$50,000 to $74,999	17.7	24.1	19.5	19.0	13.0	19.3	14.7
$75,000 to $99,999	12.3	10.5	16.9	11.8	11.5	12.1	7.9
$100,000 or more	33.5	9.9	29.5	40.6	45.3	35.6	19.5
$100,000 to $124,999	10.1	4.7	11.1	10.0	12.8	10.2	6.9
$125,000 to $149,999	6.2	1.2	4.9	6.8	9.0	7.5	4.0
$150,000 to $174,999	5.6	1.3	4.7	7.8	7.7	5.1	2.6
$175,000 to $199,999	3.2	0.0	2.3	4.1	5.1	2.9	1.9
$200,000 or more	8.5	2.7	6.4	11.8	10.7	9.8	4.1

Note: Asians are those who identify themselves as being of the race alone and those who identify themselves as being of the race in combination with other races.
Source: Bureau of the Census, 2013 Current Population Survey, Internet site http://www.census.gov/hhes/www/income/data/ incpovhlth/2012/dtables.html; calculations by New Strategist

Table 5.13 Household Income by Age of Householder, 2012: Black Households

(number and percent distribution of black households by household income and age of householder, 2012; households in thousands as of 2013)

	total	under 25	25 to 34	35 to 44	45 to 54	55 to 64	65 or older
Total black households	16,559	1,217	3,162	3,212	3,405	2,825	2,737
Under $25,000	6,469	698	1,219	958	1,129	1,103	1,362
$25,000 to $49,999	4,362	282	958	927	838	652	706
$50,000 to $74,999	2,475	132	485	536	557	462	302
$75,000 to $99,999	1,410	52	247	329	354	250	178
$100,000 or more	1,843	53	254	462	527	358	189
$100,000 to $124,999	786	23	119	206	210	145	84
$125,000 to $149,999	451	10	63	103	142	91	42
$150,000 to $174,999	220	11	32	50	66	43	18
$175,000 to $199,999	135	2	17	48	29	25	13
$200,000 or more	251	8	23	56	79	54	31
Median income	$33,718	$20,786	$32,142	$41,918	$41,197	$35,692	$25,157
Total black households	100.0%	100.0%	100.0%	100.0%	100.0%	100.0%	100.0%
Under $25,000	39.1	57.4	38.6	29.8	33.1	39.0	49.8
$25,000 to $49,999	26.3	23.1	30.3	28.8	24.6	23.1	25.8
$50,000 to $74,999	14.9	10.8	15.3	16.7	16.4	16.4	11.0
$75,000 to $99,999	8.5	4.3	7.8	10.2	10.4	8.8	6.5
$100,000 or more	11.1	4.4	8.0	14.4	15.5	12.7	6.9
$100,000 to $124,999	4.7	1.9	3.8	6.4	6.2	5.1	3.1
$125,000 to $149,999	2.7	0.8	2.0	3.2	4.2	3.2	1.5
$150,000 to $174,999	1.3	0.9	1.0	1.5	2.0	1.5	0.7
$175,000 to $199,999	0.8	0.2	0.5	1.5	0.9	0.9	0.5
$200,000 or more	1.5	0.7	0.7	1.7	2.3	1.9	1.1

Note: Blacks are those who identify themselves as being of the race alone and those who identify themselves as being of the race in combination with other races.
Source: Bureau of the Census, 2013 Current Population Survey, Internet site http://www.census.gov/hhes/www/income/data/incpovhlth/2012/dtables.html; calculations by New Strategist

Table 5.14 Household Income by Age of Householder, 2012: Hispanic Households

(number and percent distribution of Hispanic households by household income and age of householder, 2012; households in thousands as of 2013)

	total	under 25	25 to 34	35 to 44	45 to 54	55 to 64	65 or older
Total Hispanic households	**15,589**	**1,363**	**3,642**	**3,761**	**2,979**	**2,057**	**1,787**
Under $25,000	4,887	548	1,081	956	692	688	923
$25,000 to $49,999	4,577	464	1,149	1,140	857	533	434
$50,000 to $74,999	2,672	186	654	710	581	341	200
$75,000 to $99,999	1,518	74	397	418	309	207	112
$100,000 or more	1,934	91	360	538	539	287	118
$100,000 to $124,999	836	46	178	238	220	105	47
$125,000 to $149,999	397	21	81	94	118	60	23
$150,000 to $174,999	269	14	35	86	66	50	18
$175,000 to $199,999	141	6	18	42	44	27	4
$200,000 or more	291	5	48	77	92	45	25
Median income	**$39,005**	**$30,405**	**$39,648**	**$42,987**	**$47,653**	**$39,193**	**$24,122**
Total Hispanic households	**100.0%**	**100.0%**	**100.0%**	**100.0%**	**100.0%**	**100.0%**	**100.0%**
Under $25,000	31.4	40.2	29.7	25.4	23.2	33.5	51.6
$25,000 to $49,999	29.4	34.1	31.6	30.3	28.8	25.9	24.3
$50,000 to $74,999	17.1	13.7	18.0	18.9	19.5	16.6	11.2
$75,000 to $99,999	9.7	5.4	10.9	11.1	10.4	10.1	6.3
$100,000 or more	12.4	6.7	9.9	14.3	18.1	14.0	6.6
$100,000 to $124,999	5.4	3.4	4.9	6.3	7.4	5.1	2.7
$125,000 to $149,999	2.5	1.5	2.2	2.5	4.0	2.9	1.3
$150,000 to $174,999	1.7	1.0	1.0	2.3	2.2	2.5	1.0
$175,000 to $199,999	0.9	0.4	0.5	1.1	1.5	1.3	0.2
$200,000 or more	1.9	0.4	1.3	2.0	3.1	2.2	1.4

Source: Bureau of the Census, 2013 Current Population Survey, Internet site http://www.census.gov/hhes/www/income/data/incpovhlth/2012/dtables.html; calculations by New Strategist

Table 5.15 Household Income by Age of Householder, 2012: Non-Hispanic White Households

(number and percent distribution of non-Hispanic white households by household income and age of householder, 2012; households in thousands as of 2013)

	total	under 25	25 to 34	35 to 44	45 to 54	55 to 64	65 or older
Total non-Hispanic white households	**83,792**	**3,346**	**11,888**	**12,943**	**16,337**	**16,882**	**22,395**
Under $25,000	17,619	1,256	1,901	1,583	2,276	3,092	7,510
$25,000 to $49,999	19,514	937	2,842	2,393	2,902	3,419	7,022
$50,000 to $74,999	15,118	580	2,655	2,508	2,892	3,124	3,359
$75,000 to $99,999	10,577	291	1,879	2,098	2,238	2,329	1,744
$100,000 or more	20,963	283	2,611	4,361	6,029	4,919	2,759
$100,000 to $124,999	7,219	140	1,126	1,518	1,882	1,530	1,022
$125,000 to $149,999	4,519	46	623	926	1,263	1,030	631
$150,000 to $174,999	3,033	31	356	628	940	705	373
$175,000 to $199,999	1,787	37	188	344	582	419	218
$200,000 or more	4,404	30	319	944	1,361	1,235	515
Median income	**$57,009**	**$33,656**	**$60,504**	**$74,814**	**$75,863**	**$65,126**	**$35,559**
Total non-Hispanic white households	**100.0%**	**100.0%**	**100.0%**	**100.0%**	**100.0%**	**100.0%**	**100.0%**
Under $25,000	21.0	37.5	16.0	12.2	13.9	18.3	33.5
$25,000 to $49,999	23.3	28.0	23.9	18.5	17.8	20.3	31.4
$50,000 to $74,999	18.0	17.3	22.3	19.4	17.7	18.5	15.0
$75,000 to $99,999	12.6	8.7	15.8	16.2	13.7	13.8	7.8
$100,000 or more	25.0	8.5	22.0	33.7	36.9	29.1	12.3
$100,000 to $124,999	8.6	4.2	9.5	11.7	11.5	9.1	4.6
$125,000 to $149,999	5.4	1.4	5.2	7.2	7.7	6.1	2.8
$150,000 to $174,999	3.6	0.9	3.0	4.9	5.8	4.2	1.7
$175,000 to $199,999	2.1	1.1	1.6	2.7	3.6	2.5	1.0
$200,000 or more	5.3	0.9	2.7	7.3	8.3	7.3	2.3

Note: Non-Hispanic whites are those who identify themselves as being white alone and not Hispanic.
Source: Bureau of the Census, 2013 Current Population Survey, Internet site http://www.census.gov/hhes/www/income/data/ incpovhlth/2012/dtables.html; calculations by New Strategist

More than 4 Million Couples Have Incomes of $200,000 or More

Married couples are by far the most-affluent household type.

Most married couples are dual earners, which accounts for their higher incomes. More than one-third of couples had an income of $100,000 or more in 2012. Seven percent had an income of $200,000 or more, accounting for 81 percent of all households with incomes that high.

Married couples are the only household type whose median income is significantly above the all-household average of $51,017. Female-headed families had a median income of just $34,002, while male-headed families had a median income only slightly below the national median, at $48,634. Sixteen percent of male-headed families had an income of $100,000 or more in 2012 compared with only 9 percent of female-headed families.

Women who live alone have the lowest incomes, a median of $22,794 in 2012. Most women who live alone are older widows, which accounts for their low incomes. Men who live alone have much higher incomes than their female counterparts—a median of $31,212—because most are under age 55 and in the labor force.

■ The incomes of women who live alone are likely to rise in the decades ahead as career-oriented baby-boom women become widows.

Women who live alone have the lowest incomes

(median income of people who live alone, by sex, 2012)

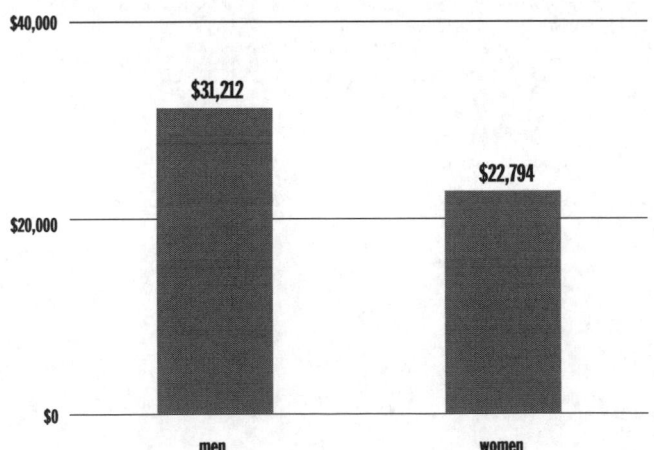

Table 5.16 Household Income by Household Type, 2012: Total Households

(number and percent distribution of households by household income and type of householder, 2012; households in thousands as of 2013)

| | | | family households | | nonfamily households | | | |
| | | | female householder, no spouse present | male householder, no spouse present | female householder | | male householder | |
	total households	married couples			total	living alone	total	living alone
Total households	**122,459**	**59,204**	**15,469**	**6,229**	**21,810**	**18,568**	**19,747**	**15,002**
Under $25,000	30,204	5,799	5,694	1,351	10,552	9,980	6,808	6,081
$25,000 to $49,999	29,728	11,950	4,656	1,847	5,614	4,801	5,660	4,583
$50,000 to $74,999	21,418	11,491	2,546	1,305	2,887	2,219	3,190	2,216
$75,000 to $99,999	14,284	9,348	1,212	712	1,251	819	1,760	970
$100,000 or more	26,825	20,616	1,361	1,013	1,506	749	2,329	1,152
$100,000 to $124,999	9,490	6,913	642	437	639	351	859	467
$125,000 to $149,999	5,759	4,363	299	223	350	156	525	261
$150,000 to $174,999	3,870	3,096	164	144	171	87	295	130
$175,000 to $199,999	2,247	1,807	84	66	108	27	181	63
$200,000 or more	5,460	4,437	172	144	238	128	470	232
Median income	**$51,017**	**$75,694**	**$34,002**	**$48,634**	**$26,016**	**$22,794**	**$36,989**	**$31,212**
Total households	**100.0%**	**100.0%**	**100.0%**	**100.0%**	**100.0%**	**100.0%**	**100.0%**	**100.0%**
Under $25,000	24.7	9.8	36.8	21.7	48.4	53.7	34.5	40.5
$25,000 to $49,999	24.3	20.2	30.1	29.7	25.7	25.9	28.7	30.5
$50,000 to $74,999	17.5	19.4	16.5	20.9	13.2	11.9	16.2	14.8
$75,000 to $99,999	11.7	15.8	7.8	11.4	5.7	4.4	8.9	6.5
$100,000 or more	21.9	34.8	8.8	16.3	6.9	4.0	11.8	7.7
$100,000 to $124,999	7.7	11.7	4.2	7.0	2.9	1.9	4.3	3.1
$125,000 to $149,999	4.7	7.4	1.9	3.6	1.6	0.8	2.7	1.7
$150,000 to $174,999	3.2	5.2	1.1	2.3	0.8	0.5	1.5	0.9
$175,000 to $199,999	1.8	3.1	0.5	1.1	0.5	0.1	0.9	0.4
$200,000 or more	4.5	7.5	1.1	2.3	1.1	0.7	2.4	1.5

Source: Bureau of the Census, 2013 Current Population Survey, Internet site http://www.census.gov/hhes/www/income/data/ incpovhlth/2012/dtables.html; calculations by New Strategist

From Young to Old, Incomes Vary by Household Type

In all but the youngest age group, married couples have the highest incomes.

Married couples are the most-affluent household type, while the middle-aged are the most-affluent age group. Combine those characteristics and you have the most-affluent households in the country. Married couples in the 45-to-54 age group had a median income of $94,191 in 2012, 47 percent having an income of $100,000 or more and 11 percent having an income of $200,000 or more. Among couples aged 35 to 44 and 55 to 64, a substantial 41 and 39 percent, respectively, have an income of $100,000 or more.

Only 15 percent of households headed by people under age 25 are married couples, which is one reason for the low incomes of the age group. Among householders under age 25, male-headed families have the highest incomes, a median of $45,184 versus $39,127 for married couples.

■ Earners generate income. Because most married couples are dual-earners, their incomes typically are much higher than the incomes of other household types.

Many married couples have incomes of $100,000 or more

(percent of married couples with household incomes of $100,000 or more, by age of householder, 2012)

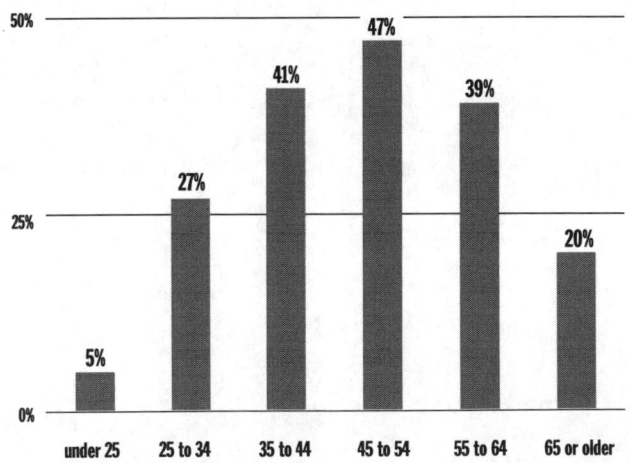

Table 5.17 Household Income by Household Type, 2012: Householders under Age 25

(number and percent distribution of households headed by people under age 25 by household income and type of householder, 2012; households in thousands as of 2013)

	total households	married couples	family households female householder, no spouse present	male householder, no spouse present	nonfamily households female householder total	living alone	male householder total	living alone
Householder under age 25	**6,314**	**970**	**1,394**	**921**	**1,493**	**788**	**1,536**	**760**
Under $25,000	2,648	251	708	226	748	567	715	506
$25,000 to $49,999	1,766	363	332	286	389	166	395	181
$50,000 to $74,999	982	205	158	193	201	43	225	49
$75,000 to $99,999	459	100	88	89	68	7	114	19
$100,000 or more	460	51	108	127	87	4	88	5
$100,000 to $124,999	219	31	51	49	49	2	40	3
$125,000 to $149,999	83	7	13	29	16	2	17	1
$150,000 to $174,999	62	7	14	18	8	0	15	1
$175,000 to $199,999	45	3	12	14	10	0	6	0
$200,000 or more	51	3	18	17	4	0	10	0
Median income	**$30,604**	**$39,127**	**$24,445**	**$45,184**	**$24,947**	**$18,507**	**$26,832**	**$17,126**
Householder under age 25	**100.0%**	**100.0%**	**100.0%**	**100.0%**	**100.0%**	**100.0%**	**100.0%**	**100.0%**
Under $25,000	41.9	25.9	50.8	24.5	50.1	72.0	46.5	66.5
$25,000 to $49,999	28.0	37.5	23.8	31.1	26.1	21.1	25.7	23.8
$50,000 to $74,999	15.6	21.1	11.4	21.0	13.5	5.5	14.6	6.5
$75,000 to $99,999	7.3	10.3	6.3	9.7	4.6	0.9	7.4	2.6
$100,000 or more	7.3	5.2	7.7	13.7	5.8	0.5	5.7	0.7
$100,000 to $124,999	3.5	3.2	3.6	5.3	3.3	0.3	2.6	0.4
$125,000 to $149,999	1.3	0.8	1.0	3.1	1.1	0.2	1.1	0.2
$150,000 to $174,999	1.0	0.7	1.0	1.9	0.6	0.0	1.0	0.1
$175,000 to $199,999	0.7	0.3	0.9	1.6	0.7	0.0	0.4	0.0
$200,000 or more	0.8	0.3	1.3	1.8	0.3	0.0	0.6	0.0

Source: Bureau of the Census, 2013 Current Population Survey, Internet site http://www.census.gov/hhes/www/income/data/ incpovhlth/2012/dtables.html; calculations by New Strategist

Table 5.18 Household Income by Household Type, 2012: Householders Aged 25 to 34

(number and percent distribution of households headed by people aged 25 to 34 by household income and type of householder, 2012; households in thousands as of 2013)

| | | family households | | | nonfamily households | | | |
| | | | female householder, no spouse present | male householder, no spouse present | female householder | | male householder | |
	total households	married couples			total	living alone	total	living alone
Householder aged 25 to 34	**20,017**	**8,551**	**3,373**	**1,416**	**2,686**	**1,818**	**3,992**	**2,433**
Under $25,000	4,410	921	1,647	292	707	606	841	681
$25,000 to $49,999	5,197	1,743	1,004	402	842	660	1,206	902
$50,000 to $74,999	4,051	2,029	400	298	497	317	827	478
$75,000 to $99,999	2,736	1,571	151	187	303	139	524	197
$100,000 or more	3,624	2,287	170	237	336	95	593	175
$100,000 to $124,999	1,581	1,004	85	107	158	48	228	86
$125,000 to $149,999	832	517	44	57	75	24	140	24
$150,000 to $174,999	483	314	30	27	36	10	76	20
$175,000 to $199,999	252	172	4	14	21	0	42	12
$200,000 or more	475	280	8	33	47	14	107	34
Median income	**$51,381**	**$69,727**	**$25,525**	**$50,660**	**$43,653**	**$35,477**	**$48,425**	**$37,730**
Householder aged 25 to 34	**100.0%**	**100.0%**	**100.0%**	**100.0%**	**100.0%**	**100.0%**	**100.0%**	**100.0%**
Under $25,000	22.0	10.8	48.8	20.7	26.3	33.4	21.1	28.0
$25,000 to $49,999	26.0	20.4	29.8	28.4	31.3	36.3	30.2	37.1
$50,000 to $74,999	20.2	23.7	11.9	21.0	18.5	17.5	20.7	19.6
$75,000 to $99,999	13.7	18.4	4.5	13.2	11.3	7.6	13.1	8.1
$100,000 or more	18.1	26.7	5.0	16.7	12.5	5.2	14.9	7.2
$100,000 to $124,999	7.9	11.7	2.5	7.5	5.9	2.6	5.7	3.5
$125,000 to $149,999	4.2	6.0	1.3	4.0	2.8	1.3	3.5	1.0
$150,000 to $174,999	2.4	3.7	0.9	1.9	1.4	0.6	1.9	0.8
$175,000 to $199,999	1.3	2.0	0.1	1.0	0.8	0.0	1.1	0.5
$200,000 or more	2.4	3.3	0.2	2.3	1.7	0.8	2.7	1.4

Source: Bureau of the Census, 2013 Current Population Survey, Internet site http://www.census.gov/hhes/www/income/data/incpovhlth/2012/dtables.html; calculations by New Strategist

Table 5.19 Household Income by Household Type, 2012: Householders Aged 35 to 44

(number and percent distribution of households headed by people aged 35 to 44 by household income and type of householder, 2012; households in thousands as of 2013)

		family households			nonfamily households			
			female householder, no spouse present	male householder, no spouse present	female householder		male householder	
	total households	married couples			total	living alone	total	living alone
Householder aged 35 to 44	21,334	11,985	3,605	1,258	1,627	1,296	2,859	2,161
Under $25,000	3,634	881	1,309	254	487	426	703	625
$25,000 to $49,999	4,698	1,860	1,119	389	441	383	889	727
$50,000 to $74,999	4,035	2,228	648	271	366	296	522	395
$75,000 to $99,999	3,015	2,149	247	159	140	80	321	196
$100,000 or more	5,952	4,867	282	184	194	111	425	217
$100,000 to $124,999	2,112	1,655	128	90	76	44	164	103
$125,000 to $149,999	1,223	1,031	47	37	46	23	63	31
$150,000 to $174,999	874	728	36	22	21	12	67	29
$175,000 to $199,999	494	411	21	13	12	2	37	13
$200,000 or more	1,249	1,042	50	22	40	30	94	40
Median income	**$63,629**	**$85,448**	**$34,776**	**$48,828**	**$42,687**	**$37,517**	**$45,500**	**$39,579**
Householder aged 35 to 44	100.0%	100.0%	100.0%	100.0%	100.0%	100.0%	100.0%	100.0%
Under $25,000	17.0	7.4	36.3	20.2	29.9	32.9	24.6	28.9
$25,000 to $49,999	22.0	15.5	31.0	30.9	27.1	29.5	31.1	33.6
$50,000 to $74,999	18.9	18.6	18.0	21.6	22.5	22.8	18.2	18.3
$75,000 to $99,999	14.1	17.9	6.8	12.7	8.6	6.2	11.2	9.1
$100,000 or more	27.9	40.6	7.8	14.6	11.9	8.6	14.9	10.1
$100,000 to $124,999	9.9	13.8	3.5	7.1	4.7	3.4	5.7	4.8
$125,000 to $149,999	5.7	8.6	1.3	3.0	2.8	1.8	2.2	1.5
$150,000 to $174,999	4.1	6.1	1.0	1.7	1.3	1.0	2.3	1.3
$175,000 to $199,999	2.3	3.4	0.6	1.1	0.7	0.2	1.3	0.6
$200,000 or more	5.9	8.7	1.4	1.7	2.5	2.3	3.3	1.9

Source: Bureau of the Census, 2013 Current Population Survey, Internet site http://www.census.gov/hhes/www/income/data/ incpovhlth/2012/dtables.html; calculations by New Strategist

Table 5.20 Household Income by Household Type, 2012: Householders Aged 45 to 54

(number and percent distribution of households headed by people aged 45 to 54 by household income and type of householder, 2012; households in thousands as of 2013)

| | | family households | | | nonfamily households | | | |
| | | | female householder, no spouse present | male householder, no spouse present | female householder | | male householder | |
	total households	married couples			total	living alone	total	living alone
Householder aged 45 to 54	**24,068**	**13,237**	**3,099**	**1,204**	**2,913**	**2,432**	**3,615**	**2,880**
Under $25,000	4,311	906	889	254	1,114	1,035	1,148	1,048
$25,000 to $49,999	4,836	1,786	918	368	764	633	1,000	837
$50,000 to $74,999	4,217	2,239	626	239	523	445	590	445
$75,000 to $99,999	3,053	2,112	302	127	213	158	300	204
$100,000 or more	7,650	6,194	363	216	299	162	578	346
$100,000 to $124,999	2,474	1,875	172	90	111	79	226	143
$125,000 to $149,999	1,637	1,310	80	47	64	20	135	76
$150,000 to $174,999	1,166	986	42	36	42	24	60	38
$175,000 to $199,999	708	598	22	15	26	10	46	20
$200,000 or more	1,667	1,424	46	28	57	29	111	69
Median income	**$66,411**	**$94,191**	**$41,492**	**$48,389**	**$34,791**	**$30,782**	**$40,998**	**$35,860**
Householder aged 45 to 54	**100.0%**	**100.0%**	**100.0%**	**100.0%**	**100.0%**	**100.0%**	**100.0%**	**100.0%**
Under $25,000	17.9	6.8	28.7	21.1	38.2	42.5	31.7	36.4
$25,000 to $49,999	20.1	13.5	29.6	30.6	26.2	26.0	27.7	29.1
$50,000 to $74,999	17.5	16.9	20.2	19.8	18.0	18.3	16.3	15.5
$75,000 to $99,999	12.7	16.0	9.7	10.5	7.3	6.5	8.3	7.1
$100,000 or more	31.8	46.8	11.7	17.9	10.3	6.6	16.0	12.0
$100,000 to $124,999	10.3	14.2	5.5	7.5	3.8	3.3	6.2	5.0
$125,000 to $149,999	6.8	9.9	2.6	3.9	2.2	0.8	3.7	2.6
$150,000 to $174,999	4.8	7.4	1.4	3.0	1.4	1.0	1.7	1.3
$175,000 to $199,999	2.9	4.5	0.7	1.3	0.9	0.4	1.3	0.7
$200,000 or more	6.9	10.8	1.5	2.3	2.0	1.2	3.1	2.4

Source: Bureau of the Census, 2013 Current Population Survey, Internet site http://www.census.gov/hhes/www/income/data/incpovhlth/2012/dtables.html; calculations by New Strategist

Table 5.21 Household Income by Household Type, 2012: Householders Aged 55 to 64

(number and percent distribution of households headed by people aged 55 to 64 by household income and type of householder, 2012; households in thousands as of 2013)

| | total households | family households | | | nonfamily households | | | |
| | | married couples | female householder, no spouse present | male householder, no spouse present | female householder | | male householder | |
					total	living alone	total	living alone
Householder aged 55 to 64	**22,802**	**12,043**	**1,969**	**812**	**4,308**	**3,805**	**3,669**	**3,110**
Under $25,000	5,064	1,085	544	171	1,830	1,751	1,434	1,335
$25,000 to $49,999	4,809	1,923	571	221	1,140	1,043	955	855
$50,000 to $74,999	4,123	2,314	368	177	663	549	601	492
$75,000 to $99,999	2,913	1,992	219	89	324	252	288	192
$100,000 or more	5,893	4,729	268	154	351	210	392	236
$100,000 to $124,999	1,883	1,446	122	61	129	96	124	78
$125,000 to $149,999	1,252	969	68	27	97	49	91	65
$150,000 to $174,999	846	716	23	25	33	17	49	23
$175,000 to $199,999	497	417	16	7	24	8	34	17
$200,000 or more	1,416	1,181	38	34	68	41	94	54
Median income	**$58,626**	**$82,959**	**$43,657**	**$51,458**	**$31,038**	**$27,990**	**$35,463**	**$31,192**
Householder aged 55 to 64	**100.0%**	**100.0%**	**100.0%**	**100.0%**	**100.0%**	**100.0%**	**100.0%**	**100.0%**
Under $25,000	22.2	9.0	27.6	21.0	42.5	46.0	39.1	42.9
$25,000 to $49,999	21.1	16.0	29.0	27.2	26.5	27.4	26.0	27.5
$50,000 to $74,999	18.1	19.2	18.7	21.8	15.4	14.4	16.4	15.8
$75,000 to $99,999	12.8	16.5	11.1	11.0	7.5	6.6	7.8	6.2
$100,000 or more	25.8	39.3	13.6	19.0	8.1	5.5	10.7	7.6
$100,000 to $124,999	8.3	12.0	6.2	7.5	3.0	2.5	3.4	2.5
$125,000 to $149,999	5.5	8.0	3.5	3.3	2.3	1.3	2.5	2.1
$150,000 to $174,999	3.7	5.9	1.2	3.1	0.8	0.5	1.3	0.7
$175,000 to $199,999	2.2	3.5	0.8	0.8	0.5	0.2	0.9	0.5
$200,000 or more	6.2	9.8	1.9	4.2	1.6	1.1	2.6	1.7

Source: Bureau of the Census, 2013 Current Population Survey, Internet site http://www.census.gov/hhes/www/income/data/incpovhlth/2012/dtables.html; calculations by New Strategist

Table 5.22 Household Income by Household Type, 2012: Householders Aged 65 or Older

(number and percent distribution of households headed by people aged 65 or older by household income and type of householder, 2012; households in thousands as of 2013)

| | total households | family households | | | nonfamily households | | | |
| | | | female householder, no spouse present | male householder, no spouse present | female householder | | male householder | |
		married couples			total	living alone	total	living alone
Householder aged 65 or older	**27,924**	**12,418**	**2,029**	**619**	**8,783**	**8,429**	**4,075**	**3,658**
Under $25,000	10,138	1,754	597	153	5,666	5,595	1,967	1,886
$25,000 to $49,999	8,421	4,274	712	182	2,038	1,916	1,215	1,082
$50,000 to $74,999	4,010	2,476	345	127	637	569	425	356
$75,000 to $99,999	2,108	1,425	205	61	203	183	214	162
$100,000 or more	3,247	2,489	170	96	238	166	253	172
$100,000 to $124,999	1,221	902	85	41	117	82	76	53
$125,000 to $149,999	732	528	46	26	52	39	79	64
$150,000 to $174,999	440	346	19	16	31	23	28	19
$175,000 to $199,999	252	206	9	3	16	7	17	1
$200,000 or more	602	506	11	10	22	14	53	34
Median income	**$33,848**	**$51,416**	**$37,715**	**$44,566**	**$19,192**	**$18,663**	**$25,944**	**$24,084**
Householder aged 65 or older	**100.0%**	**100.0%**	**100.0%**	**100.0%**	**100.0%**	**100.0%**	**100.0%**	**100.0%**
Under $25,000	36.3	14.1	29.4	24.8	64.5	66.4	48.3	51.6
$25,000 to $49,999	30.2	34.4	35.1	29.4	23.2	22.7	29.8	29.6
$50,000 to $74,999	14.4	19.9	17.0	20.5	7.3	6.7	10.4	9.7
$75,000 to $99,999	7.5	11.5	10.1	9.8	2.3	2.2	5.3	4.4
$100,000 or more	11.6	20.0	8.4	15.5	2.7	2.0	6.2	4.7
$100,000 to $124,999	4.4	7.3	4.2	6.6	1.3	1.0	1.9	1.5
$125,000 to $149,999	2.6	4.3	2.3	4.2	0.6	0.5	1.9	1.7
$150,000 to $174,999	1.6	2.8	0.9	2.5	0.4	0.3	0.7	0.5
$175,000 to $199,999	0.9	1.7	0.4	0.5	0.2	0.1	0.4	0.0
$200,000 or more	2.2	4.1	0.5	1.7	0.3	0.2	1.3	0.9

Source: Bureau of the Census, 2013 Current Population Survey, Internet site http://www.census.gov/hhes/www/income/data/incpovhlth/2012/dtables.html; calculations by New Strategist

Asian Married Couples Have the Highest Income

Hispanic women who live alone have the lowest.

Married couples are the most-affluent household type, and Asians are the most-affluent racial or ethnic group. Combine those characteristics and you have the most-affluent households in the country. Asian married couples had a median income of $87,675 in 2012, 44 percent having an income of $100,000 or more. Twelve percent of Asian couples have an income of $200,000 or more. Black couples have higher incomes than Hispanic couples—a median of $64,594 compared with $50,398 for Hispanics. Twenty-six percent of black couples have an income of $100,000 or more compared with only 18 percent of Hispanic couples.

Hispanic women who live alone have the lowest incomes, a median of just $15,675 in 2012. Women who live alone account for only 9 percent of Hispanic households. In contrast, women who live alone constitute a much larger 16 percent of non-Hispanic white households. Their median income is $24,233.

■ Black couples have much higher incomes than Hispanic couples because they are better educated and more likely to be employed as managers or professionals.

Asian married couples are most likely to have incomes of $100,000 or more

(percent of married couples with household incomes of $100,000 or more, by race and Hispanic origin of householder, 2012)

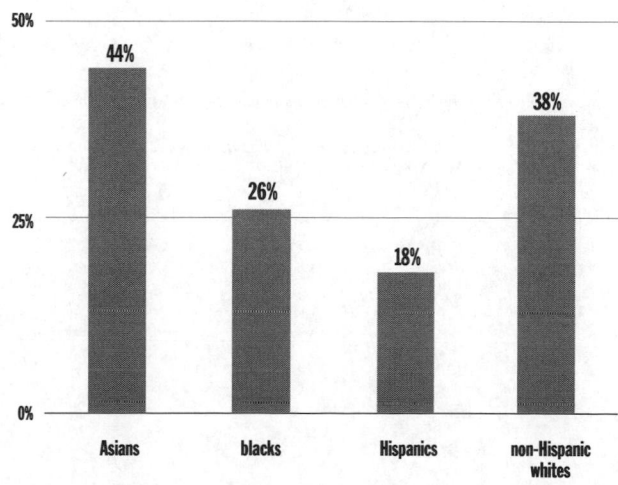

Table 5.23 Household Income by Household Type, 2012: Asian Households

(number and percent distribution of Asian households by household income and type of householder, 2012; households in thousands as of 2013)

| | | | family households | | nonfamily households | | | |
| | | | female householder, no spouse present | male householder, no spouse present | female householder | | male householder | |
	total households	married couples			total	living alone	total	living alone
Asian households	5,872	3,409	565	346	758	610	794	539
Under $25,000	1,037	320	147	51	307	279	211	186
$25,000 to $49,999	1,103	530	143	84	159	134	187	126
$50,000 to $74,999	1,041	584	101	79	125	102	152	103
$75,000 to $99,999	722	461	58	44	58	49	101	66
$100,000 or more	1,970	1,514	116	88	109	46	143	58
$100,000 to $124,999	591	413	52	37	39	15	51	26
$125,000 to $149,999	364	277	29	12	26	13	19	7
$150,000 to $174,999	329	251	18	18	18	6	24	11
$175,000 to $199,999	185	160	0	3	13	4	9	2
$200,000 or more	500	412	17	19	12	8	40	12
Median income	$68,182	$87,675	$49,010	$60,792	$32,409	$27,372	$49,928	$40,711
Asian households	100.0%	100.0%	100.0%	100.0%	100.0%	100.0%	100.0%	100.0%
Under $25,000	17.7	9.4	26.1	14.8	40.6	45.8	26.5	34.4
$25,000 to $49,999	18.8	15.6	25.3	24.2	20.9	22.0	23.6	23.3
$50,000 to $74,999	17.7	17.1	17.9	23.0	16.5	16.7	19.2	19.2
$75,000 to $99,999	12.3	13.5	10.2	12.6	7.7	8.0	12.8	12.2
$100,000 or more	33.5	44.4	20.5	25.5	14.4	7.5	18.0	10.8
$100,000 to $124,999	10.1	12.1	9.2	10.6	5.1	2.5	6.4	4.8
$125,000 to $149,999	6.2	8.1	5.1	3.6	3.4	2.1	2.4	1.2
$150,000 to $174,999	5.6	7.4	3.2	5.1	2.4	1.0	3.0	2.1
$175,000 to $199,999	3.2	4.7	0.0	0.7	1.8	0.6	1.2	0.3
$200,000 or more	8.5	12.1	3.0	5.5	1.6	1.4	5.0	2.3

Note: Asians are those who identify themselves as being of the race alone and those who identify themselves as being of the race in combination with other races.
Source: Bureau of the Census, 2013 Current Population Survey, Internet site http://www.census.gov/hhes/www/income/data/incpovhlth/2012/dtables.html; calculations by New Strategist

Table 5.24 Household Income by Household Type, 2012: Black Households

(number and percent distribution of black households by household income and type of householder, 2012; households in thousands as of 2013)

| | total households | family households | | | nonfamily households | | | |
| | | married couples | female householder, no spouse present | male householder, no spouse present | female householder | | male householder | |
					total	living alone	total	living alone
Black households	**16,559**	**4,700**	**4,473**	**1,105**	**3,424**	**3,042**	**2,856**	**2,370**
Under $25,000	6,469	678	2,092	363	1,951	1,835	1,386	1,241
$25,000 to $49,999	4,362	1,058	1,299	310	860	751	836	710
$50,000 to $74,999	2,475	1,004	600	216	345	275	310	219
$75,000 to $99,999	1,410	759	251	100	141	101	159	105
$100,000 or more	1,843	1,202	232	116	127	81	166	95
$100,000 to $124,999	786	491	123	60	50	31	62	34
$125,000 to $149,999	451	324	41	12	39	23	34	19
$150,000 to $174,999	220	139	30	18	11	9	22	10
$175,000 to $199,999	135	86	11	9	10	2	19	11
$200,000 or more	251	162	26	16	18	15	29	22
Median income	**$33,718**	**$64,954**	**$27,064**	**$40,301**	**$20,733**	**$19,165**	**$25,820**	**$23,163**
Black households	**100.0%**	**100.0%**	**100.0%**	**100.0%**	**100.0%**	**100.0%**	**100.0%**	**100.0%**
Under $25,000	39.1	14.4	46.8	32.8	57.0	60.3	48.5	52.4
$25,000 to $49,999	26.3	22.5	29.0	28.1	25.1	24.7	29.3	30.0
$50,000 to $74,999	14.9	21.4	13.4	19.6	10.1	9.0	10.8	9.3
$75,000 to $99,999	8.5	16.1	5.6	9.0	4.1	3.3	5.6	4.4
$100,000 or more	11.1	25.6	5.2	10.5	3.7	2.7	5.8	4.0
$100,000 to $124,999	4.7	10.4	2.8	5.4	1.4	1.0	2.2	1.4
$125,000 to $149,999	2.7	6.9	0.9	1.1	1.1	0.8	1.2	0.8
$150,000 to $174,999	1.3	3.0	0.7	1.7	0.3	0.3	0.8	0.4
$175,000 to $199,999	0.8	1.8	0.3	0.8	0.3	0.1	0.7	0.4
$200,000 or more	1.5	3.5	0.6	1.5	0.5	0.5	1.0	0.9

Note: Blacks are those who identify themselves as being of the race alone and those who identify themselves as being of the race in combination with other races.
Source: Bureau of the Census, 2013 Current Population Survey, Internet site http://www.census.gov/hhes/www/income/data/incpovhlth/2012/dtables.html; calculations by New Strategist

Table 5.25 Household Income by Household Type, 2012: Hispanic Households

(number and percent distribution of Hispanic households by household income and type of householder, 2012; households in thousands as of 2013)

| | | | family households | | nonfamily households | | | |
| | | | female householder, no spouse present | male householder, no spouse present | female householder | | male householder | |
	total households	married couples			total	living alone	total	living alone
Hispanic households	**15,589**	**7,455**	**3,106**	**1,391**	**1,683**	**1,367**	**1,954**	**1,345**
Under $25,000	4,887	1,479	1,360	322	984	904	742	633
$25,000 to $49,999	4,577	2,211	969	439	342	262	615	439
$50,000 to $74,999	2,672	1,496	404	304	179	106	289	155
$75,000 to $99,999	1,518	944	193	133	85	46	164	74
$100,000 or more	1,934	1,325	181	192	92	49	144	43
$100,000 to $124,999	836	541	98	94	33	21	69	23
$125,000 to $149,999	397	284	33	43	16	3	21	8
$150,000 to $174,999	269	194	26	21	11	6	17	3
$175,000 to $199,999	141	96	7	13	6	2	18	3
$200,000 or more	291	211	17	21	25	17	18	6
Median income	**$39,005**	**$50,398**	**$28,075**	**$45,015**	**$20,041**	**$15,675**	**$31,895**	**$26,517**
Hispanic households	**100.0%**	**100.0%**	**100.0%**	**100.0%**	**100.0%**	**100.0%**	**100.0%**	**100.0%**
Under $25,000	31.4	19.8	43.8	23.2	58.5	66.2	38.0	47.1
$25,000 to $49,999	29.4	29.7	31.2	31.6	20.3	19.2	31.5	32.7
$50,000 to $74,999	17.1	20.1	13.0	21.8	10.7	7.7	14.8	11.5
$75,000 to $99,999	9.7	12.7	6.2	9.6	5.1	3.3	8.4	5.5
$100,000 or more	12.4	17.8	5.8	13.8	5.5	3.6	7.3	3.2
$100,000 to $124,999	5.4	7.3	3.2	6.8	2.0	1.5	3.5	1.7
$125,000 to $149,999	2.5	3.8	1.1	3.1	1.0	0.2	1.1	0.6
$150,000 to $174,999	1.7	2.6	0.8	1.5	0.7	0.5	0.9	0.2
$175,000 to $199,999	0.9	1.3	0.2	1.0	0.4	0.1	0.9	0.2
$200,000 or more	1.9	2.8	0.5	1.5	1.5	1.3	0.9	0.5

Source: Bureau of the Census, 2013 Current Population Survey, Internet site http://www.census.gov/hhes/www/income/data/incpovhlth/2012/dtables.html; calculations by New Strategist

Table 5.26 Household Income by Household Type, 2012: Non-Hispanic White Households

(number and percent distribution of non-Hispanic white households by household income and type of householder, 2012; households in thousands as of 2013)

| | | family households | | | nonfamily households | | | |
| | | | | | female householder | | male householder | |
	total households	married couples	female householder, no spouse present	male householder, no spouse present	total	living alone	total	living alone
Non-Hispanic white households	**83,792**	**43,299**	**7,317**	**3,388**	**15,833**	**13,476**	**13,955**	**10,609**
Under $25,000	17,619	3,270	2,102	600	7,285	6,934	4,362	3,932
$25,000 to $49,999	19,514	8,082	2,233	1,015	4,187	3,614	3,997	3,288
$50,000 to $74,999	15,118	8,346	1,437	704	2,228	1,733	2,403	1,710
$75,000 to $99,999	10,577	7,136	708	435	961	625	1,338	730
$100,000 or more	20,963	16,465	837	635	1,172	570	1,854	949
$100,000 to $124,999	7,219	5,419	370	257	511	280	662	381
$125,000 to $149,999	4,519	3,447	198	155	267	117	451	226
$150,000 to $174,999	3,033	2,496	93	89	131	66	224	103
$175,000 to $199,999	1,787	1,471	64	41	77	19	134	48
$200,000 or more	4,404	3,632	112	92	185	89	383	191
Median income	**$57,009**	**$80,903**	**$41,206**	**$51,640**	**$27,414**	**$24,233**	**$40,457**	**$34,191**
Non-Hispanic white households	**100.0%**	**100.0%**	**100.0%**	**100.0%**	**100.0%**	**100.0%**	**100.0%**	**100.0%**
Under $25,000	21.0	7.6	28.7	17.7	46.0	51.5	31.3	37.1
$25,000 to $49,999	23.3	18.7	30.5	30.0	26.4	26.8	28.6	31.0
$50,000 to $74,999	18.0	19.3	19.6	20.8	14.1	12.9	17.2	16.1
$75,000 to $99,999	12.6	16.5	9.7	12.8	6.1	4.6	9.6	6.9
$100,000 or more	25.0	38.0	11.4	18.7	7.4	4.2	13.3	8.9
$100,000 to $124,999	8.6	12.5	5.1	7.6	3.2	2.1	4.7	3.6
$125,000 to $149,999	5.4	8.0	2.7	4.6	1.7	0.9	3.2	2.1
$150,000 to $174,999	3.6	5.8	1.3	2.6	0.8	0.5	1.6	1.0
$175,000 to $199,999	2.1	3.4	0.9	1.2	0.5	0.1	1.0	0.4
$200,000 or more	5.3	8.4	1.5	2.7	1.2	0.7	2.7	1.8

Note: Non-Hispanic whites are those who identify themselves as being white alone and not Hispanic.
Source: Bureau of the Census, 2013 Current Population Survey, Internet site http://www.census.gov/hhes/www/income/data/incpovhlth/2012/dtables.html; calculations by New Strategist

Dual-Earner Couples Have the Highest Incomes

Most have incomes of $100,000 or more, and many have incomes of $200,000 or more.

The median income of all married-couple families stood at $75,535 in 2012. Among dual-earner couples, median income was a much higher $110,357. Thirteen percent of dual-earner couples have an income of $200,000 or more. Twenty-eight percent of the nation's couples are dual-earners, in which both husband and wife work full-time.

Among all married couples, those with children under age 18 at home have higher incomes than those without children—$81,455 versus $70,902. Those with children at home have higher incomes because they are more likely to be in the labor force, and many are in their peak earning years. Couples without children at home have lower incomes because many are older and retired.

Among couples in which both husband and wife work full-time, however, those without children at home—many of them empty-nesters—have a higher income than those with children at home, a median of $111,124 in 2012. Dual-earner couples with children have a lower median income of $109,070.

■ The incomes of married couples without children at home should continue to grow in the years ahead as aging boomers postpone retirement.

Dual-earner married couples without children at home have the highest incomes

(median income of married couples by work status and presence of children under age 18 at home, 2012)

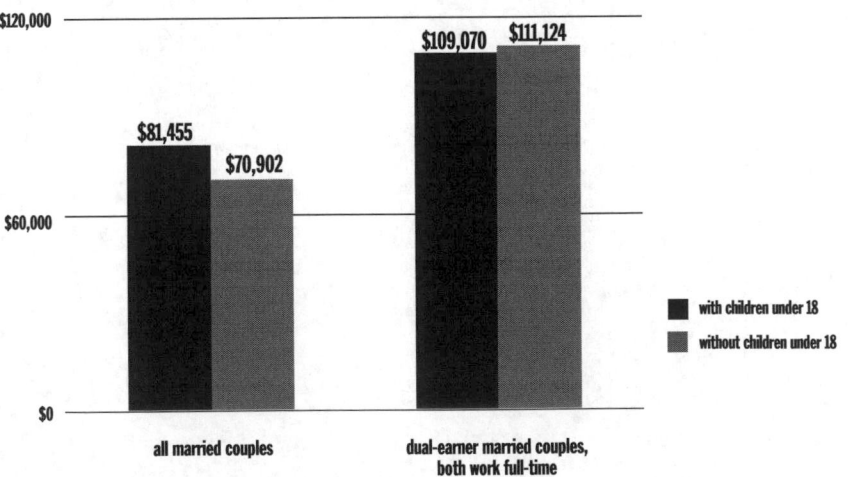

Table 5.27 Income of Married Couples by Presence of Children, 2012

(number and percent distribution of married-couple families by income and presence and age of related children under age 18 at home, 2012; couples in thousands as of 2013)

			with one or more children			
	total	no children	total	all under 6	some under 6, some 6 to 17	all 6 to 17
Total couples	59,224	33,955	25,269	5,913	5,360	13,996
Under $25,000	5,849	3,647	2,202	567	647	988
$25,000 to $49,999	12,000	7,617	4,383	1,101	1,087	2,195
$50,000 to $74,999	11,484	6,700	4,784	1,194	1,035	2,555
$75,000 to $99,999	9,331	5,091	4,241	999	866	2,376
$100,000 or more	20,560	10,900	9,660	2,051	1,725	5,883
$100,000 to $124,999	6,921	3,655	3,266	756	605	1,906
$125,000 to $149,999	4,340	2,319	2,022	411	343	1,267
$150,000 to $174,999	3,081	1,631	1,449	327	253	869
$175,000 to $199,999	1,795	945	850	158	155	538
$200,000 or more	4,422	2,350	2,072	399	369	1,303
Median income	$75,535	$70,902	$81,455	$76,508	$71,646	$87,102
Total couples	100.0%	100.0%	100.0%	100.0%	100.0%	100.0%
Under $25,000	9.9	10.7	8.7	9.6	12.1	7.1
$25,000 to $49,999	20.3	22.4	17.3	18.6	20.3	15.7
$50,000 to $74,999	19.4	19.7	18.9	20.2	19.3	18.3
$75,000 to $99,999	15.8	15.0	16.8	16.9	16.2	17.0
$100,000 or more	34.7	32.1	38.2	34.7	32.2	42.0
$100,000 to $124,999	11.7	10.8	12.9	12.8	11.3	13.6
$125,000 to $149,999	7.3	6.8	8.0	7.0	6.4	9.1
$150,000 to $174,999	5.2	4.8	5.7	5.5	4.7	6.2
$175,000 to $199,999	3.0	2.8	3.4	2.7	2.9	3.8
$200,000 or more	7.5	6.9	8.2	6.8	6.9	9.3

Note: The median income of married couples in this table is slightly different from the figure shown in the household income tables because this figure includes the incomes only of the family members and not any unrelated members of the household. Source: Bureau of the Census, 2013 Current Population Survey, Internet site http://www.census.gov/hhes/www/income/data/incpovhlth/2012/dtables.html; calculations by New Strategist

Table 5.28 Income of Dual-Earner Married Couples by Presence of Children, 2012

(number and percent distribution of married couples in which both husband and wife work full-time, year-round, by income and presence and age of related children under age 18 at home, 2012; couples in thousands as of 2013)

	total	no children	with one or more children			
			total	all under 6	some under 6, some 6 to 17	all 6 to 17
Total dual-earner couples	16,868	8,550	8,319	1,900	1,474	4,945
Under $25,000	65	45	21	3	3	15
$25,000 to $49,999	950	462	489	114	91	284
$50,000 to $74,999	2,693	1,370	1,323	336	265	722
$75,000 to $99,999	3,394	1,656	1,739	414	327	998
$100,000 or more	9,765	5,018	4,747	1,033	788	2,927
$100,000 to $124,999	2,998	1,514	1,485	342	235	907
$125,000 to $149,999	2,126	1,081	1,045	211	171	663
$150,000 to $174,999	1,482	788	694	178	118	397
$175,000 to $199,999	975	486	489	79	82	327
$200,000 or more	2,184	1,149	1,035	222	181	632
Median income	$110,357	$111,124	$109,070	$106,591	$103,148	$111,254
Total dual-earner couples	100.0%	100.0%	100.0%	100.0%	100.0%	100.0%
Under $25,000	0.4	0.5	0.3	0.1	0.2	0.3
$25,000 to $49,999	5.6	5.4	5.9	6.0	6.2	5.7
$50,000 to $74,999	16.0	16.0	15.9	17.7	17.9	14.6
$75,000 to $99,999	20.1	19.4	20.9	21.8	22.2	20.2
$100,000 or more	57.9	58.7	57.1	54.4	53.5	59.2
$100,000 to $124,999	17.8	17.7	17.8	18.0	16.0	18.3
$125,000 to $149,999	12.6	12.6	12.6	11.1	11.6	13.4
$150,000 to $174,999	8.8	9.2	8.3	9.4	8.0	8.0
$175,000 to $199,999	5.8	5.7	5.9	4.2	5.6	6.6
$200,000 or more	12.9	13.4	12.4	11.7	12.3	12.8

Source: Bureau of the Census, 2013 Current Population Survey, Internet site http://www.census.gov/hhes/www/income/data/ incpovhlth/2012/dtables.html; calculations by New Strategist

Single Parents Have Low Incomes

But many male- and female-headed families have incomes close to the average.

Single-parent families are those with children under age 18 and headed by a man or woman without a spouse. Single parents account for 65 percent of female-headed families and 51 percent of families headed by men. The incomes of single-parent families are lower than those of other male- and female-headed families. Female-headed single-parent families had a median income of $25,493 in 2012, while their male counterparts had a median income of $36,471.

Male- and female-headed families without children under age 18 at home have substantially higher incomes. Many of these men and women live with other adults such as parents, brothers, or sisters—which adds earners to the household. The median income of male-headed families without children under age 18 at home stood at $49,338, close to the national median. A substantial 16 percent had incomes of $100,000 or more. Their female counterparts had a median income of $42,147.

■ Both male- and female-headed families have seen their incomes fall because of the Great Recession.

Female-headed families with children have lower incomes

(median income of female- and male-headed families by presence of children under age 18 at home, 2012)

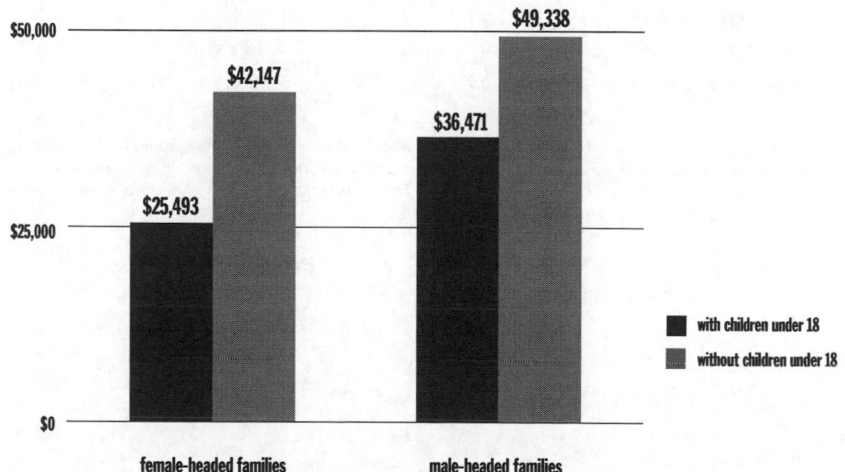

| | with children under 18 |
| | without children under 18 |

female-headed families   male-headed families

Table 5.29 Income of Female- and Male-Headed Families by Presence of Children, 2012

(number and percent distribution of female- and male-headed families with no spouse present, by family income and presence of children under age 18 at home, 2012; families in thousands as of 2013)

	female-headed families			male-headed families		
	total	no children	one or more children	total	no children	one or more children
Total families	**15,489**	**5,456**	**10,033**	**6,231**	**3,062**	**3,169**
Under $25,000	6,381	1,449	4,931	1,668	671	996
$25,000 to $49,999	4,647	1,720	2,927	1,924	882	1,043
$50,000 to $74,999	2,294	1,069	1,225	1,214	683	531
$75,000 to $99,999	1,045	592	453	625	343	282
$100,000 or more	1,122	626	496	800	483	317
$100,000 to $124,999	531	289	242	336	201	134
$125,000 to $149,999	261	161	100	163	115	49
$150,000 to $174,999	115	59	57	122	69	52
$175,000 to $199,999	72	45	27	58	37	21
$200,000 or more	143	73	70	122	61	61
Median income	**$30,686**	**$42,147**	**$25,493**	**$42,358**	**$49,338**	**$36,471**
Total families	**100.0%**	**100.0%**	**100.0%**	**100.0%**	**100.0%**	**100.0%**
Under $25,000	41.2	26.6	49.2	26.8	21.9	31.4
$25,000 to $49,999	30.0	31.5	29.2	30.9	28.8	32.9
$50,000 to $74,999	14.8	19.6	12.2	19.5	22.3	16.7
$75,000 to $99,999	6.7	10.9	4.5	10.0	11.2	8.9
$100,000 or more	7.2	11.5	4.9	12.8	15.8	10.0
$100,000 to $124,999	3.4	5.3	2.4	5.4	6.6	4.2
$125,000 to $149,999	1.7	3.0	1.0	2.6	3.7	1.5
$150,000 to $174,999	0.7	1.1	0.6	2.0	2.3	1.7
$175,000 to $199,999	0.5	0.8	0.3	0.9	1.2	0.7
$200,000 or more	0.9	1.3	0.7	2.0	2.0	1.9

Note: Median incomes in this table are slightly different from the figures shown in the household income tables because these figures include the incomes only of the family members and not any unrelated members of the household.
Source: Bureau of the Census, 2013 Current Population Survey, Internet site http://www.census.gov/hhes/www/income/data/incpovhlth/2012/dtables.html; calculations by New Strategist

Most Women Who Live Alone Have Low Incomes

Among people under age 25 who live alone, men have lower incomes than women.

Among the nation's 34 million single-person households, women head the 55 percent majority. The median income of all women who live alone was just $22,794 in 2012. The median income of all men who live alone was a higher $31,212. The gap in median incomes can be explained largely by the age differences between men and women who live alone. The 66 percent majority of women who live alone are aged 55 or older, many of them elderly widows dependent on Social Security. Fifty-five percent of men who live alone are under age 55, many in their peak earning years.

For both men and women who live alone, income is lowest in the youngest age group. Women under age 25 who live alone had a median income of $18,507. Men under age 25 who live alone had an even lower median income of $17,126. For people who live alone, income peaks in the 35-to-44 age group. The median income of women in the age group who live alone was $37,517 in 2012. For their male counterparts, it was a slightly larger $39,579.

■ Men and women who live alone had a lower median income in 2012 than in 2000, after adjusting for inflation.

Among women who live alone, those aged 35 to 44 have the highest median income

(median income of women who live alone, by age, 2012)

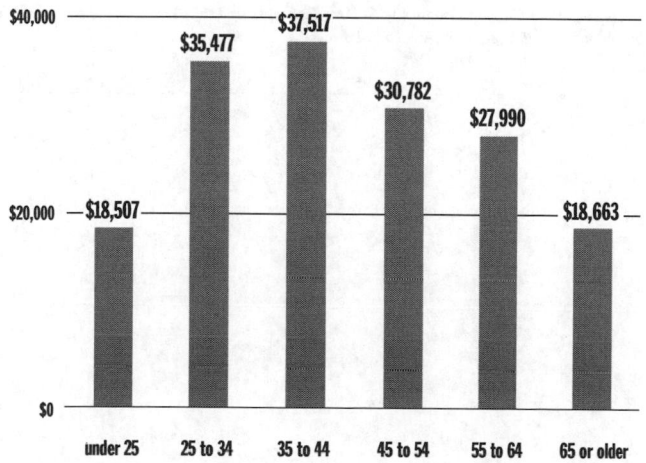

Table 5.30 Household Income of Men Who Live Alone, 2012

(number and percent distribution of male-headed single-person households by household income and age of householder, 2012; households in thousands as of 2013)

	total	under 25	25 to 34	35 to 44	45 to 54	55 to 64	65 or older
Total men living alone	**15,002**	**760**	**2,433**	**2,161**	**2,880**	**3,110**	**3,658**
Under $25,000	6,081	506	681	625	1,048	1,335	1,886
$25,000 to $49,999	4,583	181	902	727	837	855	1,082
$50,000 to $74,999	2,216	49	478	395	445	492	356
$75,000 to $99,999	970	19	197	196	204	192	162
$100,000 or more	1,152	5	175	217	346	236	172
$100,000 to $124,999	467	3	86	103	143	78	53
$125,000 to $149,999	261	1	24	31	76	65	64
$150,000 to $174,999	130	1	20	29	38	23	19
$175,000 to $199,999	63	0	12	13	20	17	1
$200,000 or more	232	0	34	40	69	54	34
Median income	**$31,212**	**$17,126**	**$37,730**	**$39,579**	**$35,860**	**$31,192**	**$24,084**
Total men living alone	**100.0%**	**100.0%**	**100.0%**	**100.0%**	**100.0%**	**100.0%**	**100.0%**
Under $25,000	40.5	66.5	28.0	28.9	36.4	42.9	51.6
$25,000 to $49,999	30.5	23.8	37.1	33.6	29.1	27.5	29.6
$50,000 to $74,999	14.8	6.5	19.6	18.3	15.5	15.8	9.7
$75,000 to $99,999	6.5	2.6	8.1	9.1	7.1	6.2	4.4
$100,000 or more	7.7	0.7	7.2	10.1	12.0	7.6	4.7
$100,000 to $124,999	3.1	0.4	3.5	4.8	5.0	2.5	1.5
$125,000 to $149,999	1.7	0.2	1.0	1.5	2.6	2.1	1.7
$150,000 to $174,999	0.9	0.1	0.8	1.3	1.3	0.7	0.5
$175,000 to $199,999	0.4	0.0	0.5	0.6	0.7	0.5	0.0
$200,000 or more	1.5	0.0	1.4	1.9	2.4	1.7	0.9

Source: Bureau of the Census, 2013 Current Population Survey, Internet site http://www.census.gov/hhes/www/income/data/ incpovhlth/2012/dtables.html; calculations by New Strategist

Table 5.31 Household Income of Women Who Live Alone, 2012

(number and percent distribution of female-headed single-person households by household income and age of householder, 2012; households in thousands as of 2013)

	total	under 25	25 to 34	35 to 44	45 to 54	55 to 64	65 or older
Total women living alone	**18,568**	**788**	**1,818**	**1,296**	**2,432**	**3,805**	**8,429**
Under $25,000	9,980	567	606	426	1,035	1,751	5,595
$25,000 to $49,999	4,801	166	660	383	633	1,043	1,916
$50,000 to $74,999	2,219	43	317	296	445	549	569
$75,000 to $99,999	819	7	139	80	158	252	183
$100,000 or more	749	4	95	111	162	210	166
$100,000 to $124,999	351	2	48	44	79	96	82
$125,000 to $149,999	156	2	24	23	20	49	39
$150,000 to $174,999	87	0	10	12	24	17	23
$175,000 to $199,999	27	0	0	2	10	8	7
$200,000 or more	128	0	14	30	29	41	14
Median income	**$22,794**	**$18,507**	**$35,477**	**$37,517**	**$30,782**	**$27,990**	**$18,663**
Total women living alone	**100.0%**	**100.0%**	**100.0%**	**100.0%**	**100.0%**	**100.0%**	**100.0%**
Under $25,000	53.7	72.0	33.4	32.9	42.5	46.0	66.4
$25,000 to $49,999	25.9	21.1	36.3	29.5	26.0	27.4	22.7
$50,000 to $74,999	11.9	5.5	17.5	22.8	18.3	14.4	6.7
$75,000 to $99,999	4.4	0.9	7.6	6.2	6.5	6.6	2.2
$100,000 or more	4.0	0.5	5.2	8.6	6.6	5.5	2.0
$100,000 to $124,999	1.9	0.3	2.6	3.4	3.3	2.5	1.0
$125,000 to $149,999	0.8	0.2	1.3	1.8	0.8	1.3	0.5
$150,000 to $174,999	0.5	0.0	0.6	1.0	1.0	0.5	0.3
$175,000 to $199,999	0.1	0.0	0.0	0.2	0.4	0.2	0.1
$200,000 or more	0.7	0.0	0.8	2.3	1.2	1.1	0.2

Source: Bureau of the Census, 2013 Current Population Survey, Internet site http://www.census.gov/hhes/www/income/data/ incpovhlth/2012/dtables.html; calculations by New Strategist

College-Educated Householders Have the Highest Incomes

Median income of households headed by college graduates is 66 percent higher than the national average.

The higher the degree, the greater the household income. At the top are householders with professional degrees, such as doctors or lawyers. Their median household income was $129,588 in 2012, 29 percent having household incomes of $200,000 or more.

Thirty-three percent of householders aged 25 or older have at least a bachelor's degree. Their median income stood at $86,419 in 2012. In contrast, householders who went no further than high school had a median income that was far below average at just $39,845. Those who did not graduate from high school had a median household income of less than $24,000.

■ Households headed by college graduates account for 79 percent of all households with incomes of $200,000 or more.

Incomes rise with education

(median income of householders aged 25 or older by educational attainment, 2012)

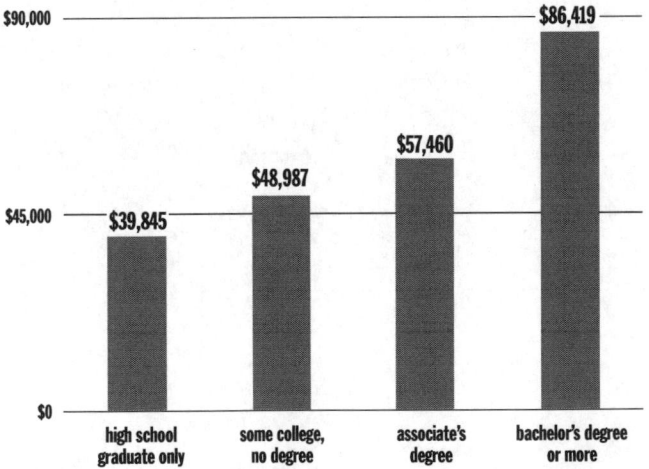

Table 5.32 Household Income by Education of Householder, 2012

(number and percent distribution of householders aged 25 or older by household income and educational attainment of householder, 2012; households in thousands as of 2013)

	total	less than 9th grade	9th to 12th grade, no diploma	high school graduate	some college, no degree	associate's degree	bachelor's degree or more total	bachelor's degree	master's degree	professional degree	doctoral degree
Total households	**116,145**	**4,903**	**8,054**	**32,308**	**21,211**	**11,760**	**37,910**	**23,782**	**10,247**	**1,826**	**2,055**
Under $25,000	27,556	2,675	4,283	9,868	4,992	2,132	3,607	2,499	831	137	139
$25,000 to $49,999	27,962	1,397	2,130	9,594	5,822	2,971	6,048	4,308	1,356	163	221
$50,000 to $74,999	20,436	495	923	5,934	4,213	2,490	6,382	4,083	1,834	214	250
$75,000 to $99,999	13,825	199	423	3,175	2,513	1,740	5,775	3,801	1,516	200	257
$100,000 or more	26,366	136	295	3,735	3,671	2,428	16,099	9,090	4,709	1,112	1,188
$100,000 to $124,999	9,271	62	162	1,820	1,593	1,091	4,542	2,860	1,284	168	230
$125,000 to $149,999	5,676	31	59	835	909	571	3,271	1,970	941	157	203
$150,000 to $174,999	3,808	10	33	449	498	335	2,482	1,418	734	150	180
$175,000 to $199,999	2,202	6	15	222	229	177	1,552	812	507	106	126
$200,000 or more	5,409	26	27	409	442	253	4,252	2,030	1,243	531	449
Median income	**$52,119**	**$22,496**	**$23,347**	**$39,845**	**$48,987**	**$57,460**	**$86,419**	**$80,549**	**$92,362**	**$129,588**	**$116,983**
Total households	**100.0%**	**100.0%**	**100.0%**	**100.0%**	**100.0%**	**100.0%**	**100.0%**	**100.0%**	**100.0%**	**100.0%**	**100.0%**
Under $25,000	23.7	54.6	53.2	30.5	23.5	18.1	9.5	10.5	8.1	7.5	6.8
$25,000 to $49,999	24.1	28.5	26.4	29.7	27.4	25.3	16.0	18.1	13.2	8.9	10.7
$50,000 to $74,999	17.6	10.1	11.5	18.4	19.9	21.2	16.8	17.2	17.9	11.7	12.2
$75,000 to $99,999	11.9	4.1	5.3	9.8	11.8	14.8	15.2	16.0	14.8	11.0	12.5
$100,000 or more	22.7	2.8	3.7	11.6	17.3	20.6	42.5	38.2	46.0	60.9	57.8
$100,000 to $124,999	8.0	1.3	2.0	5.6	7.5	9.3	12.0	12.0	12.5	9.2	11.2
$125,000 to $149,999	4.9	0.6	0.7	2.6	4.3	4.9	8.6	8.3	9.2	8.6	9.9
$150,000 to $174,999	3.3	0.2	0.4	1.4	2.3	2.9	6.5	6.0	7.2	8.2	8.8
$175,000 to $199,999	1.9	0.1	0.2	0.7	1.1	1.5	4.1	3.4	5.0	5.8	6.1
$200,000 or more	4.7	0.5	0.3	1.3	2.1	2.2	11.2	8.5	12.1	29.1	21.8

Source: Bureau of the Census, 2013 Current Population Survey, Internet site http://www.census.gov/hhes/www/income/data/incpovhlth/2012/dtables.html; calculations by New Strategist

Incomes Have Plummeted among Men under Age 65

Most women under age 65 are also losing ground.

Between 2007 and 2012, older men and women made gains in income—in contrast to everyone else. Among men and women aged 65 or older, median income climbed 3 percent during those years, after adjusting for inflation. Younger men and women lost ground, and among men the losses started well before the Great Recession. Men under age 55 experienced double-digit declines in median income between 2000 and 2012.

Women's median income stood at $21,520 in 2012, well below the $33,904 median income of men. Men's incomes are higher than women's in part because men are more likely to work full-time. Incomes peak among men aged 45 to 54 at $46,466. Women's income peak is in the 35-to-44 age group at $30,061—including both full- and part-time workers.

■ The median income of women aged 55 to 64 grew rapidly between 2000 and 2012 as career-oriented baby boomers filled the age group.

Median income of men aged 45 to 54 fell 8 percent between 2007 and 2012

(median income of men aged 25 to 64 by age, 2007 and 2012; in 2012 dollars)

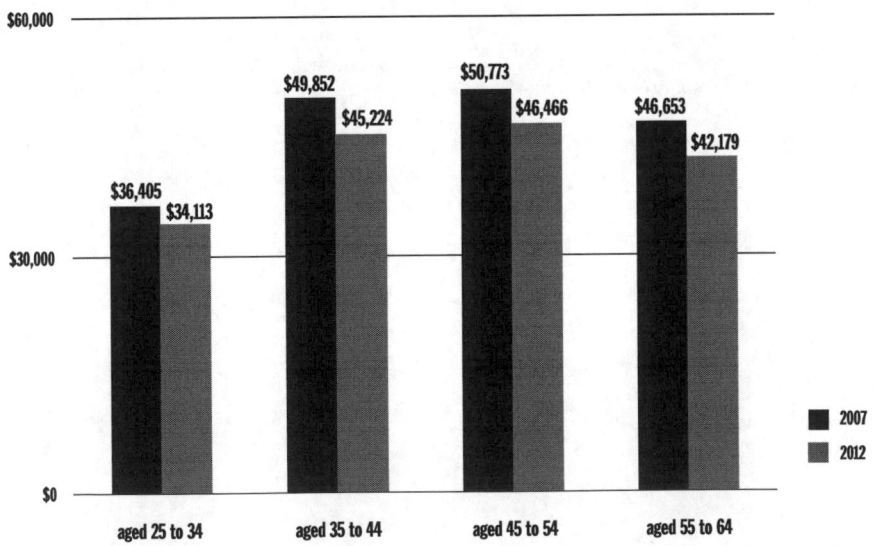

Table 5.33 Median Income of Men by Age, 2000 to 2012

(median income of men aged 15 or older with income by age, 2000 to 2012; percent change in income for selected years; in 2012 dollars)

	total men	under 25	25 to 34	35 to 44	45 to 54	55 to 64	65 or older total	65 to 74	75 or older
2012	$33,904	$10,869	$34,113	$45,224	$46,466	$42,176	$27,612	$31,762	$23,570
2011	33,675	10,738	33,262	44,885	46,910	42,418	28,286	31,888	24,115
2010	33,915	10,433	33,637	44,474	47,861	43,432	27,096	30,878	23,165
2009	34,452	10,743	34,163	45,200	47,883	44,206	27,701	30,992	24,366
2008	35,363	11,494	35,634	47,124	48,564	44,530	27,197	30,919	23,366
2007	36,761	12,413	36,405	49,852	50,773	46,653	26,935	30,770	23,033
2006	36,744	12,486	36,591	48,555	52,035	47,234	26,762	29,920	23,504
2005	36,784	12,313	36,650	48,179	51,312	47,815	25,621	28,605	22,867
2004	37,094	12,255	37,673	49,272	50,890	47,757	25,686	29,433	22,763
2003	37,367	12,436	38,154	48,932	52,533	48,583	25,422	28,915	22,197
2002	37,317	12,306	39,153	48,362	52,289	46,301	24,806	27,174	22,346
2001	37,742	12,063	39,569	49,724	53,309	46,218	25,534	28,137	22,723
2000	37,791	12,728	40,339	50,563	54,719	45,585	25,881	28,621	22,925

PERCENT CHANGE

	total men	under 25	25 to 34	35 to 44	45 to 54	55 to 64	65 or older total	65 to 74	75 or older
2007 to 2012	−7.8%	−12.4%	−6.3%	−9.3%	−8.5%	−9.6%	2.5%	3.2%	2.3%
2000 to 2007	−2.7	−2.5	−9.8	−1.4	−7.2	2.3	4.1	7.5	0.5
2000 to 2012	−10.3	−14.6	−15.4	−10.6	−15.1	−7.5	6.7	11.0	2.8

Source: Bureau of the Census, Historical Income Data, Internet site http://www.census.gov/hhes/www/income/; calculations by New Strategist

Table 5.34 Median Income of Women by Age, 2000 to 2012

(median income of women aged 15 or older with income by age, 2000 to 2012; percent change in income for selected years; in 2012 dollars)

	total women	under 25	25 to 34	35 to 44	45 to 54	55 to 64	65 or older total	65 to 74	75 or older
2012	$21,520	$9,581	$26,173	$30,061	$29,784	$26,684	$16,040	$17,236	$14,916
2011	21,543	9,297	26,260	29,703	29,055	26,465	15,683	16,818	14,895
2010	21,878	9,159	26,919	30,826	29,142	26,817	15,888	16,961	15,157
2009	22,434	9,581	27,015	29,860	30,634	26,882	16,359	17,243	15,750
2008	22,253	9,492	27,250	29,189	30,111	27,210	15,526	15,816	15,333
2007	23,169	9,921	28,664	30,677	32,616	27,975	15,527	15,993	15,168
2006	22,792	9,854	27,535	30,028	31,709	27,543	15,491	16,033	15,148
2005	21,848	9,668	26,834	29,915	31,140	26,019	14,696	15,102	14,456
2004	21,476	9,364	26,824	29,662	31,887	25,286	14,685	14,936	14,516
2003	21,547	9,282	27,455	29,303	32,292	25,428	14,788	15,160	14,524
2002	21,457	9,677	27,631	28,490	32,118	24,460	14,558	14,395	14,681
2001	21,547	9,684	27,849	29,143	31,301	23,115	14,672	14,527	14,780
2000	21,417	9,813	28,065	29,436	31,643	22,560	14,697	14,544	14,813

PERCENT CHANGE

2007 to 2012	−7.1%	−3.4%	−8.7%	−2.0%	−8.7%	−4.6%	3.3%	7.8%	−1.7%
2000 to 2007	8.2	1.1	2.1	4.2	3.1	24.0	5.6	10.0	2.4
2000 to 2012	0.5	−2.4	−6.7	2.1	−5.9	18.3	9.1	18.5	0.7

Source: Bureau of the Census, Historical Income Data, Internet site http://www.census.gov/hhes/www/income/; calculations by New Strategist

Every Race and Hispanic Origin Group Lost Ground during the Great Recession

Women fared no better than men.

No race or Hispanic origin group was immune from the Great Recession. The median income of black men fell 13 percent between 2007 and 2012, after adjusting for inflation. The median income of Hispanic men fell 9 percent, non-Hispanic white men's income was down 6 percent, and Asians lost 3 percent. The story was the same for women. Between 2007 and 2012, Asian women saw their median income decline 13 percent, Hispanic women lost 10 percent, black women 9 percent, and non-Hispanic white women 5 percent.

Among both men and women, Hispanics have the lowest median income—just $16,725 for women and $24,592 for men in 2012. Asians have the highest income among men, a median of just under $40,000. Asians also have the highest median income among women, at $23,290 in 2012.

■ In every race and Hispanic origin group, men's median income was lower in 2012 than in 2000, after adjusting for inflation.

The Great Recession hurt men and women regardless of race or Hispanic origin group

(percent change in median income of people aged 15 or older, by sex, race, and Hispanic origin, 2007 to 2012; in 2012 dollars)

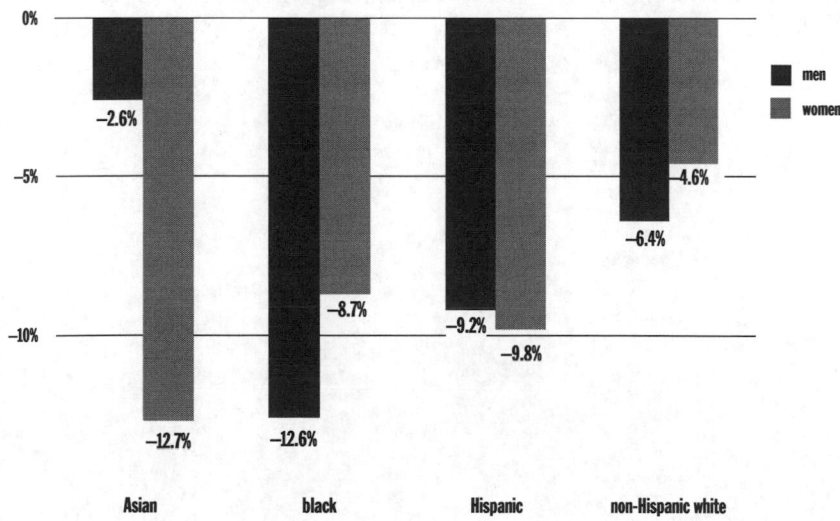

Table 5.35 Median Income of Men by Race and Hispanic Origin, 2000 to 2012

(median income of men aged 15 or older with income by race and Hispanic origin, 2000 to 2012; percent change in income for selected years; in 2012 dollars)

	total men	Asian	black	Hispanic	non-Hispanic white
2012	$33,904	$39,606	$24,959	$24,592	$38,751
2011	33,675	36,584	24,077	24,227	38,945
2010	33,915	36,986	24,312	23,610	39,127
2009	34,452	39,486	25,342	23,825	39,377
2008	35,363	38,608	26,786	25,597	39,893
2007	36,761	40,673	28,562	27,077	41,386
2006	36,744	42,255	28,556	26,707	41,639
2005	36,784	38,855	26,591	25,980	41,571
2004	37,094	39,465	27,609	26,203	40,938
2003	37,367	39,621	27,384	26,283	40,363
2002	37,317	39,360	27,452	26,422	40,885
2001	37,742	40,329	27,840	26,184	41,230
2000	37,791	41,111	28,457	25,997	42,011

PERCENT CHANGE

	total men	Asian	black	Hispanic	non-Hispanic white
2007 to 2012	−7.8%	−2.6%	−12.6%	−9.2%	−6.4%
2000 to 2007	−2.7	−1.1	0.4	4.2	−1.5
2000 to 2012	−10.3	−3.7	−12.3	−5.4	−7.8

Note: Beginning in 2002, Asians and blacks are those who identify themselves as being of the race alone and those who identify themselves as being of the race in combination with other races. Hispanics may be of any race. Beginning in 2002, non-Hispanic whites are those who identify themselves as being white alone and not Hispanic.
Source: Bureau of the Census, Historical Income Data, Internet site http://www.census.gov/hhes/www/income/; calculations by New Strategist

Table 5.36 Median Income of Women by Race and Hispanic Origin, 2000 to 2012

(median income of women aged 15 or older with income by race and Hispanic origin, 2000 to 2012; percent change in income for selected years; in 2012 dollars)

	total women	Asian	black	Hispanic	non-Hispanic white
2012	$21,520	$23,290	$19,925	$16,725	$22,902
2011	21,543	22,473	19,970	17,181	22,690
2010	21,878	24,802	20,586	17,157	22,868
2009	22,434	25,873	20,781	17,352	23,485
2008	22,253	24,544	21,545	17,507	23,193
2007	23,169	26,683	21,829	18,547	24,016
2006	22,792	25,147	21,711	17,945	23,604
2005	21,848	25,432	20,694	17,684	22,877
2004	21,476	25,060	21,087	17,567	22,409
2003	21,547	22,321	20,649	17,031	22,847
2002	21,457	22,843	21,277	17,057	22,194
2001	21,547	24,026	21,117	16,319	22,345
2000	21,417	23,141	21,175	16,331	22,220

PERCENT CHANGE

2007 to 2012	−7.1%	−12.7%	−8.7%	−9.8%	−4.6%
2000 to 2007	8.2	15.3	3.1	13.6	8.1
2000 to 2012	0.5	0.6	−5.9	2.4	3.1

Note: Beginning in 2002, Asians and blacks are those who identify themselves as being of the race alone and those who identify themselves as being of the race in combination with other races. Hispanics may be of any race. Beginning in 2002, non-Hispanic whites are those who identify themselves as being white alone and not Hispanic.
Source: Bureau of the Census, Historical Income Data, Internet site http://www.census.gov/hhes/www/income/; calculations by New Strategist

Incomes of Men and Women Peak in Middle Age

Men's income peak is much higher than women's.

Men aged 45 to 54 have the highest incomes—a median of $46,466 in 2012. Their female counterparts had a median income of $29,784, just 64 percent as much as men's. The income gap between men and women is somewhat smaller when comparing only full-time workers. Among full-time workers aged 45 to 54, women's income was 72 percent as high as men's ($41,804 versus $57,954)

A substantial 17 percent of men aged 45 to 54 had an income of $100,000 or more in 2012. Incomes are lowest for men under age 25, a median of just $10,869, because many are college students working part-time. Among young men who work full-time, median income was a higher $25,316.

Women are much less likely than men to have high incomes. Only 6 percent of women aged 45 to 54 had an income of $100,000 or more. Older women have much lower incomes than their male counterparts because fewer are covered by pensions. Women aged 65 or older had a median income of just $16,040 versus $27,612 for men.

■ The percentage of men who work full-time peaks at 72 percent in the 35-to-44 age group. Among women, the peak is 51 percent in the 45-to-54 age group.

Even among full-time workers, men's incomes are much higher

(median income of people aged 45 to 54, by work status and sex, 2012)

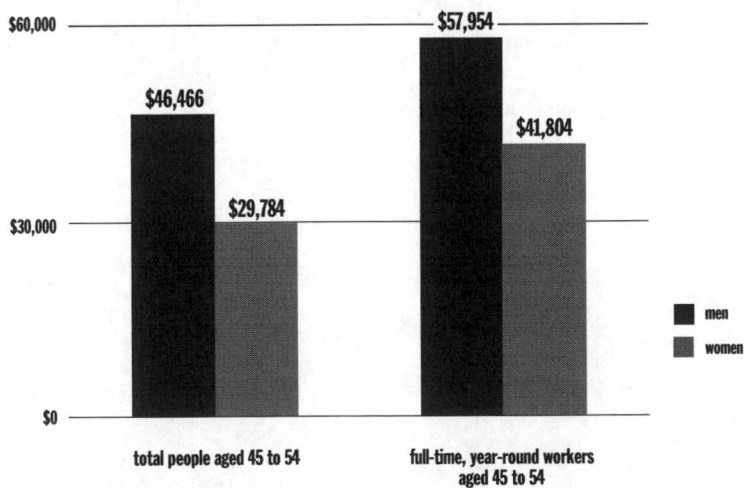

Table 5.37 Income of Men by Age, 2012

(number and percent distribution of men aged 15 or older by income and age, 2012; median income of men with income and of men working full-time, year-round; percent working full-time, year-round; men in thousands as of 2013)

	total	under 25	25 to 34	35 to 44	45 to 54	55 to 64	65 or older total	65 to 74	75 or older
Total men	**121,111**	**21,806**	**20,816**	**19,623**	**21,244**	**18,323**	**19,298**	**11,604**	**7,693**
Without income	13,577	8,534	1,634	1,040	1,061	808	500	285	214
With income	107,534	13,271	19,183	18,583	20,183	17,515	18,798	11,319	7,479
Under $5,000	7,050	3,884	870	549	688	676	383	232	151
$5,000 to $9,999	7,122	2,344	1,128	662	964	945	1,078	624	454
$10,000 to $14,999	8,706	1,814	1,359	1,029	1,149	1,211	2,144	1,090	1,053
$15,000 to $19,999	9,103	1,442	1,446	1,161	1,088	1,261	2,705	1,325	1,380
$20,000 to $24,999	8,370	1,153	1,637	1,218	1,209	1,007	2,146	1,204	942
$25,000 to $29,999	7,276	768	1,618	1,086	1,198	1,059	1,547	853	694
$30,000 to $34,999	7,032	542	1,683	1,314	1,230	990	1,273	738	536
$35,000 to $39,999	5,975	327	1,375	1,096	1,073	1,016	1,088	671	417
$40,000 to $44,999	5,584	273	1,213	1,121	1,141	988	847	559	288
$45,000 to $49,999	4,666	160	1,065	954	961	817	709	478	231
$50,000 to $54,999	4,886	168	1,024	1,021	1,050	932	691	472	219
$55,000 to $59,999	3,028	68	629	642	615	580	494	376	118
$60,000 to $64,999	3,640	71	737	761	827	734	509	359	150
$65,000 to $69,999	2,653	26	434	621	652	563	357	231	127
$70,000 to $74,999	2,627	43	512	561	668	509	334	240	95
$75,000 to $79,999	2,112	29	374	550	506	360	293	212	81
$80,000 to $84,999	2,113	21	338	507	551	482	215	167	48
$85,000 to $89,999	1,447	17	211	323	391	314	191	127	64
$90,000 to $94,999	1,684	27	279	427	460	292	200	136	64
$95,000 to $99,999	929	7	148	269	221	151	133	98	35
$100,000 or more	11,531	88	1,103	2,711	3,541	2,628	1,459	1,126	333
Median income									
Men with income	$33,904	$10,869	$34,113	$45,224	$46,466	$42,176	$27,612	$31,762	$23,570
Working full-time	50,683	25,316	41,648	52,442	57,954	60,076	67,148	69,024	63,969
Percent full-time	48.7%	17.5%	65.0%	72.2%	69.2%	55.5%	13.7%	18.7%	6.1%
PERCENT DISTRIBUTION									
Total men	**100.0%**	**100.0%**	**100.0%**	**100.0%**	**100.0%**	**100.0%**	**100.0%**	**100.0%**	**100.0%**
Without income	11.2	39.1	7.8	5.3	5.0	4.4	2.6	2.5	2.8
With income	88.8	60.9	92.2	94.7	95.0	95.6	97.4	97.5	97.2
Under $15,000	18.9	36.9	16.1	11.4	13.2	15.5	18.7	16.8	21.6
$15,000 to $24,999	14.4	11.9	14.8	12.1	10.8	12.4	25.1	21.8	30.2
$25,000 to $34,999	11.8	6.0	15.9	12.2	11.4	11.2	14.6	13.7	16.0
$35,000 to $49,999	13.4	3.5	17.5	16.2	14.9	15.4	13.7	14.7	12.2
$50,000 to $74,999	13.9	1.7	16.0	18.4	17.9	18.1	12.4	14.5	9.2
$75,000 to $99,999	6.8	0.5	6.5	10.6	10.0	8.7	5.3	6.4	3.8
$100,000 or more	9.5	0.4	5.3	13.8	16.7	14.3	7.6	9.7	4.3

Source: Bureau of the Census, 2013 Current Population Survey, Internet site http://www.census.gov/hhes/www/income/data/incpovhlth/2012/dtables.html; calculations by New Strategist

Table 5.38 Income of Women by Age, 2012

(number and percent distribution of women aged 15 or older by income and age, 2012; median income of women with income and of women working full-time, year-round; percent working full-time, year-round; women in thousands as of 2013)

	total	under 25	25 to 34	35 to 44	45 to 54	55 to 64	65 or older total	65 to 74	75 or older
Total women	**128,912**	**21,318**	**20,981**	**20,254**	**22,202**	**20,168**	**23,990**	**13,098**	**10,892**
Without income	19,529	8,191	3,165	2,712	2,445	2,071	945	561	384
With income	109,383	13,127	17,815	17,542	19,757	18,097	23,045	12,537	10,508
Under $5,000	12,544	4,186	1,877	1,872	1,806	1,632	1,171	599	571
$5,000 to $9,999	13,589	2,553	1,628	1,381	1,722	1,885	4,420	2,185	2,235
$10,000 to $14,999	13,957	1,926	1,727	1,452	1,758	2,025	5,070	2,581	2,489
$15,000 to $19,999	10,988	1,437	1,601	1,410	1,547	1,408	3,585	1,662	1,923
$20,000 to $24,999	9,643	1,067	1,628	1,442	1,718	1,588	2,200	1,149	1,052
$25,000 to $29,999	7,488	678	1,528	1,193	1,367	1,225	1,497	844	654
$30,000 to $34,999	6,840	396	1,455	1,241	1,450	1,242	1,056	663	393
$35,000 to $39,999	5,504	244	1,271	1,125	1,186	952	725	506	219
$40,000 to $44,999	4,849	207	988	1,029	1,110	879	637	391	246
$45,000 to $49,999	3,756	146	834	774	824	748	430	287	143
$50,000 to $54,999	3,687	84	778	826	886	668	445	306	140
$55,000 to $59,999	2,223	58	410	528	513	453	261	194	67
$60,000 to $64,999	2,496	32	405	565	612	588	295	224	71
$65,000 to $69,999	1,688	36	333	391	355	351	221	158	63
$70,000 to $74,999	1,677	17	223	400	499	373	166	122	44
$75,000 to $79,999	1,193	8	239	219	331	278	118	92	26
$80,000 to $84,999	1,144	1	144	235	336	301	126	97	29
$85,000 to $89,999	698	6	99	163	171	165	94	69	25
$90,000 to $94,999	735	4	118	157	203	183	71	59	12
$95,000 to $99,999	488	4	67	118	129	115	55	48	7
$100,000 or more	4,196	38	462	1,023	1,233	1,039	401	300	101
Median income									
Women with income	$21,520	$9,581	$26,173	$30,061	$29,784	$26,684	$16,040	$17,236	$14,916
Working full-time	40,019	22,469	36,641	41,682	41,804	43,024	46,718	47,957	41,357
Percent full-time	34.2%	12.8%	47.0%	49.7%	51.4%	41.4%	6.9%	10.8%	2.2%
PERCENT DISTRIBUTION									
Total women	**100.0%**	**100.0%**	**100.0%**	**100.0%**	**100.0%**	**100.0%**	**100.0%**	**100.0%**	**100.0%**
Without income	15.1	38.4	15.1	13.4	11.0	10.3	3.9	4.3	3.5
With income	84.9	61.6	84.9	86.6	89.0	89.7	96.1	95.7	96.5
Under $15,000	31.1	40.6	24.9	23.2	23.8	27.5	44.4	41.0	48.6
$15,000 to $24,999	16.0	11.7	15.4	14.1	14.7	14.9	24.1	21.5	27.3
$25,000 to $34,999	11.1	5.0	14.2	12.0	12.7	12.2	10.6	11.5	9.6
$35,000 to $49,999	10.9	2.8	14.7	14.5	14.1	12.8	7.5	9.0	5.6
$50,000 to $74,999	9.1	1.1	10.2	13.4	12.9	12.1	5.8	7.7	3.5
$75,000 to $99,999	3.3	0.1	3.2	4.4	5.3	5.2	1.9	2.8	0.9
$100,000 or more	3.3	0.2	2.2	5.0	5.6	5.2	1.7	2.3	0.9

Source: Bureau of the Census, 2013 Current Population Survey, Internet site http://www.census.gov/hhes/www/income/data/incpovhlth/2012/dtables.html; calculations by New Strategist

Among Both Men and Women, Asians Have the Highest Incomes

Asian men are most likely to work full-time.

Among full-time workers, Asian men have the highest incomes, a median of $59,531 in 2012. Non-Hispanic white men have a median income of $56,247. Black men who work full-time had a median income of $39,975, and Hispanic men with full-time jobs have the lowest median income—just $32,516. Asian men are most likely to work full-time (54 percent), and black men the least (40 percent).

Among women who work full-time, Asians again have the highest incomes, a median of $46,241. Non-Hispanic white women rank second, with a median of $42,171. Black women who work full-time have a median income of $35,105, while Hispanic women with full-time jobs have the lowest incomes—a median of just $29,508. Asian women are most likely to work full-time (37 percent), and Hispanic women the least (31 percent).

■ More than one in 10 Asian and non-Hispanic white men had an income of $100,000 or more in 2012.

Blacks have higher incomes than their Hispanic counterparts

(median income of people aged 15 or older who work full-time, year-round, by sex, race, and Hispanic origin, 2012)

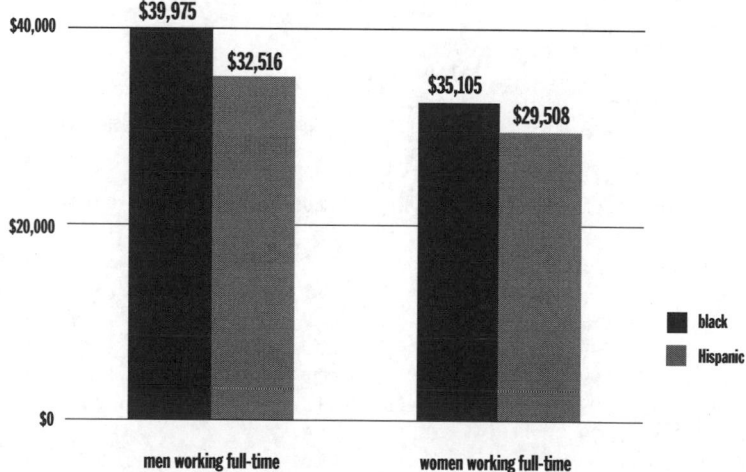

Table 5.39 Men's Income by Race and Hispanic Origin, 2012

(number and percent distribution of men aged 15 or older by income, race, and Hispanic origin, 2012; median income of men with income and of men working full-time, year-round; percent working full-time, year-round; men in thousands as of 2013)

	total	Asian	black	Hispanic	non-Hispanic white
Total men	**121,111**	**6,729**	**14,895**	**19,187**	**79,740**
Without income	13,577	920	2,934	3,182	6,500
With income	107,534	5,810	11,961	16,005	73,240
Under $5,000	7,050	422	1,070	1,130	4,385
$5,000 to $9,999	7,122	392	1,475	1,403	3,816
$10,000 to $14,999	8,706	405	1,343	1,897	5,033
$15,000 to $19,999	9,103	420	1,128	1,933	5,582
$20,000 to $24,999	8,370	382	971	1,738	5,220
$25,000 to $29,999	7,276	334	904	1,373	4,657
$30,000 to $34,999	7,032	335	853	1,225	4,593
$35,000 to $39,999	5,975	228	636	1,033	4,061
$40,000 to $44,999	5,584	275	574	790	3,929
$45,000 to $49,999	4,666	225	444	548	3,423
$50,000 to $54,999	4,886	229	458	544	3,618
$55,000 to $59,999	3,028	169	266	259	2,313
$60,000 to $64,999	3,640	201	277	335	2,798
$65,000 to $69,999	2,653	127	257	232	2,023
$70,000 to $74,999	2,627	171	206	201	2,041
$75,000 to $79,999	2,112	131	151	204	1,615
$80,000 to $84,999	2,113	138	144	193	1,635
$85,000 to $89,999	1,447	86	105	123	1,123
$90,000 to $94,999	1,684	136	117	137	1,284
$95,000 to $99,999	929	91	81	90	660
$100,000 or more	11,531	913	504	617	9,430
Median income					
Men with income	$33,904	$39,606	$24,959	$24,592	$38,751
Working full-time	50,683	59,531	39,975	32,516	56,247
Percent full-time	48.7%	54.0%	39.5%	49.1%	50.1%
PERCENT DISTRIBUTION					
Total men	**100.0%**	**100.0%**	**100.0%**	**100.0%**	**100.0%**
Without income	11.2	13.7	19.7	16.6	8.2
With income	88.8	86.3	80.3	83.4	91.8
Under $15,000	18.9	18.1	26.1	23.1	16.6
$15,000 to $24,999	14.4	11.9	14.1	19.1	13.5
$25,000 to $34,999	11.8	10.0	11.8	13.5	11.6
$35,000 to $49,999	13.4	10.8	11.1	12.4	14.3
$50,000 to $74,999	13.9	13.3	9.8	8.2	16.0
$75,000 to $99,999	6.8	8.6	4.0	3.9	7.9
$100,000 or more	9.5	13.6	3.4	3.2	11.8

Note: Asians and blacks are those who identify themselves as being of the race alone and those who identify themselves as being of the race in combination with other races. Non-Hispanic whites are those who identify themselves as being white alone and not Hispanic. Numbers do not add to total because some people identify themselves as being of more than one race, not all races are shown, and Hispanics may be of any race.
Source: Bureau of the Census, 2013 Current Population Survey, Internet site http://www.census.gov/hhes/www/income/data/incpovhlth/2012/dtables.html; calculations by New Strategist

Table 5.40 Women's Income by Race and Hispanic Origin, 2012

(number and percent distribution of women aged 15 or older by income, race, and Hispanic origin, 2012; median income of women with income and of women working full-time, year-round; percent working full-time, year-round; women in thousands as of 2013)

	total	Asian	black	Hispanic	non-Hispanic white
Total women	**128,912**	**7,649**	**17,837**	**19,039**	**83,919**
Without income	19,529	1,677	3,115	5,350	9,390
With income	109,383	5,972	14,722	13,689	74,529
Under $5,000	12,544	820	1,523	1,896	8,186
$5,000 to $9,999	13,589	726	2,214	2,170	8,374
$10,000 to $14,999	13,957	567	2,085	2,110	9,156
$15,000 to $19,999	10,988	502	1,558	1,602	7,307
$20,000 to $24,999	9,643	483	1,396	1,411	6,363
$25,000 to $29,999	7,488	323	1,039	939	5,138
$30,000 to $34,999	6,840	291	990	771	4,768
$35,000 to $39,999	5,504	267	782	585	3,840
$40,000 to $44,999	4,849	256	608	442	3,511
$45,000 to $49,999	3,756	218	471	350	2,708
$50,000 to $54,999	3,687	207	418	333	2,724
$55,000 to $59,999	2,223	138	281	202	1,607
$60,000 to $64,999	2,496	193	252	187	1,854
$65,000 to $69,999	1,688	118	184	91	1,273
$70,000 to $74,999	1,677	111	162	111	1,282
$75,000 to $79,999	1,193	77	111	89	918
$80,000 to $84,999	1,144	79	125	66	877
$85,000 to $89,999	698	48	79	34	531
$90,000 to $94,999	735	74	73	51	543
$95,000 to $99,999	488	49	48	14	371
$100,000 or more	4,196	426	324	235	3,200
Median income					
Women with income	$21,520	$23,290	$19,925	$16,725	$22,902
Working full-time	40,019	46,241	35,105	29,508	42,171
Percent full-time	34.2%	36.6%	35.0%	31.2%	34.5%
PERCENT DISTRIBUTION					
Total women	**100.0%**	**100.0%**	**100.0%**	**100.0%**	**100.0%**
Without income	15.1	21.9	17.5	28.1	11.2
With income	84.9	78.1	82.5	71.9	88.8
Under $15,000	31.1	27.6	32.6	32.4	30.6
$15,000 to $24,999	16.0	12.9	16.6	15.8	16.3
$25,000 to $34,999	11.1	8.0	11.4	9.0	11.8
$35,000 to $49,999	10.9	9.7	10.4	7.2	12.0
$50,000 to $74,999	9.1	10.0	7.3	4.8	10.4
$75,000 to $99,999	3.3	4.3	2.4	1.3	3.9
$100,000 or more	3.3	5.6	1.8	1.2	3.8

Note: Asians and blacks are those who identify themselves as being of the race alone and those who identify themselves as being of the race in combination with other races. Non-Hispanic whites are those who identify themselves as being white alone and not Hispanic. Numbers do not add to total because some people identify themselves as being of more than one race, not all races are shown, and Hispanics may be of any race.
Source: Bureau of the Census, 2013 Current Population Survey, Internet site http://www.census.gov/hhes/www/income/data/incpovhlth/2012/dtables.html; calculations by New Strategist

Women Lost Ground during the Great Recession

Women's earnings fell more than men's between 2007 and 2012.

Among people working full-time, year-round in 2012, men's median earnings stood at $49,398. Among their female counterparts, median earnings were a smaller $37,791—or 77 percent as high as men's. The earnings gap between women and men narrowed somewhat between 2000 and 2007, but since then women have made no progress.

The earnings gap between women and men had been closing because women's earnings were growing faster than men's. Among full-time workers, women's median earnings grew 6 percent between 2000 and 2007, after adjusting for inflation. Men's earnings grew by a tiny 0.6 percent during those years. Between 2007 and 2012, however, women's incomes fell 2.8 percent, which was well more than double the 1.1 percent loss experienced by men.

■ With women's earnings declining, households are feeling the pinch.

The gap between the sexes

(women's median earnings as a percent of men's median earnings among full-time, year-round workers, 2000 to 2012)

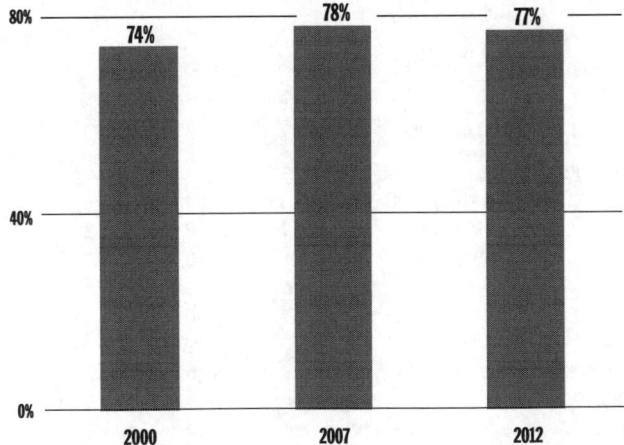

Table 5.41 Median Earnings of Full-Time Workers by Sex, 2000 to 2012

(median earnings of people aged 15 or older who work full-time, year-round, by sex, and index of women's earnings to men's, 2000 to 2012; percent change in earnings for selected years; in 2012 dollars)

	men	women	index of women's earnings to men's
2012	$49,398	$37,791	77
2011	49,209	37,893	77
2010	50,497	38,846	77
2009	50,448	38,835	77
2008	49,446	38,119	77
2007	49,958	38,872	78
2006	48,127	37,028	77
2005	48,676	37,470	77
2004	49,591	37,975	77
2003	50,771	38,357	76
2002	50,323	38,548	77
2001	49,640	37,890	76
2000	49,669	36,616	74

PERCENT CHANGE

	men	women	
2007 to 2012	–1.1%	–2.8%	
2000 to 2007	0.6	6.2	–
2000 to 2012	–0.5	3.2	–

Note: The index is calculated by dividing the median earnings of women by the median earnings of men and multiplying by 100. "–" means not applicable.
Source: Bureau of the Census, Historical Income Data, Internet site http://www.census.gov/hhes/www/income/; calculations by New Strategist

Education Boosts Earnings

Although college costs are soaring, the payback has been worth the investment.

Among full-time workers, men with at least a bachelor's degree earned a median of $75,320 in 2012. Those who went no further than high school earned just $40,351. Women with at least a bachelor's degree earned a median of $53,686 versus the $30,406 earned by those who went no further than high school. Women's earnings are lower than men's partly because the average working woman is younger than the average working man, and job experience boosts earnings.

The highest-paid men are those with professional degrees, such as doctors or lawyers. Their median earnings stood at $116,355 in 2012. The highest-paid women are also those with professional degrees, with median earnings of $94,473.

■ The enormous increase in the cost of getting a college degree may reduce the economic return of a college education.

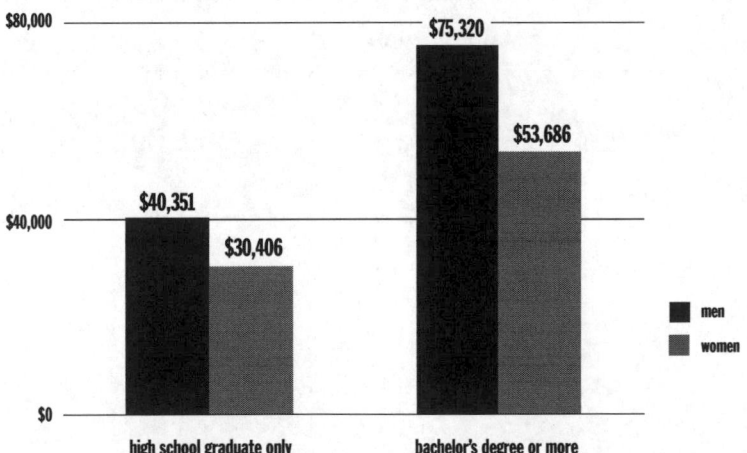

Earnings are much higher for college graduates

(median earnings of full-time, year-round workers, by educational attainment and sex, 2012)

Table 5.42 Earnings of Men Who Work Full-Time by Education, 2012

(number and percent distribution of men aged 25 or older working full-time, year-round by earnings and educational attainment, and median earnings of those with earnings, 2012; men in thousands as of 2013)

	total	less than 9th grade	9th to 12th grade, no diploma	high school graduate	some college, no degree	associate's degree	bachelor's degree or more total	bachelor's degree	master's degree	professional degree	doctoral degree
Men with earnings	55,208	1,793	2,671	15,295	8,974	5,423	21,052	13,315	5,003	1,301	1,433
Under $5,000	325	18	25	85	65	50	82	51	17	4	11
$5,000 to $9,999	334	32	49	117	40	25	71	55	13	2	1
$10,000 to $14,999	1,237	167	156	510	146	75	183	120	46	10	7
$15,000 to $19,999	2,130	334	357	814	264	121	240	187	39	5	9
$20,000 to $24,999	3,332	336	427	1,329	576	232	432	355	60	9	8
$25,000 to $29,999	3,631	292	290	1,404	740	344	561	420	110	12	18
$30,000 to $34,999	4,343	174	312	1,753	796	457	850	674	131	24	22
$35,000 to $39,999	3,765	111	241	1,466	739	394	813	686	103	18	7
$40,000 to $44,999	3,989	96	225	1,442	718	445	1,063	833	160	21	48
$45,000 to $49,999	3,278	59	94	985	665	411	1,064	779	209	34	42
$50,000 to $54,999	3,818	52	124	1,205	682	505	1,250	920	245	35	50
$55,000 to $59,999	2,171	25	68	574	414	247	843	589	178	26	50
$60,000 to $64,999	3,000	18	68	774	545	423	1,170	802	259	51	59
$65,000 to $69,999	2,066	22	53	519	385	268	818	522	223	31	41
$70,000 to $74,999	2,089	14	49	440	356	237	994	646	236	49	62
$75,000 to $79,999	1,719	7	28	299	317	216	851	592	211	20	28
$80,000 to $84,999	1,704	11	17	321	301	167	888	527	254	51	55
$85,000 to $89,999	1,070	5	15	174	146	115	615	382	171	30	33
$90,000 to $94,999	1,377	2	14	241	155	152	815	519	214	32	49
$95,000 to $99,999	675	2	11	97	113	77	374	220	97	32	26
$100,000 or more	9,156	17	48	745	810	463	7,073	3,436	2,027	806	805
Median earnings	$50,955	$25,131	$30,329	$40,351	$47,187	$50,961	$75,320	$66,153	$85,116	$116,355	$106,467

PERCENT DISTRIBUTION

	total	less than 9th grade	9th to 12th grade, no diploma	high school graduate	some college, no degree	associate's degree	bachelor's degree or more total	bachelor's degree	master's degree	professional degree	doctoral degree
Men with earnings	100.0%	100.0%	100.0%	100.0%	100.0%	100.0%	100.0%	100.0%	100.0%	100.0%	100.0%
Under $15,000	3.4	12.1	8.6	4.7	2.8	2.7	1.6	1.7	1.5	1.1	1.4
$15,000 to $24,999	9.9	37.3	29.3	14.0	9.4	6.5	3.2	4.1	2.0	1.1	1.2
$25,000 to $34,999	14.4	26.0	22.5	20.6	17.1	14.8	6.7	8.2	4.8	2.8	2.8
$35,000 to $49,999	20.0	14.9	21.0	25.5	23.6	23.0	14.0	17.3	9.4	5.6	6.8
$50,000 to $74,999	23.8	7.3	13.5	23.0	26.5	31.0	24.1	26.1	22.8	14.8	18.3
$75,000 to $99,999	11.9	1.5	3.2	7.4	11.5	13.4	16.8	16.8	18.9	12.7	13.4
$100,000 or more	16.6	0.9	1.8	4.9	9.0	8.5	33.6	25.8	40.5	61.9	56.2

Source: Bureau of the Census, 2013 Current Population Survey, Internet site http://www.census.gov/hhes/www/income/data/incpovhlth/2012/dtables.html; calculations by New Strategist

Table 5.43 Earnings of Women Who Work Full-Time by Education, 2012

(number and percent distribution of women aged 25 or older working full-time, year-round by earnings and educational attainment, and median earnings of those with earnings, 2012; women in thousands as of 2013)

	total	less than 9th grade	9th to 12th grade, no diploma	high school graduate	some college, no degree	associate's degree	bachelor's degree or more total	bachelor's degree	master's degree	professional degree	doctoral degree
Women with earnings	41,319	690	1,351	9,870	6,899	5,246	17,263	10,961	4,887	670	745
Under $5,000	266	18	10	77	60	31	70	51	15	0	3
$5,000 to $9,999	497	34	66	172	68	36	121	101	19	1	0
$10,000 to $14,999	1,621	123	225	587	314	163	208	176	26	4	3
$15,000 to $19,999	2,624	167	262	1,044	509	313	329	266	52	7	4
$20,000 to $24,999	3,890	164	310	1,470	771	527	648	539	88	12	9
$25,000 to $29,999	3,784	79	179	1,414	793	542	777	637	112	12	15
$30,000 to $34,999	4,174	43	101	1,334	921	651	1,125	892	201	13	18
$35,000 to $39,999	3,813	23	67	1,052	846	533	1,292	961	294	14	22
$40,000 to $44,999	3,242	9	43	784	551	481	1,375	977	345	19	34
$45,000 to $49,999	2,695	12	30	458	446	425	1,324	825	433	26	40
$50,000 to $54,999	2,779	8	9	491	406	354	1,510	958	466	44	42
$55,000 to $59,999	1,462	0	4	244	178	180	856	540	281	20	15
$60,000 to $64,999	1,932	3	16	227	289	219	1,178	702	395	24	57
$65,000 to $69,999	1,150	0	0	93	142	191	724	444	223	27	31
$70,000 to $74,999	1,274	1	7	101	138	158	870	488	310	25	47
$75,000 to $79,999	851	0	4	60	55	72	660	406	184	33	37
$80,000 to $84,999	902	0	0	67	103	102	630	326	232	30	42
$85,000 to $89,999	449	0	0	26	52	37	333	184	122	9	19
$90,000 to $94,999	561	0	2	15	35	45	464	258	160	16	30
$95,000 to $99,999	328	0	1	11	39	39	238	126	83	13	16
$100,000 or more	3,027	6	14	143	182	150	2,532	1,104	845	322	262
Median earnings	$39,977	$20,060	$21,387	$30,406	$35,058	$37,321	$53,686	$50,173	$60,927	$94,473	$77,902

PERCENT DISTRIBUTION

	total	less than 9th grade	9th to 12th grade, no diploma	high school graduate	some college, no degree	associate's degree	bachelor's degree or more total	bachelor's degree	master's degree	professional degree	doctoral degree
Women with earnings	100.0%	100.0%	100.0%	100.0%	100.0%	100.0%	100.0%	100.0%	100.0%	100.0%	100.0%
Under $15,000	5.8	25.4	22.3	8.5	6.4	4.4	2.3	3.0	1.2	0.8	0.8
$15,000 to $24,999	15.8	47.9	42.3	25.5	18.6	16.0	5.7	7.3	2.9	2.8	1.7
$25,000 to $34,999	19.3	17.6	20.8	27.8	24.8	22.7	11.0	14.0	6.4	3.7	4.5
$35,000 to $49,999	23.6	6.5	10.4	23.2	26.7	27.4	23.1	25.2	22.0	8.8	12.8
$50,000 to $74,999	20.8	1.8	2.7	11.7	16.7	21.0	29.8	28.6	34.3	20.9	25.8
$75,000 to $99,999	7.5	0.0	0.5	1.8	4.1	5.6	13.5	11.9	16.0	15.0	19.3
$100,000 or more	7.3	0.9	1.0	1.4	2.6	2.9	14.7	10.1	17.3	48.1	35.2

Source: Bureau of the Census, 2013 Current Population Survey, Internet site http://www.census.gov/hhes/www/income/data/incpovhlth/2012/dtables.html; calculations by New Strategist

Among Full-Time Workers, Women Earn 77 Percent as Much as Men

The gap varies greatly by occupation, however.

Although a substantial gap exists between the earnings of men and women who work full-time, in some occupations women make close to or even more than men. Women in management and in business and financial occupations earn only 73 percent as much as their male counterparts. For women in professional occupations, the figure is 71 percent. Among computer scientists, however, women earn 84 percent as much as men. Among lawyers, judges, and magistrates, women's earnings are equal to men's.

A big earnings gap exists in some occupations. Among physicians, women earn only 64 percent as much as men. This is largely because the average male doctor is older and more experienced than the average female doctor.

■ One reason for the earnings gap between men and women is that the average male worker has been on the job longer than the average female worker.

In most occupations, women earn less than men

(women's median annual earnings as a percent of men's among full-time wage and salary workers, by occupation, 2012)

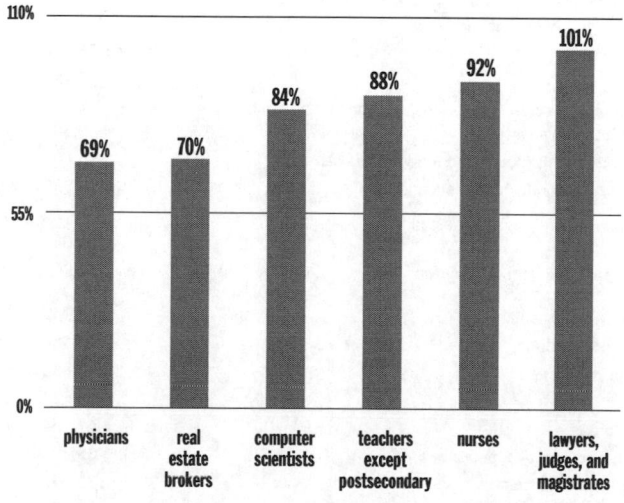

Table 5.44 Median Earnings of Full-Time Workers by Occupation and Sex, 2012

(median earnings of full-time, year-round workers aged 15 or older by occupation and sex, and index of women's to men's earnings, 2012)

	men	women	index, women's earnings to men's
TOTAL FULL-TIME WORKERS AGED 15 OR OLDER	**$49,398**	**$37,791**	**77**
Management, science, and arts occupations	**71,550**	**51,304**	**72**
Management, business and financial operations occupations	71,837	52,438	73
Management occupations	72,811	55,719	77
Chief executives, general and operations managers	100,199	82,167	82
All other managers	69,906	52,078	74
Business and financial operations occupations	67,413	51,350	76
Business operations specialists	66,847	51,688	77
Financial specialists	68,628	51,128	75
Professional and related occupations	71,298	50,605	71
Computer and mathematical occupations	80,068	67,203	84
Computer scientists, analysts, programmers, engineers, and administrators	80,262	67,114	84
Mathematicians, statisticians, operations research, and other math occupations	76,004	67,314	89
Architecture and engineering occupations	79,163	66,232	84
Architects, except naval	71,151	–	–
Engineers	86,959	79,532	91
Drafters, engineering technicians, and surveying and mapping technicians	58,807	–	–
Life, physical, and social science occupations	71,675	61,119	85
Psychologists and sociologists	–	64,843	–
All other scientists	75,467	61,484	81
Science technicians	49,042	46,468	95
Community and social services occupations	42,297	41,364	98
Legal occupations	102,216	58,468	57
Lawyers, judges, and magistrates	116,237	117,311	101
Paralegals, legal assistants, and legal support workers	50,532	43,443	86
Education, training, and library occupations	56,306	44,159	78
Postsecondary teachers	76,212	60,192	79
All other teachers	51,783	45,683	88
Archivists, curators, museum technicians, librarians, and other technicians and assistants	38,563	22,723	59
Arts, design, entertainment, sports, and media occupations	55,805	44,724	80
Health care practitioner and technical occupations	79,339	55,583	70
Doctors	162,129	111,891	69
Nurses	64,037	59,223	92
All other health and technical occupations	51,962	47,416	91
Service occupations	**31,331**	**23,927**	**76**
Health care support occupations	30,586	26,624	87
Protective service occupations	53,836	42,215	78
Supervisors	63,524	–	–
Firefighters and police	67,764	66,239	98
All other protective service occupations	35,097	35,326	101
Food preparation and serving–related occupations	23,672	20,739	88
Supervisors	31,676	26,963	85
Chefs and cooks	23,288	20,542	88
All other food preparation occupations	21,933	19,897	91
Building and grounds cleaning and maintenance occupations	28,340	21,078	74
Supervisors	45,062	30,110	67
All other maintenance occupations	26,890	20,681	77

	men	women	index, women's earnings to men's
Personal care and service occupations	$31,544	$22,824	72
Supervisors	41,365	31,750	77
All other personal care and service occupations	29,610	22,070	75
Sales and office occupations	**45,117**	**32,991**	**73**
Sales and related occupations	47,401	30,495	64
Supervisors	47,360	33,632	71
Cashiers	21,947	19,165	87
Insurance sales agents	61,920	41,065	66
Real estate brokers and sales agents	50,804	35,689	70
All other sales and related occupations	50,984	31,432	62
Office and administrative support occupations	40,696	35,084	86
Supervisors	51,395	41,185	80
Postal workers	58,429	52,993	91
All other office and administrative support occupations	36,905	33,678	91
Natural resources, construction, and maintenance occupations	**40,421**	**31,678**	**78**
Farming, fishing, and forestry occupations	25,711	20,587	80
Farming, fishing, and forestry occupations, except supervisors	25,404	20,265	80
Construction and extraction occupations	38,295	27,494	72
Construction	37,360	27,348	73
Supervisors	50,685	–	–
Brickmasons, blockmasons, and stonemasons	30,986	–	–
Carpenters	32,215	–	–
Electricians	53,993	–	–
Painters and paperhangers	31,849	–	–
All other construction trades	34,467	–	–
Extraction workers	62,399	–	–
Installation, maintenance, and repair occupations	43,100	42,773	99
Supervisors	56,873	–	–
Aircraft mechanics and service	57,730	–	–
Auto, bus, truck, heavy equipment mechanics	41,021	–	–
Heating, air conditioning, and refrigeration mechanics and installers	41,059	–	–
Electrical power-line and telecommunications line installers and repairers	51,455	–	–
All other installation, maintenance, and repair occupations	42,142	41,981	100
Production, transportation, and material moving occupations	**40,100**	**27,381**	**68**
Production occupations	40,595	27,324	67
Supervisors	52,177	39,761	76
All other production occupations	38,624	26,808	69
Transportation and material moving occupations	38,405	27,511	72
Supervisors	56,708	–	–
Auto, bus, truck, ambulance, taxi drivers	41,454	30,780	74
Rail and subway workers	65,901	–	–
All other transportation occupations	31,585	25,852	82
Armed Forces	**45,977**	–	–

Note: The index is calculated by dividing women's median earnings by men's median earnings and multiplying by 100.
"–" means sample is too small to make a reliable estimate.
Source: Bureau of the Census, 2013 Current Population Survey, Internet site http://www.census.gov/hhes/www/income/data/incpovhlth/2012/dtables.html; calculations by New Strategist

Incomes Are Highest in the Suburbs

Households in nonmetropolitan areas have the lowest incomes.

Households in the suburbs of the nation's metropolitan areas (outside principal cities) have the highest incomes, a median of $58,780 in 2012—15 percent higher than the national median. Many suburban householders are middle-aged married couples in their peak earning years. Nonmetropolitan households have the lowest incomes, a median of $41,198 in 2012, or just 81 percent of the national average. The elderly head a disproportionate share of households in nonmetro areas.

Households in the Northeast and West have above-average incomes, while those in the Midwest have average incomes and those in the South have incomes well below average. Among the 50 states, Maryland has the highest household income, with a 2012 median of $71,836—41 percent above average. Mississippi has the lowest median household income, just $36,641 in 2012, or 28 percent below average. The gap in the median household income of Maryland and Mississippi was more than $35,000 in 2012.

■ The Great Recession has not reduced the income gap between the richest and poorest states.

Households in the South have the lowest incomes

(median household income by region, 2012)

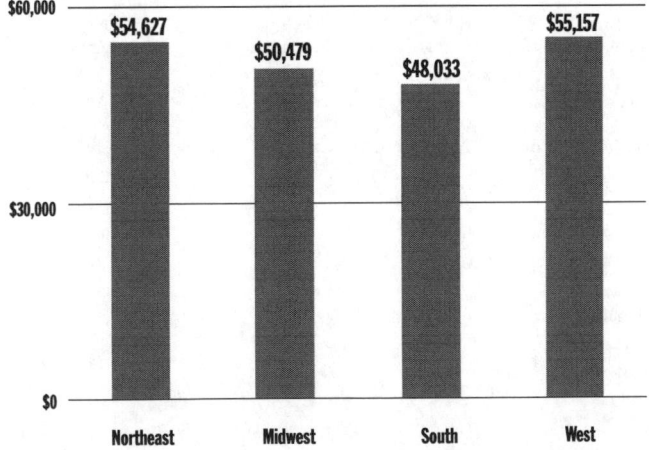

Table 5.45 Median Household Income by Metropolitan Status and Region of Residence, 2012

(number of households, median household income, and index of category median to national median, by metropolitan status, and region and division of residence, 2012; households in thousands as of 2013)

	number of households	median income	index
Total households	**122,459**	**$51,017**	**100**
Metropolitan status			
Inside metropolitan areas	102,784	52,988	104
Inside principal cities	41,152	45,902	90
Outside principal cities	61,631	58,780	115
Outside metropolitan areas	19,676	41,198	81
Region			
Northeast	22,125	54,627	107
New England	5,777	61,175	120
Middle Atlantic	16,348	52,075	102
Midwest	27,093	50,479	99
East North Central	18,701	49,139	96
West North Central	8,392	53,041	104
South	45,938	48,033	94
South Atlantic	24,424	49,532	97
East South Central	7,489	41,551	81
West South Central	14,025	49,020	96
West	27,303	55,157	108
Mountain	8,817	50,705	99
Pacific	18,486	57,398	113

Note: The index is calculated by dividing the median for each metropolitan status and region by the national median and multiplying by 100.
Source: Bureau of the Census, 2013 Current Population Survey, Internet site http://www.census.gov/hhes/www/income/data/incpovhlth/2012/dtables.html; calculations by New Strategist

Table 5.46 Median Household Income by State, 2012

(median income of households by state, state rank, and index to national median, 2012)

	median household income	rank among 50 states	index to national median
United States	**$51,017**	–	**100**
Alabama	43,464	44	85
Alaska	63,648	8	125
Arizona	47,044	37	92
Arkansas	39,018	50	76
California	57,020	14	112
Colorado	57,255	13	112
Connecticut	64,247	6	126
Delaware	48,972	31	96
District of Columbia	65,246	4	128
Florida	46,071	39	90
Georgia	48,121	33	94
Hawaii	56,263	15	110
Idaho	47,922	34	94
Illinois	51,738	25	101
Indiana	46,158	38	90
Iowa	53,442	19	105
Kansas	50,003	27	98
Kentucky	41,086	48	81
Louisiana	39,085	49	77
Maine	49,158	30	96
Maryland	71,836	1	141
Massachusetts	63,656	7	125
Michigan	50,015	26	98
Minnesota	61,795	10	121
Mississippi	36,641	51	72
Missouri	49,764	28	98
Montana	45,088	40	88
Nebraska	52,196	21	102
Nevada	47,333	36	93
New Hampshire	67,819	2	133
New Jersey	66,692	3	131
New Mexico	43,424	45	85
New York	47,680	35	93
North Carolina	41,553	47	81
North Dakota	55,766	17	109
Ohio	44,375	42	87
Oklahoma	48,407	32	95
Oregon	51,775	24	101
Pennsylvania	51,904	23	102

	median household income	rank among 50 states	index to national median
Rhode Island	$56,065	16	110
South Carolina	44,401	41	87
South Dakota	49,415	29	97
Tennessee	42,995	46	84
Texas	51,926	22	102
Utah	58,341	11	114
Vermont	55,582	18	109
Virginia	64,632	5	127
Washington	62,187	9	122
West Virginia	43,553	43	85
Wisconsin	53,079	20	104
Wyoming	57,512	12	113

Note: The index is calculated by dividing the median income of each state by the national median and multiplying by 100.
"–" means not applicable.
Source: Bureau of the Census, 2013 Current Population Survey, Internet site http://www.census.gov/hhes/www/income/data/ incpovhlth/2012/dtables.html; calculations by New Strategist

Table 5.47 Median Household Income by State, 2007 and 2012

(median income of households by state, 2007 and 2012; percent change, 2007–12; in 2012 dollars)

	2012	2007	percent change 2007–12
United States	**$51,017**	**$55,627**	**–8.3%**
Alabama	43,464	46,745	–7.0
Alaska	63,648	69,758	–8.8
Arizona	47,044	52,285	–10.0
Arkansas	39,018	45,176	–13.6
California	57,020	61,719	–7.6
Colorado	57,255	67,707	–15.4
Connecticut	64,247	71,029	–9.5
Delaware	48,972	60,451	–19.0
District of Columbia	65,246	56,237	16.0
Florida	46,071	50,712	–9.2
Georgia	48,121	53,865	–10.7
Hawaii	56,263	70,897	–20.6
Idaho	47,922	54,466	–12.0
Illinois	51,738	58,145	–11.0
Indiana	46,158	52,549	–12.2
Iowa	53,442	54,160	–1.3
Kansas	50,003	53,705	–6.9
Kentucky	41,086	43,689	–6.0
Louisiana	39,085	45,750	–14.6
Maine	49,158	53,037	–7.3
Maryland	71,836	72,678	–1.2
Massachusetts	63,656	64,741	–1.7
Michigan	50,015	54,672	–8.5
Minnesota	61,795	64,293	–3.9
Mississippi	36,641	41,282	–11.2
Missouri	49,764	50,945	–2.3
Montana	45,088	48,343	–6.7
Nebraska	52,196	54,455	–4.1
Nevada	47,333	59,863	–20.9
New Hampshire	67,819	74,833	–9.4
New Jersey	66,692	67,006	–0.5
New Mexico	43,424	49,119	–11.6
New York	47,680	54,200	–12.0
North Carolina	41,553	48,186	–13.8
North Dakota	55,766	52,274	6.7
Ohio	44,375	54,372	–18.4
Oklahoma	48,407	47,857	1.1
Oregon	51,775	55,631	–6.9
Pennsylvania	$51,904	$53,639	–3.2

	2012	2007	percent change 2007–12
Rhode Island	$56,065	$60,032	–6.6%
South Carolina	44,401	48,961	9.3
South Dakota	49,415	51,403	–3.9
Tennessee	42,995	45,619	–5.8
Texas	51,926	50,999	1.8
Utah	58,341	59,277	–1.6
Vermont	55,582	52,479	5.9
Virginia	64,632	65,514	–1.3
Washington	62,187	64,317	–3.3
West Virginia	43,553	46,611	–6.6
Wisconsin	53,079	56,784	–6.5
Wyoming	57,512	53,979	6.5

Source: Bureau of the Census, 2013 Current Population Survey, Internet site http://www.census.gov/hhes/www/income/data/ incpovhlth/2012/dtables.html; calculations by New Strategist

Wages and Salaries Rank Number One

Wages and salaries are the most important source of income for the largest share of Americans.

Among the 217 million Americans aged 15 or older with income in 2012, slightly more than 72 percent received income from earnings—such as wages and salaries (68 percent), nonfarm self-employment income (6 percent), or farm self-employment income (less than 1 percent). Among those with income from earnings, the median amount received was $31,921. Twenty-two percent of Americans received Social Security income, averaging $13,247 per person.

Forty-three percent of the population received property income in 2012, such as interest, dividends, rent, or royalties. Nearly 88 million people received interest income in 2012, pocketing a median of $1,413 from this source. Fourteen percent of the population received dividend income (a median of $1,710). Ten percent received retirement income, and 8 percent received pensions. (Note: These figures do not include withdrawals from IRAs or 401(k)s unless they are taken as annuities.)

■ While most people of working age are dependent primarily on wages and salaries, older Americans depend on a wider variety of income sources—from Social Security and pensions to interest and dividends.

Social Security is the third largest source of income

(percent of people aged 15 or older receiving income by source, for the five most common sources of income, 2012)

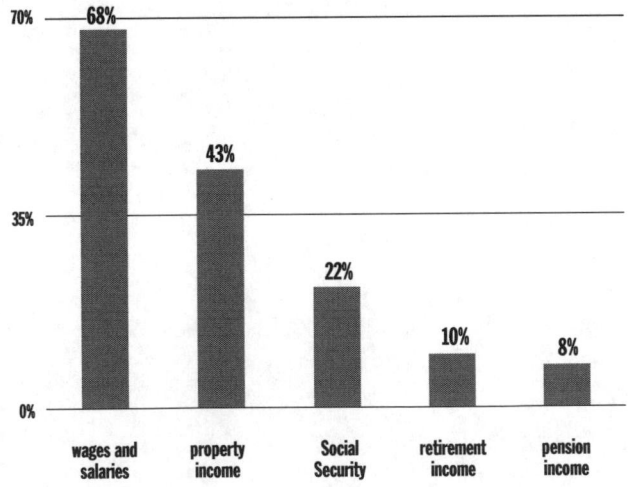

68%	43%	22%	10%	8%
wages and salaries	property income	Social Security	retirement income	pension income

Table 5.48 Sources of Income, 2012

(number and percent of people aged 15 or older with income by source and median income for those with income, 2012; people in thousands as of 2013; ranked by number receiving income)

	number with income	percent with income	median amount received by those with income
Total	**216,917**	**100.0%**	**$26,989**
Earnings	157,191	72.5	31,921
Wages and salary	148,308	68.4	32,196
Nonfarm self-employment	11,946	5.5	15,765
Farm self-employment	1,939	0.9	2,180
Property income	94,030	43.3	1,610
Interest	87,603	40.4	1,413
Dividends	30,892	14.2	1,710
Rents, royalties, estates, or trusts	11,504	5.3	2,300
Social Security	47,824	22.0	13,247
Retirement income	21,615	10.0	13,069
Company or union retirement	11,437	5.3	9,163
State or local government retirement	5,029	2.3	19,195
Federal government retirement	1,905	0.9	23,520
Military retirement	1,235	0.6	19,930
Annuities	227	0.1	19,230
IRA, Keogh, or 401(k)	618	0.3	7,164
Railroad retirement	882	0.4	10,096
Pension income	17,672	8.1	13,925
Company or union retirement	10,018	4.6	9,479
State or local government retirement	4,514	2.1	20,503
Federal government retirement	1,521	0.7	27,616
Military retirement	1,028	0.5	20,897
Annuities	243	0.1	9,100
Railroad retirement	174	0.1	18,431
Educational assistance	9,563	4.4	4,897
Unemployment compensation	8,644	4.0	4,349
SSI (Supplemental Security Income)	5,999	2.8	8,051
Child support	4,915	2.3	3,781
Veterans benefits	3,223	1.5	9,806
Survivor benefits	2,859	1.3	7,474
Financial assistance from other household	2,596	1.2	3,979
Public assistance	2,150	1.0	2,263
Disability benefits	1,673	0.8	10,379
Workers compensation	1,617	0.7	3,182
Alimony	937	0.4	1,702
Other income	385	0.2	8,041

Source: Bureau of the Census, 2013 Current Population Survey, Internet site http://www.census.gov/hhes/www/income/data/incpovhlth/2012/dtables.html; calculations by New Strategist

Minorities Account for Most of the Poor

Among the nation's 46 million poor, most are Asian, black, or Hispanic.

Poverty rates have grown sharply during the Great Recession. In 2012, 15.0 percent of Americans were poor, up from 11.3 percent in 2000. The number of poor expanded by 47 percent between 2000 and 2012.

Overall, 41 percent of the nation's poor are non-Hispanic white and 59 percent are Asian, black, Hispanic, or another minority. Some segments of the population are poorer than others. Only 9.7 percent of non-Hispanic whites are poor versus 27.1 percent of blacks and 25.6 percent of Hispanics. Overall, 21.8 percent of the nation's children are poor. The figure is 36.7 percent among black children and 33.8 percent among Hispanic children.

The poverty rate varies sharply by family type. Regardless of race or Hispanic origin, the poverty rate is low among married couples. Overall, only 6.3 percent of married couples are poor compared with 30.9 percent of female-headed families. Among female-headed families with children, the poverty rate is an even higher 40.9 percent.

■ Childhood poverty will remain a chronic problem until single parents become a smaller share of all families.

Poverty rate is low for married couples

(percent of families in poverty by race, Hispanic origin, and family type, 2012)

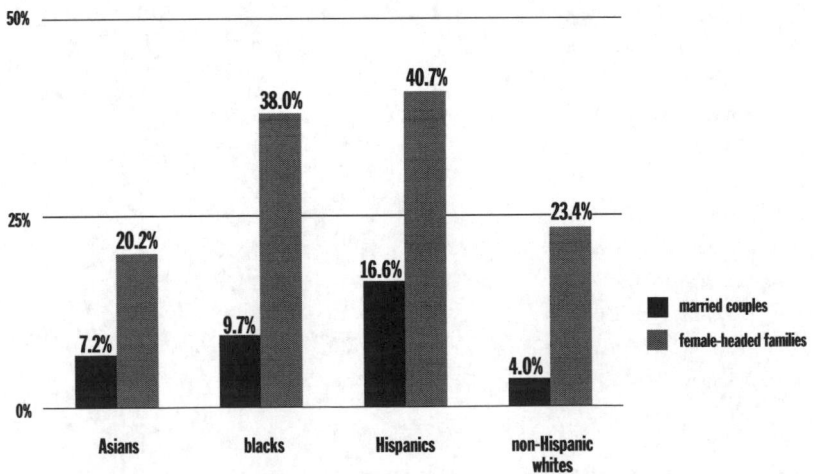

Table 5.49 People in Poverty, 2000 to 2012

(number and percent of people below poverty level, 2000 to 2012; percent and percentage point change for selected years; people in thousands as of the following year)

	number	percent
2012	46,496	15.0%
2011	46,247	15.0
2010	46,343	15.1
2009	43,569	14.3
2008	39,829	13.2
2007	37,276	12.5
2006	36,460	12.3
2005	36,950	12.6
2004	37,040	12.7
2003	35,861	12.5
2002	34,570	12.1
2001	32,907	11.7
2000	31,581	11.3

	percent change	percentage point change
2007 to 2012	24.7%	2.5
2000 to 2007	18.0	1.2
2000 to 2012	47.2	3.7

Source: Bureau of the Census, Current Population Surveys, Internet site http://www.census.gov/hhes/www/poverty/data/ historical/people.html; calculations by New Strategist

Table 5.50 People in Poverty by Age, Race, and Hispanic Origin, 2012

(number and percent of people in poverty and percent distribution of poor, by age, race, and Hispanic origin, 2012; people in thousands as of 2013)

	total	Asian	black	Hispanic	non-Hispanic white
NUMBER OF POOR					
Total people in poverty	**46,496**	**2,072**	**11,809**	**13,616**	**18,940**
Under age 18	16,073	570	4,815	5,976	4,782
Aged 18 to 24	6,117	360	1,493	1,614	2,608
Aged 25 to 34	6,633	318	1,575	2,032	2,727
Aged 35 to 44	4,960	213	1,137	1,650	1,946
Aged 45 to 54	4,675	235	1,132	971	2,270
Aged 55 to 59	2,230	78	547	378	1,209
Aged 60 to 64	1,882	87	381	332	1,074
Aged 65 or older	3,926	211	730	663	2,324
PERCENT IN POVERTY					
Total people	**15.0%**	**11.4%**	**27.1%**	**25.6%**	**9.7%**
Under age 18	21.8	12.5	36.7	33.8	12.3
Aged 18 to 24	20.4	19.2	29.5	25.6	15.6
Aged 25 to 34	15.9	10.6	26.2	23.6	11.3
Aged 35 to 44	12.4	7.4	20.9	21.6	8.2
Aged 45 to 54	10.8	10.1	20.2	16.3	7.8
Aged 55 to 59	10.7	7.7	22.4	17.5	8.0
Aged 60 to 64	10.7	10.6	19.7	21.0	8.2
Aged 65 or older	9.1	12.4	18.3	20.6	6.8
PERCENT DISTRIBUTION OF POOR BY RACE AND HISPANIC ORIGIN					
Total people in poverty	**100.0**	**4.5**	**25.4**	**29.3**	**40.7**
Under age 18	100.0	3.5	30.0	37.2	29.8
Aged 18 to 24	100.0	5.9	24.4	26.4	42.6
Aged 25 to 34	100.0	4.8	23.7	30.6	41.1
Aged 35 to 44	100.0	4.3	22.9	33.3	39.2
Aged 45 to 54	100.0	5.0	24.2	20.8	48.6
Aged 55 to 59	100.0	3.5	24.5	17.0	54.2
Aged 60 to 64	100.0	4.6	20.2	17.6	57.1
Aged 65 or older	100.0	5.4	18.6	16.9	59.2

Note: Numbers do not add to total because Asians and blacks are those who identify themselves as being of the race alone and those who identify themselves as being of the race in combination with other races. Non-Hispanic whites are those who identify themselves as being white alone and not Hispanic. Hispanics may be of any race.
Source: Bureau of the Census, Poverty Data, Internet site http://www.census.gov/hhes/www/poverty/data/index.html; calculations by New Strategist

Table 5.51 Families in Poverty by Family Type, Race, and Hispanic Origin, 2012

(number and percent of families in poverty, and percent distribution of families in poverty, by type of family and race and Hispanic origin of householder, 2012; families in thousands as of 2013)

	total	Asian	black	Hispanic	non-Hispanic white
NUMBER IN POVERTY					
Total families in poverty	**9,520**	**409**	**2,439**	**2,807**	**3,835**
Married couples	3,705	245	458	1,238	1,735
Female householders, no spouse present	4,793	115	1,707	1,266	1,713
Male householders, no spouse present	1,023	49	274	303	387
PERCENT IN POVERTY					
Total families	**11.8%**	**9.5%**	**23.7%**	**23.5%**	**7.1%**
Married couples	6.3	7.2	9.7	16.6	4.0
Female householders, no spouse present	30.9	20.2	38.0	40.7	23.4
Male householders, no spouse present	16.4	14.2	24.8	21.7	11.4
PERCENT DISTRIBUTION OF FAMILIES IN POVERTY BY RACE AND HISPANIC ORIGIN					
Total families in poverty	**100.0**	**4.3**	**25.6**	**29.5**	**40.3**
Married couples	100.0	6.6	12.4	33.4	46.8
Female householders, no spouse present	100.0	2.4	35.6	26.4	35.7
Male householders, no spouse present	100.0	4.8	26.8	29.6	37.8
PERCENT DISTRIBUTION OF FAMILIES IN POVERTY BY FAMILY TYPE					
Total families in poverty	**100.0**	**100.0**	**100.0**	**100.0**	**100.0**
Married couples	38.9	59.9	18.8	44.1	45.2
Female householders, no spouse present	50.3	28.1	70.0	45.1	44.7
Male householders, no spouse present	10.7	12.0	11.2	10.8	10.1

Note: Numbers do not add to total because Asians and blacks are those who identify themselves as being of the race alone and those who identify themselves as being of the race in combination with other races. Non-Hispanic whites are those who identify themselves as being white alone and not Hispanic. Hispanics may be of any race.
Source: Bureau of the Census, Poverty Data, Internet site http://www.census.gov/hhes/www/poverty/data/index.html; calculations by New Strategist

Table 5.52 Families with Children in Poverty by Family Type, Race, and Hispanic Origin, 2012

(number and percent of families with children under age 18 in poverty, and percent distribution of families with children in poverty, by type of family and race and Hispanic origin of householder, 2012; families in thousands as of 2013)

	total	Asian	black	Hispanic	non-Hispanic white
NUMBER IN POVERTY					
Total families with children in poverty	7,063	265	1,944	2,341	2,510
Married couples	2,246	154	286	973	820
Female householders, no spouse present	4,099	82	1,479	1,133	1,415
Male householders, no spouse present	717	29	179	235	274
PERCENT IN POVERTY					
Total families with children	18.4%	11.8%	32.1%	30.1%	11.2%
Married couples	8.9	8.4	12.5	20.9	5.0
Female householders, no spouse present	40.9	27.5	46.8	48.6	33.1
Male householders, no spouse present	22.6	24.5	29.5	30.1	16.3
PERCENT DISTRIBUTION OF FAMILIES IN POVERTY BY RACE AND HISPANIC ORIGIN					
Total families with children in poverty	100.0	3.8	27.5	33.1	35.5
Married couples	100.0	6.9	12.7	43.3	36.5
Female householders, no spouse present	100.0	2.0	36.1	27.6	34.5
Male householders, no spouse present	100.0	4.0	25.0	32.8	38.2
PERCENT DISTRIBUTION OF FAMILIES IN POVERTY BY FAMILY TYPE					
Total families with children in poverty	100.0	100.0	100.0	100.0	100.0
Married couples	31.8	58.1	14.7	41.6	32.7
Female householders, no spouse present	58.0	30.9	76.1	48.4	56.4
Male householders, no spouse present	10.2	10.9	9.2	10.0	10.9

Note: Numbers do not add to total because Asians and blacks are those who identify themselves as being of the race alone and those who identify themselves as being of the race in combination with other races. Non-Hispanic whites are those who identify themselves as being white alone and not Hispanic. Hispanics may be of any race.
Source: Bureau of the Census, Poverty Data, Internet site http://www.census.gov/hhes/www/poverty/data/index.html; calculations by New Strategist

6

Labor Force

Trends

Older Americans are increasingly likely to work.

Twenty-four percent of men aged 65 or older are in the labor force, up from 16 percent in 1990.

Unemployment remains high.

More than 12 million Americans were unemployed in 2012, 8.1 percent of the labor force.

Many workers have part-time jobs.

Thirty-four million workers are part-timers, including 19 percent of men and 32 percent of women. Many part-time workers want full-time jobs.

Long-term employment is more common among older workers.

As older men postpone retirement, the proportion of workers aged 65 or older who have been with their employer for 10 or more years climbed from 48.6 to 55.5 percent between 2000 and 2012.

Few Americans are self-employed.

Those aged 65 or older are most likely to be self-employed (17 percent), in part because they have health insurance through Medicare.

Big gains for older workers.

The labor force as a whole will grow 7 percent between 2010 and 2020, but the number of workers aged 65 or older is projected to expand by 80 percent.

Labor Force Participation Fell between 2000 and 2012

Older men and women are more likely to work, however.

Both men's and women's labor force participation rate fell between 2000 and 2012, with the decline greater for men than for women. One factor behind the decline was the economic downturn, although participation rates include people who are looking for a job. Many Americans were too discouraged by the troubled economy to even look for work, pushing the labor force participation rate down.

The labor force participation rate fell for men and women under age 55, the steepest decline occurring among teenagers. One reason for the decline in the labor force participation rate of teenagers is the increase in extracurricular activities among high school students and the rise in college enrollment rates among recent high school graduates.

The labor force participation rate of older men and women increased significantly between 2000 and 2012. Among women and men aged 65 or older, labor force participation climbed 5.0 and 5.9 percentage points, respectively. In 2012, a substantial 23.6 percent of men aged 65 or older were in the labor force. The labor force participation rate of men aged 65 or older has not been that high since 1972.

■ As older Americans postpone retirement, it becomes more difficult for young and middle-aged adults to find jobs.

More older men are working

(percent of men aged 65 or older in the civilian labor force, 2000 and 2012)

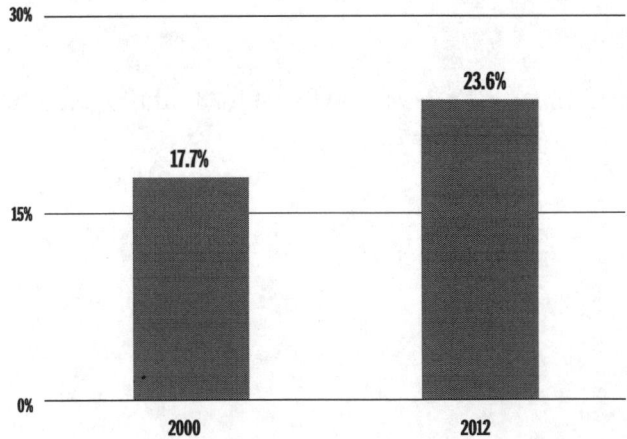

Table 6.1 Labor Force Participation Rate by Sex and Age, 1950 to 2012

(percent of people aged 16 or older in the civilian labor force by sex and age, 1950 to 2012; percentage point change for selected years)

	2012	2010	2000	1990	1980	1970	1960	1950	percentage point change 2000–12	1950–2012
Total people	**63.7%**	**64.7%**	**67.1%**	**66.4%**	**63.8%**	**60.4%**	**59.4%**	**59.2%**	**–3.4**	**4.5**
Aged 16 to 24	54.9	55.2	65.8	67.3	68.1	59.8	56.4	59.9	–10.9	–5.0
Aged 25 to 34	81.7	82.2	84.6	83.6	79.9	69.7	65.4	63.5	–2.9	18.2
Aged 35 to 44	82.6	83.2	84.8	85.2	80.0	73.1	69.4	67.5	–2.2	15.1
Aged 45 to 54	80.2	81.2	82.5	80.7	74.9	73.5	72.2	66.4	–2.3	13.8
Aged 55 to 64	64.5	64.9	59.2	55.9	55.7	61.8	60.9	56.7	5.3	7.8
Aged 65 or older	18.5	17.4	12.9	11.8	12.5	17.0	20.8	26.7	5.6	–8.2
Total men	**70.2**	**71.2**	**74.8**	**76.1**	**77.4**	**79.7**	**83.3**	**86.4**	**–4.6**	**–16.2**
Aged 16 to 24	56.5	56.7	68.6	71.5	74.4	69.4	71.7	77.3	–12.1	–20.8
Aged 25 to 34	89.5	89.7	93.4	94.2	95.2	96.4	97.5	96.0	–3.9	–6.5
Aged 35 to 44	90.7	91.5	92.7	94.4	95.5	96.8	97.7	97.6	–2.0	–6.9
Aged 45 to 54	86.1	86.8	88.6	90.7	91.2	94.3	95.7	95.8	–2.5	–9.7
Aged 55 to 64	69.9	70.0	67.3	67.7	72.1	83.0	87.3	86.9	2.6	–17.0
Aged 65 or older	23.6	22.1	17.7	16.4	19.0	26.8	33.1	45.8	5.9	–22.2
Total women	**57.7**	**58.6**	**59.9**	**57.5**	**51.5**	**43.3**	**37.7**	**33.9**	**–2.2**	**23.8**
Aged 16 to 24	53.2	53.6	63.0	63.1	61.9	51.3	42.8	43.9	–9.8	9.3
Aged 25 to 34	74.1	74.7	76.1	73.6	65.5	45.0	36.0	34.0	–2.0	40.1
Aged 35 to 44	74.8	75.2	77.2	76.5	65.5	51.1	43.4	39.1	–2.4	35.7
Aged 45 to 54	74.7	75.7	76.8	71.2	59.9	54.4	49.9	37.9	–2.1	36.8
Aged 55 to 64	59.4	60.2	51.9	45.3	41.3	43.0	37.2	27.0	7.5	32.4
Aged 65 or older	14.4	13.8	9.4	8.7	8.1	9.7	10.8	9.7	5.0	4.7

Source: Bureau of Labor Statistics, Labor Force Statistics from the Current Population Survey, Internet site http://www.bls .gov/cps/tables.htm#empstat; and Monthly Labor Review, December 1999; calculations by New Strategist

Sixty-Four Percent of Americans Are in the Labor Force

Women account for 47 percent of the labor force.

Of the nation's 243 million people aged 16 or older, 155 million were in the civilian labor force in 2012. Labor force statistics include both the employed and the unemployed. In 2012, a substantial 12.5 million people were unemployed—8.1 percent of the labor force.

Labor force participation peaks at 91 percent among men in their thirties. Women's participation rate peaks at 76 percent in the 40-to-49 age group. Both men's and women's participation falls in the 55-to-64 age group as some workers retire, although most in the age group work. A significant 24 percent of men and 14 percent of women aged 65 or older are in the labor force.

Unemployment is highest among the youngest workers. The unemployment rate among 16-to-17-year-olds was nearly 31 percent among men and 24 percent among women in 2012.

■ The economic downturn forced some aging boomers to postpone retirement and drove others to retire earlier than they had planned.

Men are the majority of workers

(percent distribution of the labor force by sex, 2012)

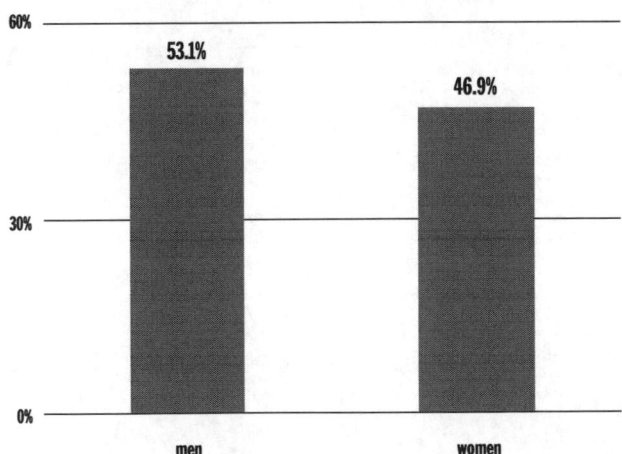

Table 6.2 Employment Status by Sex and Age, 2012

(number and percent of people aged 16 or older in the civilian labor force by sex, age, and employment status, 2012; numbers in thousands)

	civilian noninstitutional population	civilian labor force				
		total	percent of population	employed	unemployed number	percent
Total people	243,284	154,975	63.7%	142,469	12,506	8.1%
Aged 16 to 17	8,891	1,952	22.0	1,419	533	27.3
Aged 18 to 19	8,093	3,870	47.8	3,007	863	22.3
Aged 20 to 24	21,799	15,462	70.9	13,408	2,054	13.3
Aged 25 to 29	20,653	16,792	81.3	15,293	1,500	8.9
Aged 30 to 34	20,322	16,673	82.0	15,408	1,265	7.6
Aged 35 to 39	19,025	15,658	82.3	14,560	1,098	7.0
Aged 40 to 44	20,617	17,076	82.8	16,016	1,060	6.2
Aged 45 to 49	21,359	17,456	81.7	16,371	1,086	6.2
Aged 50 to 54	22,339	17,598	78.8	16,503	1,095	6.2
Aged 55 to 59	20,574	14,908	72.5	14,015	892	6.0
Aged 60 to 64	17,743	9,802	55.2	9,224	578	5.9
Aged 65 or older	41,869	7,727	18.5	7,245	482	6.2
Aged 65 to 69	13,801	4,427	32.1	4,133	295	6.7
Aged 70 to 74	9,853	1,917	19.5	1,794	124	6.4
Aged 75 or older	18,216	1,383	7.6	1,319	64	4.6
Total men	117,343	82,327	70.2	75,555	6,771	8.2
Aged 16 to 17	4,550	950	20.9	659	291	30.6
Aged 18 to 19	4,107	1,990	48.5	1,493	497	25.0
Aged 20 to 24	10,889	8,110	74.5	6,948	1,163	14.3
Aged 25 to 29	10,216	9,027	88.4	8,219	808	9.0
Aged 30 to 34	9,989	9,055	90.7	8,387	668	7.4
Aged 35 to 39	9,309	8,502	91.3	7,930	572	6.7
Aged 40 to 44	10,107	9,106	90.1	8,553	552	6.1
Aged 45 to 49	10,449	9,205	88.1	8,633	572	6.2
Aged 50 to 54	10,890	9,157	84.1	8,588	570	6.2
Aged 55 to 59	9,922	7,737	78.0	7,243	494	6.4
Aged 60 to 64	8,495	5,142	60.5	4,826	317	6.2
Aged 65 or older	18,422	4,345	23.6	4,077	268	6.2
Aged 65 to 69	6,499	2,412	37.1	2,252	159	6.6
Aged 70 to 74	4,537	1,096	24.2	1,025	71	6.5
Aged 75 or older	7,386	837	11.3	800	37	4.4
Total women	125,941	72,648	57.7	66,914	5,734	7.9
Aged 16 to 17	4,341	1,003	23.1	760	242	24.2
Aged 18 to 19	3,986	1,880	47.2	1,514	367	19.5
Aged 20 to 24	10,910	7,352	67.4	6,460	891	12.1
Aged 25 to 29	10,437	7,765	74.4	7,073	692	8.9
Aged 30 to 34	10,333	7,617	73.7	7,021	597	7.8
Aged 35 to 39	9,716	7,156	73.7	6,630	526	7.3
Aged 40 to 44	10,510	7,970	75.8	7,462	508	6.4
Aged 45 to 49	10,909	8,251	75.6	7,738	513	6.2
Aged 50 to 54	11,449	8,440	73.7	7,915	525	6.2
Aged 55 to 59	10,653	7,171	67.3	6,773	398	5.6
Aged 60 to 64	9,249	4,660	50.4	4,399	261	5.6
Aged 65 or older	23,447	3,383	14.4	3,168	214	6.3
Aged 65 to 69	7,301	2,015	27.6	1,880	135	6.7
Aged 70 to 74	5,316	821	15.4	769	52	6.4
Aged 75 or older	10,830	546	5.0	519	27	4.9

Note: The civilian labor force equals the number of the employed plus the number of the unemployed. The civilian population equals the number in the labor force plus the number not in the labor force.
Source: Bureau of Labor Statistics, Labor Force Statistics from the Current Population Survey, Internet site http://www.bls .gov/cps/tables.htm#empstat

Labor Force Participation Varies by Race and Hispanic Origin

Unemployment rate is highest among the young.

Among men, the labor force participation rate ranges from a high of 76 percent among Hispanics to a low of 64 percent among blacks (the labor force includes both the employed and the unemployed). The labor force participation rate varies little by race and Hispanic origin among women.

During and after the Great Recession, every racial and ethnic group experienced a surge in unemployment. The rate of unemployment remains elevated, although the economic recovery is several years old. In 2012, the unemployment rate ranged from a high of 13.8 percent among blacks to a low of 5.9 percent among Asians. Young black men have the highest unemployment rate of all. Among black men aged 16 to 19, fully 41.3 percent were unemployed in 2012.

■ Among Asians and Hispanics, women have a higher unemployment rate than men.

Blacks have the highest unemployment rate

(percentage of the civilian labor force aged 16 or older who are unemployed, by race and Hispanic origin, 2012)

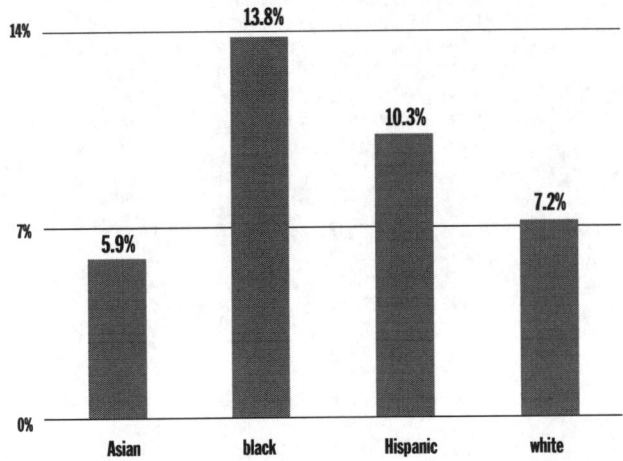

Table 6.3 Employment Status of Asians by Sex and Age, 2012

(number and percent of Asians aged 16 or older in the civilian labor force by sex, age, and employment status, 2012; numbers in thousands)

	civilian noninstitutional population	civilian labor force				
		total	percent of population	employed	unemployed number	unemployed percent
Total Asians	**12,815**	**8,188**	**63.9%**	**7,705**	**483**	**5.9%**
Aged 16 to 19	802	162	20.1	128	34	20.8
Aged 20 to 24	1,151	608	52.8	544	64	10.5
Aged 25 to 34	2,699	2,067	76.6	1,956	111	5.4
Aged 35 to 44	2,632	2,129	80.9	2,038	90	4.2
Aged 45 to 54	2,195	1,782	81.2	1,684	98	5.5
Aged 55 to 64	1,719	1,144	66.5	1,071	73	6.4
Aged 65 or older	1,617	296	18.3	283	12	4.2
Asian men	**6,000**	**4,334**	**72.2**	**4,085**	**249**	**5.8**
Aged 16 to 19	411	77	18.7	59	18	22.8
Aged 20 to 24	576	328	57.0	295	34	10.2
Aged 25 to 34	1,279	1,117	87.3	1,066	51	4.6
Aged 35 to 44	1,228	1,135	92.4	1,090	44	3.9
Aged 45 to 54	1,024	928	90.6	871	57	6.1
Aged 55 to 64	772	580	75.2	543	38	6.5
Aged 65 or older	708	170	23.9	161	8	4.9
Asian women	**6,815**	**3,853**	**56.5**	**3,620**	**234**	**6.1**
Aged 16 to 19	391	85	21.7	69	16	19.0
Aged 20 to 24	575	280	48.7	250	31	10.9
Aged 25 to 34	1,419	950	67.0	890	60	6.3
Aged 35 to 44	1,404	994	70.8	948	46	4.7
Aged 45 to 54	1,171	855	73.0	813	41	4.9
Aged 55 to 64	947	563	59.5	528	35	6.3
Aged 65 or older	909	126	13.9	122	4	3.2

Note: The civilian labor force equals the number of the employed plus the number of the unemployed. The civilian population equals the number in the labor force plus the number not in the labor force.
Source: Bureau of Labor Statistics, Labor Force Statistics from the Current Population Survey, Internet site http://www.bls .gov/cps/tables.htm#empstat

Table 6.4 Employment Status of Blacks by Sex and Age, 2012

(number and percent of blacks aged 16 or older in the civilian labor force by sex, age, and employment status, 2012; numbers in thousands)

| | civilian noninstitutional population | civilian labor force | | | | |
| | | total | percent of population | employed | unemployed | |
					number	percent
Total blacks	**29,907**	**18,400**	**61.5%**	**15,856**	**2,544**	**13.8%**
Aged 16 to 19	2,643	711	26.9	438	272	38.3
Aged 20 to 24	3,326	2,210	66.5	1,700	510	23.1
Aged 25 to 34	5,455	4,333	79.4	3,693	640	14.8
Aged 35 to 44	5,107	4,120	80.7	3,662	457	11.1
Aged 45 to 54	5,446	4,057	74.5	3,660	397	9.8
Aged 55 to 64	4,281	2,369	55.3	2,161	209	8.8
Aged 65 or older	3,650	599	16.4	540	59	9.8
Black men	**13,508**	**8,594**	**63.6**	**7,302**	**1,292**	**15.0**
Aged 16 to 19	1,319	338	25.6	198	140	41.3
Aged 20 to 24	1,586	1,054	66.4	784	269	25.6
Aged 25 to 34	2,461	2,030	82.5	1,723	308	15.2
Aged 35 to 44	2,286	1,908	83.5	1,667	241	12.6
Aged 45 to 54	2,484	1,884	75.9	1,693	191	10.2
Aged 55 to 64	1,923	1,099	57.1	988	110	10.1
Aged 65 or older	1,449	281	19.4	249	32	11.5
Black women	**16,400**	**9,805**	**59.8**	**8,553**	**1,252**	**12.8**
Aged 16 to 19	1,324	373	28.2	240	133	35.6
Aged 20 to 24	1,740	1,157	66.5	916	241	20.8
Aged 25 to 34	2,994	2,303	76.9	1,970	333	14.4
Aged 35 to 44	2,821	2,212	78.4	1,995	216	9.8
Aged 45 to 54	2,963	2,173	73.3	1,968	205	9.4
Aged 55 to 64	2,358	1,271	53.9	1,173	98	7.7
Aged 65 or older	2,201	317	14.4	291	26	8.2

Note: The civilian labor force equals the number of the employed plus the number of the unemployed. The civilian population equals the number in the labor force plus the number not in the labor force.
Source: Bureau of Labor Statistics, Labor Force Statistics from the Current Population Survey, Internet site http://www.bls.gov/cps/tables.htm#empstat

Table 6.5 Employment Status of Hispanics by Sex and Age, 2012

(number and percent of Hispanics aged 16 or older in the civilian labor force by sex, age, and employment status, 2012; numbers in thousands)

| | civilian noninstitutional population | civilian labor force | | | | |
| | | total | percent of population | employed | unemployed | |
					number	percent
Total Hispanics	**36,759**	**24,391**	**66.4%**	**21,878**	**2,514**	**10.3%**
Aged 16 to 19	3,656	1,131	30.9	808	324	28.6
Aged 20 to 24	4,502	3,205	71.2	2,761	444	13.8
Aged 25 to 34	8,512	6,736	79.1	6,119	618	9.2
Aged 35 to 44	7,551	6,053	80.2	5,552	502	8.3
Aged 45 to 54	5,831	4,569	78.4	4,188	381	8.3
Aged 55 to 64	3,613	2,185	60.5	1,983	201	9.2
Aged 65 or older	3,094	512	16.5	467	44	8.7
Hispanic men	**18,434**	**14,026**	**76.1**	**12,643**	**1,383**	**9.9**
Aged 16 to 19	1,879	620	33.0	431	189	30.5
Aged 20 to 24	2,341	1,837	78.5	1,584	254	13.8
Aged 25 to 34	4,424	4,053	91.6	3,714	339	8.4
Aged 35 to 44	3,822	3,480	91.1	3,229	251	7.2
Aged 45 to 54	2,911	2,542	87.3	2,334	208	8.2
Aged 55 to 64	1,729	1,215	70.3	1,097	119	9.8
Aged 65 or older	1,329	280	21.1	256	24	8.6
Hispanic women	**18,324**	**10,365**	**56.6**	**9,235**	**1,130**	**10.9**
Aged 16 to 19	1,776	512	28.8	377	135	26.4
Aged 20 to 24	2,161	1,368	63.3	1,178	190	13.9
Aged 25 to 34	4,088	2,683	65.6	2,405	278	10.4
Aged 35 to 44	3,729	2,574	69.0	2,323	251	9.7
Aged 45 to 54	2,920	2,027	69.4	1,854	173	8.5
Aged 55 to 64	1,884	969	51.4	887	83	8.5
Aged 65 or older	1,765	232	13.2	212	20	8.8

Note: The civilian labor force equals the number of the employed plus the number of the unemployed. The civilian population equals the number in the labor force plus the number not in the labor force.
Source: Bureau of Labor Statistics, Labor Force Statistics from the Current Population Survey, Internet site http://www.bls.gov/cps/tables.htm#empstat

Table 6.6 Employment Status of Whites by Sex and Age, 2012

(number and percent of whites aged 16 or older in the civilian labor force by sex, age, and employment status, 2012; numbers in thousands)

| | | civilian labor force | | | | |
	civilian noninstitutional population	total	percent of population	employed	unemployed number	unemployed percent
Total whites	**193,204**	**123,684**	**64.0%**	**114,769**	**8,915**	**7.2%**
Aged 16 to 19	12,658	4,669	36.9	3,665	1,004	21.5
Aged 20 to 24	16,289	11,914	73.1	10,561	1,353	11.4
Aged 25 to 34	31,242	25,806	82.6	23,925	1,881	7.3
Aged 35 to 44	30,597	25,445	83.2	23,931	1,514	5.9
Aged 45 to 54	34,935	28,384	81.2	26,769	1,614	5.7
Aged 55 to 64	31,511	20,752	65.9	19,608	1,144	5.5
Aged 65 or older	35,973	6,714	18.7	6,309	405	6.0
White men	**94,266**	**66,921**	**71.0**	**61,990**	**4,931**	**7.4**
Aged 16 to 19	6,486	2,382	36.7	1,797	584	24.5
Aged 20 to 24	8,211	6,339	77.2	5,547	792	12.5
Aged 25 to 34	15,691	14,256	90.9	13,212	1,044	7.3
Aged 35 to 44	15,263	14,018	91.8	13,224	794	5.7
Aged 45 to 54	17,287	15,121	87.5	14,264	856	5.7
Aged 55 to 64	15,333	10,970	71.6	10,334	637	5.8
Aged 65 or older	15,995	3,835	24.0	3,611	224	5.8
White women	**98,938**	**56,763**	**57.4**	**52,779**	**3,985**	**7.0**
Aged 16 to 19	6,172	2,288	37.1	1,868	420	18.4
Aged 20 to 24	8,078	5,575	69.0	5,014	561	10.1
Aged 25 to 34	15,550	11,550	74.3	10,713	837	7.2
Aged 35 to 44	15,334	11,428	74.5	10,708	720	6.3
Aged 45 to 54	17,648	13,263	75.2	12,505	758	5.7
Aged 55 to 64	16,179	9,782	60.5	9,274	508	5.2
Aged 65 or older	19,978	2,879	14.4	2,698	181	6.3

Note: The civilian labor force equals the number of the employed plus the number of the unemployed. The civilian population equals the number in the labor force plus the number not in the labor force.
Source: Bureau of Labor Statistics, Labor Force Statistics from the Current Population Survey, Internet site http://www.bls.gov/cps/tables.htm#empstat

Working Mothers Are the Norm

Most working mothers have full-time jobs.

Working mothers are the norm—even among women with infants. Fifty-seven percent of mothers with children under age 1 were in the labor force in 2012. Among the employed, most had full-time jobs.

Labor force participation is higher for mothers with school-aged children than for those with preschoolers. Seventy-five percent of women with children aged 6 to 17 were in the labor force in 2012. This compares with 65 percent of women with children under age 6. Among workers in both groups, the majority has a full-time job.

Fifty-nine percent of the nation's married couples with children under age 18 are dual-earners, with both mother and father employed. In just 30 percent of couples, only the father is employed. Even among couples with preschoolers, the 55 percent majority are dual-earners.

■ With most parents working, day care has become a substantial expense for families with preschoolers.

Most mothers are in the labor force

(percent of women in the labor force by age of children at home, 2012)

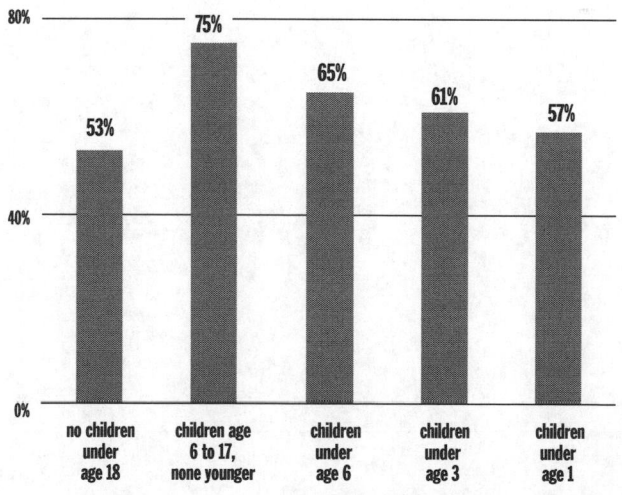

Table 6.7 Labor Force Status of Women by Presence of Children, 2012

(number and percent distribution of women by labor force status and presence and age of own children under age 18 at home, 2012; numbers in thousands)

	civilian population	civilian labor force total	employed total	full-time	part-time
Total women	**125,940**	**72,648**	**66,914**	**49,331**	**17,582**
No children under age 18	90,033	47,334	43,707	32,008	11,699
With children under age 18	35,907	25,314	23,207	17,323	5,883
Children aged 6 to 17, none younger	19,814	14,887	13,801	10,602	3,199
Children under age 6	16,094	10,427	9,406	6,721	2,684
Children under age 3	9,134	5,612	5,047	3,552	1,495
Children under age 1	3,049	1,737	1,546	1,102	444
Total women	**100.0%**	**57.7%**	**53.1%**	**39.2%**	**14.0%**
No children under age 18	100.0	52.6	48.5	35.6	13.0
With children under age 18	100.0	70.5	64.6	48.2	16.4
Children aged 6 to 17, none younger	100.0	75.1	69.7	53.5	16.1
Children under age 6	100.0	64.8	58.4	41.8	16.7
Children under age 3	100.0	61.4	55.3	38.9	16.4
Children under age 1	100.0	57.0	50.7	36.1	14.6

Source: Bureau of Labor Statistics, Employment Characteristics of Families, Internet site http://www.bls.gov/new.release/famee .toc.htm

Table 6.8 Labor Force Status of Families with Children under Age 18, 2012

(number and percent distribution of families by employment status of parent and age of youngest own child under age 18 at home, by family type, 2012; numbers in thousands)

NUMBER	total	youngest child aged 6 to 17	youngest child under age 6
Married couples with children under age 18	**23,297**	**12,982**	**10,315**
One or both parents employed	22,429	12,471	9,958
Mother employed	15,243	9,028	6,215
Both parents employed	13,739	8,104	5,635
Mother employed, not father	1,503	924	580
Father employed, not mother	7,086	3,443	3,744
Neither parent employed	868	511	357
Female-headed families with children under age 18	**8,757**	**5,149**	**3,609**
Mother employed	5,872	3,711	2,161
Mother not employed	2,885	1,437	1,448
Male-headed families with children under age 18	**2,512**	**1,447**	**1,065**
Father employed	2,050	1,173	877
Father not employed	462	274	188
PERCENT DISTRIBUTION			
Married couples with children under age 18	**100.0%**	**100.0%**	**100.0%**
One or both parents employed	96.3	96.1	96.5
Mother employed	65.4	69.5	60.3
Both parents employed	59.0	62.4	54.6
Mother employed, not father	6.5	7.1	5.6
Father employed, not mother	30.4	26.5	36.3
Neither parent employed	3.7	3.9	3.5
Female-headed families with children under age 18	**100.0**	**100.0**	**100.0**
Mother employed	67.1	72.1	59.9
Mother not employed	32.9	27.9	40.1
Male-headed families with children under age 18	**100.0**	**100.0**	**100.0**
Father employed	81.6	81.1	82.3
Father not employed	18.4	18.9	17.7

Source: Bureau of Labor Statistics, Employment Characteristics of Families, Internet site http://www.bls.gov/news.release/famee.toc.htm

More than Half of Couples Are Dual-Earners

In just 23 percent of married couples, only the husband is in the labor force.

Dual incomes are by far the norm among married couples. Both husband and wife are in the labor force in 52 percent of married couples. In another 23 percent, the husband is the only worker. Not far behind are the 18 percent of couples in which neither spouse is in the labor force. The wife is the sole worker among 8 percent of couples.

At least two-thirds of couples aged 30 to 54 are dual-earners. This lifestyle accounts for half of couples aged 55 to 64. The wife is the only spouse employed in a substantial 13 percent of couples aged 55 to 64. In these homes, typically, the older husband is retired while the younger wife is still at work. For 54 percent of couples aged 65 to 74 and 82 percent of those aged 75 or older, neither husband nor wife is working.

■ As boomers retire, the number of couples in which neither spouse is in the labor force may surpass the number in which only the husband is employed.

Dual-earners outnumber single-earners

(percent distribution of married couples by labor force status of husband and wife, 2012)

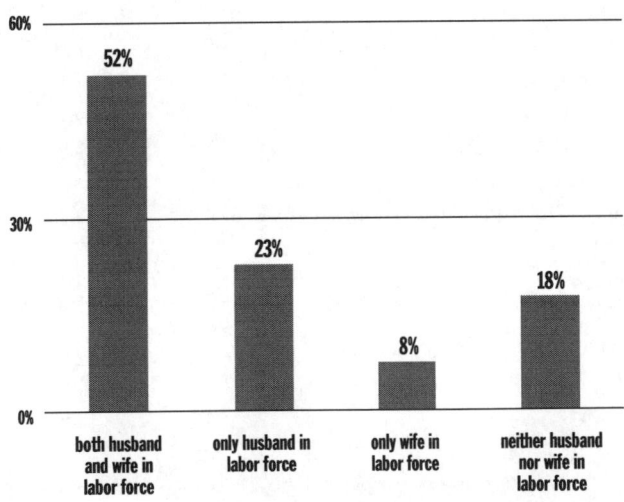

Table 6.9 Labor Force Status of Married-Couple Family Groups, 2012

(number and percent distribution of married-couple family groups aged 20 or older by age of householder and labor force status of husband and wife, 2012; numbers in thousands)

		husband and/or wife in labor force			neither husband nor wife in labor force
	total	husband and wife	husband only	wife only	
Married couples	**61,047**	**31,803**	**13,820**	**4,595**	**10,830**
Under age 25	1,247	653	491	52	51
Aged 25 to 29	3,576	2,217	1,118	149	91
Aged 30 to 34	5,482	3,618	1,564	195	105
Aged 35 to 39	5,727	3,803	1,616	203	104
Aged 40 to 44	6,622	4,593	1,583	257	189
Aged 45 to 54	13,822	9,335	3,071	834	582
Aged 55 to 64	12,431	6,188	2,726	1,625	1,891
Aged 65 to 74	7,751	1,208	1,288	1,059	4,197
Aged 75 or older	4,391	188	364	220	3,619
Married couples	**100.0%**	**52.1%**	**22.6%**	**7.5%**	**17.7%**
Under age 25	100.0	52.4	39.4	4.2	4.1
Aged 25 to 29	100.0	62.0	31.3	4.2	2.5
Aged 30 to 34	100.0	66.0	28.5	3.6	1.9
Aged 35 to 39	100.0	66.4	28.2	3.5	1.8
Aged 40 to 44	100.0	69.4	23.9	3.9	2.9
Aged 45 to 54	100.0	67.5	22.2	6.0	4.2
Aged 55 to 64	100.0	49.8	21.9	13.1	15.2
Aged 65 to 74	100.0	15.6	16.6	13.7	54.1
Aged 75 or older	100.0	4.3	8.3	5.0	82.4

Source: Bureau of the Census, America's Families and Living Arrangements: 2012, Detailed Tables, Internet site http://www.census.gov/hhes/families/data/cps2012.html; calculations by New Strategist

Most Preschoolers Are in Day Care

The children of affluent, educated parents are most likely to be in day care.

Among the nation's preschoolers, 60 percent are in nonparental care arrangements (day care) at least once a week. Only 40 percent are not in day care at least weekly. Among children in nonparental care on a weekly basis, more than half spend time in center-based care, 42 percent in relative care, and 24 percent in nonrelative care (many parents use more than one type of nonparental care arrangement).

Affluent and educated parents are most likely to have their preschooler in day care. By parent's educational attainment, the percentage of preschoolers in day care ranges from a low of 45 percent among those with a parent who did not graduate from high school to a high of 73 percent among those with a parent who has a graduate degree. By household income, the percentage ranges from a low of 48 percent for preschoolers in the poorest families to a high of 73 percent for those in the most affluent families.

■ Day care is most popular among the affluent and educated because they can afford the high fees.

The higher the income, the more likely a preschooler is to be in day care

(percent of children aged 0 to 5 in a nonparental care arrangement at least weekly, by household income, 2012)

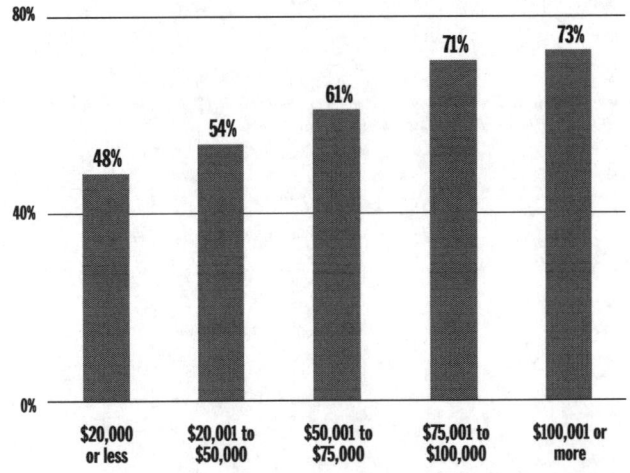

Table 6.10 Day Care Arrangements of Preschoolers, 2012

(percent distribution of children aged 0 to 5 not yet in kindergarten by type of care, child and family characteristics, 2012)

	total	at least one weekly nonparental care arrangement total	relative	nonrelative	center	no weekly nonparental care arrangement
TOTAL CHILDREN	100.0%	60%	42%	24%	56%	40%
Age						
Aged less than 1	100.0	46	60	30	23	54
Aged 1 to 2	100.0	54	49	31	40	46
Aged 3 to 5	100.0	76	31	16	80	24
Race and Hispanic origin of child						
Asian	100.0	54	37	15	65	46
Black, non-Hispanic	100.0	69	46	16	61	31
Hispanic	100.0	55	52	21	49	45
White, non-Hispanic	100.0	62	37	28	57	38
Family type						
Two parents	100.0	58	36	25	57	42
One parent	100.0	66	54	21	53	34
No parents	100.0	74	77	14	54	26
Parent's educational attainment						
Less than high school	100.0	45	57	21	43	55
High school graduate/GED	100.0	53	53	17	50	47
Vocational/technical/some college	100.0	60	46	23	53	40
Bachelor's degree	100.0	67	35	24	63	33
Graduate or professional degree	100.0	73	29	31	64	27
Parent's labor force status						
Two-parent family						
Both full-time	100.0	89	40	31	51	11
One full-time, one part-time	100.0	78	38	27	55	22
One full-time, one not in labor force	100.0	34	29	14	70	66
Single-parent family						
Full-time	100.0	83	50	23	57	17
Part-time	100.0	77	58	23	48	23
Not in labor force	100.0	45	65	19	50	55
Region						
Northeast	100.0	67	40	25	57	33
Midwest	100.0	61	40	19	63	39
South	100.0	62	40	29	54	38
West	100.0	55	49	25	48	45
Household income						
$20,000 or less	100.0	48	53	19	51	52
$20,001 to $50,000	100.0	54	49	18	53	46
$50,001 to $75,000	100.0	61	42	21	56	39
$75,001 to $100,000	100.0	71	38	28	56	29
$100,001 or more	100.0	73	31	31	62	27
Poverty status						
At or above poverty threshold	100.0	65	39	25	58	35
Below poverty threshold	100.0	47	53	17	50	53

Note: Nonparental care arrangements by type do not sum to total because more than one arrangement may be used. Center-based care includes day care centers, prekindergartens, nursery schools, Head Start programs, and other early childhood education programs.
Source: National Center for Education Statistics, Early Childhood Program Participation from the National Household Education Surveys Program of 2012, Internet site http://nces.ed.gov/pubsearch/pubsinfo.asp?pubid=2013029

One in Four Workers Is a Part-Timer

Among women workers, nearly one-third work part-time.

Most of the nation's workers have full-time jobs. Part-timers outnumber those with full-time jobs only among teenagers. Seventy-seven percent of workers aged 16 to 19 are part-timers. Among 20-to-24-year-olds, a smaller 42 percent work part-time. The figure drops to 19 percent among 25-to-54-year-olds, then rises again to 28 percent among those aged 55 or older.

Many part-time workers would rather have a full-time job. Among the 34 million part-time workers, 29 percent of men and 20 percent of women are working part-time for economic reasons—meaning either their hours have been reduced or they cannot find a full-time job. The proportion of part-timers who would rather work full-time peaks at 37 percent among men aged 25 to 54.

■ The Great Recession forced many Americans into part-time employment to make ends meet.

Part-time work is most common among teens and young adults

(percent of people aged 16 or older in nonagricultural industries who work part-time, by age, 2012)

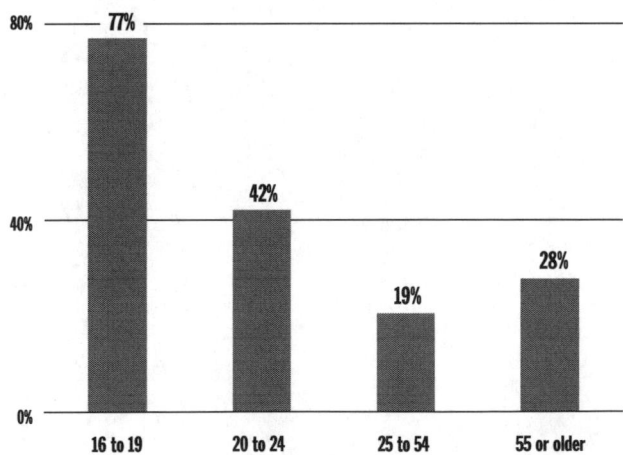

Table 6.11 Full-Time and Part-Time Workers by Sex and Age, 2012

(number and percent distribution of employed men aged 16 or older by age and full- or part-time employment status, 2012; numbers in thousands)

	total	full-time		part-time	
		number	percent	number	percent
Total employed	**135,235**	**101,383**	**75.0%**	**33,852**	**25.0%**
Aged 16 to 19	4,160	975	23.4	3,184	76.5
Aged 20 to 24	12,881	7,447	57.8	5,434	42.2
Aged 25 or older	118,195	92,961	78.7	25,234	21.3
Aged 25 to 54	89,901	72,671	80.8	17,230	19.2
Aged 55 or older	28,294	20,290	71.7	8,004	28.3
Employed men	**71,765**	**58,149**	**81.0**	**13,616**	**19.0**
Aged 16 to 19	2,004	567	28.3	1,437	71.7
Aged 20 to 24	6,660	4,213	63.3	2,447	36.7
Aged 25 or older	63,100	53,369	84.6	9,731	15.4
Aged 25 to 54	48,174	41,828	86.8	6,346	13.2
Aged 55 or older	14,926	11,541	77.3	3,385	22.7
Employed women	**63,470**	**43,233**	**68.1**	**20,236**	**31.9**
Aged 16 to 19	2,155	408	18.9	1,747	81.1
Aged 20 to 24	6,220	3,233	52.0	2,987	48.0
Aged 25 or older	55,094	39,592	71.9	15,503	28.1
Aged 25 to 54	41,727	30,843	73.9	10,884	26.1
Aged 55 or older	13,367	8,749	65.5	4,618	34.5

Note: "Full-time" is defined as 35 hours or more per week. "Part-time" is defined as less than 35 hours per week.
Source: Bureau of Labor Statistics, Labor Force Statistics from the Current Population Survey, Internet site http://www.bls .gov/cps/tables.htm#empstat; calculations by New Strategist

Table 6.12 Part-Time Workers for Economic Reasons, 2012

(number of people aged 16 or older who work part-time, and number and percent who work-part-time for economic reasons, by sex and age, 2012; numbers in thousands)

		for economic reasons	
	total	number	share of total
Total who work part-time	**33,852**	**8,003**	**23.6%**
Aged 16 to 19	3,184	419	13.2
Aged 20 to 24	5,434	1,489	27.4
Aged 25 or older	25,234	6,095	24.2
Aged 25 to 54	17,230	4,790	27.8
Aged 55 or older	8,004	1,305	16.3
Men who work part-time	**13,616**	**3,981**	**29.2%**
Aged 16 to 19	1,437	225	15.7
Aged 20 to 24	2,447	758	31.0
Aged 25 or older	9,731	2,997	30.8
Aged 25 to 54	6,346	2,372	37.4
Aged 55 or older	3,385	626	18.5
Women who work part-time	**20,236**	**4,022**	**19.9**
Aged 16 to 19	1,747	194	11.1
Aged 20 to 24	2,987	730	24.4
Aged 25 or older	15,503	3,098	20.0
Aged 25 to 54	10,884	2,418	22.2
Aged 55 or older	4,618	680	14.7

Note: "Part-time" is defined as less than 35 hours per week. Part-time for economic reasons are people who work part-time because of slack work or poor business conditions, people who cannot find full-time jobs, and people who have seasonal jobs. Source: Bureau of Labor Statistics, Labor Force Statistics from the Current Population Survey, Internet site http://www.bls .gov/cps/tables.htm#empstat; calculations by New Strategist

Occupations Differ for Men and Women

Occupational differences are also considerable by race and Hispanic origin.

Women are more likely than men to work in education or health care occupations. Men are more likely than women to work in computer, construction, and production occupations. Occupational differences are even greater by race and Hispanic origin. While 48 percent of Asians work in management or professional occupations, the proportion is just 21 percent among Hispanics. Nine percent of Hispanics work in construction versus 1 percent of Asians.

Women account for the majority of workers in many occupations, including human resource managers, education administrators, registered nurses, librarians, and secretaries. Asians are well represented in many professional occupations. Although they account for only 5 percent of all workers, Asians are 29 percent of software developers. Blacks are 11 percent of all workers, but a larger 23 percent of social workers and licensed practical nurses. Hispanics are 15 percent of all workers but 43 percent of maids and housekeepers, 53 percent of cement masons, and 62 percent of drywall installers.

■ Women account for 31 percent of lawyers and 34 percent of doctors, but only 14 percent of civil engineers.

Thirty percent of blacks work in management or professional jobs

(percent of workers in management or professional occupations, by race and Hispanic origin, 2012)

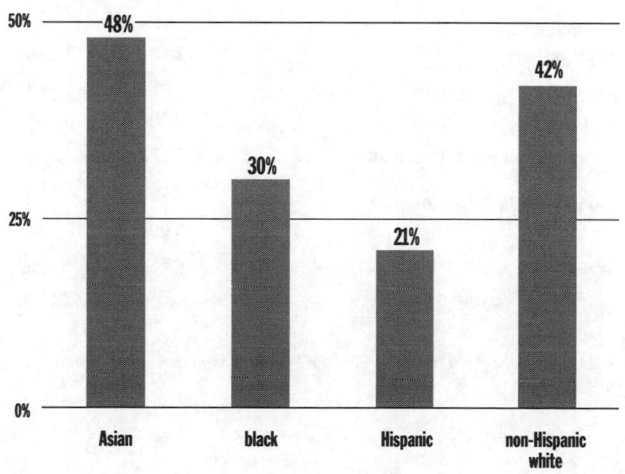

Table 6.13 Workers by Occupation and Sex, 2012

(number of employed people aged 16 or older in the civilian labor force, by occupation and sex, 2012; numbers in thousands)

	total	men	women
TOTAL EMPLOYED	**142,469**	**75,555**	**66,914**
Management, professional and related occupations	**54,043**	**26,208**	**27,834**
Management, business and financial operations occupations	22,678	12,779	9,899
Management occupations	16,042	9,849	6,194
Business and financial operations occupations	6,636	2,931	3,705
Professional and related occupations	31,365	13,429	17,936
Computer and mathematical occupations	3,816	2,841	976
Architecture and engineering occupations	2,846	2,457	390
Life, physical, and social science occupations	1,316	720	596
Community and social services occupations	2,265	819	1,446
Legal occupations	1,786	885	901
Education, training, and library occupations	8,543	2,253	6,290
Art, design, entertainment, sports, and media occupations	2,814	1,456	1,358
Health care practitioner and technical occupations	7,977	1,998	5,979
Service occupations	**25,459**	**11,135**	**14,324**
Health care support occupations	3,496	434	3,062
Protective service occupations	3,096	2,449	647
Food preparation and serving–related occupations	8,018	3,648	4,370
Building and grounds cleaning and maintenance occupations	5,591	3,430	2,160
Personal care and service occupations	5,258	1,173	4,085
Sales and office occupations	**33,152**	**12,653**	**20,500**
Sales and related occupations	15,457	7,922	7,535
Office and administrative support occupations	17,695	4,730	12,965
Natural resources, construction, and maintenance occupations	**12,821**	**12,266**	**554**
Farming, fishing, and forestry occupations	994	768	226
Construction and extraction occupations	7,005	6,832	173
Installation, maintenance, and repair occupations	4,821	4,666	156
Production, transportation, and material moving occupations	**16,994**	**13,294**	**3,701**
Production occupations	8,455	6,109	2,346
Transportation and material moving occupations	8,540	7,185	1,355

Source: Bureau of Labor Statistics, Labor Force Statistics from the Current Population Survey, Internet site http://www.bls .gov/cps/tables.htm#empstat

Table 6.14 Occupational Distribution of Workers by Sex, 2012

(occupational distribution of employed people aged 16 or older in the civilian labor force, by sex, 2012)

	total	men	women
TOTAL EMPLOYED	**100.0%**	**100.0%**	**100.0%**
Management, professional and related occupations	**37.9**	**34.7**	**41.6**
Management, business and financial operations occupations	15.9	16.9	14.8
Management occupations	11.3	13.0	9.3
Business and financial operations occupations	4.7	3.9	5.5
Professional and related occupations	22.0	17.8	26.8
Computer and mathematical occupations	2.7	3.8	1.5
Architecture and engineering occupations	2.0	3.3	0.6
Life, physical, and social science occupations	0.9	1.0	0.9
Community and social services occupations	1.6	1.1	2.2
Legal occupations	1.3	1.2	1.3
Education, training, and library occupations	6.0	3.0	9.4
Art, design, entertainment, sports, and media occupations	2.0	1.9	2.0
Health care practitioner and technical occupations	5.6	2.6	8.9
Service occupations	**17.9**	**14.7**	**21.4**
Health care support occupations	2.5	0.6	4.6
Protective service occupations	2.2	3.2	1.0
Food preparation and serving–related occupations	5.6	4.8	6.5
Building and grounds cleaning and maintenance occupations	3.9	4.5	3.2
Personal care and service occupations	3.7	1.6	6.1
Sales and office occupations	**23.3**	**16.7**	**30.6**
Sales and related occupations	10.8	10.5	11.3
Office and administrative support occupations	12.4	6.3	19.4
Natural resources, construction, and maintenance occupations	**9.0**	**16.2**	**0.8**
Farming, fishing, and forestry occupations	0.7	1.0	0.3
Construction and extraction occupations	4.9	9.0	0.3
Installation, maintenance, and repair occupations	3.4	6.2	0.2
Production, transportation, and material moving occupations	**11.9**	**17.6**	**5.5**
Production occupations	5.9	8.1	3.5
Transportation and material moving occupations	6.0	9.5	2.0

Source: Bureau of Labor Statistics, Labor Force Statistics from the Current Population Survey, Internet site http://www.bls.gov/cps/tables.htm#empstat

Table 6.15 Distribution of Men and Women by Occupation, 2012

(percent distribution of employed people aged 16 or older in occupations by sex, 2012)

	total	men	women
TOTAL EMPLOYED	100.0%	53.0%	47.0%
Management, professional and related occupations	100.0	48.5	51.5
Management, business and financial operations occupations	100.0	56.3	43.7
Management occupations	100.0	61.4	38.6
Business and financial operations occupations	100.0	44.2	55.8
Professional and related occupations	100.0	42.8	57.2
Computer and mathematical occupations	100.0	74.4	25.6
Architecture and engineering occupations	100.0	86.3	13.7
Life, physical, and social science occupations	100.0	54.7	45.3
Community and social services occupations	100.0	36.2	63.8
Legal occupations	100.0	49.6	50.4
Education, training, and library occupations	100.0	26.4	73.6
Art, design, entertainment, sports, and media occupations	100.0	51.7	48.3
Health care practitioner and technical occupations	100.0	25.0	75.0
Service occupations	100.0	43.7	56.3
Health care support occupations	100.0	12.4	87.6
Protective service occupations	100.0	79.1	20.9
Food preparation and serving–related occupations	100.0	45.5	54.5
Building and grounds cleaning and maintenance occupations	100.0	61.3	38.6
Personal care and service occupations	100.0	22.3	77.7
Sales and office occupations	100.0	38.2	61.8
Sales and related occupations	100.0	51.3	48.7
Office and administrative support occupations	100.0	26.7	73.3
Natural resources, construction, and maintenance occupations	100.0	95.7	4.3
Farming, fishing, and forestry occupations	100.0	77.3	22.7
Construction and extraction occupations	100.0	97.5	2.5
Installation, maintenance, and repair occupations	100.0	96.8	3.2
Production, transportation, and material moving occupations	100.0	78.2	21.8
Production occupations	100.0	72.3	27.7
Transportation and material moving occupations	100.0	84.1	15.9

Source: Bureau of Labor Statistics, Labor Force Statistics from the Current Population Survey, Internet site http://www.bls.gov/cps/tables.htm#empstat

Table 6.16 Workers by Occupation, Race, and Hispanic Origin, 2012

(number of employed people aged 16 or older in the civilian labor force, by occupation, race, and Hispanic origin, 2012; numbers in thousands)

	total	Asian	black	Hispanic	non-Hispanic white
TOTAL EMPLOYED	**142,469**	**7,705**	**15,856**	**21,878**	**97,030**
Management, professional and related occupations	**54,043**	**3,735**	**4,678**	**4,516**	**41,114**
Management, business and financial operations occ.	22,678	1,305	1,766	1,940	17,667
Management occupations	16,042	814	1,114	1,410	12,704
Business and financial operations occupations	6,636	491	651	530	4,964
Professional and related occupations	31,365	2,431	2,912	2,576	23,446
Computer and mathematical occupations	3,816	666	284	234	2,632
Architecture and engineering occupations	2,846	308	159	212	2,167
Life, physical, and social science occupations	1,316	130	85	88	1,013
Community and social services occupations	2,265	71	425	251	1,518
Legal occupations	1,786	70	127	133	1,456
Education, training, and library occupations	8,543	368	814	829	6,532
Art, design, entertainment, sports, and media occ.	2,814	145	170	250	2,249
Health care practitioner and technical occupations	7,977	671	847	579	5,880
Service occupations	**25,459**	**1,415**	**4,039**	**5,754**	**14,251**
Health care support occupations	3,496	156	925	536	1,879
Protective service occupations	3,096	83	532	425	2,056
Food preparation and serving–related occupations	8,018	495	968	1,911	4,644
Building and grounds cleaning and maintenance occ.	5,591	184	839	2,020	2,548
Personal care and service occupations	5,258	497	774	862	3,125
Sales and office occupations	**33,152**	**1,564**	**3,907**	**4,650**	**23,031**
Sales and related occupations	15,457	815	1,627	2,091	10,924
Office and administrative support occupations	17,695	749	2,280	2,559	12,107
Natural resources, construction, and maintenance occupations	**12,821**	**274**	**892**	**3,268**	**8,387**
Farming, fishing, and forestry occupations	994	18	53	440	483
Construction and extraction occupations	7,005	110	434	2,027	4,434
Installation, maintenance, and repair occupations	4,821	146	405	801	3,469
Production, transportation, and material moving occupations	**16,994**	**716**	**2,341**	**3,690**	**10,247**
Production occupations	8,455	488	985	1,838	5,144
Transportation and material moving occupations	8,540	229	1,356	1,852	5,103

Note: Non-Hispanic whites are estimated by subtracting Asians, blacks, and Hispanics from the total.
Source: Bureau of Labor Statistics, Labor Force Statistics from the Current Population Survey, Internet site http://www.bls .gov/cps/tables.htm#empstat

Table 6.17 Occupational Distribution of Workers by Race and Hispanic Origin, 2012

(occupational distribution of employed people aged 16 or older by race and Hispanic origin, 2012)

	total	Asian	black	Hispanic	non-Hispanic white
TOTAL EMPLOYED	**100.0%**	**100.0%**	**100.0%**	**100.0%**	**100.0%**
Management, professional and related occupations	**37.9**	**48.5**	**29.5**	**20.6**	**42.4**
Management, business and financial operations occ.	15.9	16.9	11.1	8.9	18.2
Management occupations	11.3	10.6	7.0	6.4	13.1
Business and financial operations occupations	4.7	6.4	4.1	2.4	5.1
Professional and related occupations	22.0	31.6	18.4	11.8	24.2
Computer and mathematical occupations	2.7	8.6	1.8	1.1	2.7
Architecture and engineering occupations	2.0	4.0	1.0	1.0	2.2
Life, physical, and social science occupations	0.9	1.7	0.5	0.4	1.0
Community and social services occupations	1.6	0.9	2.7	1.1	1.6
Legal occupations	1.3	0.9	0.8	0.6	1.5
Education, training, and library occupations	6.0	4.8	5.1	3.8	6.7
Art, design, entertainment, sports, and media occupations	2.0	1.9	1.1	1.1	2.3
Health care practitioner and technical occupations	5.6	8.7	5.3	2.6	6.1
Service occupations	**17.9**	**18.4**	**25.5**	**26.3**	**14.7**
Health care support occupations	2.5	2.0	5.8	2.4	1.9
Protective service occupations	2.2	1.1	3.4	1.9	2.1
Food preparation and serving–related occupations	5.6	6.4	6.1	8.7	4.8
Building and grounds cleaning and maintenance occ.	3.9	2.4	5.3	9.2	2.6
Personal care and service occupations	3.7	6.5	4.9	3.9	3.2
Sales and office occupations	**23.3**	**20.3**	**24.6**	**21.3**	**23.7**
Sales and related occupations	10.8	10.6	10.3	9.6	11.3
Office and administrative support occupations	12.4	9.7	14.4	11.7	12.5
Natural resources, construction, and maintenance occupations	**9.0**	**3.6**	**5.6**	**14.9**	**8.6**
Farming, fishing, and forestry occupations	0.7	0.2	0.3	2.0	0.5
Construction and extraction occupations	4.9	1.4	2.7	9.3	4.6
Installation, maintenance, and repair occupations	3.4	1.9	2.6	3.7	3.6
Production, transportation, and material moving occupations	**11.9**	**9.3**	**14.8**	**16.9**	**10.6**
Production occupations	5.9	6.3	6.2	8.4	5.3
Transportation and material moving occupations	6.0	3.0	8.6	8.5	5.3

Note: Non-Hispanic whites are estimated by subtracting Asians, blacks, and Hispanics from the total.
Source: Bureau of Labor Statistics, Labor Force Statistics from the Current Population Survey, Internet site http://www.bls
.gov/cps/tables.htm#empstat

Table 6.18 Race and Hispanic Origin Distributions of Occupations, 2012

(percent distribution by occupation of employed people aged 16 or older by race and Hispanic origin, 2012)

	total	Asian	black	Hispanic	non-Hispanic white
TOTAL EMPLOYED	**100.0%**	**5.4%**	**11.1%**	**15.4%**	**68.1%**
Management, professional and related occupations	**100.0**	**6.9**	**8.7**	**8.4**	**76.1**
Management, business and financial operations occ.	100.0	5.8	7.8	8.6	77.9
Management occupations	100.0	5.1	6.9	8.8	79.2
Business and financial operations occupations	100.0	7.4	9.8	8.0	74.8
Professional and related occupations	100.0	7.8	9.3	8.2	74.8
Computer and mathematical occupations	100.0	17.5	7.4	6.1	69.0
Architecture and engineering occupations	100.0	10.8	5.6	7.4	76.1
Life, physical, and social science occupations	100.0	9.9	6.5	6.7	77.0
Community and social services occupations	100.0	3.1	18.8	11.1	67.0
Legal occupations	100.0	3.9	7.1	7.4	81.5
Education, training, and library occupations	100.0	4.3	9.5	9.7	76.5
Art, design, entertainment, sports, and media occ.	100.0	5.2	6.0	8.9	79.9
Health care practitioner and technical occupations	100.0	8.4	10.6	7.3	73.7
Service occupations	**100.0**	**5.6**	**15.9**	**22.6**	**56.0**
Health care support occupations	100.0	4.5	26.5	15.3	53.7
Protective service occupations	100.0	2.7	17.2	13.7	66.4
Food preparation and serving–related occupations	100.0	6.2	12.1	23.8	57.9
Building and grounds cleaning and maintenance occ.	100.0	3.3	15.0	36.1	45.6
Personal care and service occupations	100.0	9.5	14.7	16.4	59.4
Sales and office occupations	**100.0**	**4.7**	**11.8**	**14.0**	**69.5**
Sales and related occupations	100.0	5.3	10.5	13.5	70.7
Office and administrative support occupations	100.0	4.2	12.9	14.5	68.4
Natural resources, construction, and maintenance occupations	**100.0**	**2.1**	**7.0**	**25.5**	**65.4**
Farming, fishing, and forestry occupations	100.0	1.8	5.3	44.3	48.6
Construction and extraction occupations	100.0	1.6	6.2	28.9	63.3
Installation, maintenance, and repair occupations	100.0	3.0	8.4	16.6	72.0
Production, transportation, and material moving occupations	**100.0**	**4.2**	**13.8**	**21.7**	**60.3**
Production occupations	100.0	5.8	11.6	21.7	60.8
Transportation and material moving occupations	100.0	2.7	15.9	21.7	59.8

Note: Non-Hispanic whites are estimated by subtracting Asians, blacks, and Hispanics from the total.
Source: Bureau of Labor Statistics, Labor Force Statistics from the Current Population Survey, Internet site http://www.bls
.gov/cps/tables.htm#empstat

Table 6.19 Workers by Detailed Occupation, Sex, Race, and Hispanic Origin, 2012

(percentage of employed civilians aged 16 or older who are women, Asians, blacks, or Hispanics, by selected detailed occupation, 2012)

	women	Asian	black	Hispanic	non-Hispanic white
TOTAL EMPLOYED	**47.0%**	**5.4%**	**11.1%**	**15.4%**	**68.1%**
Management, professional, and related occupations	**51.5**	**6.9**	**8.7**	**8.4**	**76.0**
Management, business and financial operations occupations	43.6	5.8	7.8	8.6	77.8
Management occupations	38.6	5.1	6.9	8.8	79.2
Chief executives	27.4	4.2	3.7	4.7	87.4
General and operations managers	29.1	4.7	6.2	9.3	79.8
Advertising and promotions managers	49.4	4.3	6.7	10.0	79.0
Marketing and sales managers	45.2	6.0	4.2	6.1	83.7
Public relations and fundraising managers	69.3	3.4	5.8	8.0	82.8
Administrative services managers	44.1	4.4	6.4	9.5	79.7
Computer and information systems managers	26.8	14.5	5.6	5.8	74.1
Financial managers	53.5	5.7	8.6	10.3	75.4
Human resources managers	72.7	2.4	11.3	9.5	76.8
Industrial production managers	17.6	5.1	3.4	11.4	80.1
Purchasing managers	50.9	4.6	8.4	10.4	76.6
Transportation, storage, and distribution managers	15.6	3.3	11.1	11.3	74.3
Farmers, ranchers, and other agricultural managers	24.5	1.2	0.8	4.0	94.0
Construction managers	6.4	2.2	3.7	9.4	84.7
Education administrators	64.4	2.2	13.8	7.9	76.1
Architectural and engineering managers	10.9	7.7	2.8	2.9	86.6
Food service managers	47.2	9.5	8.8	16.5	65.2
Lodging managers	45.0	13.9	8.0	11.5	66.6
Medical and health services managers	69.7	5.1	10.9	8.1	75.9
Property, real estate, and community association managers	50.7	3.4	8.5	11.4	76.7
Social and community service managers	70.5	3.7	14.6	8.5	73.2
Managers, all other	35.0	5.0	7.3	9.3	78.4
Business and financial operations occupations	55.8	7.4	9.8	8.0	74.8
Wholesale and retail buyers, except farm products	55.2	7.7	7.1	10.9	74.3
Purchasing agents, except wholesale, retail, and farm products	55.1	4.4	6.1	9.8	79.7
Claims adjusters, appraisers, examiners, and investigators	63.4	3.1	17.5	10.3	69.1
Compliance officers	50.6	3.3	9.1	8.2	79.4
Cost estimators	11.7	2.0	1.5	6.8	89.7
Human resources workers	71.8	4.4	15.4	11.8	68.4
Compensation, benefits, and job analysis specialists	81.1	4.2	6.9	11.8	77.1
Training and development specialists	56.4	0.8	15.9	10.8	72.5
Logisticians	36.8	2.2	12.3	11.9	73.6
Management analysts	39.8	8.8	6.8	4.4	80.0
Meeting, convention, and event planners	73.3	4.2	8.1	10.3	77.4
Fundraisers	75.3	4.6	5.1	3.4	86.9
Market research analysts and marketing specialists	54.2	9.1	5.4	4.7	80.8
Business operations specialists, all other	67.3	5.6	14.2	9.2	71.0
Accountants and auditors	60.9	12.0	9.7	6.8	71.5
Appraisers and assessors of real estate	40.6	2.7	9.8	1.0	86.5
Budget analysts	52.5	8.7	11.5	8.2	71.6
Financial analysts	36.8	9.0	3.7	6.3	81.0

	women	Asian	black	Hispanic	non-Hispanic white
Personal financial advisors	31.2%	6.2%	4.8%	4.5%	84.5%
Insurance underwriters	70.4	0.7	10.7	10.2	78.4
Credit counselors and loan officers	59.2	6.0	13.2	9.3	71.5
Tax examiners and collectors, and revenue agents	62.4	11.5	13.9	13.9	60.7
Tax preparers	59.6	7.1	10.4	15.9	66.6
Financial specialists, all other	66.5	8.4	10.9	11.5	69.2
Professional and related occupations	57.2	7.8	9.3	8.2	74.7
Computer and mathematical occupations	25.6	17.5	7.4	6.1	69.0
Computer systems analysts	30.9	15.8	8.8	4.5	70.9
Information security analysts	15.1	14.2	11.8	4.0	70.0
Computer programmers	22.5	17.3	5.9	5.3	71.5
Software developers, applications and systems software	19.7	29.4	4.0	5.2	61.4
Web developers	33.7	8.0	4.1	5.6	82.3
Computer support specialists	27.1	7.7	12.0	9.7	70.6
Database administrators	36.6	10.0	4.1	9.8	76.1
Network and computer systems administrators	25.0	11.0	10.0	10.7	68.3
Computer network architects	8.1	14.6	10.0	4.6	70.8
Computer occupations, all other	24.4	11.7	11.4	5.9	71.0
Operations research analysts	54.9	9.3	8.3	6.5	75.9
Architecture and engineering occupations	13.7	10.8	5.6	7.4	76.2
Architects, except naval	23.5	6.2	1.3	8.2	84.3
Surveyors, cartographers, and photogrammetrists	27.8	5.4	4.3	8.1	82.2
Aerospace engineers	9.0	13.4	1.8	4.6	80.2
Chemical engineers	17.7	9.3	5.9	6.7	78.1
Civil engineers	13.7	9.0	5.4	3.7	81.9
Computer hardware engineers	15.1	20.8	8.5	6.5	64.2
Electrical and electronics engineers	9.0	16.6	3.5	6.7	73.2
Industrial engineers, including health and safety	18.8	9.6	6.2	10.5	73.7
Mechanical engineers	4.5	12.3	6.3	4.9	76.5
Engineers, all other	13.2	15.4	3.9	5.9	74.8
Drafters	16.6	7.7	3.0	9.9	79.4
Engineering technicians, except drafters	16.3	5.0	10.8	12.3	71.9
Surveying and mapping technicians	4.3	2.5	5.3	13.5	78.7
Life, physical, and social science occupations	45.3	9.9	6.5	6.7	76.9
Biological scientists	50.1	11.7	3.7	7.2	77.4
Medical scientists	52.8	22.4	5.3	5.8	66.5
Chemists and materials scientists	44.2	9.2	4.0	9.4	77.4
Environmental scientists and geoscientists	25.7	1.3	7.0	1.7	90.0
Physical scientists, all other	35.1	20.4	2.7	3.8	73.1
Psychologists	72.7	3.9	6.0	6.3	83.8
Miscellaneous social scientists and related workers	54.3	5.5	10.8	7.0	76.7
Chemical technicians	29.9	4.8	15.4	7.4	72.4
Miscellaneous life, physical, and social science technicians	52.8	14.4	12.8	10.4	62.4
Community and social service occupations	63.8	3.2	18.8	11.1	66.9
Counselors	69.3	2.9	19.4	10.7	67.0
Social workers	80.6	3.1	23.0	12.6	61.3
Probation officers and correctional treatment specialists	47.5	1.3	20.7	15.0	63.0
Social and human service assistants	77.1	3.8	24.4	15.5	56.3
Miscellaneous community and social service specialists, including health educators and community health workers	75.7	2.4	16.9	18.4	62.3

	women	Asian	black	Hispanic	non-Hispanic white
Clergy	20.5%	4.2%	11.2%	6.1%	78.5%
Directors, religious activities and education	66.3	2.1	7.4	5.9	84.6
Religious workers, all other	62.4	2.8	10.0	8.9	78.3
Legal occupations	50.4	3.9	7.1	7.4	81.6
Lawyers	31.1	4.3	4.4	4.0	87.3
Judges, magistrates, and other judicial workers	39.0	0.7	12.8	4.5	82.0
Paralegals and legal assistants	85.9	4.6	10.7	17.0	67.7
Miscellaneous legal support workers	79.0	1.4	11.9	7.0	79.7
Education, training, and library occupations	73.6	4.3	9.5	9.7	76.5
Postsecondary teachers	48.2	11.3	7.9	6.2	74.6
Preschool and kindergarten teachers	98.1	4.2	11.8	12.0	72.0
Elementary and middle school teachers	81.4	2.1	9.8	10.3	77.8
Secondary school teachers	57.3	3.1	6.0	7.6	83.3
Special education teachers	86.2	1.1	6.9	9.4	82.6
Other teachers and instructors	65.6	5.9	10.7	9.5	73.9
Librarians	86.8	2.5	7.9	2.8	86.8
Teacher assistants	91.1	2.7	14.5	15.7	67.1
Other education, training, and library workers	67.3	2.5	11.7	11.8	74.0
Arts, design, entertainment, sports, and media occupations	48.3	5.2	6.0	8.9	79.9
Artists and related workers	51.6	9.3	4.0	6.6	80.1
Designers	55.3	5.9	3.9	8.9	81.3
Producers and directors	40.8	3.3	8.2	4.9	83.6
Athletes, coaches, umpires, and related workers	36.5	1.4	6.4	9.0	83.2
Musicians, singers, and related workers	35.5	2.8	10.9	6.7	79.6
Announcers	23.6	8.3	12.0	15.3	64.4
News analysts, reporters, and correspondents	45.7	6.1	9.2	5.9	78.8
Public relations specialists	58.2	5.8	7.3	8.0	78.9
Editors	50.7	3.2	4.8	6.5	85.5
Technical writers	55.5	6.7	2.7	3.7	86.9
Writers and authors	55.6	4.2	5.4	2.9	87.5
Miscellaneous media and communication workers	79.2	15.0	5.6	35.0	44.4
Broadcast and sound engineering technicians and radio operators	8.4	1.6	4.1	12.6	81.7
Photographers	52.2	4.3	6.2	10.7	78.8
Television, video, and motion picture camera operators and editors	21.4	5.6	4.4	10.7	79.3
Health care practitioners and technical occupations	75.0	8.4	10.6	7.3	73.7
Chiropractors	22.3	3.5	0.0	4.0	92.5
Dentists	24.2	10.6	1.7	2.5	85.2
Dietitians and nutritionists	93.3	5.1	13.7	7.2	74.0
Pharmacists	53.7	18.5	6.8	5.1	69.6
Physicians and surgeons	34.3	18.1	7.2	5.2	69.5
Physician assistants	69.4	9.0	8.2	8.8	74.0
Occupational therapists	94.0	4.0	2.5	5.8	87.7
Physical therapists	70.7	9.1	4.4	9.4	77.1
Respiratory therapists	60.4	5.6	12.1	10.6	71.7
Speech–language pathologists	95.2	1.7	3.1	8.3	86.9
Therapists, all other	83.6	2.9	10.3	8.7	78.1
Veterinarians	54.7	1.3	1.9	6.1	90.7
Registered nurses	90.6	7.3	11.5	6.2	75.0
Nurse practitioners	86.1	4.6	4.5	2.9	88.0

	women	Asian	black	Hispanic	non-Hispanic white
Clinical laboratory technologists and technicians	72.8%	14.0%	13.5%	10.7%	61.8%
Dental hygienists	99.3	5.6	3.3	8.1	83.0
Diagnostic-related technologists and technicians	74.5	4.1	9.0	7.8	79.1
Emergency medical technicians and paramedics	31.2	1.6	5.0	8.1	85.3
Health practitioner support technologists and technicians	83.6	5.9	15.8	12.2	66.1
Licensed practical and licensed vocational nurses	94.2	5.1	23.3	9.4	62.2
Medical records and health information technicians	89.3	4.3	17.1	15.6	63.0
Opticians, dispensing	59.6	3.8	8.2	4.1	83.9
Miscellaneous health technologists and technicians	60.2	11.0	18.7	10.0	60.3
Other health care practitioners and technical occupations	50.3	3.1	8.8	5.6	82.5
Service occupations	**56.3**	**5.6**	**15.9**	**22.6**	**55.9**
Health care support occupations	87.6	4.5	26.5	15.3	53.7
Nursing, psychiatric, and home health aides	87.9	4.6	34.5	14.2	46.7
Physical therapist assistants and aides	66.4	3.6	14.7	5.6	76.1
Massage therapists	81.5	7.7	5.4	12.0	74.9
Dental assistants	97.9	3.6	9.6	21.2	65.6
Medical assistants	93.8	3.8	15.0	22.9	58.3
Medical transcriptionists	98.2	0.3	7.0	4.0	88.7
Phlebotomists	80.2	4.8	26.5	15.7	53.0
Miscellaneous health care support occupations, including medical equipment preparers	69.0	4.0	21.9	9.9	64.2
Protective service occupations	20.9	2.7	17.2	13.7	66.4
First-line supervisors of police and detectives	15.2	4.4	9.2	10.6	75.8
First-line supervisors of fire fighting and prevention workers	0.5	0.0	10.7	6.6	82.7
First-line supervisors of protective service workers, all other	29.9	0.4	17.4	12.5	69.7
Firefighters	3.4	1.1	7.7	9.9	81.3
Bailiffs, correctional officers, and jailers	28.0	1.1	22.7	18.3	57.9
Detectives and criminal investigators	24.8	3.5	9.8	10.4	76.3
Police and sheriff's patrol officers	12.6	3.1	12.8	13.8	70.3
Private detectives and investigators	44.0	2.2	8.0	11.1	78.7
Security guards and gaming surveillance officers	18.5	4.1	26.6	15.8	53.5
Crossing guards	55.3	1.8	19.7	16.1	62.4
Lifeguards and other recreational, and all other protective service workers	52.6	1.2	7.8	9.2	81.8
Food preparation and serving–related occupations	54.5	6.2	12.1	23.8	57.9
Chefs and head cooks	21.5	14.2	11.9	18.6	55.3
First-line supervisors of food preparation and serving workers	59.3	4.0	13.9	17.2	64.9
Cooks	37.7	6.0	16.6	31.7	45.7
Food preparation workers	58.0	5.7	12.1	27.5	54.7
Bartenders	59.9	3.5	5.2	13.2	78.1
Combined food preparation and serving workers, including fast food	64.9	3.1	14.1	18.0	64.8
Counter attendants, cafeteria, food concession, and coffee shop	70.8	4.8	10.9	16.6	67.7
Waiters and waitresses	71.2	7.1	7.9	19.6	65.4
Food servers, nonrestaurant	64.9	6.4	22.2	20.1	51.3
Dining room and cafeteria attendants and bartender helpers	43.4	5.5	10.0	31.7	52.8
Dishwashers	18.7	5.5	12.9	40.5	41.1
Hosts and hostesses, restaurant, lounge, and coffee shop	81.5	5.4	10.2	14.8	69.6

	women	Asian	black	Hispanic	non-Hispanic white
Building and grounds cleaning and maintenance occupations	38.6%	3.3%	15.0%	36.1%	45.6%
First-line supervisors of housekeeping and janitorial workers	47.1	3.3	16.9	21.7	58.1
First-line supervisors of landscaping, lawn service, and groundskeeping workers	7.6	1.1	6.6	19.8	72.5
Janitors and building cleaners	29.7	3.6	18.4	30.9	47.1
Maids and housekeeping cleaners	88.1	4.8	17.2	43.3	34.7
Pest control workers	4.7	0.1	7.7	20.4	71.8
Grounds maintenance workers	5.1	1.7	8.7	44.4	45.2
Personal care and service occupations	77.7	9.5	14.7	16.4	59.4
First-line supervisors of gaming workers	43.0	9.2	5.2	10.1	75.5
First-line supervisors of personal service workers	70.3	19.8	10.7	9.3	60.2
Nonfarm animal caretakers	74.2	1.8	4.3	12.2	81.7
Gaming services workers	51.0	24.3	9.4	13.5	52.8
Miscellaneous entertainment attendants and related workers	45.4	5.1	14.0	17.6	63.3
Barbers	21.9	2.5	38.2	24.1	35.2
Hairdressers, hairstylists, and cosmetologists	92.8	6.5	13.2	15.0	65.3
Miscellaneous personal appearance workers	81.5	59.6	5.3	9.5	25.6
Baggage porters, bellhops, and concierges	25.0	13.1	20.8	18.0	48.1
Tour and travel guides	36.9	7.1	3.6	15.1	74.2
Childcare workers	94.1	3.3	15.3	20.3	61.1
Personal care aides	84.7	7.9	21.8	21.2	49.1
Recreation and fitness workers	66.5	4.5	10.0	9.7	75.8
Residential advisors	61.4	1.4	29.1	5.4	64.1
Personal care and service workers, all other	45.7	3.3	5.5	17.5	73.7
Sales and office occupations	**61.8**	**4.7**	**11.8**	**14.0**	**69.5**
Sales and related occupations	48.7	5.3	10.5	13.5	70.7
First-line supervisors of retail sales workers	43.4	5.9	8.6	11.3	74.2
First-line supervisors of nonretail sales workers	24.7	5.0	7.2	10.4	77.4
Cashiers	71.8	7.3	17.2	19.9	55.6
Counter and rental clerks	53.4	5.2	8.9	19.6	66.3
Parts salespersons	13.3	4.1	8.3	12.3	75.3
Retail salespersons	50.2	4.4	12.5	15.3	67.8
Advertising sales agents	47.4	2.3	9.9	7.6	80.2
Insurance sales agents	44.1	1.8	8.1	10.3	79.8
Securities, commodities, and financial services sales agents	27.9	8.3	3.4	8.9	79.4
Travel agents	79.0	9.3	2.5	4.8	83.4
Sales representatives, services, all other	31.0	3.7	7.9	10.1	78.3
Sales representatives, wholesale and manufacturing	27.0	3.7	3.7	9.4	83.2
Models, demonstrators, and product promoters	83.4	4.0	19.4	10.6	66.0
Real estate brokers and sales agents	57.1	4.7	4.0	8.7	82.6
Telemarketers	50.3	1.1	23.0	14.7	61.2
Door-to-door sales workers, news and street vendors, and related workers	62.2	3.8	10.2	13.5	72.5
Sales and related workers, all other	47.9	4.7	7.7	10.3	77.3
Office and administrative support occupations	73.3	4.2	12.9	14.5	68.4
First-line supervisors of office and administrative support workers	68.5	3.5	11.3	11.9	73.3
Bill and account collectors	69.1	3.6	15.3	17.6	63.5
Billing and posting clerks	90.1	4.0	11.8	16.2	68.0
Bookkeeping, accounting, and auditing clerks	89.1	5.0	7.6	9.0	78.4

	women	Asian	black	Hispanic	non-Hispanic white
Payroll and timekeeping clerks	92.6%	4.6%	9.5%	15.1%	70.8%
Tellers	87.3	5.7	11.6	18.6	64.1
Financial clerks, all other	68.4	4.1	17.1	16.6	62.2
Court, municipal, and license clerks	77.2	1.2	23.0	13.4	62.4
Customer service representatives	67.8	4.2	16.2	18.0	61.6
Eligibility interviewers, government programs	81.4	2.1	19.8	23.1	55.0
File clerks	81.3	4.6	14.1	16.4	64.9
Hotel, motel, and resort desk clerks	64.6	6.3	18.4	18.6	56.7
Interviewers, except eligibility and loan	83.7	6.0	20.0	12.1	61.9
Library assistants, clerical	84.0	3.2	7.0	5.8	84.0
Loan interviewers and clerks	81.2	4.0	10.9	10.4	74.7
Order clerks	58.2	4.1	5.8	21.3	68.8
Human resources assistants, except payroll and timekeeping	82.7	1.9	18.3	7.9	71.9
Receptionists and information clerks	91.5	4.3	12.1	17.9	65.7
Reservation and transportation ticket agents and travel clerks	58.6	10.9	21.8	21.5	45.8
Information and record clerks, all other	80.2	2.5	17.0	13.4	67.1
Couriers and messengers	15.5	2.4	13.0	16.9	67.7
Dispatchers	61.5	2.3	13.5	16.7	67.5
Postal service clerks	50.0	9.5	21.3	12.0	57.2
Postal service mail carriers	37.7	6.7	16.5	8.8	68.0
Postal service mail sorters, processors, and processing machine operators	47.6	12.7	28.6	9.8	48.9
Production, planning, and expediting clerks	55.0	3.2	11.0	12.5	73.3
Shipping, receiving, and traffic clerks	27.8	3.6	15.6	23.7	57.1
Stock clerks and order fillers	35.5	4.5	16.7	18.1	60.7
Weighers, measurers, checkers, and samplers, recordkeeping	49.1	2.8	19.9	21.9	55.4
Secretaries and administrative assistants	95.3	3.2	8.6	10.3	77.9
Computer operators	50.7	6.5	12.2	10.7	70.6
Data entry keyers	77.0	5.1	14.0	13.8	67.1
Word processors and typists	88.7	2.8	12.4	12.9	71.9
Insurance claims and policy processing clerks	81.9	3.6	12.7	13.7	70.0
Mail clerks and mail machine operators, except postal service	41.2	10.6	18.1	10.1	61.2
Office clerks, general	83.4	5.0	12.4	16.9	65.7
Office and administrative support workers, all other	77.3	3.9	14.1	11.0	71.0
Natural resources, construction, and maintenance occupations	**4.3**	**2.1**	**7.0**	**25.5**	**65.4**
Farming, fishing, and forestry occupations	22.7	1.8	5.3	44.2	48.7
First-line supervisors of farming, fishing, and forestry workers	14.1	4.2	7.8	23.9	64.1
Graders and sorters, agricultural products	59.8	2.1	16.6	58.0	23.3
Miscellaneous agricultural workers	18.9	1.5	3.2	48.9	46.4
Construction and extraction occupations	2.5	1.6	6.2	28.9	63.3
First-line supervisors of construction trades and extraction workers	2.8	1.3	4.5	14.0	80.2
Brickmasons, blockmasons, and stonemasons	0.1	0.3	5.8	43.2	50.7
Carpenters	1.6	1.9	4.2	29.0	64.9
Carpet, floor, and tile installers and finishers	2.2	0.4	8.8	37.8	53.0
Cement masons, concrete finishers, and terrazzo workers	2.7	3.1	5.8	53.3	37.8
Construction laborers	2.9	2.0	8.4	41.2	48.4

	women	Asian	black	Hispanic	non-Hispanic white
Operating engineers and other construction equipment operators	1.3%	0.2%	6.0%	17.1%	76.7%
Drywall installers, ceiling tile installers, and tapers	0.3	0.0	2.7	62.0	35.3
Electricians	1.8	2.3	6.0	14.8	76.9
Painters, construction and maintenance	5.5	2.0	5.5	42.6	49.9
Pipelayers, plumbers, pipefitters, and steamfitters	1.3	1.5	6.6	20.9	71.0
Roofers	1.5	0.5	7.0	45.1	47.4
Sheet metal workers	4.6	1.7	3.2	12.1	83.0
Structural iron and steel workers	2.8	0.0	6.5	15.8	77.7
Helpers, construction trades	4.5	1.3	12.1	38.4	48.2
Construction and building inspectors	7.8	2.1	5.5	7.7	84.7
Highway maintenance workers	1.5	0.1	11.0	12.4	76.5
Mining machine operators	0.3	0.0	3.8	17.2	79.0
Other extraction workers	4.5	1.0	5.6	26.2	67.2
Installation, maintenance, and repair occupations	3.2	3.0	8.4	16.6	72.0
First-line supervisors of mechanics, installers, and repairers	5.9	1.0	11.3	10.4	77.3
Computer, automated teller, and office machine repairers	10.7	7.2	10.8	9.9	72.1
Radio and telecommunications equipment installers and repairers	5.8	3.2	11.2	13.8	71.8
Electronic home entertainment equipment installers and repairers	0.5	4.3	11.6	13.2	70.9
Aircraft mechanics and service technicians	1.6	5.4	7.5	14.3	72.8
Automotive body and related repairers	1.8	2.3	5.7	25.3	66.7
Automotive service technicians and mechanics	1.2	4.7	9.6	21.3	64.4
Bus and truck mechanics and diesel engine specialists	0.5	1.3	8.6	13.4	76.7
Heavy vehicle and mobile equipment service technicians and mechanics	1.0	2.0	5.4	17.3	75.3
Small engine mechanics	1.4	0.2	4.9	12.2	82.7
Miscellaneous vehicle and mobile equipment mechanics, installers, and repairers	1.8	0.0	8.0	31.4	60.6
Heating, air conditioning, and refrigeration mechanics and installers	1.6	3.2	7.1	16.2	73.5
Industrial and refractory machinery mechanics	1.9	2.9	4.5	13.3	79.3
Maintenance and repair workers, general	2.2	3.2	8.4	19.4	69.0
Millwrights	6.4	1.4	2.1	6.7	89.8
Electrical power-line installers and repairers	2.4	0.3	7.8	7.9	84.0
Telecommunications line installers and repairers	4.8	1.9	11.2	15.7	71.2
Precision instrument and equipment repairers	16.0	1.1	9.1	13.3	76.5
Other installation, maintenance, and repair workers	3.6	1.4	5.9	21.2	71.5
Production, transportation, and material moving occupations	**21.8**	**4.2**	**13.8**	**21.7**	**60.3**
Production occupations	27.7	5.8	11.6	21.7	60.9
First-line supervisors of production and operating workers	19.5	5.8	9.4	13.9	70.9
Electrical, electronics, and electromechanical assemblers	52.8	16.3	13.4	24.0	46.3
Miscellaneous assemblers and fabricators	38.4	6.9	15.8	19.3	58.0
Bakers	53.9	5.1	15.6	28.4	50.9
Butchers and other meat, poultry, and fish processing workers	23.0	7.9	13.5	41.6	37.0
Food batchmakers	59.6	5.7	12.2	33.5	48.6
Food processing workers, all other	29.5	5.9	15.9	34.6	43.6
Computer control programmers and operators	8.4	3.3	6.4	17.1	73.2

	women	Asian	black	Hispanic	non-Hispanic white
Cutting, punching, and press machine setters, operators, and tenders, metal and plastic	18.9%	3.3%	8.4%	22.9%	65.4%
Grinding, lapping, polishing, and buffing machine tool setters, operators, and tenders, metal and plastic	6.6	0.7	13.7	21.8	63.8
Machinists	3.8	4.9	4.5	11.7	78.9
Tool and die makers	0.8	5.6	3.1	4.3	87.0
Welding, soldering, and brazing workers	4.8	2.6	8.7	23.0	65.7
Metal workers and plastic workers, all other	19.5	6.6	14.4	26.0	53.0
Printing press operators	17.2	3.4	10.1	15.6	70.9
Laundry and dry-cleaning workers	53.3	10.3	20.8	37.1	31.8
Pressers, textile, garment, and related materials	70.6	3.5	17.0	47.9	31.6
Sewing machine operators	74.2	11.4	5.6	43.8	39.2
Tailors, dressmakers, and sewers	77.1	19.5	5.9	24.9	49.7
Stationary engineers and boiler operators	5.5	4.3	10.4	13.8	71.5
Water and wastewater treatment plant and system operators	4.5	1.7	8.4	19.6	70.3
Chemical processing machine setters, operators, and tenders	16.2	0.8	4.5	10.7	84.0
Crushing, grinding, polishing, mixing, and blending workers	15.0	6.8	14.5	18.4	60.3
Cutting workers	19.2	3.5	14.1	15.8	66.6
Inspectors, testers, sorters, samplers, and weighers	33.4	6.7	11.5	13.6	68.2
Medical, dental, and ophthalmic laboratory technicians	50.7	8.9	1.6	15.9	73.6
Packaging and filling machine operators and tenders	52.3	8.8	14.1	38.0	39.1
Painting workers	15.1	4.3	5.7	34.9	55.1
Photographic process workers and processing machine operators	45.6	4.9	13.3	18.7	63.1
Helpers—production workers	34.8	2.9	19.8	30.6	46.7
Production workers, all other	26.3	4.0	13.7	21.5	60.8
Transportation and material moving occupations	15.9	2.7	15.9	21.7	59.7
Supervisors of transportation and material moving workers	23.0	4.4	13.5	18.4	63.7
Aircraft pilots and flight engineers	4.1	2.5	2.7	5.0	89.8
Flight attendants	77.6	5.9	11.8	10.5	71.8
Bus drivers	45.5	2.3	25.3	12.9	59.5
Driver/sales workers and truck drivers	5.4	1.6	14.0	19.3	65.1
Taxi drivers and chauffeurs	13.2	13.8	24.8	16.0	45.4
Motor vehicle operators, all other	13.3	1.4	14.4	10.5	73.7
Railroad conductors and yardmasters	5.6	0.7	16.2	12.5	70.6
Parking lot attendants	11.6	5.3	23.5	35.5	35.7
Automotive and watercraft service attendants	9.2	5.2	12.9	12.5	69.4
Crane and tower operators	4.0	0.9	12.3	12.2	74.6
Industrial truck and tractor operators	7.4	1.6	18.4	31.3	48.7
Cleaners of vehicles and equipment	15.2	2.7	16.8	35.9	44.6
Laborers and freight, stock, and material movers, hand	18.7	2.5	15.9	23.0	58.6
Packers and packagers, hand	53.1	3.5	14.0	42.0	40.5
Refuse and recyclable material collectors	6.6	1.4	24.9	29.4	44.3

Note: Non-Hispanic whites are estimated by subtracting Asians, blacks, and Hispanics from the total.
Source: Bureau of Labor Statistics, Labor Force Statistics from the Current Population Survey, Internet site http://www.bls
.gov/cps/tables.htm#empstat; calculations by New Strategist

One in Four Men Works in Manufacturing or Construction

More than one-third of women work in the educational and health services industry.

While women account for slightly less than half of all workers, the share varies greatly by industry. In some industries, workers are overwhelmingly female, while in others women account for few of the employed. Women account for just 9 percent of workers in the construction industry and 29 percent of workers in the manufacturing industry, for example. But they are 74 percent of workers in the educational and health services industry, which includes teachers and nurses.

Men dominate a number of industries. They account for 91 percent of construction industry workers, 87 percent of those employed in the mining industry, and 71 percent of workers in the manufacturing industry.

■ The rapid growth of the educational and health services industry over the past few decades has drawn millions of women into the workforce.

Women dominate educational and health services, men manufacturing and construction

(percent distribution of workers in selected industries, by sex, 2012)

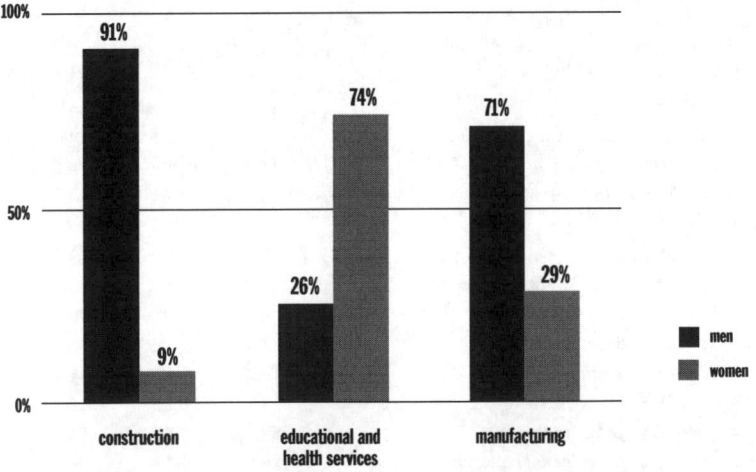

Table 6.20 Workers by Industry and Sex, 2012

(number, percent distribution, and share of employed aged 16 or older by industry and sex, 2012; numbers in thousands)

	total	men			women		
		number	percent distribution	share of total	number	percent distribution	share of total
TOTAL EMPLOYED	**142,469**	**75,555**	**100.0%**	**53.0%**	**66,914**	**100.0%**	**47.0%**
Agriculture, forestry, fishing, and hunting	2,186	1,626	2.2	74.4	560	0.8	25.6
Mining	957	831	1.1	86.8	126	0.2	13.2
Construction	8,964	8,162	10.8	91.1	802	1.2	8.9
Manufacturing	14,686	10,432	13.8	71.0	4,255	6.4	29.0
Durable goods	9,244	6,932	9.2	75.0	2,311	3.5	25.0
Nondurable goods	5,443	3,499	4.6	64.3	1,943	2.9	35.7
Wholesale/retail trade	19,876	11,004	14.6	55.4	8,871	13.3	44.6
Wholesale trade	3,694	2,638	3.5	71.4	1,056	1.6	28.6
Retail trade	16,182	8,367	11.1	51.7	7,815	11.7	48.3
Transportation and utilities	7,271	5,581	7.4	76.8	1,691	2.5	23.3
Information	2,971	1,838	2.4	61.9	1,134	1.7	38.2
Financial activities	9,590	4,482	5.9	46.7	5,108	7.6	53.3
Professional and business services	16,539	9,741	12.9	58.9	6,798	10.2	41.1
Educational and health services	32,350	8,263	10.9	25.5	24,087	36.0	74.5
Leisure and hospitality	13,193	6,487	8.6	49.2	6,706	10.0	50.8
Other services	7,168	3,439	4.6	48.0	3,728	5.6	52.0
Other services except private households	6,430	3,357	4.4	52.2	3,072	4.6	47.8
Private households	738	82	0.1	11.1	656	1.0	88.9
Public administration	6,717	3,669	4.9	54.6	3,048	4.6	45.4

Source: Bureau of Labor Statistics, Labor Force Statistics from the Current Population Survey, Internet site http://www.bls .gov/cps/tables.htm#empstat

Job Tenure Has Increased

A growing share of older workers have been with their current employer for 10 or more years.

The number of years the average worker has been with his or her current employer has increased. Overall, workers aged 25 or older had been with their current employer for a median of 5.4 years in 2012, up from 4.7 years in 2000. Behind the rise in job tenure is the aging of the labor force and the postponement of retirement among older men. Median job tenure for men aged 65 or older climbed from 9.0 to 10.2 years between 2000 and 2012.

Long-term employment (defined as 10 or more years) has dropped among middle-aged men and women, but has soared in the older age groups as workers postpone retirement. Among men ranging in age from 35 to 49, the share with a long-term job fell 3 to 4 percentage points between 2000 and 2012. But among men aged 55 or older, the share with a long-term job increased. Among men aged 65 or older, the figure climbed from 49 to well over 50 percent. Long-term employment also climbed among older women.

■ The rise in long-term employment among older Americans is evidence of an end to early retirement.

Long-term employment has increased sharply among men aged 65 or older

(percentage of men aged 65 or older who have been with their current employer for 10 or more years, 2000 and 2012)

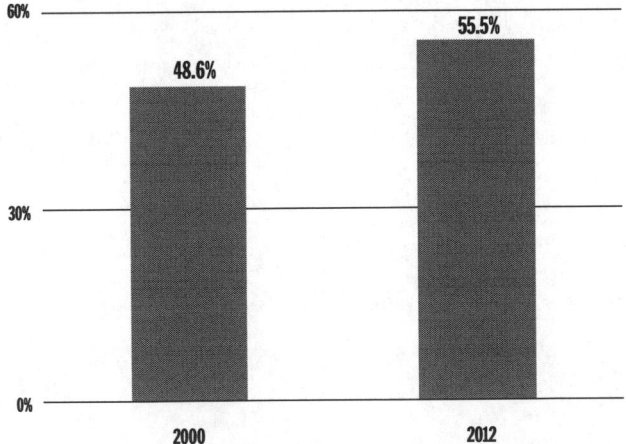

Table 6.21 Tenure with Current Employer by Sex and Age, 2000 to 2012

(median number of years workers aged 25 or older have been with their current employer by sex and age 2000 to 2012; change in years, 2000–12)

	2012	2010	2000	change in years, 2000–12
Total, aged 25 or older	**5.4 yrs.**	**5.2 yrs.**	**4.7 yrs.**	**0.7 yrs.**
Aged 25 to 34	3.2	3.1	2.6	0.6
Aged 35 to 44	5.3	5.1	4.8	0.5
Aged 45 to 54	7.8	7.8	8.2	–0.4
Aged 55 to 64	10.3	10.0	10.0	0.3
Aged 65 or older	10.3	9.9	9.4	0.9
Men, aged 25 or older	**5.5**	**5.3**	**4.9**	**0.6**
Aged 25 to 34	3.2	3.2	2.7	0.5
Aged 35 to 44	5.4	5.3	5.3	0.1
Aged 45 to 54	8.5	8.5	9.5	–1.0
Aged 55 to 64	10.7	10.4	10.2	0.5
Aged 65 or older	10.2	9.7	9.0	1.2
Women, aged 25 or older	**5.4**	**5.1**	**4.4**	**1.0**
Aged 25 to 34	3.1	3.0	2.5	0.6
Aged 35 to 44	5.2	4.9	4.3	0.9
Aged 45 to 54	7.3	7.1	7.3	0.0
Aged 55 to 64	10.0	9.7	9.9	0.1
Aged 65 or older	10.5	10.1	9.7	0.8

Source: Bureau of Labor Statistics, Employee Tenure, Internet site http://www.bls.gov/news.release/tenure.nr0.htm; calculations by New Strategist

Table 6.22 Long-Term Employment by Sex and Age, 2000 to 2012

(percent of workers aged 25 or older who have worked for their current employer 10 years or more by sex and age, 2000 to 2012; percentage point change, 2000–12)

	2012	2010	2000	percentage point change, 2000–12
Total, aged 25 or older	**33.7%**	**33.1%**	**31.5%**	**2.2**
Aged 25 to 29	2.5	2.3	2.5	0.0
Aged 30 to 34	12.5	12.8	13.9	–1.4
Aged 35 to 39	25.2	25.7	26.1	–0.9
Aged 40 to 44	35.1	35.3	35.8	–0.7
Aged 45 to 49	41.6	40.8	45.2	–3.6
Aged 50 to 54	48.4	48.9	48.7	–0.3
Aged 55 to 59	54.1	52.4	53.1	1.0
Aged 60 to 64	55.1	54.5	53.0	2.1
Aged 65 or older	55.5	53.1	49.8	5.7
Men, aged 25 or older	**34.6**	**34.3**	**33.4**	**1.2**
Aged 25 to 29	2.6	3.1	3.0	–0.4
Aged 30 to 34	13.2	14.3	15.1	–1.9
Aged 35 to 39	25.7	27.2	29.4	–3.7
Aged 40 to 44	36.9	37.5	40.2	–3.3
Aged 45 to 49	44.8	43.7	49.0	–4.2
Aged 50 to 54	51.4	51.3	51.6	–0.2
Aged 55 to 59	55.7	53.6	53.7	2.0
Aged 60 to 64	56.2	56.8	52.4	3.8
Aged 65 or older	55.5	51.9	48.6	6.9
Women, aged 25 or older	**32.8**	**31.9**	**29.5**	**3.3**
Aged 25 to 29	2.3	1.6	1.9	0.4
Aged 30 to 34	11.8	11.1	12.5	–0.7
Aged 35 to 39	24.7	24.0	22.3	2.4
Aged 40 to 44	33.2	32.9	31.2	2.0
Aged 45 to 49	38.3	38.0	41.4	–3.1
Aged 50 to 54	45.5	46.5	45.8	–0.3
Aged 55 to 59	52.6	51.2	52.5	0.1
Aged 60 to 64	54.0	52.2	53.6	0.4
Aged 65 or older	55.6	54.3	51.0	4.6

Source: Bureau of Labor Statistics, Employee Tenure, Internet site http://www.bls.gov/news.release/tenure.nr0.htm; calculations by New Strategist

Self-Employment Rises with Age

One in five employed men aged 65 or older is self-employed.

Many Americans say they would like to be their own boss. But few people actually attain this goal—only 7 percent of workers are self-employed.

The self-employment rate rises with age. Only 2 percent of workers under age 25 are self-employed. Among workers aged 25 to 54, only 4 to 8 percent are self-employed. The rate rises slightly to 10 percent among workers aged 55 to 64 as some begin to make the transition from work to partial retirement. A larger 17 percent of workers aged 65 or older are self-employed as the Medicare health insurance program frees them from the need to find a job with health insurance coverage.

Men are more likely than women to be self-employed, especially among older workers. Twenty percent of working men aged 65 or older are self-employed compared with 14 percent of their female counterparts.

■ The self-employment rate among older Americans is likely to grow as more boomers reach their 65th birthday and look for ways to earn money while they postpone retirement.

Older workers are most likely to be self-employed

(percent of workers who are self-employed, by age, 2012)

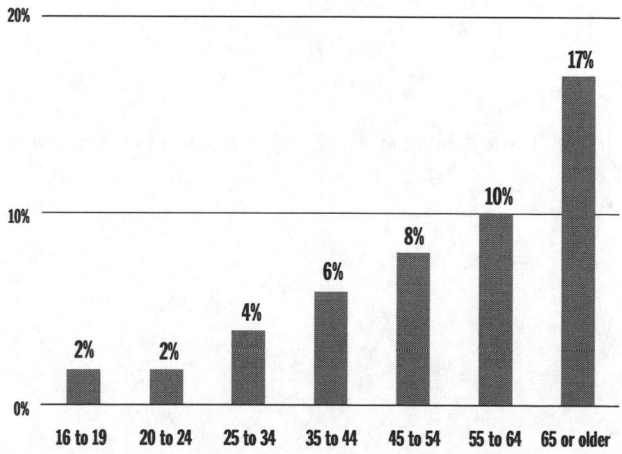

Table 6.23 Self-Employed Workers by Sex and Age, 2012

(number of people aged 16 or older in the labor force, number and percent who are self-employed, and percent distribution of self-employed, by sex and age, 2012; numbers in thousands)

	total employed	self-employed number	self-employed percent of total	self-employed percent distribution
Total people	**142,469**	**9,529**	**6.7%**	**100.0%**
Aged 16 to 19	4,426	76	1.7	0.8
Aged 20 to 24	13,408	255	1.9	2.7
Aged 25 to 34	30,701	1,293	4.2	13.6
Aged 35 to 44	30,576	1,936	6.3	20.3
Aged 45 to 54	32,874	2,511	7.6	26.4
Aged 55 to 64	23,239	2,215	9.5	23.2
Total men	**75,556**	**5,828**	**7.7**	**100.0**
Aged 16 to 19	2,152	55	2.6	0.9
Aged 20 to 24	6,948	150	2.2	2.6
Aged 25 to 34	16,606	758	4.6	13.0
Aged 35 to 44	16,483	1,171	7.1	20.1
Aged 45 to 54	17,220	1,508	8.8	25.9
Aged 55 to 64	12,068	1,376	11.4	23.6
Aged 65 or older	4,077	812	19.9	13.9
Total women	**66,913**	**3,701**	**5.5**	**100.0**
Aged 16 to 19	2,274	22	1.0	0.6
Aged 20 to 24	6,460	105	1.6	2.8
Aged 25 to 34	14,094	535	3.8	14.5
Aged 35 to 44	14,093	765	5.4	20.7
Aged 45 to 54	15,653	1,003	6.4	27.1
Aged 55 to 64	11,171	840	7.5	22.7
Aged 65 or older	3,168	431	13.6	11.6

Source: Bureau of Labor Statistics, Current Population Survey, Internet site http://www.bls.gov/cps/tables.htm#empstat; calculations by New Strategist

Few Workers Are Represented by Unions

The differences are greatest by occupation.

Union representation has fallen sharply over the past few decades. In 1970, 30 percent of nonagricultural workers were represented by labor unions. In 2012, the figure was just 12 percent.

Union representation is about the same for men and women. It is higher for blacks than for Asians, Hispanics, or whites. The biggest differences are by occupation. Thirty-nine percent of workers in education, training, and library occupations are represented by unions, as are 36 percent of protective service workers. In contrast, unions represent only 4 percent of food preparation workers and farm workers.

■ Union representation has declined in part because the global economy makes it increasingly risky for American workers to make demands on their employers.

Union representation is much greater in some occupations

(percent of employed wage and salary workers aged 16 or older who are represented by unions, by occupation, 2012)

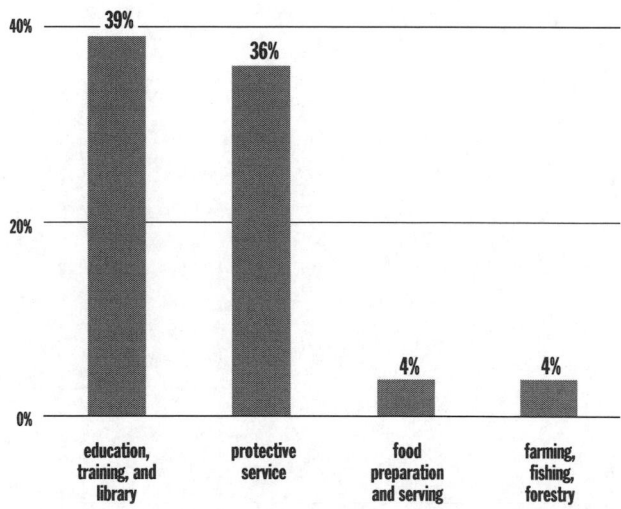

Table 6.24 Workers Represented by Unions by Sex, Age, Race, and Hispanic Origin, 2012

(number of employed wage and salary workers aged 16 or older, and number and percent who are represented by unions, by sex, age, race, and Hispanic origin, 2012; numbers in thousands)

		represented by unions	
	total	number	percent
Total employed	**127,577**	**15,922**	**12.5%**
Men	65,898	8,611	13.1
Women	61,679	7,311	11.9
Aged 16 to 24	17,417	869	5.0
Aged 25 to 34	28,875	3,083	10.7
Aged 35 to 44	27,442	3,746	13.6
Aged 45 to 54	28,765	4,437	15.4
Aged 55 to 64	19,694	3,233	16.4
Aged 65 or older	5,385	554	10.3
Asians	6,953	758	10.9
Blacks	14,975	2,220	14.8
Hispanics	20,144	2,197	10.9
Whites	101,851	12,517	12.3

Note: Workers represented by unions are either members of a labor union or similar employee association or workers who report no union affiliation but whose jobs are covered by a union or an employee association contract.
Source: Bureau of Labor Statistics, Current Population Survey, Internet site http://www.bls.gov/cps/tables.htm#empstat

Table 6.25 Workers Represented by Unions by Occupation, 2012

(number of employed wage and salary workers aged 16 or older, and number and percent who are represented by unions, by occupation, 2012; numbers in thousands)

	total	represented by unions number	represented by unions percent
TOTAL EMPLOYED	**127,577**	**15,922**	**12.5%**
Management, professional and related occupations	**46,897**	**6,514**	**13.9**
Management, business and financial operations occupations	18,153	1,009	5.6
Management occupations	12,259	610	5.0
Business and financial operations occupations	5,894	399	6.8
Professional and related occupations	28,743	5,505	19.2
Computer and mathematical occupations	3,578	173	4.8
Architecture and engineering occupations	2,701	240	8.9
Life, physical, and social science occupations	1,219	150	12.3
Community and social services occupations	2,239	406	18.1
Legal occupations	1,428	87	6.1
Education, training, and library occupations	8,325	3,267	39.2
Art, design, entertainment, sports, and media occupations	1,943	159	8.2
Health care practitioner and technical occupations	7,309	1,023	14.0
Service occupations	**23,095**	**2,630**	**11.4**
Health care support occupations	3,340	321	9.6
Protective service occupations	3,078	1,122	36.5
Food preparation and serving–related occupations	7,966	358	4.5
Building and grounds cleaning and maintenance occupations	4,729	540	11.4
Personal care and service occupations	3,983	289	7.3
Sales and office occupations	**30,685**	**2,357**	**7.7**
Sales and related occupations	13,366	465	3.5
Office and administrative support occupations	17,319	1,892	10.9
Natural resources, construction, and maintenance occupations	**10,863**	**1,876**	**17.3**
Farming, fishing, and forestry occupations	949	38	4.1
Construction and extraction occupations	5,567	1,108	19.9
Installation, maintenance, and repair occupations	4,347	729	16.8
Production, transportation, and material moving occupations	**16,038**	**2,546**	**15.9**
Production occupations	8,116	1,084	13.4
Transportation and material moving occupations	7,922	1,462	18.5

Note: Workers represented by unions are either members of a labor union or similar employee association or workers who report no union affiliation but whose jobs are covered by a union or an employee association contract.
Source: Bureau of Labor Statistics, Current Population Survey, Internet site http://www.bls.gov/cps/tables.htm#empstat

More than Three Million Earn Minimum Wage or Less

Many who earn minimum wage are food service workers.

Among the nation's 75 million workers who are paid hourly rates, 3.6 million (4.7 percent) earn minimum wage or less, according to the Bureau of Labor Statistics. Of minimum-wage workers, more than half are under age 25.

Women are more likely than men to earn minimum wage or less, and they account for 64 percent of the nation's minimum-wage workers. Part-time workers also dominate the minimum-wage labor force, accounting for 64 percent of the total. By occupation, 44 percent of minimum-wage workers are in food service occupations. Twenty-two percent of those with food-service jobs are paid minimum wage or less.

■ One in eight service workers earns minimum wage or less.

Young adults account for most minimum wage workers

(percent distribution of workers making minimum wage or less by age, 2012)

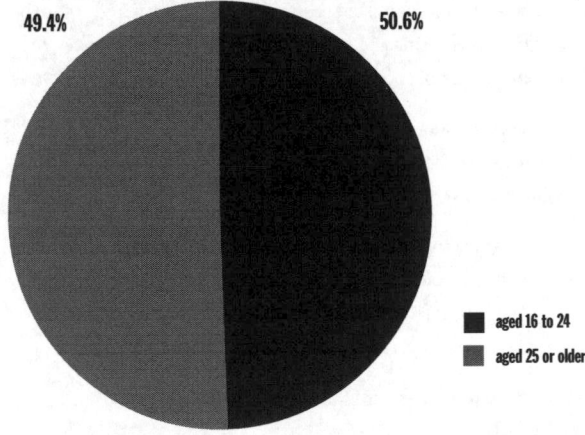

49.4%   50.6%

■ aged 16 to 24
■ aged 25 or older

Table 6.26 Workers Earning Minimum Wage by Selected Characteristics, 2012

(number and percent distribution of employed wage and salary workers paid hourly rates at or below minimum wage, by selected characteristics, 2012; numbers in thousands)

	total employed	paid at or below minimum wage number	percent of total	percent distribution
Total aged 16 or older	75,276	3,550	4.7%	100.0%
Aged 16 to 24	14,909	1,796	12.0	50.6
Aged 25 or older	60,367	1,754	2.9	49.4
Sex				
Men	37,113	1,264	3.4	35.6
Women	38,163	2,286	6.0	64.4
Race and Hispanic origin				
Asian	3,403	117	3.4	3.3
Black	10,049	533	5.3	15.0
Hispanic	14,404	717	5.0	20.2
White	59,180	2,760	4.7	77.7
Work status				
Full-time workers	54,745	1,261	2.3	35.5
Part-time workers	20,411	2,286	11.2	64.4
TOTAL EMPLOYED	**75,276**	**3,550**	**4.7**	**100.0**
Management, professional and related occupations	**15,962**	**145**	**0.9**	**4.1**
Management, business and financial operations occ.	4,609	33	0.7	0.9
Management occupations	2,705	25	0.9	0.7
Business and financial operations occupations	1,904	8	0.4	0.2
Professional and related occupations	11,353	112	1.0	3.2
Computer and mathematical occupations	919	3	0.4	0.1
Architecture and engineering occupations	922	5	0.6	0.1
Life, physical, and social science occupations	419	5	1.2	0.1
Community and social services occupations	835	8	1.0	0.2
Legal occupations	350	2	0.6	0.1
Education, training, and library occupations	2,454	59	2.4	1.7
Art, design, entertainment, sports, and media occ.	791	8	1.1	0.2
Health care practitioner and technical occupations	4,662	20	0.4	0.6
Service occupations	**18,277**	**2,203**	**12.1**	**62.1**
Health care support occupations	2,835	100	3.5	2.8
Protective service occupations	1,935	49	2.5	1.4
Food preparation and serving–related occupations	6,971	1,554	22.3	43.8
Building and grounds cleaning and maintenance occ.	3,772	232	6.1	6.5
Personal care and service occupations	2,764	268	9.7	7.5

	total employed	paid at or below minimum wage		
		number	percent of total	percent distribution
Sales and office occupations	**20,123**	**773**	**3.8%**	**21.8%**
Sales and related occupations	7,956	546	6.9	15.4
Office and administrative support occupations	12,167	227	1.9	6.4
Natural resources, construction, and maintenance occupations	**8,217**	**79**	**1.0**	**2.2**
Farming, fishing, and forestry occupations	683	40	5.9	1.1
Construction and extraction occupations	4,330	23	0.5	0.6
Installation, maintenance, and repair occupations	3,204	16	0.5	0.5
Production, transportation, and material moving occupations	**12,697**	**350**	**2.8**	**9.9**
Production occupations	6,740	109	1.6	3.1
Transportation and material moving occupations	5,957	240	4.0	6.8

Source: Bureau of Labor Statistics, 2012 Current Population Survey, Internet site http://www.bls.gov/cps/tables.htm#empstat; calculations by New Strategist

Millions Work at Home

College graduates are most likely to report working at home.

The Bureau of Labor Statistics' American Time Use Survey reveals just how many Americans work at home. Among the 103 million people who work on an average day, 23 percent reported working at least part of their day at home. Those who worked at home logged an average of 3.01 work hours at home.

Interestingly, there is not much variation in the percentage of workers who work at home by full- or part-time status or by sex. Twenty-two percent of full-time workers work at home on an average day, as do 27 percent of part-time workers. Twenty-three percent of men and women report working at home. There are substantial differences by education, however. Fully 38 percent of college graduates work at home on an average day versus only 13 percent of those who went no further than high school. Not surprisingly, the self-employed are far more likely to work at home (56 percent) than wage and salary workers (20 percent).

■ The percentage of people who work at home has been fairly stable through the sluggish economic recovery.

More than one-third of college graduates work at home on an average day

(percent of workers aged 25 or older who reported working at home on an average day, by educational attainment, 2012)

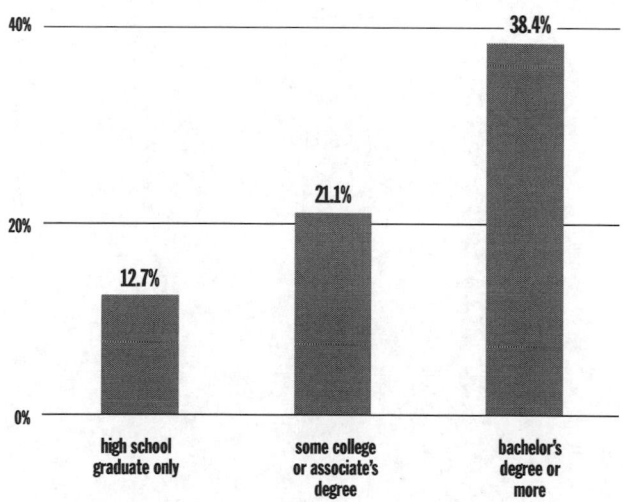

Table 6.27 People Who Work at Home, 2012

(total number of employed workers aged 15 or older, number and percent who worked on diary day and average hours of work, number and percent who worked at home on diary day and average number of hours worked at home, by selected characteristics, 2012)

	total employed	total who worked on an average day			total who worked at home on an average day		
		number	percent of employed	hours of work	number	percent of those who worked	hours of work
Total workers	150,877	102,817	68.1%	7.65 hrs.	23,878	23.2%	3.01 hrs.
Full-time	114,136	83,117	72.8	8.22	18,502	22.3	3.19
Part-time	36,741	19,701	53.6	5.24	5,376	27.3	2.38
Sex of worker							
Men	79,458	55,361	69.7	8.07	12,828	23.2	3.07
Women	71,419	47,456	66.4	7.16	11,050	23.3	2.93
Educational attainment, aged 25+							
Not a high school graduate	9,879	6,563	66.4	7.76	357	5.4	3.18
High school graduate only	36,749	24,589	66.9	7.97	3,118	12.7	3.56
Some college or associate's degree	33,843	22,569	66.7	7.86	4,769	21.1	3.17
Bachelor's degree or more	49,670	36,252	73.0	7.57	13,914	38.4	2.87
Class of worker							
Wage and salary	139,487	93,584	67.1	7.65	18,428	19.7	2.58
Self-employed	11,135	7,611	68.4	6.87	4,270	56.1	4.86

Note: Time spent working excludes travel time related to work. Working at home includes any time the respondent reported doing activities that were identified as "part of one's job," and is not restricted to persons whose usual workplace is their home.
Source: Bureau of Labor Statistics, American Time Use Survey, Internet site http://www.bls.gov/news.release/atus.toc.htm; calculations by New Strategist

Most Workers Drive to Work Alone

Public transportation is most popular in the Northeast.

Despite the efforts of many to encourage carpooling and the use of public transportation during the commute to work, the great majority of workers drive to work alone. In 2011, fully 76 percent of workers aged 16 or older drove alone. Only 10 percent carpool, while just 5 percent use public transportation. Three percent of workers walk to work, and 4 percent work at home.

Workers in the Northeast are least likely to drive to work alone, with 68 percent doing so. Fourteen percent of workers in the Northeast take public transportation to work. In the Midwest and South, 80 percent of workers drive to work alone. Only 2 percent of workers in the South use public transportation for their commute, in part because public transportation is unavailable in many areas of the South.

■ Cars will continue to dominate the journey to work because many Americans do not have access to public transportation.

Driving to work alone is most common in the Midwest and South

(percent of workers who drive alone to work, by region, 2011)

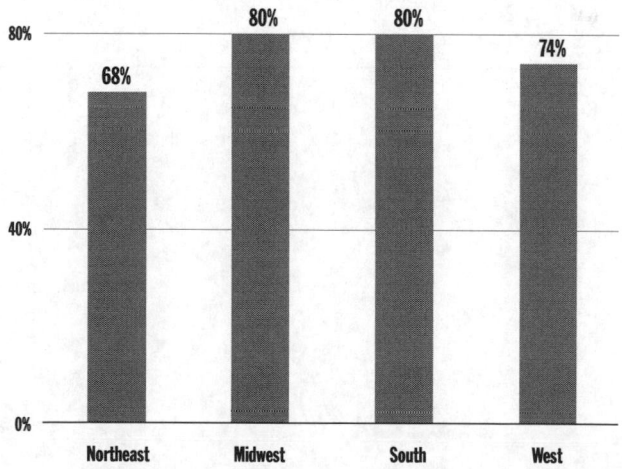

Table 6.28 Journey to Work by Region, 2011

(number and percent distribution of workers aged 16 or older by principal means of transportation to work, by region, 2011; numbers in thousands)

	total	Northeast	Midwest	South	West
Total workers	**138,270**	**25,611**	**30,679**	**50,303**	**31,677**
Drove car, truck, or van alone	105,639	17,368	24,537	40,278	23,456
Carpooled in car, truck, or van	13,388	2,059	2,751	5,109	3,468
Public transportation (including taxis)	6,956	3,522	915	1,175	1,344
Walked	3,889	1,204	815	932	937
Other means	2,405	411	423	796	775
Worked at home	5,994	1,048	1,238	2,012	1,696
Average travel time to work (minutes)	**25.5**	**28.6**	**23.4**	**25.3**	**25.3**
PERCENT DISTRIBUTION					
Total workers	**100.0%**	**100.0%**	**100.0%**	**100.0%**	**100.0%**
Drove car, truck, or van alone	76.4	67.8	80.0	80.1	74.0
Carpooled in car, truck, or van	9.7	8.0	9.0	10.2	10.9
Public transportation (including taxis)	5.0	13.8	3.0	2.3	4.2
Walked	2.8	4.7	2.7	1.9	3.0
Other means	1.7	1.6	1.4	1.6	2.4
Worked at home	4.3	4.1	4.0	4.0	5.4

Source: Bureau of the Census, 2011 American Community Survey, Internet site http://factfinder2.census.gov/faces/nav/jsf/pages/index.xhtml; calculations by New Strategist

Number of Older Workers Will Expand Rapidly

Early retirement will become less common.

As the baby-boom generation enters its late 60s and early 70s during the next decade, the number of workers aged 65 or older will surge. While the labor force as a whole is projected to increase 7 percent between 2010 and 2020, the number of working men aged 65 or older will grow by 73 percent. The number of working women in the age group will expand by 90 percent. In contrast, the number of workers aged 45 to 54 will decline.

The Bureau of Labor Statistics projects an increase in the labor force participation rate of men aged 65 or older, with the rate rising by nearly 5 percentage points to 26.7 percent. The government foresees declines in labor force participation among men under age 55.

Women's labor force participation should also climb in the older age groups between 2010 and 2020. Among women aged 55 to 64, labor force participation is projected to rise by 6 percentage points.

■ If older workers retire sooner than planned (as many do), then labor force participation rates among Americans aged 65 or older may rise more slowly than projected.

Rapid growth is projected for workers aged 65 or older

(percent change in number of total workers and workers aged 65 or older, by sex, 2010–20)

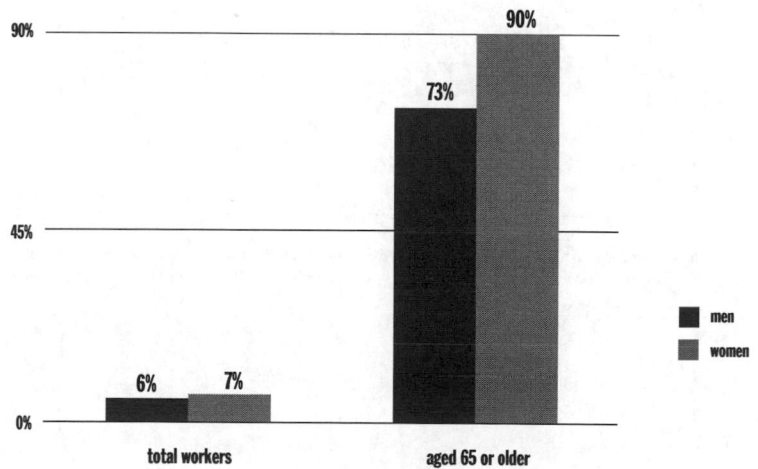

Table 6.29 Labor Force Projections by Sex and Age, 2010 and 2020

(number and percent of people aged 16 or older in the civilian labor force by sex and age, 2010 and 2020; percent change in number and percentage point change in rate 2010–20; numbers in thousands)

	participation rate			number		
	2010	2020	percent change	2010	2020	percentage point change
Total labor force	**153,889**	**164,360**	**6.8%**	**64.7%**	**62.5%**	**–2.2**
Aged 16 to 19	5,906	4,548	–23.0	34.9	26.5	–8.4
Aged 20 to 24	15,028	13,783	–8.3	71.4	65.9	–5.5
Aged 25 to 34	33,614	36,421	8.4	82.2	80.6	–1.6
Aged 35 to 44	33,366	35,147	5.3	83.2	82.6	–0.6
Aged 45 to 54	35,960	33,051	–8.1	81.2	80.8	–0.4
Aged 55 to 64	23,297	29,298	25.8	64.9	68.8	3.9
Aged 65 or older	6,717	12,113	80.3	17.4	22.6	5.2
Aged 65 to 74	5,424	9,945	83.4	25.7	31.0	5.3
Aged 75 or older	1,293	2,168	67.7	7.4	10.0	2.6
Men in labor force	**81,985**	**87,128**	**6.3**	**71.2**	**68.2**	**–3.0**
Aged 16 to 19	2,991	2,413	–19.3	34.9	27.9	–7.0
Aged 20 to 24	7,864	7,276	–7.5	74.5	69.4	–5.1
Aged 25 to 34	18,352	19,667	7.2	90.3	86.9	–3.4
Aged 35 to 44	18,119	19,303	6.5	91.5	91.3	–0.2
Aged 45 to 54	18,856	17,415	–7.6	86.8	86.0	–0.8
Aged 55 to 64	12,103	14,662	21.1	70.0	71.1	1.1
Aged 65 or older	3,700	6,391	72.7	22.1	26.7	4.6
Aged 65 to 74	2,971	5,236	76.2	30.4	35.1	4.7
Aged 75 or older	729	1,155	58.4	10.4	12.8	2.4
Women in labor force	**71,904**	**77,232**	**7.4**	**58.6**	**57.1**	**–1.5**
Aged 16 to 19	2,914	2,134	–26.8	35.0	25.2	–9.8
Aged 20 to 24	7,164	6,506	–9.2	68.3	62.3	–6.0
Aged 25 to 34	15,263	16,754	9.8	74.7	74.2	–0.5
Aged 35 to 44	15,247	15,844	3.9	75.2	74.0	–1.2
Aged 45 to 54	17,104	15,635	–8.6	75.7	75.7	0.0
Aged 55 to 64	11,194	14,637	30.8	60.2	66.6	6.4
Aged 65 or older	3,017	5,721	89.6	13.8	19.2	5.4
Aged 65 to 74	2,453	4,709	92.0	21.6	27.5	5.9
Aged 75 or older	564	1,012	79.4	5.3	8.0	2.7

Source: Bureau of Labor Statistics, Labor Force Projections to 2020: A More Slowly Growing Workforce, Monthly Labor Review, January 2012, Internet site http://www.bls.gov/opub/mlr/2012/01/home.htm; calculations by New Strategist

Numbers of Asian and Hispanic Workers Will Expand the Most

Non-Hispanic whites will decline as a share of workers.

Between 2010 and 2020, the labor force will grow by 7 percent—to 164 million, according to projections by the Bureau of Labor Statistics. The number of minority workers will grow much faster than the number of non-Hispanic whites. Asian and Hispanic workers will expand by 30 and 34 percent, respectively, during those years. The black labor force will grow by 10 percent. The non-Hispanic white labor force is projected to decline by nearly 2 percent.

The non-Hispanic white share of the labor force will fall from 68 to 62 percent between 2010 and 2020. In contrast, the Hispanic share will climb from 15 to 19 percent during those years. The black share of the labor force will remain stable at 12 percent, and the Asian share will increase from 5 to 6 percent.

■ The ability to manage a diverse workforce will become increasingly important as the minority share of American workers grows.

The labor force is becoming increasingly diverse

(percent distribution of the labor force by race and Hispanic origin, 2010 and 2020)

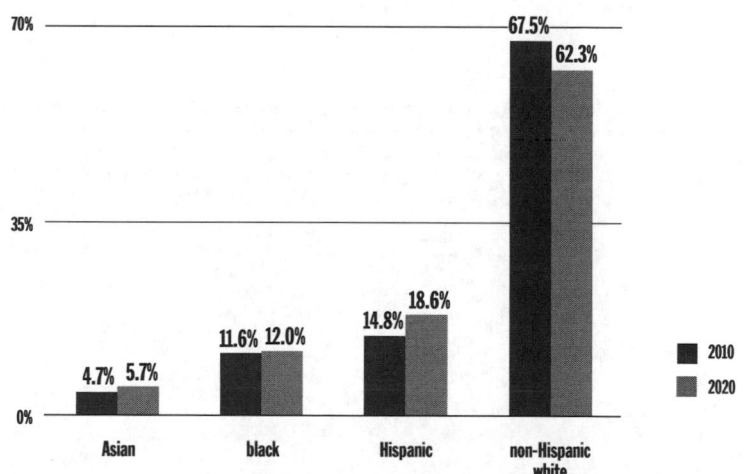

Table 6.30 Labor Force Projections by Race and Hispanic Origin, 2010 and 2020

(number and percent of people aged 16 or older in the civilian labor force by sex, race, and Hispanic origin, 2010 and 2020; percent change in number, 2010–20; numbers in thousands)

	2010 number	2010 participation rate	2020 number	2020 participation rate	percent change in number, 2010–20
Total in labor force	**153,889**	**64.7%**	**164,360**	**62.5%**	**6.8%**
Asian	7,248	64.7	9,430	63.1	30.1
Black	17,862	62.2	19,676	60.3	10.2
Hispanic	22,748	67.5	30,493	66.2	34.0
Non-Hispanic white	103,947	64.6	102,371	62.0	−1.5
Other racial groups	3,694	63.2	4,738	61.4	28.3
Men in labor force	**81,985**	**71.2**	**87,128**	**68.2**	**6.3**
Asian	3,893	73.2	4,968	71.0	27.6
Black	8,415	65.0	9,393	63.1	11.6
Hispanic	13,511	77.8	17,859	75.9	32.2
Non-Hispanic white	55,116	70.7	53,867	67.2	−2.3
Other racial groups	1,949	68.7	2,388	63.4	22.5
Women in labor force	**71,904**	**58.6**	**77,232**	**57.1**	**7.4**
Asian	3,355	57.0	4,462	56.1	33.0
Black	9,447	59.9	10,283	57.9	8.8
Hispanic	9,238	56.5	12,634	56.1	36.8
Non-Hispanic white	48,831	58.9	48,504	57.2	−0.7
Other racial groups	1,746	58.0	2,350	59.5	34.6

Note: Numbers do not add to total because Hispanics may be of any race. Asians and blacks are those who identify themselves as being of the race alone. Non-Hispanic whites are those who identify themselves as being white alone and not Hispanic. "Other racial groups" are those of more than one race, American Indians, and Native Hawaiians.
Source: Bureau of Labor Statistics, Labor Force Projections to 2020: A More Slowly Growing Workforce, Monthly Labor Review, January 2012, Internet site http://www.bls.gov/opub/mlr/2012/01/home.htm

Table 6.31 Distribution of the Labor Force by Race and Hispanic Origin, 2010 and 2020

(number and percent distribution of people aged 16 or older in the civilian labor force by sex, race, and Hispanic origin, 2010 and 2020; percentage point change in distribution, 2010–20; numbers in thousands)

	2010		2020		percentage point change, 2010–20
	number	percent distribution	number	percent distribution	
Total in labor force	**153,889**	**100.0%**	**164,360**	**100.0%**	–
Asian	7,248	4.7	9,430	5.7	1.0
Black	17,862	11.6	19,676	12.0	0.4
Hispanic	22,748	14.8	30,493	18.6	3.8
Non-Hispanic white	103,947	67.5	102,371	62.3	−5.3
Other racial groups	3,694	2.4	4,738	2.9	0.5
Men in labor force	**81,985**	**100.0**	**87,128**	**100.0**	–
Asian	3,893	4.7	4,968	5.7	1.0
Black	8,415	10.3	9,393	10.8	0.5
Hispanic	13,511	16.5	17,859	20.5	4.0
Non-Hispanic white	55,116	67.2	53,867	61.8	−5.4
Other racial groups	1,949	2.4	2,388	2.7	0.4
Women in labor force	**71,904**	**100.0**	**77,232**	**100.0**	–
Asian	3,355	4.7	4,462	5.8	1.1
Black	9,447	13.1	10,283	13.3	0.2
Hispanic	9,238	12.8	12,634	16.4	3.5
Non-Hispanic white	48,831	67.9	48,504	62.8	−5.1
Other racial groups	1,746	2.4	2,350	3.0	0.6

Note: Numbers do not add to total because Hispanics may be of any race. Asians and blacks are those who identify themselves as being of the race alone. Non-Hispanic whites are those who identify themselves as being white alone and not Hispanic. "Other racial groups" are those of more than one race, American Indians, and Native Hawaiians. "–" means not applicable.
Source: Bureau of Labor Statistics, Labor Force Projections to 2020: A More Slowly Growing Workforce, Monthly Labor Review, January 2012, Internet site http://www.bls.gov/opub/mlr/2012/01/home.htm

Construction and Health Care Lead the Pack

The postal service will see big job declines.

Every two years, the Bureau of Labor Statistics produces occupational projections that look 10 years ahead, based on demographic and technological change. The most recent set of projections offers a few surprises. While health care continues to appear in the list of occupations projected to either grow the fastest or gain the most jobs, many blue-collar positions also appear on the lists. Brickmasons, rebar workers, and carpenter's helpers, for example, are among the occupations projected to grow the fastest. The reason for this growth is recovery from the Great Recession. A number of postal service jobs are among those projected to decline the most.

Among the fastest growing occupations, personal care aide is at the top of the list, with a 70 percent increase in employment projected for the 2010-to-2020 time period. The median annual wage for this occupation was just $19,640 in 2010. Other occupations projected to be among the fastest growing are biomedical engineer, veterinary technologist, and physical therapy assistant.

The jobs expected to offer the largest number of employment opportunities include registered nurse, retail salesperson, home health aide, personal care aide, office clerk, food prep worker, customer service representative, and college teacher. Quite a few of the occupations forecast to make big gains are relatively low paying.

■ Employment is expected to grow by at least 25 percent in three industries between 2010 and 2020: construction; educational services; and health care and social assistance.

Gains for nurses, losses for postal workers

(change in employment of registered nurses and postal service mail sorters, 2010 to 2020)

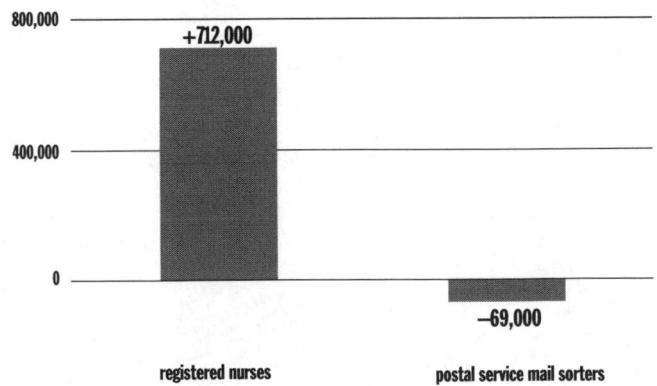

Table 6.32 Employment by Major Occupational Group, 2010 and 2020

(number of employed people aged 16 or older by major occupational group, 2010 and 2020; percent change in number, 2010–20; median annual wage in 2010; ranked by percent change in employment; numbers in thousands)

	2010	2020	percent change, 2010–20	median annual wage in 2010
Total employed	**143,068**	**163,537**	**14.3%**	**$33,840**
Health care support occupations	4,190	5,634	34.5	24,760
Personal care and service occupations	4,995	6,331	26.8	20,640
Health care practitioner and technical occupations	7,799	9,819	25.9	58,490
Community and social services occupations	2,403	2,985	24.2	39,280
Construction and extraction occupations	6,328	7,735	22.2	39,080
Computer and mathematical occupations	3,543	4,321	22.0	73,720
Business and financial operations occupations	6,789	7,962	17.3	60,670
Life, physical, and social science occupations	1,229	1,420	15.5	58,530
Education, training, and library occupations	9,194	10,597	15.3	45,690
Transportation and material moving occupations	9,005	10,333	14.8	28,400
Installation, maintenance, and repair occupations	5,429	6,229	14.7	40,120
Art, design, entertainment, sports, and media occupations	2,709	3,051	12.6	42,870
Sales and related occupations	14,916	16,785	12.5	24,370
Building and grounds cleaning and maintenance occ.	5,499	6,163	12.1	22,490
Protective service occupations	3,303	3,667	11.0	36,660
Legal occupations	1,212	1,343	10.8	74,580
Architecture and engineering occupations	2,433	2,686	10.4	70,610
Office and administrative support occupations	22,603	24,938	10.3	30,710
Food preparation and serving–related occupations	11,150	12,243	9.8	18,770
Management occupations	8,776	9,392	7.0	91,440
Production occupations	8,594	8,951	4.2	30,330
Farming, fishing, and forestry occupations	972	953	–2.0	19,630

Source: Bureau of Labor Statistics, Employment Projections, Internet site http://www.bls.gov/emp/; calculations by New Strategist

Table 6.33 Fastest Growing Occupations, 2010 to 2020

(number of employed people aged 16 or older by detailed occupational group, 2010 and 2020; percent change in number, 2010–20; median annual wage in 2010; ranked by percent change in employment; numbers in thousands)

	2010	2020	change, 2010–20 number	change, 2010–20 percent	median annual wage in 2010
Personal care aides	861	1,468	607	70.5%	$19,640
Home health aides	1,018	1,724	706	69.4	20,560
Biomedical engineers	16	25	10	61.7	81,540
Helpers for brickmasons, blockmasons, and stonemasons	29	47	18	60.1	27,780
Helpers for carpenters	47	72	26	55.7	25,760
Veterinary technologists and technicians	80	122	42	52.0	29,710
Reinforcing iron and rebar workers	19	28	9	48.6	38,430
Physical therapist assistants	67	98	31	45.7	49,690
Helpers for pipelayers, plumbers, pipefitters, and steamfitters	58	84	26	45.4	26,740
Meeting, convention, and event planners	72	103	31	43.7	45,260
Diagnostic medical sonographers	54	77	23	43.5	64,380
Occupational therapy assistants	29	41	12	43.3	51,010
Physical therapist aides	47	67	20	43.1	23,680
Glaziers	42	60	18	42.4	36,640
Interpreters and translators	58	83	25	42.2	43,300
Medical secretaries	509	719	210	41.3	30,530
Market research analysts and marketing specialists	283	399	117	41.2	60,570
Marriage and family therapists	36	51	15	41.2	45,720
Brickmasons and blockmasons	89	125	36	40.5	46,930
Physical therapists	199	276	77	39.0	76,310
Dental hygienists	182	250	69	37.7	68,250
Bicycle repairers	10	14	4	37.6	23,660
Audiologists	13	18	5	36.8	66,660
Health educators	63	87	23	36.5	45,830
Stonemasons	16	21	6	36.5	37,180
Cost estimators	185	253	68	36.4	57,860
Medical scientists, except epidemiologists	100	137	36	36.4	76,700
Mental health counselors	120	164	44	36.3	38,150
Pile-driver operators	4	6	2	36.0	47,860
Veterinarians	61	83	22	35.9	82,040

Source: Bureau of Labor Statistics, Employment Projections, Internet site http://www.bls.gov/emp/; calculations by New Strategist

Table 6.34 Occupations with the Largest Job Growth, 2010 to 2020

(number of people aged 16 or older employed in the 30 occupations with the largest projected job growth, 2010 to 2020; numerical and percent change, 2010–20; median annual wage in 2010; ranked by numerical change in employment; numbers in thousands)

	2010	2020	change, 2010–20		median annual wage in 2010
			number	percent	
Registered nurses	2,737	3,449	712	26.0%	$64,690
Retail salespersons	4,262	4,968	707	16.6	20,670
Home health aides	1,018	1,724	706	69.4	20,560
Personal care aides	861	1,468	607	70.5	19,640
Office clerks, general	2,951	3,440	490	16.6	26,610
Combined food preparation and serving workers, including fast food	2,682	3,080	398	14.8	17,950
Customer service representatives	2,187	2,526	338	15.5	30,460
Heavy and tractor-trailer truck drivers	1,605	1,935	330	20.6	37,770
Laborers and freight, stock, and material movers, hand	2,068	2,387	319	15.4	23,460
Postsecondary teachers	1,756	2,062	306	17.4	45,690
Nursing aides, orderlies, and attendants	1,505	1,807	302	20.1	24,010
Childcare workers	1,282	1,544	262	20.4	19,300
Bookkeeping, accounting, and auditing clerks	1,898	2,157	259	13.6	34,030
Cashiers	3,363	3,613	250	7.4	18,500
Elementary school teachers, except special education	1,477	1,725	249	16.8	51,660
Receptionists and information clerks	1,049	1,297	249	23.7	25,240
Janitors and cleaners, except maids and housekeeping cleaners	2,310	2,557	246	10.7	22,210
Landscaping and groundskeeping workers	1,152	1,392	241	20.9	23,400
Sales representatives, wholesale and manufacturing, except technical and scientific products	1,430	1,653	223	15.6	52,440
Construction laborers	999	1,211	212	21.3	29,280
Medical secretaries	509	719	210	41.3	30,530
First-line supervisors of office and administrative support workers	1,424	1,628	203	14.3	47,460
Carpenters	1,002	1,198	196	19.6	39,530
Waiters and waitresses	2,260	2,456	196	8.7	18,330
Security guards	1,036	1,231	195	18.8	23,920
Teacher assistants	1,288	1,479	191	14.8	23,220
Accountants and auditors	1,217	1,408	191	15.7	61,690
Licensed practical and licensed vocational nurses	752	921	169	22.4	40,380
Physicians and surgeons	691	859	168	24.4	111,570
Medical assistants	528	690	163	30.9	28,860

Source: Bureau of Labor Statistics, Employment Projections, Internet site http://www.bls.gov/emp/; calculations by New Strategist

Table 6.35 Occupations with the Largest Job Declines, 2010 to 2020

(number of people aged 16 or older employed in the 10 occupations with the largest projected employment declines, 2010 to 2020; numerical and percent change, 2010–20; median annual wage in 2010; ranked by percent change in employment; numbers in thousands)

	2010	2020	change, 2010–20 number	change, 2010–20 percent	median annual wage in 2010
Shoe machine operators and tenders	3	2	–2	–53.4%	$26,280
Postal service mail sorters, processors, and processing machine operators	142	73	–69	–48.5	53,080
Postal service clerks	66	34	–32	–48.2	53,100
Fabric and apparel patternmakers	6	4	–2	–35.6	38,970
Postmasters and mail superintendents	25	18	–7	–27.8	60,300
Sewing machine operators	163	121	–42	–25.8	20,600
Switchboard operators, including answering service	143	109	–33	–23.3	24,920
Textile cutting machine setters, operators, and tenders	15	12	–3	–21.8	23,490
Textile knitting and weaving machine setters, operators, and tenders	23	18	–4	–18.2	25,870
Semiconductor processors	21	17	–4	–17.9	33,130

Source: Bureau of Labor Statistics, Employment Projections, Internet site http://www.bls.gov/emp/; calculations by New Strategist

Table 6.36 Employment by Major Industry, 2010 and 2020

(number of employed people aged 16 or older by major industry, 2010 and 2020; percent change, 2010–20; numbers in thousands)

	2010	2020	percent change, 2010–20
Total employed	**143,068**	**163,537**	**14.3%**
Nonagriculture wage and salary	130,436	150,177	15.1
Goods producing	17,706	19,497	10.1
Mining	656	681	3.8
Construction	5,526	7,365	33.3
Manufacturing	11,524	11,451	–0.6
Services providing	112,730	130,680	15.9
Utilities	552	516	–6.5
Wholesale trade	5,456	6,200	13.6
Retail trade	14,414	16,182	12.3
Transportation and warehousing	4,183	5,036	20.4
Information	2,711	2,851	5.2
Financial activities	7,630	8,411	10.2
Professional and business services	16,688	20,497	22.8
Educational services	3,150	3,969	26.0
Health care and social assistance	16,415	22,054	34.4
Leisure and hospitality	13,020	14,362	10.3
Other services	6,031	6,851	13.6
Federal government	2,968	2,596	–12.5
State and local government	19,513	21,155	8.4
Agriculture, forestry, fishing, and hunting	2,136	2,005	–6.1
Agriculture wage and salary	1,282	1,236	–3.6
Agriculture self-employed and unpaid family workers	853	769	–9.9
Nonagricultural self-employed and unpaid family workers	8,944	9,721	8.7
Secondary wage and salary jobs in agriculture, forestry, fishing, or private households	112	113	1.0
Secondary jobs as self-employed or unpaid family workers	1,442	1,522	5.5

Source: Bureau of Labor Statistics, Employment Projections, Internet site http://www.bls.gov/emp/; calculations by New Strategist

Table 6.37 Industries with the Fastest Wage and Salary Employment Growth, 2010 to 2020

(number of people aged 16 or older employed in the 10 industries with the fastest wage and salary employment growth, 2010 to 2020; numerical and percent change in employment, 2010–20; ranked by percent change in employment; numbers in thousands)

	2010	2020	change, 2010–20	
			number	percent
Home health care services	1,081	1,952	872	80.7%
Individual and family services	1,215	2,066	851	70.1
Management, scientific, and technical consulting services	991	1,567	576	58.1
Veneer, plywood, and engineered wood product manufacturing	65	95	30	46.7
Computer systems design and related services	1,442	2,113	671	46.6
Cement and concrete product manufacturing	172	236	64	37.4
Outpatient, laboratory, and other ambulatory care services	1,077	1,471	394	36.6
Offices of health practitioners	3,818	5,210	1,391	36.4
Software publishers	260	352	92	35.3
Construction	5,526	7,365	1,840	33.3

Source: Bureau of Labor Statistics, Employment Projections, Internet site http://www.bls.gov/emp/; calculations by New Strategist

7

Living Arrangements

Trends

Married couples are slipping as a share of households.

Married couples account for only 48 percent of households, and couples with children under age 18 are just 21 percent of the total.

Households headed by older adults are growing rapidly.

Between 2000 and 2013, the number of households headed by 55-to-64-year-olds grew by 68 percent. In contrast, the number of households headed by 35-to-44-year-olds fell 11 percent.

The non-Hispanic white share of households varies by household type.

Non-Hispanic whites head 73 percent of the nation's married-couple households, but only 47 of female-headed families.

Only 59 percent of children live with two married biological parents.

The figure ranges from a low of 29 percent among black children to a high of 76 percent among Asian children.

Hispanic households are more likely to include children.

The 58 percent majority of Hispanic households include children of any age versus only 35 percent of non-Hispanic white households.

Young adults are postponing marriage.

The median age at first marriage is at a record high for both men and women.

Same-sex couples head more than 600,000 households.

Same-sex couples are far better educated than opposite-sex married couples and much more affluent than opposite-sex unmarried couples.

Married Couples Account for Fewer than Half of Households

The number of married couples with children under age 18 is declining.

Household growth slowed to a crawl during the Great Recession. During the three years from 2007 (the start of the Great Recession) and 2010, the number of households in the United States grew by only 1.5 million. During the three years between 2010 and 2013, the number of households grew by a much larger 4.9 million. But the number of nuclear families (married couples with children under age 18) continued to decline, falling by nearly 1 million between 2010 and 2013.

The married couple share of households slipped from the 53 percent majority in 2000 to a 48 percent minority in 2013. Nuclear families now account for only about one in five households, down from one in four in 2000. Households headed by people who live alone are more common than nuclear families (27 versus 21 percent).

■ The Great Recession temporarily slowed the increase in single-person households, but growth has now resumed.

Married couples are still the most common type of household

(percent distribution of households by type, 2013; ranked by share of households)

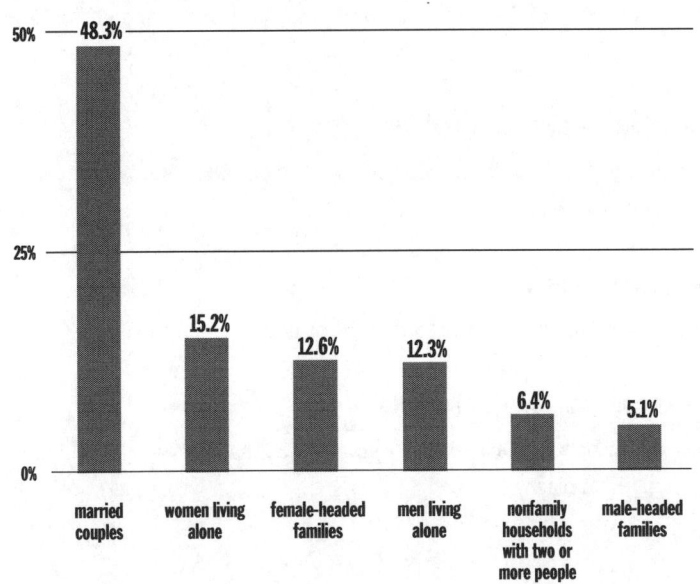

Table 7.1 Households by Type, 2000 to 2013

(number and percent distribution of households by household type, 2000 to 2013; percent change in number for selected years; numbers in thousands)

NUMBER	2013	2010	2007	2000	percent change 2007–13	percent change 2000–13
TOTAL HOUSEHOLDS	122,459	117,538	116,011	104,705	5.6%	17.0%
Family households	80,902	78,833	78,425	72,025	3.2	12.3
Married couples	59,204	58,410	58,945	55,311	0.4	7.0
With children under age 18	25,269	26,171	27,350	26,359	−7.6	−4.1
Female householders, no spouse present	15,469	14,843	14,416	12,687	7.3	21.9
With children under age 18	10,033	9,867	9,883	8,727	1.5	15.0
Male householders, no spouse present	6,229	5,580	5,063	4,028	23.0	54.6
With children under age 18	3,169	2,851	2,587	2,164	22.5	46.4
Nonfamily households	41,558	38,705	37,587	32,680	10.6	27.2
Female householders	21,810	20,442	20,249	18,039	7.7	20.9
Living alone	18,568	17,428	17,604	15,543	5.5	19.5
Male householders	19,747	18,263	17,338	14,641	13.9	34.9
Living alone	15,002	13,971	13,528	11,181	10.9	34.2

PERCENT DISTRIBUTION	2013	2010	2007	2000	percentage point change 2007–13	percentage point change 2000–13
TOTAL HOUSEHOLDS	100.0%	100.0%	100.0%	100.0%	–	–
Family households	66.1	67.1	67.6	68.8	−1.5	−2.7
Married couples	48.3	49.7	50.8	52.8	−2.5	−4.5
With children under age 18	20.6	22.3	23.6	25.2	−2.9	−4.5
Female householders, no spouse present	12.6	12.6	12.4	12.1	0.2	0.5
With children under age 18	8.2	8.4	8.5	8.3	−0.3	−0.1
Male householders, no spouse present	5.1	4.7	4.4	3.8	0.7	1.2
With children under age 18	2.6	2.4	2.2	2.1	0.4	0.5
Nonfamily households	33.9	32.9	32.4	31.2	1.5	2.7
Female householders	17.8	17.4	17.5	17.2	0.4	0.6
Living alone	15.2	14.8	15.2	14.8	0.0	0.3
Male householders	16.1	15.5	14.9	14.0	1.2	2.1
Living alone	12.3	11.9	11.7	10.7	0.6	1.6

Note: "–" means not applicable.
*Source: Bureau of the Census, Current Population Survey Annual Social and Economic Supplement, Internet site http://www
.census.gov/hhes/www/income/dinctabs.html; calculations by New Strategist*

Households Headed by Older Americans Are Growing Rapidly

Number of households headed by 35-to-44-year-olds declined between 2000 and 2013.

Between 2000 and 2013, the number of households headed by 55-to-64-year-olds grew 68 percent, four times as fast as the 17 percent gain for all households during those years. Behind the rapid growth was the aging of the baby-boom generation.

The 35-to-44 age group was the only one to see its household numbers decline between 2000 and 2013. As the small generation X entered its late thirties and early forties, the number of householders aged 35 to 44 fell 11 percent. The Great Recession is behind the decline in the number of households headed by people under age 25 between 2007 and 2013. Unemployment forced many young adults to live with their parents rather than establish their own households.

■ The number of households headed by people aged 65 or older will grow rapidly as boomers enter the age group.

The number of households headed by Americans aged 65 or older is about to expand rapidly

(percent change in number of households by age of householder, 2000–13)

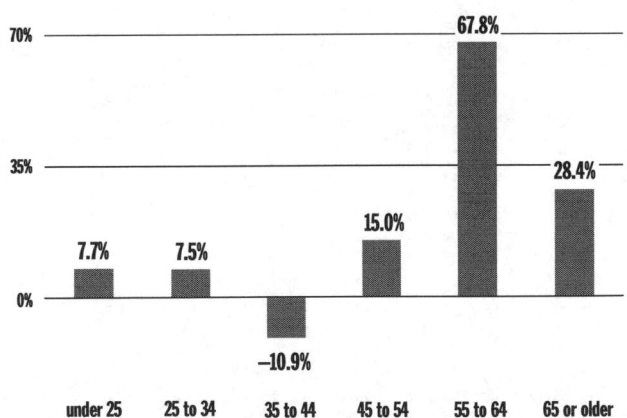

Table 7.2 Households by Age of Householder, 2000 to 2013

(number and percent distribution of households by age of householder, 2000 to 2013; percent change in number for selected years; numbers in thousands)

NUMBER	2013	2010	2007	2000	percent change 2007–13	percent change 2000–13
TOTAL HOUSEHOLDS	**122,459**	**117,538**	**116,011**	**104,705**	**5.6%**	**17.0%**
Under age 25	6,314	6,233	6,662	5,860	–5.2	7.7
Aged 25 to 34	20,017	19,257	19,435	18,627	3.0	7.5
Aged 35 to 44	21,334	21,519	22,779	23,955	–6.3	–10.9
Aged 45 to 54	24,068	24,871	24,140	20,927	–0.3	15.0
Aged 55 to 64	22,802	20,387	19,266	13,592	18.4	67.8
Aged 65 or older	27,924	25,270	23,729	21,745	17.7	28.4

PERCENT DISTRIBUTION	2013	2010	2007	2000	percentage point change 2007–13	percentage point change 2000–13
TOTAL HOUSEHOLDS	**100.0%**	**100.0%**	**100.0%**	**100.0%**	–	–
Under age 25	5.2	5.3	5.7	5.6	–0.6	–0.4
Aged 25 to 34	16.3	16.4	16.8	17.8	–0.4	–1.4
Aged 35 to 44	17.4	18.3	19.6	22.9	–2.2	–5.5
Aged 45 to 54	19.7	21.2	20.8	20.0	–1.2	–0.3
Aged 55 to 64	18.6	17.3	16.6	13.0	2.0	5.6
Aged 65 or older	22.8	21.5	20.5	20.8	2.3	2.0

Note: "–" means not applicable.
Source: Bureau of the Census, Current Population Survey Annual Social and Economic Supplement, Internet site http://www.census.gov/hhes/www/income/dinctabs.html; calculations by New Strategist

Lifestyles Change with Age

The households of young adults differ from those of older Americans.

Married couples are far less common among the youngest and oldest householders than they are among the middle aged. Only 15 percent of households headed by people under age 25 are married couples. Among the elderly, married couples head a 44 percent minority of households. In contrast, couples account for the 53 to 56 percent majority of households headed by people ranging in age from 35 to 64.

Female-headed families are most common among the youngest householders, at 22 percent. They account for less than 9 percent of households headed by people aged 55 or older. Women who live alone are most common among the oldest householders, at 30 percent of households. They are least common among 35-to-44-year-olds, at 6 percent. Men who live alone account for 10 to 14 percent of households regardless of age.

■ With the baby-boom generation now filling the 65-plus age group, expect to see many more single-person households.

Married couples head most households in the 35-to-64 age groups

(percent of households headed by married couples, by age of householder, 2013)

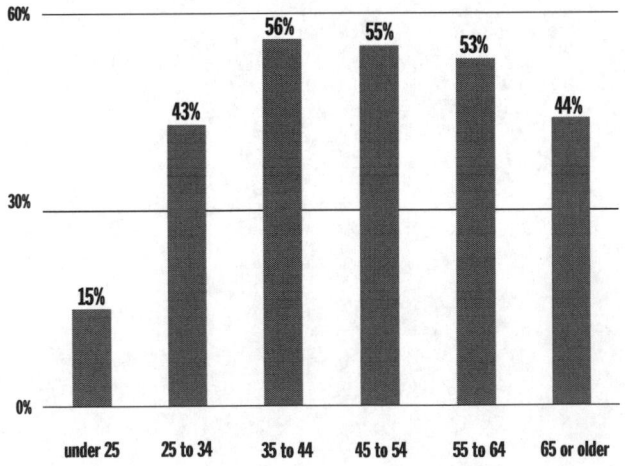

Table 7.3 Households by Household Type and Age of Householder, 2013

(number and percent distribution of households by household type and age of householder, 2013; numbers in thousands)

	total	under 25	25 to 34	35 to 44	45 to 54	55 to 64	65 or older
TOTAL HOUSEHOLDS	**122,459**	**6,314**	**20,017**	**21,334**	**24,068**	**22,802**	**27,924**
Family households	**80,902**	**3,285**	**13,340**	**16,848**	**17,539**	**14,825**	**15,066**
Married couples	59,204	970	8,551	11,985	13,237	12,043	12,418
Female householders, no spouse present	15,469	1,394	3,373	3,605	3,099	1,969	2,029
Male householders, no spouse present	6,229	921	1,416	1,258	1,204	812	619
Nonfamily households	**41,558**	**3,029**	**6,678**	**4,486**	**6,528**	**7,978**	**12,858**
Female householders	21,810	1,493	2,686	1,627	2,913	4,308	8,783
Living alone	18,568	788	1,818	1,296	2,432	3,805	8,429
Male householders	19,747	1,536	3,992	2,859	3,615	3,669	4,075
Living alone	15,002	760	2,433	2,161	2,880	3,110	3,658
PERCENT DISTRIBUTION BY HOUSEHOLD TYPE							
TOTAL HOUSEHOLDS	**100.0%**	**100.0%**	**100.0%**	**100.0%**	**100.0%**	**100.0%**	**100.0%**
Family households	**66.1**	**52.0**	**66.6**	**79.0**	**72.9**	**65.0**	**54.0**
Married couples	48.3	15.4	42.7	56.2	55.0	52.8	44.5
Female householders, no spouse present	12.6	22.1	16.8	16.9	12.9	8.6	7.3
Male householders, no spouse present	5.1	14.6	7.1	5.9	5.0	3.6	2.2
Nonfamily households	**33.9**	**48.0**	**33.4**	**21.0**	**27.1**	**35.0**	**46.0**
Female householders	17.8	23.6	13.4	7.6	12.1	18.9	31.5
Living alone	15.2	12.5	9.1	6.1	10.1	16.7	30.2
Male householders	16.1	24.3	19.9	13.4	15.0	16.1	14.6
Living alone	12.3	12.0	12.2	10.1	12.0	13.6	13.1

	total	under 25	25 to 34	35 to 44	45 to 54	55 to 64	65 or older
PERCENT DISTRIBUTION BY AGE OF HOUSEHOLDER							
TOTAL HOUSEHOLDS	**100.0%**	**5.2%**	**16.3%**	**17.4%**	**19.7%**	**18.6%**	**22.8%**
Family households	**100.0**	**4.1**	**16.5**	**20.8**	**21.7**	**18.3**	**18.6**
Married couples	100.0	1.6	14.4	20.2	22.4	20.3	21.0
Female householders, no spouse present	100.0	9.0	21.8	23.3	20.0	12.7	13.1
Male householders, no spouse present	100.0	14.8	22.7	20.2	19.3	13.0	9.9
Nonfamily households	**100.0**	**7.3**	**16.1**	**10.8**	**15.7**	**19.2**	**30.9**
Female householders	100.0	6.8	12.3	7.5	13.4	19.8	40.3
Living alone	100.0	4.2	9.8	7.0	13.1	20.5	45.4
Male householders	100.0	7.8	20.2	14.5	18.3	18.6	20.6
Living alone	100.0	5.1	16.2	14.4	19.2	20.7	24.4

Source: Bureau of the Census, 2012 Current Population Survey Annual Social and Economic Supplement, Internet site http://www.census.gov/hhes/www/cpstables/032012/hhinc/toc.htm; calculations by New Strategist

Households Differ by Race and Hispanic Origin

Married couples head the majority of Asian and non-Hispanic white households.

Although the Hispanic population is now larger than the black population, black households outnumbered Hispanic households by nearly 1 million in 2013. But Hispanic married couples greatly outnumber black married couples—7 million to 5 million. There are more than 3 million Asian married couples.

Among blacks, married couples outnumber female-headed families by only 227,000, with married couples accounting for 28 percent of black households and female-headed families for 27 percent. Among Hispanics, married couples account for 48 percent of households and female-headed families for a much smaller 20 percent. Female-headed families account for only 10 percent of Asian and 9 percent of non-Hispanic white households.

Among all households, people who live alone head a substantial 27 percent. The proportion varies greatly by race and Hispanic origin, from a low of 17 percent among Hispanics to a high of 33 percent among blacks.

■ Blacks have lower incomes than Asians and non-Hispanic whites in part because a much smaller share of their households is headed by married couples.

Married couples head a minority of black and Hispanic households

(percent of households headed by married couples, by race and Hispanic origin, 2013)

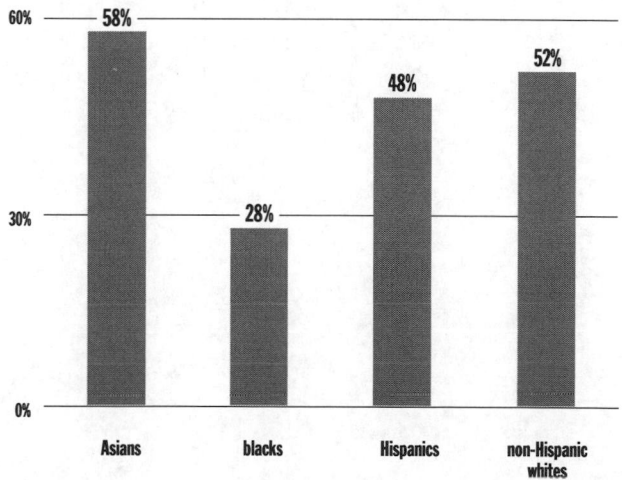

Table 7.4 Households by Household Type, Race, and Hispanic Origin of Householder, 2013

(number and percent distribution of households by household type, race, and Hispanic origin of householder, 2013; numbers in thousands)

	total	Asian	black	Hispanic	non-Hispanic white
TOTAL HOUSEHOLDS	**122,459**	**5,872**	**16,559**	**15,589**	**83,792**
Family households	**80,902**	**4,320**	**10,279**	**11,952**	**54,004**
Married couples	59,204	3,409	4,700	7,455	43,299
Female householders, no spouse present	15,469	565	4,473	3,106	7,317
Male householders, no spouse present	6,229	346	1,105	1,391	3,388
Nonfamily households	**41,558**	**1,552**	**6,280**	**3,637**	**29,787**
Female householders	21,810	758	3,424	1,683	15,833
Living alone	18,568	610	3,042	1,367	13,476
Male householders	19,747	794	2,856	1,954	13,955
Living alone	15,002	539	2,370	1,345	10,609

PERCENT DISTRIBUTION BY HOUSEHOLD TYPE

	total	Asian	black	Hispanic	non-Hispanic white
TOTAL HOUSEHOLDS	**100.0%**	**100.0%**	**100.0%**	**100.0%**	**100.0%**
Family households	**66.1**	**73.6**	**62.1**	**76.7**	**64.5**
Married couples	48.3	58.1	28.4	47.8	51.7
Female householders, no spouse present	12.6	9.6	27.0	19.9	8.7
Male householders, no spouse present	5.1	5.9	6.7	8.9	4.0
Nonfamily households	**33.9**	**26.4**	**37.9**	**23.3**	**35.5**
Female householders	17.8	12.9	20.7	10.8	18.9
Living alone	15.2	10.4	18.4	8.8	16.1
Male householders	16.1	13.5	17.2	12.5	16.7
Living alone	12.3	9.2	14.3	8.6	12.7

	total	Asian	black	Hispanic	non-Hispanic white
PERCENT DISTRIBUTION BY RACE AND HISPANIC ORIGIN					
TOTAL HOUSEHOLDS	**100.0%**	**4.8%**	**13.5%**	**12.7%**	**68.4%**
Family households	**100.0**	**5.3**	**12.7**	**14.8**	**66.8**
Married couples	100.0	5.8	7.9	12.6	73.1
Female householders, no spouse present	100.0	3.7	28.9	20.1	47.3
Male householders, no spouse present	100.0	5.5	17.7	22.3	54.4
Nonfamily households	**100.0**	**3.7**	**15.1**	**8.8**	**71.7**
Female householders	100.0	3.5	15.7	7.7	72.6
Living alone	100.0	3.3	16.4	7.4	72.6
Male householders	100.0	4.0	14.5	9.9	70.7
Living alone	100.0	3.6	15.8	9.0	70.7

Note: Numbers do not add to total because Hispanics may be of any race, not all races are shown, and some householders may be of more than one race. Asians and blacks are those who identify themselves as being of the race alone and those who identify themselves as being of the race in combination with other races. Non-Hispanic whites are those who identify themselves as being white alone and not Hispanic.
Source: Bureau of the Census, Current Population Survey Annual Social and Economic Supplement, Internet site http://www .census.gov/hhes/www/income/dinctabs.html; calculations by New Strategist

Most Households Are Small

The number of single-person households is climbing.

Sixty-one percent of the nation's households are home to only one or two people. The number of single-person households increased by 26 percent between 2000 and 2013, significantly faster than the 17 percent growth in households overall.

Single-person households accounted for 27 percent of the nation's 122 million households in 2013. Two-person households are most common, accounting for 34 percent of the total. Only 23 percent of households have four or more people. Overall, the average household in the United States was home to 2.54 people in 2013, down from 2.62 in 2000.

■ Household size will continue to shrink as the baby-boom generation ages.

Two-person households are most common

(percent distribution of households by size, 2013)

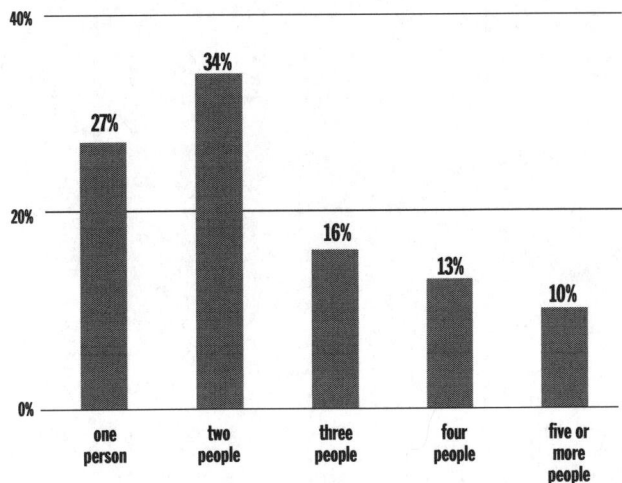

Table 7.5 Households by Size, 2000 to 2013

(number and percent distribution of households by size, 2000 to 2013; percent and percentage point change for selected years; number of households in thousands)

NUMBER	2013	2010	2007	2000	percent change 2007–13	percent change 2000–13
TOTAL HOUSEHOLDS	**122,459**	**117,538**	**116,011**	**104,705**	**5.6%**	**17.0%**
One person	33,570	31,399	31,132	26,724	7.8	25.6
Two people	41,503	39,487	38,580	34,666	7.6	19.7
Three people	19,283	18,638	18,808	17,152	2.5	12.4
Four people	16,361	16,122	16,172	15,309	1.2	6.9
Five people	7,425	7,367	7,202	6,981	3.1	6.4
Six people	2,735	2,784	2,702	2,445	1.2	11.9
Seven or more people	1,581	1,740	1,415	1,428	11.7	10.7
Average number of persons per household	2.54	2.59	2.56	2.62	–	–

PERCENT DISTRIBUTION	2013	2010	2007	2000	percentage point change 2007–13	percentage point change 2000–13
TOTAL HOUSEHOLDS	**100.0%**	**100.0%**	**100.0%**	**100.0%**	–	–
One person	27.4	26.7	26.8	25.5	0.6	1.9
Two people	33.9	33.6	33.3	33.1	0.6	0.8
Three people	15.7	15.9	16.2	16.4	–0.5	–0.6
Four people	13.4	13.7	13.9	14.6	–0.6	–1.3
Five people	6.1	6.3	6.2	6.7	–0.1	–0.6
Six people	2.2	2.4	2.3	2.3	–0.1	–0.1
Seven or more people	1.3	1.5	1.2	1.4	0.1	–0.1

Note: "–" means not applicable.
Source: Bureau of the Census, Current Population Survey Annual Social and Economic Supplement, Internet site http://www
.census.gov/hhes/www/income/dinctabs.html; calculations by New Strategist

More than 8 Million Elderly Women Live Alone

Nearly half the women who live alone are 65 or older.

Among the nation's 34 million single-person households, older Americans (aged 55 or older) head the 57 percent majority. Women account for the 55 percent majority of single-person households.

There are substantial differences in the ages of men and women who live alone. Most men who live alone are under age 55, while most women who live alone are aged 55 or older. Among men, those aged 75 or older are most likely to live alone, but the proportion is only 23 percent. In contrast, 45 percent of their female counterparts live by themselves. Most men live alone before marriage or after divorce. Most women live alone following the death of their spouse.

■ The number of single-person households will rise as boomers age.

Women are increasingly likely to live alone after middle age

(percent of women who live alone by age, 2013)

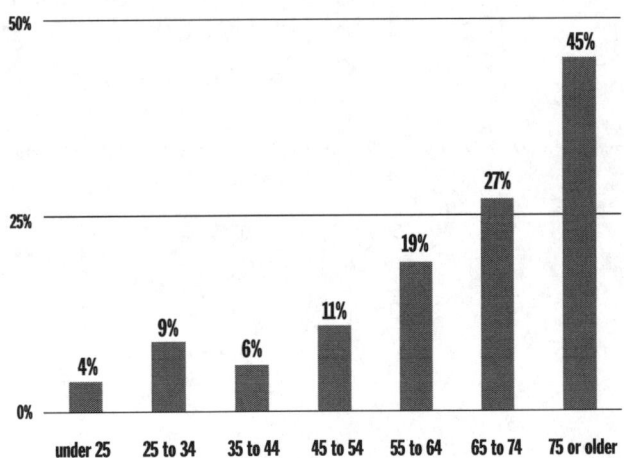

Table 7.6 People Living Alone by Sex and Age, 2013

(total number of people aged 15 or older, number and percent living alone, and percent distribution of people who live alone, by sex and age, 2013; numbers in thousands)

		living alone		
	total	number	percent of total	percent distribution
Total people	**250,023**	**33,570**	**13.4%**	**100.0%**
Under age 25	43,124	1,548	3.6	4.6
Aged 25 to 34	41,797	4,250	10.2	12.7
Aged 35 to 44	39,877	3,457	8.7	10.3
Aged 45 to 54	43,446	5,312	12.2	15.8
Aged 55 to 64	38,491	6,915	18.0	20.6
Aged 65 or older	43,287	12,087	27.9	36.0
Aged 65 to 74	24,702	5,423	22.0	16.2
Aged 75 or older	18,585	6,665	35.9	19.9
Total men	**121,111**	**15,002**	**12.4**	**100.0**
Under age 25	21,806	760	3.5	5.1
Aged 25 to 34	20,816	2,433	11.7	16.2
Aged 35 to 44	19,623	2,161	11.0	14.4
Aged 45 to 54	21,244	2,880	13.6	19.2
Aged 55 to 64	18,323	3,110	17.0	20.7
Aged 65 or older	19,298	3,658	19.0	24.4
Aged 65 to 74	11,604	1,888	16.3	12.6
Aged 75 or older	7,693	1,770	23.0	11.8
Total women	**128,912**	**18,568**	**14.4**	**100.0**
Under age 25	21,318	788	3.7	4.2
Aged 25 to 34	20,981	1,818	8.7	9.8
Aged 35 to 44	20,254	1,296	6.4	7.0
Aged 45 to 54	22,202	2,432	11.0	13.1
Aged 55 to 64	20,168	3,805	18.9	20.5
Aged 65 or older	23,990	8,429	35.1	45.4
Aged 65 to 74	13,098	3,534	27.0	19.0
Aged 75 or older	10,892	4,895	44.9	26.4

Source: Bureau of the Census, Current Population Survey Annual Social and Economic Supplement, Internet site http://www .census.gov/hhes/www/income/dinctabs.html; calculations by New Strategist

Households Are Growing in Every Region

The South is home to the majority of black households.

Household growth slowed considerably during the Great Recession, but growth has picked up in recent years in every region. Household growth is fastest in the South and West. Between 2007 and 2013, the number of households in the South grew by 7.9 percent. In the West, the increase was 6.4 percent.

The 55 percent majority of black households are in the South. Forty-five percent of Asian households are in the West. The West is also home to 39 percent of Hispanic households, while the South claims another 38 percent. Among all households in the South, blacks head 20 percent and are the largest minority. Hispanics are the largest minority in the West, accounting for 22 percent of the region's households. The Asian presence is also greatest in the West, where they head 10 percent of households.

■ The nation's markets and politics will increasingly be shaped by the concentration of Asians, blacks, and Hispanics in certain regions and states.

Only 40 percent of the nation's households are in the Northeast and Midwest

(percent distribution of households by region, 2013)

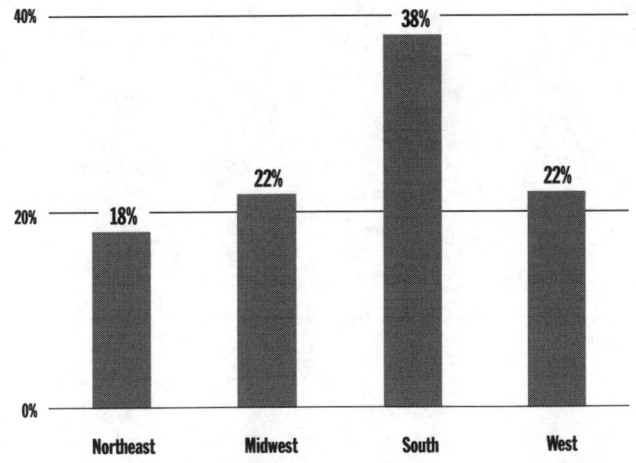

Table 7.7 Households by Region, 2000 to 2013

(number and percent distribution of households by region, 2000 to 2013; percent and percentage point change for selected years; numbers in thousands)

NUMBER	2013	2010	2007	2000	percent change 2007–13	2000–13
TOTAL HOUSEHOLDS	**122,459**	**117,538**	**116,011**	**104,705**	**5.6%**	**17.0%**
Northeast	22,125	21,479	21,261	20,087	4.1	10.1
Midwest	27,093	26,390	26,508	24,508	2.2	10.5
South	45,938	43,611	42,587	37,303	7.9	23.1
West	27,303	26,058	25,656	22,808	6.4	19.7

PERCENT DISTRIBUTION					percentage point change 2007–13	2000–13
TOTAL HOUSEHOLDS	**100.0%**	**100.0%**	**100.0%**	**100.0%**	–	–
Northeast	18.1	18.3	18.3	19.2	–0.3	–1.1
Midwest	22.1	22.5	22.8	23.4	–0.7	–1.3
South	37.5	37.1	36.7	35.6	0.8	1.9
West	22.3	22.2	22.1	21.8	0.2	0.5

Note: "–" means not applicable.
Source: Bureau of the Census, Current Population Survey Annual Social and Economic Supplement, Internet site http://www .census.gov/hhes/www/income/dinctabs.html; calculations by New Strategist

Table 7.8 Households by Region, Race, and Hispanic Origin, 2013

(number and percent distribution of households by household type, race, and Hispanic origin of householder, 2013; numbers in thousands)

	total	Asian	black	Hispanic	non-Hispanic white
Total households	122,459	5,872	16,559	15,589	83,792
Northeast	22,125	1,174	2,880	2,295	16,036
Midwest	27,093	687	2,971	1,310	21,933
South	45,938	1,342	9,059	5,899	29,369
West	27,303	2,669	1,649	6,085	16,454

PERCENT DISTRIBUTION BY REGION

Total households	100.0%	100.0%	100.0%	100.0%	100.0%
Northeast	18.1	20.0	17.4	14.7	19.1
Midwest	22.1	11.7	17.9	8.4	26.2
South	37.5	22.9	54.7	37.8	35.0
West	22.3	45.5	10.0	39.0	19.6

PERCENT DISTRIBUTION BY RACE AND HISPANIC ORIGIN OF HOUSEHOLDER

Total households	100.0%	4.8%	13.5%	12.7%	68.4%
Northeast	100.0	5.3	13.0	10.4	72.5
Midwest	100.0	2.5	11.0	4.8	81.0
South	100.0	2.9	19.7	12.8	63.9
West	100.0	9.8	6.0	22.3	60.3

Note: Numbers do not add to total because Hispanics may be of any race, not all races are shown, and some householders may be of more than one race. Asians and blacks are those who identify themselves as being of the race alone and those who identify themselves as being of the race in combination with other races. Non-Hispanic whites are those who identify themselves as being white alone and not Hispanic.
Source: Bureau of the Census, Current Population Survey Annual Social and Economic Supplement, Internet site http://www .census.gov/hhes/www/income/dinctabs.html; calculations by New Strategist

More than 80 Percent of Households Are in Metropolitan Areas

Non-Hispanic whites dominate households in nonmetropolitan areas.

Of the nation's 122 million households, 84 percent are in metropolitan areas, defined as counties with a city of 50,000 or more population plus any adjacent counties with economic ties to the core county. Only 16 percent of households are in nonmetropolitan areas. Asians, blacks, and Hispanics are much more likely than non-Hispanic whites to live in a metropolitan area.

About half of the nation's Asian, black, and Hispanic households are in the principal cities (central cities) of metropolitan areas. The figure is a much smaller 26 percent among non-Hispanic whites. The 54 percent majority of non-Hispanic white households are in the suburbs of metropolitan areas (outside principal cities) compared with 39 to 45 percent of Asian, black, and Hispanic households. Nineteen percent of non-Hispanic white households are in nonmetropolitan areas versus only 3 percent of Asian households.

■ Non-Hispanic whites head 53 percent of principal city households and 82 percent of households in nonmetropolitan areas.

Few non-Hispanic white households are in principal cities of metro areas

(percent of households in the principal cities of metropolitan areas, by race and Hispanic origin, 2013)

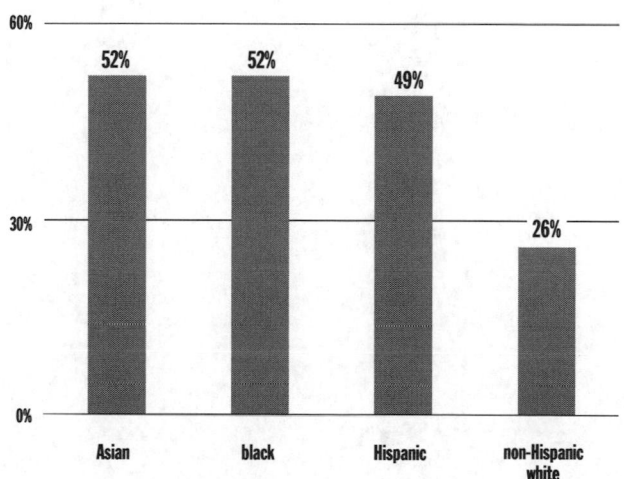

Table 7.9 Households by Metropolitan Status, 2000 to 2013

(number and percent distribution of households by metropolitan status, 2000 to 2013; percent and percentage point change for selected years; numbers in thousands)

NUMBER	2013	2010	2007	2000	percent change 2007–13	percent change 2000–13
TOTAL HOUSEHOLDS	**122,459**	**117,538**	**116,011**	**104,705**	**5.6%**	**17.0%**
Inside metropolitan areas	102,784	98,379	96,739	84,259	6.2	22.0
Inside principal cities	41,152	38,850	38,488	31,825	6.9	29.3
Outside principal cities	61,631	59,529	58,251	52,433	5.8	17.5
Outside metropolitan areas	19,676	19,159	19,272	20,447	2.1	–3.8

PERCENT DISTRIBUTION					percentage point change 2007–13	percentage point change 2000–13
TOTAL HOUSEHOLDS	**100.0%**	**100.0%**	**100.0%**	**100.0%**	–	–
Inside metropolitan areas	83.9	83.7	83.4	80.5	0.5	3.5
Inside principal cities	33.6	33.1	33.2	30.4	0.4	3.2
Outside principal cities	50.3	50.6	50.2	50.1	0.1	0.3
Outside metropolitan areas	16.1	16.3	16.6	19.5	–0.5	–3.5

Note: "–" means not applicable.
Source: Bureau of the Census, Current Population Survey Annual Social and Economic Supplement, Internet site http://www
.census.gov/hhes/www/income/dinctabs.html; calculations by New Strategist

Table 7.10 Households by Metropolitan Status, Race, and Hispanic Origin, 2013

(number and percent distribution of households by metropolitan status, race, and Hispanic origin, 2013; numbers in thousands)

	total	Asian	black	Hispanic	non-Hispanic white
Total households	**122,459**	**5,872**	**16,559**	**15,589**	**83,792**
Inside metropolitan areas	102,784	5,675	14,953	14,393	67,651
Inside principal cities	41,152	3,034	8,568	7,635	21,998
Outside principal cities	61,631	2,641	6,385	6,757	45,652
Outside metropolitan areas	19,676	197	1,607	1,196	16,141

PERCENT DISTRIBUTION BY METROPOLITAN STATUS

	total	Asian	black	Hispanic	non-Hispanic white
Total households	**100.0%**	**100.0%**	**100.0%**	**100.0%**	**100.0%**
Inside metropolitan areas	83.9	96.6	90.3	92.3	80.7
Inside principal cities	33.6	51.7	51.7	49.0	26.3
Outside principal cities	50.3	45.0	38.6	43.3	54.5
Outside metropolitan areas	16.1	3.4	9.7	7.7	19.3

PERCENT DISTRIBUTION BY RACE AND HISPANIC ORIGIN OF HOUSEHOLDER

	total	Asian	black	Hispanic	non-Hispanic white
Total households	**100.0%**	**4.8%**	**13.5%**	**12.7%**	**68.4%**
Inside metropolitan areas	100.0	5.5	14.5	14.0	65.8
Inside principal cities	100.0	7.4	20.8	18.6	53.5
Outside principal cities	100.0	4.3	10.4	11.0	74.1
Outside metropolitan areas	100.0	1.0	8.2	6.1	82.0

Note: Numbers do not add to total because Hispanics may be of any race, not all races are shown, and some householders may be of more than one race. Asians and blacks are those who identify themselves as being of the race alone and those who identify themselves as being of the race in combination with other races. Non-Hispanic whites are those who identify themselves as being white alone and not Hispanic.
Source: Bureau of the Census, Current Population Survey Annual Social and Economic Supplement, Internet site http://www .census.gov/hhes/www/income/dinctabs.html; calculations by New Strategist

Nearly One in Four Children Live with Their Mother Only

Only 4 percent live with their father only.

Among the nation's 74 million children under age 18, only 68 percent live with two parents. The proportion of children who live with two parents (married or unmarried) ranges from a low of 40 percent among black children to a high of 83 percent among Asian children. A smaller share of children lives with two married biological parents, ranging from 29 percent of blacks to 76 percent of Asians.

Fifty-three percent of the nation's children are non-Hispanic white. By living arrangement, however, the non-Hispanic white share varies greatly. Just 36 percent of children living with their mother only are non-Hispanic white. Among children living with two married biological parents, 61 percent are non-Hispanic white.

■ The poverty rate among children is unlikely to decline significantly until fewer children live in single-parent families.

Children's living arrangements vary greatly by race and Hispanic origin

(percent of children living with two married, biological parents, by race and Hispanic origin, 2012)

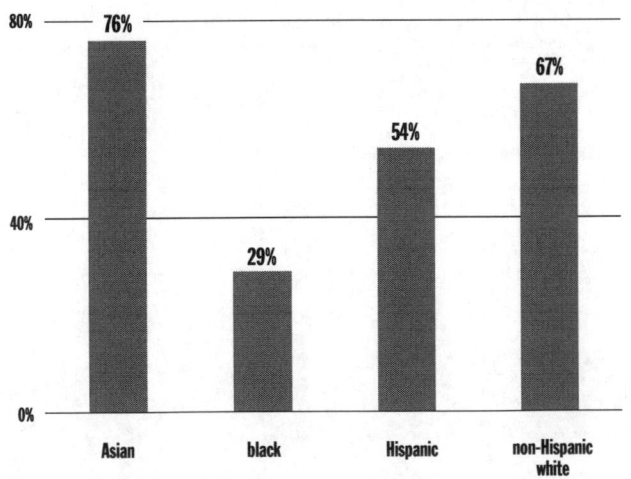

Table 7.11 Children's Living Arrangements: Number by Race and Hispanic Origin, 2012

(number of children under age 18 by living arrangement, race, and Hispanic origin, 2012; numbers in thousands)

	total	Asian	black	Hispanic	non-Hispanic white
TOTAL CHILDREN	**73,817**	**4,542**	**13,012**	**17,570**	**39,062**
Living with two parents	**50,267**	**3,785**	**5,200**	**11,542**	**29,881**
Married parents	47,330	3,657	4,537	10,364	28,806
Unmarried parents	2,937	129	663	1,178	1,075
Biological mother and father	45,221	3,554	4,364	10,589	26,888
Married parents	42,691	3,431	3,816	9,528	25,997
Biological mother and stepfather	3,016	73	518	680	1,742
Biological father and stepmother	919	29	160	125	587
Biological mother and adoptive father	185	10	22	29	118
Biological father and adoptive mother	34	2	3	1	28
Adoptive mother and father	661	109	101	86	364
Other	231	8	32	31	154
Living with one parent	**20,916**	**662**	**6,958**	**5,465**	**8,090**
Mother only	17,991	548	6,414	4,926	6,423
Father only	2,924	114	545	539	1,667
Living with no parents	**2,634**	**95**	**853**	**563**	**1,091**
Grandparents	1,454	29	494	265	627
Other	1,180	66	360	298	463
Living with at least one biological parent	**69,941**	**4,290**	**11,907**	**16,822**	**37,339**
Living with at least one stepparent	**4,287**	**121**	**750**	**864**	**2,519**
Living with at least one adoptive parent	**1,126**	**150**	**205**	**160**	**600**

Note: Asians and blacks are those who identify themselves as being of the race alone and those who identify themselves as being of the race in combination with other races. Non-Hispanic whites are those who identify themselves as being white alone and not Hispanic.
Source: Bureau of the Census, America's Families and Living Arrangements: 2012, Detailed Tables, Internet site http://www .census.gov/hhes/families/data/cps2012.html; calculations by New Strategist

Table 7.12 Children's Living Arrangements: Distribution by Living Arrangement, 2012

(percent distribution of children under age 18 by living arrangement, by race and Hispanic origin, 2012; numbers in thousands)

	total	Asian	black	Hispanic	non-Hispanic white
TOTAL CHILDREN	100.0%	100.0%	100.0%	100.0%	100.0%
Living with two parents	**68.1**	**83.3**	**40.0**	**65.7**	**76.5**
Married parents	64.1	80.5	34.9	59.0	73.7
Unmarried parents	4.0	2.8	5.1	6.7	2.8
Biological mother and father	61.3	78.2	33.5	60.3	68.8
Married parents	57.8	75.5	29.3	54.2	66.6
Biological mother and stepfather	4.1	1.6	4.0	3.9	4.5
Biological father and stepmother	1.2	0.6	1.2	0.7	1.5
Biological mother and adoptive father	0.3	0.2	0.2	0.2	0.3
Biological father and adoptive mother	0.0	0.0	0.0	0.0	0.1
Adoptive mother and father	0.9	2.4	0.8	0.5	0.9
Other	0.3	0.2	0.2	0.2	0.4
Living with one parent	**28.3**	**14.6**	**53.5**	**31.1**	**20.7**
Mother only	24.4	12.1	49.3	28.0	16.4
Father only	4.0	2.5	4.2	3.1	4.3
Living with no parents	**3.6**	**2.1**	**6.6**	**3.2**	**2.8**
Grandparents	2.0	0.6	3.8	1.5	1.6
Other	1.6	1.5	2.8	1.7	1.2
Living with at least one biological parent	**94.7**	**94.5**	**91.5**	**95.7**	**95.6**
Living with at least one stepparent	**5.8**	**2.7**	**5.8**	**4.9**	**6.4**
Living with at least one adoptive parent	**1.5**	**3.3**	**1.6**	**0.9**	**1.5**

Note: Asians and blacks are those who identify themselves as being of the race alone and those who identify themselves as being of the race in combination with other races. Non-Hispanic whites are those who identify themselves as being white alone and not Hispanic.
Source: Bureau of the Census, America's Families and Living Arrangements: 2012, Detailed Tables, Internet site http://www .census.gov/hhes/families/data/cps2012.html; calculations by New Strategist

Table 7.13 Children's Living Arrangement: Distribution by Race and Hispanic Origin, 2012

(percent distribution of children under age 18 by race and Hispanic origin, by living arrangement, 2012)

	total	Asian	black	Hispanic	non-Hispanic white
TOTAL CHILDREN	100.0%	6.2%	17.6%	23.8%	52.9%
Living with two parents	100.0	7.5	10.3	23.0	59.4
Married parents	100.0	7.7	9.6	21.9	60.9
Unmarried parents	100.0	4.4	22.6	40.1	36.6
Biological mother and father	100.0	7.9	9.7	23.4	59.5
Married parents	100.0	8.0	8.9	22.3	60.9
Biological mother and stepfather	100.0	2.4	17.2	22.5	57.8
Biological father and stepmother	100.0	3.2	17.4	13.6	63.9
Biological mother and adoptive father	100.0	5.4	11.9	15.7	63.8
Biological father and adoptive mother	100.0	5.9	8.8	2.9	82.4
Adoptive mother and father	100.0	16.5	15.3	13.0	55.1
Other	100.0	3.5	13.9	13.4	66.7
Living with one parent	100.0	3.2	33.3	26.1	38.7
Mother only	100.0	3.0	35.7	27.4	35.7
Father only	100.0	3.9	18.6	18.4	57.0
Living with no parents	100.0	3.6	32.4	21.4	41.4
Grandparents	100.0	2.0	34.0	18.2	43.1
Other	100.0	5.6	30.5	25.3	39.2
At least one biological parent	100.0	6.1	17.0	24.1	53.4
At least one stepparent	100.0	2.8	17.5	20.2	58.8
At least one adoptive parent	100.0	13.3	18.2	14.2	53.3

Note: Asians and blacks are those who identify themselves as being of the race alone and those who identify themselves as being of the race in combination with other races. Non-Hispanic whites are those who identify themselves as being white alone and not Hispanic.
Source: Bureau of the Census, America's Families and Living Arrangements: 2012, Detailed Tables, Internet site http://www .census.gov/hhes/families/data/cps2012.html; calculations by New Strategist

Most Married Couples Have Children at Home

Most do not have children under age 18 at home, however.

Among the nation's 121 million households in 2012, only 29 percent included children under age 18. When adult children are also considered in the calculation, a larger 40 percent of households include children. Among married couples, 52 percent have children of any age living with them versus 40 percent with children under age 18.

Hispanics are most likely to be living with children. Forty-six percent of Hispanic households include children under age 18 and 58 percent have children of any age at home. Non-Hispanic whites are least likely to live with children. Only 25 percent of non-Hispanic white households include children under age 18 and 35 percent have children of any age at home.

■ Householders aged 35 to 39 are most likely to have children under age 18 in their home.

Most Hispanic households include children

(percent of households with children of any age at home, by race and Hispanic origin of householder, 2012)

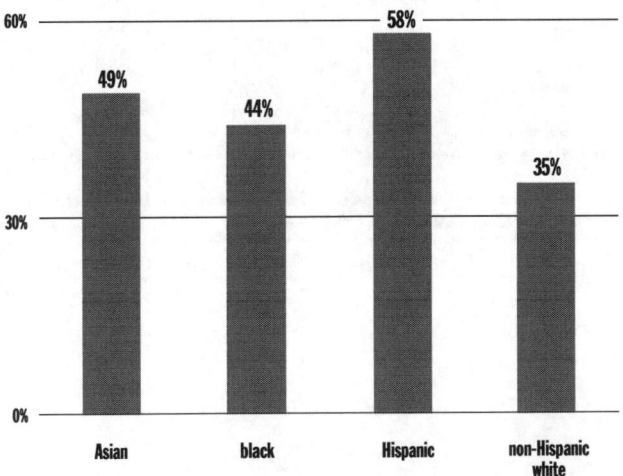

Table 7.14 Households by Age of Householder, Type of Household, and Presence of Children under Age 18, 2012

(number and percent distribution of households by age of householder, type of household, and presence of own children under age 18, 2012; numbers in thousands)

	all households		married couples		female-headed families		male-headed families	
	total	with children under 18	total	with children under 18	total	with children under 18	total	with children under 18
Total households	121,084	34,989	58,949	23,704	15,669	8,869	5,888	2,415
Under age 25	6,180	1,737	1,059	597	1,456	970	819	171
Aged 25 to 29	9,208	3,820	3,366	2,063	1,611	1,401	768	356
Aged 30 to 34	10,638	6,176	5,292	4,090	1,809	1,676	665	409
Aged 35 to 39	10,111	6,772	5,557	4,690	1,871	1,666	560	415
Aged 40 to 44	11,129	6,686	6,397	4,953	1,801	1,344	596	389
Aged 45 to 49	11,763	5,213	6,438	3,872	1,722	998	605	343
Aged 50 to 54	12,433	2,880	6,861	2,176	1,414	533	506	171
Aged 55 to 64	22,779	1,428	12,093	1,079	2,013	224	795	124
Aged 65 or older	26,843	277	11,886	183	1,972	57	573	37

PERCENT OF HOUSEHOLDS WITH CHILDREN UNDER AGE 18

	all households		married couples		female-headed families		male-headed families	
Total households	100.0%	28.9%	100.0%	40.2%	100.0%	56.6%	100.0%	41.0%
Under age 25	100.0	28.1	100.0	56.4	100.0	66.6	100.0	20.9
Aged 25 to 29	100.0	41.5	100.0	61.3	100.0	87.0	100.0	46.4
Aged 30 to 34	100.0	58.1	100.0	77.3	100.0	92.6	100.0	61.5
Aged 35 to 39	100.0	67.0	100.0	84.4	100.0	89.0	100.0	74.1
Aged 40 to 44	100.0	60.1	100.0	77.4	100.0	74.6	100.0	65.3
Aged 45 to 49	100.0	44.3	100.0	60.1	100.0	58.0	100.0	56.7
Aged 50 to 54	100.0	23.2	100.0	31.7	100.0	37.7	100.0	33.8
Aged 55 to 64	100.0	6.3	100.0	8.9	100.0	11.1	100.0	15.6
Aged 65 or older	100.0	1.0	100.0	1.5	100.0	2.9	100.0	6.5

Source: Bureau of the Census, America's Families and Living Arrangements: 2012, Detailed Tables, Internet site http://www .census.gov/hhes/families/data/cps2012.html; calculations by New Strategist

Table 7.15 Households by Age of Householder, Type of Household, and Presence of Children of Any Age, 2012

(number and percent distribution of households by age of householder, type of household, and presence of own children of any age, 2012; numbers in thousands)

	all households		married couples		female-headed families		male-headed families	
	total	with children of any age	total	with children of any age	total	with children of any age	total	with children of any age
Total households	121,084	47,912	58,949	30,882	15,669	13,397	5,888	3,633
Under age 25	6,180	1,749	1,059	598	1,456	980	819	171
Aged 25 to 29	9,208	3,854	3,366	2,072	1,611	1,411	768	371
Aged 30 to 34	10,638	6,226	5,292	4,127	1,809	1,689	665	411
Aged 35 to 39	10,111	6,959	5,557	4,765	1,871	1,763	560	431
Aged 40 to 44	11,129	7,463	6,397	5,327	1,801	1,691	596	445
Aged 45 to 49	11,763	6,915	6,438	4,871	1,722	1,571	605	473
Aged 50 to 54	12,433	5,542	6,861	3,914	1,414	1,251	506	378
Aged 55 to 64	22,779	5,794	12,093	3,754	2,013	1,536	795	504
Aged 65 or older	26,843	3,411	11,886	1,454	1,972	1,506	573	451

PERCENT OF HOUSEHOLDS WITH CHILDREN OF ANY AGE

	all households		married couples		female-headed families		male-headed families	
Total households	100.0%	39.6%	100.0%	52.4%	100.0%	85.5%	100.0%	61.7%
Under age 25	100.0	28.3	100.0	56.5	100.0	67.3	100.0	20.9
Aged 25 to 29	100.0	41.9	100.0	61.6	100.0	87.6	100.0	48.3
Aged 30 to 34	100.0	58.5	100.0	78.0	100.0	93.4	100.0	61.8
Aged 35 to 39	100.0	68.8	100.0	85.7	100.0	94.2	100.0	77.0
Aged 40 to 44	100.0	67.1	100.0	83.3	100.0	93.9	100.0	74.7
Aged 45 to 49	100.0	58.8	100.0	75.7	100.0	91.2	100.0	78.2
Aged 50 to 54	100.0	44.6	100.0	57.0	100.0	88.5	100.0	74.7
Aged 55 to 64	100.0	25.4	100.0	31.0	100.0	76.3	100.0	63.4
Aged 65 or older	100.0	12.7	100.0	12.2	100.0	76.4	100.0	78.7

Source: Bureau of the Census, America's Families and Living Arrangements: 2012, Detailed Tables, Internet site http://www.census.gov/hhes/families/data/cps2012.html; calculations by New Strategist

Table 7.16 Households by Age, Race, and Hispanic Origin of Householder and Presence of Children under Age 18, 2012

(number and percent distribution of households by age, race, and Hispanic origin of householder and presence of own children under age 18, 2012; numbers in thousands)

	Asian		black		Hispanic		non-Hispanic white	
	total	with children under 18	total	with children under 18	total	with children under 18	total	with children under 18
Total households	5,705	2,069	16,165	5,163	14,939	6,912	83,573	20,790
Under age 25	407	42	1,119	397	1,288	469	3,367	826
Aged 25 to 29	554	120	1,402	731	1,621	936	5,626	2,049
Aged 30 to 34	695	336	1,628	1,038	1,933	1,386	6,333	3,402
Aged 35 to 39	717	486	1,511	968	1,842	1,407	6,015	3,912
Aged 40 to 44	607	428	1,664	858	1,777	1,181	7,050	4,197
Aged 45 to 49	629	392	1,623	610	1,598	858	7,847	3,357
Aged 50 to 54	509	161	1,709	321	1,345	438	8,742	1,926
Aged 55 to 64	855	93	2,910	179	1,935	190	16,886	958
Aged 65 or older	731	12	2,599	60	1,600	46	21,708	163

PERCENT OF HOUSEHOLDS WITH CHILDREN UNDER AGE 18

	Asian		black		Hispanic		non-Hispanic white	
Total households	100.0%	36.3%	100.0%	31.9%	100.0%	46.3%	100.0%	24.9%
Under age 25	100.0	10.3	100.0	35.5	100.0	36.4	100.0	24.5
Aged 25 to 29	100.0	21.7	100.0	52.1	100.0	57.7	100.0	36.4
Aged 30 to 34	100.0	48.3	100.0	63.8	100.0	71.7	100.0	53.7
Aged 35 to 39	100.0	67.8	100.0	64.1	100.0	76.4	100.0	65.0
Aged 40 to 44	100.0	70.5	100.0	51.6	100.0	66.5	100.0	59.5
Aged 45 to 49	100.0	62.3	100.0	37.6	100.0	53.7	100.0	42.8
Aged 50 to 54	100.0	31.6	100.0	18.8	100.0	32.6	100.0	22.0
Aged 55 to 64	100.0	10.9	100.0	6.2	100.0	9.8	100.0	5.7
Aged 65 or older	100.0	1.6	100.0	2.3	100.0	2.9	100.0	0.8

Note: Asians and blacks are those who identify themselves as being of the race alone and those who identify themselves as being of the race in combination with other races. Non-Hispanic whites are those who identify themselves as being white alone and not Hispanic.
Source: Bureau of the Census, America's Families and Living Arrangements: 2012, Detailed Tables, Internet site http://www .census.gov/hhes/families/data/cps2012.html; calculations by New Strategist

Table 7.17 Households by Age, Race, and Hispanic Origin of Householder and Presence of Children of Any Age, 2012

(number and percent distribution of households by age, race, and Hispanic origin of householder and presence of own children of any age, 2012; numbers in thousands)

	Asian		black		Hispanic		non-Hispanic white	
	total	with children of any age	total	with children of any age	total	with children of any age	total	with children of any age
Total households	5,705	2,805	16,165	7,192	14,939	8,611	83,573	29,138
Under age 25	407	42	1,119	397	1,288	469	3,367	826
Aged 25 to 29	554	120	1,402	731	1,621	936	5,626	2,049
Aged 30 to 34	695	336	1,628	1,038	1,933	1,386	6,333	3,402
Aged 35 to 39	717	486	1,511	968	1,842	1,407	6,015	3,912
Aged 40 to 44	607	428	1,664	858	1,777	1,181	7,050	4,197
Aged 45 to 49	629	392	1,623	610	1,598	858	7,847	3,357
Aged 50 to 54	509	161	1,709	321	1,345	438	8,742	1,926
Aged 55 to 64	855	93	2,910	179	1,935	190	16,886	958
Aged 65 or older	731	12	2,599	60	1,600	46	21,708	163

PERCENT OF HOUSEHOLDS WITH CHILDREN OF ANY AGE

	Asian		black		Hispanic		non-Hispanic white	
Total households	100.0%	49.2%	100.0%	44.5%	100.0%	57.6%	100.0%	34.9%
Under age 25	100.0	10.3	100.0	35.7	100.0	37.0	100.0	24.6
Aged 25 to 29	100.0	22.4	100.0	52.6	100.0	57.9	100.0	36.8
Aged 30 to 34	100.0	48.9	100.0	64.6	100.0	71.9	100.0	54.2
Aged 35 to 39	100.0	69.0	100.0	67.8	100.0	78.7	100.0	66.3
Aged 40 to 44	100.0	73.6	100.0	63.3	100.0	75.1	100.0	65.2
Aged 45 to 49	100.0	73.3	100.0	54.8	100.0	69.9	100.0	56.5
Aged 50 to 54	100.0	64.4	100.0	38.1	100.0	60.1	100.0	42.3
Aged 55 to 64	100.0	46.9	100.0	28.8	100.0	38.1	100.0	22.3
Aged 65 or older	100.0	22.7	100.0	20.9	100.0	22.4	100.0	10.7

Note: Asians and blacks are those who identify themselves as being of the race alone and those who identify themselves as being of the race in combination with other races. Non-Hispanic whites are those who identify themselves as being white alone and not Hispanic.
Source: Bureau of the Census, America's Families and Living Arrangements: 2012, Detailed Tables, Internet site http://www .census.gov/hhes/families/data/cps2012.html; calculations by New Strategist

Most Men and Women Are Householders

Many young men live with their parents.

Among the nation's 120 million men aged 15 or older, 70 percent head households as a married-couple householder or spouse, a male family head, a single-person householder, or as a householder who lives with nonrelatives. Among women aged 15 or older, an even larger 75 percent are householders or the spouse of a married-couple householder.

Being a married-couple householder or spouse is the most common living arrangement for both men and women. Among women, the second most common arrangement is living alone, with 14 percent of women aged 15 or older heading a single-person household. Ranking third among women is being the child of the householder (13 percent). Among men, the second most common living arrangement is child of householder (18 percent), and 12 percent live alone.

■ Among young adults, men are more likely than women to live with their parents because men marry at an older age.

Nearly half of men are married-couple householders or spouses

(percent distribution of men aged 15 or older by householder status, 2012)

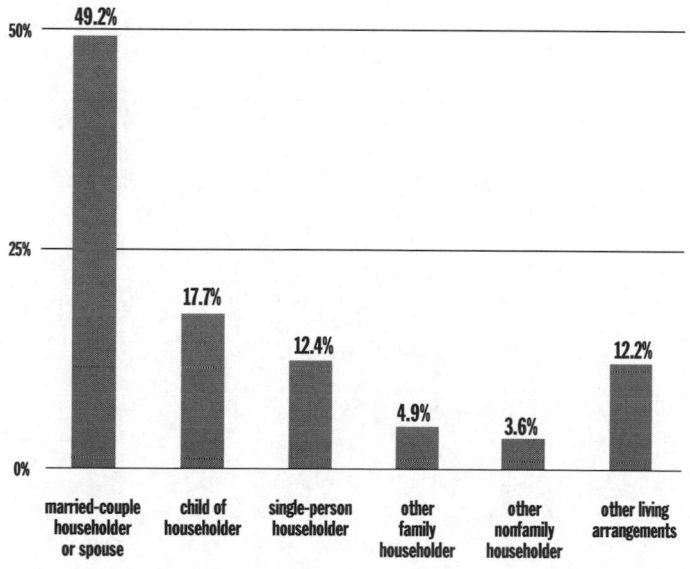

Table 7.18 Living Arrangements of Women by Age, 2012

(number and percent distribution of women aged 15 or older by living arrangement and age, 2012; numbers in thousands)

	total	under 20	20 to 24	25 to 29	30 to 34	35 to 44	45 to 54	55 to 64	65 or older
TOTAL WOMEN	127,695	10,393	10,888	10,459	10,284	20,244	22,459	19,808	23,160
Householder	96,000	397	3,910	7,126	8,492	17,669	19,814	17,919	20,675
Married-couple householder or spouse	58,949	69	1,355	4,030	5,619	12,344	13,701	11,765	10,068
Other family householder	15,668	231	1,224	1,610	1,809	3,672	3,136	2,013	1,973
Living alone	18,354	51	673	947	811	1,319	2,501	3,697	8,356
Living with nonrelatives	3,029	46	658	539	253	334	476	444	278
Not a householder	31,695	9,996	6,979	3,333	1,792	2,575	2,644	1,888	2,485
Child of householder	17,120	8,682	4,595	1,494	661	859	550	228	47
Other relative of householder	7,730	910	825	513	330	775	1,156	1,093	2,130
In nonfamily household	6,845	404	1,559	1,326	801	941	938	567	308

PERCENT DISTRIBUTION BY LIVING ARRANGEMENT

	total	under 20	20 to 24	25 to 29	30 to 34	35 to 44	45 to 54	55 to 64	65 or older
TOTAL WOMEN	100.0%	100.0%	100.0%	100.0%	100.0%	100.0%	100.0%	100.0%	100.0%
Householder	75.2	3.8	35.9	68.1	82.6	87.3	88.2	90.5	89.3
Married-couple householder or spouse	46.2	0.7	12.4	38.5	54.6	61.0	61.0	59.4	43.5
Other family householder	12.3	2.2	11.2	15.4	17.6	18.1	14.0	10.2	8.5
Living alone	14.4	0.5	6.2	9.1	7.9	6.5	11.1	18.7	36.1
Living with nonrelatives	2.4	0.4	6.0	5.2	2.5	1.6	2.1	2.2	1.2
Not a householder	24.8	96.2	64.1	31.9	17.4	12.7	11.8	9.5	10.7
Child of householder	13.4	83.5	42.2	14.3	6.4	4.2	2.4	1.2	0.2
Other relative of householder	6.1	8.8	7.6	4.9	3.2	3.8	5.1	5.5	9.2
In nonfamily household	5.4	3.9	14.3	12.7	7.8	4.6	4.2	2.9	1.3

Source: Bureau of the Census, America's Families and Living Arrangements: 2012, Detailed Tables, Internet site http://www .census.gov/hhes/families/data/cps2012.html; calculations by New Strategist

Table 7.19 Living Arrangements of Men by Age, 2012

(number and percent distribution of men aged 15 or older by living arrangement and age, 2012; numbers in thousands)

	total	under 20	20 to 24	25 to 29	30 to 34	35 to 44	45 to 54	55 to 64	65 or older
TOTAL MEN	119,877	10,836	10,982	10,430	10,028	19,670	21,463	18,137	18,332
Householder	96,000	397	3,910	7,126	8,492	17,669	19,814	17,919	20,675
Married-couple householder or spouse	58,949	33	763	2,960	4,912	11,888	13,425	12,123	12,846
Other family householder	5,888	273	546	767	665	1,157	1,111	795	573
Living alone	14,835	58	596	1,147	1,176	2,137	3,052	3,206	3,462
Living with nonrelatives	4,360	61	706	830	632	668	619	530	316
Not a householder	35,844	10,412	8,370	4,725	2,643	3,820	3,255	1,483	1,135
Child of householder	21,195	9,194	5,896	2,321	1,138	1,407	997	206	33
Other relative of householder	6,720	905	1,022	804	455	936	1,099	699	802
In nonfamily household	7,929	313	1,452	1,600	1,050	1,477	1,159	578	300

PERCENT DISTRIBUTION BY LIVING ARRANGEMENT

	total	under 20	20 to 24	25 to 29	30 to 34	35 to 44	45 to 54	55 to 64	65 or older
TOTAL MEN	100.0%	100.0%	100.0%	100.0%	100.0%	100.0%	100.0%	100.0%	100.0%
Householder	70.1	3.9	23.8	54.7	73.6	80.6	84.8	91.8	93.8
Married-couple householder or spouse	49.2	0.3	6.9	28.4	49.0	60.4	62.5	66.8	70.1
Other family householder	4.9	2.5	5.0	7.4	6.6	5.9	5.2	4.4	3.1
Living alone	12.4	0.5	5.4	11.0	11.7	10.9	14.2	17.7	18.9
Living with nonrelatives	3.6	0.6	6.4	8.0	6.3	3.4	2.9	2.9	1.7
Not a householder	29.9	96.1	76.2	45.3	26.4	19.4	15.2	8.2	6.2
Child of householder	17.7	84.8	53.7	22.3	11.3	7.2	4.6	1.1	0.2
Other relative of householder	5.6	8.4	9.3	7.7	4.5	4.8	5.1	3.9	4.4
In nonfamily household	6.6	2.9	13.2	15.3	10.5	7.5	5.4	3.2	1.6

Source: Bureau of the Census, America's Families and Living Arrangements: 2012, Detailed Tables, Internet site http://www .census.gov/hhes/families/data/cps2012.html; calculations by New Strategist

Many Young Adults Are Postponing Marriage

Cohabitation is common before marrying.

Men and women are remaining single longer than ever as more attend college and establish themselves in a career before tying the knot. Among women aged 20 to 24, fully 81 percent have not yet married. Among their male counterparts, the figure is 89 percent. In the 25-to-29 age group, 51 percent of women and 63 percent of men are still unmarried. The median age at first marriage is at a record high of 28.6 years for men and 26.6 years for women.

Just because young adults are unmarried does not mean they are living the single life. Many live together outside of marriage. Nearly one in five women aged 20 to 24 and men aged 25 to 29 are currently cohabiting. Once married, many divorce. Among women aged 40 to 44, only half are currently in their first marriage. One in three has been married more than once or is single but formerly married.

■ Cohabitation is particularly common among the least educated.

Most women have married by their early thirties

(percentage of women aged 20 or older who have never married, by age, 2012)

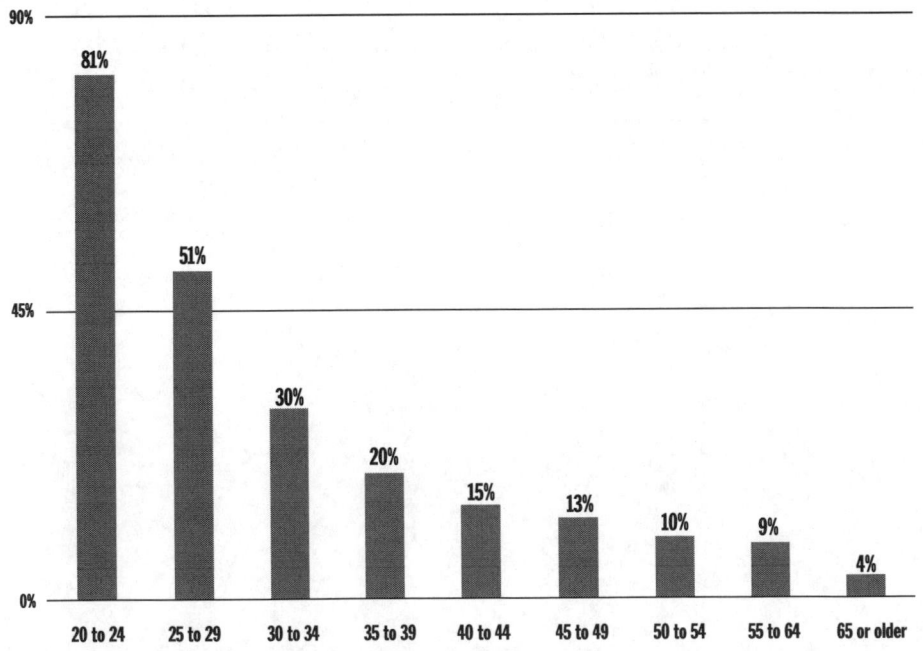

Table 7.20 Never-Married People by Age and Sex, 2012

(percent of people aged 20 or older who have never married, by age and sex, 2012)

	total	men	women
Total people	**25.0%**	**27.9%**	**22.3%**
Aged 20 to 24	85.3	89.2	81.3
Aged 25 to 29	57.2	63.5	51.0
Aged 30 to 34	34.4	39.1	29.7
Aged 35 to 39	22.2	24.4	20.1
Aged 40 to 44	17.5	20.1	15.0
Aged 45 to 49	15.2	17.5	13.0
Aged 50 to 54	11.4	12.4	10.5
Aged 55 to 64	9.0	9.4	8.7
Aged 65 or older	4.4	4.5	4.3

Source: Bureau of the Census, America's Families and Living Arrangements: 2012, Detailed Tables, Internet site http://www .census.gov/hhes/families/data/cps2012.html; calculations by New Strategist

Table 7.21 Median Age at First Marriage by Sex, 1950 to 2012

(median age at first marriage by sex, 1950 to 2012; change in years for selected years)

	men	women
2012	28.6 yrs.	26.6 yrs.
2011	28.4	26.4
2010	28.2	26.1
2009	28.1	25.9
2008	27.6	25.9
2007	27.5	25.6
2006	27.5	25.5
2005	27.1	25.3
2004	27.4	25.3
2003	27.1	25.3
2002	26.9	25.3
2001	26.9	25.1
2000	26.8	25.1
1990	26.1	23.9
1980	24.7	22.0
1970	23.2	20.8
1960	22.8	20.3
1950	22.8	20.3

Change in years

	men	women
2000 to 2012	1.8 yrs.	1.5 yrs.
1950 to 2012	5.8	6.3

Source: Bureau of the Census, Families and Living Arrangements, Historical Time Series, Internet site http://www.census.gov/ hhes/families/data/historical.html; calculations by New Strategist

Table 7.22 Marital Status by Sex, 2012

(number and percent distribution of people aged 15 or older by marital status and sex, 2012; numbers in thousands)

	total	men	women
Total people	**247,573**	**119,877**	**127,695**
Never married	77,273	41,035	36,238
Married, spouse present	122,095	61,047	61,047
Married, spouse absent	3,568	1,759	1,809
Separated	5,668	2,475	3,193
Divorced	24,911	10,696	14,215
Widowed	14,058	2,864	11,193

PERCENT DISTRIBUTION BY MARITAL STATUS

Total people	**100.0%**	**100.0%**	**100.0%**
Never married	31.2	34.2	28.4
Married, spouse present	49.3	50.9	47.8
Married, spouse absent	1.4	1.5	1.4
Separated	2.3	2.1	2.5
Divorced	10.1	8.9	11.1
Widowed	5.7	2.4	8.8

PERCENT DISTRIBUTION BY SEX

Total people	**100.0**	**48.4**	**51.6**
Never married	100.0	53.1	46.9
Married, spouse present	100.0	50.0	50.0
Married, spouse absent	100.0	49.3	50.7
Separated	100.0	43.7	56.3
Divorced	100.0	42.9	57.1
Widowed	100.0	20.4	79.6

Source: Bureau of the Census, America's Families and Living Arrangements: 2012, Current Population Survey Annual Social and Economic Supplement, Internet site http://www.census.gov/hhes/families/data/cps2012.html; calculations by New Strategist

Table 7.23 Current Marital Status of Men, 2006–2010

(total number of men aged 15 to 44, and percent distribution by current marital status, by selected characteristics, 2006–2010; numbers in thousands)

| | total | | in a union | | | | not in a union | |
	number	percent	total	first marriage	second or higher marriage	cohabiting	never married	formerly married
Total men aged 15 to 44	**62,128**	**100.0%**	**49.8%**	**32.8%**	**4.8%**	**12.2%**	**45.0%**	**5.2%**
Aged 15 to 19	10,816	100.0	2.6	0.3	0.0	2.3	97.3	–
Aged 20 to 24	10,394	100.0	26.3	11.3	–	15.0	72.6	0.8
Aged 25 to 29	10,758	100.0	53.7	32.8	1.4	19.5	43.1	3.1
Aged 30 to 34	9,228	100.0	71.1	50.9	5.2	15.0	22.0	7.0
Aged 35 to 39	10,405	100.0	74.3	54.1	7.9	12.3	16.0	9.7
Aged 40 to 44	10,526	100.0	74.2	50.2	14.6	9.4	14.8	11.1
Number of biologial children								
None	34,307	100.0	23.5	13.3	0.8	9.4	74.1	2.4
One or more children	27,821	100.0	82.1	56.7	9.8	15.6	9.1	8.7
Race and Hispanic origin								
Asian	2,406	100.0	50.0	44.7	1.9	3.4	49.4	0.7
Black	7,341	100.0	39.7	24.2	2.7	12.8	55.1	5.2
Hispanic	11,847	100.0	52.5	31.7	3.2	17.6	42.0	5.4
Non-Hispanic white	37,283	100.0	50.5	34.3	5.9	10.3	44.0	5.6
Education								
Not a high school graduate	9,004	100.0	70.1	37.7	5.8	26.6	23.3	6.7
High school graduate or GED	12,068	100.0	61.5	40.6	8.3	12.6	28.6	9.9
Some college, no degree	13,206	100.0	59.1	37.8	7.2	14.1	34.7	6.3
Bachelor's degree	8,924	100.0	62.3	48.6	4.1	9.6	32.9	4.7
Master's degree or more	3,857	100.0	74.9	65.7	4.2	5.0	20.7	4.3
Family structure at age 14								
Living with both parents	43,070	100.0	51.1	35.5	4.6	11.0	44.2	4.7
Other	19,058	100.0	46.7	26.4	5.4	14.9	46.8	6.5

Note: Asians and blacks are those who identify themselves as being of the race alone. Education categories include only people aged 22 to 44. "–" means sample is too small to make a reliable estimate.
Source: National Center for Health Statistics, First Marriages in the United States: Data from the 2006–2010 National Survey of Family Growth, National Health Statistics Reports, No. 49, 2012, Internet site http://www.cdc.gov/nchs/nsfg/new_nsfg.htm

Table 7.24 Current Marital Status of Women, 2006–2010

(total number of women aged 15 to 44, and percent distribution by current marital status, by selected characteristics, 2006–2010; numbers in thousands)

| | total | | in a union | | | | not in a union | |
	number	percent	total	first marriage	second or higher marriage	cohabiting	never married	formerly married
Total women aged 15 to 44	**61,755**	**100.0%**	**52.7%**	**36.4%**	**5.1%**	**11.2%**	**38.2%**	**9.2%**
Aged 15 to 19	10,478	100.0	5.9	1.1	0.0	4.8	94.1	0.0
Aged 20 to 24	10,365	100.0	36.0	17.3	–	18.7	60.8	2.9
Aged 25 to 29	10,535	100.0	61.3	42.3	2.2	16.8	31.3	7.4
Aged 30 to 34	9,188	100.0	71.4	53.7	5.6	12.1	18.1	10.5
Aged 35 to 39	10,538	100.0	72.4	55.9	8.7	7.8	13.0	14.6
Aged 40 to 44	10,652	100.0	70.4	49.6	13.6	7.2	10.2	19.4
Number of biologial children								
None	27,401	100.0	27.6	17.0	1.3	9.3	69.1	3.2
One or more births	34,353	100.0	72.6	51.8	8.1	12.7	13.5	13.9
Race and Hispanic origin								
Asian	2,456	100.0	56.2	48.5	4.2	3.5	38.7	5.2
Black	8,451	100.0	33.3	21.3	2.7	9.3	55.1	11.6
Hispanic	10,474	100.0	55.2	35.9	4.2	15.1	35.5	9.3
Non-Hispanic white	37,384	100.0	56.8	40.2	5.9	10.7	34.3	8.9
Education								
Not a high school graduate	6,844	100.0	64.5	36.6	7.7	20.2	19.1	16.5
High school graduate or GED	11,578	100.0	64.2	39.5	9.2	15.5	20.3	15.6
Some college, no degree	13,702	100.0	61.1	42.1	7.4	11.6	26.4	12.6
Bachelor's degree	11,024	100.0	68.4	58.3	3.3	6.8	25.5	6.1
Master's degree or more	4,059	100.0	72.9	63.0	4.4	5.5	20.1	7.0
Family structure at age 14								
Living with both parents	40,463	100.0	55.3	40.6	5.2	9.5	36.7	8.0
Other	21,291	100.0	47.7	28.3	5.0	14.4	41.0	11.3

Note: Asians and blacks are those who identify themselves as being of the race alone. Education categories include only people aged 22 to 44. "–" means sample is too small to make a reliable estimate.
Source: National Center for Health Statistics, First Marriages in the United States: Data from the 2006–2010 National Survey of Family Growth, National Health Statistics Reports, No. 49, 2012, Internet site http://www.cdc.gov/nchs/nsfg/new_nsfg.htm

Husbands and Wives Are Alike in Many Ways

Most couples are close in age and of the same race.

Men usually marry slightly younger women, but most husbands and wives are close in age. Thirty-three percent are within one year of each other in age, and in another 34 percent the husband is only two to five years older than the wife.

Both husband and wife are non-Hispanic white in 69 percent of the nation's married couples. In 11 percent both are Hispanic, in 6 percent both are non-Hispanic black, and in another 6 percent both are non-Hispanic "other" (primarily Asian). No single mixed race/Hispanic origin combination accounts for more than about 2 percent of couples.

In the 54 percent majority of married couples, neither husband nor wife has a bachelor's degree. Both have a bachelor's degree in 24 percent. There are bigger differences between spouses by earnings. Only 25 percent of couples are within $4,999 of one another's earnings. For 55 percent of couples, the husband earns at least $5,000 more than his wife.

■ The similarities between husbands and wives mean that high earners tend to marry one another, boosting incomes.

Most husbands and wives are close in age

(percent distribution of married couples by age difference between husband and wife, 2012)

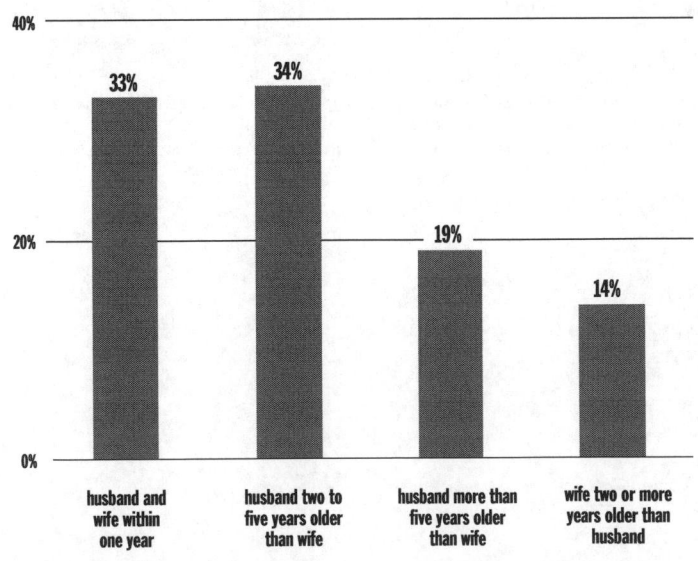

Table 7.25 Age Difference between Husbands and Wives, 2012

(number and percent distribution of married-couple family groups by age difference between husband and wife, 2012; numbers in thousands)

AGE DIFFERENCE	number	percent distribution
Total married couples	**61,047**	**100.0%**
Husband 20 or more years older than wife	590	1.0
Husband 15 to 19 years older than wife	962	1.6
Husband 10 to 14 years older than wife	3,024	5.0
Husband 6 to 9 years older than wife	6,935	11.4
Husband 4 to 5 years older than wife	8,083	13.2
Husband 2 to 3 years older than wife	12,433	20.4
Husband and wife within 1 year	20,344	33.3
Wife 2 to 3 years older than husband	3,983	6.5
Wife 4 to 5 years older than husband	1,998	3.3
Wife 6 to 9 years older than husband	1,682	2.8
Wife 10 to 14 years older than husband	631	1.0
Wife 15 to 19 years older than husband	182	0.3
Wife 20 or more years older than husband	200	0.3

Note: Married-couple family groups include married-couple householders and married couples living in households headed by others.
Source: Bureau of the Census, America's Families and Living Arrangements: 2012, Current Population Survey Annual Social and Economic Supplement, Internet site http://www.census.gov/hhes/families/data/cps2012.html; calculations by New Strategist

Table 7.26 Race and Hispanic Origin Difference between Husband and Wife, 2012

(number and percent distribution of married-couple family groups by race and Hispanic origin difference between husband and wife, 2012; numbers in thousands)

RACE AND HISPANIC ORIGIN DIFFERENCE	number	percent distribution
Total married-couple family groups	**61,047**	**100.0%**
Both white	41,996	68.8
Both Hispanic	6,730	11.0
Both black	3,860	6.3
Both other	3,616	5.9
Mixed race/Hispanic origin couples	4,507	7.4
Husband white, wife black	144	0.2
Husband white, wife Hispanic	1,098	1.8
Husband white, wife other	1,084	1.8
Husband black, wife white	315	0.5
Husband black, wife Hispanic	166	0.3
Husband black, wife other	85	0.1
Husband Hispanic, wife white	977	1.6
Husband Hispanic, wife black	36	0.1
Husband Hispanic, wife other	132	0.2
Husband other, wife white	644	1.1
Husband other, wife black	43	0.1
Husband other, wife Hispanic	121	0.2

Note: Whites, blacks, and "others" are not Hispanic. "Other" includes Asians and American Indians. Hispanics may be of any race. Married-couple family groups include married-couple householders and married couples living in households headed by others.
Source: Bureau of the Census, America's Families and Living Arrangements: 2012, Current Population Survey Annual Social and Economic Supplement, Internet site http://www.census.gov/hhes/families/data/cps2012.html; calculations by New Strategist

Table 7.27 Educational Difference between Husbands and Wives, 2012

(number and percent distribution of married-couple family groups by educational difference between husband and wife, 2012; numbers in thousands)

EDUCATIONAL DIFFERENCE	number	percent distribution
Total married-couple family groups	**61,047**	**100.0%**
Neither has bachelor's degree	33,034	54.1
One has bachelor's degree, other has less	13,665	22.4
Both have bachelor's degree	14,348	23.5

Note: Married-couple family groups include married-couple householders and married couples living in households headed by others.
Source: Bureau of the Census, America's Families and Living Arrangements: 2012, Current Population Survey Annual Social and Economic Supplement, Internet site http://www.census.gov/hhes/families/data/cps2012.html; calculations by New Strategist

Table 7.28 Earnings Difference between Husbands and Wives, 2012

(number and percent distribution of married-couple family groups by earnings difference between husbands and wives, 2012; numbers in thousands)

EARNINGS DIFFERENCE	number	percent distribution
Total married-couple family groups	**61,047**	**100.0%**
Husband earns at least $50,000 more than wife	13,232	21.7
Husband earns $30,000 to $49,999 more than wife	7,495	12.3
Husband earns $10,000 to $29,999 more than wife	10,126	16.6
Husband earns $5,000 to $9,999 more than wife	2,458	4.0
Husband earns within $4,999 of wife	15,495	25.4
Wife earns $5,000 to $9,999 more than husband	1,780	2.9
Wife earns $10,000 to $29,999 more than husband	5,230	8.6
Wife earns $30,000 to $49,999 more than husband	2,508	4.1
Wife earns at least $50,000 more than husband	2,723	4.5

Note: Married-couple family groups include married-couple householders and married couples living in households headed by others.
Source: Bureau of the Census, America's Families and Living Arrangements: 2012, Current Population Survey Annual Social and Economic Supplement, Internet site http://www.census.gov/hhes/families/data/cps2012.html; calculations by New Strategist

Divorce Is Highest among Women in Their Fifties

One in four women aged 50 to 59 has married at least twice.

Fully 37 percent of women aged 50 to 59 have experienced divorce, according to a Census Bureau study of marriage and divorce through 2009. The share of the ever-divorced exceeds 35 percent among men ranging in age from 50 to 69. Despite the high level of divorce, most men aged 30 or older have married only once and are still married to their first wife.

Among ever-married women and men aged 15 to 44, the 52 to 56 percent majority of marriages have lasted 20 years. Those most likely to have a lasting marriage are the more educated, those who have been married only once, and those who did not have children before marrying.

■ One reason for the high divorce rate among baby-boom men and women is the revolutionary change in women's roles, which occurred as boomers were entering adulthood.

Divorce is less common among the oldest women

(percent of women aged 25 or older who have ever divorced, by age, 2009)

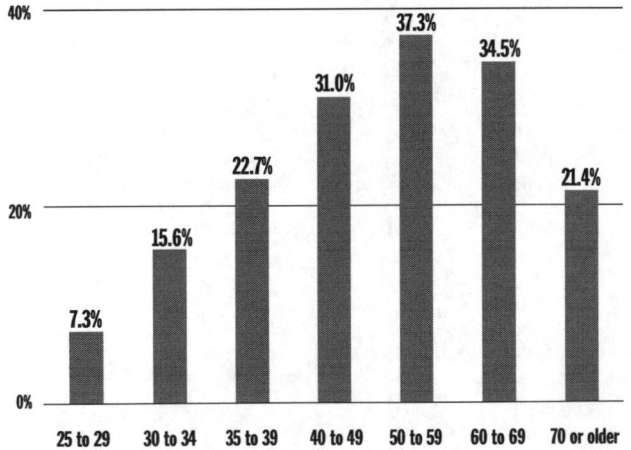

Table 7.29 Marital History of Men by Age, 2009

(number of men aged 15 or older and percent distribution by marital history and age, 2009; numbers in thousands)

	total	15–19	20–24	25–29	30–34	35–39	40–49	50–59	60–69	70+
Total men, number	115,797	10,870	10,152	10,567	9,518	9,995	21,504	19,568	12,774	10,849
Total men, percent	100.0%	100.0%	100.0%	100.0%	100.0%	100.0%	100.0%	100.0%	100.0%	100.0%
Never married	33.0	98.0	87.5	59.7	35.6	23.5	16.4	10.8	4.6	3.4
Ever married	67.0	2.0	12.5	40.3	64.4	76.5	83.6	89.2	95.4	96.6
Married once	52.3	1.9	12.5	38.8	59.4	66.9	65.8	63.4	64.8	72.3
Still married	42.5	1.3	11.2	34.2	52.2	56.1	52.2	50.4	53.5	54.0
Married twice	11.6	0.1	0.0	1.5	4.8	8.7	14.8	20.0	22.1	18.9
Still married	9.0	0.1	0.0	1.3	4.0	7.4	11.3	15.5	17.5	13.2
Married three or more times	3.1	0.0	0.0	0.1	0.2	1.0	3.0	5.8	8.5	5.4
Still married	2.3	0.0	0.0	0.1	0.2	0.8	2.2	4.3	6.5	3.8
Ever divorced	20.5	0.3	0.8	5.0	10.5	17.9	28.5	35.7	36.5	23.4
Currently divorced	9.1	0.2	0.7	3.7	6.2	9.5	14.2	15.5	12.4	7.2
Ever widowed	3.6	0.4	0.1	0.3	0.2	0.5	1.3	2.5	6.4	22.6
Currently widowed	2.6	0.3	0.1	0.3	0.1	0.3	0.9	1.6	3.9	17.4

Source: Bureau of the Census, Number, Timing, and Duration of Marriages and Divorces: 2009, Current Population Reports P70-125, 2011, Internet site http://www.census.gov/hhes/socdemo/marriage/data/sipp/index.html; calculations by New Strategist

Table 7.30 Marital History of Women by Age, 2009

(number of women aged 15 or older and percent distribution by marital history and age, 2009; numbers in thousands)

	total	15–19	20–24	25–29	30–34	35–39	40–49	50–59	60–69	70+
Total women, number	123,272	10,478	10,158	10,408	9,645	10,267	22,119	20,702	14,288	15,207
Total women, percent	100.0%	100.0%	100.0%	100.0%	100.0%	100.0%	100.0%	100.0%	100.0%	100.0%
Never married	27.2	97.5	77.3	46.8	26.7	17.3	13.0	9.1	6.0	4.3
Ever married	72.8	2.5	22.7	53.2	73.3	82.7	87.0	90.9	94.0	95.7
Married once	57.5	2.5	22.4	50.8	64.5	69.3	67.4	65.5	67.7	76.1
Still married	40.6	1.9	19.7	43.2	54.5	55.8	51.6	47.5	45.7	30.1
Married twice	12.1	0.1	0.3	2.3	8.0	11.6	15.8	19.5	20.1	15.2
Still married	7.9	0.6	0.2	2.0	6.9	9.1	11.3	13.4	13.2	5.2
Married three or more times	3.2	0.0	0.0	0.0	0.8	1.9	3.8	5.9	6.2	4.4
Still married	1.9	0.0	0.0	0.0	0.7	1.4	2.5	4.1	3.6	1.4
Ever divorced	22.4	0.2	1.8	7.3	15.6	22.7	31.0	37.3	34.5	21.4
Currently divorced	11.3	0.1	1.5	5.3	8.1	11.8	16.4	18.6	16.0	9.9
Ever widowed	10.0	0.3	0.1	0.2	0.6	1.4	2.6	6.5	17.0	51.2
Currently widowed	8.9	0.3	0.1	0.1	0.4	0.8	1.8	4.9	13.9	48.3

Source: Bureau of the Census, Number, Timing, and Duration of Marriages and Divorces: 2009, Current Population Reports P70-125, 2011, Internet site http://www.census.gov/hhes/socdemo/marriage/data/sipp/index.html; calculations by New Strategist

Table 7.31 Probability of Reaching Marriage Anniversary, 2006–10: Women

(percent of ever-married women aged 15 to 44 whose first marriage survived for specified number of years, by selected characteristics 2006–10)

	percent of first marriages surviving			
	5 years	10 years	15 years	20 years
Total ever-married women aged 15 to 44	**80%**	**68%**	**60%**	**52%**
Age at first marriage				
Under age 20	70	54	46	37
Aged 20 to 24	81	69	60	55
Aged 25 or older	86	78	73	–
Race and Hispanic origin				
Asian	91	83	78	69
Black	72	56	45	37
Hispanic	84	73	64	53
Non-Hispanic white	80	68	61	54
Education				
Not a high school graduate	76	60	53	39
High school graduate or GED	75	60	51	41
Some college, no degree	76	63	54	49
Bachelor's degree	90	85	79	78
Master's degree or more	88	82	78	–
Family structure at age 14				
Living with both parents	83	73	66	58
Other	73	57	47	38
Religion raised				
None	73	61	58	43
Protestant	77	65	56	50
Catholic	84	73	63	53
Other religions	86	75	68	65
Births at time of first marriage				
No births	82	71	64	56
One or more births	74	56	44	33

	percent of first marriages surviving			
	5 years	10 years	15 years	20 years
First birth timing relative to first marriage				
No first birth	72%	56%	50%	–
Birth before marriage	74	56	44	33%
Birth 0 to 7 months after marriage	76	55	48	41
Birth 8 or more months after marriage	93	85	77	68
Cohabitation with first husband before marriage				
Yes, cohabited and engaged	81	67	58	46
Yes, cohabited but not engaged	78	61	53	45
No, did not cohabit with first husband	80	71	63	57
First husband ever married before this marriage				
Yes	75	62	53	38
No	81	69	61	54
First husband had children from previous relationship				
Yes	72	57	48	37
No	82	70	62	54

Note: Asians and blacks are those who identify themselves as being of the race alone. Education categories include only people aged 22 to 44. "–" means sample is too small to make a reliable estimate.
Source: National Center for Health Statistics, First Marriages in the United States: Data from the 2006–2010 National Survey of Family Growth, National Health Statistics Reports, No. 49, 2012, Internet site http://www.cdc.gov/nchs/nsfg/new_nsfg.htm

Table 7.32 Probability of Reaching Marriage Anniversary, 2006–10: Men

(percent of ever-married men aged 15 to 44 whose first marriage survived for specified number of years, by selected characteristics 2006–10)

	percent of first marriages surviving			
	5 years	10 years	15 years	20 years
Total ever-married men aged 15 to 44	**81%**	**70%**	**62%**	**56%**
Age at first marriage				
Under age 20	66	48	46	41
Aged 20 to 24	81	70	60	54
Aged 25 or older	84	76	68	–
Race and Hispanic origin				
Black	75	64	55	53
Hispanic	82	73	67	62
Non-Hispanic white	82	70	61	54
Education				
Not a high school graduate	79	66	56	54
High school graduate or GED	80	66	54	47
Some college, no degree	76	64	57	54
Bachelor's degree	87	80	75	65
Master's degree or more	90	88	83	–
Family structure at age 14				
Living with both parents	84	74	66	60
Other	75	60	49	44
Religion raised				
None	79	68	54	–
Protestant	80	67	58	53
Catholic	83	74	67	59
Other religions	83	73	72	–
Births at time of first marriage				
No children	83	74	65	59
One or more children	74	55	48	43

	percent of first marriages surviving			
	5 years	10 years	15 years	20 years
First birth timing relative to first marriage				
No first birth	73%	63%	52%	–
Birth before marriage	74	55	48	43%
Birth 0 to 7 months after marriage	78	68	55	42
Birth 8 or more months after marriage	95	86	78	74
Cohabitation with first wife before marriage				
Yes, cohabited and engaged	81	71	63	57
Yes, cohabited but not engaged	79	66	55	49
No, did not cohabit with first wife	82	73	65	60
First wife ever married before this marriage				
Yes	76	59	50	–
No	82	72	64	58
First wife had children from previous relationship				
Yes	72	55	39	–
No	84	74	67	61

Note: Asians and blacks are those who identify themselves as being of the race alone. Education categories include only people aged 22 to 44. "–" means sample is too small to make a reliable estimate.
Source: National Center for Health Statistics, First Marriages in the United States: Data from the 2006–2010 National Survey of Family Growth, National Health Statistics Reports, No. 49, 2012, Internet site http://www.cdc.gov/nchs/nsfg/new_nsfg.htm

Same-Sex Couples Have High Incomes

Unmarried, opposite-sex couples have the lowest incomes.

According to the 2012 American Community Survey, there were 639,440 same-sex couples in the United States. Among same-sex couples, most identify themselves as unmarried partners. But 101,195 females and 80,727 males say they are spouses of a same-sex partner.

On average, same-sex couples are younger than married couples, but older than unmarried opposite-sex couples. They are far more educated and equally or even more affluent than opposite-sex married couples. The average household income of male same-sex couples was a substantial $129,069 in 2012, and female same-sex couples had an average income of $95,913. These figures compare with an average income of $97,682 for opposite-sex married couples and $66,516 for opposite-sex unmarried couples.

■ Same-sex couples who identify themselves as spouses are older than same-sex unmarried partners. They are also more likely to have children and be homeowners.

Same-sex couples are affluent

(average income of couples by type, 2012)

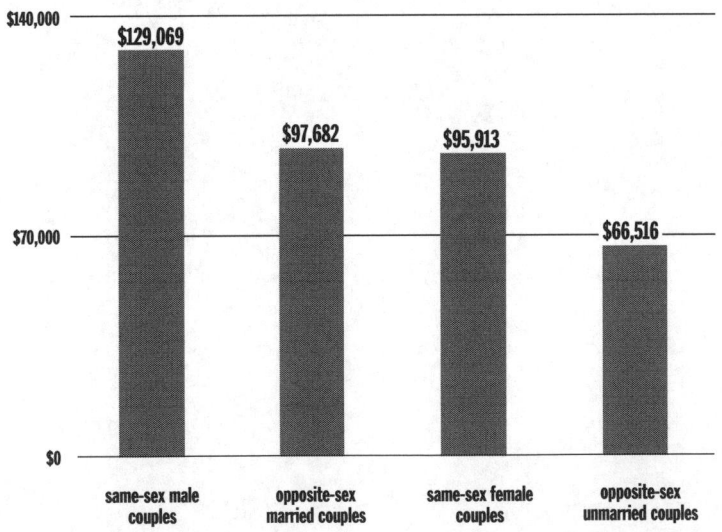

Table 7.33 Characteristics of Opposite-Sex and Same-Sex Couple Households, 2012

(number of households with opposite and same-sex spouses or partners and percent distribution by selected characteristics, 2012)

	opposite-sex couples		same-sex couples		
	married	unmarried	total	male	female
Total couples (number)	55,754,450	6,288,791	639,440	305,794	333,646
Total couples (percent)	100.0%	100.0%	100.0%	100.0%	100.0%
Age of householder					
Under age 25	1.4%	12.8%	4.1%	3.1%	5.0%
Aged 25 to 34	13.4	35.1	17.6	16.0	19.1
Aged 35 to 44	20.4	21.3	20.7	21.3	20.2
Aged 45 to 54	23.0	16.4	26.5	28.7	24.5
Aged 55 to 64	21.0	9.4	17.8	18.0	17.7
Aged 65 or older	20.9	5.1	13.3	13.0	13.6
Average age of householder (years)	**51.5**	**38.6**	**47.8**	**48.2**	**47.4**
Average age of spouse/partner (years)	**50.6**	**37.7**	**45.9**	**45.8**	**45.9**
Race and Hispanic origin of householder					
Asian	5.2%	2.3%	2.5%	2.8%	2.1%
Black	6.9	11.4	6.5	5.2	7.6
Hispanic	12.0	18.6	10.3	10.8	9.8
Non-Hispanic white	74.3	64.9	78.1	78.9	77.3
Educational attainment of householder					
Householder has at least a bachelor's degree	36.5	22.9	48.9	52.2	45.9
Both partners have at least a bachelor's degree	22.8	11.7	31.6	32.4	30.9
Employment status					
Householder employed	67.8	76.2	74.4	75.8	73.1
Both partners employed	47.4	56.4	59.3	60.7	58.0
Children in the household	**40.3**	**41.6**	**18.1**	**11.4**	**24.3**
Household income					
Under $35,000	16.5	30.6	15.9	13.0	18.7
$35,000 to $49,999	12.3	16.4	10.4	8.9	11.8
$50,000 to $74,999	20.2	21.5	17.8	15.9	19.6
$75,000 to $99,999	16.3	13.4	14.9	14.9	14.9
$100,000 or more	34.7	18.1	40.9	47.3	35.0
Average household income	**$97,682**	**$66,516**	**$111,769**	**$129,069**	**$95,913**
Housing tenure					
Owner	79.9%	42.0%	68.4%	69.3%	67.7%
Renter	20.1	58.0	31.6	30.7	32.3

Note: Asians and blacks are those who identify themselves as being of the race alone.
Source: Census Bureau, 2012 American Community Survey, Internet site http://www.census.gov/hhes/samesex/

Table 7.34 Characteristics of Same-Sex Couple Households by Marital Status, 2012

(number of same-sex couple households by marital status and percent distribution by selected characteristics, 2012)

	couples reported as spouses		unmarried partners	
	male–male	female–female	male–male	female–female
Total couples (number)	80,727	101,195	225,067	232,451
Total couples (percent)	100.0%	100.0%	100.0%	100.0%
Age of householder				
Under age 25	1.1%	2.0%	3.8%	6.2%
Aged 25 to 34	12.0	13.9	17.4	21.3
Aged 35 to 44	19.2	16.4	22.0	21.9
Aged 45 to 54	27.7	20.0	29.0	26.4
Aged 55 to 64	18.0	19.0	18.0	17.1
Aged 65 or older	22.0	28.7	9.7	7.0
Average age of householder (years)	**52.4**	**54.2**	**46.7**	**44.5**
Average age of spouse/partner (years)	**50.4**	**52.3**	**44.2**	**43.2**
Race and Hispanic origin of householder				
Asian	3.9%	3.1%	2.5%	1.7%
Black	6.8	9.2	4.6	7.0
Hispanic	11.3	9.4	10.7	10.0
Non-Hispanic white	75.9	75.6	80.0	78.0
Educational attainment of householder				
Householder has at least a bachelor's degree	45.1	40.9	54.7	48.1
Both partners have at least a bachelor's degree	30.2	28.5	33.2	31.9
Employment status				
Householder employed	66.4	60.3	79.2	78.7
Both partners employed	49.1	46.6	64.8	63.0
Children in household	**25.3**	**27.7**	**6.4**	**22.8**
Household income				
Under $35,000	16.7	21.3	11.6	17.5
$35,000 to $49,999	9.7	11.6	8.6	11.9
$50,000 to $74,999	16.1	18.9	15.8	19.9
$75,000 to $99,999	13.2	13.7	15.5	15.4
$100,000 or more	44.3	34.4	48.4	35.3
Average household income	**$125,410**	**$96,075**	**$130,382**	**$95,843**
Housing tenure				
Owner	76.7%	77.6%	66.6%	63.3%
Renter	23.3	22.4	33.4	36.7

Note: Asians and blacks are those who identify themselves as being of the race alone.
Source: Census Bureau, 2012 American Community Survey, Internet site http://www.census.gov/hhes/samesex/

Population

Trends

The number of people in their sixties is growing rapidly.

The 60-to-64 age group grew the fastest between 2000 and 2012—up 64 percent as the oldest boomers entered the age group.

The non-Hispanic white population is growing slowly.

Between 2000 and 2012, the number of non-Hispanic whites increased by just 1 percent. Sixty-three percent of Americans are non-Hispanic white, down from 69 percent in 2000.

Minorities will become the majority in 2043, the Census Bureau projects.

In 2050 Hispanics will account for 28 percent of the population, blacks for 17 percent, and Asians 10 percent.

More than 80 percent of Americans live in a metropolitan area.

The population of large metropolitan areas is growing faster than the rest of the nation.

The mobility rate is close to a record low.

Among homeowners, the mobility rate has never been lower. Only 4.7 percent of homeowners moved between 2011 and 2012.

Most immigrants settle in only five states.

California, New York, Florida, Texas, and New Jersey receive most of the nation's immigrants.

U.S. Population Is Aging

Boomers are behind the rapid growth of the 60-plus age group.

Between 2000 and 2012, the resident population of the United States grew by 11 percent to 314 million. The 60-to-64 age group grew the fastest during those years, rising by 64 percent as the oldest boomers aged into their sixties. The aging of the small generation X into its thirties and early forties is behind the decline in the number of people aged 35 to 44.

Although there are more females than males in the population, males outnumber females until the 35-to-39 age group. Among people aged 85 or older, there are only 50 men for every 100 women. Males slightly outnumber females at younger ages because boys outnumber girls at birth. Women outnumber men at older ages because, throughout life, males have the higher death rate.

■ Because the death rate is higher for males than for females, women will always greatly outnumber men in old age.

Median age of U.S. population is rising

(median age of U.S. population, 2000 and 2012)

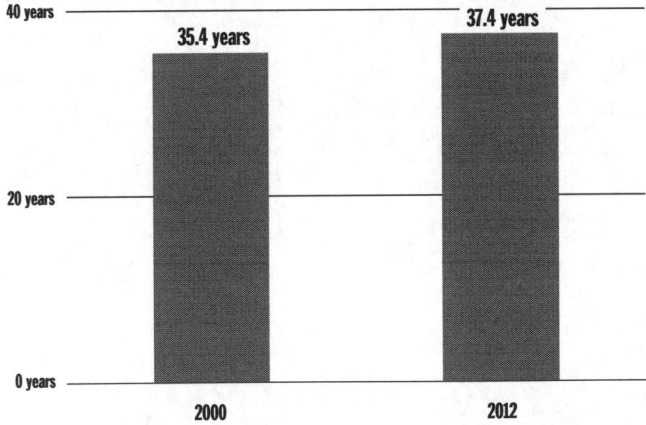

Table 8.1 Population by Age, 2000 to 2012

(number of people by age, 2000 to 2012; percent change, 2000–12)

	2012	2010	2000	percent change 2000–12
Total people	**313,914,040**	**309,326,225**	**282,162,411**	**11.3%**
Under age 5	19,999,344	20,189,418	19,178,293	4.3
Aged 5 to 9	20,475,536	20,331,865	20,463,852	0.1
Aged 10 to 14	20,669,218	20,680,465	20,637,696	0.2
Aged 15 to 19	21,360,702	21,979,234	20,294,955	5.3
Aged 20 to 24	22,583,203	21,701,492	19,116,667	18.1
Aged 25 to 29	21,398,326	21,144,251	19,280,263	11.0
Aged 30 to 34	20,910,995	20,068,672	20,524,234	1.9
Aged 35 to 39	19,488,199	20,077,504	22,650,852	−14.0
Aged 40 to 44	21,028,221	20,904,159	22,517,991	−6.6
Aged 45 to 49	21,689,479	22,635,688	20,219,527	7.3
Aged 50 to 54	22,579,259	22,352,471	17,779,447	27.0
Aged 55 to 59	20,772,517	19,794,508	13,565,937	53.1
Aged 60 to 64	17,813,685	16,989,649	10,863,129	64.0
Aged 65 to 69	13,977,353	12,520,917	9,523,909	46.8
Aged 70 to 74	10,008,039	9,335,704	8,860,028	13.0
Aged 75 to 79	7,489,583	7,319,122	7,438,619	0.7
Aged 80 to 84	5,783,051	5,758,589	4,984,540	16.0
Aged 85 or older	5,887,330	5,542,517	4,262,472	38.1
Aged 18 to 24	31,359,915	30,761,907	27,315,274	14.8
Aged 18 or older	240,185,952	235,205,658	209,786,222	14.5
Aged 65 or older	43,145,356	40,476,849	35,069,568	23.0
Median age (years)	37.4	37.2	35.4	–

Note: Numbers are for July 1 of each year. "–" means not applicable.
Source: Bureau of the Census, Population Estimates, Internet site http://www.census.gov/popest/index.html; calculations by New Strategist

Table 8.2 Population by Age and Sex, 2012

(number of people by age and sex, and sex ratio by age, 2012)

	total	male	female	sex ratio
Total people	**313,914,040**	**154,492,067**	**159,421,973**	**97**
Under age 5	19,999,344	10,216,135	9,783,209	104
Aged 5 to 9	20,475,536	10,459,193	10,016,343	104
Aged 10 to 14	20,669,218	10,567,214	10,102,004	105
Aged 15 to 19	21,360,702	10,962,861	10,397,841	105
Aged 20 to 24	22,583,203	11,549,456	11,033,747	105
Aged 25 to 29	21,398,326	10,844,886	10,553,440	103
Aged 30 to 34	20,910,995	10,493,906	10,417,089	101
Aged 35 to 39	19,488,199	9,714,613	9,773,586	99
Aged 40 to 44	21,028,221	10,458,994	10,569,227	99
Aged 45 to 49	21,689,479	10,726,625	10,962,854	98
Aged 50 to 54	22,579,259	11,080,245	11,499,014	96
Aged 55 to 59	20,772,517	10,068,409	10,704,108	94
Aged 60 to 64	17,813,685	8,534,485	9,279,200	92
Aged 65 to 69	13,977,353	6,606,856	7,370,497	90
Aged 70 to 74	10,008,039	4,596,006	5,412,033	85
Aged 75 to 79	7,489,583	3,291,452	4,198,131	78
Aged 80 to 84	5,783,051	2,356,698	3,426,353	69
Aged 85 or older	5,887,330	1,964,033	3,923,297	50
Aged 18 to 24	31,359,915	16,065,251	15,294,664	105
Aged 18 or older	240,185,952	116,802,459	123,383,493	95
Aged 65 or older	43,145,356	18,815,045	24,330,311	77
Median age (years)	37.4	36.1	38.8	–

Note: The sex ratio is the number of men per 100 women. "–" means not applicable.
Source: Bureau of the Census, Population Estimates, Internet site http://www.census.gov/popest/index.html; calculations by New Strategist

Non-Hispanic White Population Is Growing Slowly

Minorities account for half of preschoolers.

The U.S. population is diverse. Only 63 percent of Americans are non-Hispanic white, down from 69 percent in 2000. The non-Hispanic white population grew by only 1 percent between 2000 and 2012. This compares with a 56 percent increase in the Asian (alone or in combination) population and a 49 percent increase in the Hispanic population. The black (alone or in combination) population grew by 19 percent.

Hispanic origin is an ethnic identity, not a race. In fact, Hispanics may be of any race. In 2012, fully 88 percent of Hispanics were white (alone), 5 percent were black (alone). Three percent of Hispanics are of mixed race.

The non-Hispanic white share of the population rises with age. Only 50 percent of children under age 5 are non-Hispanic white. Among 18-to-24-year-olds, the figure is 56 percent. It exceeds 60 percent in the 40-to-44 age group, and surpasses 70 percent among 55-to-59-year-olds. Among people aged 80 or older, more than 80 percent are non-Hispanic white.

■ The nation's political schisms are caused in part by racial and ethnic differences between young and old.

The non-Hispanic white population barely grew between 2000 and 2012

(percent change in population by race and Hispanic origin, 2000–12)

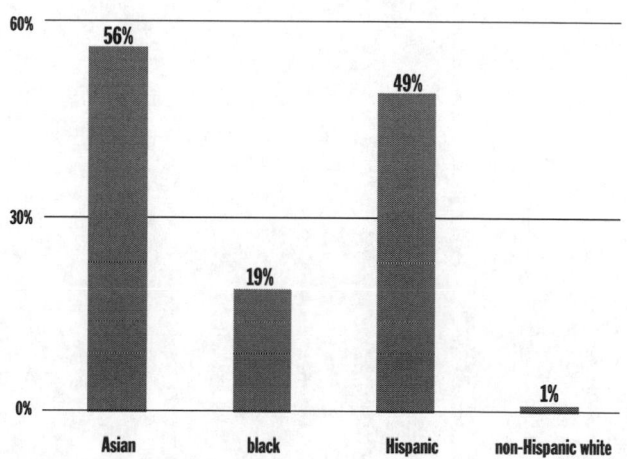

Table 8.3 Population by Race and Hispanic Origin, 2000 to 2012

(number of people by race and Hispanic origin, 2000, 2010, and 2012; numerical and percent change, 2000–12)

	2012 number	2012 percent distribution	2010 number	2010 percent distribution	2000 number	2000 percent distribution	change, 2000–2012 numerical	change, 2000–2012 percent
Total population	313,914,040	100.0%	309,326,225	100.0%	282,162,411	100.0%	31,751,629	11.3%
Race alone								
American Indian	3,857,495	1.2	3,753,225	1.2	2,684,491	1.0	1,173,004	43.7
Asian	16,145,821	5.1	15,264,207	4.9	10,705,839	3.8	5,439,982	50.8
Black	41,204,793	13.1	40,352,963	13.0	35,814,706	12.7	5,390,087	15.0
Native Hawaiian	707,228	0.2	678,205	0.2	467,339	0.2	239,889	51.3
White	244,495,567	77.9	242,236,526	78.3	228,530,479	81.0	15,965,088	7.0
Two or more races	**7,503,136**	**2.4**	**7,041,099**	**2.3**	**3,959,557**	**1.4**	**3,543,579**	**89.5**
Race alone or in combination								
American Indian	6,348,956	2.0	6,162,542	2.0	4,243,551	1.5	2,105,405	49.6
Asian	18,855,104	6.0	17,802,502	5.8	12,119,307	4.3	6,735,797	55.6
Black	44,456,009	14.2	43,346,604	14.0	37,225,810	13.2	7,230,199	19.4
Native Hawaiian	1,400,269	0.4	1,339,933	0.4	912,989	0.3	487,280	53.4
White	251,106,806	80.0	248,419,741	80.3	231,963,847	82.2	19,142,959	8.3
Hispanic	**53,027,708**	**16.9**	**50,747,840**	**16.4**	**35,661,885**	**12.6**	**17,365,823**	**48.7**
Non-Hispanic white	**197,705,655**	**63.0**	**197,389,398**	**63.8**	**195,701,752**	**69.4**	**2,003,903**	**1.0**

Note: Numbers by race in combination do not add to total because they include those who identify themselves as being of the race alone and those who identify themselves as being of the race in combination with other races. Hispanics may be of any race. Non-Hispanic whites are those who identify themselves as being white alone and not Hispanic. Numbers are for July 1 of each year.
Source: Bureau of the Census, Population Estimates, Internet site http://www.census.gov/popest/index.html; calculations by New Strategist

Table 8.4 Hispanics and Non-Hispanics by Race, 2012

(number and percent distribution of Hispanics and non-Hispanics by race, 2012)

	Hispanics		non-Hispanics	
	number	percent distribution	number	percent distribution
Total population	**53,027,708**	**100.0%**	**260,886,332**	**100.0%**
Race alone				
American Indian	1,548,383	2.9	2,309,112	0.9
Asian	525,824	1.0	15,619,997	6.0
Black	2,477,730	4.7	38,727,063	14.8
Native Hawaiian	186,541	0.4	520,687	0.2
White	46,789,912	88.2	197,705,655	75.8
Two or more races	**1,499,318**	**2.8**	**6,003,818**	**2.3**

Source: Bureau of the Census, Population Estimates, Internet site http://www.census.gov/popest/index.html; calculations by New Strategist

Table 8.5 Population by Age, Race, and Hispanic Origin, 2012

(number and percent distribution of people by age, race, and Hispanic origin, 2012)

	total	Asian	black	Hispanic	non-Hispanic white
Total people	**313,914,040**	**18,855,104**	**44,456,009**	**53,027,708**	**197,705,655**
Under age 5	19,999,344	1,401,164	3,677,294	5,155,033	10,022,740
Aged 5 to 9	20,475,536	1,388,532	3,567,425	5,024,590	10,678,902
Aged 10 to 14	20,669,218	1,281,933	3,583,032	4,694,112	11,220,688
Aged 15 to 19	21,360,702	1,265,656	3,729,374	4,580,695	11,845,921
Aged 20 to 24	22,583,203	1,465,184	3,839,396	4,584,841	12,745,541
Aged 25 to 29	21,398,326	1,548,977	3,196,995	4,369,337	12,332,092
Aged 30 to 34	20,910,995	1,554,906	3,056,143	4,302,215	12,047,330
Aged 35 to 39	19,488,199	1,506,551	2,765,295	3,982,806	11,256,200
Aged 40 to 44	21,028,221	1,447,108	2,881,061	3,666,104	13,006,639
Aged 45 to 49	21,689,479	1,261,818	2,923,552	3,206,468	14,224,590
Aged 50 to 54	22,579,259	1,145,716	2,896,014	2,682,905	15,738,510
Aged 55 to 59	20,772,517	1,020,051	2,506,795	2,088,602	15,036,536
Aged 60 to 64	17,813,685	843,832	1,966,975	1,546,288	13,349,576
Aged 65 to 69	13,977,353	598,824	1,348,297	1,100,124	10,847,397
Aged 70 to 74	10,008,039	432,600	948,781	768,337	7,803,417
Aged 75 to 79	7,489,583	305,461	681,397	556,201	5,912,325
Aged 80 to 84	5,783,051	205,517	454,711	390,115	4,711,317
Aged 85 or older	5,887,330	181,274	433,472	328,935	4,925,934
Aged 18 to 24	31,359,915	1,978,121	5,402,658	6,441,839	17,607,512
Aged 18 or older	240,185,952	14,030,756	31,462,146	35,430,276	158,799,375
Aged 65 or older	43,145,356	1,723,676	3,866,658	3,143,712	34,200,390
Median age (years)	37.4	33.4	31.0	27.8	42.6

Note: Numbers by race and Hispanic origin do not add to total because Asians and blacks are those who identify themselves as being of the race alone and those who identify themselves as being of the race in combination with other races. Hispanics may be of any race. Non-Hispanic whites are those who identify themselves as being white alone and not Hispanic.
Source: Bureau of the Census, Population Estimates, Internet site http://www.census.gov/popest/index.html; calculations by New Strategist

Table 8.6 Distribution of Population by Age, Race, and Hispanic Origin, 2012

(percent distribution of people by age, race, and Hispanic origin, 2012)

	total	Asian	black	Hispanic	non-Hispanic white
Total people	**100.0%**	**6.0%**	**14.2%**	**16.9%**	**63.0%**
Under age 5	100.0	7.0	18.4	25.8	50.1
Aged 5 to 9	100.0	6.8	17.4	24.5	52.2
Aged 10 to 14	100.0	6.2	17.3	22.7	54.3
Aged 15 to 19	100.0	5.9	17.5	21.4	55.5
Aged 20 to 24	100.0	6.5	17.0	20.3	56.4
Aged 25 to 29	100.0	7.2	14.9	20.4	57.6
Aged 30 to 34	100.0	7.4	14.6	20.6	57.6
Aged 35 to 39	100.0	7.7	14.2	20.4	57.8
Aged 40 to 44	100.0	6.9	13.7	17.4	61.9
Aged 45 to 49	100.0	5.8	13.5	14.8	65.6
Aged 50 to 54	100.0	5.1	12.8	11.9	69.7
Aged 55 to 59	100.0	4.9	12.1	10.1	72.4
Aged 60 to 64	100.0	4.7	11.0	8.7	74.9
Aged 65 to 69	100.0	4.3	9.6	7.9	77.6
Aged 70 to 74	100.0	4.3	9.5	7.7	78.0
Aged 75 to 79	100.0	4.1	9.1	7.4	78.9
Aged 80 to 84	100.0	3.6	7.9	6.7	81.5
Aged 85 or older	100.0	3.1	7.4	5.6	83.7
Aged 18 to 24	100.0	6.3	17.2	20.5	56.1
Aged 18 or older	100.0	5.8	13.1	14.8	66.1
Aged 65 or older	100.0	4.0	9.0	7.3	79.3

Note: Numbers by race and Hispanic origin do not add to total because Asians and blacks are those who identify themselves as being of the race alone and those who identify themselves as being of the race in combination with other races. Hispanics may be of any race. Non-Hispanic whites are those who identify themselves as being white alone and not Hispanic.
Source: Bureau of the Census, Population Estimates, Internet site http://www.census.gov/popest/index.html; calculations by New Strategist

U.S. Population Will Number Nearly 400 Million by 2050

Minorities will become the majority in 2043, according to Census Bureau projections.

The U.S. population is projected to grow by 27 percent between 2012 and 2050, from 314 million to nearly 400 million. The minority share of the population will rise from 37 to 53 percent during those years. The non-Hispanic white share of the population will fall below 50 percent in 2043.

The number of Hispanics will more than double between 2012 and 2050, growing from 53 million to 112 million and accounting for 28 percent of the total population. The number of Asians is also projected to more than double during those years, and the black population will grow by 56 percent. Meanwhile, the non-Hispanic white population will shrink 6 percent. The number of non-Hispanic whites will fall by more than 11 million between 2012 and 2050.

■ The 65-plus age group will grow faster than any other between 2012 and 2050, nearly doubling during those years.

Non-Hispanic whites will fall below 50 percent in 2043

(non-Hispanic white share of U.S. population, for selected years, 2012 to 2050)

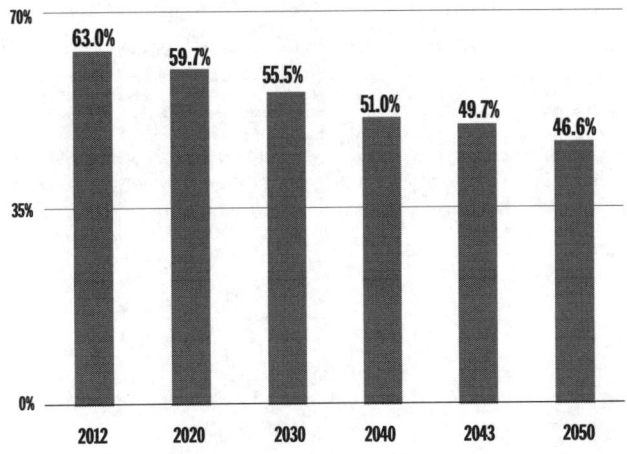

Table 8.7 Projections of the Population by Age, 2012 to 2050

(projected number of people by age, 2012 to 2050; percent change for selected years; numbers in thousands)

	2012	2020	2030	2040	2050
Total people	**314,004**	**333,896**	**358,471**	**380,016**	**399,803**
Under age 5	20,274	21,808	22,252	23,004	24,115
Aged 5 to 9	20,457	21,307	22,451	22,886	23,983
Aged 10 to 14	20,639	20,616	22,365	22,893	23,682
Aged 15 to 19	21,326	20,806	21,946	23,174	23,642
Aged 20 to 24	22,554	21,651	21,940	23,863	24,463
Aged 25 to 29	21,375	23,366	22,712	24,151	25,493
Aged 30 to 34	20,901	22,906	23,340	23,924	25,949
Aged 35 to 39	19,479	21,869	24,423	24,002	25,513
Aged 40 to 44	21,017	20,361	23,403	24,000	24,655
Aged 45 to 49	21,678	20,008	21,935	24,595	24,262
Aged 50 to 54	22,572	20,467	20,083	23,176	23,866
Aged 55 to 59	20,769	21,747	19,393	21,384	24,094
Aged 60 to 64	17,808	21,017	19,454	19,242	22,348
Aged 65 or older	43,155	55,969	72,774	79,719	83,739

PERCENT CHANGE	2012–20	2020–30	2030–40	2040–50	2012 to 2050
Total people	**6.3%**	**7.4%**	**6.0%**	**5.2%**	**27.3%**
Under age 5	7.6	2.0	3.4	4.8	18.9
Aged 5 to 9	4.2	5.4	1.9	4.8	17.2
Aged 10 to 14	–0.1	8.5	2.4	3.4	14.7
Aged 15 to 19	–2.4	5.5	5.6	2.0	10.9
Aged 20 to 24	–4.0	1.3	8.8	2.5	8.5
Aged 25 to 29	9.3	–2.8	6.3	5.6	19.3
Aged 30 to 34	9.6	1.9	2.5	8.5	24.1
Aged 35 to 39	12.3	11.7	–1.7	6.3	31.0
Aged 40 to 44	–3.1	14.9	2.6	2.7	17.3
Aged 45 to 49	–7.7	9.6	12.1	–1.4	11.9
Aged 50 to 54	–9.3	–1.9	15.4	3.0	5.7
Aged 55 to 59	4.7	–10.8	10.3	12.7	16.0
Aged 60 to 64	18.0	–7.4	–1.1	16.1	25.5
Aged 65 or older	29.7	30.0	9.5	5.0	94.0

Note: Numbers are for July 1 of each year.
Source: Bureau of the Census, Population Projections, Internet site http://www.census.gov/population/projections/; calculations by New Strategist

Table 8.8 Projections of the Minority Population, 2012 to 2050

(projected number of total people, non-Hispanic whites, and minorities, and non-Hispanic white and minority share of total, 2012 to 2050; numbers in thousands)

		non-Hispanics whites		minorities	
	total	number	share of total	number	share of total
2012	314,004	197,762	63.0%	116,242	37.0%
2013	316,439	198,003	62.6	118,436	37.4
2014	318,892	198,232	62.2	120,661	37.8
2015	321,363	198,449	61.8	122,914	38.2
2016	323,849	198,654	61.3	125,195	38.7
2017	326,348	198,845	60.9	127,503	39.1
2018	328,857	199,020	60.5	129,838	39.5
2019	331,375	199,177	60.1	132,198	39.9
2020	333,896	199,313	59.7	134,583	40.3
2021	336,416	199,424	59.3	136,991	40.7
2022	338,930	199,508	58.9	139,423	41.1
2023	341,436	199,560	58.4	141,877	41.6
2024	343,929	199,577	58.0	144,352	42.0
2025	346,407	199,557	57.6	146,850	42.4
2026	348,867	199,497	57.2	149,369	42.8
2027	351,304	199,395	56.8	151,909	43.2
2028	353,718	199,248	56.3	154,470	43.7
2029	356,107	199,056	55.9	157,051	44.1
2030	358,471	198,817	55.5	159,654	44.5
2031	360,792	198,528	55.0	162,264	45.0
2032	363,070	198,190	54.6	164,880	45.4
2033	365,307	197,802	54.1	167,505	45.9
2034	367,503	197,367	53.7	170,137	46.3
2035	369,662	196,886	53.3	172,776	46.7
2036	371,788	196,361	52.8	175,427	47.2
2037	373,883	195,796	52.4	178,087	47.6
2038	375,950	195,192	51.9	180,758	48.1
2039	377,993	194,555	51.5	183,438	48.5
2040	380,016	193,887	51.0	186,129	49.0
2041	382,021	193,192	50.6	188,829	49.4
2042	384,012	192,474	50.1	191,537	49.9
2043	385,992	191,737	49.7	194,255	50.3
2044	387,965	190,985	49.2	196,980	50.8
2045	389,934	190,221	48.8	199,713	51.2
2046	391,902	189,449	48.3	202,453	51.7
2047	393,869	188,671	47.9	205,198	52.1
2048	395,841	187,891	47.5	207,950	52.5
2049	397,818	187,111	47.0	210,707	53.0
2050	399,803	186,334	46.6	213,469	53.4

Note: Minorities are those who do not identify themselves as being white alone and not Hispanic.
Source: Bureau of the Census, Population Projections, Internet site http://www.census.gov/population/projections/; calculations by New Strategist

Table 8.9 Projections of the Population by Race and Hispanic Origin, 2012 to 2050

(projected number and percent distribution of people by race and Hispanic origin, 2012 to 2050; percent change in number and percentage point change in share, 2012–50; numbers in thousands)

NUMBER	total	Asian	black	Hispanic	non-Hispanic white
2012	314,004	18,647	44,462	53,274	197,762
2015	321,363	20,007	46,246	57,075	198,449
2020	333,896	22,384	49,338	63,784	199,313
2025	346,407	24,878	52,512	70,973	199,557
2030	358,471	27,482	55,727	78,655	198,817
2035	369,662	30,159	58,987	86,659	196,886
2040	380,016	32,876	62,350	94,876	193,887
2045	389,934	35,628	65,859	103,259	190,221
2050	399,803	38,407	69,525	111,732	186,334
PERCENT CHANGE					
2012 to 2050	27.3%	106.0%	56.4%	109.7%	−5.8%
PERCENT DISTRIBUTION					
2012	100.0	5.9	14.2	17.0	63.0
2015	100.0	6.2	14.4	17.8	61.8
2020	100.0	6.7	14.8	19.1	59.7
2025	100.0	7.2	15.2	20.5	57.6
2030	100.0	7.7	15.5	21.9	55.5
2035	100.0	8.2	16.0	23.4	53.3
2040	100.0	8.7	16.4	25.0	51.0
2045	100.0	9.1	16.9	26.5	48.8
2050	100.0	9.6	17.4	27.9	46.6
PERCENTAGE POINT CHANGE					
2012 to 2050	–	3.7	3.2	11.0	−16.4

Note: Numbers by race and Hispanic origin do not add to total because Asians and blacks are those who identify themselves as being of the race alone and those who identify themselves as being of the race in combination with other races. Hispanics may be of any race. Non-Hispanic whites are those who identify themselves as being white alone and not Hispanic. "–" means not applicable.
Source: Bureau of the Census, Population Projections, Internet site http://www.census.gov/population/projections/; calculations by New Strategist

The South Is the Most Populous Region

The West is the most diverse.

The South is by far the most populous region. Slightly more than 37 percent of Americans lived in the South in 2012. The Northeast is the least populous region, home to 18 percent of the total. Between 2000 and 2012, the South grew by 16.6 percent, slightly faster than the 16.0 percent growth in the West. The Midwest grew by only 4.4 percent and the Northeast by an even slower 3.9 percent.

The West is the most diverse region, with minorities accounting for 48 percent of its population. The Midwest is the least diverse region, with minorities accounting for only 23 percent of its population.

The South is home to the 54 percent majority of the nation's blacks. Within the region, blacks account for more than one-fifth of the population. Forty percent of Hispanics live in the West, where they account for 29 percent of the population. Forty-six percent of Asians live in the West, and they account for one in eight Western residents.

■ Asians, blacks, and Hispanics will soon account for the majority of the population in the Western states.

The Midwest is the least diverse region

(minority share of population by region, 2012)

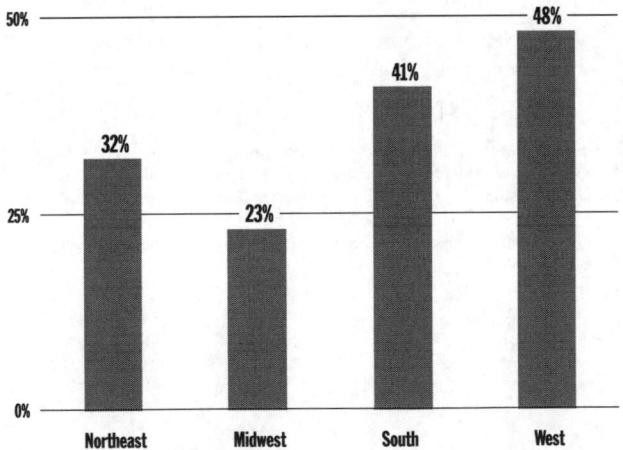

Table 8.10 Population by Region, 2000 to 2012

(number and percent distribution of population by region, 2000, 2010, and 2012; percent and percentage point change, 2000–12)

	2012	2010	2000	percent change, 2000–12
Total population	**313,914,040**	**309,326,225**	**282,162,411**	**11.3%**
Northeast	55,761,091	55,376,926	53,666,295	3.9
Midwest	67,316,297	66,972,135	64,491,431	4.4
South	117,257,221	114,853,800	100,565,549	16.6
West	73,579,431	72,123,364	63,439,136	16.0
				percentage point change, 2000–12
PERCENT DISTRIBUTION				
Total population	**100.0%**	**100.0%**	**100.0%**	–
Northeast	17.8	17.9	19.0	–1.3
Midwest	21.4	21.7	22.9	–1.4
South	37.4	37.1	35.6	1.7
West	23.4	23.3	22.5	1.0

Note: Numbers are for July 1 of each year. "–" means not applicable.
Source: Bureau of the Census, Population Estimates, Internet site http://www.census.gov/popest/index.html; calculations by New Strategist

Table 8.11 Minority Population by Region, 2012

(number of total people, and number and percent distribution of non-Hispanic whites and minorities, by region, 2012)

	total	non-Hispanic white	minority
Total population	**313,914,040**	**197,705,655**	**116,208,385**
Northeast	55,761,091	37,899,436	17,861,655
Midwest	67,316,297	52,059,292	15,257,005
South	117,257,221	69,412,944	47,844,277
West	73,579,431	38,333,983	35,245,448

PERCENT DISTRIBUTION BY RACE AND HISPANIC ORIGIN

	total	non-Hispanic white	minority
Total population	**100.0%**	**63.0%**	**37.0%**
Northeast	100.0	68.0	32.0
Midwest	100.0	77.3	22.7
South	100.0	59.2	40.8
West	100.0	52.1	47.9

PERCENT DISTRIBUTION BY REGION

	total	non-Hispanic white	minority
Total population	**100.0**	**100.0**	**100.0**
Northeast	17.8	19.2	15.4
Midwest	21.4	26.3	13.1
South	37.4	35.1	41.2
West	23.4	19.4	30.3

Note: Minorities are those who do not identify themselves as being white alone and not Hispanic.
Source: Bureau of the Census, Population Estimates, Internet site http://www.census.gov/popest/index.html; calculations by New Strategist

Table 8.12 Population by Region, Race, and Hispanic Origin, 2012

(number and percent distribution of people by region, race, and Hispanic origin, 2012)

	total	Asian	black	Hispanic	non-Hispanic white
Total population	**313,914,040**	**18,855,104**	**44,456,009**	**53,027,708**	**197,705,655**
Northeast	55,761,091	3,724,263	7,881,002	7,367,346	37,899,436
Midwest	67,316,297	2,224,979	7,822,278	4,895,277	52,059,292
South	117,257,221	4,256,868	24,196,010	19,321,511	69,412,944
West	73,579,431	8,648,994	4,556,719	21,443,574	38,333,983
PERCENT DISTRIBUTION BY RACE AND HISPANIC ORIGIN					
Total population	**100.0%**	**6.0%**	**14.2%**	**16.9%**	**63.0%**
Northeast	100.0	6.7	14.1	13.2	68.0
Midwest	100.0	3.3	11.6	7.3	77.3
South	100.0	3.6	20.6	16.5	59.2
West	100.0	11.8	6.2	29.1	52.1
PERCENT DISTRIBUTION BY REGION					
Total population	**100.0**	**100.0**	**100.0**	**100.0**	**100.0**
Northeast	17.8	19.8	17.7	13.9	19.2
Midwest	21.4	11.8	17.6	9.2	26.3
South	37.4	22.6	54.4	36.4	35.1
West	23.4	45.9	10.2	40.4	19.4

Note: Asians and blacks are those who identify themselves as being of the race alone and those who identify themselves as being of the race in combination with other races. Hispanics may be of any race. Non-Hispanic whites are those who identify themselves as being white alone and not Hispanic.
Source: Bureau of the Census, Population Estimates, Internet site http://www.census.gov/popest/index.html; calculations by New Strategist

Washington, D.C. Is Growing the Fastest

Nevada has fallen to 14th place.

Between 2000 and 2010, Nevada's population grew the fastest—a 34 percent gain. Arizona and Utah ranked second and third during those years, with a 24 percent increase. Idaho and Texas also grew by more than 20 percent. Michigan was the only state that lost population during the decade.

More recently, state population growth patterns have shifted because of the Great Recession and the collapse of the housing market. In the two years between 2010 and 2012, the District of Columbia grew faster than any of the states, its population increasing by 4.5 percent. North Dakota was second in growth as oil industry jobs lured people to the plains. Michigan grew by a tiny 0.1 percent, and Rhode Island was the only loser.

■ California, the most populous state, grew 1.9 percent between 2010 and 2012, slightly faster than the 1.5 percent gain for the United States as a whole.

North Dakota is number two in growth

(percent change in population in the five fastest growing states, 2010 to 2012)

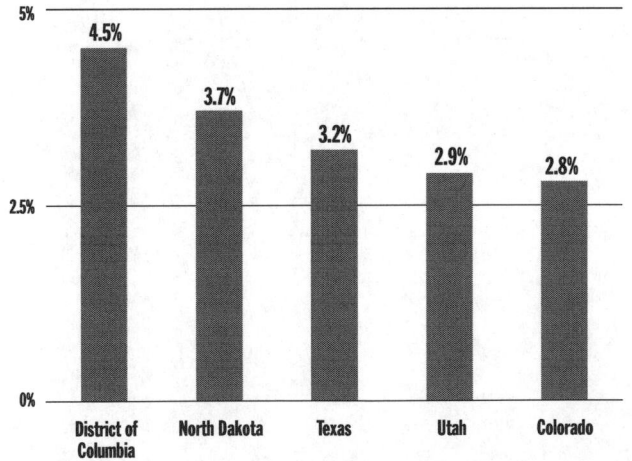

Table 8.13 Population by State, 2000 to 2012

(number of people by state, 2000, 2010, and 2012; percent change for selected years)

	2012	2010	2000	percentage change 2010–12	percentage change 2000–10
United States	**313,914,040**	**309,326,225**	**282,162,411**	**1.5%**	**9.6%**
Alabama	4,822,023	4,784,762	4,452,173	0.8	7.5
Alaska	731,449	714,046	627,963	2.4	13.7
Arizona	6,553,255	6,410,810	5,160,586	2.2	24.2
Arkansas	2,949,131	2,922,750	2,678,588	0.9	9.1
California	38,041,430	37,334,410	33,987,977	1.9	9.8
Colorado	5,187,582	5,048,472	4,326,921	2.8	16.7
Connecticut	3,590,347	3,576,616	3,411,777	0.4	4.8
Delaware	917,092	899,824	786,373	1.9	14.4
District of Columbia	632,323	604,989	572,046	4.5	5.8
Florida	19,317,568	18,845,967	16,047,515	2.5	17.4
Georgia	9,919,945	9,714,748	8,227,303	2.1	18.1
Hawaii	1,392,313	1,364,274	1,213,519	2.1	12.4
Idaho	1,595,728	1,570,784	1,299,430	1.6	20.9
Illinois	12,875,255	12,840,459	12,434,161	0.3	3.3
Indiana	6,537,334	6,489,856	6,091,866	0.7	6.5
Iowa	3,074,186	3,050,321	2,929,067	0.8	4.1
Kansas	2,885,905	2,858,837	2,693,681	0.9	6.1
Kentucky	4,380,415	4,346,655	4,049,021	0.8	7.4
Louisiana	4,601,893	4,544,125	4,471,885	1.3	1.6
Maine	1,329,192	1,327,585	1,277,072	0.1	4.0
Maryland	5,884,563	5,787,998	5,311,034	1.7	9.0
Massachusetts	6,646,144	6,563,259	6,361,104	1.3	3.2
Michigan	9,883,360	9,877,670	9,952,450	0.1	–0.8
Minnesota	5,379,139	5,310,737	4,933,692	1.3	7.6
Mississippi	2,984,926	2,969,137	2,848,353	0.5	4.2
Missouri	6,021,988	5,996,092	5,607,285	0.4	6.9
Montana	1,005,141	990,735	903,773	1.5	9.6
Nebraska	1,855,525	1,829,696	1,713,820	1.4	6.8
Nevada	2,758,931	2,703,758	2,018,741	2.0	33.9
New Hampshire	1,320,718	1,316,843	1,239,882	0.3	6.2
New Jersey	8,864,590	8,803,388	8,430,621	0.7	4.4
New Mexico	2,085,538	2,064,767	1,821,204	1.0	13.4
New York	19,570,261	19,399,242	19,001,780	0.9	2.1
North Carolina	9,752,073	9,559,048	8,081,614	2.0	18.3
North Dakota	699,628	674,363	642,023	3.7	5.0
Ohio	11,544,225	11,538,290	11,363,543	0.1	1.5
Oklahoma	3,814,820	3,759,482	3,454,365	1.5	8.8
Oregon	3,899,353	3,838,212	3,429,708	1.6	11.9
Pennsylvania	12,763,536	12,711,308	12,284,173	0.4	3.5

	2012	2010	2000	percentage change 2010–12	percentage change 2000–10
Rhode Island	1,050,292	1,052,769	1,050,268	–0.2%	0.2%
South Carolina	4,723,723	4,635,835	4,024,223	1.9	15.2
South Dakota	833,354	816,223	755,844	2.1	8.0
Tennessee	6,456,243	6,356,673	5,703,719	1.6	11.4
Texas	26,059,203	25,242,683	20,944,499	3.2	20.5
Utah	2,855,287	2,775,093	2,244,502	2.9	23.6
Vermont	626,011	625,916	609,618	0.0	2.7
Virginia	8,185,867	8,025,105	7,105,817	2.0	12.9
Washington	6,897,012	6,743,636	5,910,512	2.3	14.1
West Virginia	1,855,413	1,854,019	1,807,021	0.1	2.6
Wisconsin	5,726,398	5,689,591	5,373,999	0.6	5.9
Wyoming	576,412	564,367	494,300	2.1	14.2

Note: Numbers are as of July 1 of each year.
Source: Bureau of the Census, Population Estimates, Internet site http://www.census.gov/popest/index.html; calculations by New Strategist

Four States Have Minority Majorities

Four states are more than 90 percent non-Hispanic white.

Among the 50 states, Hawaii has the smallest share of non-Hispanic whites—only 23 percent of its population is non-Hispanic white and 57 percent is Asian. In New Mexico, non-Hispanic whites account for 40 percent of the population and Hispanics for a larger 47 percent. In California, the nation's most populous state, 38 percent of residents are Hispanic, 16 percent are Asian, and 39 percent are non-Hispanic white. In the nation's second most populous state, Texas, non-Hispanic whites account for 44 percent of the population. Thirty-eight percent of Texas residents are Hispanic and 13 percent are black.

At the other extreme, non-Hispanic whites account for more than 90 percent of the population of New Hampshire, West Virginia, Vermont, and Maine. In 13 additional states, minorities account for less than 20 percent of the population.

■ Although Hispanics and Asians are growing in number, their political power is muted by low voter participation rates.

California is one of the nation's most diverse states

(percent distribution of population in California, by race and Hispanic origin, 2012)

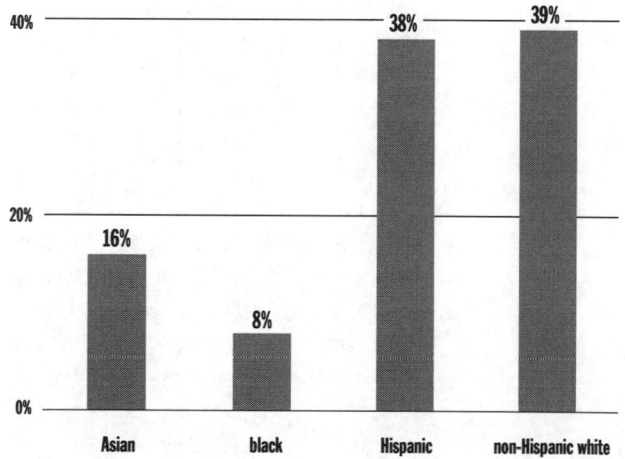

Table 8.14 Minority Population by State, 2012

(number of total people, non-Hispanic whites, and minorities by state, and minority share of total, 2012)

	total	non-Hispanic white	minority number	share of total
United States	**313,914,040**	**197,705,655**	**116,208,385**	**37.0%**
Alabama	4,822,023	3,210,178	1,611,845	33.4
Alaska	731,449	461,208	270,241	36.9
Arizona	6,553,255	3,739,038	2,814,217	42.9
Arkansas	2,949,131	2,180,732	768,399	26.1
California	38,041,430	14,971,342	23,070,088	60.6
Colorado	5,187,582	3,608,087	1,579,495	30.4
Connecticut	3,590,347	2,522,870	1,067,477	29.7
Delaware	917,092	592,014	325,078	35.4
District of Columbia	632,323	224,327	407,996	64.5
Florida	19,317,568	11,008,396	8,309,172	43.0
Georgia	9,919,945	5,469,942	4,450,003	44.9
Hawaii	1,392,313	318,118	1,074,195	77.2
Idaho	1,595,728	1,331,650	264,078	16.5
Illinois	12,875,255	8,114,559	4,760,696	37.0
Indiana	6,537,334	5,295,511	1,241,823	19.0
Iowa	3,074,186	2,705,594	368,592	12.0
Kansas	2,885,905	2,235,436	650,469	22.5
Kentucky	4,380,415	3,761,002	619,413	14.1
Louisiana	4,601,893	2,755,571	1,846,322	40.1
Maine	1,329,192	1,251,365	77,827	5.9
Maryland	5,884,563	3,170,288	2,714,275	46.1
Massachusetts	6,646,144	5,037,923	1,608,221	24.2
Michigan	9,883,360	7,533,928	2,349,432	23.8
Minnesota	5,379,139	4,429,871	949,268	17.6
Mississippi	2,984,926	1,720,045	1,264,881	42.4
Missouri	6,021,988	4,856,485	1,165,503	19.4
Montana	1,005,141	876,823	128,318	12.8
Nebraska	1,855,525	1,510,296	345,229	18.6
Nevada	2,758,931	1,458,379	1,300,552	47.1
New Hampshire	1,320,718	1,213,106	107,612	8.1
New Jersey	8,864,590	5,161,886	3,702,704	41.8
New Mexico	2,085,538	830,454	1,255,084	60.2
New York	19,570,261	11,272,085	8,298,176	42.4
North Carolina	9,752,073	6,309,775	3,442,298	35.3
North Dakota	699,628	616,336	83,292	11.9
Ohio	11,544,225	9,321,104	2,223,121	19.3
Oklahoma	3,814,820	2,588,845	1,225,975	32.1
Oregon	3,899,353	3,033,807	865,546	22.2
Pennsylvania	12,763,536	10,054,425	2,709,111	21.2

	total	non-Hispanic white	minority number	minority share of total
Rhode Island	1,050,292	797,099	253,193	24.1%
South Carolina	4,723,723	3,021,140	1,702,583	36.0
South Dakota	833,354	698,668	134,686	16.2
Tennessee	6,456,243	4,848,546	1,607,697	24.9
Texas	26,059,203	11,583,831	14,475,372	55.5
Utah	2,855,287	2,281,568	573,719	20.1
Vermont	626,011	588,677	37,334	6.0
Virginia	8,185,867	5,245,511	2,940,356	35.9
Washington	6,897,012	4,935,687	1,961,325	28.4
West Virginia	1,855,413	1,722,801	132,612	7.1
Wisconsin	5,726,398	4,741,504	984,894	17.2
Wyoming	576,412	487,822	88,590	15.4

Note: Minorities are those who do not identify themselves as being white alone and not Hispanic.
Source: Bureau of the Census, Population Estimates, Internet site http://www.census.gov/popest/index.html; calculations by New Strategist

Table 8.15 Population by State, Race, and Hispanic Origin, 2012

(number of people by state, race, and Hispanic origin, 2012)

	total	Asian	black	Hispanic	non-Hispanic white
United States	**313,914,040**	**18,855,104**	**44,456,009**	**53,027,708**	**197,705,655**
Alabama	4,822,023	74,107	1,312,795	196,032	3,210,178
Alaska	731,449	55,126	38,054	44,869	461,208
Arizona	6,553,255	263,383	361,946	1,976,106	3,739,038
Arkansas	2,949,131	50,859	480,534	199,693	2,180,732
California	38,041,430	6,008,218	2,916,166	14,537,666	14,971,342
Colorado	5,187,582	205,623	277,484	1,088,744	3,608,087
Connecticut	3,590,347	171,813	446,009	510,645	2,522,870
Delaware	917,092	37,301	216,664	78,813	592,014
District of Columbia	632,323	30,403	326,178	62,726	224,327
Florida	19,317,568	631,542	3,408,788	4,484,199	11,008,396
Georgia	9,919,945	403,991	3,200,755	909,902	5,469,942
Hawaii	1,392,313	791,778	48,532	131,744	318,118
Idaho	1,595,728	33,671	19,088	185,160	1,331,650
Illinois	12,875,255	716,337	2,012,093	2,101,208	8,114,559
Indiana	6,537,334	141,323	683,756	412,609	5,295,511
Iowa	3,074,186	71,919	123,260	162,894	2,705,594
Kansas	2,885,905	91,537	215,646	317,061	2,235,436
Kentucky	4,380,415	69,077	395,892	142,028	3,761,002
Louisiana	4,601,893	92,485	1,527,711	208,325	2,755,571
Maine	1,329,192	19,904	24,049	18,599	1,251,365
Maryland	5,884,563	404,223	1,854,705	512,010	3,170,288
Massachusetts	6,646,144	433,436	598,730	674,073	5,037,923
Michigan	9,883,360	311,839	1,525,561	456,330	7,533,928
Minnesota	5,379,139	268,922	356,237	264,359	4,429,871
Mississippi	2,984,926	35,587	1,135,322	85,260	1,720,045
Missouri	6,021,988	133,772	763,966	225,314	4,856,485
Montana	1,005,141	12,054	10,136	31,552	876,823
Nebraska	1,855,525	45,468	106,146	179,970	1,510,296
Nevada	2,758,931	267,558	282,482	752,049	1,458,379
New Hampshire	1,320,718	37,445	25,616	40,042	1,213,106
New Jersey	8,864,590	857,930	1,396,938	1,641,398	5,161,886
New Mexico	2,085,538	46,560	66,014	979,722	830,454
New York	19,570,261	1,713,859	3,690,417	3,552,781	11,272,085
North Carolina	9,752,073	285,348	2,258,700	850,853	6,309,775
North Dakota	699,628	10,439	14,133	17,230	616,336
Ohio	11,544,225	257,584	1,581,085	377,119	9,321,104
Oklahoma	3,814,820	93,721	346,971	356,300	2,588,845
Oregon	3,899,353	205,453	110,608	474,157	3,033,807
Pennsylvania	12,763,536	438,034	1,595,749	781,202	10,054,425

	total	Asian	black	Hispanic	non-Hispanic white
Rhode Island	1,050,292	40,282	93,177	138,549	797,099
South Carolina	4,723,723	85,264	1,366,615	249,712	3,021,140
South Dakota	833,354	11,880	19,015	25,715	698,668
Tennessee	6,456,243	126,377	1,152,737	312,732	4,848,546
Texas	26,059,203	1,245,279	3,409,917	9,960,900	11,583,831
Utah	2,855,287	88,762	52,715	379,436	2,281,568
Vermont	626,011	11,560	10,317	10,057	588,677
Virginia	8,185,867	573,230	1,720,834	687,496	5,245,511
Washington	6,897,012	663,071	362,000	807,599	4,935,687
West Virginia	1,855,413	18,074	80,892	24,530	1,722,801
Wisconsin	5,726,398	163,959	421,380	355,468	4,741,504
Wyoming	576,412	7,737	11,494	54,770	487,822

Note: Asians and blacks are those who identify themselves as being of the race alone and those who identify themselves as being of the race in combination with other races. Hispanics may be of any race. Non-Hispanic whites are those who identify themselves as being white alone and not Hispanic.
Source: Bureau of the Census, Population Estimates, Internet site http://www.census.gov/popest/index.html; calculations by New Strategist

Table 8.16 Distribution of Population by State, Race, and Hispanic Origin, 2012

(percent distribution of people by state, race, and Hispanic origin, 2012)

	total	Asian	black	Hispanic	non-Hispanic white
United States	**100.0%**	**6.0%**	**14.2%**	**16.9%**	**63.0%**
Alabama	100.0	1.5	27.2	4.1	66.6
Alaska	100.0	7.5	5.2	6.1	63.1
Arizona	100.0	4.0	5.5	30.2	57.1
Arkansas	100.0	1.7	16.3	6.8	73.9
California	100.0	15.8	7.7	38.2	39.4
Colorado	100.0	4.0	5.3	21.0	69.6
Connecticut	100.0	4.8	12.4	14.2	70.3
Delaware	100.0	4.1	23.6	8.6	64.6
District of Columbia	100.0	4.8	51.6	9.9	35.5
Florida	100.0	3.3	17.6	23.2	57.0
Georgia	100.0	4.1	32.3	9.2	55.1
Hawaii	100.0	56.9	3.5	9.5	22.8
Idaho	100.0	2.1	1.2	11.6	83.5
Illinois	100.0	5.6	15.6	16.3	63.0
Indiana	100.0	2.2	10.5	6.3	81.0
Iowa	100.0	2.3	4.0	5.3	88.0
Kansas	100.0	3.2	7.5	11.0	77.5
Kentucky	100.0	1.6	9.0	3.2	85.9
Louisiana	100.0	2.0	33.2	4.5	59.9
Maine	100.0	1.5	1.8	1.4	94.1
Maryland	100.0	6.9	31.5	8.7	53.9
Massachusetts	100.0	6.5	9.0	10.1	75.8
Michigan	100.0	3.2	15.4	4.6	76.2
Minnesota	100.0	5.0	6.6	4.9	82.4
Mississippi	100.0	1.2	38.0	2.9	57.6
Missouri	100.0	2.2	12.7	3.7	80.6
Montana	100.0	1.2	1.0	3.1	87.2
Nebraska	100.0	2.5	5.7	9.7	81.4
Nevada	100.0	9.7	10.2	27.3	52.9
New Hampshire	100.0	2.8	1.9	3.0	91.9
New Jersey	100.0	9.7	15.8	18.5	58.2
New Mexico	100.0	2.2	3.2	47.0	39.8
New York	100.0	8.8	18.9	18.2	57.6
North Carolina	100.0	2.9	23.2	8.7	64.7
North Dakota	100.0	1.5	2.0	2.5	88.1
Ohio	100.0	2.2	13.7	3.3	80.7
Oklahoma	100.0	2.5	9.1	9.3	67.9
Oregon	100.0	5.3	2.8	12.2	77.8
Pennsylvania	100.0	3.4	12.5	6.1	78.8

	total	Asian	black	Hispanic	non-Hispanic white
Rhode Island	100.0%	3.8%	8.9%	13.2%	75.9%
South Carolina	100.0	1.8	28.9	5.3	64.0
South Dakota	100.0	1.4	2.3	3.1	83.8
Tennessee	100.0	2.0	17.9	4.8	75.1
Texas	100.0	4.8	13.1	38.2	44.5
Utah	100.0	3.1	1.8	13.3	79.9
Vermont	100.0	1.8	1.6	1.6	94.0
Virginia	100.0	7.0	21.0	8.4	64.1
Washington	100.0	9.6	5.2	11.7	71.6
West Virginia	100.0	1.0	4.4	1.3	92.9
Wisconsin	100.0	2.9	7.4	6.2	82.8
Wyoming	100.0	1.3	2.0	9.5	84.6

Note: Numbers by race and Hispanic origin do not add to total because Asians and blacks are those who identify themselves as being of the race alone and those who identify themselves as being of the race in combination with other races. Hispanics may be of any race. Non-Hispanic whites are those who identify themselves as being white alone and not Hispanic.
Source: Bureau of the Census, Population Estimates, Internet site http://www.census.gov/popest/index.html; calculations by New Strategist

Most People Live in Metropolitan Areas

New York is the largest.

Eighty-three percent of Americans live in a metropolitan area, according to the 2010 census. In 1950, only 56 percent were metropolitan residents. The nonmetropolitan share of the population fell from a substantial 44 to just 17 percent over the past six decades.

Among the nation's largest metropolitan areas, New York is by far the most populous, with 20 million people. Overall, 52 metropolitan areas are home to at least 1 million people. In the past few years, large metropolitan areas have been growing faster than average. Between 2010 and 2012, the nation's metros with 1 million or more people grew by 2 percent. This compares with population growth of just 0.9 percent in the rest of the country.

The minority share of the nation's metropolitan areas varies greatly, from 4 percent in Parkersburg–Marietta–Vienna, West Virginia–Ohio, to 97 percent in Laredo, Texas. In a substantial 46 metropolitan areas, minorities are the majority. These include Houston, Los Angeles, Miami, New York, San Francisco, and Washington, D.C.

■ The New York metropolitan area is growing more slowly than many other large metros, but it will remain the largest for decades to come.

Minorities are the majority in New York and Los Angeles

(minority share of the population of the five most populous metropolitan areas, 2010)

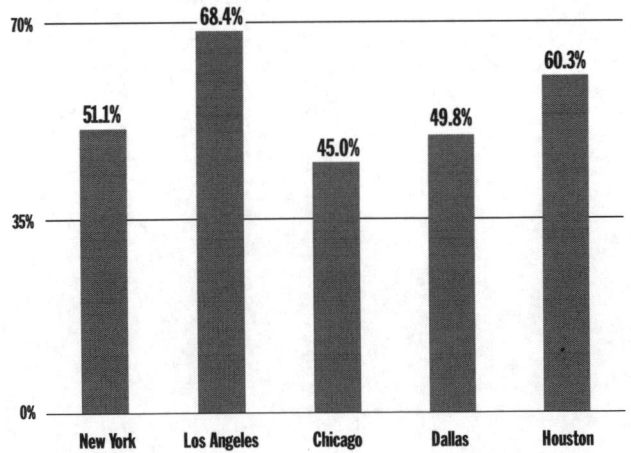

Table 8.17 Population by Metropolitan Status, 1950 to 2010

(number and percent distribution of people by metropolitan status, 1950 to 2010; numbers in thousands; metropolitan areas as defined at the respective time periods)

NUMBER	total	live in a metropolitan area	live in a nonmetropolitan area
2010	308,746	258,318	50,428
2000	281,422	225,968	55,454
1990	249,464	198,249	51,215
1980	227,225	177,361	49,864
1970	203,212	139,480	63,732
1960	179,323	112,885	66,438
1950	150,697	84,501	66,196
PERCENT DISTRIBUTION			
2010	100.0%	82.8%	17.2%
2000	100.0	80.3	19.7
1990	100.0	77.5	22.5
1980	100.0	74.8	25.2
1970	100.0	69.0	31.0
1960	100.0	63.3	36.7
1950	100.0	56.1	43.9

Note: For the definition of metropolitan statistical area, see the glossary.
Source: Bureau of the Census, Population Distributon and Change: 2000 to 2010, 2010 Census Briefs; 2000 Census, Table DP-1: Profile of General Demographic Characteristics: 2000; and Metropolitan Areas and Cities, 1990 Census Profile, No. 3, 1991; and Historical Statistics of the United States, Colonial Times to 1970, Part 1, 1975; calculations by New Strategist

Table 8.18 Population of Large Metropolitan Areas, 2010 and 2012

(number of people in metropolitan areas with at least 1 million residents, 2010 and 2012; percent change, 2010–12)

	2012	2010	percent change
Total U.S. population	**313,914,040**	**309,326,225**	**1.5%**
In metropolitan areas of 1 million or more	173,283,025	169,907,459	2.0
Outside metropolitan areas of 1 million or more	140,631,015	139,418,766	0.9
New York–Newark–Jersey City, NY–NJ–PA	19,831,858	19,598,491	1.2
Los Angeles–Long Beach–Anaheim, CA	13,052,921	12,843,942	1.6
Chicago–Naperville–Elgin, IL–IN–WI	9,522,434	9,471,608	0.5
Dallas–Fort Worth–Arlington, TX	6,700,991	6,452,764	3.8
Houston–The Woodlands–Sugar Land, TX	6,177,035	5,948,300	3.8
Philadelphia–Camden–Wilmington, PA–NJ–DE–MD	6,018,800	5,972,025	0.8
Washington–Arlington–Alexandria, DC–VA–MD–WV	5,860,342	5,665,604	3.4
Miami–Fort Lauderdale–West Palm Beach, FL	5,762,717	5,581,600	3.2
Atlanta–Sandy Springs–Roswell, GA	5,457,831	5,304,665	2.9
Boston–Cambridge–Newton, MA–NH	4,640,802	4,563,863	1.7
San Francisco–Oakland–Hayward, CA	4,455,560	4,345,156	2.5
Riverside–San Bernardino–Ontario, CA	4,350,096	4,243,987	2.5
Phoenix–Mesa–Scottsdale, AZ	4,329,534	4,209,375	2.9
Detroit–Warren–Dearborn, MI	4,292,060	4,291,828	0.0
Seattle–Tacoma–Bellevue, WA	3,552,157	3,448,919	3.0
Minneapolis–St. Paul–Bloomington, MN–WI	3,422,264	3,355,674	2.0
San Diego–Carlsbad, CA	3,177,063	3,103,933	2.4
Tampa–St. Petersburg–Clearwater, FL	2,842,878	2,788,833	1.9
St. Louis, MO–IL	2,795,794	2,789,873	0.2
Baltimore–Columbia–Towson, MD	2,753,149	2,715,586	1.4
Denver–Aurora–Lakewood, CO	2,645,209	2,554,118	3.6
Pittsburgh, PA	2,360,733	2,356,827	0.2
Charlotte–Concord–Gastonia, NC–SC	2,296,569	2,223,685	3.3
Portland–Vancouver–Hillsboro, OR–WA	2,289,800	2,232,717	2.6
San Antonio–New Braunfels, TX	2,234,003	2,153,140	3.8
Orlando–Kissimmee–Sanford, FL	2,223,674	2,139,583	3.9
Sacramento–Roseville–Arden-Arcade, CA	2,196,482	2,154,776	1.9
Cincinnati, OH–KY–IN	2,128,603	2,116,811	0.6
Cleveland–Elyria, OH	2,063,535	2,076,016	–0.6
Kansas City, MO–KS	2,038,724	2,013,864	1.2
Las Vegas–Henderson–Paradise, NV	2,000,759	1,953,422	2.4
Columbus, OH	1,944,002	1,906,295	2.0
Indianapolis–Carmel–Anderson, IN	1,928,982	1,892,368	1.9
San Jose–Sunnyvale–Santa Clara, CA	1,894,388	1,842,123	2.8
Austin–Round Rock, TX	1,834,303	1,727,661	6.2

	2012	2010	percent change
Nashville–Davidson–Murfreesboro–Franklin, TN	1,726,693	1,675,886	3.0%
Virginia Beach–Norfolk–Newport News, VA–NC	1,699,925	1,680,394	1.2
Providence–Warwick, RI–MA	1,601,374	1,601,992	0.0
Milwaukee–Waukesha–West Allis, WI	1,566,981	1,556,711	0.7
Jacksonville, FL	1,377,850	1,349,103	2.1
Memphis, TN–MS–AR	1,341,690	1,326,570	1.1
Oklahoma City, OK	1,296,565	1,257,927	3.1
Louisville/Jefferson County, KY–IN	1,251,351	1,237,847	1.1
Richmond, VA	1,231,980	1,210,180	1.8
New Orleans–Metairie, LA	1,227,096	1,195,466	2.6
Hartford–West Hartford–East Hartford, CT	1,214,400	1,212,839	0.1
Raleigh, NC	1,188,564	1,137,352	4.5
Birmingham–Hoover, AL	1,136,650	1,129,038	0.7
Buffalo–Cheektowaga–Niagara Falls, NY	1,134,210	1,135,610	–0.1
Salt Lake City, UT	1,123,712	1,091,718	2.9
Rochester, NY	1,082,284	1,079,913	0.2
Grand Rapids–Wyoming, MI	1,005,648	989,481	1.6

Source: Bureau of the Census, Population Estimates, Internet site http://www.census.gov/popest/index.html; calculations by New Strategist

Table 8.19 Minority Population of Metropolitan Areas, 2010

(number of total people, non-Hispanic whites, and minorities by metropolitan area, and minority share of total, 2010)

			minorities	
	total	non-Hispanic white	number	percent of total
Abilene, TX	165,252	112,735	52,517	31.8%
Akron, OH	703,200	579,151	124,049	17.6
Albany–Schenectady–Troy, NY	870,716	721,505	149,211	17.1
Albany, GA	157,308	68,820	88,488	56.3
Albuquerque, NM	887,077	374,214	512,863	57.8
Alexandria, LA	153,922	98,984	54,938	35.7
Allentown–Bethlehem–Easton, PA–NJ	821,173	645,741	175,432	21.4
Altoona, PA	127,089	121,495	5,594	4.4
Amarillo, TX	249,881	160,881	89,000	35.6
Ames, IA	89,542	77,812	11,730	13.1
Anchorage, AK	380,821	256,490	124,331	32.6
Anderson, IN	131,636	113,577	18,059	13.7
Anderson, SC	187,126	147,362	39,764	21.2
Ann Arbor, MI	344,791	248,675	96,116	27.9
Anniston–Oxford, AL	118,572	87,285	31,287	26.4
Appleton, WI	225,666	203,691	21,975	9.7
Asheville, NC	424,858	366,448	58,410	13.7
Athens–Clarke County, GA	192,541	130,515	62,026	32.2
Atlanta–Sandy Springs–Marietta, GA	5,268,860	2,671,757	2,597,103	49.3
Atlantic City–Hammonton, NJ	274,549	160,871	113,678	41.4
Auburn–Opelika, AL	140,247	97,900	42,347	30.2
Augusta–Richmond County, GA–SC	556,877	314,669	242,208	43.5
Austin–Round Rock–San Marcos, TX	1,716,289	938,474	777,815	45.3
Bakersfield–Delano, CA	839,631	323,794	515,837	61.4
Baltimore–Towson, MD	2,710,489	1,626,199	1,084,290	40.0
Bangor, ME	153,923	145,700	8,223	5.3
Barnstable Town, MA	215,888	197,327	18,561	8.6
Baton Rouge, LA	802,484	465,308	337,176	42.0
Battle Creek, MI	136,146	108,664	27,482	20.2
Bay City, MI	107,771	98,241	9,530	8.8
Beaumont–Port Arthur, TX	388,745	228,486	160,259	41.2
Bellingham, WA	201,140	164,675	36,465	18.1
Bend, OR	157,733	139,470	18,263	11.6
Billings, MT	158,050	140,131	17,919	11.3
Binghamton, NY	251,725	222,179	29,546	11.7
Birmingham–Hoover, AL	1,128,047	733,656	394,391	35.0
Bismarck, ND	108,779	100,591	8,188	7.5
Blacksburg–Christiansburg–Radford, VA	162,958	143,718	19,240	11.8
Bloomington–Normal, IL	169,572	138,835	30,737	18.1
Bloomington, IN	192,714	172,163	20,551	10.7

	total	non-Hispanic white	minorities number	percent of total
Boise City–Nampa, ID	616,561	505,202	111,359	18.1%
Boston–Cambridge–Quincy, MA–NH	4,552,402	3,408,585	1,143,817	25.1
Boulder, CO	294,567	233,741	60,826	20.6
Bowling Green, KY	125,953	104,540	21,413	17.0
Bremerton–Silverdale, WA	251,133	198,745	52,388	20.9
Bridgeport–Stamford–Norwalk, CT	916,829	606,716	310,113	33.8
Brownsville–Harlingen, TX	406,220	43,427	362,793	89.3
Brunswick, GA	112,370	77,516	34,854	31.0
Buffalo–Niagara Falls, NY	1,135,509	903,063	232,446	20.5
Burlington–South Burlington, VT	211,261	194,738	16,523	7.8
Burlington, NC	151,131	101,718	49,413	32.7
Canton–Massillon, OH	404,422	357,541	46,881	11.6
Cape Coral–Fort Myers, FL	618,754	439,048	179,706	29.0
Cape Girardeau–Jackson, MO–IL	96,275	83,552	12,723	13.2
Carson City, NV	55,274	39,083	16,191	29.3
Casper, WY	75,450	67,191	8,259	10.9
Cedar Rapids, IA	257,940	233,695	24,245	9.4
Champaign–Urbana, IL	231,891	172,266	59,625	25.7
Charleston–North Charleston–Summerville, SC	664,607	420,240	244,367	36.8
Charleston, WV	304,284	279,242	25,042	8.2
Charlotte–Gastonia–Rock Hill, NC–SC	1,758,038	1,076,021	682,017	38.8
Charlottesville, VA	201,559	154,343	47,216	23.4
Chattanooga, TN–GA	528,143	420,172	107,971	20.4
Cheyenne, WY	91,738	74,120	17,618	19.2
Chicago–Joliet–Naperville, IL–IN–WI	9,461,105	5,204,489	4,256,616	45.0
Chico, CA	220,000	165,416	54,584	24.8
Cincinnati–Middletown, OH–KY–IN	2,130,151	1,738,775	391,376	18.4
Clarksville, TN–KY	273,949	191,406	82,543	30.1
Cleveland–Elyria–Mentor, OH	2,077,240	1,490,074	587,166	28.3
Cleveland, TN	115,788	103,851	11,937	10.3
Coeur d'Alene, ID	138,494	127,454	11,040	8.0
College Station–Bryan, TX	228,660	136,769	91,891	40.2
Colorado Springs, CO	645,613	469,095	176,518	27.3
Columbia, MO	172,786	140,917	31,869	18.4
Columbia, SC	767,598	447,927	319,671	41.6
Columbus, GA–AL	294,865	147,518	147,347	50.0
Columbus, IN	76,794	66,817	9,977	13.0
Columbus, OH	1,836,536	1,394,399	442,137	24.1
Corpus Christi, TX	428,185	155,550	272,635	63.7
Corvallis, OR	85,579	71,552	14,027	16.4
Crestview–Fort Walton Beach–Destin, FL	180,822	139,500	41,322	22.9
Cumberland, MD–WV	103,299	92,937	10,362	10.0
Dallas–Fort Worth–Arlington, TX	6,371,773	3,201,677	3,170,096	49.8

	total	non-Hispanic white	minorities number	percent of total
Dalton, GA	142,227	97,484	44,743	31.5%
Danville, IL	81,625	65,590	16,035	19.6
Danville, VA	106,561	67,357	39,204	36.8
Davenport–Moline–Rock Island, IA–IL	379,690	311,053	68,637	18.1
Dayton, OH	841,502	663,353	178,149	21.2
Decatur, AL	153,829	119,005	34,824	22.6
Decatur, IL	110,768	86,822	23,946	21.6
Deltona–Daytona Beach–Ormond Beach, FL	494,593	372,982	121,611	24.6
Denver–Aurora–Broomfield, CO	2,543,482	1,673,709	869,773	34.2
Des Moines–West Des Moines, IA	569,633	476,434	93,199	16.4
Detroit–Warren–Livonia, MI	4,296,250	2,916,144	1,380,106	32.1
Dothan, AL	145,639	104,154	41,485	28.5
Dover, DE	162,310	105,891	56,419	34.8
Dubuque, IA	93,653	86,981	6,672	7.1
Duluth, MN–WI	279,771	257,081	22,690	8.1
Durham–Chapel Hill, NC	504,357	278,907	225,450	44.7
Eau Claire, WI	161,151	149,946	11,205	7.0
El Centro, CA	174,528	23,927	150,601	86.3
El Paso, TX	800,647	105,246	695,401	86.9
Elizabethtown, KY	119,736	95,235	24,501	20.5
Elkhart–Goshen, IN	197,559	152,555	45,004	22.8
Elmira, NY	88,830	77,643	11,187	12.6
Erie, PA	280,566	242,787	37,779	13.5
Eugene–Springfield, OR	351,715	297,808	53,907	15.3
Evansville, IN–KY	358,676	318,979	39,697	11.1
Fairbanks, AK	97,581	72,259	25,322	25.9
Fargo, ND–MN	208,777	188,964	19,813	9.5
Farmington, NM	130,044	55,254	74,790	57.5
Fayetteville–Springdale–Rogers, AR–MO	463,204	353,302	109,902	23.7
Fayetteville, NC	366,383	169,891	196,492	53.6
Flagstaff, AZ	134,421	74,231	60,190	44.8
Flint, MI	425,790	309,683	116,107	27.3
Florence–Muscle Shoals, AL	147,137	122,562	24,575	16.7
Florence, SC	205,566	112,098	93,468	45.5
Fond du Lac, WI	101,633	93,398	8,235	8.1
Fort Collins–Loveland, CO	299,630	253,047	46,583	15.5
Fort Smith, AR–OK	298,592	226,828	71,764	24.0
Fort Wayne, IN	416,257	330,540	85,717	20.6
Fresno, CA	930,450	304,522	625,928	67.3
Gadsden, AL	104,430	82,789	21,641	20.7
Gainesville, FL	264,275	172,348	91,927	34.8
Gainesville, GA	179,684	114,300	65,384	36.4
Glens Falls, NY	128,923	121,581	7,342	5.7

	total	non-Hispanic white	minorities number	percent of total
Goldsboro, NC	122,623	68,216	54,407	44.4%
Grand Forks, ND–MN	98,461	87,768	10,693	10.9
Grand Junction, CO	146,723	121,944	24,779	16.9
Grand Rapids–Wyoming, MI	774,160	615,337	158,823	20.5
Great Falls, MT	81,327	71,100	10,227	12.6
Greeley, CO	252,825	170,827	81,998	32.4
Green Bay, WI	306,241	263,593	42,648	13.9
Greensboro–High Point, NC	723,801	449,177	274,624	37.9
Greenville–Mauldin–Easley, SC	636,986	467,055	169,931	26.7
Greenville, NC	189,510	106,076	83,434	44.0
Gulfport–Biloxi, MS	248,820	177,475	71,345	28.7
Hagerstown–Martinsburg, MD–WV	269,140	229,076	40,064	14.9
Hanford–Corcoran, CA	152,982	53,879	99,103	64.8
Harrisburg–Carlisle, PA	549,475	442,343	107,132	19.5
Harrisonburg, VA	125,228	105,031	20,197	16.1
Hartford–West Hartford–East Hartford, CT	1,212,381	868,016	344,365	28.4
Hattiesburg, MS	142,842	95,576	47,266	33.1
Hickory–Lenoir–Morganton, NC	365,497	302,096	63,401	17.3
Hinesville–Fort Stewart, GA	77,917	35,576	42,341	54.3
Holland–Grand Haven, MI	263,801	226,156	37,645	14.3
Honolulu, HI	953,207	181,684	771,523	80.9
Hot Springs, AR	96,024	80,621	15,403	16.0
Houma–Bayou Cane–Thibodaux, LA	208,178	151,869	56,309	27.0
Houston–Sugar Land–Baytown, TX	5,946,800	2,360,472	3,586,328	60.3
Huntington–Ashland, WV–KY–OH	287,702	270,988	16,714	5.8
Huntsville, AL	417,593	286,557	131,036	31.4
Idaho Falls, ID	130,374	111,798	18,576	14.2
Indianapolis–Carmel, IN	1,756,241	1,310,092	446,149	25.4
Iowa City, IA	152,586	128,881	23,705	15.5
Ithaca, NY	101,564	81,490	20,074	19.8
Jackson, MI	160,248	137,588	22,660	14.1
Jackson, MS	539,057	260,512	278,545	51.7
Jackson, TN	115,425	71,897	43,528	37.7
Jacksonville, FL	1,345,596	885,040	460,556	34.2
Jacksonville, NC	177,772	122,558	55,214	31.1
Janesville, WI	160,331	135,526	24,805	15.5
Jefferson City, MO	149,807	131,411	18,396	12.3
Johnson City, TN	198,716	183,099	15,617	7.9
Johnstown, PA	143,679	134,073	9,606	6.7
Jonesboro, AR	121,026	98,641	22,385	18.5
Joplin, MO	175,518	151,986	23,532	13.4
Kalamazoo–Portage, MI	326,589	263,075	63,514	19.4
Kankakee–Bradley, IL	113,449	83,218	30,231	26.6

	total	non-Hispanic white	minorities number	percent of total
Kansas City, MO–KS	2,035,334	1,514,888	520,446	25.6%
Kennewick–Pasco–Richland, WA	253,340	164,241	89,099	35.2
Killeen–Temple–Fort Hood, TX	405,300	218,901	186,399	46.0
Kingsport–Bristol–Bristol, TN–VA	309,544	293,968	15,576	5.0
Kingston, NY	182,493	149,099	33,394	18.3
Knoxville, TN	698,030	606,269	91,761	13.1
Kokomo, IN	98,688	87,446	11,242	11.4
La Crosse, WI–MN	133,665	122,899	10,766	8.1
Lafayette, IN	201,789	166,341	35,448	17.6
Lafayette, LA	273,738	182,803	90,935	33.2
Lake Charles, LA	199,607	140,168	59,439	29.8
Lake Havasu City–Kingman, AZ	200,186	159,378	40,808	20.4
Lakeland–Winter Haven, FL	602,095	388,769	213,326	35.4
Lancaster, PA	519,445	440,969	78,476	15.1
Lansing–East Lansing, MI	464,036	363,242	100,794	21.7
Laredo, TX	250,304	8,345	241,959	96.7
Las Cruces, NM	209,233	62,992	146,241	69.9
Las Vegas–Paradise, NV	1,951,269	935,955	1,015,314	52.0
Lawrence, KS	110,826	90,532	20,294	18.3
Lawton, OK	124,098	73,122	50,976	41.1
Lebanon, PA	133,568	116,010	17,558	13.1
Lewiston–Auburn, ME	107,702	98,931	8,771	8.1
Lewiston, ID–WA	60,888	54,861	6,027	9.9
Lexington–Fayette, KY	472,099	372,839	99,260	21.0
Lima, OH	106,331	87,708	18,623	17.5
Lincoln, NE	302,157	256,854	45,303	15.0
Little Rock–North Little Rock–Conway, AR	699,757	487,009	212,748	30.4
Logan, UT–ID	125,442	108,026	17,416	13.9
Longview, TX	214,369	141,499	72,870	34.0
Longview, WA	102,410	87,825	14,585	14.2
Los Angeles–Long Beach–Santa Ana, CA	12,828,837	4,056,820	8,772,017	68.4
Louisville/Jefferson County, KY–IN	1,283,566	1,012,081	271,485	21.2
Lubbock, TX	284,890	162,440	122,450	43.0
Lynchburg, VA	252,634	194,849	57,785	22.9
Macon, GA	232,293	119,766	112,527	48.4
Madera–Chowchilla, CA	150,865	57,380	93,485	62.0
Madison, WI	568,593	476,020	92,573	16.3
Manchester–Nashua, NH	400,721	351,224	49,497	12.4
Manhattan, KS	127,081	96,848	30,233	23.8
Mankato–North Mankato, MN	96,740	88,338	8,402	8.7
Mansfield, OH	124,475	107,726	16,749	13.5
McAllen–Edinburg–Mission, TX	774,769	60,553	714,216	92.2
Medford, OR	203,206	170,023	33,183	16.3

	total	non-Hispanic white	minorities number	percent of total
Memphis, TN–MS–AR	1,316,100	608,449	707,651	53.8%
Merced, CA	255,793	81,599	174,194	68.1
Miami–Fort Lauderdale–Pompano Beach, FL	5,564,635	1,937,939	3,626,696	65.2
Michigan City–La Porte, IN	111,467	90,695	20,772	18.6
Midland, TX	136,872	72,822	64,050	46.8
Milwaukee–Waukesha–West Allis, WI	1,555,908	1,073,109	482,799	31.0
Minneapolis–St. Paul–Bloomington, MN–WI	3,279,833	2,578,117	701,716	21.4
Missoula, MT	109,299	99,489	9,810	9.0
Mobile, AL	412,992	243,904	169,088	40.9
Modesto, CA	514,453	240,423	274,030	53.3
Monroe, LA	176,441	106,971	69,470	39.4
Monroe, MI	152,021	140,609	11,412	7.5
Montgomery, AL	374,536	192,543	181,993	48.6
Morgantown, WV	129,709	118,855	10,854	8.4
Morristown, TN	136,608	121,337	15,271	11.2
Mount Vernon–Anacortes, WA	116,901	89,694	27,207	23.3
Muncie, IN	117,671	103,721	13,950	11.9
Muskegon–Norton Shores, MI	172,188	133,132	39,056	22.7
Myrtle Beach–North Myrtle Beach–Conway, SC	269,291	208,096	61,195	22.7
Napa, CA	136,484	76,967	59,517	43.6
Naples–Marco Island, FL	321,520	211,156	110,364	34.3
Nashville-Davidson–Murfreesboro–Franklin, TN	1,589,934	1,176,069	413,865	26.0
New Haven–Milford, CT	862,477	582,384	280,093	32.5
New Orleans–Metairie–Kenner, LA	1,167,764	628,878	538,886	46.1
New York–Northern New Jersey–Long Island, NY–NJ–PA	18,897,109	9,233,812	9,663,297	51.1
Niles–Benton Harbor, MI	156,813	119,389	37,424	23.9
North Port–Bradenton–Sarasota, FL	702,281	558,928	143,353	20.4
Norwich–New London, CT	274,055	214,605	59,450	21.7
Ocala, FL	331,298	245,136	86,162	26.0
Ocean City, NJ	97,265	84,522	12,743	13.1
Odessa, TX	137,130	56,306	80,824	58.9
Ogden–Clearfield, UT	547,184	452,785	94,399	17.3
Oklahoma City, OK	1,252,987	845,104	407,883	32.6
Olympia, WA	252,264	199,019	53,245	21.1
Omaha–Council Bluffs, NE–IA	865,350	681,172	184,178	21.3
Orlando–Kissimmee–Sanford, FL	2,134,411	1,136,863	997,548	46.7
Oshkosh–Neenah, WI	166,994	151,509	15,485	9.3
Owensboro, KY	114,752	104,565	10,187	8.9
Oxnard–Thousand Oaks–Ventura, CA	823,318	400,868	422,450	51.3
Palm Bay–Melbourne–Titusville, FL	543,376	421,466	121,910	22.4
Palm Coast, FL	95,696	72,860	22,836	23.9
Panama City–Lynn Haven–Panama City Beach, FL	168,852	133,790	35,062	20.8

	total	non-Hispanic white	minorities number	percent of total
Parkersburg–Marietta–Vienna, WV–OH	162,056	155,597	6,459	4.0%
Pascagoula, MS	162,246	117,679	44,567	27.5
Pensacola–Ferry Pass–Brent, FL	448,991	325,627	123,364	27.5
Peoria, IL	379,186	319,493	59,693	15.7
Philadelphia–Camden–Wilmington, PA–NJ–DE–MD	5,965,343	3,875,845	2,089,498	35.0
Phoenix–Mesa–Glendale, AZ	4,192,887	2,460,541	1,732,346	41.3
Pine Bluff, AR	100,258	48,740	51,518	51.4
Pittsburgh, PA	2,356,285	2,051,163	305,122	12.9
Pittsfield, MA	131,219	118,926	12,293	9.4
Pocatello, ID	90,656	76,730	13,926	15.4
Port St. Lucie, FL	424,107	287,564	136,543	32.2
Portland–South Portland–Biddeford, ME	514,098	480,553	33,545	6.5
Portland–Vancouver–Hillsboro, OR–WA	2,226,009	1,698,126	527,883	23.7
Poughkeepsie–Newburgh–Middletown, NY	670,301	476,071	194,230	29.0
Prescott, AZ	211,033	172,968	38,065	18.0
Providence–New Bedford–Fall River, RI–MA	1,600,852	1,273,029	327,823	20.5
Provo–Orem, UT	526,810	444,339	82,471	15.7
Pueblo, CO	159,063	86,054	73,009	45.9
Punta Gorda, FL	159,978	137,628	22,350	14.0
Racine, WI	195,408	145,414	49,994	25.6
Raleigh–Cary, NC	1,130,490	716,883	413,607	36.6
Rapid City, SD	126,382	105,389	20,993	16.6
Reading, PA	411,442	316,406	95,036	23.1
Redding, CA	177,223	146,044	31,179	17.6
Reno–Sparks, NV	425,417	281,745	143,672	33.8
Richmond, VA	1,258,251	754,328	503,923	40.0
Riverside–San Bernardino–Ontario, CA	4,224,851	1,546,666	2,678,185	63.4
Roanoke, VA	308,707	248,968	59,739	19.4
Rochester, MN	186,011	159,840	26,171	14.1
Rochester, NY	1,054,323	824,425	229,898	21.8
Rockford, IL	349,431	254,953	94,478	27.0
Rocky Mount, NC	152,392	73,130	79,262	52.0
Rome, GA	96,317	70,959	25,358	26.3
Sacramento–Arden-Arcade–Roseville, CA	2,149,127	1,197,389	951,738	44.3
Saginaw–Saginaw Township North, MI	200,169	141,187	58,982	29.5
Salem, OR	390,738	277,460	113,278	29.0
Salinas, CA	415,057	136,435	278,622	67.1
Salisbury, MD	125,203	79,563	45,640	36.5
Salt Lake City, UT	1,124,197	842,071	282,126	25.1
San Angelo, TX	111,823	64,952	46,871	41.9
San Antonio–New Braunfels, TX	2,142,508	773,807	1,368,701	63.9
San Diego–Carlsbad–San Marcos, CA	3,095,313	1,500,047	1,595,266	51.5
San Francisco–Oakland–Fremont, CA	4,335,391	1,840,372	2,495,019	57.6

	total	non-Hispanic white	minorities	
			number	percent of total
San Jose–Sunnyvale–Santa Clara, CA	1,836,911	648,063	1,188,848	64.7%
San Luis Obispo–Paso Robles, CA	269,637	191,696	77,941	28.9
Sandusky, OH	77,079	65,463	11,616	15.1
Santa Barbara–Santa Maria–Goleta, CA	423,895	203,122	220,773	52.1
Santa Cruz–Watsonville, CA	262,382	156,397	105,985	40.4
Santa Fe, NM	144,170	63,291	80,879	56.1
Santa Rosa–Petaluma, CA	483,878	320,027	163,851	33.9
Savannah, GA	347,611	199,249	148,362	42.7
Scranton–Wilkes-Barre, PA	563,631	502,578	61,053	10.8
Seattle–Tacoma–Bellevue, WA	3,439,809	2,340,274	1,099,535	32.0
Sebastian–Vero Beach, FL	138,028	106,780	31,248	22.6
Sheboygan, WI	115,507	100,520	14,987	13.0
Sherman–Denison, TX	120,877	95,103	25,774	21.3
Shreveport–Bossier City, LA	398,604	218,052	180,552	45.3
Sioux City, IA–NE–SD	143,577	109,779	33,798	23.5
Sioux Falls, SD	228,261	202,388	25,873	11.3
South Bend–Mishawaka, IN–MI	319,224	247,405	71,819	22.5
Spartanburg, SC	284,307	199,184	85,123	29.9
Spokane, WA	471,221	408,629	62,592	13.3
Springfield, IL	210,170	175,307	34,863	16.6
Springfield, MA	692,942	516,073	176,869	25.5
Springfield, MO	436,712	399,431	37,281	8.5
Springfield, OH	138,333	117,976	20,357	14.7
St. Cloud, MN	189,093	172,353	16,740	8.9
St. George, UT	138,115	118,282	19,833	14.4
St. Joseph, MO–KS	127,329	111,905	15,424	12.1
St. Louis, MO–IL	2,812,896	2,112,954	699,942	24.9
State College, PA	153,990	135,427	18,563	12.1
Steubenville–Weirton, OH–WV	124,454	115,903	8,551	6.9
Stockton, CA	685,306	245,919	439,387	64.1
Sumter, SC	107,456	50,423	57,033	53.1
Syracuse, NY	662,577	555,047	107,530	16.2
Tallahassee, FL	367,413	211,958	155,455	42.3
Tampa–St. Petersburg–Clearwater, FL	2,783,243	1,879,437	903,806	32.5
Terre Haute, IN	172,425	155,488	16,937	9.8
Texarkana–Texarkana, TX–AR	136,027	92,034	43,993	32.3
Toledo, OH	651,429	503,966	147,463	22.6
Topeka, KS	233,870	186,502	47,368	20.3
Trenton–Ewing, NJ	366,513	199,909	166,604	45.5
Tucson, AZ	980,263	541,700	438,563	44.7
Tulsa, OK	937,478	635,628	301,850	32.2
Tuscaloosa, AL	219,461	134,386	85,075	38.8
Tyler, TX	209,714	130,246	79,468	37.9

	total	non-Hispanic white	minorities number	minorities percent of total
Utica–Rome, NY	299,397	260,944	38,453	12.8%
Valdosta, GA	139,588	80,113	59,475	42.6
Vallejo–Fairfield, CA	413,344	168,628	244,716	59.2
Victoria, TX	115,384	55,695	59,689	51.7
Vineland–Millville–Bridgeton, NJ	156,898	78,931	77,967	49.7
Virginia Beach–Norfolk–Newport News, VA–NC	1,671,683	955,896	715,787	42.8
Visalia–Porterville, CA	442,179	143,935	298,244	67.4
Waco, TX	234,906	138,295	96,611	41.1
Warner Robins, GA	139,900	84,703	55,197	39.5
Washington–Arlington–Alexandria, DC–VA–MD–WV	5,582,170	2,711,258	2,870,912	51.4
Waterloo–Cedar Falls, IA	167,819	145,617	22,202	13.2
Wausau, WI	134,063	121,007	13,056	9.7
Wenatchee–East Wenatchee, WA	110,884	77,272	33,612	30.3
Wheeling, WV–OH	147,950	139,308	8,642	5.8
Wichita Falls, TX	151,306	108,124	43,182	28.5
Wichita, KS	623,061	459,730	163,331	26.2
Williamsport, PA	116,111	106,710	9,401	8.1
Wilmington, NC	362,315	281,017	81,298	22.4
Winchester, VA–WV	128,472	108,821	19,651	15.3
Winston-Salem, NC	477,717	317,660	160,057	33.5
Worcester, MA	798,552	644,299	154,253	19.3
Yakima, WA	243,231	116,024	127,207	52.3
York–Hanover, PA	434,972	374,779	60,193	13.8
Youngstown–Warren–Boardman, OH–PA	565,773	476,794	88,979	15.7
Yuba City, CA	166,892	90,198	76,694	46.0
Yuma, AZ	195,751	69,022	126,729	64.7

Note: Minorities are those who do not identify themselves as being white alone and not Hispanic.
Source: Bureau of the Census, 2010 census, Internet site, http://factfinder2.census.gov/faces/nav/jsf/pages/index.xhtml; calculations by New Strategist

Americans Are Moving Less

The mobility rate of homeowners is the lowest ever recorded.

Only 12.0 percent of Americans moved between March 2011 and March 2012, down from 14.2 percent in 2000–01 and 21.2 percent in 1950–51. The 2011–12 mobility rate was slightly higher than the all-time low of 11.6 percent in 2010–11. Among homeowners, however, the 2011–12 mobility rate matched the previous year's record low of 4.7 percent. Mobility among renters was a much higher 26.7 percent but close to its all-time low.

Most moves are local, motivated by housing needs rather than job relocations. Among movers between 2011 and 2012, the 64 percent majority remained in the same county. Only 14 percent moved to a different state. In 2000–01, a larger 20 percent moved to a different state.

Young adults are most likely to move, many of them graduating from college and looking for work. One in four 20-to-29-year-olds moved between 2011 and 2012. The mobility rate falls with age to less than 10 percent among people aged 40 or older and to less than 5 percent among people aged 65 or older.

■ There is pent-up demand for moving because millions of Americans have been stuck in place, waiting for the housing market to improve.

Mobility has fallen

(percent of people aged 1 or older who moved in a 12-month period, selected years, 1950–51 to 2011–12)

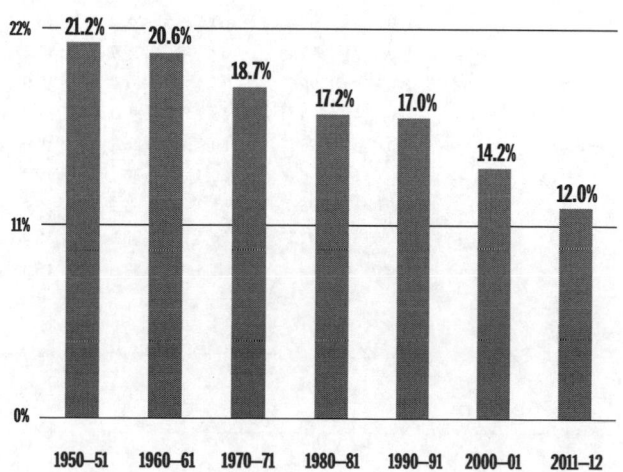

Table 8.20 Geographical Mobility, 1950 to 2012

(number and percent distribution of people aged 1 or older by mobility status, 1950–51 to 2011–12; numbers in thousands)

	total people aged 1+	same house (nonmovers)	total movers	total	same county	total	same state	different state	movers from abroad
				different house in United States					
						different county			
2011–12	304,924	268,436	36,488	35,334	23,493	11,842	6,782	5,059	1,154
2010–11	302,640	267,602	35,038	33,953	23,330	10,623	5,868	4,756	1,084
2009–10	300,419	262,975	37,445	36,459	25,910	10,549	6,227	4,323	985
2008–09	297,182	260,077	37,105	36,017	24,984	11,034	6,374	4,660	1,087
2007–08	294,851	259,685	35,167	34,022	23,013	11,009	6,282	4,728	1,145
2000–01	275,611	236,605	39,006	37,251	21,918	15,333	7,550	7,783	1,756
1990–91	244,884	203,345	41,539	40,154	25,151	15,003	7,881	7,122	1,385
1980–81	221,641	183,442	38,199	36,887	23,097	13,789	7,614	6,175	1,313
1970–71	201,506	163,800	37,706	36,161	23,018	13,143	6,197	6,946	1,544
1960–61	177,354	140,821	36,533	35,535	24,289	11,246	5,493	5,753	998
1950–51	148,400	116,936	31,464	31,158	20,694	10,464	5,276	5,188	306

PERCENT DISTRIBUTION OF POPULATION BY MOBILITY STATUS

2011–12	100.0%	88.0%	12.0%	11.6%	7.7%	3.9%	2.2%	1.7%	0.4%
2010–11	100.0	88.4	11.6	11.2	7.7	3.5	1.9	1.6	0.4
2009–10	100.0	87.5	12.5	12.1	8.6	3.5	2.1	1.4	0.3
2008–09	100.0	87.5	12.5	12.1	8.4	3.7	2.1	1.6	0.4
2007–08	100.0	88.1	11.9	11.5	7.8	3.7	2.1	1.6	0.4
2000–01	100.0	85.8	14.2	13.5	8.0	5.6	2.7	2.8	0.6
1990–91	100.0	83.0	17.0	16.4	10.3	6.1	3.2	2.9	0.6
1980–81	100.0	82.8	17.2	16.6	10.4	6.2	3.4	2.8	0.6
1970–71	100.0	81.3	18.7	17.9	11.4	6.5	3.1	3.4	0.8
1960–61	100.0	79.4	20.6	20.0	13.7	6.3	3.1	3.2	0.6
1950–51	100.0	78.8	21.2	21.0	13.9	7.1	3.6	3.5	0.2

PERCENT DISTRIBUTION OF MOVERS BY TYPE OF MOVE

2011–12	–	–	100.0%	96.8%	64.4%	32.5%	18.6%	13.9%	3.2%
2010–11	–	–	100.0	96.9	66.6	30.3	16.7	13.6	3.1
2009–10	–	–	100.0	97.4	69.2	28.2	16.6	11.5	2.6
2008–09	–	–	100.0	97.1	67.3	29.7	17.2	12.6	2.9
2007–08	–	–	100.0	96.7	65.4	31.3	17.9	13.4	3.3
2000–01	–	–	100.0	95.5	56.2	39.3	19.4	20.0	4.5
1990–91	–	–	100.0	96.7	60.5	36.1	19.0	17.1	3.3
1980–81	–	–	100.0	96.6	60.5	36.1	19.9	16.2	3.4
1970–71	–	–	100.0	95.9	61.0	34.9	16.4	18.4	4.1
1960–61	–	–	100.0	97.3	66.5	30.8	15.0	15.7	2.7
1950–51	–	–	100.0	99.0	65.8	33.3	16.8	16.5	1.0

Note: "–" means not applicable.
Source: Bureau of the Census, Geographical Mobility/Migration, Internet site http://www.census.gov/hhes/migration/data/cps/ historical.html; calculations by New Strategist

Table 8.21 Geographical Mobility of Homeowners, 2000 to 2012

(number and percent distribution of people aged 1 or older living in owner-occupied homes by mobility status, 2000–01 to 2011–12; numbers in thousands)

	total aged 1+ in owner-occupied housing	same house (nonmovers)	total movers	different house in United States		different county			movers from abroad
				total	same county	total	same state	different state	
2011–2012	204,716	195,015	9,701	9,480	5,940	3,540	2,203	1,337	221
2010–2011	205,493	195,826	9,667	9,395	5,929	3,466	1,946	1,520	272
2009–2010	206,520	195,798	10,722	10,419	6,959	3,460	2,044	1,416	303
2008–2009	206,924	196,146	10,778	10,445	6,873	3,572	2,013	1,559	333
2007–2008	208,212	197,055	11,157	10,875	6,850	4,025	2,306	1,719	283
2006–2007	207,774	194,014	13,760	13,378	8,467	4,911	2,881	2,030	381
2005–2006	206,136	191,579	14,558	14,214	8,708	5,506	3,414	2,092	344
2004–2005	206,955	191,509	15,446	15,018	8,494	6,524	3,477	3,048	427
2003–2004	203,302	188,461	14,841	14,525	8,303	6,222	3,398	2,824	316
2002–2003	200,627	185,686	14,942	14,641	8,549	6,092	3,195	2,897	301
2001–2002	196,488	180,518	15,971	15,692	9,142	6,550	3,563	2,987	279
2000–2001	194,329	179,990	14,339	13,920	7,737	6,183	3,284	2,899	420

PERCENT DISTRIBUTION OF POPULATION BY MOBILITY STATUS

2011–2012	100.0%	95.3%	4.7%	4.6%	2.9%	1.7%	1.1%	0.7%	0.1%
2010–2011	100.0	95.3	4.7	4.6	2.9	1.7	0.9	0.7	0.1
2009–2010	100.0	94.8	5.2	5.0	3.4	1.7	1.0	0.7	0.1
2008–2009	100.0	94.8	5.2	5.0	3.3	1.7	1.0	0.8	0.2
2007–2008	100.0	94.6	5.4	5.2	3.3	1.9	1.1	0.8	0.1
2006–2007	100.0	93.4	6.6	6.4	4.1	2.4	1.4	1.0	0.2
2005–2006	100.0	92.9	7.1	6.9	4.2	2.7	1.7	1.0	0.2
2004–2005	100.0	92.5	7.5	7.3	4.1	3.2	1.7	1.5	0.2
2003–2004	100.0	92.7	7.3	7.1	4.1	3.1	1.7	1.4	0.2
2002–2003	100.0	92.6	7.4	7.3	4.3	3.0	1.6	1.4	0.2
2001–2002	100.0	91.9	8.1	8.0	4.7	3.3	1.8	1.5	0.1
2000–2001	100.0	92.6	7.4	7.2	4.0	3.2	1.7	1.5	0.2

PERCENT DISTRIBUTION OF MOVERS BY TYPE OF MOVE

2011–2012	–	–	100.0%	97.7%	61.2%	36.5%	22.7%	13.8%	2.3%
2010–2011	–	–	100.0	97.2	61.3	35.9	20.1	15.7	2.8
2009–2010	–	–	100.0	97.2	64.9	32.3	19.1	13.2	2.8
2008–2009	–	–	100.0	96.9	63.8	33.1	18.7	14.5	3.1
2007–2008	–	–	100.0	97.5	61.4	36.1	20.7	15.4	2.5
2006–2007	–	–	100.0	97.2	61.5	35.7	20.9	14.8	2.8
2005–2006	–	–	100.0	97.6	59.8	37.8	23.5	14.4	2.4
2004–2005	–	–	100.0	97.2	55.0	42.2	22.5	19.7	2.8
2003–2004	–	–	100.0	97.9	55.9	41.9	22.9	19.0	2.1
2002–2003	–	–	100.0	98.0	57.2	40.8	21.4	19.4	2.0
2001–2002	–	–	100.0	98.3	57.2	41.0	22.3	18.7	1.7
2000–2001	–	–	100.0	97.1	54.0	43.1	22.9	20.2	2.9

Note: "–" means not applicable.
Source: Bureau of the Census, Geographical Mobility/Migration, Internet site http://www.census.gov/hhes/migration/data/cps/historical.html; calculations by New Strategist

Table 8.22 Geographical Mobility of Renters, 2000 to 2012

(number and percent distribution of people aged 1 or older living in renter-occupied homes by mobility status, 2000–01 to 2011–12; numbers in thousands)

| | total aged 1+ in renter-occupied housing | same house (nonmovers) | total movers | different house in United States | | | different state | | | movers from abroad |
				total	same county	total	same state	different state	
2011–2012	100,208	73,421	26,787	25,854	17,553	8,301	4,579	3,722	933
2010–2011	97,147	71,776	25,370	24,558	17,401	7,157	3,921	3,236	812
2009–2010	93,899	67,177	26,722	26,040	18,951	7,089	4,183	2,906	682
2008–2009	90,257	63,931	26,326	25,572	18,111	7,461	4,361	3,101	754
2007–2008	86,639	62,630	24,010	23,147	16,163	6,984	3,976	3,009	862
2006–2007	84,975	60,053	24,922	24,111	16,725	7,386	4,555	2,831	809
2005–2006	83,646	58,366	25,280	24,327	16,143	8,184	4,596	3,588	953
2004–2005	80,193	55,752	24,442	23,004	14,242	8,763	4,370	4,393	1,437
2003–2004	81,065	56,911	24,153	23,196	14,248	8,948	4,443	4,505	957
2002–2003	81,929	56,777	25,151	24,183	14,919	9,264	4,533	4,731	968
2001–2002	81,673	56,532	25,142	23,857	14,570	9,287	4,504	4,783	1,285
2000–2001	81,282	56,615	24,667	23,329	14,181	9,148	4,265	4,883	1,337

PERCENT DISTRIBUTION OF POPULATION BY MOBILITY STATUS

2011–2012	100.0%	73.3%	26.7%	25.8%	17.5%	8.3%	4.6%	3.7%	0.9%
2010–2011	100.0	73.9	26.1	25.3	17.9	7.4	4.0	3.3	0.8
2009–2010	100.0	71.5	28.5	27.7	20.2	7.5	4.5	3.1	0.7
2008–2009	100.0	70.8	29.2	28.3	20.1	8.3	4.8	3.4	0.8
2007–2008	100.0	72.3	27.7	26.7	18.7	8.1	4.6	3.5	1.0
2006–2007	100.0	70.7	29.3	28.4	19.7	8.7	5.4	3.3	1.0
2005–2006	100.0	69.8	30.2	29.1	19.3	9.8	5.5	4.3	1.1
2004–2005	100.0	69.5	30.5	28.7	17.8	10.9	5.4	5.5	1.8
2003–2004	100.0	70.2	29.8	28.6	17.6	11.0	5.5	5.6	1.2
2002–2003	100.0	69.3	30.7	29.5	18.2	11.3	5.5	5.8	1.2
2001–2002	100.0	69.2	30.8	29.2	17.8	11.4	5.5	5.9	1.6
2000–2001	100.0	69.7	30.3	28.7	17.4	11.3	5.2	6.0	1.6

PERCENT DISTRIBUTION OF MOVERS BY TYPE OF MOVE

2011–2012	–	–	100.0	96.5	65.5	31.0	17.1	13.9	3.5
2010–2011	–	–	100.0	96.8	68.6	28.2	15.5	12.8	3.2
2009–2010	–	–	100.0	97.4	70.9	26.5	15.7	10.9	2.6
2008–2009	–	–	100.0	97.1	68.8	28.3	16.6	11.8	2.9
2007–2008	–	–	100.0	96.4	67.3	29.1	16.6	12.5	3.6
2006–2007	–	–	100.0	96.7	67.1	29.6	18.3	11.4	3.2
2005–2006	–	–	100.0	96.2	63.9	32.4	18.2	14.2	3.8
2004–2005	–	–	100.0	94.1	58.3	35.9	17.9	18.0	5.9
2003–2004	–	–	100.0	96.0	59.0	37.0	18.4	18.7	4.0
2002–2003	–	–	100.0	96.2	59.3	36.8	18.0	18.8	3.8
2001–2002	–	–	100.0	94.9	58.0	36.9	17.9	19.0	5.1
2000–2001	–	–	100.0	94.6	57.5	37.1	17.3	19.8	5.4

Note: "–" means not applicable.
Source: Bureau of the Census, Geographical Mobility/Migration, Internet site http://www.census.gov/hhes/migration/data/cps/historical.html; calculations by New Strategist

Table 8.23 Geographical Mobility by Age and Type of Move, 2011–12

(total number of people aged 1 or older, and number and percent who moved between March 2011 and March 2012, by age and type of move; numbers in thousands)

	total	same house (nonmovers)	total movers	same county	different county, same state	different state total	different state same region	different state different region	movers from abroad
Total, aged 1 or older	**304,924**	**268,436**	**36,488**	**23,493**	**6,782**	**5,059**	**2,319**	**2,740**	**1,154**
Aged 1 to 4	16,207	13,117	3,090	2,086	521	400	178	222	83
Aged 5 to 9	20,416	17,532	2,884	1,993	496	332	142	190	62
Aged 10 to 14	20,605	18,221	2,384	1,612	403	308	144	164	60
Aged 15 to 17	12,977	11,666	1,311	880	225	172	90	82	34
Aged 18 to 19	8,262	7,109	1,153	744	249	117	48	69	43
Aged 20 to 24	21,878	16,491	5,387	3,486	957	732	334	398	213
Aged 25 to 29	20,893	15,756	5,137	3,204	912	795	410	385	226
Aged 30 to 34	20,326	16,663	3,663	2,341	674	522	236	286	126
Aged 35 to 39	19,140	16,606	2,534	1,657	434	377	141	236	66
Aged 40 to 44	20,787	18,770	2,017	1,237	420	270	113	157	90
Aged 45 to 49	21,583	19,807	1,776	1,139	341	249	113	136	47
Aged 50 to 54	22,372	20,746	1,626	1,004	345	249	105	144	27
Aged 55 to 59	20,470	19,275	1,195	729	276	153	87	66	38
Aged 60 to 61	7,344	6,970	374	223	84	56	23	33	10
Aged 62 to 64	10,157	9,625	532	334	102	92	37	55	3
Aged 65 to 69	13,599	13,111	488	259	146	78	35	43	6
Aged 70 to 74	9,784	9,399	385	230	92	56	34	22	6
Aged 75 to 79	7,331	7,118	213	113	48	49	24	25	4
Aged 80 to 84	5,786	5,620	166	119	17	23	10	13	7
Aged 85 or older	5,006	4,832	174	102	41	28	15	13	2

PERCENT DISTRIBUTION OF POPULATION BY MOBILITY STATUS

	total	same house (nonmovers)	total movers	same county	different county, same state	different state total	different state same region	different state different region	movers from abroad
Total, aged 1 or older	**100.0%**	**88.0%**	**12.0%**	**7.7%**	**2.2%**	**1.7%**	**0.8%**	**0.9%**	**0.4%**
Aged 1 to 4	100.0	80.9	19.1	12.9	3.2	2.5	1.1	1.4	0.5
Aged 5 to 9	100.0	85.9	14.1	9.8	2.4	1.6	0.7	0.9	0.3
Aged 10 to 14	100.0	88.4	11.6	7.8	2.0	1.5	0.7	0.8	0.3
Aged 15 to 17	100.0	89.9	10.1	6.8	1.7	1.3	0.7	0.6	0.3
Aged 18 to 19	100.0	86.0	14.0	9.0	3.0	1.4	0.6	0.8	0.5
Aged 20 to 24	100.0	75.4	24.6	15.9	4.4	3.3	1.5	1.8	1.0
Aged 25 to 29	100.0	75.4	24.6	15.3	4.4	3.8	2.0	1.8	1.1
Aged 30 to 34	100.0	82.0	18.0	11.5	3.3	2.6	1.2	1.4	0.6
Aged 35 to 39	100.0	86.8	13.2	8.7	2.3	2.0	0.7	1.2	0.3
Aged 40 to 44	100.0	90.3	9.7	6.0	2.0	1.3	0.5	0.8	0.4
Aged 45 to 49	100.0	91.8	8.2	5.3	1.6	1.2	0.5	0.6	0.2
Aged 50 to 54	100.0	92.7	7.3	4.5	1.5	1.1	0.5	0.6	0.1
Aged 55 to 59	100.0	94.2	5.8	3.6	1.3	0.7	0.4	0.3	0.2
Aged 60 to 61	100.0	94.9	5.1	3.0	1.1	0.8	0.3	0.4	0.1
Aged 62 to 64	100.0	94.8	5.2	3.3	1.0	0.9	0.4	0.5	0.0
Aged 65 to 69	100.0	96.4	3.6	1.9	1.1	0.6	0.3	0.3	0.0
Aged 70 to 74	100.0	96.1	3.9	2.4	0.9	0.6	0.3	0.2	0.1
Aged 75 to 79	100.0	97.1	2.9	1.5	0.7	0.7	0.3	0.3	0.1
Aged 80 to 84	100.0	97.1	2.9	2.1	0.3	0.4	0.2	0.2	0.1
Aged 85 or older	100.0	96.5	3.5	2.0	0.8	0.6	0.3	0.3	0.0

Source: Bureau of the Census, Geographical Mobility: 2011 to 2012, Internet site http://www.census.gov/hhes/migration/data/cps/cps2012.html; calculations by New Strategist

Table 8.24 Movers by Age and Type of Move, 2011–12

(number and percent distribution of people aged 1 or older who moved between March 2011 and March 2012, by age and type of move; numbers in thousands)

	total movers	same county	different county, same state	different state total	different state same region	different state different region	movers from abroad
Total, aged 1 or older	36,488	23,493	6,782	5,059	2,319	2,740	1,154
Aged 1 to 4	3,090	2,086	521	400	178	222	83
Aged 5 to 9	2,884	1,993	496	332	142	190	62
Aged 10 to 14	2,384	1,612	403	308	144	164	60
Aged 15 to 17	1,311	880	225	172	90	82	34
Aged 18 to 19	1,153	744	249	117	48	69	43
Aged 20 to 24	5,387	3,486	957	732	334	398	213
Aged 25 to 29	5,137	3,204	912	795	410	385	226
Aged 30 to 34	3,663	2,341	674	522	236	286	126
Aged 35 to 39	2,534	1,657	434	377	141	236	66
Aged 40 to 44	2,017	1,237	420	270	113	157	90
Aged 45 to 49	1,776	1,139	341	249	113	136	47
Aged 50 to 54	1,626	1,004	345	249	105	144	27
Aged 55 to 59	1,195	729	276	153	87	66	38
Aged 60 to 61	374	223	84	56	23	33	10
Aged 62 to 64	532	334	102	92	37	55	3
Aged 65 to 69	488	259	146	78	35	43	6
Aged 70 to 74	385	230	92	56	34	22	6
Aged 75 to 79	213	113	48	49	24	25	4
Aged 80 to 84	166	119	17	23	10	13	7
Aged 85 or older	174	102	41	28	15	13	2

PERCENT DISTRIBUTION BY TYPE OF MOVE

	total movers	same county	different county, same state	different state total	different state same region	different state different region	movers from abroad
Total, aged 1 or older	100.0%	64.4%	18.6%	13.9%	6.4%	7.5%	3.2%
Aged 1 to 4	100.0	67.5	16.9	12.9	5.8	7.2	2.7
Aged 5 to 9	100.0	69.1	17.2	11.5	4.9	6.6	2.1
Aged 10 to 14	100.0	67.6	16.9	12.9	6.0	6.9	2.5
Aged 15 to 17	100.0	67.1	17.2	13.1	6.9	6.3	2.6
Aged 18 to 19	100.0	64.5	21.6	10.1	4.2	6.0	3.7
Aged 20 to 24	100.0	64.7	17.8	13.6	6.2	7.4	4.0
Aged 25 to 29	100.0	62.4	17.8	15.5	8.0	7.5	4.4
Aged 30 to 34	100.0	63.9	18.4	14.3	6.4	7.8	3.4
Aged 35 to 39	100.0	65.4	17.1	14.9	5.6	9.3	2.6
Aged 40 to 44	100.0	61.3	20.8	13.4	5.6	7.8	4.5
Aged 45 to 49	100.0	64.1	19.2	14.0	6.4	7.7	2.6
Aged 50 to 54	100.0	61.7	21.2	15.3	6.5	8.9	1.7
Aged 55 to 59	100.0	61.0	23.1	12.8	7.3	5.5	3.2
Aged 60 to 61	100.0	59.6	22.5	15.0	6.1	8.8	2.7
Aged 62 to 64	100.0	62.8	19.2	17.3	7.0	10.3	0.6
Aged 65 to 69	100.0	53.1	29.9	16.0	7.2	8.8	1.2
Aged 70 to 74	100.0	59.7	23.9	14.5	8.8	5.7	1.6
Aged 75 to 79	100.0	53.1	22.5	23.0	11.3	11.7	1.9
Aged 80 to 84	100.0	71.7	10.2	13.9	6.0	7.8	4.2
Aged 85 or older	100.0	58.6	23.6	16.1	8.6	7.5	1.1

Source: Bureau of the Census, Geographic Mobility: 2011 to 2012, Internet site http://www.census.gov/hhes/migration/data/cps/cps2012.html; calculations by New Strategist

Legal Immigration Adds Millions to the Population

Illegal immigration adds even more, especially in California.

During the 2000–09 decade, more than 10 million immigrants were granted permanent legal residence in the United States, more than in any other decade in the nation's history. In 2010, 2011, and 2012, another 1 million legal immigrants were admitted to the United States each year. As of 2011, there were also an estimated 11.5 million undocumented immigrants living in the United States, 36 percent more than in 2000.

The impact of immigration varies dramatically by state. The 58 percent majority of legal immigrants who came to the United States in 2012 settled in just five states: California, New York, Florida, Texas, and New Jersey. California is the number-one state for immigrants, both legal and illegal. Nineteen percent of legal immigrants admitted to the United States in 2012 settled in California. Twenty-five percent of unauthorized immigrants live in California.

Mexico sends the largest number of legal immigrants to the United States, accounting for 14 percent of the total in 2012. Mexico has also sent the largest number of undocumented immigrants to the United States, accounting for 59 percent of the undocumented population in 2011.

■ Although unauthorized immigration to the United States has slowed because of the Great Recession, legal immigration remains high.

Mexico sends the largest number of legal immigrants to the United States

(share of total legal immigrants admitted to the United States accounted for by the top five countries, 2012)

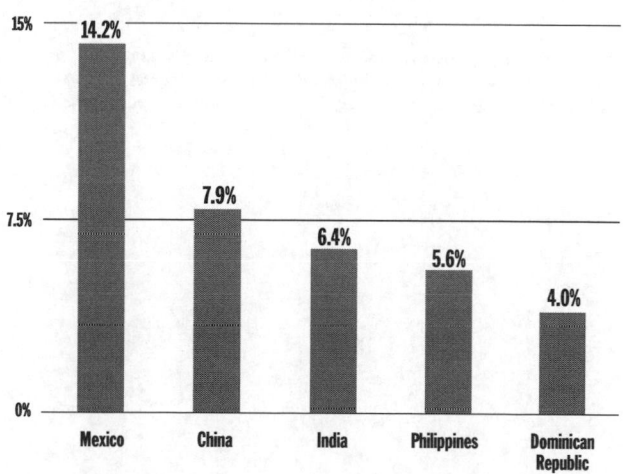

Table 8.25 Legal Immigration to the United States, 1900 to 2012

(number of legal immigrants granted permanent residence in the United States by single year, 2000 to 2012, and by decade, 1900–09 to 2000–09)

SINGLE YEAR

2012	1,031,631
2011	1,062,040
2010	1,042,625
2009	1,130,818
2008	1,107,126
2007	1,052,415
2006	1,266,129
2005	1,122,257
2004	957,883
2003	703,542
2002	1,059,356
2001	1,058,902
2000	841,002

DECADE

2000–09	10,299,430
1990–99	9,775,398
1980–89	6,244,379
1970–79	4,248,203
1960–69	3,213,749
1950–59	2,499,268
1940–49	856,608
1930–39	699,375
1920–29	4,295,510
1910–19	6,347,380
1900–09	8,202,388

Note: Immigrants are those granted legal permanent residence in the United States. They either arrive in the United States with immigrant visas issued abroad or adjust their status in the United States from temporary to permanent residence.
Source: Department of Homeland Security, 2012 Yearbook of Immigration Statistics, Internet site http://www.dhs.gov/yearbook-immigration-statistics

Table 8.26 Legal Immigrants by Country of Birth and State of Residence, 2012

(number and percent distribution of legal immigrants admitted to the United States from the 10 leading countries of birth and percent distribution by state of residence, 2012; for the five states receiving the largest total number of legal immigrants in 2012)

	total	total in top five states	California	New York	Florida	Texas	New Jersey
Total legal immigrants	**1,031,631**	**595,521**	**196,622**	**149,505**	**103,047**	**95,557**	**50,790**
Total from top 10 countries	**519,236**	**334,116**	**126,580**	**64,576**	**59,732**	**57,331**	**25,897**
Mexico	146,406	93,695	49,595	1,910	3,505	37,852	833
China, People's Republic	81,784	54,504	22,424	24,956	1,755	3,203	2,166
India	66,434	33,976	13,951	4,621	1,937	5,844	7,623
Philippines	57,327	33,184	22,484	3,231	2,372	2,778	2,319
Dominican Republic	41,566	29,492	171	19,920	3,067	220	6,114
Cuba	32,820	28,953	350	396	26,422	1,043	742
Vietnam	28,304	15,630	9,714	528	1,278	3,691	419
Haiti	22,818	17,899	107	4,038	11,860	107	1,787
Colombia	20,931	15,000	1,163	3,069	7,160	1,380	2,228
South Korea	20,846	11,783	6,621	1,907	376	1,213	1,666

PERCENT DISTRIBUTION BY STATE OF RESIDENCE

	total	total in top five states	California	New York	Florida	Texas	New Jersey
Total legal immigrants	**100.0%**	**57.7%**	**19.1%**	**14.5%**	**10.0%**	**9.3%**	**4.9%**
Total from top 10 countries	**100.0**	**64.3**	**24.4**	**12.4**	**11.5**	**11.0**	**5.0**
Mexico	100.0	64.0	33.9	1.3	2.4	25.9	0.6
China, People's Republic	100.0	66.6	27.4	30.5	2.1	3.9	2.6
India	100.0	51.1	21.0	7.0	2.9	8.8	11.5
Philippines	100.0	57.9	39.2	5.6	4.1	4.8	4.0
Dominican Republic	100.0	71.0	0.4	47.9	7.4	0.5	14.7
Cuba	100.0	88.2	1.1	1.2	80.5	3.2	2.3
Vietnam	100.0	55.2	34.3	1.9	4.5	13.0	1.5
Haiti	100.0	78.4	0.5	17.7	52.0	0.5	7.8
Colombia	100.0	71.7	5.6	14.7	34.2	6.6	10.6
South Korea	100.0	56.5	31.8	9.1	1.8	5.8	8.0

PERCENT DISTRIBUTION BY COUNTRY OF BIRTH

	total	total in top five states	California	New York	Florida	Texas	New Jersey
Total legal immigrants	**100.0**	**100.0**	**100.0**	**100.0**	**100.0**	**100.0**	**100.0**
Total from top 10 countries	**50.3**	**56.1**	**64.4**	**43.2**	**58.0**	**60.0**	**51.0**
Mexico	14.2	15.7	25.2	1.3	3.4	39.6	1.6
China, People's Republic	7.9	9.2	11.4	16.7	1.7	3.4	4.3
India	6.4	5.7	7.1	3.1	1.9	6.1	15.0
Philippines	5.6	5.6	11.4	2.2	2.3	2.9	4.6
Dominican Republic	4.0	5.0	0.1	13.3	3.0	0.2	12.0
Cuba	3.2	4.9	0.2	0.3	25.6	1.1	1.5
Vietnam	2.7	2.6	4.9	0.4	1.2	3.9	0.8
Haiti	2.2	3.0	0.1	2.7	11.5	0.1	3.5
Colombia	2.0	2.5	0.6	2.1	6.9	1.4	4.4
South Korea	2.0	2.0	3.4	1.3	0.4	1.3	3.3

Note: Total includes immigrants from other countries not shown separately. Immigrants are people granted legal permanent residence in the United States. They either arrive in the United States with immigrant visas issued abroad or adjust their status in the United States from temporary to permanent residence.
Source: Department of Homeland Security, 2012 Yearbook of Immigration Statistics, Internet site http://www.dhs.gov/yearbook-immigration-statistics; calculations by New Strategist

Table 8.27 Unauthorized Immigrant Population, 2000 and 2011

(number and percent distribution of unauthorized immigrants residing in the United States by country of birth and state of residence, 2000 and 2011; numerical and percent change, 2000–11; numbers in thousands)

	2011 number	2011 percent distribution	2000 number	2000 percent distribution	change, 2000–2011 numerical	change, 2000–2011 percent
COUNTRY OF BIRTH						
Total unauthorized immigrants	**11,510**	**100.0%**	**8,460**	**100.0%**	**3,050**	**36.1%**
Mexico	6,800	59.1	4,680	55.3	2,120	45.3
El Salvador	660	5.7	430	5.1	230	53.5
Guatemala	520	4.5	290	3.4	230	79.3
Honduras	380	3.3	160	1.9	220	137.5
China	280	2.4	190	2.2	90	47.4
Philippines	270	2.3	200	2.4	70	35.0
India	240	2.1	120	1.4	120	100.0
Korea	230	2.0	180	2.1	50	27.8
Ecuador	210	1.8	110	1.3	100	90.9
Vietnam	170	1.5	160	1.9	10	6.3
Other countries	1,750	15.2	1,940	22.9	–190	–9.8
STATE OF RESIDENCE						
Total unauthorized immigrants	**11,510**	**100.0%**	**8,460**	**100.0%**	**3,050**	**36.1%**
California	2,830	24.6	2,510	29.7	320	12.7
Texas	1,790	15.6	1,090	12.9	700	64.2
Florida	740	6.4	800	9.5	–60	–7.5
New York	630	5.5	540	6.4	90	16.7
Illinois	550	4.8	440	5.2	110	25.0
Georgia	440	3.8	220	2.6	220	100.0
New Jersey	420	3.6	350	4.1	70	20.0
North Carolina	400	3.5	260	3.1	140	53.8
Arizona	360	3.1	330	3.9	30	9.1
Washington	260	2.3	170	2.0	90	52.9
Other states	3,100	26.9	1,750	20.7	1,350	77.1

Note: Percent change calculations are based on unrounded figures.
Source: Department of Homeland Security, Estimates of the Unauthorized Immigrant Population Residing in the United States: January 2011, Internet site http://www.dhs.gov/estimates-unauthorized-immigrant-population-residing-united-states-january-2011

Many U.S. Residents Are Foreign-Born

One in eight was born in another country.

Americans are known for their mobility, but most of us live in our state of birth. In 2012, well more than half (59 percent) of U.S. residents lived in their state of birth, 27 percent lived in another state, and 13 percent were born outside the United States.

More than 40 million U.S. residents were born in a foreign country, according to the Census Bureau's 2012 American Community Survey. Among the foreign-born, a substantial 46 percent are naturalized citizens. The 52 percent majority of the foreign-born are from Mexico or Latin America. Twenty-nine percent are from Asia, and only 12 percent are from Europe.

Thanks to immigration, the population of the United States is a diverse mixture of ancestries. German is the most common ancestry, reported by 15 percent of Americans, or 47 million people. The second most common ancestry is Irish, specified by 11 percent. Twenty-four million people say their ancestry is "American."

■ The number of foreign-born in the United States will continue to expand as long as immigration remains high, creating a dynamic multicultural market.

More than 45 percent of the foreign-born are naturalized citizens

(percent distribution of foreign-born by citizenship status, 2012)

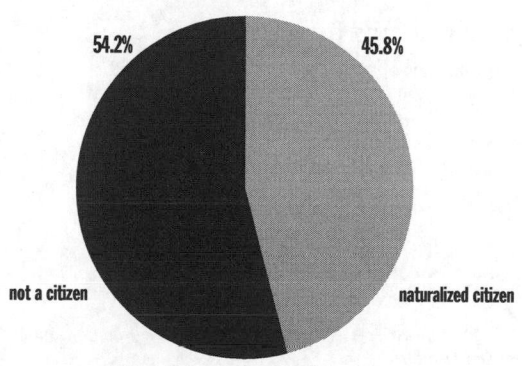

Table 8.28 Place of Birth, 2012

(number and percent distribution of U.S. residents by place of birth, 2012)

	number	percent
Total population	**313,914,040**	**100.0%**
Native-born	273,089,382	87.0
Born in state of residence	184,556,088	58.8
Born in other state in United States	84,147,291	26.8
Born outside United States	4,386,003	1.4
Foreign-born	40,824,658	13.0
Naturalized U.S. citizen	18,686,237	6.0
Not a U.S. citizen	22,138,421	7.1

Note: The native-born born outside the United States were born in Puerto Rico, U.S. Island areas, or abroad to American parents.
Source: Bureau of the Census, 2012 American Community Survey, Internet site http://factfinder2.census.gov/faces/nav/jsf/pages/index.xhtml; calculations by New Strategist

Table 8.29 Foreign-Born by World Region of Birth, 2012

(number and percent distribution of the foreign-born population by naturalization status and world region of birth, 2012)

	number	percent distribution
Total foreign-born	**40,824,658**	**100.0%**
Naturalized citizen	18,686,237	45.8
Not a U.S. citizen	22,138,421	54.2
WORLD REGION OF BIRTH		
Total foreign-born	**40,824,658**	**100.0**
Europe	4,809,392	11.8
Asia	11,931,658	29.2
Africa	1,723,895	4.2
Oceania	239,861	0.6
Latin America	21,311,457	52.2
Northern America	808,290	2.0

Source: Bureau of the Census, 2012 American Community Survey, Internet site http://factfinder2.census.gov/faces/nav/jsf/pages/index.xhtml; calculations by New Strategist

Table 8.30 Ancestry of the U.S. Population, 2012

(number and percent distribution of U.S. residents by selected ancestry group, 2012)

	number	percent
Total population	**313,914,040**	**100.0%**
German	46,875,013	14.9
Irish	34,148,645	10.9
English	25,261,814	8.0
American	23,567,147	7.5
Italian	17,343,394	5.5
Polish	9,500,696	3.0
French (except Basque)	8,475,331	2.7
Scottish	5,379,735	1.7
Norwegian	4,398,608	1.4
Dutch	4,350,633	1.4
Swedish	3,980,614	1.3
Scotch-Irish	3,117,627	1.0
Subsaharan African	3,008,961	1.0
Russian	2,895,912	0.9
West Indian	2,758,050	0.9
French Canadian	1,992,174	0.6
Arab	1,798,991	0.6
Welsh	1,780,002	0.6
Czech	1,507,815	0.5
Hungarian	1,427,110	0.5
Portuguese	1,380,877	0.4
Danish	1,296,751	0.4
Greek	1,296,119	0.4
Ukrainian	968,769	0.3
Swiss	941,692	0.3
Slovak	742,738	0.2
Lithuanian	680,912	0.2

Note: Ancestry is self-reported and excludes Hispanic origin (such as Spanish), which is considered an ethnic group.
Source: Bureau of the Census, 2012 American Community Survey, Internet site http://factfinder2.census.gov/faces/nav/jsf/pages/index.xhtml; calculations by New Strategist

Millions of U.S. Residents Speak Spanish at Home

Most Spanish speakers also speak English very well.

Nearly 62 million U.S. residents speak a language other than English at home—21 percent of the population aged 5 or older, according to the Census Bureau's 2012 American Community Survey. Spanish is by far the most common non-English language spoken at home, with 38 million speaking Spanish. Spanish speakers account for 62 percent of all those who speak a language other than English at home.

Among people who speak Spanish at home, 42 percent say they do not speak English very well. Among people who speak a Chinese language at home, a larger 56 percent say they do not speak English very well.

■ The number of Spanish speakers in the United States will continue to grow rapidly because of immigration from Mexico and Latin America.

Spanish is much more likely to be spoken than other non-English languages

(number of people aged 5 or older who speak a language other than English at home, 2012; in millions)

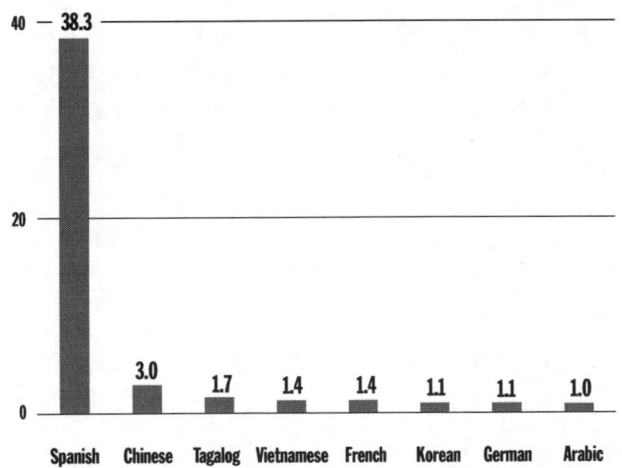

Table 8.31 Language Spoken at Home, 2012

(number and percent distribution of people aged 5 or older by language spoken at home and ability to speak English, 2012; languages shown are those with at least 1 million home speakers)

	number	percent distribution
Total population aged 5 or older	**294,003,714**	**100.0%**
Speak only English at home	232,126,499	79.0
Speak a language other than English at home	61,877,215	21.0
Total who speak a language other than English at home	**61,877,215**	**100.0**
Speak Spanish	38,325,155	61.9
Speak Chinese	2,964,393	4.8
Speak Tagalog	1,672,406	2.7
Speak Vietnamese	1,425,803	2.3
Speak French (including Patois, Cajun)	1,350,201	2.2
Speak Korean	1,131,096	1.8
Speak German	1,063,188	1.7
Speak Arabic	1,010,748	1.6
Total who speak Spanish at home	**38,325,155**	**100.0**
Speak English less than very well	16,149,456	42.1
Total who speak Chinese at home	**2,964,393**	**100.0**
Speak English less than very well	1,645,458	55.5
Total who speak Tagalog at home	**1,672,406**	**100.0**
Speak English less than very well	528,159	31.6
Total who speak Vietnamese at home	**1,425,803**	**100.0**
Speak English less than very well	834,656	58.5
Total who speak French (including Patois, Cajun) at home	**1,350,201**	**100.0**
Speak English less than very well	279,266	20.7
Total who speak Korean at home	**1,131,096**	**100.0**
Speak English less than very well	619,814	54.8
Total who speak German at home	**1,063,188**	**100.0**
Speak English less than very well	173,607	16.3
Total who speak Arabic at home	**1,010,748**	**100.0**
Speak English less than very well	375,021	37.1

Source: Bureau of the Census, 2012 American Community Survey, Internet site http://factfinder2.census.gov/faces/nav/jsf/pages/ index.xhtml; calculations by New Strategist

Non-Hispanic Whites Are a Shrinking Share of Voters

Voter participation is highest among blacks.

In the 2012 presidential election, blacks were more likely to vote than non-Hispanic whites. Among black citizens aged 18 or older, 65.9 percent reported voting. Among non-Hispanic whites, the figure was a smaller 64.1 percent. This marks the first time that black voter participation has exceeded that of non-Hispanic whites. Voter participation among Hispanics and Asians is low, with fewer than half of citizens going to the polls.

Non-Hispanic white voters greatly outnumbered minority voters in the 2012 presidential election—98 million to 35 million. But older non-Hispanic white voters were a 48 percent minority of all those who went to the polls, possibly explaining the ease with which the first black president was reelected. Among the 133 million voters in 2012, only 64 million were non-Hispanic whites aged 45 or older. A larger 70 million were minorities or non-Hispanic whites under age 45.

■ The political power of Hispanics would be much greater if their voter participation rate were higher.

The political power of older whites is declining

(percent distribution of voters by age, race, and Hispanic origin, 2012 presidential election)

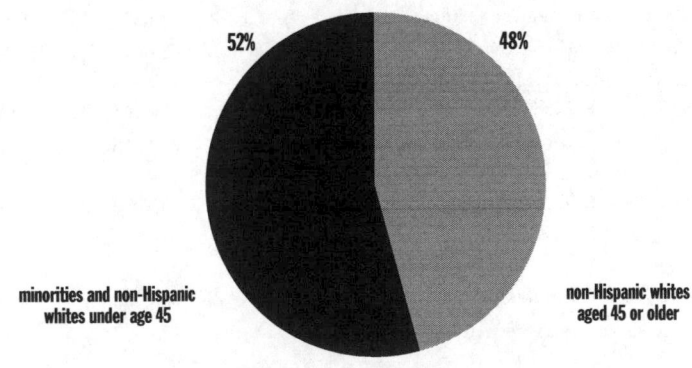

52%

48%

minorities and non-Hispanic
whites under age 45

non-Hispanic whites
aged 45 or older

Table 8.32 Voting Rate in Presidential Elections by Race and Hispanic Origin, 1992 to 2012

(percent of citizens aged 18 or older who reported voting in presidential elections by race and Hispanic origin, 1992 to 2012)

	total	Asian	black	Hispanic	non-Hispanic white
2012	61.8%	47.9%	65.9%	48.0%	64.1%
2008	63.6	47.6	64.7	49.9	66.1
2004	63.8	44.6	59.9	47.2	67.1
2000	59.5	43.4	56.8	45.1	61.8
1996	58.4	45.0	53.0	44.0	60.7
1992	67.7	53.9	59.2	51.6	70.2

Note: Asians and blacks are those who identify themselves as being of the race alone and those who identify themselves as being of the race in combination with other races. Non-Hispanic whites are those who identify themselves as being white alone and not Hispanic.
Source: Bureau of the Census, Voting and Registration, Internet site http://www.census.gov/hhes/www/socdemo/voting/index .html; calculations by New Strategist

Table 8.33 Voters by Age, Race, and Hispanic Origin, 2012

(number and percent distribution of people who reported voting in the presidential election by age, race, and Hispanic origin, 2012; numbers in thousands)

	total	Asian	black	Hispanic	non-Hispanic white
Total voters	**132,948**	**4,331**	**18,558**	**11,188**	**98,041**
Aged 18 to 24	11,353	408	2,306	1,677	6,933
Aged 25 to 44	39,942	1,652	6,595	4,365	27,216
Aged 45 to 64	52,013	1,522	6,890	3,609	39,507
Aged 65 or older	29,641	748	2,767	1,537	24,385
Total voters	**100.0%**	**3.3%**	**14.0%**	**8.4%**	**73.7%**
Aged 18 to 24	100.0	3.6	20.3	14.8	61.1
Aged 25 to 44	100.0	4.1	16.5	10.9	68.1
Aged 45 to 64	100.0	2.9	13.2	6.9	76.0
Aged 65 or older	100.0	2.5	9.3	5.2	82.3

Note: Asians and blacks are those who identify themselves as being of the race alone and those who identify themselves as being of the race in combination with other races. Non-Hispanic whites are those who identify themselves as being white alone and not Hispanic.
Source: Bureau of the Census, Voting and Registration, Internet site http://www.census.gov/hhes/www/socdemo/voting/index .html; calculations by New Strategist

9

Spending

Trends

Average household spending grew 1.6 percent between 2010 and 2012, to $51,442 after adjusting for inflation.

Spending in 2012 was still 6.7 percent below the $55,119 of 2006, which was the peak spending year.

Households headed by people aged 45 to 54 spend the most—$62,103 in 2012.

The youngest householders, under age 25, spend the least—only $31,411.

Households with incomes of $100,000 or more spend twice as much as the average household.

While the affluent represent only 19 percent of households, they control 37 percent of spending.

Married couples with children spend much more than average.

In 2012, couples with kids spent $72,814 versus the $51,442 spent by the average household.

Asians spend the most, substantially more than non-Hispanic whites.

Hispanics and blacks spend more than average on children's clothes and rent.

Spending is highest in the West.

Households in the West spent $56,782 in 2012, or 10 percent more than average.

Households with college graduates spend much more than average.

In 2012, households with members who had a bachelor's degree spent $71,151—38 percent more than average.

Average Household Spending Is Growing Again

Household spending declined during the Great Recession and its aftermath, bottoming out in 2010. Then things began to get better. Between 2010 and 2012, average annual household spending climbed 1.6 percent to $51,442, after adjusting for inflation. The 2012 figure was still 6.7 percent below the 2006 peak, however, when the average household spent $55,119.

Although household spending is growing again, the average household is spending less than it did in 2006 on most items. Spending on alcoholic beverages is an example. Although the average household spent 4 percent more on beer, wine, and other alcoholic beverages in 2012 ($451) than in 2010 ($434), the 2012 figure is 20 percent below the 2006 figure ($566). Many categories show a similar pattern. The average household spent 5 percent more on furniture in 2012 ($391) than in 2010 ($374), but the amount the average household spends on furniture in 2012 was 26 percent below the spending of 2006 ($527). Spending on new cars and trucks increased by a substantial 28 percent between 2010 and 2012, but the 2012 figure was still 20 percent below the level of 2006.

Households are spending more, but still less than they once did

(percent change in spending by the average household on selected products and services, 2006, 2010, and 2012; in 2012 dollars)

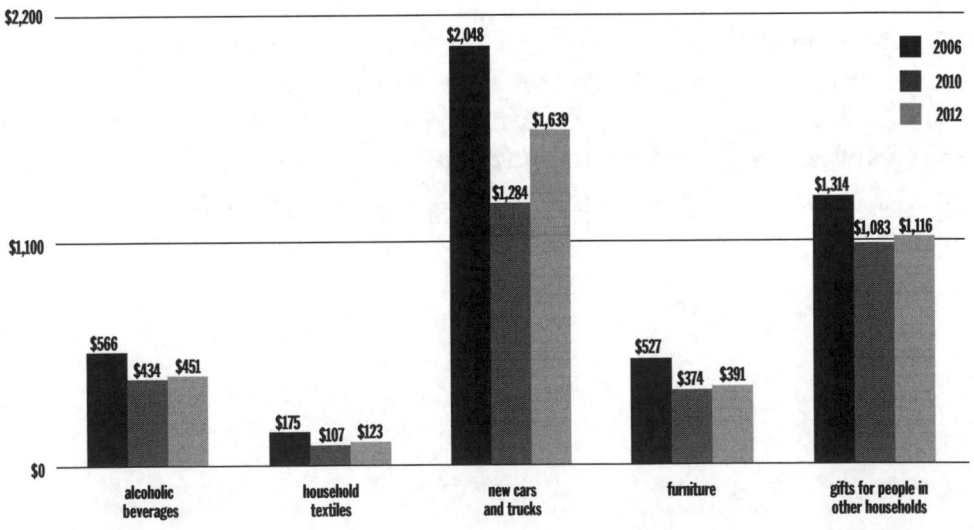

Other categories continued their decline in the 2010-to-2012 time period, despite the overall spending recovery. Average household spending on mortgage interest fell 13 percent between 2010 and 2012, after adjusting for inflation, as more Americans chose to rent rather than buy a home. Spending on apparel continued its long-term decline. Conversely, a handful of spending categories have grown steadily despite the Great Recession, including health insurance, medical services, education, and the category "pets, toys, and playground equipment" (which is dominated by pet spending).

Although household spending is beginning to recover from the Great Recession, the recovery is slow and spending on many categories continues to decline. But those who have been eagerly awaiting good economic news should take heart at the spending boost for items such as new cars and trucks, household textiles, reading material, footwear, personal care products and services, cash contributions, and gifts for people in other households. Americans may be starting to open their wallets, at least a bit.

Table 9.1 Household Spending Trends, 2000 to 2012

(average annual spending of total consumer units [CU], 2000, 2006, 2010, and 2012; percent change for selected years; in 2012 dollars)

	2012	2010	2006	2000	2010–12	2006–12	2000–06	2000–12
Number of consumer units (in 000s)	124,416	121,107	118,843	109,367	2.7%	4.7%	8.7%	13.8%
Average annual spending of CU	$51,442	$50,655	$55,119	$50,725	1.6	–6.7	8.7	1.4
FOOD	6,599	6,453	6,960	6,877	2.3	–5.2	1.2	–4.0
Food at home	3,921	3,816	3,892	4,028	2.8	0.8	–3.4	–2.7
Cereals and bakery products	538	529	508	604	1.8	5.9	–15.9	–10.9
Cereals and cereal products	182	174	163	208	4.8	11.8	–21.7	–12.5
Bakery products	356	355	346	396	0.3	2.8	–12.6	–10.1
Meats, poultry, fish, and eggs	852	825	908	1,060	3.2	–6.1	–14.4	–19.6
Beef	226	228	269	317	–1.1	–15.9	–15.3	–28.8
Pork	166	157	179	223	5.8	–7.2	–19.7	–25.4
Other meats	122	123	120	135	–1.0	2.0	–11.2	–9.4
Poultry	159	145	161	193	9.4	–1.0	–16.9	–17.8
Fish and seafood	126	123	139	147	2.3	–9.3	–5.3	–14.1
Eggs	53	48	42	45	9.4	25.8	–7.0	16.9
Dairy products	419	400	419	433	4.7	0.0	–3.3	–3.3
Fresh milk and cream	152	148	159	175	2.4	–4.7	–8.7	–13.0
Other dairy products	267	253	260	257	5.7	2.8	0.9	3.8
Fruits and vegetables	731	715	674	695	2.2	8.4	–2.9	5.2
Fresh fruits	261	244	222	217	6.8	17.5	2.2	20.1
Fresh vegetables	226	221	220	212	2.2	2.8	3.7	6.6
Processed fruits	114	119	124	153	–4.2	–8.2	–19.0	–25.6
Processed vegetables	130	131	108	112	–0.4	20.2	–3.4	16.1
Other food at home	1,380	1,346	1,380	1,236	2.6	0.0	11.7	11.7
Sugar and other sweets	147	139	142	156	5.8	3.3	–8.7	–5.8
Fats and oils	114	108	98	111	5.1	16.4	–11.5	3.0
Miscellaneous foods	699	702	714	583	–0.5	–2.1	22.6	20.0
Nonalcoholic beverages	370	351	378	333	5.5	–2.1	13.4	11.0
Food prepared by consumer unit on trips	50	45	49	53	10.4	2.1	–8.2	–6.2
Food away from home	2,678	2,638	3,068	2,849	1.5	–12.7	7.7	–6.0
ALCOHOLIC BEVERAGES	451	434	566	496	4.0	–20.3	14.1	–9.1
HOUSING	16,887	17,433	18,639	16,425	–3.1	–9.4	13.5	2.8
Shelter	9,891	10,331	11,016	9,485	–4.3	–10.2	16.1	4.3
Owned dwellings	6,056	6,609	7,421	6,136	–8.4	–18.4	20.9	–1.3
Mortgage interest and charges	3,067	3,528	4,274	3,519	–13.1	–28.2	21.5	–12.8
Property taxes	1,836	1,910	1,878	1,519	–3.9	–2.2	23.7	20.9
Maintenance, repair, insurance, other expenses	1,153	1,171	1,270	1,100	–1.5	–9.2	15.4	4.8
Rented dwellings	3,186	3,053	2,950	2,712	4.3	8.0	8.8	17.5
Other lodging	649	669	646	637	–2.9	0.5	1.3	1.8
Utilities, fuels, and public services	3,648	3,854	3,869	3,319	–5.3	–5.7	16.6	9.9
Natural gas	359	463	580	409	–22.5	–38.1	41.6	–12.3
Electricity	1,388	1,488	1,442	1,215	–6.7	–3.7	18.7	14.3
Fuel oil and other fuels	137	147	157	129	–7.1	–12.8	21.5	5.9
Telephone services	1,239	1,240	1,238	1,169	–0.1	0.1	5.9	6.0
Water and other public services	525	515	452	395	2.0	16.1	14.6	33.0

	2012	2010	2006	2000	2010–12	2006–12	2000–06	2000–12
Household services	$1,159	$1,060	$1,080	$912	9.3%	7.3%	18.4%	27.1%
Personal services	368	358	448	435	2.8	–17.8	3.0	–15.3
Other household services	791	702	632	477	12.6	25.1	32.4	65.7
Housekeeping supplies	**610**	**644**	**729**	**643**	**–5.3**	**–16.3**	**13.4**	**–5.1**
Laundry and cleaning supplies	155	158	172	175	–1.9	–9.9	–1.5	–11.3
Other household products	319	346	376	301	–7.9	–15.1	24.7	5.9
Postage and stationery	136	139	181	168	–2.1	–24.9	7.8	–19.0
Household furnishings and equipment	**1,580**	**1,545**	**1,945**	**2,065**	**2.3**	**–18.8**	**–5.8**	**–23.5**
Household textiles	123	107	175	141	14.5	–29.9	24.1	–13.0
Furniture	391	374	527	521	4.6	–25.8	1.1	–25.0
Floor coverings	16	38	55	59	–57.8	–70.7	–6.8	–72.7
Major appliances	197	220	274	252	–10.5	–28.2	8.9	–21.8
Small appliances and miscellaneous housewares	98	113	124	116	–13.0	–21.1	7.0	–15.5
Miscellaneous household equipment	754	692	789	975	9.0	–4.5	–19.0	–22.6
APPAREL AND RELATED SERVICES	**1,736**	**1,790**	**2,134**	**2,475**	**–3.0**	**–18.7**	**–13.8**	**–29.8**
Men and boys	**408**	**402**	**506**	**587**	**1.4**	**–19.3**	**–13.8**	**–30.5**
Men, aged 16 or older	320	320	402	459	0.0	–20.4	–12.3	–30.2
Boys, aged 2 to 15	88	82	104	128	7.1	–15.1	–19.0	–31.2
Women and girls	**688**	**698**	**855**	**967**	**–1.4**	**–19.6**	**–11.5**	**–28.8**
Women, aged 16 or older	573	592	716	809	–3.2	–20.0	–11.5	–29.2
Girls, aged 2 to 15	116	106	139	157	9.1	–16.5	–11.7	–26.3
Children under age 2	**63**	**96**	**109**	**109**	**–34.2**	**–42.4**	**0.0**	**–42.4**
Footwear	**347**	**319**	**346**	**457**	**8.8**	**0.2**	**–24.3**	**–24.1**
Other apparel products and services	**230**	**275**	**319**	**355**	**–16.3**	**–27.9**	**–10.1**	**–35.1**
TRANSPORTATION	**8,998**	**8,083**	**9,690**	**9,889**	**11.3**	**–7.1**	**–2.0**	**–9.0**
Vehicle purchases	**3,210**	**2,725**	**3,896**	**4,557**	**17.8**	**–17.6**	**–14.5**	**–29.6**
Cars and trucks, new	1,639	1,284	2,048	2,140	27.7	–20.0	–4.3	–23.4
Cars and trucks, used	1,516	1,388	1,786	2,360	9.2	–15.1	–24.3	–35.8
Gasoline and motor oil	**2,756**	**2,245**	**2,536**	**1,721**	**22.8**	**8.7**	**47.3**	**60.1**
Other vehicle expenses	**2,490**	**2,594**	**2,682**	**3,041**	**–4.0**	**–7.2**	**–11.8**	**–18.1**
Vehicle finance charges	223	256	339	437	–12.8	–34.3	–22.4	–49.0
Maintenance and repairs	814	829	784	832	–1.8	3.9	–5.8	–2.2
Vehicle insurance	1,018	1,063	1,009	1,037	–4.3	0.9	–2.7	–1.9
Vehicle rentals, leases, licenses, other charges	434	445	549	735	–2.6	–20.9	–25.3	–40.9
Public transportation	**542**	**519**	**575**	**569**	**4.4**	**–5.8**	**1.0**	**–4.8**
HEALTH CARE	**3,556**	**3,324**	**3,150**	**2,755**	**7.0**	**12.9**	**14.4**	**29.1**
Health insurance	2,061	1,928	1,668	1,311	6.9	23.5	27.3	57.3
Medical services	839	760	763	757	10.4	10.0	0.8	10.8
Drugs	515	511	585	555	0.8	–12.0	5.5	–7.1
Medical supplies	142	125	133	132	13.3	6.6	0.9	7.6
ENTERTAINMENT	**2,605**	**2,637**	**2,706**	**2,484**	**–1.2**	**–3.7**	**8.9**	**4.9**
Fees and admissions	614	612	690	687	0.4	–11.0	0.5	–10.6
Audio and visual equipment and services	979	1,004	1,032	829	–2.5	–5.1	24.4	18.1
Pets, toys, and playground equipment	648	638	469	445	1.6	38.1	5.4	45.5
Other entertainment products and services	363	383	514	524	–5.3	–29.3	–2.0	–30.7
PERSONAL CARE PRODUCTS AND SERVICES	**628**	**613**	**666**	**752**	**2.5**	**–5.7**	**–11.4**	**–16.5**
READING	**109**	**105**	**133**	**195**	**3.5**	**–18.2**	**–31.5**	**–44.0**
EDUCATION	**1,207**	**1,131**	**1,011**	**843**	**6.7**	**19.3**	**20.0**	**43.2**
TOBACCO PRODUCTS AND SMOKING SUPPLIES	**332**	**381**	**372**	**425**	**–12.9**	**–10.9**	**–12.4**	**–21.9**

	2012	2010	2006	2000	2010–12	2006–12	2000–06	2000–12
MISCELLANEOUS	$829	$894	$963	$1,035	–7.3%	–14.0%	–6.9%	–19.9%
CASH CONTRIBUTIONS	1,913	1,719	2,129	1,589	11.3	–10.1	33.9	20.4
PERSONAL INSURANCE AND PENSIONS	5,591	5,657	6,002	4,487	–1.2	–6.8	33.8	24.6
Life and other personal insurance	353	335	367	532	5.4	–3.7	–31.1	–33.6
Pensions and Social Security*	5,238	5,321	5,635	–	–1.6	–7.0	–	–
PERSONAL TAXES	2,226	1,863	2,770	4,156	19.5	–19.6	–33.4	–46.4
Federal income taxes	1,568	1,196	1,949	3,212	31.1	–19.5	–39.3	–51.2
State and local income taxes	526	508	591	749	3.6	–11.0	–21.1	–29.8
Other taxes	132	159	230	195	–17.0	–42.6	18.2	–32.2
GIFTS FOR PEOPLE IN OTHER HOUSEHOLDS	1,116	1,083	1,314	1,444	3.0	–15.1	–9.0	–22.7

*Recent spending on pensions and Social Security is not comparable with 2000 because of changes in methodology.
Note: Spending by category does not add to total spending because gift spending is also included in the preceding product and service categories and personal taxes are not included in the total. "–" means data are not comparable.
Source: Bureau of Labor Statistics, 2000, 2006, 2010, and 2012 Consumer Expenditure Surveys, Internet site http://www.bls.gov/cex/; calculations by New Strategist

Householders Aged 45 to 54 Spend the Most

The youngest householders spend the least.

Households headed by people aged 45 to 54 spent an average of $62,103 in 2012—21 percent more than the average household. In second place are householders aged 35 to 44, who spent an average of $58,069. Not far behind are householders aged 55 to 64, who spent an average of $55,636. Middle-aged households spend more than younger or older households because they are in their peak earning years and have higher incomes.

Households headed by people under age 25 spend less than any other age group, an average of just $31,411 in 2012. This figure is slightly below the average spending of householders aged 75 or older, which stood at $33,530 in 2012.

The Indexed Spending table shows spending by age of householder in comparison to what the average household spends. An index of 100 means households in the age group spend an average amount on the item. An index above 100 means households in the age group spend more than average on the item, while an index below 100 reveals below-average spending.

Spending peaks in middle age

(average annual spending of consumer units by age of consumer unit reference person, 2012)

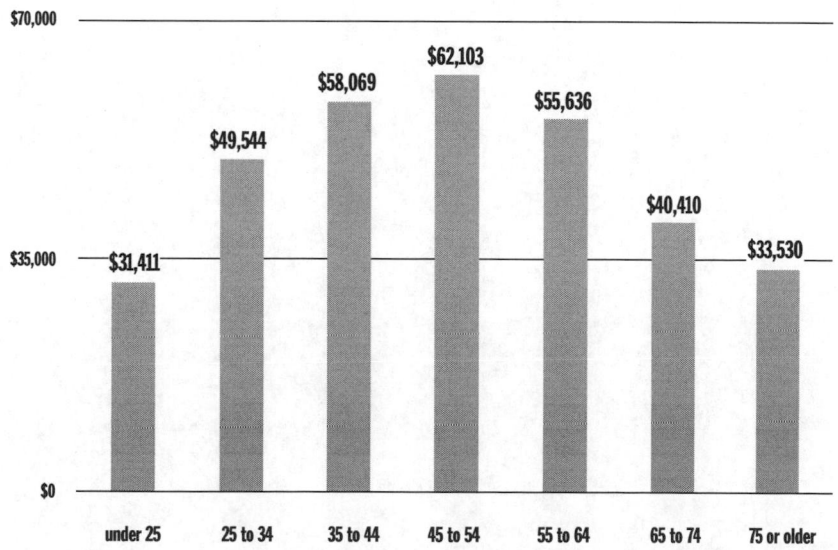

A look at Table 9.3 shows that spending is below average on most items for households headed by the youngest and the oldest householders—those under age 25 and those aged 75 or older. Spending is much closer to the average on most items for households headed by 25-to-34-year-olds and 65-to-74-year-olds. Spending is above average in most categories for householders spanning the ages from 35 to 64. There are some exceptions, however. Householders under age 25 spend 80 percent more than average on rent (with an index of 180). They spend 78 percent more than average on baby clothes and 56 percent more than average on education because many are in college. The oldest householders spend 25 percent more than the average household on reading material, 39 percent more on cash contributions, and 51 percent more on drugs.

The Market Share table shows how much of total spending by category is accounted for by each age group. Householders aged 45 to 54 account for the largest share of spending—24 percent of aggregate household expenditures in 2012. Interestingly, for the first time in 2012, the market share of spending controlled by householders aged 55 to 64 surpassed the share controlled by householders aged 35 to 44. Demographics are behind this trend. Boomers have filled the older age group, and many have postponed retirement and are spending more. Nevertheless, the 35-to-44 age group accounts for a larger share of spending than the older age group on many items such as children's clothes, mortgage interest, fees and admissions to entertainment events, and food away from home.

■ The share of spending controlled by householders aged 65 to 74 will grow as boomers fill the age group.

Table 9.2 Average Spending by Age of Householder, 2012

(average annual spending of consumer units [CU] by product and service category and age of consumer unit reference person, 2012)

	total consumer units	under 25	25 to 34	35 to 44	45 to 54	55 to 64	aged 65 or older total	65 to 74	75 or older
Number of consumer units (in 000s)	124,416	8,159	20,112	21,598	24,624	22,770	27,154	14,993	12,161
Average number of persons per CU	2.5	2.0	2.8	3.4	2.7	2.1	1.7	1.8	1.5
Average annual spending	$51,442	$31,411	$49,544	$58,069	$62,103	$55,636	$40,410	$45,968	$33,530
FOOD	6,599	4,412	6,513	7,701	7,917	6,800	5,059	5,793	4,141
Food at home	3,921	2,529	3,680	4,490	4,707	4,012	3,273	3,719	2,716
Cereals and bakery products	538	355	512	632	633	527	459	490	421
Cereals and cereal products	182	143	187	223	228	159	134	143	122
Bakery products	356	211	325	409	405	369	326	347	299
Meats, poultry, fish, and eggs	852	573	755	999	1,047	887	686	804	539
Beef	226	160	192	264	288	241	174	202	137
Pork	166	110	145	198	195	175	138	167	103
Other meats	122	77	111	148	144	121	105	122	84
Poultry	159	114	163	180	207	159	109	123	92
Fish and seafood	126	73	93	150	154	138	112	137	81
Eggs	53	39	50	60	60	53	47	52	41
Dairy products	419	251	394	497	498	433	342	385	289
Fresh milk and cream	152	100	150	190	182	142	119	126	111
Other dairy products	267	152	244	307	316	291	223	259	178
Fruits and vegetables	731	456	683	808	872	733	659	723	580
Fresh fruits	261	162	237	297	308	258	242	260	219
Fresh vegetables	226	128	208	243	269	234	210	242	169
Processed fruits	114	77	112	124	135	111	101	100	103
Processed vegetables	130	89	126	144	159	130	107	121	88
Other food at home	1,380	894	1,335	1,555	1,657	1,432	1,127	1,318	887
Sugar and other sweets	147	91	135	170	163	160	129	141	114
Fats and oils	114	82	98	133	137	113	100	109	90
Miscellaneous foods	699	441	732	786	835	711	549	650	424
Nonalcoholic beverages	370	272	331	419	455	384	301	353	235
Food prepared by consumer unit on trips	50	8	40	47	66	64	47	65	24
Food away from home	2,678	1,883	2,833	3,210	3,210	2,788	1,785	2,074	1,426
ALCOHOLIC BEVERAGES	451	354	564	501	454	493	315	407	201
HOUSING	16,887	10,957	17,157	19,858	19,076	17,247	13,833	15,076	12,298
Shelter	9,891	7,285	10,458	11,849	11,244	9,728	7,605	8,372	6,659
Owned dwellings	6,056	1,307	4,552	7,676	7,625	6,991	5,101	5,970	4,030
Mortgage interest and charges	3,067	728	3,010	4,794	4,077	3,228	1,387	1,980	657
Property taxes	1,836	318	1,024	1,910	2,332	2,310	1,986	2,148	1,787
Maintenance, repair, insurance, other expenses	1,153	261	518	973	1,216	1,453	1,728	1,843	1,587
Rented dwellings	3,186	5,748	5,603	3,691	2,712	1,788	1,828	1,557	2,162
Other lodging	649	230	304	483	907	949	676	845	467
Utilities, fuels, and public services	3,648	1,879	3,130	4,077	4,304	3,992	3,340	3,595	3,025
Natural gas	359	162	279	402	432	390	352	365	337
Electricity	1,388	737	1,191	1,522	1,593	1,516	1,329	1,429	1,206
Fuel oil and other fuels	137	22	70	128	143	164	200	194	208
Telephone services	1,239	764	1,190	1,455	1,519	1,319	926	1,049	775
Water and other public services	525	194	400	570	617	603	532	558	500

	total consumer units	under 25	25 to 34	35 to 44	45 to 54	55 to 64	aged 65 or older total	65 to 74	75 or older
Household services	$1,159	$538	$1,338	$1,559	$1,080	$1,029	$1,076	$1,004	$1,164
Personal services	368	195	728	793	206	88	198	83	340
Other household services	791	343	609	767	874	941	878	921	825
Housekeeping supplies	610	303	538	618	668	736	597	670	507
Laundry and cleaning supplies	155	103	160	175	176	160	129	145	109
Other household products	319	141	272	312	351	410	309	347	262
Postage and stationery	136	59	106	131	141	165	159	178	136
Household furnishings and equipment	1,580	952	1,693	1,755	1,780	1,763	1,215	1,436	942
Household textiles	123	50	104	134	123	160	119	152	79
Furniture	391	325	431	527	473	378	212	259	155
Floor coverings	16	4	12	18	24	18	13	12	14
Major appliances	197	83	164	249	241	202	172	224	108
Small appliances, miscellaneous housewares	98	50	89	90	104	150	77	101	48
Miscellaneous household equipment	754	440	893	737	816	855	621	689	538
APPAREL AND RELATED SERVICES	1,736	1,246	2,061	2,264	2,041	1,622	1,022	1,287	691
Men and boys	408	306	421	616	512	365	199	258	124
Men, aged 16 or older	320	279	295	423	419	315	179	230	115
Boys, aged 2 to 15	88	27	126	193	93	50	20	28	9
Women and girls	688	421	801	800	809	693	481	591	343
Women, aged 16 or older	573	399	649	558	676	629	437	522	332
Girls, aged 2 to 15	116	22	152	243	133	64	43	69	11
Children under age 2	63	112	141	95	32	34	16	25	4
Footwear	347	222	411	493	435	285	185	226	134
Other apparel products and services	230	185	288	260	253	244	142	187	86
TRANSPORTATION	8,998	6,410	9,724	9,991	10,644	9,519	6,538	8,214	4,468
Vehicle purchases	3,210	2,867	4,175	3,610	3,537	2,895	2,250	2,993	1,333
Cars and trucks, new	1,639	809	1,842	1,551	1,976	1,714	1,438	1,903	865
Cars and trucks, used	1,516	1,851	2,260	1,990	1,512	1,141	805	1,078	469
Gasoline and motor oil	2,756	1,931	2,822	3,342	3,421	2,887	1,775	2,222	1,224
Other vehicle expenses	2,490	1,322	2,238	2,532	3,046	3,046	2,041	2,414	1,579
Vehicle finance charges	223	129	297	302	281	202	100	147	42
Maintenance and repairs	814	486	707	834	988	998	667	840	453
Vehicle insurance	1,018	471	785	911	1,268	1,372	934	1,007	843
Vehicle rentals, leases, licenses, other charges	434	236	450	485	508	474	340	420	242
Public transportation	542	291	489	506	640	691	472	585	332
HEALTH CARE	3,556	1,024	2,047	2,948	3,687	4,377	5,118	5,259	4,944
Health insurance	2,061	458	1,227	1,751	2,109	2,271	3,186	3,299	3,047
Medical services	839	406	525	720	892	1,210	935	974	887
Drugs	515	114	213	363	527	724	798	813	779
Medical supplies	142	47	82	114	159	172	200	174	231
ENTERTAINMENT	2,605	1,257	2,382	3,232	3,051	2,911	2,020	2,413	1,532
Fees and admissions	614	249	541	865	751	665	413	534	263
Audio and visual equipment and services	979	588	951	1,105	1,095	1,045	854	943	743
Pets, toys, hobbies, and playground equipment	648	261	571	690	733	844	554	704	368
Other entertainment products and services	363	159	319	573	471	358	198	231	157
PERSONAL CARE PRODUCTS AND SERVICES	628	360	574	694	707	696	569	652	465
READING	109	44	72	93	118	133	142	148	136
EDUCATION	1,207	1,886	1,021	1,050	2,426	1,118	236	245	223
TOBACCO PRODUCTS AND SMOKING SUPPLIES	332	262	351	358	431	372	193	249	124

	total consumer units	under 25	25 to 34	35 to 44	45 to 54	55 to 64	aged 65 or older total	65 to 74	75 or older
MISCELLANEOUS	$829	$372	$660	$876	$924	$908	$902	$1,031	$743
CASH CONTRIBUTIONS	1,913	488	1,104	1,469	2,430	2,353	2,454	2,289	2,658
PERSONAL INSURANCE AND PENSIONS	5,591	2,339	5,313	7,033	8,196	7,088	2,009	2,904	906
Life and other personal insurance	353	50	144	325	446	517	397	484	290
Pensions and Social Security	5,238	2,289	5,169	6,709	7,749	6,571	1,612	2,420	616
PERSONAL TAXES	2,226	2,969	1,395	1,793	2,845	4,205	744	1,011	413
Federal income taxes	1,568	2,481	871	1,144	2,027	3,098	449	663	187
State and local income taxes	526	478	460	542	680	911	115	160	59
Other taxes	132	10	64	108	138	196	179	189	167
GIFTS FOR PEOPLE IN OTHER HOUSEHOLDS	1,116	340	529	752	1,627	1,972	902	994	787

Note: Spending by category does not add to total spending because gift spending is also included in the preceding product and service categories and personal taxes are not included in the total.
Source: Bureau of Labor Statistics, 2012 Consumer Expenditure Survey, Internet site http://www.bls.gov/cex/

Table 9.3 Indexed Spending by Age of Householder, 2012

(indexed average annual spending of consumer units by product and service category and age of consumer unit reference person, 2012; index definition: an index of 100 is the average for all consumer units; an index of 125 means that spending by consumer units in that group is 25 percent above the average for all consumer units; an index of 75 indicates spending that is 25 percent below the average for all consumer units)

	total consumer units	under 25	25 to 34	35 to 44	45 to 54	55 to 64	aged 65 or older total	65 to 74	75 or older
Average spending of consumer units	$51,442	$31,411	$49,544	$58,069	$62,103	$55,636	$40,410	$45,968	$33,530
Indexed spending of consumer units	100	61	96	113	121	108	79	89	65
FOOD	100	67	99	117	120	103	77	88	63
Food at home	100	64	94	115	120	102	83	95	69
Cereals and bakery products	100	66	95	117	118	98	85	91	78
Cereals and cereal products	100	79	103	123	125	87	74	79	67
Bakery products	100	59	91	115	114	104	92	97	84
Meats, poultry, fish, and eggs	100	67	89	117	123	104	81	94	63
Beef	100	71	85	117	127	107	77	89	61
Pork	100	66	87	119	117	105	83	101	62
Other meats	100	63	91	121	118	99	86	100	69
Poultry	100	72	103	113	130	100	69	77	58
Fish and seafood	100	58	74	119	122	110	89	109	64
Eggs	100	74	94	113	113	100	89	98	77
Dairy products	100	60	94	119	119	103	82	92	69
Fresh milk and cream	100	66	99	125	120	93	78	83	73
Other dairy products	100	57	91	115	118	109	84	97	67
Fruits and vegetables	100	62	93	111	119	100	90	99	79
Fresh fruits	100	62	91	114	118	99	93	100	84
Fresh vegetables	100	57	92	108	119	104	93	107	75
Processed fruits	100	68	98	109	118	97	89	88	90
Processed vegetables	100	68	97	111	122	100	82	93	68
Other food at home	100	65	97	113	120	104	82	96	64
Sugar and other sweets	100	62	92	116	111	109	88	96	78
Fats and oils	100	72	86	117	120	99	88	96	79
Miscellaneous foods	100	63	105	112	119	102	79	93	61
Nonalcoholic beverages	100	74	89	113	123	104	81	95	64
Food prepared by consumer unit on trips	100	16	80	94	132	128	94	130	48
Food away from home	100	70	106	120	120	104	67	77	53
ALCOHOLIC BEVERAGES	100	78	125	111	101	109	70	90	45
HOUSING	100	65	102	118	113	102	82	89	73
Shelter	100	74	106	120	114	98	77	85	67
Owned dwellings	100	22	75	127	126	115	84	99	67
Mortgage interest and charges	100	24	98	156	133	105	45	65	21
Property taxes	100	17	56	104	127	126	108	117	97
Maintenance, repair, insurance, other expenses	100	23	45	84	105	126	150	160	138
Rented dwellings	100	180	176	116	85	56	57	49	68
Other lodging	100	35	47	74	140	146	104	130	72
Utilities, fuels, and public services	100	52	86	112	118	109	92	99	83
Natural gas	100	45	78	112	120	109	98	102	94
Electricity	100	53	86	110	115	109	96	103	87
Fuel oil and other fuels	100	16	51	93	104	120	146	142	152
Telephone services	100	62	96	117	123	106	75	85	63
Water and other public services	100	37	76	109	118	115	101	106	95

	total consumer units	under 25	25 to 34	35 to 44	45 to 54	55 to 64	aged 65 or older		
							total	65 to 74	75 or older
Household services	100	46	115	135	93	89	93	87	100
Personal services	100	53	198	215	56	24	54	23	92
Other household services	100	43	77	97	110	119	111	116	104
Housekeeping supplies	100	50	88	101	110	121	98	110	83
Laundry and cleaning supplies	100	66	103	113	114	103	83	94	70
Other household products	100	44	85	98	110	129	97	109	82
Postage and stationery	100	43	78	96	104	121	117	131	100
Household furnishings and equipment	100	60	107	111	113	112	77	91	60
Household textiles	100	41	85	109	100	130	97	124	64
Furniture	100	83	110	135	121	97	54	66	40
Floor coverings	100	25	75	113	150	113	81	75	88
Major appliances	100	42	83	126	122	103	87	114	55
Small appliances, miscellaneous housewares	100	51	91	92	106	153	79	103	49
Miscellaneous household equipment	100	58	118	98	108	113	82	91	71
APPAREL AND RELATED SERVICES	100	72	119	130	118	93	59	74	40
Men and boys	100	75	103	151	125	89	49	63	30
Men, aged 16 or older	100	87	92	132	131	98	56	72	36
Boys, aged 2 to 15	100	31	143	219	106	57	23	32	10
Women and girls	100	61	116	116	118	101	70	86	50
Women, aged 16 or older	100	70	113	97	118	110	76	91	58
Girls, aged 2 to 15	100	19	131	209	115	55	37	59	9
Children under age 2	100	178	224	151	51	54	25	40	6
Footwear	100	64	118	142	125	82	53	65	39
Other apparel products and services	100	80	125	113	110	106	62	81	37
TRANSPORTATION	100	71	108	111	118	106	73	91	50
Vehicle purchases	100	89	130	112	110	90	70	93	42
Cars and trucks, new	100	49	112	95	121	105	88	116	53
Cars and trucks, used	100	122	149	131	100	75	53	71	31
Gasoline and motor oil	100	70	102	121	124	105	64	81	44
Other vehicle expenses	100	53	90	102	122	122	82	97	63
Vehicle finance charges	100	58	133	135	126	91	45	66	19
Maintenance and repairs	100	60	87	102	121	123	82	103	56
Vehicle insurance	100	46	77	89	125	135	92	99	83
Vehicle rentals, leases, licenses, other charges	100	54	104	112	117	109	78	97	56
Public transportation	100	54	90	93	118	127	87	108	61
HEALTH CARE	100	29	58	83	104	123	144	148	139
Health insurance	100	22	60	85	102	110	155	160	148
Medical services	100	48	63	86	106	144	111	116	106
Drugs	100	22	41	70	102	141	155	158	151
Medical supplies	100	33	58	80	112	121	141	123	163
ENTERTAINMENT	100	48	91	124	117	112	78	93	59
Fees and admissions	100	41	88	141	122	108	67	87	43
Audio and visual equipment and services	100	60	97	113	112	107	87	96	76
Pets, toys, hobbies, and playground equipment	100	40	88	106	113	130	85	109	57
Other entertainment products and services	100	44	88	158	130	99	55	64	43
PERSONAL CARE PRODUCTS AND SERVICES	100	57	91	111	113	111	91	104	74
READING	100	40	66	85	108	122	130	136	125
EDUCATION	100	156	85	87	201	93	20	20	18
TOBACCO PRODUCTS AND SMOKING SUPPLIES	100	79	106	108	130	112	58	75	37

	total consumer units	under 25	25 to 34	35 to 44	45 to 54	55 to 64	aged 65 or older		
							total	65 to 74	75 or older
MISCELLANEOUS	100	45	80	106	111	110	109	124	90
CASH CONTRIBUTIONS	100	26	58	77	127	123	128	120	139
PERSONAL INSURANCE AND PENSIONS	100	42	95	126	147	127	36	52	16
Life and other personal insurance	100	14	41	92	126	146	112	137	82
Pensions and Social Security	100	44	99	128	148	125	31	46	12
PERSONAL TAXES	100	133	63	81	128	189	33	45	19
Federal income taxes	100	158	56	73	129	198	29	42	12
State and local income taxes	100	91	87	103	129	173	22	30	11
Other taxes	100	8	48	82	105	148	136	143	127
GIFTS FOR PEOPLE IN OTHER HOUSEHOLDS	100	30	47	67	146	177	81	89	71

Source: Calculations by New Strategist based on the Bureau of Labor Statistics 2012 Consumer Expenditure Survey, Internet site http://www.bls.gov/cex/home.htm

Table 9.4 Market Shares by Age of Householder, 2012

(share of total household spending accounted for by age group, 2012)

	total consumer units	under 25	25 to 34	35 to 44	45 to 54	55 to 64	aged 65 or older		
							total	65 to 74	75 or older
Share of total consumer units	100.0%	6.6%	16.2%	17.4%	19.8%	18.3%	21.8%	12.1%	9.8%
Share of total spending	100.0	4.0	15.6	19.6	23.9	19.8	17.1	10.8	6.4
FOOD	100.0	4.4	16.0	20.3	23.7	18.9	16.7	10.6	6.1
Food at home	100.0	4.2	15.2	19.9	23.8	18.7	18.2	11.4	6.8
Cereals and bakery products	100.0	4.3	15.4	20.4	23.3	17.9	18.6	11.0	7.6
Cereals and cereal products	100.0	5.2	16.6	21.3	24.8	16.0	16.1	9.5	6.6
Bakery products	100.0	3.9	14.8	19.9	22.5	19.0	20.0	11.7	8.2
Meats, poultry, fish, and eggs	100.0	4.4	14.3	20.4	24.3	19.1	17.6	11.4	6.2
Beef	100.0	4.6	13.7	20.3	25.2	19.5	16.8	10.8	5.9
Pork	100.0	4.3	14.1	20.7	23.2	19.3	18.1	12.1	6.1
Other meats	100.0	4.1	14.7	21.1	23.4	18.2	18.8	12.1	6.7
Poultry	100.0	4.7	16.6	19.7	25.8	18.3	15.0	9.3	5.7
Fish and seafood	100.0	3.8	11.9	20.7	24.2	20.0	19.4	13.1	6.3
Eggs	100.0	4.8	15.3	19.7	22.4	18.3	19.4	11.8	7.6
Dairy products	100.0	3.9	15.2	20.6	23.5	18.9	17.8	11.1	6.7
Fresh milk and cream	100.0	4.3	16.0	21.7	23.7	17.1	17.1	10.0	7.1
Other dairy products	100.0	3.7	14.8	20.0	23.4	19.9	18.2	11.7	6.5
Fruits and vegetables	100.0	4.1	15.1	19.2	23.6	18.4	19.7	11.9	7.8
Fresh fruits	100.0	4.1	14.7	19.8	23.4	18.1	20.2	12.0	8.2
Fresh vegetables	100.0	3.7	14.9	18.7	23.6	18.9	20.3	12.9	7.3
Processed fruits	100.0	4.4	15.9	18.9	23.4	17.8	19.3	10.6	8.8
Processed vegetables	100.0	4.5	15.7	19.2	24.2	18.3	18.0	11.2	6.6
Other food at home	100.0	4.2	15.6	19.6	23.8	19.0	17.8	11.5	6.3
Sugar and other sweets	100.0	4.1	14.8	20.1	21.9	19.9	19.2	11.6	7.6
Fats and oils	100.0	4.7	13.9	20.3	23.8	18.1	19.1	11.5	7.7
Miscellaneous foods	100.0	4.1	16.9	19.5	23.6	18.6	17.1	11.2	5.9
Nonalcoholic beverages	100.0	4.8	14.5	19.7	24.3	19.0	17.8	11.5	6.2
Food prepared by consumer unit on trips	100.0	1.0	12.9	16.3	26.1	23.4	20.5	15.7	4.7
Food away from home	100.0	4.6	17.1	20.8	23.7	19.1	14.5	9.3	5.2
ALCOHOLIC BEVERAGES	100.0	5.1	20.2	19.3	19.9	20.0	15.2	10.9	4.4
HOUSING	100.0	4.3	16.4	20.4	22.4	18.7	17.9	10.8	7.1
Shelter	100.0	4.8	17.1	20.8	22.5	18.0	16.8	10.2	6.6
Owned dwellings	100.0	1.4	12.2	22.0	24.9	21.1	18.4	11.9	6.5
Mortgage interest and charges	100.0	1.6	15.9	27.1	26.3	19.3	9.9	7.8	2.1
Property taxes	100.0	1.1	9.0	18.1	25.1	23.0	23.6	14.1	9.5
Maintenance, repair, insurance, other expenses	100.0	1.5	7.3	14.6	20.9	23.1	32.7	19.3	13.5
Rented dwellings	100.0	11.8	28.4	20.1	16.8	10.3	12.5	5.9	6.6
Other lodging	100.0	2.3	7.6	12.9	27.7	26.8	22.7	15.7	7.0
Utilities, fuels, and public services	100.0	3.4	13.9	19.4	23.4	20.0	20.0	11.9	8.1
Natural gas	100.0	3.0	12.6	19.4	23.8	19.9	21.4	12.3	9.2
Electricity	100.0	3.5	13.9	19.0	22.7	20.0	20.9	12.4	8.5
Fuel oil and other fuels	100.0	1.1	8.3	16.2	20.7	21.9	31.9	17.1	14.8
Telephone services	100.0	4.0	15.5	20.4	24.3	19.5	16.3	10.2	6.1
Water and other public services	100.0	2.4	12.3	18.8	23.3	21.0	22.1	12.8	9.3

	total consumer units	under 25	25 to 34	35 to 44	45 to 54	55 to 64	aged 65 or older total	65 to 74	75 or older
Household services	100.0%	3.0%	18.7%	23.4%	18.4%	16.2%	20.3%	10.4%	9.8%
Personal services	100.0	3.5	32.0	37.4	11.1	4.4	11.7	2.7	9.0
Other household services	100.0	2.8	12.4	16.8	21.9	21.8	24.2	14.0	10.2
Housekeeping supplies	100.0	3.3	14.3	17.6	21.7	22.1	21.4	13.2	8.1
Laundry and cleaning supplies	100.0	4.4	16.7	19.6	22.5	18.9	18.2	11.3	6.9
Other household products	100.0	2.9	13.8	17.0	21.8	23.5	21.1	13.1	8.0
Postage and stationery	100.0	2.8	12.6	16.7	20.5	22.2	25.5	15.8	9.8
Household furnishings and equipment	100.0	4.0	17.3	19.3	22.3	20.4	16.8	11.0	5.8
Household textiles	100.0	2.7	13.7	18.9	19.8	23.8	21.1	14.9	6.3
Furniture	100.0	5.5	17.8	23.4	23.9	17.7	11.8	8.0	3.9
Floor coverings	100.0	1.6	12.1	19.5	29.7	20.6	17.7	9.0	8.6
Major appliances	100.0	2.8	13.5	21.9	24.2	18.8	19.1	13.7	5.4
Small appliances, miscellaneous housewares	100.0	3.3	14.7	15.9	21.0	28.0	17.1	12.4	4.8
Miscellaneous household equipment	100.0	3.8	19.1	17.0	21.4	20.8	18.0	11.0	7.0
APPAREL AND RELATED SERVICES	100.0	4.7	19.2	22.6	23.3	17.1	12.8	8.9	3.9
Men and boys	100.0	4.9	16.7	26.2	24.8	16.4	10.6	7.6	3.0
Men, aged 16 or older	100.0	5.7	14.9	22.9	25.9	18.0	12.2	8.7	3.5
Boys, aged 2 to 15	100.0	2.0	23.1	38.1	20.9	10.4	5.0	3.8	1.0
Women and girls	100.0	4.0	18.8	20.2	23.3	18.4	15.3	10.4	4.9
Women, aged 16 or older	100.0	4.6	18.3	16.9	23.3	20.1	16.6	11.0	5.7
Girls, aged 2 to 15	100.0	1.2	21.2	36.4	22.7	10.1	8.1	7.2	0.9
Children under age 2	100.0	11.7	36.2	26.2	10.1	9.9	5.5	4.8	0.6
Footwear	100.0	4.2	19.1	24.7	24.8	15.0	11.6	7.8	3.8
Other apparel products and services	100.0	5.3	20.2	19.6	21.8	19.4	13.5	9.8	3.7
TRANSPORTATION	100.0	4.7	17.5	19.3	23.4	19.4	15.9	11.0	4.9
Vehicle purchases	100.0	5.9	21.0	19.5	21.8	16.5	15.3	11.2	4.1
Cars and trucks, new	100.0	3.2	18.2	16.4	23.9	19.1	19.1	14.0	5.2
Cars and trucks, used	100.0	8.0	24.1	22.8	19.7	13.8	11.6	8.6	3.0
Gasoline and motor oil	100.0	4.6	16.6	21.1	24.6	19.2	14.1	9.7	4.3
Other vehicle expenses	100.0	3.5	14.5	17.7	24.2	22.4	17.9	11.7	6.2
Vehicle finance charges	100.0	3.8	21.5	23.5	24.9	16.6	9.8	7.9	1.8
Maintenance and repairs	100.0	3.9	14.0	17.8	24.0	22.4	17.9	12.4	5.4
Vehicle insurance	100.0	3.0	12.5	15.5	24.7	24.7	20.0	11.9	8.1
Vehicle rentals, leases, licenses, other charges	100.0	3.6	16.8	19.4	23.2	20.0	17.1	11.7	5.5
Public transportation	100.0	3.5	14.6	16.2	23.4	23.3	19.0	13.0	6.0
HEALTH CARE	100.0	1.9	9.3	14.4	20.5	22.5	31.4	17.8	13.6
Health insurance	100.0	1.5	9.6	14.7	20.3	20.2	33.7	19.3	14.5
Medical services	100.0	3.2	10.1	14.9	21.0	26.4	24.3	14.0	10.3
Drugs	100.0	1.5	6.7	12.2	20.3	25.7	33.8	19.0	14.8
Medical supplies	100.0	2.2	9.3	13.9	22.2	22.2	30.7	14.8	15.9
ENTERTAINMENT	100.0	3.2	14.8	21.5	23.2	20.5	16.9	11.2	5.7
Fees and admissions	100.0	2.7	14.2	24.5	24.2	19.8	14.7	10.5	4.2
Audio and visual equipment and services	100.0	3.9	15.7	19.6	22.1	19.5	19.0	11.6	7.4
Pets, toys, hobbies, and playground equipment	100.0	2.6	14.2	18.5	22.4	23.8	18.7	13.1	5.6
Other entertainment products and services	100.0	2.9	14.2	27.4	25.7	18.0	11.9	7.7	4.2
PERSONAL CARE PRODUCTS AND SERVICES	100.0	3.8	14.8	19.2	22.3	20.3	19.8	12.5	7.2
READING	100.0	2.6	10.7	14.8	21.4	22.3	28.4	16.4	12.2
EDUCATION	100.0	10.2	13.7	15.1	39.8	17.0	4.3	2.4	1.8
TOBACCO PRODUCTS AND SMOKING SUPPLIES	100.0	5.2	17.1	18.7	25.7	20.5	12.7	9.0	3.7

	total consumer units	under 25	25 to 34	35 to 44	45 to 54	55 to 64	aged 65 or older		
							total	65 to 74	75 or older
MISCELLANEOUS	**100.0%**	**2.9%**	**12.9%**	**18.3%**	**22.1%**	**20.0%**	**23.7%**	**15.0%**	**8.8%**
CASH CONTRIBUTIONS	**100.0**	**1.7**	**9.3**	**13.3**	**25.1**	**22.5**	**28.0**	**14.4**	**13.6**
PERSONAL INSURANCE AND PENSIONS	**100.0**	**2.7**	**15.4**	**21.8**	**29.0**	**23.2**	**7.8**	**6.3**	**1.6**
Life and other personal insurance	100.0	0.9	6.6	16.0	25.0	26.8	24.5	16.5	8.0
Pensions and Social Security	100.0	2.9	16.0	22.2	29.3	23.0	6.7	5.6	1.1
PERSONAL TAXES	**100.0**	**8.7**	**10.1**	**14.0**	**25.3**	**34.6**	**7.3**	**5.5**	**1.8**
Federal income taxes	100.0	10.4	9.0	12.7	25.6	36.2	6.2	5.1	1.2
State and local income taxes	100.0	6.0	14.1	17.9	25.6	31.7	4.8	3.7	1.1
Other taxes	100.0	0.5	7.8	14.2	20.7	27.2	29.6	17.3	12.4
GIFTS FOR PEOPLE IN OTHER HOUSEHOLDS	**100.0**	**2.0**	**7.7**	**11.7**	**28.9**	**32.3**	**17.6**	**10.7**	**6.9**

Source: Calculations by New Strategist based on the Bureau of Labor Statistics 2012 Consumer Expenditure Survey, Internet site http://www.bls.gov/cex/home.htm

Spending Rises with Income

Households with incomes of $100,000 or more spend twice as much as the average household.

Households with incomes of $100,000 or more spent an average of $101,423 in 2012—about twice the $51,442 spent by the average household. The most-affluent households are also the largest, with an average of 3.2 people according to the Bureau of Labor Statistics' Consumer Expenditure Survey. This compares with 2.5 people in the average household. Households with incomes of $150,000 or more spent $129,211 in 2012. They spend almost as much on restaurant meals ($6,585) as they do on groceries ($6,790).

Tables 9.6 and 9.9 show spending by household income in comparison with what the average household spends. An index of 100 means households in the income group spend an average amount on the item. An index above 100 means households in the income group spend more than average on the item, while an index below 100 reveals below-average spending.

A look at tables 9.6 and 9.9 shows that spending is below average on most items for households with incomes below $50,000, about average for those with incomes between $50,000 and $70,000, and above

High-income households account for a disproportionate share of spending

(share of spending accounted for by consumer unit income groups, 2012)

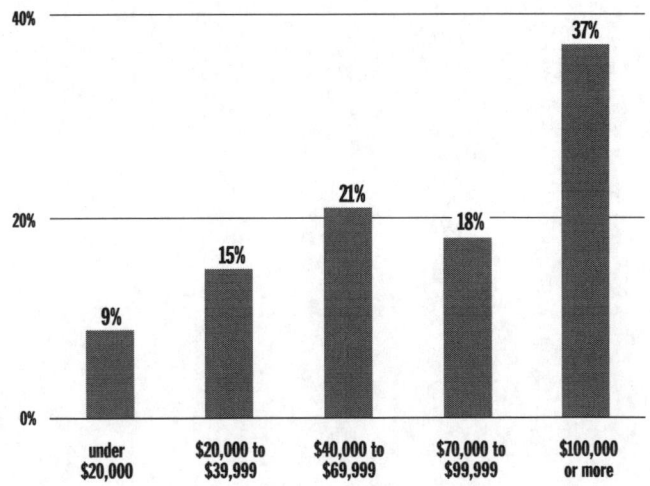

average for households with incomes of $70,000 or more. There are some exceptions, however. Households with incomes below $50,000 spend more than average on rent. Households with incomes of $100,000 or more spend less than average on tobacco. The most-affluent households—those with incomes of $150,000 or more—spend at least four times the average on items such as "other" lodging (which includes college dorm rooms as well as hotels and motels), fees and admissions to entertainment events, and education.

The Market Share tables show how much of total spending by category is accounted for by each income group. Table 9.10 shows how much high-income households dominate spending. While 19 percent of households have annual incomes of $100,000 or more, they control 37 percent of household spending. Households with incomes of $150,000 or more account for only 7 percent of households but they control 18 percent of total household spending. These most-affluent households control more than one-third of spending on "other lodging" and education. They control more than one-fourth of spending on public transportation and fees and admissions to entertainment events.

■ As the cost of necessities rises, high-income households are often the only ones able to devote a substantial sum to discretionary products and services.

Table 9.5 Average Spending by Household Income, 2012

(average annual spending of consumer units [CU] by product and service category and before-tax income of consumer unit, 2012)

	total consumer units	under $10,000	$10,000–$19,999	$20,000–$29,999	$30,000–$39,999	$40,000–$49,999	$50,000–$69,999	$70,000 or more
Number of consumer units (in 000s)	124,416	10,077	16,100	14,515	13,526	11,010	17,972	41,216
Average number of persons per CU	2.5	1.8	1.7	2.1	2.4	2.5	2.6	3.0
Average annual spending	**$51,442**	**$21,574**	**$22,925**	**$30,869**	**$36,229**	**$41,567**	**$49,982**	**$85,410**
FOOD	**6,599**	**3,382**	**3,583**	**4,271**	**4,962**	**5,698**	**6,518**	**10,205**
Food at home	**3,921**	**2,276**	**2,497**	**2,877**	**3,216**	**3,621**	**3,910**	**5,560**
Cereals and bakery products	538	318	350	400	421	521	549	750
Cereals and cereal products	182	107	124	127	152	176	177	256
Bakery products	356	211	227	273	269	345	372	494
Meats, poultry, fish, and eggs	852	535	563	626	752	791	825	1,185
Beef	226	132	130	164	199	231	222	318
Pork	166	128	113	129	145	145	168	221
Other meats	122	72	74	99	111	117	117	169
Poultry	159	97	113	113	146	149	152	219
Fish and seafood	126	71	90	77	102	99	115	191
Eggs	53	37	41	43	50	50	51	68
Dairy products	419	216	259	299	337	374	414	614
Fresh milk and cream	152	90	107	121	133	142	152	204
Other dairy products	267	125	151	178	204	232	263	410
Fruits and vegetables	731	400	461	536	599	655	719	1,055
Fresh fruits	261	125	152	181	191	233	261	395
Fresh vegetables	226	121	145	161	192	209	217	326
Processed fruits	114	73	66	88	103	95	113	161
Processed vegetables	130	81	96	106	112	118	128	173
Other food at home	1,380	806	864	1,016	1,108	1,281	1,403	1,956
Sugar and other sweets	147	82	94	116	111	131	152	207
Fats and oils	114	74	79	87	102	114	115	151
Miscellaneous foods	699	413	435	499	558	654	706	999
Nonalcoholic beverages	370	219	242	285	311	348	387	504
Food prepared by consumer unit on trips	50	18	13	30	26	33	43	95
Food away from home	**2,678**	**1,106**	**1,086**	**1,394**	**1,746**	**2,077**	**2,608**	**4,645**
ALCOHOLIC BEVERAGES	**451**	**148**	**155**	**219**	**335**	**352**	**420**	**804**
HOUSING	**16,887**	**8,667**	**9,142**	**11,728**	**13,224**	**14,645**	**16,278**	**25,809**
Shelter	**9,891**	**5,523**	**5,518**	**6,686**	**7,703**	**8,384**	**9,551**	**15,063**
Owned dwellings	6,056	1,629	1,865	2,815	3,564	4,500	5,585	11,355
Mortgage interest and charges	3,067	660	589	959	1,637	2,126	3,039	6,099
Property taxes	1,836	573	711	1,037	1,091	1,344	1,560	3,360
Maintenance, repair, insurance, other expenses	1,153	397	564	820	835	1,030	986	1,896
Rented dwellings	3,186	3,629	3,492	3,651	3,909	3,569	3,541	2,300
Other lodging	649	265	161	220	230	316	424	1,408
Utilities, fuels, and public services	**3,648**	**1,923**	**2,384**	**2,894**	**3,225**	**3,557**	**3,823**	**4,917**
Natural gas	359	179	223	261	305	351	344	518
Electricity	1,388	865	1,027	1,192	1,295	1,367	1,417	1,749
Fuel oil and other fuels	137	65	72	119	86	119	139	207
Telephone services	1,239	581	719	930	1,097	1,207	1,383	1,705
Water and other public services	525	233	343	393	442	512	540	738

	total consumer units	under $10,000	$10,000–$19,999	$20,000–$29,999	$30,000–$39,999	$40,000–$49,999	$50,000–$69,999	$70,000 or more
Household services	**$1,159**	**$351**	**$407**	**$701**	**$768**	**$899**	**$923**	**$2,112**
Personal services	368	39	92	194	196	247	212	775
Other household services	791	313	315	507	572	652	710	1,337
Housekeeping supplies	**610**	**311**	**309**	**483**	**490**	**527**	**557**	**930**
Laundry and cleaning supplies	155	78	93	130	155	143	140	217
Other household products	319	167	151	245	239	266	288	501
Postage and stationery	136	67	64	108	96	118	128	212
Household furnishings and equipment	**1,580**	**558**	**523**	**964**	**1,038**	**1,278**	**1,425**	**2,787**
Household textiles	123	87	30	82	69	97	99	219
Furniture	391	117	118	203	272	368	323	707
Floor coverings	16	4	4	7	7	9	12	34
Major appliances	197	57	88	102	140	154	202	336
Small appliances, miscellaneous housewares	98	34	37	55	66	75	95	171
Miscellaneous household equipment	754	260	245	515	483	576	693	1,322
APPAREL AND RELATED SERVICES	**1,736**	**843**	**769**	**1,064**	**1,163**	**1,398**	**1,559**	**2,932**
Men and boys	**408**	**195**	**156**	**216**	**250**	**264**	**371**	**736**
Men, aged 16 or older	320	167	111	158	175	202	280	597
Boys, aged 2 to 15	88	28	45	58	75	62	91	140
Women and girls	**688**	**342**	**250**	**458**	**453**	**580**	**658**	**1,148**
Women, aged 16 or older	573	263	200	373	368	482	556	964
Girls, aged 2 to 15	116	80	51	84	85	97	101	184
Children under age 2	**63**	**45**	**40**	**49**	**44**	**70**	**60**	**88**
Footwear	**347**	**151**	**209**	**223**	**266**	**329**	**312**	**539**
Other apparel products and services	**230**	**110**	**115**	**118**	**149**	**155**	**158**	**420**
TRANSPORTATION	**8,998**	**3,317**	**3,554**	**4,991**	**6,311**	**7,531**	**9,928**	**14,781**
Vehicle purchases	**3,210**	**1,167**	**897**	**1,425**	**1,751**	**2,197**	**3,855**	**5,711**
Cars and trucks, new	1,639	726	438	487	659	1,101	1,711	3,169
Cars and trucks, used	1,516	439	458	918	1,081	1,075	2,089	2,415
Gasoline and motor oil	**2,756**	**1,106**	**1,340**	**1,896**	**2,337**	**2,651**	**3,091**	**4,034**
Other vehicle expenses	**2,490**	**816**	**1,157**	**1,450**	**1,941**	**2,365**	**2,533**	**3,968**
Vehicle finance charges	223	37	54	93	174	197	242	396
Maintenance and repairs	814	319	385	517	640	722	881	1,261
Vehicle insurance	1,018	305	581	628	845	1,136	997	1,521
Vehicle rentals, leases, licenses, other charges	434	153	136	211	282	310	413	789
Public transportation	**542**	**228**	**160**	**220**	**281**	**318**	**449**	**1,068**
HEALTH CARE	**3,556**	**1,340**	**1,962**	**2,844**	**2,906**	**3,244**	**3,689**	**5,212**
Health insurance	2,061	754	1,162	1,664	1,696	1,926	2,235	2,951
Medical services	839	297	396	592	653	689	778	1,358
Drugs	515	247	327	503	461	526	527	667
Medical supplies	142	42	76	86	96	103	150	236
ENTERTAINMENT	**2,605**	**908**	**1,057**	**1,481**	**1,816**	**1,934**	**2,438**	**4,534**
Fees and admissions	614	127	112	205	245	378	476	1,318
Audio and visual equipment and services	979	487	568	734	824	919	982	1,413
Pets, toys, hobbies, and playground equipment	648	249	242	435	602	443	636	1,058
Other entertainment products and services	363	45	135	107	145	194	345	745
PERSONAL CARE PRODUCTS AND SERVICES	**628**	**236**	**269**	**412**	**423**	**479**	**606**	**1,058**
READING	**109**	**42**	**46**	**65**	**77**	**87**	**103**	**185**
EDUCATION	**1,207**	**923**	**420**	**319**	**589**	**571**	**647**	**2,515**
TOBACCO PRODUCTS AND SMOKING SUPPLIES	**332**	**310**	**293**	**336**	**384**	**364**	**374**	**306**

	total consumer units	under $10,000	$10,000– $19,999	$20,000– $29,999	$30,000– $39,999	$40,000– $49,999	$50,000– $69,999	$70,000 or more
MISCELLANEOUS	$829	$402	$357	$766	$557	$666	$727	$1,316
CASH CONTRIBUTIONS	1,913	774	672	1,104	1,130	1,193	1,819	3,450
PERSONAL INSURANCE AND PENSIONS	5,591	281	643	1,271	2,353	3,407	4,875	12,302
Life and other personal insurance	353	77	111	133	188	209	266	722
Pensions and Social Security	5,238	204	532	1,137	2,164	3,198	4,609	11,580
PERSONAL TAXES	2,226	–139	–219	–232	–45	483	1,084	6,335
Federal income taxes	1,568	–204	–267	–351	–210	158	625	4,766
State and local income taxes	526		11	37	82	202	361	1,332
Other taxes	132	64	37	81	83	123	98	237
GIFTS FOR PEOPLE IN OTHER HOUSEHOLDS	1,116	700	394	487	569	608	716	2,218

Note: Spending by category does not add to total spending because gift spending is also included in the preceding product and service categories and personal taxes are not included in the total.
Source: Bureau of Labor Statistics, 2012 Consumer Expenditure Survey, Internet site http://www.bls.gov/cex/; calculations by New Strategist

Table 9.6 Indexed Spending by Household Income, 2012

(indexed average annual spending of consumer units by product and service category and before tax income of consumer unit reference person, 2012; index definition: an index of 100 is the average for all consumer units; an index of 125 means that spending by consumer units in that group is 25 percent above the average for all consumer units; an index of 75 indicates spending that is 25 percent below the average for all consumer units)

	total consumer units	under $10,000	$10,000–$19,999	$20,000–$29,999	$30,000–$39,999	$40,000–$49,999	$50,000–$69,999	$70,000 or more
Average spending of consumer units	$51,442	$21,574	$22,925	$30,869	$36,229	$41,567	$49,982	$85,410
Indexed spending of consumer units	100	42	45	60	70	81	97	166
FOOD	100	51	54	65	75	86	99	155
Food at home	100	58	64	73	82	92	100	142
Cereals and bakery products	100	59	65	74	78	97	102	139
Cereals and cereal products	100	59	68	70	84	97	97	141
Bakery products	100	59	64	77	76	97	104	139
Meats, poultry, fish, and eggs	100	63	66	73	88	93	97	139
Beef	100	58	58	73	88	102	98	141
Pork	100	77	68	78	87	87	101	133
Other meats	100	59	61	81	91	96	96	139
Poultry	100	61	71	71	92	94	96	138
Fish and seafood	100	56	71	61	81	79	91	152
Eggs	100	69	78	81	94	94	96	128
Dairy products	100	51	62	71	80	89	99	147
Fresh milk and cream	100	59	71	80	88	93	100	134
Other dairy products	100	47	57	67	76	87	99	154
Fruits and vegetables	100	55	63	73	82	90	98	144
Fresh fruits	100	48	58	69	73	89	100	151
Fresh vegetables	100	53	64	71	85	92	96	144
Processed fruits	100	64	58	77	90	83	99	141
Processed vegetables	100	62	74	82	86	91	98	133
Other food at home	100	58	63	74	80	93	102	142
Sugar and other sweets	100	56	64	79	76	89	103	141
Fats and oils	100	65	69	76	89	100	101	132
Miscellaneous foods	100	59	62	71	80	94	101	143
Nonalcoholic beverages	100	59	66	77	84	94	105	136
Food prepared by consumer unit on trips	100	36	27	60	52	66	86	190
Food away from home	100	41	41	52	65	78	97	173
ALCOHOLIC BEVERAGES	100	33	34	49	74	78	93	178
HOUSING	100	51	54	69	78	87	96	153
Shelter	100	56	56	68	78	85	97	152
Owned dwellings	100	27	31	46	59	74	92	188
Mortgage interest and charges	100	22	19	31	53	69	99	199
Property taxes	100	31	39	56	59	73	85	183
Maintenance, repair, insurance, other expenses	100	34	49	71	72	89	86	164
Rented dwellings	100	114	110	115	123	112	111	72
Other lodging	100	41	25	34	35	49	65	217
Utilities, fuels, and public services	100	53	65	79	88	98	105	135
Natural gas	100	50	62	73	85	98	96	144
Electricity	100	62	74	86	93	98	102	126
Fuel oil and other fuels	100	48	53	87	63	87	101	151
Telephone services	100	47	58	75	89	97	112	138
Water and other public services	100	44	65	75	84	98	103	141

	total consumer units	under $10,000	$10,000–$19,999	$20,000–$29,999	$30,000–$39,999	$40,000–$49,999	$50,000–$69,999	$70,000 or more
Household services	100	30	35	60	66	78	80	182
Personal services	100	11	25	53	53	67	58	211
Other household services	100	40	40	64	72	82	90	169
Housekeeping supplies	100	51	51	79	80	86	91	152
Laundry and cleaning supplies	100	50	60	84	100	92	90	140
Other household products	100	52	47	77	75	83	90	157
Postage and stationery	100	49	47	79	71	87	94	156
Household furnishings and equipment	100	35	33	61	66	81	90	176
Household textiles	100	71	25	67	56	79	80	178
Furniture	100	30	30	52	70	94	83	181
Floor coverings	100	28	25	44	44	56	75	213
Major appliances	100	29	45	52	71	78	103	171
Small appliances, miscellaneous housewares	100	34	38	56	67	77	97	174
Miscellaneous household equipment	100	34	32	68	64	76	92	175
APPAREL AND RELATED SERVICES	100	49	44	61	67	81	90	169
Men and boys	100	48	38	53	61	65	91	180
Men, aged 16 or older	100	52	35	49	55	63	88	187
Boys, aged 2 to 15	100	32	52	66	85	70	103	159
Women and girls	100	50	36	67	66	84	96	167
Women, aged 16 or older	100	46	35	65	64	84	97	168
Girls, aged 2 to 15	100	69	44	72	73	84	87	159
Children under age 2	100	72	63	78	70	111	95	140
Footwear	100	43	60	64	77	95	90	155
Other apparel products and services	100	48	50	51	65	67	69	183
TRANSPORTATION	100	37	40	55	70	84	110	164
Vehicle purchases	100	36	28	44	55	68	120	178
Cars and trucks, new	100	44	27	30	40	67	104	193
Cars and trucks, used	100	29	30	61	71	71	138	159
Gasoline and motor oil	100	40	49	69	85	96	112	146
Other vehicle expenses	100	33	46	58	78	95	102	159
Vehicle finance charges	100	17	24	42	78	88	109	178
Maintenance and repairs	100	39	47	64	79	89	108	155
Vehicle insurance	100	30	57	62	83	112	98	149
Vehicle rentals, leases, licenses, other charges	100	35	31	49	65	71	95	182
Public transportation	100	42	30	41	52	59	83	197
HEALTH CARE	100	38	55	80	82	91	104	147
Health insurance	100	37	56	81	82	93	108	143
Medical services	100	35	47	71	78	82	93	162
Drugs	100	48	64	98	90	102	102	130
Medical supplies	100	30	54	61	68	73	106	166
ENTERTAINMENT	100	35	41	57	70	74	94	174
Fees and admissions	100	21	18	33	40	62	78	215
Audio and visual equipment and services	100	50	58	75	84	94	100	144
Pets, toys, hobbies, and playground equipment	100	38	37	67	93	68	98	163
Other entertainment products and services	100	12	37	29	40	53	95	205
PERSONAL CARE PRODUCTS AND SERVICES	100	38	43	66	67	76	96	168
READING	100	39	43	60	71	80	94	170
EDUCATION	100	76	35	26	49	47	54	208
TOBACCO PRODUCTS AND SMOKING SUPPLIES	100	93	88	101	116	110	113	92

	total consumer units	under $10,000	$10,000–$19,999	$20,000–$29,999	$30,000–$39,999	$40,000–$49,999	$50,000–$69,999	$70,000 or more
MISCELLANEOUS	100	49	43	92	67	80	88	159
CASH CONTRIBUTIONS	100	40	35	58	59	62	95	180
PERSONAL INSURANCE AND PENSIONS	100	5	12	23	42	61	87	220
Life and other personal insurance	100	22	31	38	53	59	75	205
Pensions and Social Security	100	4	10	22	41	61	88	221
PERSONAL TAXES	100	–6	–10	–10	–2	22	49	285
Federal income taxes	100	–13	–17	–22	–13	10	40	304
State and local income taxes	100	0	2	7	16	38	69	253
Other taxes	100	48	28	61	63	93	74	180
GIFTS FOR PEOPLE IN OTHER HOUSEHOLDS	100	63	35	44	51	54	64	199

Source: Calculations by New Strategist based on the Bureau of Labor Statistics 2012 Consumer Expenditure Survey, Internet site http://www.bls.gov/cex/home.htm

Table 9.7 Market Shares by Household Income, 2012

(share of total household spending accounted for by household income group, 2012)

	total consumer units	under $10,000	$10,000–$19,999	$20,000–$29,999	$30,000–$39,999	$40,000–$49,999	$50,000–$69,999	$70,000 or more
Share of total consumer units	100.0%	8.1%	12.9%	11.7%	10.9%	8.8%	14.4%	33.1%
Share of total spending	100.0	3.4	5.8	7.0	7.7	7.2	14.0	55.0
FOOD	100.0	4.2	7.0	7.6	8.2	7.6	14.3	51.2
Food at home	100.0	4.7	8.2	8.6	8.9	8.2	14.4	47.0
Cereals and bakery products	100.0	4.8	8.4	8.7	8.5	8.6	14.7	46.2
Cereals and cereal products	100.0	4.8	8.8	8.1	9.1	8.6	14.0	46.6
Bakery products	100.0	4.8	8.2	8.9	8.2	8.6	15.1	46.0
Meats, poultry, fish, and eggs	100.0	5.1	8.5	8.6	9.6	8.2	14.0	46.1
Beef	100.0	4.7	7.4	8.5	9.6	9.0	14.2	46.6
Pork	100.0	6.3	8.8	9.1	9.5	7.7	14.6	44.1
Other meats	100.0	4.8	7.9	9.5	9.9	8.5	13.9	45.9
Poultry	100.0	4.9	9.2	8.3	10.0	8.3	13.8	45.6
Fish and seafood	100.0	4.5	9.2	7.1	8.8	7.0	13.2	50.2
Eggs	100.0	5.6	10.1	9.5	10.3	8.3	13.9	42.5
Dairy products	100.0	4.2	8.0	8.3	8.7	7.9	14.3	48.5
Fresh milk and cream	100.0	4.8	9.1	9.3	9.5	8.3	14.4	44.5
Other dairy products	100.0	3.8	7.3	7.8	8.3	7.7	14.2	50.9
Fruits and vegetables	100.0	4.4	8.2	8.6	8.9	7.9	14.2	47.8
Fresh fruits	100.0	3.9	7.6	8.1	8.0	7.9	14.4	50.1
Fresh vegetables	100.0	4.3	8.3	8.3	9.2	8.2	13.9	47.8
Processed fruits	100.0	5.2	7.5	9.0	9.8	7.4	14.3	46.8
Processed vegetables	100.0	5.0	9.6	9.5	9.4	8.0	14.2	44.1
Other food at home	100.0	4.7	8.1	8.6	8.7	8.2	14.7	47.0
Sugar and other sweets	100.0	4.5	8.3	9.2	8.2	7.9	14.9	46.6
Fats and oils	100.0	5.3	9.0	8.9	9.7	8.8	14.6	43.9
Miscellaneous foods	100.0	4.8	8.1	8.3	8.7	8.3	14.6	47.3
Nonalcoholic beverages	100.0	4.8	8.5	9.0	9.1	8.3	15.1	45.1
Food prepared by consumer unit on trips	100.0	2.9	3.5	7.0	5.7	5.8	12.4	62.9
Food away from home	100.0	3.3	5.2	6.1	7.1	6.9	14.1	57.5
ALCOHOLIC BEVERAGES	100.0	2.7	4.4	5.7	8.1	6.9	13.5	59.1
HOUSING	100.0	4.2	7.0	8.1	8.5	7.7	13.9	50.6
Shelter	100.0	4.5	7.2	7.9	8.5	7.5	13.9	50.4
Owned dwellings	100.0	2.2	4.0	5.4	6.4	6.6	13.3	62.1
Mortgage interest and charges	100.0	1.7	2.5	3.6	5.8	6.1	14.3	65.9
Property taxes	100.0	2.5	5.0	6.6	6.5	6.5	12.3	60.6
Maintenance, repair, insurance, other expenses	100.0	2.8	6.3	8.3	7.9	7.9	12.4	54.5
Rented dwellings	100.0	9.2	14.2	13.4	13.3	9.9	16.1	23.9
Other lodging	100.0	3.3	3.2	4.0	3.9	4.3	9.4	71.9
Utilities, fuels, and public services	100.0	4.3	8.5	9.3	9.6	8.6	15.1	44.7
Natural gas	100.0	4.0	8.1	8.5	9.2	8.7	13.8	47.8
Electricity	100.0	5.0	9.6	10.0	10.1	8.7	14.7	41.7
Fuel oil and other fuels	100.0	3.9	6.8	10.1	6.8	7.7	14.7	50.1
Telephone services	100.0	3.8	7.5	8.8	9.6	8.6	16.1	45.6
Water and other public services	100.0	3.6	8.4	8.7	9.2	8.6	14.9	46.6

	total consumer units	under $10,000	$10,000– $19,999	$20,000– $29,999	$30,000– $39,999	$40,000– $49,999	$50,000– $69,999	$70,000 or more
Household services	100.0%	2.5%	4.5%	7.1%	7.2%	6.9%	11.5%	60.4%
Personal services	100.0	0.9	3.2	6.2	5.8	5.9	8.3	69.8
Other household services	100.0	3.2	5.2	7.5	7.9	7.3	13.0	56.0
Housekeeping supplies	100.0	4.1	6.6	9.2	8.7	7.6	13.2	50.5
Laundry and cleaning supplies	100.0	4.1	7.8	9.8	10.9	8.2	13.0	46.4
Other household products	100.0	4.2	6.1	9.0	8.1	7.4	13.0	52.0
Postage and stationery	100.0	4.0	6.1	9.3	7.7	7.7	13.6	51.6
Household furnishings and equipment	100.0	2.9	4.3	7.1	7.1	7.2	13.0	58.4
Household textiles	100.0	5.7	3.2	7.8	6.1	7.0	11.6	59.0
Furniture	100.0	2.4	3.9	6.1	7.6	8.3	11.9	59.9
Floor coverings	100.0	2.3	3.2	5.1	4.8	5.0	10.8	70.4
Major appliances	100.0	2.3	5.8	6.0	7.7	6.9	14.8	56.5
Small appliances, miscellaneous housewares	100.0	2.8	4.9	6.5	7.3	6.8	14.0	57.8
Miscellaneous household equipment	100.0	2.8	4.2	8.0	7.0	6.8	13.3	58.1
APPAREL AND RELATED SERVICES	100.0	3.9	5.7	7.2	7.3	7.1	13.0	56.0
Men and boys	100.0	3.9	5.0	6.2	6.7	5.7	13.1	59.8
Men, aged 16 or older	100.0	4.2	4.5	5.8	5.9	5.6	12.6	61.8
Boys, aged 2 to 15	100.0	2.6	6.7	7.7	9.3	6.2	14.9	52.7
Women and girls	100.0	4.0	4.7	7.8	7.2	7.5	13.8	55.3
Women, aged 16 or older	100.0	3.7	4.5	7.6	7.0	7.4	14.0	55.7
Girls, aged 2 to 15	100.0	5.6	5.7	8.4	8.0	7.4	12.6	52.5
Children under age 2	100.0	5.8	8.2	9.1	7.6	9.8	13.8	46.3
Footwear	100.0	3.5	7.8	7.5	8.3	8.4	13.0	51.5
Other apparel products and services	100.0	3.9	6.5	6.0	7.0	6.0	9.9	60.5
TRANSPORTATION	100.0	3.0	5.1	6.5	7.6	7.4	15.9	54.4
Vehicle purchases	100.0	2.9	3.6	5.2	5.9	6.1	17.3	58.9
Cars and trucks, new	100.0	3.6	3.5	3.5	4.4	5.9	15.1	64.1
Cars and trucks, used	100.0	2.3	3.9	7.1	7.8	6.3	19.9	52.8
Gasoline and motor oil	100.0	3.3	6.3	8.0	9.2	8.5	16.2	48.5
Other vehicle expenses	100.0	2.7	6.0	6.8	8.5	8.4	14.7	52.8
Vehicle finance charges	100.0	1.4	3.1	4.9	8.5	7.8	15.7	58.8
Maintenance and repairs	100.0	3.2	6.1	7.4	8.5	7.8	15.6	51.3
Vehicle insurance	100.0	2.4	7.4	7.2	9.0	9.9	14.1	49.5
Vehicle rentals, leases, licenses, other charges	100.0	2.9	4.1	5.7	7.1	6.3	13.7	60.2
Public transportation	100.0	3.4	3.8	4.7	5.6	5.2	12.0	65.3
HEALTH CARE	100.0	3.1	7.1	9.3	8.9	8.1	15.0	48.6
Health insurance	100.0	3.0	7.3	9.4	8.9	8.3	15.7	47.4
Medical services	100.0	2.9	6.1	8.2	8.5	7.3	13.4	53.6
Drugs	100.0	3.9	8.2	11.4	9.7	9.0	14.8	42.9
Medical supplies	100.0	2.4	7.0	7.1	7.3	6.4	15.3	55.1
ENTERTAINMENT	100.0	2.8	5.3	6.6	7.6	6.6	13.5	57.7
Fees and admissions	100.0	1.7	2.4	3.9	4.3	5.4	11.2	71.1
Audio and visual equipment and services	100.0	4.0	7.5	8.7	9.2	8.3	14.5	47.8
Pets, toys, hobbies, and playground equipment	100.0	3.1	4.8	7.8	10.1	6.0	14.2	54.1
Other entertainment products and services	100.0	1.0	4.8	3.4	4.3	4.7	13.7	68.0
PERSONAL CARE PRODUCTS AND SERVICES	100.0	3.0	5.6	7.7	7.3	6.7	13.9	55.8
READING	100.0	3.1	5.5	7.0	7.7	7.1	13.6	56.2
EDUCATION	100.0	6.2	4.5	3.1	5.3	4.2	7.7	69.0
TOBACCO PRODUCTS AND SMOKING SUPPLIES	100.0	7.6	11.4	11.8	12.6	9.7	16.3	30.5

	total consumer units	under $10,000	$10,000–$19,999	$20,000–$29,999	$30,000–$39,999	$40,000–$49,999	$50,000–$69,999	$70,000 or more
MISCELLANEOUS	100.0%	3.9%	5.6%	10.8%	7.3%	7.1%	12.7%	52.6%
CASH CONTRIBUTIONS	100.0	3.3	4.5	6.7	6.4	5.5	13.7	59.7
PERSONAL INSURANCE AND PENSIONS	100.0	0.4	1.5	2.7	4.6	5.4	12.6	72.9
Life and other personal insurance	100.0	1.8	4.1	4.4	5.8	5.2	10.9	67.8
Pensions and Social Security	100.0	0.3	1.3	2.5	4.5	5.4	12.7	73.2
PERSONAL TAXES	100.0	–	–	–	–	1.9	7.0	–
Federal income taxes	100.0	–	–	–	–	0.9	5.8	–
State and local income taxes	100.0	0.0	0.3	0.8	1.7	3.4	9.9	83.9
Other taxes	100.0	3.9	3.6	7.2	6.8	8.2	10.7	59.5
GIFTS FOR PEOPLE IN OTHER HOUSEHOLDS	100.0	5.1	4.6	5.1	5.5	4.8	9.3	65.8

Note: "–" means a refund was received.
Source: Calculations by New Strategist based on the Bureau of Labor Statistics 2012 Consumer Expenditure Survey, Internet site http://www.bls.gov/cex/home.htm

Table 9.8 Average Spending by High-Income Households, 2012

(average annual spending of consumer units by product and service category and before-tax income of consumer unit, 2012)

	total consumer units	less than $70,000	$70,000– $79,999	$80,000– $99,999	$100,000 or more total	$100,000– $119,999	$120,000– $149,999	$150,000 or more
Number of consumer units (in 000s)	124,416	83,200	6,946	10,977	23,293	7,183	6,947	9,162
Average number of persons per consumer unit	2.5	2.2	2.8	2.9	3.2	3.1	3.2	3.2
Average annual spending	**$51,442**	**$34,679**	**$59,984**	**$67,418**	**$101,423**	**$77,966**	**$89,521**	**$129,211**
FOOD	**6,599**	**4,842**	**8,250**	**8,612**	**11,527**	**9,599**	**11,287**	**13,375**
Food at home	**3,921**	**3,124**	**4,945**	**4,865**	**6,060**	**5,279**	**6,003**	**6,790**
Cereals and bakery products	538	435	669	664	814	720	797	909
Cereals and cereal products	182	146	234	228	276	254	272	297
Bakery products	356	289	435	436	538	465	526	612
Meats, poultry, fish, and eggs	852	691	1,074	1,086	1,264	1,127	1,204	1,430
Beef	226	182	272	285	347	320	277	425
Pork	166	139	217	212	226	205	219	249
Other meats	122	100	156	145	183	151	178	215
Poultry	159	130	208	200	231	193	265	239
Fish and seafood	126	94	157	183	205	190	193	227
Eggs	53	46	64	61	72	68	73	76
Dairy products	419	324	541	533	673	581	654	767
Fresh milk and cream	152	127	193	185	215	194	205	242
Other dairy products	267	198	349	348	457	387	449	526
Fruits and vegetables	731	574	878	906	1,176	985	1,172	1,347
Fresh fruits	261	196	306	333	451	363	457	524
Fresh vegetables	226	178	268	273	368	293	370	433
Processed fruits	114	91	150	141	173	150	165	198
Processed vegetables	130	109	155	160	184	179	181	191
Other food at home	1,380	1,100	1,783	1,676	2,134	1,867	2,175	2,336
Sugar and other sweets	147	117	195	166	229	198	226	258
Fats and oils	114	96	141	128	163	152	180	161
Miscellaneous foods	699	554	877	869	1,095	952	1,129	1,196
Nonalcoholic beverages	370	305	502	432	536	478	545	580
Food prepared by consumer unit on trips	50	28	68	79	111	87	95	141
Food away from home	**2,678**	**1,718**	**3,306**	**3,747**	**5,467**	**4,320**	**5,284**	**6,585**
ALCOHOLIC BEVERAGES	**451**	**279**	**583**	**659**	**937**	**737**	**899**	**1,140**
HOUSING	**16,887**	**12,476**	**18,456**	**21,039**	**30,243**	**23,410**	**27,330**	**37,877**
Shelter	**9,891**	**7,328**	**10,437**	**12,293**	**17,748**	**13,796**	**15,837**	**22,296**
Owned dwellings	6,056	3,431	6,721	8,888	13,898	10,653	12,588	17,436
Mortgage interest and charges	3,067	1,565	3,618	4,954	7,378	5,904	6,710	9,040
Property taxes	1,836	1,080	2,002	2,471	4,184	3,124	3,651	5,421
Maintenance, repair, insurance, other expenses	1,153	786	1,102	1,464	2,336	1,625	2,228	2,975
Rented dwellings	3,186	3,625	3,065	2,708	1,881	2,072	1,752	1,828
Other lodging	649	272	650	697	1,969	1,070	1,498	3,032
Utilities, fuels, and public services	**3,648**	**3,020**	**4,149**	**4,432**	**5,374**	**4,795**	**5,158**	**5,992**
Natural gas	359	281	421	435	586	491	553	685
Electricity	1,388	1,209	1,538	1,580	1,891	1,722	1,787	2,103
Fuel oil and other fuels	137	102	121	177	246	202	210	309
Telephone services	1,239	1,008	1,452	1,592	1,833	1,645	1,841	1,975
Water and other public services	525	419	617	647	817	735	768	920

	total consumer units	less than $70,000	$70,000–$79,999	$80,000–$99,999	$100,000 or more total	$100,000–$119,999	$120,000–$149,999	$150,000 or more
Household services	**$1,159**	**$687**	**$1,194**	**$1,454**	**$2,696**	**$1,732**	**$2,297**	**$3,757**
Personal services	368	167	441	518	996	627	953	1,318
Other household services	791	520	754	936	1,700	1,105	1,345	2,438
Housekeeping supplies	**610**	**454**	**841**	**787**	**1,021**	**836**	**988**	**1,208**
Laundry and cleaning supplies	155	125	229	210	217	176	236	238
Other household products	319	230	436	404	564	455	523	690
Postage and stationery	136	99	176	174	240	205	229	280
Household furnishings and equipment	**1,580**	**986**	**1,835**	**2,073**	**3,404**	**2,252**	**3,050**	**4,624**
Household textiles	123	76	201	187	238	132	231	335
Furniture	391	235	322	485	926	636	676	1,344
Floor coverings	16	8	11	16	49	26	34	78
Major appliances	197	128	245	285	388	254	395	488
Small appliances, miscellaneous housewares	98	62	204	127	179	114	184	231
Miscellaneous household equipment	754	477	853	974	1,624	1,090	1,530	2,148
APPAREL AND RELATED SERVICES	**1,736**	**1,152**	**2,209**	**2,394**	**3,399**	**2,509**	**3,184**	**4,315**
Men and boys	**408**	**247**	**543**	**634**	**844**	**613**	**836**	**1,046**
Men, aged 16 or older	320	185	438	530	678	482	684	839
Boys, aged 2 to 15	88	63	105	104	166	131	152	207
Women and girls	**688**	**465**	**904**	**949**	**1,313**	**1,045**	**1,228**	**1,610**
Women, aged 16 or older	573	382	780	795	1,097	883	1,041	1,327
Girls, aged 2 to 15	116	83	125	155	216	163	187	283
Children under age 2	**63**	**51**	**65**	**96**	**92**	**70**	**80**	**120**
Footwear	**347**	**254**	**454**	**435**	**611**	**446**	**616**	**752**
Other apparel products and services	**230**	**135**	**242**	**279**	**539**	**334**	**423**	**788**
TRANSPORTATION	**8,998**	**6,139**	**11,590**	**12,953**	**16,578**	**14,841**	**14,907**	**19,217**
Vehicle purchases	**3,210**	**1,972**	**4,267**	**5,283**	**6,343**	**6,126**	**5,146**	**7,421**
Cars and trucks, new	1,639	880	2,261	2,801	3,613	3,499	3,006	4,163
Cars and trucks, used	1,516	1,071	1,876	2,419	2,573	2,456	2,098	3,025
Gasoline and motor oil	**2,756**	**2,123**	**3,432**	**3,827**	**4,311**	**4,143**	**4,363**	**4,404**
Other vehicle expenses	**2,490**	**1,763**	**3,381**	**3,203**	**4,487**	**3,775**	**4,232**	**5,248**
Vehicle finance charges	223	138	335	376	423	422	419	427
Maintenance and repairs	814	594	914	1,022	1,477	1,164	1,410	1,775
Vehicle insurance	1,018	773	1,676	1,204	1,610	1,555	1,534	1,716
Vehicle rentals, leases, licenses, other charges	434	258	456	601	977	634	868	1,329
Public transportation	**542**	**282**	**510**	**640**	**1,437**	**797**	**1,167**	**2,144**
HEALTH CARE	**3,556**	**2,737**	**4,167**	**4,535**	**5,843**	**5,277**	**5,448**	**6,593**
Health insurance	2,061	1,620	2,476	2,702	3,210	2,911	3,109	3,521
Medical services	839	581	957	1,083	1,608	1,495	1,404	1,851
Drugs	515	440	540	574	748	665	710	847
Medical supplies	142	97	194	175	277	206	226	373
ENTERTAINMENT	**2,605**	**1,655**	**3,112**	**3,202**	**5,578**	**3,934**	**4,874**	**7,456**
Fees and admissions	614	267	689	740	1,775	1,092	1,337	2,654
Audio and visual equipment and services	979	765	1,151	1,185	1,597	1,289	1,520	1,901
Pets, toys, hobbies, and playground equipment	648	448	821	865	1,217	828	1,174	1,586
Other entertainment products and services	363	176	450	412	989	724	843	1,315
PERSONAL CARE PRODUCTS AND SERVICES	**628**	**417**	**898**	**822**	**1,213**	**1,049**	**1,110**	**1,422**
READING	**109**	**72**	**141**	**148**	**216**	**162**	**204**	**267**
EDUCATION	**1,207**	**560**	**1,045**	**1,230**	**3,559**	**1,917**	**2,462**	**5,681**
TOBACCO PRODUCTS AND SMOKING SUPPLIES	**332**	**344**	**384**	**357**	**259**	**311**	**250**	**225**

	total consumer units	less than $70,000	$70,000– $79,999	$80,000– $99,999	$100,000 or more			
					total	$100,000– $119,999	$120,000– $149,999	$150,000 or more
MISCELLANEOUS	$829	$588	$794	$946	$1,648	$1,313	$1,392	$2,108
CASH CONTRIBUTIONS	1,913	1,151	1,878	2,381	4,422	2,683	3,196	6,716
PERSONAL INSURANCE AND PENSIONS	5,591	2,266	6,477	8,139	16,000	10,223	12,980	22,820
Life and other personal insurance	353	170	368	487	938	532	660	1,469
Pensions and Social Security	5,238	2,097	6,109	7,652	15,062	9,691	12,320	21,351
PERSONAL TAXES	2,226	191	1,927	2,661	9,380	3,264	4,883	17,586
Federal income taxes	1,568	–16	1,337	1,796	7,189	2,159	3,530	13,907
State and local income taxes	526	127	453	677	1,903	808	1,110	3,362
Other taxes	132	80	137	189	289	297	244	317
GIFTS FOR PEOPLE IN OTHER HOUSEHOLDS	1,116	573	1,076	1,336	2,973	1,817	2,311	4,410

Note: Spending by category does not add to total spending because gift spending is also included in the preceding product and service categories and personal taxes are not included in the total.
Source: Bureau of Labor Statistics, 2012 Consumer Expenditure Survey, Internet site http://www.bls.gov/cex/

Table 9.9 Indexed Spending by High-Income Households, 2012

(indexed average annual spending of consumer units by product and service category and before-tax income of consumer unit reference person, 2012; index definition: an index of 100 is the average for all consumer units; an index of 125 means that spending by consumer units in that group is 25 percent above the average for all consumer units; an index of 75 indicates spending that is 25 percent below the average for all consumer units)

	total consumer units	less than $70,000	$70,000–$79,999	$80,000–$99,999	$100,000 or more total	$100,000–$119,999	$120,000–$149,999	$150,000 or more
Average spending of consumer units	$51,442	$34,679	$59,984	$67,418	$101,423	$77,966	$89,521	$129,211
Indexed spending of consumer units	100	67	117	131	197	152	174	251
FOOD	100	73	125	131	175	145	171	203
Food at home	100	80	126	124	155	135	153	173
Cereals and bakery products	100	81	124	123	151	134	148	169
Cereals and cereal products	100	80	129	125	152	140	149	163
Bakery products	100	81	122	122	151	131	148	172
Meats, poultry, fish, and eggs	100	81	126	127	148	132	141	168
Beef	100	81	120	126	154	142	123	188
Pork	100	84	131	128	136	123	132	150
Other meats	100	82	128	119	150	124	146	176
Poultry	100	82	131	126	145	121	167	150
Fish and seafood	100	75	125	145	163	151	153	180
Eggs	100	87	121	115	136	128	138	143
Dairy products	100	77	129	127	161	139	156	183
Fresh milk and cream	100	84	127	122	141	128	135	159
Other dairy products	100	74	131	130	171	145	168	197
Fruits and vegetables	100	79	120	124	161	135	160	184
Fresh fruits	100	75	117	128	173	139	175	201
Fresh vegetables	100	79	119	121	163	130	164	192
Processed fruits	100	80	132	124	152	132	145	174
Processed vegetables	100	84	119	123	142	138	139	147
Other food at home	100	80	129	121	155	135	158	169
Sugar and other sweets	100	80	133	113	156	135	154	176
Fats and oils	100	84	124	112	143	133	158	141
Miscellaneous foods	100	79	125	124	157	136	162	171
Nonalcoholic beverages	100	82	136	117	145	129	147	157
Food prepared by consumer unit on trips	100	56	136	158	222	174	190	282
Food away from home	100	64	123	140	204	161	197	246
ALCOHOLIC BEVERAGES	100	62	129	146	208	163	199	253
HOUSING	100	74	109	125	179	139	162	224
Shelter	100	74	106	124	179	139	160	225
Owned dwellings	100	57	111	147	229	176	208	288
Mortgage interest and charges	100	51	118	162	241	193	219	295
Property taxes	100	59	109	135	228	170	199	295
Maintenance, repair, insurance, other expenses	100	68	96	127	203	141	193	258
Rented dwellings	100	114	96	85	59	65	55	57
Other lodging	100	42	100	107	303	165	231	467
Utilities, fuels, and public services	100	83	114	121	147	131	141	164
Natural gas	100	78	117	121	163	137	154	191
Electricity	100	87	111	114	136	124	129	152
Fuel oil and other fuels	100	74	88	129	180	147	153	226
Telephone services	100	81	117	128	148	133	149	159
Water and other public services	100	80	118	123	156	140	146	175

	total consumer units	less than $70,000	$70,000–$79,999	$80,000–$99,999	$100,000 or more			
					total	$100,000–$119,999	$120,000–$149,999	$150,000 or more
Household services	100	59	103	125	233	149	198	324
Personal services	100	45	120	141	271	170	259	358
Other household services	100	66	95	118	215	140	170	308
Housekeeping supplies	100	74	138	129	167	137	162	198
Laundry and cleaning supplies	100	81	148	135	140	114	152	154
Other household products	100	72	137	127	177	143	164	216
Postage and stationery	100	73	129	128	176	151	168	206
Household furnishings and equipment	100	62	116	131	215	143	193	293
Household textiles	100	62	163	152	193	107	188	272
Furniture	100	60	82	124	237	163	173	344
Floor coverings	100	50	69	100	306	163	213	488
Major appliances	100	65	124	145	197	129	201	248
Small appliances, miscellaneous housewares	100	63	208	130	183	116	188	236
Miscellaneous household equipment	100	63	113	129	215	145	203	285
APPAREL AND RELATED SERVICES	100	66	127	138	196	145	183	249
Men and boys	100	61	133	155	207	150	205	256
Men, aged 16 or older	100	58	137	166	212	151	214	262
Boys, aged 2 to 15	100	72	119	118	189	149	173	235
Women and girls	100	68	131	138	191	152	178	234
Women, aged 16 or older	100	67	136	139	191	154	182	232
Girls, aged 2 to 15	100	72	108	134	186	141	161	244
Children under age 2	100	81	103	152	146	111	127	190
Footwear	100	73	131	125	176	129	178	217
Other apparel products and services	100	59	105	121	234	145	184	343
TRANSPORTATION	100	68	129	144	184	165	166	214
Vehicle purchases	100	61	133	165	198	191	160	231
Cars and trucks, new	100	54	138	171	220	213	183	254
Cars and trucks, used	100	71	124	160	170	162	138	200
Gasoline and motor oil	100	77	125	139	156	150	158	160
Other vehicle expenses	100	71	136	129	180	152	170	211
Vehicle finance charges	100	62	150	169	190	189	188	191
Maintenance and repairs	100	73	112	126	181	143	173	218
Vehicle insurance	100	76	165	118	158	153	151	169
Vehicle rentals, leases, licenses, other charges	100	59	105	138	225	146	200	306
Public transportation	100	52	94	118	265	147	215	396
HEALTH CARE	100	77	117	128	164	148	153	185
Health insurance	100	79	120	131	156	141	151	171
Medical services	100	69	114	129	192	178	167	221
Drugs	100	85	105	111	145	129	138	164
Medical supplies	100	68	137	123	195	145	159	263
ENTERTAINMENT	100	64	119	123	214	151	187	286
Fees and admissions	100	43	112	121	289	178	218	432
Audio and visual equipment and services	100	78	118	121	163	132	155	194
Pets, toys, hobbies, and playground equipment	100	69	127	133	188	128	181	245
Other entertainment products and services	100	48	124	113	272	199	232	362
PERSONAL CARE PRODUCTS AND SERVICES	100	66	143	131	193	167	177	226
READING	100	66	129	136	198	149	187	245
EDUCATION	100	46	87	102	295	159	204	471
TOBACCO PRODUCTS AND SMOKING SUPPLIES	100	104	116	108	78	94	75	68

	total consumer units	less than $70,000	$70,000–$79,999	$80,000–$99,999	$100,000 or more			
					total	$100,000–$119,999	$120,000–$149,999	$150,000 or more
MISCELLANEOUS	100	71	96	114	199	158	168	254
CASH CONTRIBUTIONS	100	60	98	124	231	140	167	351
PERSONAL INSURANCE AND PENSIONS	100	41	116	146	286	183	232	408
Life and other personal insurance	100	48	104	138	266	151	187	416
Pensions and Social Security	100	40	117	146	288	185	235	408
PERSONAL TAXES	100	9	87	120	421	147	219	790
Federal income taxes	100	–1	85	115	458	138	225	887
State and local income taxes	100	24	86	129	362	154	211	639
Other taxes	100	61	104	143	219	225	185	240
GIFTS FOR PEOPLE IN OTHER HOUSEHOLDS	100	51	96	120	266	163	207	395

Source: Calculations by New Strategist based on the Bureau of Labor Statistics 2012 Consumer Expenditure Survey, Internet site http://www.bls.gov/cex/home.htm

Table 9.10 Market Shares of High-Income Households, 2012

(share of total household spending accounted for by income groups, 2012)

	total consumer units	less than $70,000	$70,000–$79,999	$80,000–$99,999	$100,000 or more total	$100,000–$119,999	$120,000–$149,999	$150,000 or more
Share of total consumer units	100.0%	66.9%	5.6%	8.8%	18.7%	5.8%	5.6%	7.4%
Share of total spending	100.0	45.1	6.5	11.6	36.9	8.8	9.7	18.5
FOOD	100.0	49.1	7.0	11.5	32.7	8.4	9.6	14.9
Food at home	100.0	53.3	7.0	10.9	28.9	7.8	8.5	12.8
Cereals and bakery products	100.0	54.1	6.9	10.9	28.3	7.7	8.3	12.4
Cereals and cereal products	100.0	53.6	7.2	11.1	28.4	8.1	8.3	12.0
Bakery products	100.0	54.3	6.8	10.8	28.3	7.5	8.3	12.7
Meats, poultry, fish, and eggs	100.0	54.2	7.0	11.2	27.8	7.6	7.9	12.4
Beef	100.0	53.9	6.7	11.1	28.7	8.2	6.8	13.8
Pork	100.0	56.0	7.3	11.3	25.5	7.1	7.4	11.0
Other meats	100.0	54.8	7.1	10.5	28.1	7.1	8.1	13.0
Poultry	100.0	54.7	7.3	11.1	27.2	7.0	9.3	11.1
Fish and seafood	100.0	49.9	7.0	12.8	30.5	8.7	8.6	13.3
Eggs	100.0	58.0	6.7	10.2	25.4	7.4	7.7	10.6
Dairy products	100.0	51.7	7.2	11.2	30.1	8.0	8.7	13.5
Fresh milk and cream	100.0	55.9	7.1	10.7	26.5	7.4	7.5	11.7
Other dairy products	100.0	49.6	7.3	11.5	32.0	8.4	9.4	14.5
Fruits and vegetables	100.0	52.5	6.7	10.9	30.1	7.8	9.0	13.6
Fresh fruits	100.0	50.2	6.5	11.3	32.4	8.0	9.8	14.8
Fresh vegetables	100.0	52.7	6.6	10.7	30.5	7.5	9.1	14.1
Processed fruits	100.0	53.4	7.3	10.9	28.4	7.6	8.1	12.8
Processed vegetables	100.0	56.1	6.7	10.9	26.5	7.9	7.8	10.8
Other food at home	100.0	53.3	7.2	10.7	29.0	7.8	8.8	12.5
Sugar and other sweets	100.0	53.2	7.4	10.0	29.2	7.8	8.6	12.9
Fats and oils	100.0	56.3	6.9	9.9	26.8	7.7	8.8	10.4
Miscellaneous foods	100.0	53.0	7.0	11.0	29.3	7.9	9.0	12.6
Nonalcoholic beverages	100.0	55.1	7.6	10.3	27.1	7.5	8.2	11.5
Food prepared by consumer unit on trips	100.0	37.4	7.6	13.9	41.6	10.0	10.6	20.8
Food away from home	100.0	42.9	6.9	12.3	38.2	9.3	11.0	18.1
ALCOHOLIC BEVERAGES	100.0	41.4	7.2	12.9	38.9	9.4	11.1	18.6
HOUSING	100.0	49.4	6.1	11.0	33.5	8.0	9.0	16.5
Shelter	100.0	49.5	5.9	11.0	33.6	8.1	8.9	16.6
Owned dwellings	100.0	37.9	6.2	12.9	43.0	10.2	11.6	21.2
Mortgage interest and charges	100.0	34.1	6.6	14.3	45.0	11.1	12.2	21.7
Property taxes	100.0	39.3	6.1	11.9	42.7	9.8	11.1	21.7
Maintenance, repair, insurance, other expenses	100.0	45.6	5.3	11.2	37.9	8.1	10.8	19.0
Rented dwellings	100.0	76.1	5.4	7.5	11.1	3.8	3.1	4.2
Other lodging	100.0	28.0	5.6	9.5	56.8	9.5	12.9	34.4
Utilities, fuels, and public services	100.0	55.4	6.3	10.7	27.6	7.6	7.9	12.1
Natural gas	100.0	52.3	6.5	10.7	30.6	7.9	8.6	14.1
Electricity	100.0	58.2	6.2	10.0	25.5	7.2	7.2	11.2
Fuel oil and other fuels	100.0	49.8	4.9	11.4	33.6	8.5	8.6	16.6
Telephone services	100.0	54.4	6.5	11.3	27.7	7.7	8.3	11.7
Water and other public services	100.0	53.4	6.6	10.9	29.1	8.1	8.2	12.9

	total consumer units	less than $70,000	$70,000– $79,999	$80,000– $99,999	$100,000 or more			
					total	$100,000– $119,999	$120,000– $149,999	$150,000 or more
Household services	100.0%	39.6%	5.8%	11.1%	43.5%	8.6%	11.1%	23.9%
Personal services	100.0	30.3	6.7	12.4	50.7	9.8	14.5	26.4
Other household services	100.0	44.0	5.3	10.4	40.2	8.1	9.5	22.7
Housekeeping supplies	100.0	49.8	7.7	11.4	31.3	7.9	9.0	14.6
Laundry and cleaning supplies	100.0	53.9	8.2	12.0	26.2	6.6	8.5	11.3
Other household products	100.0	48.2	7.6	11.2	33.1	8.2	9.2	15.9
Postage and stationery	100.0	48.7	7.2	11.3	33.0	8.7	9.4	15.2
Household furnishings and equipment	100.0	41.7	6.5	11.6	40.3	8.2	10.8	21.6
Household textiles	100.0	41.3	9.1	13.4	36.2	6.2	10.5	20.1
Furniture	100.0	40.2	4.6	10.9	44.3	9.4	9.7	25.3
Floor coverings	100.0	33.4	3.8	8.8	57.3	9.4	11.9	35.9
Major appliances	100.0	43.5	6.9	12.8	36.9	7.4	11.2	18.2
Small appliances, miscellaneous housewares	100.0	42.3	11.6	11.4	34.2	6.7	10.5	17.4
Miscellaneous household equipment	100.0	42.3	6.3	11.4	40.3	8.3	11.3	21.0
APPAREL AND RELATED SERVICES	100.0	44.4	7.1	12.2	36.7	8.3	10.2	18.3
Men and boys	100.0	40.5	7.4	13.7	38.7	8.7	11.4	18.9
Men, aged 16 or older	100.0	38.7	7.6	14.6	39.7	8.7	11.9	19.3
Boys, aged 2 to 15	100.0	47.9	6.7	10.4	35.3	8.6	9.6	17.3
Women and girls	100.0	45.2	7.3	12.2	35.7	8.8	10.0	17.2
Women, aged 16 or older	100.0	44.6	7.6	12.2	35.8	8.9	10.1	17.1
Girls, aged 2 to 15	100.0	47.8	6.0	11.8	34.9	8.1	9.0	18.0
Children under age 2	100.0	54.1	5.8	13.4	27.3	6.4	7.1	14.0
Footwear	100.0	48.9	7.3	11.1	33.0	7.4	9.9	16.0
Other apparel products and services	100.0	39.3	5.9	10.7	43.9	8.4	10.3	25.2
TRANSPORTATION	100.0	45.6	7.2	12.7	34.5	9.5	9.3	15.7
Vehicle purchases	100.0	41.1	7.4	14.5	37.0	11.0	9.0	17.0
Cars and trucks, new	100.0	35.9	7.7	15.1	41.3	12.3	10.2	18.7
Cars and trucks, used	100.0	47.2	6.9	14.1	31.8	9.4	7.7	14.7
Gasoline and motor oil	100.0	51.5	7.0	12.3	29.3	8.7	8.8	11.8
Other vehicle expenses	100.0	47.3	7.6	11.3	33.7	8.8	9.5	15.5
Vehicle finance charges	100.0	41.4	8.4	14.9	35.5	10.9	10.5	14.1
Maintenance and repairs	100.0	48.8	6.3	11.1	34.0	8.3	9.7	16.1
Vehicle insurance	100.0	50.8	9.2	10.4	29.6	8.8	8.4	12.4
Vehicle rentals, leases, licenses, other charges	100.0	39.8	5.9	12.2	42.1	8.4	11.2	22.6
Public transportation	100.0	34.8	5.3	10.4	49.6	8.5	12.0	29.1
HEALTH CARE	100.0	51.5	6.5	11.3	30.8	8.6	8.6	13.7
Health insurance	100.0	52.6	6.7	11.6	29.2	8.2	8.4	12.6
Medical services	100.0	46.3	6.4	11.4	35.9	10.3	9.3	16.2
Drugs	100.0	57.1	5.9	9.8	27.2	7.5	7.7	12.1
Medical supplies	100.0	45.7	7.6	10.9	36.5	8.4	8.9	19.3
ENTERTAINMENT	100.0	42.5	6.7	10.8	40.1	8.7	10.4	21.1
Fees and admissions	100.0	29.1	6.3	10.6	54.1	10.3	12.2	31.8
Audio and visual equipment and services	100.0	52.3	6.6	10.7	30.5	7.6	8.7	14.3
Pets, toys, hobbies, and playground equipment	100.0	46.2	7.1	11.8	35.2	7.4	10.1	18.0
Other entertainment products and services	100.0	32.4	6.9	10.0	51.0	11.5	13.0	26.7
PERSONAL CARE PRODUCTS AND SERVICES	100.0	44.4	8.0	11.5	36.2	9.6	9.9	16.7
READING	100.0	44.2	7.2	12.0	37.1	8.6	10.5	18.0
EDUCATION	100.0	31.0	4.8	9.0	55.2	9.2	11.4	34.7
TOBACCO PRODUCTS AND SMOKING SUPPLIES	100.0	69.3	6.5	9.5	14.6	5.4	4.2	5.0

	total consumer units	less than $70,000	$70,000–$79,999	$80,000–$99,999	$100,000 or more			
					total	$100,000–$119,999	$120,000–$149,999	$150,000 or more
MISCELLANEOUS	**100.0%**	**47.4%**	**5.3%**	**10.1%**	**37.2%**	**9.1%**	**9.4%**	**18.7%**
CASH CONTRIBUTIONS	**100.0**	**40.2**	**5.5**	**11.0**	**43.3**	**8.1**	**9.3**	**25.9**
PERSONAL INSURANCE AND PENSIONS	**100.0**	**27.1**	**6.5**	**12.8**	**53.6**	**10.6**	**13.0**	**30.1**
Life and other personal insurance	100.0	32.2	5.8	12.2	49.7	8.7	10.4	30.6
Pensions and Social Security	100.0	26.8	6.5	12.9	53.8	10.7	13.1	30.0
PERSONAL TAXES	**100.0**	**5.7**	**4.8**	**10.5**	**78.9**	**8.5**	**12.2**	**58.2**
Federal income taxes	100.0	–0.7	4.8	10.1	85.8	7.9	12.6	65.3
State and local income taxes	100.0	16.1	4.8	11.4	67.7	8.9	11.8	47.1
Other taxes	100.0	40.5	5.8	12.6	41.0	13.0	10.3	17.7
GIFTS FOR PEOPLE IN OTHER HOUSEHOLDS	**100.0**	**34.3**	**5.4**	**10.6**	**49.9**	**9.4**	**11.6**	**29.1**

Source: Calculations by New Strategist based on the Bureau of Labor Statistics 2012 Consumer Expenditure Survey, Internet site http://www.bls.gov/cex/home.htm

Couples with Children Spend the Most

Married couples with children at home spend 42 percent more than the average household.

Married couples with children spend much more than average because they have the highest incomes and the largest households. In 2012, couples with kids spent an average of $72,814 versus the $51,442 spent by the average household, according to the Bureau of Labor Statistics' Consumer Expenditure Survey.

Married couples without children at home spend 19 percent more than average. These are empty-nesters whose grown children live elsewhere or young couples who do not yet have children. Single-parent households spent an average of $38,667 in 2012, and single-person households spent the least—just $30,716.

The Indexed Spending table shows spending by household type in comparison with what the average household spends. An index of 100 means the household type spends an average amount on the item. An index above 100 means the household type spends more than average on the item, while an index below 100 reveals below-average spending.

A look at table 9.12 shows that spending is well below average for single-parent and single-person households, although single-parent households spend close to the average on most foods. Single-parent households spend 85 percent more than the average (with an index of 185) on household personal services,

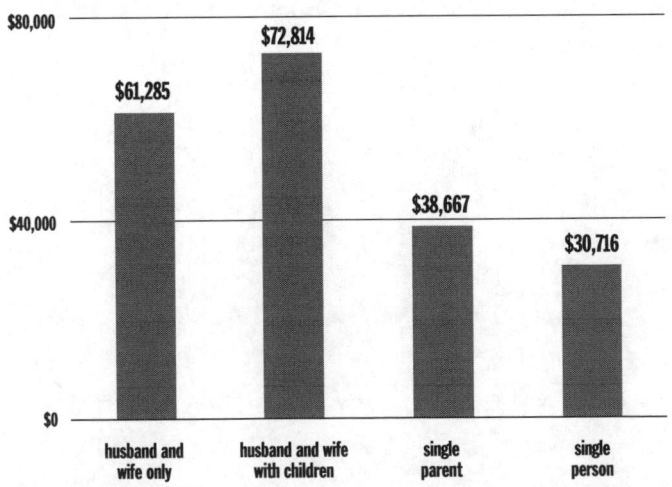

Spending is below average for single parents

(average annual spending of consumer units by type, 2012)

most of which is day care expenses. Married couples without children at home spend more than average on many items. But they spend less than average on items such as household personal services (day care), children's clothing, and education.

The Market Share table shows how much of total spending by category is accounted for by each household type. Married couples with children account for 24 percent of households and 33 percent of household spending. Single-person households account for 30 percent of households but only 18 percent of spending.

Married couples with children at home account for more than half of all household spending on some items such as household personal services (day care) and children's clothing. Married couples without children at home, who represent 21 percent of households, account for 39 percent of spending on "other" lodging (hotels and motels), 31 percent of spending on public transportation (mostly airline fares), 34 percent of spending on drugs, and 35 percent of spending on gifts for people in other households. Single parents, who represent 5 percent of households, account for less than 10 percent of spending on all but children's clothing. Single-person households account for a larger than average share of spending on rent, among other things.

■ The spending of married couples without children at home is likely to grow in the years ahead as two-income baby-boom couples postpone retirement.

Table 9.11 Average Spending by Household Type, 2012

(average annual spending of consumer units by product and service category and type of consumer unit [CU], 2012)

	total consumer units	total married couples	married couples, no children	married couples with children total	oldest child under 6	oldest child 6 to 17	oldest child 18 or older	single parent, at least one child under 18	single person
Number of consumer units (in 000s)	124,416	60,428	25,936	29,252	5,676	14,797	8,778	6,524	36,942
Average number of persons per CU	2.5	3.2	2.0	3.9	3.5	4.2	3.9	2.9	1.0
Average annual spending	**$51,442**	**$67,310**	**$61,285**	**$72,814**	**$64,103**	**$74,659**	**$75,286**	**$38,667**	**$30,716**
FOOD	**6,599**	**8,615**	**7,463**	**9,611**	**7,331**	**10,458**	**9,626**	**5,895**	**3,497**
Food at home	3,921	5,089	4,263	5,742	4,452	6,095	5,958	3,673	1,964
Cereals and bakery products	538	698	559	803	623	878	789	515	270
Cereals and cereal products	182	234	175	278	206	310	269	182	84
Bakery products	356	464	383	525	417	567	521	333	186
Meats, poultry, fish, and eggs	852	1,095	922	1,213	830	1,302	1,304	802	392
Beef	226	292	240	323	188	339	380	194	92
Pork	166	211	179	234	168	251	245	170	77
Other meats	122	160	130	184	141	195	192	121	61
Poultry	159	200	160	228	180	243	233	166	77
Fish and seafood	126	166	158	173	100	198	175	100	56
Eggs	53	66	56	72	52	76	79	51	29
Dairy products	419	561	448	656	570	693	647	353	207
Fresh milk and cream	152	198	146	240	225	248	237	145	75
Other dairy products	267	362	302	416	346	445	410	207	131
Fruits and vegetables	731	953	825	1,060	858	1,100	1,118	676	384
Fresh fruits	261	347	297	395	326	409	415	252	134
Fresh vegetables	226	298	272	317	260	330	332	177	118
Processed fruits	114	147	122	167	142	176	167	111	64
Processed vegetables	130	161	134	181	130	186	204	137	67
Other food at home	1,380	1,781	1,509	2,011	1,571	2,122	2,099	1,327	711
Sugar and other sweets	147	193	168	214	140	244	208	133	75
Fats and oils	114	145	121	163	122	167	180	109	58
Miscellaneous foods	699	906	735	1,066	929	1,108	1,081	699	354
Nonalcoholic beverages	370	462	397	502	334	525	570	361	200
Food prepared by consumer unit on trips	50	74	89	66	45	78	59	26	24
Food away from home	2,678	3,526	3,200	3,869	2,879	4,363	3,668	2,222	1,533
ALCOHOLIC BEVERAGES	**451**	**553**	**670**	**475**	**503**	**502**	**411**	**175**	**344**
HOUSING	**16,887**	**20,771**	**18,258**	**22,980**	**23,621**	**23,432**	**21,803**	**14,593**	**11,532**
Shelter	9,891	11,739	10,213	13,149	13,106	13,616	12,389	8,586	7,437
Owned dwellings	6,056	8,493	7,284	9,641	8,851	10,036	9,486	3,505	3,412
Mortgage interest and charges	3,067	4,460	3,144	5,599	5,686	5,930	4,985	2,256	1,348
Property taxes	1,836	2,583	2,504	2,725	2,270	2,765	2,951	840	1,123
Maintenance, repair, insurance, other expenses	1,153	1,450	1,637	1,318	895	1,341	1,551	409	941
Rented dwellings	3,186	2,220	1,712	2,568	3,751	2,619	1,717	4,872	3,715
Other lodging	649	1,025	1,217	940	504	961	1,186	209	311
Utilities, fuels, and public services	**3,648**	**4,487**	**3,997**	**4,752**	**3,867**	**4,797**	**5,250**	**3,298**	**2,291**
Natural gas	359	443	387	484	386	487	541	309	229
Electricity	1,388	1,676	1,521	1,738	1,449	1,772	1,867	1,345	903
Fuel oil and other fuels	137	176	187	159	138	153	182	76	98
Telephone services	1,239	1,528	1,291	1,687	1,373	1,695	1,875	1,151	736
Water and other public services	525	663	611	685	521	689	784	417	326

	total consumer units	total married couples	married couples, no children	married couples with children				single parent, at least one child under 18	single person
				total	oldest child under 6	oldest child 6 to 17	oldest child 18 or older		
Household services	$1,159	$1,562	$1,106	$2,004	$3,891	$1,785	$1,151	$1,244	$640
Personal services	368	567	93	986	3,013	756	63	679	76
Other household services	791	995	1,013	1,017	878	1,029	1,088	564	564
Housekeeping supplies	610	815	772	856	713	925	829	477	316
Laundry and cleaning supplies	155	197	165	218	182	226	226	150	81
Other household products	319	435	424	447	351	494	427	224	160
Postage and stationery	136	184	183	192	180	205	177	103	75
Household furnishings and equipment	1,580	2,169	2,170	2,220	2,044	2,309	2,183	989	848
Household textiles	123	182	197	176	153	183	178	66	67
Furniture	391	522	427	609	553	668	545	298	229
Floor coverings	16	25	21	29	47	22	29	7	7
Major appliances	197	279	254	290	249	301	297	145	100
Small appliances, miscellaneous housewares	98	131	150	124	124	123	124	44	59
Miscellaneous household equipment	754	1,030	1,121	992	918	1,011	1,010	429	386
APPAREL AND RELATED SERVICES	1,736	2,235	1,760	2,685	2,450	2,870	2,523	2,113	865
Men and boys	408	526	382	668	424	740	701	467	212
Men, aged 16 or older	320	397	353	451	299	408	618	265	198
Boys, aged 2 to 15	88	129	29	217	125	332	83	202	13
Women and girls	688	894	766	1,021	859	1,136	931	837	336
Women, aged 16 or older	573	729	707	758	696	740	828	502	322
Girls, aged 2 to 15	116	164	59	263	164	396	103	335	14
Children under age 2	63	88	24	144	488	82	31	133	8
Footwear	347	448	326	570	425	615	586	528	145
Other apparel products and services	230	279	262	282	254	297	273	148	164
TRANSPORTATION	8,998	12,163	11,254	12,786	10,925	12,522	14,424	6,353	4,599
Vehicle purchases	3,210	4,594	4,355	4,732	4,357	4,523	5,328	2,104	1,377
Cars and trucks, new	1,639	2,554	2,804	2,413	2,322	2,149	2,919	804	653
Cars and trucks, used	1,516	1,969	1,490	2,246	2,026	2,268	2,351	1,279	713
Gasoline and motor oil	2,756	3,599	3,023	3,999	3,283	4,038	4,397	2,231	1,420
Other vehicle expenses	2,490	3,214	3,058	3,322	2,710	3,205	3,903	1,767	1,472
Vehicle finance charges	223	314	240	362	402	362	337	166	92
Maintenance and repairs	814	1,040	938	1,136	900	1,156	1,256	587	525
Vehicle insurance	1,018	1,270	1,326	1,201	841	1,086	1,617	744	600
Vehicle rentals, leases, licenses, other charges	434	590	555	622	568	602	692	270	255
Public transportation	542	757	818	733	575	756	796	251	330
HEALTH CARE	3,556	4,828	5,407	4,310	3,381	4,167	5,150	1,704	2,339
Health insurance	2,061	2,860	3,251	2,518	2,119	2,439	2,909	924	1,269
Medical services	839	1,095	1,119	1,071	875	1,026	1,275	432	622
Drugs	515	682	845	526	270	513	712	278	359
Medical supplies	142	191	192	195	118	190	254	70	90
ENTERTAINMENT	2,605	3,554	3,228	3,948	3,023	4,530	3,563	1,846	1,485
Fees and admissions	614	915	728	1,156	648	1,536	842	425	300
Audio and visual equipment and services	979	1,190	1,129	1,248	1,067	1,340	1,210	856	675
Pets, toys, hobbies, and playground equipment	648	878	839	923	772	1,040	823	374	369
Other entertainment products and services	363	572	532	622	536	614	689	191	140
PERSONAL CARE PRODUCTS AND SERVICES	628	804	781	835	678	908	812	518	380
READING	109	145	172	126	96	125	148	50	83
EDUCATION	1,207	1,706	985	2,417	793	2,240	3,767	846	675
TOBACCO PRODUCTS AND SMOKING SUPPLIES	332	314	282	317	236	299	401	248	251

	total consumer units	total married couples	married couples, no children	married couples with children				single parent, at least one child under 18	single person
				total	oldest child under 6	oldest child 6 to 17	oldest child 18 or older		
MISCELLANEOUS	$829	$954	$987	$950	$936	$956	$948	$946	$647
CASH CONTRIBUTIONS	1,913	2,550	3,117	2,078	1,705	1,955	2,528	720	1,484
PERSONAL INSURANCE AND PENSIONS	5,591	8,117	6,919	9,295	8,426	9,695	9,184	2,660	2,535
Life and other personal insurance	353	554	627	505	460	501	540	142	154
Pensions and Social Security	5,238	7,562	6,291	8,790	7,966	9,194	8,643	2,518	2,382
PERSONAL TAXES	2,226	2,886	3,297	2,716	2,563	2,669	2,895	–281	1,546
Federal income taxes	1,568	2,012	2,411	1,813	1,753	1,726	1,997	–516	1,114
State and local income taxes	526	691	669	741	667	778	728	154	346
Other taxes	132	183	217	162	144	165	170	81	86
GIFTS FOR PEOPLE IN OTHER HOUSEHOLDS	1,116	1,498	1,893	1,245	517	1,247	1,711	703	825

Note: Spending by category does not add to total spending because gift spending is also included in the preceding product and service categories and personal taxes are not included in the total.
Source: Bureau of Labor Statistics, 2012 Consumer Expenditure Survey, Internet site http://www.bls.gov/cex/; calculations by New Strategist

Table 9.12 Indexed Spending by Household Type, 2012

(indexed average annual spending of consumer units by product and service category and type of consumer unit, 2012; index definition: an index of 100 is the average for all consumer units; an index of 125 means that spending by consumer units in that group is 25 percent above the average for all consumer units; an index of 75 indicates spending that is 25 percent below the average for all consumer units)

	total consumer units	total married couples	married couples, no children	married couples with children total	oldest child under 6	oldest child 6 to 17	oldest child 18 or older	single parent, at least one child under 18	single person
Average spending of consumer units	$51,442	$67,310	$61,285	$72,814	$64,103	$74,659	$75,286	$38,667	$30,716
Indexed spending of consumer units	100	131	119	142	125	145	146	75	60
FOOD	100	131	113	146	111	158	146	89	53
Food at home	100	130	109	146	114	155	152	94	50
Cereals and bakery products	100	130	104	149	116	163	147	96	50
Cereals and cereal products	100	129	96	153	113	170	148	100	46
Bakery products	100	130	108	147	117	159	146	94	52
Meats, poultry, fish, and eggs	100	129	108	142	97	153	153	94	46
Beef	100	129	106	143	83	150	168	86	41
Pork	100	127	108	141	101	151	148	102	46
Other meats	100	131	107	151	116	160	157	99	50
Poultry	100	126	101	143	113	153	147	104	48
Fish and seafood	100	132	125	137	79	157	139	79	44
Eggs	100	125	106	136	98	143	149	96	55
Dairy products	100	134	107	157	136	165	154	84	49
Fresh milk and cream	100	130	96	158	148	163	156	95	49
Other dairy products	100	136	113	156	130	167	154	78	49
Fruits and vegetables	100	130	113	145	117	150	153	92	53
Fresh fruits	100	133	114	151	125	157	159	97	51
Fresh vegetables	100	132	120	140	115	146	147	78	52
Processed fruits	100	129	107	146	125	154	146	97	56
Processed vegetables	100	124	103	139	100	143	157	105	52
Other food at home	100	129	109	146	114	154	152	96	52
Sugar and other sweets	100	131	114	146	95	166	141	90	51
Fats and oils	100	127	106	143	107	146	158	96	51
Miscellaneous foods	100	130	105	153	133	159	155	100	51
Nonalcoholic beverages	100	125	107	136	90	142	154	98	54
Food prepared by consumer unit on trips	100	148	178	132	90	156	118	52	48
Food away from home	100	132	119	144	108	163	137	83	57
ALCOHOLIC BEVERAGES	100	123	149	105	112	111	91	39	76
HOUSING	100	123	108	136	140	139	129	86	68
Shelter	100	119	103	133	133	138	125	87	75
Owned dwellings	100	140	120	159	146	166	157	58	56
Mortgage interest and charges	100	145	103	183	185	193	163	74	44
Property taxes	100	141	136	148	124	151	161	46	61
Maintenance, repair, insurance, other expenses	100	126	142	114	78	116	135	35	82
Rented dwellings	100	70	54	81	118	82	54	153	117
Other lodging	100	158	188	145	78	148	183	32	48
Utilities, fuels, and public services	100	123	110	130	106	131	144	90	63
Natural gas	100	123	108	135	108	136	151	86	64
Electricity	100	121	110	125	104	128	135	97	65
Fuel oil and other fuels	100	128	136	116	101	112	133	55	72
Telephone services	100	123	104	136	111	137	151	93	59
Water and other public services	100	126	116	130	99	131	149	79	62

	total consumer units	total married couples	married couples, no children	married couples with children				single parent, at least one child under 18	single person
				total	oldest child under 6	oldest child 6 to 17	oldest child 18 or older		
Household services	100	135	95	173	336	154	99	107	55
Personal services	100	154	25	268	819	205	17	185	21
Other household services	100	126	128	129	111	130	138	71	71
Housekeeping supplies	100	134	127	140	117	152	136	78	52
Laundry and cleaning supplies	100	127	106	141	117	146	146	97	52
Other household products	100	136	133	140	110	155	134	70	50
Postage and stationery	100	135	135	141	132	151	130	76	55
Household furnishings and equipment	100	137	137	141	129	146	138	63	54
Household textiles	100	148	160	143	124	149	145	54	54
Furniture	100	134	109	156	141	171	139	76	59
Floor coverings	100	156	131	181	294	138	181	44	44
Major appliances	100	142	129	147	126	153	151	74	51
Small appliances, miscellaneous housewares	100	134	153	127	127	126	127	45	60
Miscellaneous household equipment	100	137	149	132	122	134	134	57	51
APPAREL AND RELATED SERVICES	100	129	101	155	141	165	145	122	50
Men and boys	100	129	94	164	104	181	172	114	52
Men, aged 16 or older	100	124	110	141	93	128	193	83	62
Boys, aged 2 to 15	100	147	33	247	142	377	94	230	15
Women and girls	100	130	111	148	125	165	135	122	49
Women, aged 16 or older	100	127	123	132	121	129	145	88	56
Girls, aged 2 to 15	100	141	51	227	141	341	89	289	12
Children under age 2	100	140	38	229	775	130	49	211	13
Footwear	100	129	94	164	122	177	169	152	42
Other apparel products and services	100	121	114	123	110	129	119	64	71
TRANSPORTATION	100	135	125	142	121	139	160	71	51
Vehicle purchases	100	143	136	147	136	141	166	66	43
Cars and trucks, new	100	156	171	147	142	131	178	49	40
Cars and trucks, used	100	130	98	148	134	150	155	84	47
Gasoline and motor oil	100	131	110	145	119	147	160	81	52
Other vehicle expenses	100	129	123	133	109	129	157	71	59
Vehicle finance charges	100	141	108	162	180	162	151	74	41
Maintenance and repairs	100	128	115	140	111	142	154	72	64
Vehicle insurance	100	125	130	118	83	107	159	73	59
Vehicle rentals, leases, licenses, other charges	100	136	128	143	131	139	159	62	59
Public transportation	100	140	151	135	106	139	147	46	61
HEALTH CARE	100	136	152	121	95	117	145	48	66
Health insurance	100	139	158	122	103	118	141	45	62
Medical services	100	131	133	128	104	122	152	51	74
Drugs	100	132	164	102	52	100	138	54	70
Medical supplies	100	135	135	137	83	134	179	49	63
ENTERTAINMENT	100	136	124	152	116	174	137	71	57
Fees and admissions	100	149	119	188	106	250	137	69	49
Audio and visual equipment and services	100	122	115	127	109	137	124	87	69
Pets, toys, hobbies, and playground equipment	100	135	129	142	119	160	127	58	57
Other entertainment products and services	100	158	147	171	148	169	190	53	39
PERSONAL CARE PRODUCTS AND SERVICES	100	128	124	133	108	145	129	82	61
READING	100	133	158	116	88	115	136	46	76
EDUCATION	100	141	82	200	66	186	312	70	56
TOBACCO PRODUCTS AND SMOKING SUPPLIES	100	95	85	95	71	90	121	75	76

	total consumer units	total married couples	married couples, no children	married couples with children				single parent, at least one child under 18	single person
				total	oldest child under 6	oldest child 6 to 17	oldest child 18 or older		
MISCELLANEOUS	100	115	119	115	113	115	114	114	78
CASH CONTRIBUTIONS	100	133	163	109	89	102	132	38	78
PERSONAL INSURANCE AND PENSIONS	100	145	124	166	151	173	164	48	45
Life and other personal insurance	100	157	178	143	130	142	153	40	44
Pensions and Social Security	100	144	120	168	152	176	165	48	45
PERSONAL TAXES	100	130	148	122	115	120	130	–13	69
Federal income taxes	100	128	154	116	112	110	127	–33	71
State and local income taxes	100	131	127	141	127	148	138	29	66
Other taxes	100	139	164	123	109	125	129	61	65
GIFTS FOR PEOPLE IN OTHER HOUSEHOLDS	100	134	170	112	46	112	153	63	74

Source: Calculations by New Strategist based on the Bureau of Labor Statistics 2012 Consumer Expenditure Survey, Internet site http://www.bls.gov/cex/home.htm

Table 9.13 Market Shares by Household Type, 2012

(share of total household spending accounted for by household type, 2012)

	total consumer units	total married couples	married couples, no children	married couples with children total	oldest child under 6	oldest child 6 to 17	oldest child 18 or older	single parent, at least one child under 18	single person
Share of total consumer units	100.0%	48.6%	20.8%	23.5%	4.6%	11.9%	7.1%	5.2%	29.7%
Share of total spending	100.0	63.6	24.8	33.3	5.7	17.3	10.3	3.9	17.7
FOOD	100.0	63.4	23.6	34.2	5.1	18.8	10.3	4.7	15.7
Food at home	100.0	63.0	22.7	34.4	5.2	18.5	10.7	4.9	14.9
Cereals and bakery products	100.0	63.0	21.7	35.1	5.3	19.4	10.3	5.0	14.9
Cereals and cereal products	100.0	62.4	20.0	35.9	5.2	20.3	10.4	5.2	13.7
Bakery products	100.0	63.3	22.4	34.7	5.3	18.9	10.3	4.9	15.5
Meats, poultry, fish, and eggs	100.0	62.4	22.6	33.5	4.4	18.2	10.8	4.9	13.7
Beef	100.0	62.8	22.1	33.6	3.8	17.8	11.9	4.5	12.1
Pork	100.0	61.7	22.5	33.1	4.6	18.0	10.4	5.4	13.8
Other meats	100.0	63.7	22.2	35.5	5.3	19.0	11.1	5.2	14.8
Poultry	100.0	61.1	21.0	33.7	5.2	18.2	10.3	5.5	14.4
Fish and seafood	100.0	64.0	26.1	32.3	3.6	18.7	9.8	4.2	13.2
Eggs	100.0	60.5	22.0	31.9	4.5	17.1	10.5	5.0	16.2
Dairy products	100.0	65.0	22.3	36.8	6.2	19.7	10.9	4.4	14.7
Fresh milk and cream	100.0	63.3	20.0	37.1	6.8	19.4	11.0	5.0	14.7
Other dairy products	100.0	65.9	23.6	36.6	5.9	19.8	10.8	4.1	14.6
Fruits and vegetables	100.0	63.3	23.5	34.1	5.4	17.9	10.8	4.8	15.6
Fresh fruits	100.0	64.6	23.7	35.6	5.7	18.6	11.2	5.1	15.2
Fresh vegetables	100.0	64.0	25.1	33.0	5.2	17.4	10.4	4.1	15.5
Processed fruits	100.0	62.6	22.3	34.4	5.7	18.4	10.3	5.1	16.7
Processed vegetables	100.0	60.2	21.5	32.7	4.6	17.0	11.1	5.5	15.3
Other food at home	100.0	62.7	22.8	34.3	5.2	18.3	10.7	5.0	15.3
Sugar and other sweets	100.0	63.8	23.8	34.2	4.3	19.7	10.0	4.7	15.1
Fats and oils	100.0	61.8	22.1	33.6	4.9	17.4	11.1	5.0	15.1
Miscellaneous foods	100.0	63.0	21.9	35.9	6.1	18.9	10.9	5.2	15.0
Nonalcoholic beverages	100.0	60.6	22.4	31.9	4.1	16.9	10.9	5.1	16.0
Food prepared by consumer unit on trips	100.0	71.9	37.1	31.0	4.1	18.6	8.3	2.7	14.3
Food away from home	100.0	63.9	24.9	34.0	4.9	19.4	9.7	4.4	17.0
ALCOHOLIC BEVERAGES	100.0	59.6	31.0	24.8	5.1	13.2	6.4	2.0	22.6
HOUSING	100.0	59.7	22.5	32.0	6.4	16.5	9.1	4.5	20.3
Shelter	100.0	57.6	21.5	31.3	6.0	16.4	8.8	4.6	22.3
Owned dwellings	100.0	68.1	25.1	37.4	6.7	19.7	11.1	3.0	16.7
Mortgage interest and charges	100.0	70.6	21.4	42.9	8.5	23.0	11.5	3.9	13.1
Property taxes	100.0	68.3	28.4	34.9	5.6	17.9	11.3	2.4	18.2
Maintenance, repair, insurance, other expenses	100.0	61.1	29.6	26.9	3.5	13.8	9.5	1.9	24.2
Rented dwellings	100.0	33.8	11.2	19.0	5.4	9.8	3.8	8.0	34.6
Other lodging	100.0	76.7	39.1	34.1	3.5	17.6	12.9	1.7	14.2
Utilities, fuels, and public services	100.0	59.7	22.8	30.6	4.8	15.6	10.2	4.7	18.6
Natural gas	100.0	59.9	22.5	31.7	4.9	16.1	10.6	4.5	18.9
Electricity	100.0	58.6	22.8	29.4	4.8	15.2	9.5	5.1	19.3
Fuel oil and other fuels	100.0	62.4	28.5	27.3	4.6	13.3	9.4	2.9	21.2
Telephone services	100.0	59.9	21.7	32.0	5.1	16.3	10.7	4.9	17.6
Water and other public services	100.0	61.3	24.3	30.7	4.5	15.6	10.5	4.2	18.4

	total consumer units	total married couples	married couples, no children	married couples with children				single parent, at least one child under 18	single person
				total	oldest child under 6	oldest child 6 to 17	oldest child 18 or older		
Household services	**100.0%**	**65.5%**	**19.9%**	**40.7%**	**15.3%**	**18.3%**	**7.0%**	**5.6%**	**16.4%**
Personal services	100.0	74.8	5.3	63.0	37.4	24.4	1.2	9.7	6.1
Other household services	100.0	61.1	26.7	30.2	5.1	15.5	9.7	3.7	21.2
Housekeeping supplies	**100.0**	**64.9**	**26.4**	**33.0**	**5.3**	**18.0**	**9.6**	**4.1**	**15.4**
Laundry and cleaning supplies	100.0	61.7	22.2	33.1	5.4	17.3	10.3	5.1	15.5
Other household products	100.0	66.2	27.7	32.9	5.0	18.4	9.4	3.7	14.9
Postage and stationery	100.0	65.7	28.1	33.2	6.0	17.9	9.2	4.0	16.4
Household furnishings and equipment	**100.0**	**66.7**	**28.6**	**33.0**	**5.9**	**17.4**	**9.7**	**3.3**	**15.9**
Household textiles	100.0	71.9	33.4	33.6	5.7	17.7	10.2	2.8	16.2
Furniture	100.0	64.8	22.8	36.6	6.5	20.3	9.8	4.0	17.4
Floor coverings	100.0	75.9	27.4	42.6	13.4	16.4	12.8	2.3	13.0
Major appliances	100.0	68.8	26.9	34.6	5.8	18.2	10.6	3.9	15.1
Small appliances, miscellaneous housewares	100.0	64.9	31.9	29.7	5.8	14.9	8.9	2.4	17.9
Miscellaneous household equipment	100.0	66.3	31.0	30.9	5.6	15.9	9.5	3.0	15.2
APPAREL AND RELATED SERVICES	**100.0**	**62.5**	**21.1**	**36.4**	**6.4**	**19.7**	**10.3**	**6.4**	**14.8**
Men and boys	**100.0**	**62.6**	**19.5**	**38.5**	**4.7**	**21.6**	**12.1**	**6.0**	**15.4**
Men, aged 16 or older	100.0	60.3	23.0	33.1	4.3	15.2	13.6	4.3	18.4
Boys, aged 2 to 15	100.0	71.2	6.9	58.0	6.5	44.9	6.7	12.0	4.4
Women and girls	**100.0**	**63.1**	**23.2**	**34.9**	**5.7**	**19.6**	**9.5**	**6.4**	**14.5**
Women, aged 16 or older	100.0	61.8	25.7	31.1	5.5	15.4	10.2	4.6	16.7
Girls, aged 2 to 15	100.0	68.7	10.6	53.3	6.4	40.6	6.3	15.1	3.6
Children under age 2	**100.0**	**67.8**	**7.9**	**53.7**	**35.3**	**15.5**	**3.5**	**11.1**	**3.8**
Footwear	**100.0**	**62.7**	**19.6**	**38.6**	**5.6**	**21.1**	**11.9**	**8.0**	**12.4**
Other apparel products and services	**100.0**	**58.9**	**23.7**	**28.8**	**5.0**	**15.4**	**8.4**	**3.4**	**21.2**
TRANSPORTATION	**100.0**	**65.7**	**26.1**	**33.4**	**5.5**	**16.6**	**11.3**	**3.7**	**15.2**
Vehicle purchases	100.0	69.5	28.3	34.7	6.2	16.8	11.7	3.4	12.7
Cars and trucks, new	100.0	75.7	35.7	34.6	6.5	15.6	12.6	2.6	11.8
Cars and trucks, used	100.0	63.1	20.5	34.8	6.1	17.8	10.9	4.4	14.0
Gasoline and motor oil	**100.0**	**63.4**	**22.9**	**34.1**	**5.4**	**17.4**	**11.3**	**4.2**	**15.3**
Other vehicle expenses	**100.0**	**62.7**	**25.6**	**31.4**	**5.0**	**15.3**	**11.1**	**3.7**	**17.6**
Vehicle finance charges	100.0	68.4	22.4	38.2	8.2	19.3	10.7	3.9	12.2
Maintenance and repairs	100.0	62.1	24.0	32.8	5.0	16.9	10.9	3.8	19.2
Vehicle insurance	100.0	60.6	27.2	27.7	3.8	12.7	11.2	3.8	17.5
Vehicle rentals, leases, licenses, other charges	100.0	66.0	26.7	33.7	6.0	16.5	11.2	3.3	17.4
Public transportation	**100.0**	**67.8**	**31.5**	**31.8**	**4.8**	**16.6**	**10.4**	**2.4**	**18.1**
HEALTH CARE	**100.0**	**65.9**	**31.7**	**28.5**	**4.3**	**13.9**	**10.2**	**2.5**	**19.5**
Health insurance	100.0	67.4	32.9	28.7	4.7	14.1	10.0	2.4	18.3
Medical services	100.0	63.4	27.8	30.0	4.8	14.5	10.7	2.7	22.0
Drugs	100.0	64.3	34.2	24.0	2.4	11.8	9.8	2.8	20.7
Medical supplies	100.0	65.3	28.2	32.3	3.8	15.9	12.6	2.6	18.8
ENTERTAINMENT	**100.0**	**66.3**	**25.8**	**35.6**	**5.3**	**20.7**	**9.7**	**3.7**	**16.9**
Fees and admissions	100.0	72.4	24.7	44.3	4.8	29.8	9.7	3.6	14.5
Audio and visual equipment and services	100.0	59.0	24.0	30.0	5.0	16.3	8.7	4.6	20.5
Pets, toys, hobbies, and playground equipment	100.0	65.8	27.0	33.5	5.4	19.1	9.0	3.0	16.9
Other entertainment products and services	100.0	76.5	30.6	40.3	6.7	20.1	13.4	2.8	11.5
PERSONAL CARE PRODUCTS AND SERVICES	**100.0**	**62.2**	**25.9**	**31.3**	**4.9**	**17.2**	**9.1**	**4.3**	**18.0**
READING	**100.0**	**64.6**	**32.9**	**27.2**	**4.0**	**13.6**	**9.6**	**2.4**	**22.6**
EDUCATION	**100.0**	**68.6**	**17.0**	**47.1**	**3.0**	**22.1**	**22.0**	**3.7**	**16.6**
TOBACCO PRODUCTS AND SMOKING SUPPLIES	**100.0**	**45.9**	**17.7**	**22.4**	**3.2**	**10.7**	**8.5**	**3.9**	**22.4**

	total consumer units	total married couples	married couples, no children	married couples with children				single parent, at least one child under 18	single person
				total	oldest child under 6	oldest child 6 to 17	oldest child 18 or older		
MISCELLANEOUS	100.0%	55.9%	24.8%	26.9%	5.2%	13.7%	8.1%	6.0%	23.2%
CASH CONTRIBUTIONS	100.0	64.7	34.0	25.5	4.1	12.2	9.3	2.0	23.0
PERSONAL INSURANCE AND PENSIONS	100.0	70.5	25.8	39.1	6.9	20.6	11.6	2.5	13.5
Life and other personal insurance	100.0	76.2	37.0	33.6	5.9	16.9	10.8	2.1	13.0
Pensions and Social Security	100.0	70.1	25.0	39.5	6.9	20.9	11.6	2.5	13.5
PERSONAL TAXES	100.0	63.0	30.9	28.7	5.3	14.3	9.2	−0.7	20.6
Federal income taxes	100.0	62.3	32.1	27.2	5.1	13.1	9.0	−1.7	21.1
State and local income taxes	100.0	63.8	26.5	33.1	5.8	17.6	9.8	1.5	19.5
Other taxes	100.0	67.3	34.3	28.9	5.0	14.9	9.1	3.2	19.3
GIFTS FOR PEOPLE IN OTHER HOUSEHOLDS	100.0	65.2	35.4	26.2	2.1	13.3	10.8	3.3	21.9

Source: Calculations by New Strategist based on the Bureau of Labor Statistics 2012 Consumer Expenditure Survey, Internet site http://www.bls.gov/cex/home.htm

Asians Spend the Most

Blacks and Hispanics spend less than the average household.

Asian households have the highest incomes and they spend the most—an average of $61,399 in 2012, or 19 percent more than the average household. Non-Hispanic whites and others (a category that includes Asians and American Indians) spend 7 percent more than average. Hispanic households spent 18 percent less than average, and black households spent 25 percent less. There is great variation in spending by category, however.

The Indexed Spending table shows household spending for each racial and Hispanic origin group relative to what the average household spends. An index of 100 means households in the racial/Hispanic origin group spend an average amount on the item. An index above 100 means households in the racial/Hispanic origin group spend more than average on the item, while an index below 100 reveals below-average spending.

A look at table 9.15 shows below-average spending on most items by black and Hispanic households, close-to-average spending by non-Hispanic white households, and above-average spending by Asian households. There are some important exceptions, however. Black households spend more than average on some meats, children's clothes, and shoes. Hispanic households spend more than average on many foods and clothing, probably because their households are larger—3.3 people compared with 2.5 in the average household.

Spending of Asians surpasses spending of non-Hispanic whites

(average annual spending of consumer units by race and Hispanic origin of householder, 2012)

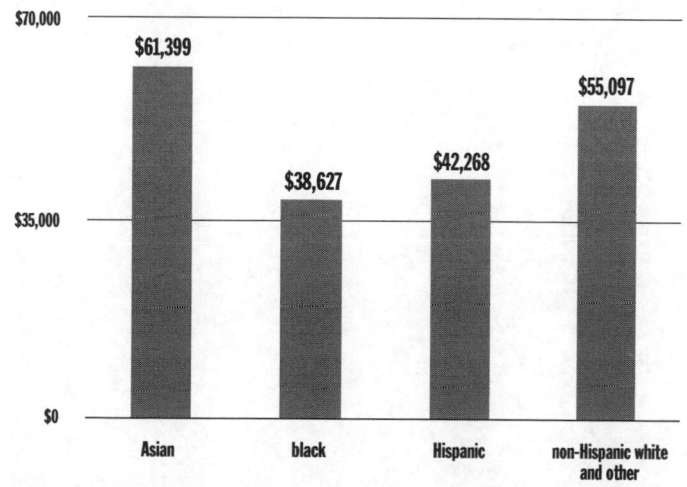

Asian households spend 35 percent more than the average household on food away from home. They spend nearly three times the average on public transportation—a category that includes airfares. They also spend nearly three times the average on education.

Because non-Hispanic whites are the majority, they dominate spending in most markets. But blacks and Hispanics together account for more than 30 percent of the market for poultry, rent, children's clothes, and shoes. Asians account for a single-digit share of the market in every product and service category except public transportation and education.

■ The spending of black households is below average because few are headed by married couples—the most-affluent household type. The spending of Hispanics is below average because many are recent immigrants with little education or earning power.

Table 9.14 Average Spending by Race and Hispanic Origin of Householder, 2012

(average annual spending of consumer units by product and service category and by race and Hispanic origin of consumer unit reference person, 2012)

	total consumer units	Asian	black	Hispanic	non-Hispanic white and other
Number of consumer units (in 000s)	124,416	5,393	15,637	15,597	93,385
Average number of persons per consumer unit	2.5	2.8	2.5	3.3	2.3
Average annual spending	**$51,442**	**$61,399**	**$38,627**	**$42,268**	**$55,097**
FOOD	**6,599**	**7,980**	**4,701**	**6,570**	**6,924**
Food at home	**3,921**	**4,367**	**2,973**	**4,116**	**4,050**
Cereals and bakery products	538	584	404	534	561
Cereals and cereal products	182	236	159	201	183
Bakery products	356	349	245	333	379
Meats, poultry, fish, and eggs	852	1,034	836	1,037	825
Beef	226	221	188	291	222
Pork	166	208	179	184	160
Other meats	122	94	97	120	127
Poultry	159	160	189	211	146
Fish and seafood	126	283	138	156	119
Eggs	53	70	45	75	51
Dairy products	419	372	254	427	446
Fresh milk and cream	152	181	96	185	156
Other dairy products	267	191	157	242	290
Fruits and vegetables	731	1,037	530	820	750
Fresh fruits	261	409	166	307	270
Fresh vegetables	226	386	149	259	234
Processed fruits	114	117	97	122	115
Processed vegetables	130	125	119	132	131
Other food at home	1,380	1,339	949	1,298	1,468
Sugar and other sweets	147	150	103	126	158
Fats and oils	114	108	92	129	115
Miscellaneous foods	699	709	467	626	751
Nonalcoholic beverages	370	319	267	389	385
Food prepared by consumer unit on trips	50	53	19	29	59
Food away from home	**2,678**	**3,613**	**1,728**	**2,454**	**2,875**
ALCOHOLIC BEVERAGES	**451**	**360**	**212**	**338**	**510**
HOUSING	**16,887**	**20,821**	**14,395**	**15,061**	**17,605**
Shelter	**9,891**	**13,841**	**8,441**	**9,215**	**10,244**
Owned dwellings	6,056	8,380	3,645	4,185	6,763
Mortgage interest and charges	3,067	4,627	2,081	2,447	3,332
Property taxes	1,836	2,610	912	1,107	2,109
Maintenance, repair, insurance, other expenses	1,153	1,143	652	632	1,322
Rented dwellings	3,186	4,770	4,521	4,843	2,694
Other lodging	649	691	275	187	787
Utilities, fuels, and public services	**3,648**	**3,456**	**3,525**	**3,325**	**3,721**
Natural gas	359	414	369	292	369
Electricity	1,388	1,145	1,437	1,218	1,407
Fuel oil and other fuels	137	76	46	48	167
Telephone services	1,239	1,250	1,211	1,272	1,238
Water and other public services	525	570	461	496	540

	total consumer units	Asian	black	Hispanic	non-Hispanic white and other
Household services	$1,159	$1,469	$810	$728	$1,288
Personal services	368	664	292	287	394
Other household services	791	805	518	440	894
Housekeeping supplies	610	497	459	568	642
Laundry and cleaning supplies	155	124	149	198	149
Other household products	319	254	224	279	341
Postage and stationery	136	119	86	91	152
Household furnishings and equipment	1,580	1,558	1,160	1,225	1,711
Household textiles	123	101	94	108	130
Furniture	391	466	345	318	413
Floor coverings	16	9	6	9	19
Major appliances	197	193	129	143	217
Small appliances, miscellaneous housewares	98	92	62	78	107
Miscellaneous household equipment	754	698	525	569	824
APPAREL AND RELATED SERVICES	1,736	2,391	1,697	2,030	1,694
Men and boys	408	605	399	478	397
Men, aged 16 or older	320	462	306	345	318
Boys, aged 2 to 15	88	143	94	133	79
Women and girls	688	837	620	770	686
Women, aged 16 or older	573	672	468	601	585
Girls, aged 2 to 15	116	165	152	169	101
Children under age 2	63	99	60	97	58
Footwear	347	473	419	461	316
Other apparel products and services	230	378	198	224	236
TRANSPORTATION	8,998	10,117	6,751	8,306	9,485
Vehicle purchases	3,210	3,339	2,155	2,890	3,439
Cars and trucks, new	1,639	2,099	815	1,102	1,862
Cars and trucks, used	1,516	1,219	1,291	1,755	1,515
Gasoline and motor oil	2,756	2,659	2,329	2,727	2,831
Other vehicle expenses	2,490	2,658	1,927	2,294	2,615
Vehicle finance charges	223	233	207	193	231
Maintenance and repairs	814	775	583	642	882
Vehicle insurance	1,018	1,096	863	1,083	1,032
Vehicle rentals, leases, licenses, other charges	434	554	274	377	470
Public transportation	542	1,461	340	395	600
HEALTH CARE	3,556	3,285	2,013	1,893	4,088
Health insurance	2,061	2,101	1,349	1,019	2,351
Medical services	839	704	307	528	978
Drugs	515	368	300	261	592
Medical supplies	142	112	57	85	166
ENTERTAINMENT	2,605	2,303	1,526	1,588	2,953
Fees and admissions	614	881	259	300	725
Audio and visual equipment and services	979	829	982	754	1,016
Pets, toys, hobbies, and playground equipment	648	259	194	375	769
Other entertainment products and services	363	334	91	158	443
PERSONAL CARE PRODUCTS AND SERVICES	628	594	565	556	651
READING	109	97	45	40	132
EDUCATION	1,207	3,295	641	488	1,423
TOBACCO PRODUCTS AND SMOKING SUPPLIES	332	161	245	157	375

	total consumer units	Asian	black	Hispanic	non-Hispanic white and other
MISCELLANEOUS	$829	$849	$563	$553	$919
CASH CONTRIBUTIONS	1,913	1,356	1,358	782	2,192
PERSONAL INSURANCE AND PENSIONS	5,591	7,789	3,914	3,905	6,146
Life and other personal insurance	353	361	321	112	398
Pensions and Social Security	5,238	7,428	3,593	3,793	5,749
PERSONAL TAXES	2,226	2,571	453	486	2,810
Federal income taxes	1,568	1,824	178	243	2,020
State and local income taxes	526	616	221	204	630
Other taxes	132	132	55	39	160
GIFTS FOR PEOPLE IN OTHER HOUSEHOLDS	1,116	1,726	474	556	1,316

Note: "Asian" and "black" include Hispanics and non-Hispanics who identify themselves as being of the respective race alone. "Hispanic" includes people of any race who identify themselves as Hispanic. "Other" includes people who identify themselves as non-Hispanic and as Alaska Native, American Indian, Asian (who are also included in the "Asian" column), Native Hawaiian or other Pacific Islander, as well as non-Hispanics reporting more than one race. Spending by category does not add to total spending because gift spending is also included in the preceding product and service categories and personal taxes are not included in the total.

Source: Bureau of Labor Statistics, 2012 Consumer Expenditure Survey, Internet site http://www.bls.gov/cex/

Table 9.15 Indexed Spending by Race and Hispanic Origin of Householder, 2012

(indexed average annual spending of consumer units by product and service category and by race and Hispanic origin of consumer unit reference person, 2012; index definition: an index of 100 is the average for all consumer units; an index of 125 means that spending by consumer units in that group is 25 percent above the average for all consumer units; an index of 75 indicates spending that is 25 percent below the average for all consumer units)

	total consumer units	Asian	black	Hispanic	non-Hispanic white and other
Average spending of consumer units	$51,442	$61,399	$38,627	$42,268	$55,097
Indexed spending of consumer units	100	119	75	82	107
FOOD	100	121	71	100	105
Food at home	100	111	76	105	103
Cereals and bakery products	100	109	75	99	104
Cereals and cereal products	100	130	87	110	101
Bakery products	100	98	69	94	106
Meats, poultry, fish, and eggs	100	121	98	122	97
Beef	100	98	83	129	98
Pork	100	125	108	111	96
Other meats	100	77	80	98	104
Poultry	100	101	119	133	92
Fish and seafood	100	225	110	124	94
Eggs	100	132	85	142	96
Dairy products	100	89	61	102	106
Fresh milk and cream	100	119	63	122	103
Other dairy products	100	72	59	91	109
Fruits and vegetables	100	142	73	112	103
Fresh fruits	100	157	64	118	103
Fresh vegetables	100	171	66	115	104
Processed fruits	100	103	85	107	101
Processed vegetables	100	96	92	102	101
Other food at home	100	97	69	94	106
Sugar and other sweets	100	102	70	86	107
Fats and oils	100	95	81	113	101
Miscellaneous foods	100	101	67	90	107
Nonalcoholic beverages	100	86	72	105	104
Food prepared by consumer unit on trips	100	106	38	58	118
Food away from home	100	135	65	92	107
ALCOHOLIC BEVERAGES	100	80	47	75	113
HOUSING	100	123	85	89	104
Shelter	100	140	85	93	104
Owned dwellings	100	138	60	69	112
Mortgage interest and charges	100	151	68	80	109
Property taxes	100	142	50	60	115
Maintenance, repair, insurance, other expenses	100	99	57	55	115
Rented dwellings	100	150	142	152	85
Other lodging	100	106	42	29	121
Utilities, fuels, and public services	100	95	97	91	102
Natural gas	100	115	103	81	103
Electricity	100	82	104	88	101
Fuel oil and other fuels	100	55	34	35	122
Telephone services	100	101	98	103	100
Water and other public services	100	109	88	94	103

	total consumer units	Asian	black	Hispanic	non-Hispanic white and other
Household services	100	127	70	63	111
Personal services	100	180	79	78	107
Other household services	100	102	65	56	113
Housekeeping supplies	100	81	75	93	105
Laundry and cleaning supplies	100	80	96	128	96
Other household products	100	80	70	87	107
Postage and stationery	100	88	63	67	112
Household furnishings and equipment	100	99	73	78	108
Household textiles	100	82	76	88	106
Furniture	100	119	88	81	106
Floor coverings	100	56	38	56	119
Major appliances	100	98	65	73	110
Small appliances, miscellaneous housewares	100	94	63	80	109
Miscellaneous household equipment	100	93	70	75	109
APPAREL AND RELATED SERVICES	100	138	98	117	98
Men and boys	100	148	98	117	97
Men, aged 16 or older	100	144	96	108	99
Boys, aged 2 to 15	100	163	107	151	90
Women and girls	100	122	90	112	100
Women, aged 16 or older	100	117	82	105	102
Girls, aged 2 to 15	100	142	131	146	87
Children under age 2	100	157	95	154	92
Footwear	100	136	121	133	91
Other apparel products and services	100	164	86	97	103
TRANSPORTATION	100	112	75	92	105
Vehicle purchases	100	104	67	90	107
Cars and trucks, new	100	128	50	67	114
Cars and trucks, used	100	80	85	116	100
Gasoline and motor oil	100	96	85	99	103
Other vehicle expenses	100	107	77	92	105
Vehicle finance charges	100	104	93	87	104
Maintenance and repairs	100	95	72	79	108
Vehicle insurance	100	108	85	106	101
Vehicle rentals, leases, licenses, other charges	100	128	63	87	108
Public transportation	100	270	63	73	111
HEALTH CARE	100	92	57	53	115
Health insurance	100	102	65	49	114
Medical services	100	84	37	63	117
Drugs	100	71	58	51	115
Medical supplies	100	79	40	60	117
ENTERTAINMENT	100	88	59	61	113
Fees and admissions	100	143	42	49	118
Audio and visual equipment and services	100	85	100	77	104
Pets, toys, hobbies, and playground equipment	100	40	30	58	119
Other entertainment products and services	100	92	25	44	122
PERSONAL CARE PRODUCTS AND SERVICES	100	95	90	89	104
READING	100	89	41	37	121
EDUCATION	100	273	53	40	118
TOBACCO PRODUCTS AND SMOKING SUPPLIES	100	48	74	47	113

	total consumer units	Asian	black	Hispanic	non-Hispanic white and other
MISCELLANEOUS	**100**	**102**	**68**	**67**	**111**
CASH CONTRIBUTIONS	**100**	**71**	**71**	**41**	**115**
PERSONAL INSURANCE AND PENSIONS	**100**	**139**	**70**	**70**	**110**
Life and other personal insurance	100	102	91	32	113
Pensions and Social Security	100	142	69	72	110
PERSONAL TAXES	**100**	**115**	**20**	**22**	**126**
Federal income taxes	100	116	11	15	129
State and local income taxes	100	117	42	39	120
Other taxes	100	100	42	30	121
GIFTS FOR PEOPLE IN OTHER HOUSEHOLDS	**100**	**155**	**42**	**50**	**118**

Note: "Asian" and "black" include Hispanics and non-Hispanics who identify themselves as being of the respective race alone. "Hispanic" includes people of any race who identify themselves as Hispanic. "Other" includes people who identify themselves as non-Hispanic and as Alaska Native, American Indian, Asian (who are also included in the "Asian" column), Native Hawaiian or other Pacific Islander, as well as non-Hispanics reporting more than one race.
Source: Calculations by New Strategist based on the Bureau of Labor Statistics 2012 Consumer Expenditure Survey, Internet site http://www.bls.gov/cex/home.htm

Table 9.16 Market Shares by Race and Hispanic Origin of Householder, 2012

(share of total household spending accounted for by race and Hispanic origin group, 2012)

	total consumer units	Asian	black	Hispanic	non-Hispanic white and other
Share of total consumer units	100.0%	4.3%	12.6%	12.5%	75.1%
Share of total spending	100.0	5.2	9.4	10.3	80.4
FOOD	100.0	5.2	9.0	12.5	78.8
Food at home	100.0	4.8	9.5	13.2	77.5
Cereals and bakery products	100.0	4.7	9.4	12.4	78.3
Cereals and cereal products	100.0	5.6	11.0	13.8	75.5
Bakery products	100.0	4.2	8.6	11.7	79.9
Meats, poultry, fish, and eggs	100.0	5.3	12.3	15.3	72.7
Beef	100.0	4.2	10.5	16.1	73.7
Pork	100.0	5.4	13.6	13.9	72.3
Other meats	100.0	3.3	10.0	12.3	78.1
Poultry	100.0	4.4	14.9	16.6	68.9
Fish and seafood	100.0	9.7	13.8	15.5	70.9
Eggs	100.0	5.7	10.7	17.7	72.2
Dairy products	100.0	3.8	7.6	12.8	79.9
Fresh milk and cream	100.0	5.2	7.9	15.3	77.0
Other dairy products	100.0	3.1	7.4	11.4	81.5
Fruits and vegetables	100.0	6.1	9.1	14.1	77.0
Fresh fruits	100.0	6.8	8.0	14.7	77.6
Fresh vegetables	100.0	7.4	8.3	14.4	77.7
Processed fruits	100.0	4.4	10.7	13.4	75.7
Processed vegetables	100.0	4.2	11.5	12.7	75.6
Other food at home	100.0	4.2	8.6	11.8	79.8
Sugar and other sweets	100.0	4.4	8.8	10.7	80.7
Fats and oils	100.0	4.1	10.1	14.2	75.7
Miscellaneous foods	100.0	4.4	8.4	11.2	80.6
Nonalcoholic beverages	100.0	3.7	9.1	13.2	78.1
Food prepared by consumer unit on trips	100.0	4.6	4.8	7.3	88.6
Food away from home	100.0	5.8	8.1	11.5	80.6
ALCOHOLIC BEVERAGES	100.0	3.5	5.9	9.4	84.9
HOUSING	100.0	5.3	10.7	11.2	78.3
Shelter	100.0	6.1	10.7	11.7	77.7
Owned dwellings	100.0	6.0	7.6	8.7	83.8
Mortgage interest and charges	100.0	6.5	8.5	10.0	81.5
Property taxes	100.0	6.2	6.2	7.6	86.2
Maintenance, repair, insurance, other expenses	100.0	4.3	7.1	6.9	86.1
Rented dwellings	100.0	6.5	17.8	19.1	63.5
Other lodging	100.0	4.6	5.3	3.6	91.0
Utilities, fuels, and public services	100.0	4.1	12.1	11.4	76.6
Natural gas	100.0	5.0	12.9	10.2	77.1
Electricity	100.0	3.6	13.0	11.0	76.1
Fuel oil and other fuels	100.0	2.4	4.2	4.4	91.5
Telephone services	100.0	4.4	12.3	12.9	75.0
Water and other public services	100.0	4.7	11.0	11.8	77.2

	total consumer units	Asian	black	Hispanic	non-Hispanic white and other
Household services	100.0%	5.5%	8.8%	7.9%	83.4%
Personal services	100.0	7.8	10.0	9.8	80.4
Other household services	100.0	4.4	8.2	7.0	84.8
Housekeeping supplies	100.0	3.5	9.5	11.7	79.0
Laundry and cleaning supplies	100.0	3.5	12.1	16.0	72.2
Other household products	100.0	3.5	8.8	11.0	80.2
Postage and stationery	100.0	3.8	7.9	8.4	83.9
Household furnishings and equipment	100.0	4.3	9.2	9.7	81.3
Household textiles	100.0	3.6	9.6	11.0	79.3
Furniture	100.0	5.2	11.1	10.2	79.3
Floor coverings	100.0	2.4	4.7	7.1	89.1
Major appliances	100.0	4.2	8.2	9.1	82.7
Small appliances, miscellaneous housewares	100.0	4.1	8.0	10.0	82.0
Miscellaneous household equipment	100.0	4.0	8.8	9.5	82.0
APPAREL AND RELATED SERVICES	100.0	6.0	12.3	14.7	73.2
Men and boys	100.0	6.4	12.3	14.7	73.0
Men, aged 16 or older	100.0	6.3	12.0	13.5	74.6
Boys, aged 2 to 15	100.0	7.0	13.4	18.9	67.4
Women and girls	100.0	5.3	11.3	14.0	74.8
Women, aged 16 or older	100.0	5.1	10.3	13.1	76.6
Girls, aged 2 to 15	100.0	6.2	16.5	18.3	65.4
Children under age 2	100.0	6.8	12.0	19.3	69.1
Footwear	100.0	5.9	15.2	16.7	68.4
Other apparel products and services	100.0	7.1	10.8	12.2	77.0
TRANSPORTATION	100.0	4.9	9.4	11.6	79.1
Vehicle purchases	100.0	4.5	8.4	11.3	80.4
Cars and trucks, new	100.0	5.6	6.2	8.4	85.3
Cars and trucks, used	100.0	3.5	10.7	14.5	75.0
Gasoline and motor oil	100.0	4.2	10.6	12.4	77.1
Other vehicle expenses	100.0	4.6	9.7	11.5	78.8
Vehicle finance charges	100.0	4.5	11.7	10.8	77.8
Maintenance and repairs	100.0	4.1	9.0	9.9	81.3
Vehicle insurance	100.0	4.7	10.7	13.3	76.1
Vehicle rentals, leases, licenses, other charges	100.0	5.5	7.9	10.9	81.3
Public transportation	100.0	11.7	7.9	9.1	83.1
HEALTH CARE	100.0	4.0	7.1	6.7	86.3
Health insurance	100.0	4.4	8.2	6.2	85.6
Medical services	100.0	3.6	4.6	7.9	87.5
Drugs	100.0	3.1	7.3	6.4	86.3
Medical supplies	100.0	3.4	5.0	7.5	87.7
ENTERTAINMENT	100.0	3.8	7.4	7.6	85.1
Fees and admissions	100.0	6.2	5.3	6.1	88.6
Audio and visual equipment and services	100.0	3.7	12.6	9.7	77.9
Pets, toys, hobbies, and playground equipment	100.0	1.7	3.8	7.3	89.1
Other entertainment products and services	100.0	4.0	3.2	5.5	91.6
PERSONAL CARE PRODUCTS AND SERVICES	100.0	4.1	11.3	11.1	77.8
READING	100.0	3.9	5.2	4.6	90.9
EDUCATION	100.0	11.8	6.7	5.1	88.5
TOBACCO PRODUCTS AND SMOKING SUPPLIES	100.0	2.1	9.3	5.9	84.8

	total consumer units	Asian	black	Hispanic	non-Hispanic white and other
MISCELLANEOUS	**100.0%**	**4.4%**	**8.5%**	**8.4%**	**83.2%**
CASH CONTRIBUTIONS	**100.0**	**3.1**	**8.9**	**5.1**	**86.0**
PERSONAL INSURANCE AND PENSIONS	**100.0**	**6.0**	**8.8**	**8.8**	**82.5**
Life and other personal insurance	100.0	4.4	11.4	4.0	84.6
Pensions and Social Security	100.0	6.1	8.6	9.1	82.4
PERSONAL TAXES	**100.0**	**5.0**	**2.6**	**2.7**	**94.8**
Federal income taxes	100.0	5.0	1.4	1.9	96.7
State and local income taxes	100.0	5.1	5.3	4.9	89.9
Other taxes	100.0	4.3	5.2	3.7	91.0
GIFTS FOR PEOPLE IN OTHER HOUSEHOLDS	**100.0**	**6.7**	**5.3**	**6.2**	**88.5**

Note: "Asian" and "black" include Hispanics and non-Hispanics who identify themselves as being of the respective race alone. "Hispanic" includes people of any race who identify themselves as Hispanic. "Other" includes people who identify themselves as non-Hispanic and as Alaska Native, American Indian, Asian (who are also included in the "Asian" column), Native Hawaiian or other Pacific Islander, as well as non-Hispanics reporting more than one race.
Source: Calculations by New Strategist based on the Bureau of Labor Statistics 2012 Consumer Expenditure Survey, Internet site http://www.bls.gov/cex/home.htm

Spending is Highest in the West

Households in the South spend the least.

The average household in the West spent $56,782 in 2012, or 10 percent more than the average household. In the Northeast, spending was 9 percent above average at $55,884. In the Midwest, households spent 6 percent less than average, and in the South they spent 7 percent less. By product and service category, however, spending varies by region.

The Indexed Spending table shows spending by the average household in each region relative to what the average household spends. An index of 100 means households in the region spend an average amount on the item. An index above 100 means households in the region spend more than average on the item, while an index below 100 reveals below-average spending.

Spending varies by region

(average annual spending of consumer units by region, 2012)

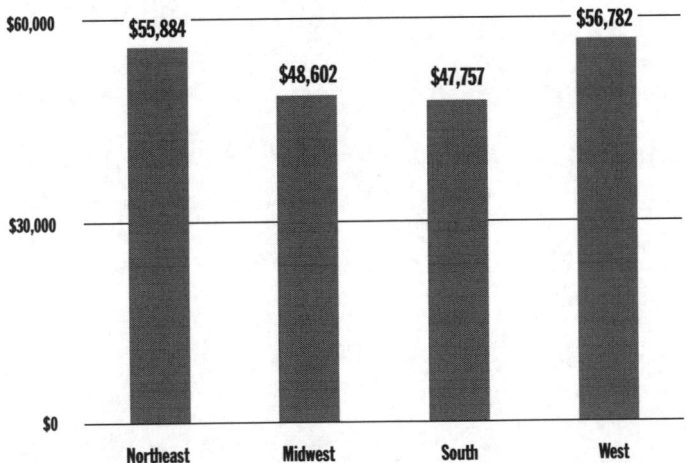

Households in the West and Northeast spend more than the average household on most foods. Spending on housing is also above average in both regions. Households in the Northeast spend 65 percent more than the average household on property taxes and 54 percent more on public transportation. In the Northeast and West, households spent 19 and 16 percent more than average, respectively, on alcoholic beverages. Households in the South spend less than the average household on most items with some exceptions such as electricity and vehicle finance charges.

The Market Share table shows how much of total spending by category is accounted for by households in each region. In most categories, spending closely matches each region's share of total households. The South, which is home to 37 percent of households, accounts for 35 percent of household spending. With 23 percent of households, the West accounts for 25 percent of household spending. There are some exceptions, however. Households in the South, for example, account for a disproportionate share of spending on electricity (44 percent), while those in the West account for only 20 percent of spending on this item.

■ Because regional spending patterns are partly determined by climate, spending by region is not likely to change much in the years ahead.

Table 9.17 Average Spending by Region, 2012

(average annual spending of consumer units by product and service category and region of residence, 2012)

	total	Northeast	Midwest	South	West
Number of consumer units (in 000s)	124,416	22,459	27,584	46,338	28,035
Average number of persons per consumer unit	2.5	2.4	2.4	2.5	2.6
Average annual spending	**$51,442**	**$55,884**	**$48,602**	**$47,757**	**$56,782**
FOOD	6,599	6,962	6,393	6,156	7,246
Food at home	3,921	4,056	3,906	3,652	4,272
Cereals and bakery products	538	586	556	488	564
Cereals and cereal products	182	195	183	165	199
Bakery products	356	391	373	324	364
Meats, poultry, fish, and eggs	852	898	797	839	893
Beef	226	218	226	229	229
Pork	166	159	155	178	161
Other meats	122	144	126	111	118
Poultry	159	178	138	154	175
Fish and seafood	126	144	104	116	150
Eggs	53	55	50	50	60
Dairy products	419	448	421	383	452
Fresh milk and cream	152	153	144	149	164
Other dairy products	267	295	277	235	288
Fruits and vegetables	731	798	728	637	836
Fresh fruits	261	285	262	218	314
Fresh vegetables	226	249	206	198	275
Processed fruits	114	127	120	97	124
Processed vegetables	130	136	140	124	123
Other food at home	1,380	1,327	1,405	1,304	1,526
Sugar and other sweets	147	136	153	138	164
Fats and oils	114	114	117	106	124
Miscellaneous foods	699	656	727	646	795
Nonalcoholic beverages	370	370	362	370	378
Food prepared by consumer unit on trips	50	50	45	44	66
Food away from home	2,678	2,906	2,486	2,504	2,974
ALCOHOLIC BEVERAGES	451	535	437	375	524
HOUSING	16,887	19,745	15,012	15,280	19,103
Shelter	9,891	12,274	8,530	8,298	11,953
Owned dwellings	6,056	7,480	5,644	5,147	6,823
Mortgage interest and charges	3,067	3,060	2,616	2,793	3,968
Property taxes	1,836	3,033	1,948	1,302	1,647
Maintenance, repair, insurance, other expenses	1,153	1,387	1,080	1,051	1,208
Rented dwellings	3,186	3,938	2,282	2,617	4,416
Other lodging	649	856	604	534	715
Utilities, fuels, and public services	3,648	3,979	3,455	3,704	3,481
Natural gas	359	504	503	211	347
Electricity	1,388	1,280	1,263	1,625	1,206
Fuel oil and other fuels	137	463	95	57	49
Telephone services	1,239	1,309	1,161	1,261	1,224
Water and other public services	525	424	433	550	655

	total	Northeast	Midwest	South	West
Household services	$1,159	$1,435	$973	$1,030	$1,333
Personal services	368	586	323	305	344
Other household services	791	850	650	726	990
Housekeeping supplies	**610**	**597**	**588**	**609**	**644**
Laundry and cleaning supplies	155	151	143	157	168
Other household products	319	310	310	322	328
Postage and stationery	136	136	135	130	147
Household furnishings and equipment	1,580	1,460	1,466	1,640	1,691
Household textiles	123	113	95	121	162
Furniture	391	382	392	400	385
Floor coverings	16	17	22	11	19
Major appliances	197	219	194	192	193
Small appliances, miscellaneous housewares	98	82	94	99	112
Miscellaneous household equipment	754	647	670	819	820
APPAREL AND RELATED SERVICES	**1,736**	**1,833**	**1,564**	**1,662**	**1,950**
Men and boys	**408**	**455**	**355**	**369**	**488**
Men, aged 16 or older	320	352	282	283	391
Boys, aged 2 to 15	88	102	72	85	96
Women and girls	**688**	**673**	**665**	**664**	**765**
Women, aged 16 or older	573	555	550	544	657
Girls, aged 2 to 15	116	118	116	120	108
Children under age 2	**63**	**72**	**60**	**67**	**54**
Footwear	**347**	**370**	**303**	**351**	**366**
Other apparel products and services	**230**	**265**	**182**	**212**	**277**
TRANSPORTATION	**8,998**	**8,857**	**8,604**	**9,080**	**9,367**
Vehicle purchases	**3,210**	**2,906**	**3,216**	**3,413**	**3,115**
Cars and trucks, new	1,639	1,598	1,528	1,708	1,664
Cars and trucks, used	1,516	1,285	1,644	1,662	1,334
Gasoline and motor oil	**2,756**	**2,503**	**2,713**	**2,863**	**2,824**
Other vehicle expenses	**2,490**	**2,612**	**2,242**	**2,434**	**2,730**
Vehicle finance charges	223	206	198	246	225
Maintenance and repairs	814	815	790	727	982
Vehicle insurance	1,018	942	863	1,119	1,066
Vehicle rentals, leases, licenses, other charges	434	649	391	341	458
Public transportation	**542**	**836**	**432**	**371**	**698**
HEALTH CARE	**3,556**	**3,572**	**3,844**	**3,234**	**3,795**
Health insurance	2,061	2,162	2,295	1,861	2,079
Medical services	839	801	858	742	1,009
Drugs	515	452	550	508	541
Medical supplies	142	156	141	122	166
ENTERTAINMENT	**2,605**	**2,723**	**2,550**	**2,407**	**2,894**
Fees and admissions	614	724	660	436	776
Audio and visual equipment and services	979	1,096	904	978	960
Pets, toys, hobbies, and playground equipment	648	628	645	624	707
Other entertainment products and services	363	274	340	368	452
PERSONAL CARE PRODUCTS AND SERVICES	**628**	**635**	**572**	**628**	**680**
READING	**109**	**134**	**107**	**82**	**137**
EDUCATION	**1,207**	**1,789**	**1,180**	**851**	**1,358**
TOBACCO PRODUCTS AND SMOKING SUPPLIES	**332**	**354**	**341**	**364**	**250**

	total	Northeast	Midwest	South	West
MISCELLANEOUS	$829	$938	$808	$665	$1,033
CASH CONTRIBUTIONS	1,913	1,798	1,851	1,699	2,417
PERSONAL INSURANCE AND PENSIONS	5,591	6,009	5,339	5,273	6,030
Life and other personal insurance	353	332	334	393	320
Pensions and Social Security	5,238	5,677	5,005	4,879	5,710
PERSONAL TAXES	2,226	2,747	2,565	1,731	2,295
Federal income taxes	1,568	1,768	1,872	1,250	1,636
State and local income taxes	526	731	603	343	588
Other taxes	132	248	89	138	71
GIFTS FOR PEOPLE IN OTHER HOUSEHOLDS	1,116	1,172	1,148	1,034	1,177

Note: Spending by category does not add to total spending because gift spending is also included in the preceding product and service categories and personal taxes are not included in the total.
Source: Bureau of Labor Statistics, 2012 Consumer Expenditure Survey, Internet site http://www.bls.gov/cex/

Table 9.18 Indexed Spending by Region, 2012

(indexed average annual spending of consumer units by product and service category and region of residence, 2012, index definition: an index of 100 is the average for all consumer units; an index of 125 means that spending by consumer units in that group is 25 percent above the average for all consumer units; an index of 75 indicates spending that is 25 percent below the average for all consumer units)

	total	Northeast	Midwest	South	West
Average spending of consumer units	$51,442	$55,884	$48,602	$47,757	$56,782
Indexed spending of consumer units	100	109	94	93	110
FOOD	100	106	97	93	110
Food at home	100	103	100	93	109
Cereals and bakery products	100	109	103	91	105
Cereals and cereal products	100	107	101	91	109
Bakery products	100	110	105	91	102
Meats, poultry, fish, and eggs	100	105	94	98	105
Beef	100	96	100	101	101
Pork	100	96	93	107	97
Other meats	100	118	103	91	97
Poultry	100	112	87	97	110
Fish and seafood	100	114	83	92	119
Eggs	100	104	94	94	113
Dairy products	100	107	100	91	108
Fresh milk and cream	100	101	95	98	108
Other dairy products	100	110	104	88	108
Fruits and vegetables	100	109	100	87	114
Fresh fruits	100	109	100	84	120
Fresh vegetables	100	110	91	88	122
Processed fruits	100	111	105	85	109
Processed vegetables	100	105	108	95	95
Other food at home	100	96	102	94	111
Sugar and other sweets	100	93	104	94	112
Fats and oils	100	100	103	93	109
Miscellaneous foods	100	94	104	92	114
Nonalcoholic beverages	100	100	98	100	102
Food prepared by consumer unit on trips	100	100	90	88	132
Food away from home	100	109	93	94	111
ALCOHOLIC BEVERAGES	100	119	97	83	116
HOUSING	100	117	89	90	113
Shelter	100	124	86	84	121
Owned dwellings	100	124	93	85	113
Mortgage interest and charges	100	100	85	91	129
Property taxes	100	165	106	71	90
Maintenance, repair, insurance, other expenses	100	120	94	91	105
Rented dwellings	100	124	72	82	139
Other lodging	100	132	93	82	110
Utilities, fuels, and public services	100	109	95	102	95
Natural gas	100	140	140	59	97
Electricity	100	92	91	117	87
Fuel oil and other fuels	100	338	69	42	36
Telephone services	100	106	94	102	99
Water and other public services	100	81	82	105	125

	total	Northeast	Midwest	South	West
Household services	**100**	**124**	**84**	**89**	**115**
Personal services	100	159	88	83	93
Other household services	100	107	82	92	125
Housekeeping supplies	**100**	**98**	**96**	**100**	**106**
Laundry and cleaning supplies	100	97	92	101	108
Other household products	100	97	97	101	103
Postage and stationery	100	100	99	96	108
Household furnishings and equipment	**100**	**92**	**93**	**104**	**107**
Household textiles	100	92	77	98	132
Furniture	100	98	100	102	98
Floor coverings	100	106	138	69	119
Major appliances	100	111	98	97	98
Small appliances, miscellaneous housewares	100	84	96	101	114
Miscellaneous household equipment	100	86	89	109	109
APPAREL AND RELATED SERVICES	**100**	**106**	**90**	**96**	**112**
Men and boys	**100**	**112**	**87**	**90**	**120**
Men, aged 16 or older	100	110	88	88	122
Boys, aged 2 to 15	100	116	82	97	109
Women and girls	**100**	**98**	**97**	**97**	**111**
Women, aged 16 or older	100	97	96	95	115
Girls, aged 2 to 15	100	102	100	103	93
Children under age 2	**100**	**114**	**95**	**106**	**86**
Footwear	**100**	**107**	**87**	**101**	**105**
Other apparel products and services	**100**	**115**	**79**	**92**	**120**
TRANSPORTATION	**100**	**98**	**96**	**101**	**104**
Vehicle purchases	**100**	**91**	**100**	**106**	**97**
Cars and trucks, new	100	97	93	104	102
Cars and trucks, used	100	85	108	110	88
Gasoline and motor oil	**100**	**91**	**98**	**104**	**102**
Other vehicle expenses	**100**	**105**	**90**	**98**	**110**
Vehicle finance charges	100	92	89	110	101
Maintenance and repairs	100	100	97	89	121
Vehicle insurance	100	93	85	110	105
Vehicle rentals, leases, licenses, other charges	100	150	90	79	106
Public transportation	**100**	**154**	**80**	**68**	**129**
HEALTH CARE	**100**	**100**	**108**	**91**	**107**
Health insurance	100	105	111	90	101
Medical services	100	95	102	88	120
Drugs	100	88	107	99	105
Medical supplies	100	110	99	86	117
ENTERTAINMENT	**100**	**105**	**98**	**92**	**111**
Fees and admissions	100	118	107	71	126
Audio and visual equipment and services	100	112	92	100	98
Pets, toys, hobbies, and playground equipment	100	97	100	96	109
Other entertainment products and services	100	75	94	101	125
PERSONAL CARE PRODUCTS AND SERVICES	**100**	**101**	**91**	**100**	**108**
READING	**100**	**123**	**98**	**75**	**126**
EDUCATION	**100**	**148**	**98**	**71**	**113**
TOBACCO PRODUCTS AND SMOKING SUPPLIES	**100**	**107**	**103**	**110**	**75**

	total	Northeast	Midwest	South	West
MISCELLANEOUS	100	113	97	80	125
CASH CONTRIBUTIONS	100	94	97	89	126
PERSONAL INSURANCE AND PENSIONS	100	107	95	94	108
Life and other personal insurance	100	94	95	111	91
Pensions and Social Security	100	108	96	93	109
PERSONAL TAXES	100	123	115	78	103
Federal income taxes	100	113	119	80	104
State and local income taxes	100	139	115	65	112
Other taxes	100	188	67	105	54
GIFTS FOR PEOPLE IN OTHER HOUSEHOLDS	100	105	103	93	105

Source: Calculations by New Strategist based on the Bureau of Labor Statistics 2012 Consumer Expenditure Survey, Internet site http://www.bls.gov/cex/home.htm

Table 9.19 Market Shares by Region, 2012

(share of total household spending accounted for by region of residence, 2012)

	total consumer units	Northeast	Midwest	South	West
Share of total consumer units	100.0%	18.1%	22.2%	37.2%	22.5%
Share of total spending	100.0	19.6	20.9	34.6	24.9
FOOD	100.0	19.0	21.5	34.7	24.7
Food at home	100.0	18.7	22.1	34.7	24.6
Cereals and bakery products	100.0	19.7	22.9	33.8	23.6
Cereals and cereal products	100.0	19.3	22.3	33.8	24.6
Bakery products	100.0	19.8	23.2	33.9	23.0
Meats, poultry, fish, and eggs	100.0	19.0	20.7	36.7	23.6
Beef	100.0	17.4	22.2	37.7	22.8
Pork	100.0	17.3	20.7	39.9	21.9
Other meats	100.0	21.3	22.9	33.9	21.8
Poultry	100.0	20.2	19.2	36.1	24.8
Fish and seafood	100.0	20.6	18.3	34.3	26.8
Eggs	100.0	18.7	20.9	35.1	25.5
Dairy products	100.0	19.3	22.3	34.0	24.3
Fresh milk and cream	100.0	18.2	21.0	36.5	24.3
Other dairy products	100.0	19.9	23.0	32.8	24.3
Fruits and vegetables	100.0	19.7	22.1	32.5	25.8
Fresh fruits	100.0	19.7	22.3	31.1	27.1
Fresh vegetables	100.0	19.9	20.2	32.6	27.4
Processed fruits	100.0	20.1	23.3	31.7	24.5
Processed vegetables	100.0	18.9	23.9	35.5	21.3
Other food at home	100.0	17.4	22.6	35.2	24.9
Sugar and other sweets	100.0	16.7	23.1	35.0	25.1
Fats and oils	100.0	18.1	22.8	34.6	24.5
Miscellaneous foods	100.0	16.9	23.1	34.4	25.6
Nonalcoholic beverages	100.0	18.1	21.7	37.2	23.0
Food prepared by consumer unit on trips	100.0	18.1	20.0	32.8	29.7
Food away from home	100.0	19.6	20.6	34.8	25.0
ALCOHOLIC BEVERAGES	100.0	21.4	21.5	31.0	26.2
HOUSING	100.0	21.1	19.7	33.7	25.5
Shelter	100.0	22.4	19.1	31.2	27.2
Owned dwellings	100.0	22.3	20.7	31.7	25.4
Mortgage interest and charges	100.0	18.0	18.9	33.9	29.2
Property taxes	100.0	29.8	23.5	26.4	20.2
Maintenance, repair, insurance, other expenses	100.0	21.7	20.8	33.9	23.6
Rented dwellings	100.0	22.3	15.9	30.6	31.2
Other lodging	100.0	23.8	20.6	30.6	24.8
Utilities, fuels, and public services	100.0	19.7	21.0	37.8	21.5
Natural gas	100.0	25.3	31.1	21.9	21.8
Electricity	100.0	16.6	20.2	43.6	19.6
Fuel oil and other fuels	100.0	61.0	15.4	15.5	8.1
Telephone services	100.0	19.1	20.8	37.9	22.3
Water and other public services	100.0	14.6	18.3	39.0	28.1

	total consumer units	Northeast	Midwest	South	West
Household services	100.0%	22.4%	18.6%	33.1%	25.9%
Personal services	100.0	28.7	19.5	30.9	21.1
Other household services	100.0	19.4	18.2	34.2	28.2
Housekeeping supplies	100.0	17.7	21.4	37.2	23.8
Laundry and cleaning supplies	100.0	17.6	20.5	37.7	24.4
Other household products	100.0	17.5	21.5	37.6	23.2
Postage and stationery	100.0	18.1	22.0	35.6	24.4
Household furnishings and equipment	100.0	16.7	20.6	38.7	24.1
Household textiles	100.0	16.6	17.1	36.6	29.7
Furniture	100.0	17.6	22.2	38.1	22.2
Floor coverings	100.0	19.2	30.5	25.6	26.8
Major appliances	100.0	20.1	21.8	36.3	22.1
Small appliances, miscellaneous housewares	100.0	15.1	21.3	37.6	25.8
Miscellaneous household equipment	100.0	15.5	19.7	40.5	24.5
APPAREL AND RELATED SERVICES	100.0	19.1	20.0	35.7	25.3
Men and boys	100.0	20.1	19.3	33.7	27.0
Men, aged 16 or older	100.0	19.9	19.5	32.9	27.5
Boys, aged 2 to 15	100.0	20.9	18.1	36.0	24.6
Women and girls	100.0	17.7	21.4	35.9	25.1
Women, aged 16 or older	100.0	17.5	21.3	35.4	25.8
Girls, aged 2 to 15	100.0	18.4	22.2	38.5	21.0
Children under age 2	100.0	20.6	21.1	39.6	19.3
Footwear	100.0	19.2	19.4	37.7	23.8
Other apparel products and services	100.0	20.8	17.5	34.3	27.1
TRANSPORTATION	100.0	17.8	21.2	37.6	23.5
Vehicle purchases	100.0	16.3	22.2	39.6	21.9
Cars and trucks, new	100.0	17.6	20.7	38.8	22.9
Cars and trucks, used	100.0	15.3	24.0	40.8	19.8
Gasoline and motor oil	100.0	16.4	21.8	38.7	23.1
Other vehicle expenses	100.0	18.9	20.0	36.4	24.7
Vehicle finance charges	100.0	16.7	19.7	41.1	22.7
Maintenance and repairs	100.0	18.1	21.5	33.3	27.2
Vehicle insurance	100.0	16.7	18.8	40.9	23.6
Vehicle rentals, leases, licenses, other charges	100.0	27.0	20.0	29.3	23.8
Public transportation	100.0	27.8	17.7	25.5	29.0
HEALTH CARE	100.0	18.1	24.0	33.9	24.0
Health insurance	100.0	18.9	24.7	33.6	22.7
Medical services	100.0	17.2	22.7	32.9	27.1
Drugs	100.0	15.8	23.7	36.7	23.7
Medical supplies	100.0	19.8	22.0	32.0	26.3
ENTERTAINMENT	100.0	18.9	21.7	34.4	25.0
Fees and admissions	100.0	21.3	23.8	26.4	28.5
Audio and visual equipment and services	100.0	20.2	20.5	37.2	22.1
Pets, toys, hobbies, and playground equipment	100.0	17.5	22.1	35.9	24.6
Other entertainment products and services	100.0	13.6	20.8	37.8	28.1
PERSONAL CARE PRODUCTS AND SERVICES	100.0	18.3	20.2	37.2	24.4
READING	100.0	22.2	21.8	28.0	28.3
EDUCATION	100.0	26.8	21.7	26.3	25.4
TOBACCO PRODUCTS AND SMOKING SUPPLIES	100.0	19.2	22.8	40.8	17.0

	total consumer units	Northeast	Midwest	South	West
MISCELLANEOUS	100.0%	20.4%	21.6%	29.9%	28.1%
CASH CONTRIBUTIONS	100.0	17.0	21.5	33.1	28.5
PERSONAL INSURANCE AND PENSIONS	100.0	19.4	21.2	35.1	24.3
Life and other personal insurance	100.0	17.0	21.0	41.5	20.4
Pensions and Social Security	100.0	19.6	21.2	34.7	24.6
PERSONAL TAXES	100.0	22.3	25.5	29.0	23.2
Federal income taxes	100.0	20.4	26.5	29.7	23.5
State and local income taxes	100.0	25.1	25.4	24.3	25.2
Other taxes	100.0	33.9	14.9	38.9	12.1
GIFTS FOR PEOPLE IN OTHER HOUSEHOLDS	100.0	19.0	22.8	34.5	23.8

Source: Calculations by New Strategist based on the Bureau of Labor Statistics 2012 Consumer Expenditure Survey, Internet site http://www.bls.gov/cex/home.htm

College Graduates Spend More

The incomes of college graduates are much higher than average, and they spend more on most items.

Households in which at least one member has a bachelor's degree have much higher incomes than households in which no one has a bachelor's degree. Consequently, they spend more. In 2012, households in which a member had a bachelor's degree spent $71,151 on average—38 percent more than the average household. Households in which no member had more than a high school diploma spent just $34,786, or 32 percent less than the average household.

The Indexed Spending table compares the spending of households by level of education with average household spending. An index of 100 means households in the educational group spend an average amount on the item. An index above 100 means households in the educational group spend more than average on the item, while an index below 100 signifies below-average spending.

College graduates spend big on many items

(indexed average annual spending of consumer units in which at least one household member has a bachelor's degree, on selected items, 2012)

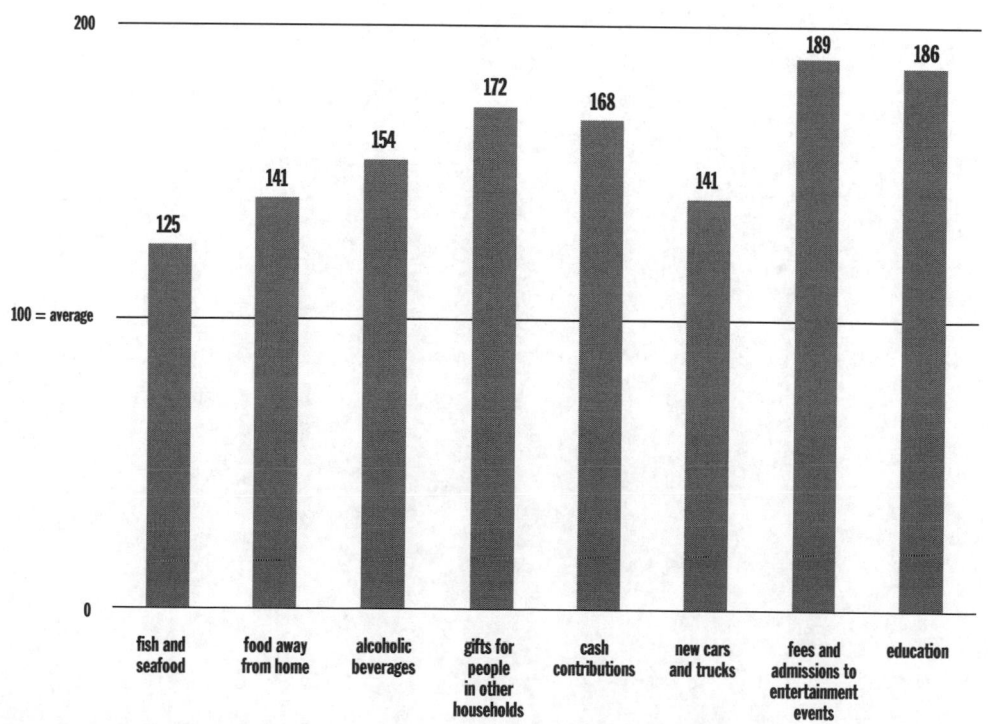

Households in which at least one member had a bachelor's degree spend like the more sophisticated consumers they are. They spend well above average on fish and seafood, fresh fruits and vegetables, restaurant meals (food away from home), and alcoholic beverages. They spend only slightly more than average on laundry and cleaning supplies, but much more than average on household textiles (bedroom and bathroom linens, for example). They spend 89 percent more than average on fees and admissions to entertainment events, but only half the average on tobacco.

The Market Share table shows how much of total household spending by category is accounted for by households in each educational group. College graduates spend disproportionately more than their share of households, while those who do not have a bachelor's degree spend less.

In 38 percent of the nation's households, at least one household member has a bachelor's degree. These households account for the 53 percent majority of consumer spending. On some items they control an even greater share of spending. They account for 71 percent of spending on other lodging, which includes dorm rooms, hotels, and motels. They account for 71 percent of spending on public transportation, which includes airline fares. They control 72 percent of spending on fees and admissions to entertainment events and 71 percent of spending on education.

■ As the educational level of the population rises, college graduates will increasingly dominate spending on a growing number of products and services.

Table 9.20 Average Spending by Education of Consumer Unit, 2012

(average annual spending of consumer units [CU] by product and service category and highest level of education of any member of the consumer unit, 2012)

	total consumer units	not a high school graduate	high school graduate	some college	associate's degree	bachelor's degree or more total	bachelor's degree	graduate degree
Number of consumer units (in 000s)	124,416	10,571	26,601	25,793	13,825	47,626	28,069	19,557
Average number of persons per CU	2.5	2.2	2.4	2.4	2.7	2.6	2.5	2.7
Average annual spending	**$51,442**	**$24,582**	**$34,786**	**$43,041**	**$50,836**	**$71,151**	**$63,135**	**$82,606**
FOOD	**6,599**	**3,913**	**4,944**	**5,749**	**6,658**	**8,435**	**7,928**	**9,143**
Food at home	**3,921**	**2,862**	**3,263**	**3,542**	**3,980**	**4,654**	**4,379**	**5,032**
Cereals and bakery products	538	383	453	481	554	637	592	700
Cereals and cereal products	182	134	153	164	194	213	203	227
Bakery products	356	250	301	317	359	425	390	473
Meats, poultry, fish, and eggs	852	672	812	772	926	930	911	957
Beef	226	175	234	201	278	231	234	226
Pork	166	145	162	167	175	169	165	174
Other meats	122	86	111	116	125	137	136	138
Poultry	159	127	151	137	173	178	169	192
Fish and seafood	126	92	105	101	121	158	152	166
Eggs	53	47	49	51	55	57	55	59
Dairy products	419	288	322	363	414	526	488	577
Fresh milk and cream	152	130	133	136	154	174	168	182
Other dairy products	267	158	189	227	260	352	320	395
Fruits and vegetables	731	550	567	626	687	919	848	1,017
Fresh fruits	261	190	187	210	229	350	317	395
Fresh vegetables	226	177	180	183	210	288	266	317
Processed fruits	114	79	85	103	107	143	130	160
Processed vegetables	130	103	115	130	141	139	135	144
Other food at home	1,380	969	1,109	1,299	1,399	1,641	1,541	1,781
Sugar and other sweets	147	103	114	130	157	178	160	204
Fats and oils	114	96	97	107	126	127	123	133
Miscellaneous foods	699	476	542	664	662	853	807	917
Nonalcoholic beverages	370	284	333	365	411	397	377	425
Food prepared by consumer unit on trips	50	11	22	33	44	86	74	103
Food away from home	**2,678**	**1,051**	**1,682**	**2,207**	**2,678**	**3,782**	**3,549**	**4,111**
ALCOHOLIC BEVERAGES	**451**	**108**	**236**	**350**	**416**	**696**	**650**	**759**
HOUSING	**16,887**	**9,388**	**12,143**	**14,241**	**16,146**	**22,815**	**20,230**	**26,512**
Shelter	**9,891**	**5,521**	**6,871**	**8,168**	**9,155**	**13,693**	**12,103**	**15,976**
Owned dwellings	6,056	2,087	3,509	4,424	5,607	9,373	8,022	11,312
Mortgage interest and charges	3,067	827	1,584	2,272	3,009	4,839	4,214	5,737
Property taxes	1,836	750	1,103	1,247	1,584	2,878	2,389	3,580
Maintenance, repair, insurance, other expenses	1,153	511	822	905	1,014	1,656	1,420	1,996
Rented dwellings	3,186	3,362	3,150	3,373	2,995	3,122	3,213	2,991
Other lodging	649	72	212	371	553	1,198	867	1,672
Utilities, fuels, and public services	**3,648**	**2,541**	**3,280**	**3,333**	**3,957**	**4,181**	**3,935**	**4,534**
Natural gas	359	244	286	317	336	456	420	507
Electricity	1,388	1,082	1,353	1,293	1,524	1,487	1,422	1,581
Fuel oil and other fuels	137	76	130	95	131	179	150	221
Telephone services	1,239	790	1,056	1,163	1,426	1,428	1,353	1,535
Water and other public services	525	348	455	465	540	631	590	691

	total consumer units	not a high school graduate	high school graduate	some college	associate's degree	bachelor's degree or more		
						total	bachelor's degree	graduate degree
Household services	$1,159	$390	$600	$845	$1,003	$1,856	$1,495	$2,373
Personal services	368	141	167	223	299	630	496	823
Other household services	791	249	433	622	704	1,226	999	1,550
Housekeeping supplies	610	382	475	564	592	753	676	859
Laundry and cleaning supplies	155	137	141	153	171	163	166	159
Other household products	319	184	252	282	303	403	350	474
Postage and stationery	136	61	82	129	117	188	160	226
Household furnishings and equipment	1,580	554	918	1,331	1,439	2,331	2,021	2,770
Household textiles	123	48	76	93	147	171	141	213
Furniture	391	144	200	284	344	626	506	797
Floor coverings	16	4	7	6	11	31	20	46
Major appliances	197	78	147	168	179	273	269	278
Small appliances, miscellaneous housewares	98	54	58	77	100	138	121	162
Miscellaneous household equipment	754	224	429	703	658	1,093	963	1,273
APPAREL AND RELATED SERVICES	1,736	1,042	1,083	1,540	1,588	2,366	2,226	2,565
Men and boys	408	285	256	324	376	566	545	596
Men, aged 16 or older	320	215	188	244	284	461	446	482
Boys, aged 2 to 15	88	71	69	80	91	105	99	114
Women and girls	688	296	429	598	675	952	887	1,043
Women, aged 16 or older	573	226	342	476	580	809	762	874
Girls, aged 2 to 15	116	70	86	122	95	143	125	169
Children under age 2	63	72	44	59	55	77	78	76
Footwear	347	241	232	389	284	422	419	426
Other apparel products and services	230	148	122	171	199	349	296	424
TRANSPORTATION	8,998	3,835	6,225	8,422	10,342	11,594	10,817	12,710
Vehicle purchases	3,210	932	1,880	3,290	4,090	4,161	3,827	4,641
Cars and trucks, new	1,639	328	638	1,593	2,320	2,315	2,022	2,736
Cars and trucks, used	1,516	598	1,192	1,593	1,762	1,787	1,758	1,830
Gasoline and motor oil	2,756	1,549	2,318	2,557	3,282	3,223	3,156	3,319
Other vehicle expenses	2,490	1,191	1,839	2,244	2,666	3,202	3,062	3,405
Vehicle finance charges	223	64	166	213	308	272	274	268
Maintenance and repairs	814	353	595	667	893	1,093	1,010	1,212
Vehicle insurance	1,018	635	847	993	1,087	1,174	1,209	1,126
Vehicle rentals, leases, licenses, other charges	434	139	232	371	378	663	569	798
Public transportation	542	162	187	331	305	1,008	773	1,345
HEALTH CARE	3,556	2,004	2,823	2,949	3,560	4,635	4,196	5,263
Health insurance	2,061	1,173	1,747	1,638	2,116	2,646	2,417	2,973
Medical services	839	354	554	734	783	1,178	1,075	1,326
Drugs	515	426	416	474	516	609	540	706
Medical supplies	142	52	106	103	146	202	164	257
ENTERTAINMENT	2,605	1,134	1,630	2,118	2,571	3,725	3,220	4,443
Fees and admissions	614	72	179	356	446	1,161	901	1,532
Audio and visual equipment and services	979	590	824	919	1,000	1,176	1,114	1,264
Pets, toys, hobbies, and playground equipment	648	329	457	621	751	799	710	923
Other entertainment products and services	363	144	170	223	373	589	494	724
PERSONAL CARE PRODUCTS AND SERVICES	628	292	388	530	627	881	769	1,039
READING	109	29	53	81	107	175	135	232
EDUCATION	1,207	120	214	892	959	2,244	1,792	2,891
TOBACCO PRODUCTS AND SMOKING SUPPLIES	332	331	497	421	372	179	219	123

	total consumer units	not a high school graduate	high school graduate	some college	associate's degree	bachelor's degree or more		
						total	bachelor's degree	graduate degree
MISCELLANEOUS	$829	$307	$691	$728	$703	$1,110	$926	$1,373
CASH CONTRIBUTIONS	1,913	599	1,012	1,214	1,473	3,213	2,411	4,364
PERSONAL INSURANCE AND PENSIONS	5,591	1,481	2,847	3,805	5,313	9,084	7,617	11,188
Life and other personal insurance	353	107	203	207	281	591	479	752
Pensions and Social Security	5,238	1,374	2,645	3,598	5,032	8,493	7,139	10,436
PERSONAL TAXES	2,226	−40	533	705	1,896	4,595	3,720	5,851
Federal income taxes	1,568	−138	252	365	1,326	3,404	2,800	4,272
State and local income taxes	526	52	203	256	455	979	753	1,303
Other taxes	132	46	78	85	115	212	167	276
GIFTS FOR PEOPLE IN OTHER HOUSEHOLDS	1,116	375	532	707	782	1,914	1,528	2,460

Note: Spending by category does not add to total spending because gift spending is also included in the preceding product and service categories and personal taxes are not included in the total.
Source: Bureau of Labor Statistics, 2012 Consumer Expenditure Survey, Internet site http://www.bls.gov/cex/

Table 9.21 Indexed Spending by Education of Consumer Unit, 2012

(indexed average annual spending of consumer units by product and service category and highest level of education of any member of the consumer unit, 2012; index definition: an index of 100 is the average for all consumer units; an index of 125 means that spending by consumer units in that group is 25 percent above the average for all consumer units; an index of 75 indicates spending that is 25 percent below the average for all consumer units)

	total consumer units	not a high school graduate	high school graduate	some college	associate's degree	bachelor's degree or more total	bachelor's degree	graduate degree
Average spending of consumer units	$51,442	$24,582	$34,786	$43,041	$50,836	$71,151	$63,135	$82,606
Indexed spending of consumer units	100	48	68	84	99	138	123	161
FOOD	100	59	75	87	101	128	120	139
Food at home	100	73	83	90	102	119	112	128
Cereals and bakery products	100	71	84	89	103	118	110	130
Cereals and cereal products	100	74	84	90	107	117	112	125
Bakery products	100	70	85	89	101	119	110	133
Meats, poultry, fish, and eggs	100	79	95	91	109	109	107	112
Beef	100	77	104	89	123	102	104	100
Pork	100	87	98	101	105	102	99	105
Other meats	100	70	91	95	102	112	111	113
Poultry	100	80	95	86	109	112	106	121
Fish and seafood	100	73	83	80	96	125	121	132
Eggs	100	89	92	96	104	108	104	111
Dairy products	100	69	77	87	99	126	116	138
Fresh milk and cream	100	86	88	89	101	114	111	120
Other dairy products	100	59	71	85	97	132	120	148
Fruits and vegetables	100	75	78	86	94	126	116	139
Fresh fruits	100	73	72	80	88	134	121	151
Fresh vegetables	100	78	80	81	93	127	118	140
Processed fruits	100	69	75	90	94	125	114	140
Processed vegetables	100	79	88	100	108	107	104	111
Other food at home	100	70	80	94	101	119	112	129
Sugar and other sweets	100	70	78	88	107	121	109	139
Fats and oils	100	84	85	94	111	111	108	117
Miscellaneous foods	100	68	78	95	95	122	115	131
Nonalcoholic beverages	100	77	90	99	111	107	102	115
Food prepared by consumer unit on trips	100	22	44	66	88	172	148	206
Food away from home	100	39	63	82	100	141	133	154
ALCOHOLIC BEVERAGES	100	24	52	78	92	154	144	168
HOUSING	100	56	72	84	96	135	120	157
Shelter	100	56	69	83	93	138	122	162
Owned dwellings	100	34	58	73	93	155	132	187
Mortgage interest and charges	100	27	52	74	98	158	137	187
Property taxes	100	41	60	68	86	157	130	195
Maintenance, repair, insurance, other expenses	100	44	71	78	88	144	123	173
Rented dwellings	100	106	99	106	94	98	101	94
Other lodging	100	11	33	57	85	185	134	258
Utilities, fuels, and public services	100	70	90	91	108	115	108	124
Natural gas	100	68	80	88	94	127	117	141
Electricity	100	78	97	93	110	107	102	114
Fuel oil and other fuels	100	55	95	69	96	131	109	161
Telephone services	100	64	85	94	115	115	109	124
Water and other public services	100	66	87	89	103	120	112	132

	total consumer units	not a high school graduate	high school graduate	some college	associate's degree	bachelor's degree or more		
						total	bachelor's degree	graduate degree
Household services	100	34	52	73	87	160	129	205
Personal services	100	38	45	61	81	171	135	224
Other household services	100	31	55	79	89	155	126	196
Housekeeping supplies	100	63	78	92	97	123	111	141
Laundry and cleaning supplies	100	88	91	99	110	105	107	103
Other household products	100	58	79	88	95	126	110	149
Postage and stationery	100	45	60	95	86	138	118	166
Household furnishings and equipment	100	35	58	84	91	148	128	175
Household textiles	100	39	62	76	120	139	115	173
Furniture	100	37	51	73	88	160	129	204
Floor coverings	100	25	44	38	69	194	125	288
Major appliances	100	40	75	85	91	139	137	141
Small appliances, miscellaneous housewares	100	55	59	79	102	141	123	165
Miscellaneous household equipment	100	30	57	93	87	145	128	169
APPAREL AND RELATED SERVICES	100	60	62	89	91	136	128	148
Men and boys	100	70	63	79	92	139	134	146
Men, aged 16 or older	100	67	59	76	89	144	139	151
Boys, aged 2 to 15	100	81	78	91	103	119	113	130
Women and girls	100	43	62	87	98	138	129	152
Women, aged 16 or older	100	39	60	83	101	141	133	153
Girls, aged 2 to 15	100	60	74	105	82	123	108	146
Children under age 2	100	114	70	94	87	122	124	121
Footwear	100	69	67	112	82	122	121	123
Other apparel products and services	100	64	53	74	87	152	129	184
TRANSPORTATION	100	43	69	94	115	129	120	141
Vehicle purchases	100	29	59	102	127	130	119	145
Cars and trucks, new	100	20	39	97	142	141	123	167
Cars and trucks, used	100	39	79	105	116	118	116	121
Gasoline and motor oil	100	56	84	93	119	117	115	120
Other vehicle expenses	100	48	74	90	107	129	123	137
Vehicle finance charges	100	29	74	96	138	122	123	120
Maintenance and repairs	100	43	73	82	110	134	124	149
Vehicle insurance	100	62	83	98	107	115	119	111
Vehicle rentals, leases, licenses, other charges	100	32	53	85	87	153	131	184
Public transportation	100	30	35	61	56	186	143	248
HEALTH CARE	100	56	79	83	100	130	118	148
Health insurance	100	57	85	79	103	128	117	144
Medical services	100	42	66	87	93	140	128	158
Drugs	100	83	81	92	100	118	105	137
Medical supplies	100	37	75	73	103	142	115	181
ENTERTAINMENT	100	44	63	81	99	143	124	171
Fees and admissions	100	12	29	58	73	189	147	250
Audio and visual equipment and services	100	60	84	94	102	120	114	129
Pets, toys, hobbies, and playground equipment	100	51	71	96	116	123	110	142
Other entertainment products and services	100	40	47	61	103	162	136	199
PERSONAL CARE PRODUCTS AND SERVICES	100	46	62	84	100	140	122	165
READING	100	27	49	74	98	161	124	213
EDUCATION	100	10	18	74	79	186	148	240
TOBACCO PRODUCTS AND SMOKING SUPPLIES	100	100	150	127	112	54	66	37

| | total consumer units | not a high school graduate | high school graduate | some college | associate's degree | bachelor's degree or more | | |
						total	bachelor's degree	graduate degree
MISCELLANEOUS	100	37	83	88	85	134	112	166
CASH CONTRIBUTIONS	100	31	53	63	77	168	126	228
PERSONAL INSURANCE AND PENSIONS	100	26	51	68	95	162	136	200
Life and other personal insurance	100	30	58	59	80	167	136	213
Pensions and Social Security	100	26	50	69	96	162	136	199
PERSONAL TAXES	100	–2	24	32	85	206	167	263
Federal income taxes	100	–9	16	23	85	217	179	272
State and local income taxes	100	10	39	49	87	186	143	248
Other taxes	100	35	59	64	87	161	127	209
GIFTS FOR PEOPLE IN OTHER HOUSEHOLDS	100	34	48	63	70	172	137	220

Source: Calculations by New Strategist based on the Bureau of Labor Statistics 2012 Consumer Expenditure Survey, Internet site http://www.bls.gov/cex/home.htm

Table 9.22 Market Shares by Education of Consumer Unit, 2012

(share of total household spending accounted for by educational group, 2012)

	total consumer units	not a high school graduate	high school graduate	some college	associate's degree	bachelor's degree or more		
						total	bachelor's degree	graduate degree
Share of total consumer units	100.0%	8.5%	21.4%	20.7%	11.1%	38.3%	22.6%	15.7%
Share of total spending	100.0	4.1	14.5	17.3	11.0	52.9	27.7	25.2
FOOD	100.0	5.0	16.0	18.1	11.2	48.9	27.1	21.8
Food at home	100.0	6.2	17.8	18.7	11.3	45.4	25.2	20.2
Cereals and bakery products	100.0	6.0	18.0	18.5	11.4	45.3	24.8	20.5
Cereals and cereal products	100.0	6.3	18.0	18.7	11.8	44.8	25.2	19.6
Bakery products	100.0	6.0	18.1	18.5	11.2	45.7	24.7	20.9
Meats, poultry, fish, and eggs	100.0	6.7	20.4	18.8	12.1	41.8	24.1	17.7
Beef	100.0	6.6	22.1	18.4	13.7	39.1	23.4	15.7
Pork	100.0	7.4	20.9	20.9	11.7	39.0	22.4	16.5
Other meats	100.0	6.0	19.5	19.7	11.4	43.0	25.1	17.8
Poultry	100.0	6.8	20.3	17.9	12.1	42.9	24.0	19.0
Fish and seafood	100.0	6.2	17.8	16.6	10.7	48.0	27.2	20.7
Eggs	100.0	7.5	19.8	19.9	11.5	41.2	23.4	17.5
Dairy products	100.0	5.8	16.4	18.0	11.0	48.1	26.3	21.6
Fresh milk and cream	100.0	7.3	18.7	18.5	11.3	43.8	24.9	18.8
Other dairy products	100.0	5.0	15.1	17.6	10.8	50.5	27.0	23.3
Fruits and vegetables	100.0	6.4	16.6	17.8	10.4	48.1	26.2	21.9
Fresh fruits	100.0	6.2	15.3	16.7	9.7	51.3	27.4	23.8
Fresh vegetables	100.0	6.7	17.0	16.8	10.3	48.8	26.6	22.0
Processed fruits	100.0	5.9	15.9	18.7	10.4	48.0	25.7	22.1
Processed vegetables	100.0	6.7	18.9	20.7	12.1	40.9	23.4	17.4
Other food at home	100.0	6.0	17.2	19.5	11.3	45.5	25.2	20.3
Sugar and other sweets	100.0	6.0	16.6	18.3	11.9	46.4	24.6	21.8
Fats and oils	100.0	7.2	18.2	19.5	12.3	42.6	24.3	18.3
Miscellaneous foods	100.0	5.8	16.6	19.7	10.5	46.7	26.0	20.6
Nonalcoholic beverages	100.0	6.5	19.2	20.5	12.3	41.1	23.0	18.1
Food prepared by consumer unit on trips	100.0	1.9	9.4	13.7	9.8	65.8	33.4	32.4
Food away from home	100.0	3.3	13.4	17.1	11.1	54.1	29.9	24.1
ALCOHOLIC BEVERAGES	100.0	2.0	11.2	16.1	10.2	59.1	32.5	26.5
HOUSING	100.0	4.7	15.4	17.5	10.6	51.7	27.0	24.7
Shelter	100.0	4.7	14.9	17.1	10.3	53.0	27.6	25.4
Owned dwellings	100.0	2.9	12.4	15.1	10.3	59.2	29.9	29.4
Mortgage interest and charges	100.0	2.3	11.0	15.4	10.9	60.4	31.0	29.4
Property taxes	100.0	3.5	12.8	14.1	9.6	60.0	29.4	30.7
Maintenance, repair, insurance, other expenses	100.0	3.8	15.2	16.3	9.8	55.0	27.8	27.2
Rented dwellings	100.0	9.0	21.1	21.9	10.4	37.5	22.8	14.8
Other lodging	100.0	0.9	7.0	11.9	9.5	70.7	30.1	40.5
Utilities, fuels, and public services	100.0	5.9	19.2	18.9	12.1	43.9	24.3	19.5
Natural gas	100.0	5.8	17.0	18.3	10.4	48.6	26.4	22.2
Electricity	100.0	6.6	20.8	19.3	12.2	41.0	23.1	17.9
Fuel oil and other fuels	100.0	4.7	20.3	14.4	10.6	50.0	24.7	25.4
Telephone services	100.0	5.4	18.2	19.5	12.8	44.1	24.6	19.5
Water and other public services	100.0	5.6	18.5	18.4	11.4	46.0	25.4	20.7

	total consumer units	not a high school graduate	high school graduate	some college	associate's degree	bachelor's degree or more		
						total	bachelor's degree	graduate degree
Household services	100.0%	2.9%	11.1%	15.1%	9.6%	61.3%	29.1%	32.2%
Personal services	100.0	3.3	9.7	12.6	9.0	65.5	30.4	35.2
Other household services	100.0	2.7	11.7	16.3	9.9	59.3	28.5	30.8
Housekeeping supplies	100.0	5.3	16.6	19.2	10.8	47.3	25.0	22.1
Laundry and cleaning supplies	100.0	7.5	19.4	20.5	12.3	40.3	24.2	16.1
Other household products	100.0	4.9	16.9	18.3	10.6	48.4	24.8	23.4
Postage and stationery	100.0	3.8	12.9	19.7	9.6	52.9	26.5	26.1
Household furnishings and equipment	100.0	3.0	12.4	17.5	10.1	56.5	28.9	27.6
Household textiles	100.0	3.3	13.2	15.7	13.3	53.2	25.9	27.2
Furniture	100.0	3.1	10.9	15.1	9.8	61.3	29.2	32.0
Floor coverings	100.0	2.1	9.4	7.8	7.6	74.2	28.2	45.2
Major appliances	100.0	3.4	16.0	17.7	10.1	53.0	30.8	22.2
Small appliances, miscellaneous housewares	100.0	4.7	12.7	16.3	11.3	53.9	27.9	26.0
Miscellaneous household equipment	100.0	2.5	12.2	19.3	9.7	55.5	28.8	26.5
APPAREL AND RELATED SERVICES	100.0	5.1	13.3	18.4	10.2	52.2	28.9	23.2
Men and boys	100.0	5.9	13.4	16.5	10.2	53.1	30.1	23.0
Men, aged 16 or older	100.0	5.7	12.6	15.8	9.9	55.1	31.4	23.7
Boys, aged 2 to 15	100.0	6.9	16.8	18.8	11.5	45.7	25.4	20.4
Women and girls	100.0	3.7	13.3	18.0	10.9	53.0	29.1	23.8
Women, aged 16 or older	100.0	3.4	12.8	17.2	11.2	54.0	30.0	24.0
Girls, aged 2 to 15	100.0	5.1	15.9	21.8	9.1	47.2	24.3	22.9
Children under age 2	100.0	9.7	14.9	19.4	9.7	46.8	27.9	19.0
Footwear	100.0	5.9	14.3	23.2	9.1	46.6	27.2	19.3
Other apparel products and services	100.0	5.5	11.3	15.4	9.6	58.1	29.0	29.0
TRANSPORTATION	100.0	3.6	14.8	19.4	12.8	49.3	27.1	22.2
Vehicle purchases	100.0	2.5	12.5	21.2	14.2	49.6	26.9	22.7
Cars and trucks, new	100.0	1.7	8.3	20.1	15.7	54.1	27.8	26.2
Cars and trucks, used	100.0	3.4	16.8	21.8	12.9	45.1	26.2	19.0
Gasoline and motor oil	100.0	4.8	18.0	19.2	13.2	44.8	25.8	18.9
Other vehicle expenses	100.0	4.1	15.8	18.7	11.9	49.2	27.7	21.5
Vehicle finance charges	100.0	2.4	15.9	19.8	15.3	46.7	27.7	18.9
Maintenance and repairs	100.0	3.7	15.6	17.0	12.2	51.4	28.0	23.4
Vehicle insurance	100.0	5.3	17.8	20.2	11.9	44.1	26.8	17.4
Vehicle rentals, leases, licenses, other charges	100.0	2.7	11.4	17.7	9.7	58.5	29.6	28.9
Public transportation	100.0	2.5	7.4	12.7	6.3	71.2	32.2	39.0
HEALTH CARE	100.0	4.8	17.0	17.2	11.1	49.9	26.6	23.3
Health insurance	100.0	4.8	18.1	16.5	11.4	49.1	26.5	22.7
Medical services	100.0	3.6	14.1	18.1	10.4	53.7	28.9	24.8
Drugs	100.0	7.0	17.3	19.1	11.1	45.3	23.7	21.5
Medical supplies	100.0	3.1	16.0	15.0	11.4	54.5	26.1	28.4
ENTERTAINMENT	100.0	3.7	13.4	16.9	11.0	54.7	27.9	26.8
Fees and admissions	100.0	1.0	6.2	12.0	8.1	72.4	33.1	39.2
Audio and visual equipment and services	100.0	5.1	18.0	19.5	11.4	46.0	25.7	20.3
Pets, toys, hobbies, and playground equipment	100.0	4.3	15.1	19.9	12.9	47.2	24.7	22.4
Other entertainment products and services	100.0	3.4	10.0	12.7	11.4	62.1	30.7	31.4
PERSONAL CARE PRODUCTS AND SERVICES	100.0	4.0	13.2	17.5	11.1	53.7	27.6	26.0
READING	100.0	2.3	10.4	15.4	10.9	61.5	27.9	33.5
EDUCATION	100.0	0.8	3.8	15.3	8.8	71.2	33.5	37.7
TOBACCO PRODUCTS AND SMOKING SUPPLIES	100.0	8.5	32.0	26.3	12.5	20.6	14.9	5.8

	total consumer units	not a high school graduate	high school graduate	some college	associate's degree	bachelor's degree or more		
						total	bachelor's degree	graduate degree
MISCELLANEOUS	100.0%	3.1%	17.8%	18.2%	9.4%	51.3%	25.2%	26.0%
CASH CONTRIBUTIONS	100.0	2.7	11.3	13.2	8.6	64.3	28.4	35.9
PERSONAL INSURANCE AND PENSIONS	100.0	2.3	10.9	14.1	10.6	62.2	30.7	31.5
Life and other personal insurance	100.0	2.6	12.3	12.2	8.8	64.1	30.6	33.5
Pensions and Social Security	100.0	2.2	10.8	14.2	10.7	62.1	30.7	31.3
PERSONAL TAXES	100.0	−0.2	5.1	6.6	9.5	79.0	37.7	41.3
Federal income taxes	100.0	−0.7	3.4	4.8	9.4	83.1	40.3	42.8
State and local income taxes	100.0	0.8	8.3	10.1	9.6	71.2	32.3	38.9
Other taxes	100.0	3.0	12.6	13.3	9.7	61.5	28.5	32.9
GIFTS FOR PEOPLE IN OTHER HOUSEHOLDS	100.0	2.9	10.2	13.1	7.8	65.7	30.9	34.6

Source: Calculations by New Strategist based on the Bureau of Labor Statistics 2012 Consumer Expenditure Survey, Internet site http://www.bls.gov/cex/home.htm

10

Time Use

Trends

Traditional sex roles are still alive and well.

On an average day, women spend more time than men doing housework. Men spend more time working and watching television.

Time use varies by age.

Older Americans watch the most television. Teenagers spend the most time playing games, and the middle aged work the most.

Women aged 25 to 34 have the least amount of leisure time.

Among men, those aged 35 to 44 have the least amount of leisure.

Asian men spend the most time at work.

On an average day in 2012, Asian men worked for 4.29 hours—15 percent more than the average man.

Hispanic women spend the most time doing housework.

Black women spend the most time participating in religious activities.

Americans Watch 2.83 Hours of Television a Day

They spend about 21 minutes a day shopping, on average.

For the past decade, the Bureau of Labor Statistics has been asking Americans how they spend their time through the American Time Use Survey. This survey asks a nationally representative sample about their activities during the past 24 hours, minute by minute. The "diary" data are combined and analyzed by type of activity and demographic characteristic.

Not surprisingly, sleep takes up the most time. The average person reported sleeping 8.73 hours per day in 2012. People work an average of 3.19 hours a day, a figure that includes those who worked on diary day, those who had the day off, and those who have no job. The 42 percent of people who worked on diary day spent an average of 7.63 hours on the job.

Traditional sex roles are abundantly evident in these statistics. On an average day, women spend much more time than men doing housework, tending children, and talking on the telephone. Men spend more time working, tending the lawn, and watching television.

■ Researchers and public policymakers use the results of the time use survey to determine how people balance work and family issues.

Women spend nearly one hour a day doing housework, on average

(average number of hours per day people spend on selected primary activities, by sex, 2012)

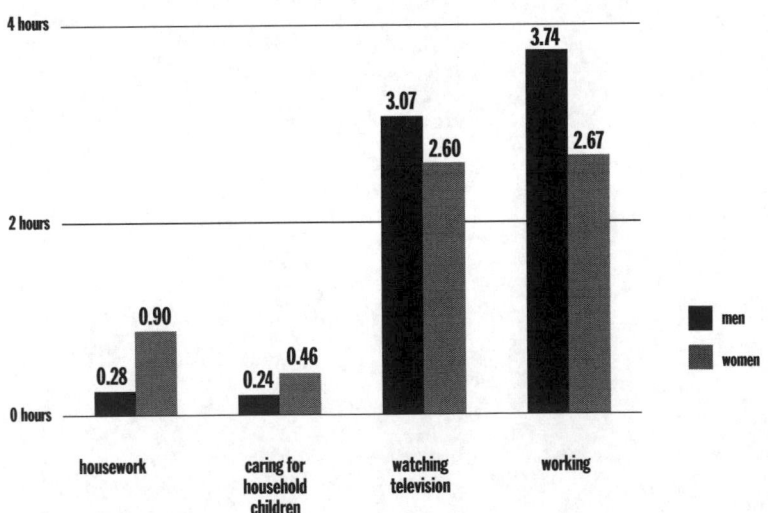

Table 10.1 Total Time Use and Percent Reporting Activity, 2012

(number and percent of total people aged 15 or older participating in primary activities on an average day, hours spent doing activity by the average person and by participants, 2012; number of people in thousands)

	total people participating		time spent in activity	
	number	percent	average person	participants
Total, all activities	**247,386**	**100.0%**	**24.00 hrs.**	**24.00 hrs.**
Personal care activities	247,307	100.0	9.47	9.47
Sleeping	247,171	99.9	8.73	8.74
Grooming	192,786	77.9	0.67	0.86
Household activities	184,544	74.6	1.75	2.34
Housework	85,574	34.6	0.60	1.73
Food preparation and cleanup	129,941	52.5	0.53	1.00
Lawn, garden, and houseplants	24,199	9.8	0.18	1.87
Animals and pets	37,443	15.1	0.10	0.65
Household management	56,770	22.9	0.18	0.77
Caring for and helping household members	60,537	24.5	0.44	1.78
Caring for and helping household children	48,918	19.8	0.36	1.80
Caring for and helping people in other households	27,456	11.1	0.12	1.09
Caring for and helping children in other households	10,829	4.4	0.06	1.37
Working and work-related activities	108,489	43.9	3.26	7.43
Working	103,467	41.8	3.19	7.63
Job search and interviewing	4,037	1.6	0.04	2.37
Education	20,951	8.5	0.46	5.45
Taking class	13,389	5.4	0.28	5.16
Research and homework	15,228	6.2	0.17	2.75
Shopping (store, telephone, Internet)	92,764	37.5	0.35	0.94
Grocery shopping	30,666	12.4	0.09	0.74
Shopping, except groceries, food, and gas	50,848	20.6	0.23	1.14
Eating and drinking	237,403	96.0	1.13	1.17
Socializing, relaxing, and leisure	235,543	95.2	4.79	5.03
Socializing and communicating	87,403	35.3	0.65	1.84
Relaxing and leisure	225,272	91.1	3.96	4.35
Watching television	197,962	80.0	2.83	3.53
Playing games (including computer)	23,614	9.5	0.21	2.18
Computer use for leisure (except games)	32,474	13.1	0.21	1.61
Reading for personal interest	51,174	20.7	0.33	1.58
Sports, exercise, and recreation	49,400	20.0	0.35	1.74
Religious and spiritual activities	22,278	9.0	0.15	1.66
Volunteering	14,273	5.8	0.13	2.18
Telephone calls	31,518	12.7	0.10	0.81
Traveling	209,446	84.7	1.20	1.42

Note: Primary activities are those respondents identified as their main activity. Other activities done simultaneously, such as eating while watching TV, are not included. Numbers may not add to total because not all categories are shown.
Source: Unpublished tables from the Bureau of Labor Statistics' 2012 American Time Use Survey, Internet site http://www.bls.gov/tus/calculations by New Strategist

Table 10.2 Men's Time Use and Percent Reporting Activity, 2012

(number and percent of total men aged 15 or older participating in primary activities on an average day, hours spent doing activity by the average man and by male participants, 2012; number of men in thousands)

	total men participating		time spent in activity	
			average man	male participants
	number	percent		
Total, all activities	**119,508**	**100.0%**	**24.00 hrs.**	**24.00 hrs.**
Personal care activities	119,438	99.9	9.20	9.20
Sleeping	119,360	99.9	8.60	8.61
Grooming	89,126	74.6	0.55	0.74
Household activities	78,420	65.6	1.29	1.97
Housework	23,696	19.8	0.28	1.40
Food preparation and cleanup	46,886	39.2	0.28	0.72
Lawn, garden, and houseplants	14,007	11.7	0.25	2.11
Animals and pets	15,708	13.1	0.09	0.65
Household management	23,694	19.8	0.15	0.75
Caring for and helping household members	23,584	19.7	0.30	1.50
Caring for and helping household children	17,973	15.0	0.24	1.59
Caring for and helping people in other households	11,714	9.8	0.10	1.05
Caring for and helping children in other households	3,905	3.3	0.04	1.18
Working and work-related activities	58,330	48.8	3.82	7.83
Working	55,586	46.5	3.74	8.05
Job search and interviewing	2,250	1.9	0.04	2.36
Education	10,467	8.8	0.49	5.62
Taking class	6,895	5.8	0.30	5.17
Research and homework	7,332	6.1	0.18	2.89
Shopping (store, telephone, Internet)	40,629	34.0	0.27	0.80
Grocery shopping	11,486	9.6	0.07	0.69
Shopping, except groceries, food, and gas	20,929	17.5	0.18	1.03
Eating and drinking	114,640	95.9	1.17	1.22
Socializing, relaxing, and leisure	114,659	95.9	5.10	5.31
Socializing and communicating	40,009	33.5	0.64	1.92
Relaxing and leisure	110,082	92.1	4.29	4.66
Watching television	96,597	80.8	3.07	3.80
Playing games (including computer)	12,883	10.8	0.27	2.53
Computer use for leisure (except games)	15,806	13.2	0.24	1.79
Reading for personal interest	20,927	17.5	0.26	1.50
Sports, exercise, and recreation	26,904	22.5	0.44	1.95
Religious and spiritual activities	8,028	6.7	0.12	1.72
Volunteering	5,570	4.7	0.11	2.29
Telephone calls	10,310	8.6	0.06	0.72
Traveling	103,682	86.8	1.26	1.45

Note: Primary activities are those respondents identified as their main activity. Other activities done simultaneously, such as eating while watching TV, are not included. Numbers may not add to total because not all categories are shown.
Source: Unpublished tables from the Bureau of Labor Statistics' 2012 American Time Use Survey, Internet site http://www.bls.gov/tus/calculations by New Strategist

Table 10.3 Women's Time Use and Percent Reporting Activity, 2012

(number and percent of total women aged 15 or older participating in primary activities on an average day, hours spent doing activity by the average woman and by female participants, 2012; number of women in thousands)

	total women participating		time spent in activity	
	number	percent	average woman	female participants
Total, all activities	**127,878**	**100.0%**	**24.00 hrs.**	**24.00 hrs.**
Personal care activities	127,869	100.0	9.72	9.72
Sleeping	127,811	99.9	8.86	8.86
Grooming	103,660	81.1	0.78	0.96
Household activities	106,124	83.0	2.17	2.62
Housework	61,879	48.4	0.90	1.86
Food preparation and cleanup	83,056	64.9	0.75	1.16
Lawn, garden, and houseplants	10,192	8.0	0.12	1.53
Animals and pets	21,735	17.0	0.11	0.65
Household management	33,076	25.9	0.20	0.78
Caring for and helping household members	36,953	28.9	0.57	1.96
Caring for and helping household children	30,944	24.2	0.46	1.91
Caring for and helping people in other households	15,742	12.3	0.14	1.13
Caring for and helping children in other households	6,925	5.4	0.08	1.47
Working and work-related activities	50,159	39.2	2.73	6.96
Working	47,881	37.4	2.67	7.13
Job search and interviewing	1,787	1.4	0.03	2.39
Education	10,484	8.2	0.43	5.29
Taking class	6,494	5.1	0.26	5.14
Research and homework	7,896	6.2	0.16	2.63
Shopping (store, telephone, Internet)	52,135	40.8	0.43	1.05
Grocery shopping	19,179	15.0	0.12	0.78
Shopping, except groceries, food, and gas	29,919	23.4	0.29	1.22
Eating and drinking	122,762	96.0	1.09	1.14
Socializing, relaxing, and leisure	120,883	94.5	4.50	4.76
Socializing and communicating	47,394	37.1	0.66	1.78
Relaxing and leisure	115,190	90.1	3.66	4.06
Watching television	101,365	79.3	2.60	3.28
Playing games (including computer)	10,731	8.4	0.15	1.77
Computer use for leisure (except games)	16,668	13.0	0.19	1.43
Reading for personal interest	30,247	23.7	0.38	1.63
Sports, exercise, and recreation	22,496	17.6	0.26	1.49
Religious and spiritual activities	14,250	11.1	0.18	1.63
Volunteering	8,703	6.8	0.14	2.11
Telephone calls	21,208	16.6	0.14	0.86
Traveling	105,764	82.7	1.15	1.39

Note: Primary activities are those respondents identified as their main activity. Other activities done simultaneously, such as eating while watching TV, are not included. Numbers may not add to total because not all categories are shown.
Source: Unpublished tables from the Bureau of Labor Statistics' 2012 American Time Use Survey, Internet site http://www.bls .gov/tus/calculations by New Strategist

Table 10.4 Time Use by Sex, 2012

(hours per day spent in primary activities by people aged 15 or older by sex, and index of women's time to men's, 2012)

	hours per day		index, women's time to men's
	men	women	
Total, all activities	**24.00 hrs.**	**24.00 hrs.**	**100**
Personal care activities	9.20	9.72	106
Sleeping	8.60	8.86	103
Grooming	0.55	0.78	142
Household activities	1.29	2.17	168
Housework	0.28	0.90	321
Food preparation and cleanup	0.28	0.75	268
Lawn, garden, and houseplants	0.25	0.12	48
Animals and pets	0.09	0.11	122
Household management	0.15	0.20	133
Caring for and helping household members	0.30	0.57	190
Caring for and helping household children	0.24	0.46	192
Caring for and helping people in other households	0.10	0.14	140
Caring for and helping children in other households	0.04	0.08	200
Working and work-related activities	3.82	2.73	71
Working	3.74	2.67	71
Job search and interviewing	0.04	0.03	75
Education	0.49	0.43	88
Taking class	0.30	0.26	87
Research and homework	0.18	0.16	89
Shopping (store, telephone, Internet)	0.27	0.43	159
Grocery shopping	0.07	0.12	171
Shopping, except groceries, food, and gas	0.18	0.29	161
Eating and drinking	1.17	1.09	93
Socializing, relaxing, and leisure	5.10	4.50	88
Socializing and communicating	0.64	0.66	103
Relaxing and leisure	4.29	3.66	85
Watching television	3.07	2.60	85
Playing games (including computer)	0.27	0.15	56
Computer use for leisure (except games)	0.24	0.19	79
Reading for personal interest	0.26	0.38	146
Sports, exercise, and recreation	0.44	0.26	59
Religious and spiritual activities	0.12	0.18	150
Volunteering	0.11	0.14	127
Telephone calls	0.06	0.14	233
Traveling	1.26	1.15	91

Note: Primary activities are those respondents identified as their main activity. Other activities done simultaneously, such as eating while watching TV, are not included. Numbers may not add to total because not all categories are shown. The index is calculated by dividing women's time by men's time and multiplying by 100.
Source: Unpublished tables from the Bureau of Labor Statistics' 2012 American Time Use Survey, Internet site http://www.bls .gov/tus/calculations by New Strategist

Women Aged 25 to 34 Have the Least Amount of Leisure Time

Men aged 45 to 54 spend the most time at work.

Time use varies sharply by age. Teenagers and older Americans have the most leisure time and the middle aged have the least. Women aged 25 to 34 spend much more time than the average person caring for household children, and men aged 45 to 54 spend much more time working.

Among men, leisure time is greatest for those aged 75 or older, with 7.53 hours of leisure a day—48 percent more than the average man. Men aged 45 to 54 spend 45 percent more time at work than the average man. Men aged 25 to 44 spend more than twice as much time as the average man caring for household children. Among males, teenagers spend the most time on the telephone.

Women aged 25 to 44 spend more than twice as much time as the average woman caring for household children. They also spend 26 to 31 percent more time than the average woman at work. That explains why women aged 25 to 44 have 20 to 22 percent less leisure time than the average woman. Women aged 75 or older spend the most time reading. Teenage girls spend the most time on the telephone.

■ Women aged 25 to 34 spend only 2.04 hours a day watching television—less time than any other demographic segment.

Women have less leisure time than men

(average number of hours per day people spend socializing, relaxing, and at leisure as a primary activity, by sex, 2012)

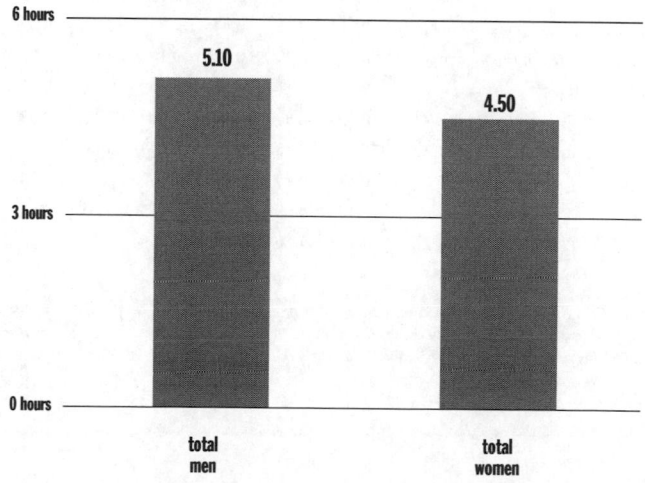

Table 10.5 Time Use by Age, 2012

(average hours per day spent in primary activities by people aged 15 or older by age, by type of activity, 2012)

	total people	15–19	20–24	25–34	35–44	45–54	55–64	65–74	75+
Total, all activities (hours)	24.00	24.00	24.00	24.00	24.00	24.00	24.00	24.00	24.00
Personal care	9.47	10.41	9.80	9.44	9.20	9.18	9.25	9.40	9.87
Sleeping	8.73	9.61	9.08	8.76	8.52	8.42	8.47	8.66	9.07
Grooming	0.67	0.78	0.70	0.66	0.63	0.69	0.66	0.62	0.64
Household activities	1.75	0.64	0.83	1.47	1.81	1.86	2.10	2.58	2.53
Housework	0.60	0.23	0.34	0.56	0.69	0.65	0.67	0.77	0.75
Food preparation and cleanup	0.53	0.15	0.27	0.55	0.62	0.56	0.56	0.66	0.72
Lawn, garden, and houseplants	0.18	0.06	0.03	0.08	0.12	0.21	0.26	0.41	0.37
Animals and pets	0.10	0.06	0.06	0.05	0.09	0.12	0.13	0.16	0.12
Household management	0.18	0.06	0.07	0.13	0.14	0.16	0.25	0.30	0.36
Caring for and helping household members	0.44	0.10	0.53	0.91	0.89	0.31	0.11	0.09	0.10
Caring for and helping household children	0.36	0.08	0.49	0.81	0.75	0.22	0.05	0.04	0.01
Caring for and helping people in other households	0.12	0.11	0.07	0.07	0.08	0.14	0.20	0.17	0.13
Caring for and helping children in other households	0.06	0.05	0.02	0.04	0.03	0.07	0.10	0.11	0.07
Work and work-related activities	3.26	0.97	3.32	4.22	4.44	4.53	3.41	1.27	0.30
Working	3.19	0.90	3.20	4.14	4.38	4.45	3.35	1.25	0.24
Job search and interviewing	0.04	0.00	0.10	0.05	0.04	0.04	0.03	0.00	0.00
Education	0.46	3.15	0.99	0.37	0.18	0.05	0.03	0.01	0.00
Taking class	0.28	2.33	0.45	0.14	0.08	0.02	0.01	0.00	0.00
Research and homework	0.17	0.76	0.50	0.21	0.10	0.04	0.02	0.00	0.00
Shopping (store, telephone, Internet)	0.35	0.27	0.25	0.37	0.38	0.34	0.39	0.41	0.34
Grocery shopping	0.09	0.03	0.04	0.11	0.10	0.09	0.10	0.12	0.12
Shopping, except groceries, food, and gas	0.23	0.22	0.19	0.23	0.25	0.23	0.26	0.27	0.20
Eating and drinking	1.13	0.91	1.03	1.10	1.09	1.09	1.18	1.29	1.40
Socializing, relaxing, and leisure	4.79	4.67	4.85	3.87	3.77	4.33	5.14	6.52	7.23
Socializing and communicating	0.65	0.85	0.95	0.58	0.58	0.57	0.57	0.71	0.69
Relaxing and leisure	3.96	3.54	3.63	3.12	3.05	3.61	4.43	5.66	6.40
Watching television	2.83	2.29	2.35	2.32	2.30	2.68	3.25	4.01	4.23
Playing games (including computer)	0.21	0.55	0.44	0.23	0.11	0.09	0.10	0.18	0.26
Computer use for leisure (excluding games)	0.21	0.29	0.41	0.18	0.17	0.20	0.18	0.22	0.12
Reading for personal interest	0.33	0.11	0.15	0.14	0.19	0.26	0.43	0.68	0.97
Sports, exercise, recreation	0.35	0.80	0.40	0.32	0.31	0.28	0.25	0.37	0.25
Religious and spiritual activities	0.15	0.15	0.08	0.09	0.11	0.14	0.20	0.19	0.31
Volunteer activities	0.13	0.09	0.07	0.07	0.14	0.13	0.14	0.24	0.15
Telephone calls	0.10	0.18	0.17	0.09	0.06	0.07	0.10	0.11	0.15
Traveling	1.20	1.20	1.29	1.32	1.30	1.26	1.21	0.96	0.78

Note: Primary activities are those respondents identified as their main activity. Other activities done simultaneously, such as eating while watching TV, are not included. Numbers may not add to total because not all categories are shown.
Source: Unpublished tables from the Bureau of Labor Statistics' 2012 American Time Use Survey, Internet site http://www.bls.gov/tus/calculations by New Strategist

Table 10.6 Index of Time Use by Age, 2012

(index of time use by age to average for total people, by type of activity, 2012)

INDEX OF TIME TO AVERAGE	total people	15–19	20–24	25–34	35–44	45–54	55–64	65–74	75+
Total, all activities	**100**	**100**	**100**	**100**	**100**	**100**	**100**	**100**	**100**
Personal care	100	110	103	100	97	97	98	99	104
Sleeping	100	110	104	100	98	96	97	99	104
Grooming	100	116	104	99	94	103	99	93	96
Household activities	100	37	47	84	103	106	120	147	145
Housework	100	38	57	93	115	108	112	128	125
Food preparation and cleanup	100	28	51	104	117	106	106	125	136
Lawn, garden, and houseplants	100	33	17	44	67	117	144	228	206
Animals and pets	100	60	60	50	90	120	130	160	120
Household management	100	33	39	72	78	89	139	167	200
Caring for and helping household members	100	23	120	207	202	70	25	20	23
Caring for and helping household children	100	22	136	225	208	61	14	11	3
Caring for and helping people in other households	100	92	58	58	67	117	167	142	108
Caring for and helping children in other households	100	83	33	67	50	117	167	183	117
Work and work-related activities	100	30	102	129	136	139	105	39	9
Working	100	28	100	130	137	139	105	39	8
Job search and interviewing	100	0	250	125	100	100	75	0	0
Education	100	685	215	80	39	11	7	2	0
Taking class	100	832	161	50	29	7	4	0	0
Research and homework	100	447	294	124	59	24	12	0	0
Shopping (store, telephone, Internet)	100	77	71	106	109	97	111	117	97
Grocery shopping	100	33	44	122	111	100	111	133	133
Shopping, except groceries, food, and gas	100	96	83	100	109	100	113	117	87
Eating and drinking	100	81	91	97	96	96	104	114	124
Socializing, relaxing, and leisure	100	97	101	81	79	90	107	136	151
Socializing and communicating	100	131	146	89	89	88	88	109	106
Relaxing and leisure	100	89	92	79	77	91	112	143	162
Watching television	100	81	83	82	81	95	115	142	149
Playing games (including computer)	100	262	210	110	52	43	48	86	124
Computer use for leisure (excluding games)	100	138	195	86	81	95	86	105	57
Reading for personal interest	100	33	45	42	58	79	130	206	294
Sports, exercise, recreation	100	229	114	91	89	80	71	106	71
Religious and spiritual activities	100	100	53	60	73	93	133	127	207
Volunteer activities	100	69	54	54	108	100	108	185	115
Telephone calls	100	180	170	90	60	70	100	110	150
Traveling	100	100	108	110	108	105	101	80	65

Note: Primary activities are those respondents identified as their main activity. Other activities done simultaneously, such as eating while watching TV, are not included. The index is calculated by dividing age group's time by total time and multiplying by 100.

Source: Unpublished tables from the Bureau of Labor Statistics' 2012 American Time Use Survey, Internet site http://www.bls.gov/tus/calculations by New Strategist

Table 10.7 Men's Time Use by Age, 2012

(average hours per day spent in primary activities by men aged 15 or older by age, by type of activity, 2012)

	total men	15–19	20–24	25–34	35–44	45–54	55–64	65–74	75+
Total, all activities (hours)	24.00	24.00	24.00	24.00	24.00	24.00	24.00	24.00	24.00
Personal care	9.20	10.07	9.41	9.16	8.92	8.99	8.92	9.21	9.77
Sleeping	8.60	9.49	8.83	8.55	8.33	8.38	8.31	8.58	9.15
Grooming	0.55	0.57	0.55	0.59	0.54	0.56	0.52	0.53	0.57
Household activities	1.29	0.58	0.62	1.03	1.20	1.34	1.68	2.09	1.99
Housework	0.28	0.17	0.21	0.29	0.35	0.30	0.32	0.25	0.19
Food preparation and cleanup	0.28	0.09	0.15	0.29	0.31	0.31	0.34	0.34	0.39
Lawn, garden, and houseplants	0.25	0.09	–	0.11	0.16	0.28	0.33	0.60	0.54
Animals and pets	0.09	0.04	0.04	0.05	0.09	0.08	0.12	0.15	0.13
Household management	0.15	0.05	0.07	0.11	0.09	0.13	0.25	0.29	0.31
Caring for and helping household members	0.30	0.06	–	0.56	0.62	0.27	0.08	0.07	0.09
Caring for and helping household children	0.24	0.04	–	0.50	0.51	0.21	0.04	0.00	–
Caring for and helping people in other households	0.10	0.12	0.07	0.08	0.05	0.10	0.16	0.15	0.11
Caring for and helping children in other households	0.04	0.05	0.00	0.04	0.01	0.03	0.05	0.09	0.04
Work and work-related activities	3.82	0.80	3.21	4.92	5.48	5.18	4.09	1.57	0.52
Working	3.74	0.71	3.06	4.81	5.44	5.11	4.02	1.54	0.47
Job search and interviewing	0.04	–	0.12	0.06	0.03	0.05	0.03	0.00	0.00
Education	0.49	3.35	0.94	0.38	0.16	0.05	–	0.00	0.00
Taking class	0.30	2.54	0.42	0.09	–	0.00	0.00	0.00	0.00
Research and homework	0.18	0.79	0.43	0.25	0.09	0.03	0.00	0.00	0.00
Shopping (store, telephone, Internet)	0.27	0.20	0.20	0.29	0.29	0.26	0.30	0.32	0.28
Grocery shopping	0.07	0.02	0.02	0.08	0.07	0.06	0.08	0.11	0.09
Shopping, except groceries, food, and gas	0.18	0.16	0.16	0.19	0.19	0.18	0.19	0.19	0.17
Eating and drinking	1.17	0.95	1.02	1.11	1.13	1.14	1.22	1.41	1.52
Socializing, relaxing, and leisure	5.10	5.03	5.78	4.24	3.94	4.58	5.46	6.85	7.53
Socializing and communicating	0.64	0.64	1.20	0.54	0.57	0.58	0.55	0.72	0.61
Relaxing and leisure	4.29	4.19	4.30	3.55	3.23	3.86	4.77	5.99	6.78
Watching television	3.07	2.38	2.62	2.60	2.49	2.94	3.60	4.39	4.61
Playing games (including computer)	0.27	0.92	0.71	0.34	0.12	0.07	0.07	0.15	0.17
Computer use for leisure (excluding games)	0.24	0.35	0.57	0.19	0.18	0.19	0.18	0.23	0.15
Reading for personal interest	0.26	0.16	0.10	0.11	0.13	0.19	0.34	0.61	0.92
Sports, exercise, recreation	0.44	1.08	0.48	0.42	0.32	0.33	0.28	0.53	0.38
Religious and spiritual activities	0.12	0.14	0.08	0.06	0.11	0.13	0.14	0.14	0.19
Volunteer activities	0.11	0.08	–	0.06	0.09	0.08	0.10	0.27	0.15
Telephone calls	0.06	0.14	0.13	0.06	0.04	0.04	0.04	0.03	0.09
Traveling	1.26	1.13	1.32	1.38	1.43	1.25	1.26	1.06	0.85

Note: Primary activities are those respondents identified as their main activity. Other activities done simultaneously, such as eating while watching TV, are not included. Numbers may not add to total because not all categories are shown. "–" means sample is too small to make a reliable estimate.
Source: Unpublished tables from the Bureau of Labor Statistics' 2012 American Time Use Survey, Internet site http://www.bls .gov/tus/calculations by New Strategist

Table 10.8 Index of Men's Time Use by Age, 2012

(index of time use by age to average for total men, by type of activity, 2012)

INDEX OF TIME TO AVERAGE FOR TOTAL MEN	total men	15–19	20–24	25–34	35–44	45–54	55–64	65–74	75+
Total, all activities	100	100	100	100	100	100	100	100	100
Personal care	100	109	102	100	97	98	97	100	106
Sleeping	100	110	103	99	97	97	97	100	106
Grooming	100	104	100	107	98	102	95	96	104
Household activities	100	45	48	80	93	104	130	162	154
Housework	100	61	75	104	125	107	114	89	68
Food preparation and cleanup	100	32	54	104	111	111	121	121	139
Lawn, garden, and houseplants	100	36	–	44	64	112	132	240	216
Animals and pets	100	44	44	56	100	89	133	167	144
Household management	100	33	47	73	60	87	167	193	207
Caring for and helping household members	100	20	–	187	207	90	27	23	30
Caring for and helping household children	100	17	–	208	213	88	17	0	–
Caring for and helping people in other households	100	120	70	80	50	100	160	150	110
Caring for and helping children in other households	100	125	0	100	25	75	125	225	100
Work and work-related activities	100	21	84	129	143	136	107	41	14
Working	100	19	82	129	145	137	107	41	13
Job search and interviewing	100	–	300	150	75	125	75	0	0
Education	100	684	192	78	33	10	–	0	0
Taking class	100	847	140	30	–	0	0	0	0
Research and homework	100	439	239	139	50	17	0	0	0
Shopping (store, telephone, Internet)	100	74	74	107	107	96	111	119	104
Grocery shopping	100	29	29	114	100	86	114	157	129
Shopping, except groceries, food, and gas	100	89	89	106	106	100	106	106	94
Eating and drinking	100	81	87	95	97	97	104	121	130
Socializing, relaxing, and leisure	100	99	113	83	77	90	107	134	148
Socializing and communicating	100	100	188	84	89	91	86	113	95
Relaxing and leisure	100	98	100	83	75	90	111	140	158
Watching television	100	78	85	85	81	96	117	143	150
Playing games (including computer)	100	341	263	126	44	26	26	56	63
Computer use for leisure (excluding games)	100	146	238	79	75	79	75	96	63
Reading for personal interest	100	62	38	42	50	73	131	235	354
Sports, exercise, recreation	100	245	109	95	73	75	64	120	86
Religious and spiritual activities	100	117	67	50	92	108	117	117	158
Volunteer activities	100	73	–	55	82	73	91	245	136
Telephone calls	100	233	217	100	67	67	67	50	150
Traveling	100	90	105	110	113	99	100	84	67

Note: Primary activities are those respondents identified as their main activity. Other activities done simultaneously, such as eating while watching TV, are not included. The index is calculated by dividing time spent by men in the age group by total men's time and multiplying by 100. "–" means sample is too small to make a reliable estimate.
Source: Unpublished tables from the Bureau of Labor Statistics' 2012 American Time Use Survey, Internet site http://www.bls .gov/tus/calculations by New Strategist

Table 10.9 Women's Time Use by Age, 2012

(average hours per day spent in primary activities by women aged 15 or older by age, by type of activity, 2012)

	total women	15–19	20–24	25–34	35–44	45–54	55–64	65–74	75+
Total, all activities (hours)	**24.00**	**24.00**	**24.00**	**24.00**	**24.00**	**24.00**	**24.00**	**24.00**	**24.00**
Personal care	9.72	10.77	10.18	9.72	9.47	9.37	9.56	9.57	9.95
Sleeping	8.86	9.74	9.33	8.97	8.69	8.46	8.61	8.74	9.02
Grooming	0.78	1.01	0.85	0.73	0.73	0.81	0.78	0.70	0.68
Household activities	2.17	0.70	1.04	1.90	2.40	2.36	2.48	3.02	2.90
Housework	0.90	0.31	0.47	0.82	1.02	0.98	0.99	1.23	1.12
Food preparation and cleanup	0.75	0.21	0.38	0.79	0.91	0.80	0.76	0.94	0.95
Lawn, garden, and houseplants	0.12	0.00	0.00	0.04	0.07	0.14	0.20	0.24	0.25
Animals and pets	0.11	0.08	0.08	0.05	0.08	0.15	0.15	0.17	0.11
Household management	0.20	0.07	0.07	0.14	0.19	0.20	0.25	0.31	0.40
Caring for and helping household members	0.57	0.14	0.80	1.26	1.15	0.34	0.14	0.11	0.11
Caring for and helping household children	0.46	0.12	0.74	1.10	0.97	0.24	0.06	0.05	0.00
Caring for and helping people in other households	0.14	0.10	0.08	0.07	0.10	0.17	0.23	0.18	0.14
Caring for and helping children in other households	0.08	0.05	0.04	0.04	0.05	0.10	0.14	0.12	0.09
Work and work-related activities	2.73	1.16	3.43	3.55	3.43	3.90	2.78	1.01	0.15
Working	2.67	1.10	3.32	3.49	3.36	3.83	2.74	0.99	0.09
Job search and interviewing	0.03	–	–	0.05	0.05	0.03	0.03	0.00	0.00
Education	0.43	2.94	1.05	0.35	0.21	0.06	0.03	0.00	0.00
Taking class	0.26	2.12	0.48	0.17	0.09	0.00	0.00	0.00	0.00
Research and homework	0.16	0.73	0.56	0.18	0.11	0.04	0.00	0.00	0.00
Shopping (store, telephone, Internet)	0.43	0.36	0.30	0.45	0.46	0.42	0.47	0.49	0.38
Grocery shopping	0.12	0.04	0.06	0.14	0.13	0.11	0.12	0.13	0.14
Shopping, except groceries, food, and gas	0.29	0.28	0.22	0.28	0.31	0.28	0.32	0.34	0.22
Eating and drinking	1.09	0.88	1.04	1.09	1.04	1.04	1.15	1.18	1.33
Socializing, relaxing, and leisure	4.50	4.29	3.92	3.51	3.61	4.10	4.84	6.23	7.04
Socializing and communicating	0.66	1.07	0.69	0.62	0.58	0.56	0.59	0.71	0.75
Relaxing and leisure	3.66	2.87	2.96	2.70	2.89	3.37	4.10	5.37	6.14
Watching television	2.60	2.19	2.09	2.04	2.11	2.44	2.93	3.68	3.97
Playing games (including computer)	0.15	0.16	0.16	0.12	0.10	0.12	0.12	0.21	0.32
Computer use for leisure (excluding games)	0.19	0.24	0.24	0.16	0.17	0.22	0.18	0.22	0.09
Reading for personal interest	0.38	0.06	0.20	0.17	0.25	0.34	0.51	0.74	1.01
Sports, exercise, recreation	0.26	0.50	0.32	0.22	0.30	0.24	0.21	0.22	0.16
Religious and spiritual activities	0.18	0.16	0.09	0.12	0.12	0.16	0.25	0.23	0.39
Volunteer activities	0.14	0.09	–	0.07	0.18	0.18	0.17	0.22	0.14
Telephone calls	0.14	0.23	0.21	0.11	0.09	0.11	0.15	0.17	0.19
Traveling	1.15	1.27	1.25	1.26	1.19	1.27	1.16	0.88	0.74

Note: Primary activities are those respondents identified as their main activity. Other activities done simultaneously, such as eating while watching TV, are not included. Numbers may not add to total because not all categories are shown. "–" means sample is too small to make a reliable estimate.
Source: Unpublished tables from the Bureau of Labor Statistics' 2012 American Time Use Survey, Internet site http://www.bls .gov/tus/calculations by New Strategist

Table 10.10 Index of Women's Time Use by Age, 2012

(index of time use by age to average for total women, by type of activity, 2012)

INDEX OF TIME TO AVERAGE FOR TOTAL WOMEN	total women	15–19	20–24	25–34	35–44	45–54	55–64	65–74	75+
Total, all activities	**100**	**100**	**100**	**100**	**100**	**100**	**100**	**100**	**100**
Personal care	100	111	105	100	97	96	98	98	102
Sleeping	100	110	105	101	98	95	97	99	102
Grooming	100	129	109	94	94	104	100	90	87
Household activities	100	32	48	88	111	109	114	139	134
Housework	100	34	52	91	113	109	110	137	124
Food preparation and cleanup	100	28	51	105	121	107	101	125	127
Lawn, garden, and houseplants	100	0	0	33	58	117	167	200	208
Animals and pets	100	73	73	45	73	136	136	155	100
Household management	100	35	35	70	95	100	125	155	200
Caring for and helping household members	100	25	140	221	202	60	25	19	19
Caring for and helping household children	100	26	161	239	211	52	13	11	0
Caring for and helping people in other households	100	71	57	50	71	121	164	129	100
Caring for and helping children in other households	100	63	50	50	63	125	175	150	113
Work and work-related activities	100	42	126	130	126	143	102	37	5
Working	100	41	124	131	126	143	103	37	3
Job search and interviewing	100	–	–	167	167	100	100	0	0
Education	100	684	244	81	49	14	7	0	0
Taking class	100	815	185	65	35	0	0	0	0
Research and homework	100	456	350	113	69	25	0	0	0
Shopping (store, telephone, Internet)	100	84	70	105	107	98	109	114	88
Grocery shopping	100	33	50	117	108	92	100	108	117
Shopping, except groceries, food, and gas	100	97	76	97	107	97	110	117	76
Eating and drinking	100	81	95	100	95	95	106	108	122
Socializing, relaxing, and leisure	100	95	87	78	80	91	108	138	156
Socializing and communicating	100	162	105	94	88	85	89	108	114
Relaxing and leisure	100	78	81	74	79	92	112	147	168
Watching television	100	84	80	78	81	94	113	142	153
Playing games (including computer)	100	107	107	80	67	80	80	140	213
Computer use for leisure (excluding games)	100	126	126	84	89	116	95	116	47
Reading for personal interest	100	16	53	45	66	89	134	195	266
Sports, exercise, recreation	100	192	123	85	115	92	81	85	62
Religious and spiritual activities	100	89	50	67	67	89	139	128	217
Volunteer activities	100	64	–	50	129	129	121	157	100
Telephone calls	100	164	150	79	64	79	107	121	136
Traveling	100	110	109	110	103	110	101	77	64

Note: Primary activities are those respondents identified as their main activity. Other activities done simultaneously, such as eating while watching TV, are not included. The index is calculated by dividing time spent by women in the age group by total women's time and multiplying by 100. "–" means sample is too small to make a reliable estimate.
Source: Unpublished tables from the Bureau of Labor Statistics' 2012 American Time Use Survey, Internet site http://www.bls .gov/tus/calculations by New Strategist

Asian Men Spend the Most Time at Work

Hispanic women spend the most time doing housework.

Time use varies by race and Hispanic origin, although not as much as it does by age. Asian men spend more time at work than either black, Hispanic, or white men. On an average day, Asian men are at work for 4.29 hours—15 percent more than the average man. Black men spend more time than the average man participating in religious activities. White men spend more time than Asian, black, or Hispanic men taking care of their lawns.

Hispanic women spend 34 percent more time than the average woman doing housework. Asian women spend more time than others on food preparation and cleanup. Asian and Hispanic women spend 26 to 46 percent more time than the average woman caring for household children. Black women spend 83 percent more time than the average woman participating in religious activities. On an average day, white women spend more time than Asian, black, or Hispanic women caring for animals and pets.

■ Because the Hispanic population is considerably younger than the black or white population, they spend more time in educational activities.

Time spent at work varies by race and Hispanic origin

(average number of hours per day people spend at work as the primary activity, by sex, race, and Hispanic origin, 2012)

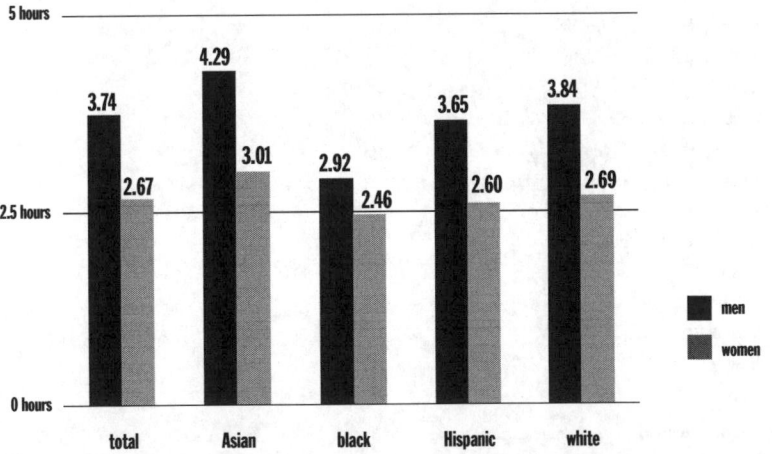

Table 10.11 Time Use by Race and Hispanic Origin, 2012

(average hours per day spent in primary activities by people aged 15 or older by race and Hispanic origin, by type of activity, 2012)

	total people	Asian	black	Hispanic	white
Total, all activities (hours)	**24.00**	**24.00**	**24.00**	**24.00**	**24.00**
Personal care	9.47	9.46	9.81	9.81	9.41
Sleeping	8.73	8.81	8.94	9.04	8.69
Grooming	0.67	0.62	0.81	0.71	0.65
Household activities	1.75	1.59	1.32	1.76	1.83
Housework	0.60	0.50	0.49	0.76	0.63
Food preparation and cleanup	0.53	0.79	0.51	0.61	0.52
Lawn, garden, and houseplants	0.18	0.10	0.09	0.11	0.20
Animals and pets	0.10	0.03	0.04	0.06	0.11
Household management	0.18	0.13	0.09	0.10	0.19
Caring for and helping household members	0.44	0.60	0.36	0.58	0.44
Caring for and helping household children	0.36	0.48	0.28	0.47	0.36
Caring for and helping people in other households	0.12	0.05	0.11	0.10	0.13
Caring for and helping children in other households	0.06	0.00	0.05	0.06	0.06
Work and work-related activities	3.26	3.73	2.77	3.19	3.31
Working	3.19	3.70	2.67	3.13	3.25
Job search and interviewing	0.04	0.00	0.07	0.02	0.04
Education	0.46	0.75	0.41	0.70	0.45
Taking class	0.28	–	0.25	0.45	0.28
Research and homework	0.17	0.42	0.15	0.23	0.16
Shopping (store, telephone, Internet)	0.35	0.36	0.37	0.36	0.35
Grocery shopping	0.09	0.11	0.08	0.09	0.09
Shopping, except groceries, food, and gas	0.23	0.22	0.26	0.25	0.23
Eating and drinking	1.13	1.47	0.84	1.08	1.15
Socializing, relaxing, and leisure	4.79	3.85	5.60	4.21	4.71
Socializing and communicating	0.65	0.46	0.67	0.62	0.66
Relaxing and leisure	3.96	3.25	4.78	3.41	3.87
Watching television	2.83	2.03	3.64	2.58	2.75
Playing games (including computer)	0.21	0.24	0.26	0.16	0.20
Computer use for leisure (excluding games)	0.21	0.50	0.17	0.14	0.20
Reading for personal interest	0.33	0.20	0.17	0.11	0.36
Sports, exercise, recreation	0.35	0.31	0.23	0.35	0.37
Religious and spiritual activities	0.15	0.15	0.27	0.17	0.13
Volunteer activities	0.13	0.06	0.11	0.07	0.13
Telephone calls	0.10	0.09	0.18	0.08	0.09
Traveling	1.20	1.24	1.24	1.21	1.20

Note: Primary activities are those respondents identified as their main activity. Other activities done simultaneously, such as eating while watching TV, are not included. Asians, blacks, and whites are those who identify themselves as being of the race alone. Hispanics may be of any race. Numbers may not add to total because not all categories are shown. "–" means sample is too small to make a reliable estimate.
Source: Unpublished tables from the Bureau of Labor Statistics' 2012 American Time Use Survey, Internet site http://www.bls .gov/tus/calculations by New Strategist

Table 10.12 Index of Time Use by Race and Hispanic Origin, 2012

(index of average hours per day people aged 15 or older spend doing primary activities by race and Hispanic origin, by type of activity, 2012)

	total people	Asian	black	Hispanic	white
INDEX OF TIME TO AVERAGE FOR TOTAL PEOPLE					
Total, all activities	**100**	**100**	**100**	**100**	**100**
Personal care	100	100	104	104	99
Sleeping	100	101	102	104	100
Grooming	100	93	121	106	97
Household activities	100	91	75	101	105
Housework	100	83	82	127	105
Food preparation and cleanup	100	149	96	115	98
Lawn, garden, and houseplants	100	56	50	61	111
Animals and pets	100	30	40	60	110
Household management	100	72	50	56	106
Caring for and helping household members	100	136	82	132	100
Caring for and helping household children	100	133	78	131	100
Caring for and helping people in other households	100	42	92	83	108
Caring for and helping children in other households	100	0	83	100	100
Work and work-related activities	100	114	85	98	102
Working	100	116	84	98	102
Job search and interviewing	100	0	175	50	100
Education	100	163	89	152	98
Taking class	100	–	89	161	100
Research and homework	100	247	88	135	94
Shopping (store, telephone, Internet)	100	103	106	103	100
Grocery shopping	100	122	89	100	100
Shopping, except groceries, food, and gas	100	96	113	109	100
Eating and drinking	100	130	74	96	102
Socializing, relaxing, and leisure	100	80	117	88	98
Socializing and communicating	100	71	103	95	102
Relaxing and leisure	100	82	121	86	98
Watching television	100	72	129	91	97
Playing games (including computer)	100	114	124	76	95
Computer use for leisure (excluding games)	100	238	81	67	95
Reading for personal interest	100	61	52	33	109
Sports, exercise, recreation	100	89	66	100	106
Religious and spiritual activities	100	100	180	113	87
Volunteer activities	100	46	85	54	100
Telephone calls	100	90	180	80	90
Traveling	100	103	103	101	100

Note: Primary activities are those respondents identified as their main activity. Other activities done simultaneously, such as eating while watching TV, are not included. Asians, blacks, and whites are those who identify themselves as being of the race alone. Hispanics may be of any race. The index is calculated by dividing time use in each race/Hispanic origin group by time use of the average person and multiplying by 100. "–" means sample is too small to make a reliable estimate.
Source: Unpublished tables from the Bureau of Labor Statistics' 2012 American Time Use Survey, Internet site http://www.bls .gov/tus/calculations by New Strategist

Table 10.13 Time Use of Men by Race and Hispanic Origin, 2012

(average hours per day spent in primary activities by men aged 15 or older by race and Hispanic origin, by type of activity, 2012)

	total men	Asian	black	Hispanic	white
Total, all activities (hours)	**24.00**	**24.00**	**24.00**	**24.00**	**24.00**
Personal care	9.20	9.16	9.48	9.56	9.16
Sleeping	8.60	8.59	8.81	8.91	8.57
Grooming	0.55	0.57	0.65	0.63	0.54
Household activities	1.29	0.94	0.95	1.13	1.37
Housework	0.28	0.24	0.24	0.32	0.29
Food preparation and cleanup	0.28	0.41	0.27	0.25	0.28
Lawn, garden, and houseplants	0.25	0.08	0.14	0.17	0.28
Animals and pets	0.09	–	0.04	0.07	0.09
Household management	0.15	0.12	0.09	0.10	0.16
Caring for and helping household members	0.30	0.48	0.22	0.37	0.29
Caring for and helping household children	0.24	0.40	0.16	0.28	0.24
Caring for and helping people in other households	0.10	0.04	0.07	0.08	0.11
Caring for and helping children in other households	0.04	–	0.01	0.04	0.04
Work and work-related activities	3.82	4.31	3.07	3.72	3.91
Working	3.74	4.29	2.92	3.65	3.84
Job search and interviewing	0.04	–	0.10	0.03	0.04
Education	0.49	0.94	0.38	0.74	0.48
Taking class	0.30	–	0.25	0.47	0.31
Research and homework	0.18	0.57	0.13	0.25	0.16
Shopping (store, telephone, Internet)	0.27	0.28	0.30	0.30	0.27
Grocery shopping	0.07	0.11	0.06	0.06	0.06
Shopping, except groceries, food, and gas	0.18	0.14	0.20	0.22	0.18
Eating and drinking	1.17	1.48	0.83	1.09	1.19
Socializing, relaxing, and leisure	5.10	4.06	6.28	4.74	4.97
Socializing and communicating	0.64	–	0.67	0.68	0.64
Relaxing and leisure	4.29	3.41	5.46	3.89	4.17
Watching television	3.07	2.02	4.11	2.85	2.98
Playing games (including computer)	0.27	0.40	0.46	0.26	0.24
Computer use for leisure (excluding games)	0.24	0.60	0.18	0.20	0.22
Reading for personal interest	0.26	0.19	0.11	0.11	0.29
Sports, exercise, recreation	0.44	0.35	0.33	0.50	0.46
Religious and spiritual activities	0.12	0.14	0.21	0.11	0.10
Volunteer activities	0.11	–	0.10	0.06	0.11
Telephone calls	0.06	0.06	0.10	0.05	0.06
Traveling	1.26	1.40	1.30	1.27	1.24

Note: Primary activities are those respondents identified as their main activity. Other activities done simultaneously, such as eating while watching TV, are not included. Asians, blacks, and whites are those who identify themselves as being of the race alone. Hispanics may be of any race. Numbers may not add to total because not all categories are shown. "–" means sample is too small to make a reliable estimate.

Source: Unpublished tables from the Bureau of Labor Statistics' 2012 American Time Use Survey, Internet site http://www.bls .gov/tus/calculations by New Strategist

Table 10.14 Index of Men's Time Use by Race and Hispanic Origin, 2012

(index of average hours per day men aged 15 or older spend doing primary activities by race and Hispanic origin, by type of activity, 2012)

INDEX OF TIME TO AVERAGE FOR TOTAL MEN	total men	Asian	black	Hispanic	white
Total, all activities	**100**	**100**	**100**	**100**	**100**
Personal care	100	100	103	104	100
Sleeping	100	100	102	104	100
Grooming	100	104	118	115	98
Household activities	100	73	74	88	106
Housework	100	86	86	114	104
Food preparation and cleanup	100	146	96	89	100
Lawn, garden, and houseplants	100	32	56	68	112
Animals and pets	100	–	44	78	100
Household management	100	80	60	67	107
Caring for and helping household members	100	160	73	123	97
Caring for and helping household children	100	167	67	117	100
Caring for and helping people in other households	100	40	70	80	110
Caring for and helping children in other households	100	–	25	100	100
Work and work-related activities	100	113	80	97	102
Working	100	115	78	98	103
Job search and interviewing	100	–	250	75	100
Education	100	192	78	151	98
Taking class	100	–	83	157	103
Research and homework	100	317	72	139	89
Shopping (store, telephone, Internet)	100	104	111	111	100
Grocery shopping	100	157	86	86	86
Shopping, except groceries, food, and gas	100	78	111	122	100
Eating and drinking	100	126	71	93	102
Socializing, relaxing, and leisure	100	80	123	93	97
Socializing and communicating	100	–	105	106	100
Relaxing and leisure	100	79	127	91	97
Watching television	100	66	134	93	97
Playing games (including computer)	100	148	170	96	89
Computer use for leisure (excluding games)	100	250	75	83	92
Reading for personal interest	100	73	42	42	112
Sports, exercise, recreation	100	80	75	114	105
Religious and spiritual activities	100	117	175	92	83
Volunteer activities	100	–	91	55	100
Telephone calls	100	100	167	83	100
Traveling	100	111	103	101	98

Note: Primary activities are those respondents identified as their main activity. Other activities done simultaneously, such as eating while watching TV, are not included. Asians, blacks, and whites are those who identify themselves as being of the race alone. Hispanics may be of any race. The index is calculated by dividing time use of men in each race/Hispanic origin group by time use of the average man and multiplying by 100. "–" means sample is too small to make a reliable estimate.
Source: Unpublished tables from the Bureau of Labor Statistics' 2012 American Time Use Survey, Internet site http://www.bls.gov/tus/calculations by New Strategist

Table 10.15 Time Use of Women by Race and Hispanic Origin, 2012

(average hours per day spent in primary activities by women aged 15 or older by race and Hispanic origin, by type of activity, 2012)

	total women	Asian	black	Hispanic	white
Total, all activities (hours)	**24.00**	**24.00**	**24.00**	**24.00**	**24.00**
Personal care	9.72	9.81	10.07	10.05	9.65
Sleeping	8.86	9.06	9.04	9.18	8.81
Grooming	0.78	0.68	0.94	0.80	0.75
Household activities	2.17	2.34	1.61	2.40	2.27
Housework	0.90	0.80	0.69	1.21	0.95
Food preparation and cleanup	0.75	1.22	0.71	0.96	0.74
Lawn, garden, and houseplants	0.12	0.13	0.06	0.05	0.13
Animals and pets	0.11	0.04	0.03	0.05	0.13
Household management	0.20	0.15	0.09	0.10	0.22
Caring for and helping household members	0.57	0.75	0.48	0.79	0.57
Caring for and helping household children	0.46	0.58	0.38	0.67	0.47
Caring for and helping people in other households	0.14	0.06	0.14	0.12	0.14
Caring for and helping children in other households	0.08	–	0.07	0.08	0.08
Work and work-related activities	2.73	3.06	2.53	2.66	2.75
Working	2.67	3.01	2.46	2.60	2.69
Job search and interviewing	0.03	–	0.05	0.02	0.03
Education	0.43	–	0.43	0.66	0.42
Taking class	0.26	–	0.25	0.43	0.26
Research and homework	0.16	–	0.17	0.21	0.15
Shopping (store, telephone, Internet)	0.43	0.45	0.44	0.42	0.43
Grocery shopping	0.12	0.11	0.10	0.12	0.12
Shopping, except groceries, food, and gas	0.29	0.32	0.31	0.28	0.28
Eating and drinking	1.09	1.45	0.84	1.06	1.11
Socializing, relaxing, and leisure	4.50	3.60	5.06	3.67	4.45
Socializing and communicating	0.66	0.40	0.67	0.56	0.67
Relaxing and leisure	3.66	3.06	4.23	2.92	3.60
Watching television	2.60	2.03	3.26	2.30	2.53
Playing games (including computer)	0.15	–	0.09	0.05	0.16
Computer use for leisure (excluding games)	0.19	–	0.16	0.08	0.18
Reading for personal interest	0.38	0.21	0.22	0.11	0.42
Sports, exercise, recreation	0.26	0.26	0.16	0.21	0.28
Religious and spiritual activities	0.18	0.17	0.33	0.23	0.16
Volunteer activities	0.14	0.05	0.13	0.08	0.15
Telephone calls	0.14	0.12	0.24	0.12	0.13
Traveling	1.15	1.06	1.19	1.16	1.15

Note: Primary activities are those respondents identified as their main activity. Other activities done simultaneously, such as eating while watching TV, are not included. Asians, blacks, and whites are those who identify themselves as being of the race alone. Hispanics may be of any race. Numbers may not add to total because not all categories are shown. "–" means sample is too small to make a reliable estimate.

Source: Unpublished tables from the Bureau of Labor Statistics' 2012 American Time Use Survey, Internet site http://www.bls .gov/tus/calculations by New Strategist

Table 10.16 Index of Women's Time Use by Race and Hispanic Origin, 2012

(index of average hours per day women aged 15 or older spend doing primary activities by race and Hispanic origin, by type of activity, 2012)

INDEX OF TIME TO AVERAGE FOR TOTAL WOMEN	total women	Asian	black	Hispanic	white
Total, all activities	**100**	**100**	**100**	**100**	**100**
Personal care	100	101	104	103	99
Sleeping	100	102	102	104	99
Grooming	100	87	121	103	96
Household activities	100	108	74	111	105
Housework	100	89	77	134	106
Food preparation and cleanup	100	163	95	128	99
Lawn, garden, and houseplants	100	108	50	42	108
Animals and pets	100	36	27	45	118
Household management	100	75	45	50	110
Caring for and helping household members	100	132	84	139	100
Caring for and helping household children	100	126	83	146	102
Caring for and helping people in other households	100	43	100	86	100
Caring for and helping children in other households	100	–	88	100	100
Work and work-related activities	100	112	93	97	101
Working	100	113	92	97	101
Job search and interviewing	100	–	167	67	100
Education	100	–	100	153	98
Taking class	100	–	96	165	100
Research and homework	100	–	106	131	94
Shopping (store, telephone, Internet)	100	105	102	98	100
Grocery shopping	100	92	83	100	100
Shopping, except groceries, food, and gas	100	110	107	97	97
Eating and drinking	100	133	77	97	102
Socializing, relaxing, and leisure	100	80	112	82	99
Socializing and communicating	100	61	102	85	102
Relaxing and leisure	100	84	116	80	98
Watching television	100	78	125	88	97
Playing games (including computer)	100	–	60	33	107
Computer use for leisure (excluding games)	100	–	84	42	95
Reading for personal interest	100	55	58	29	111
Sports, exercise, recreation	100	100	62	81	108
Religious and spiritual activities	100	94	183	128	89
Volunteer activities	100	36	93	57	107
Telephone calls	100	86	171	86	93
Traveling	100	92	103	101	100

Note: Primary activities are those respondents identified as their main activity. Other activities done simultaneously, such as eating while watching TV, are not included. Asians, blacks, and whites are those who identify themselves as being of the race alone. Hispanics may be of any race. The index is calculated by dividing time use of women in each race/Hispanic origin group by time use of the average woman and multiplying by 100. "–" means sample is too small to make a reliable estimate.
Source: Unpublished tables from the Bureau of Labor Statistics' 2012 American Time Use Survey, Internet site http://www.bls .gov/tus/calculations by New Strategist

11

Wealth

Trends

Households in every age group saw their net worth plunge between 2005 and 2011.

The median net worth of the average household was $68,828 in 2011, 36 percent lower than the $107,344 of 2005 after adjusting for inflation.

Motor vehicles are the most commonly owned asset.

The median equity of motor vehicles peaks at a modest $10,302 among married couples aged 55 to 64.

A house is the single most valuable asset owned by the largest share of Americans.

Homeownership peaks among householders aged 65 or older (79 percent) and among non-Hispanic whites (73 percent), which accounts for their higher net worth.

Retirement accounts are modest.

Fewer than half of households have 401(k) accounts, and those accounts were worth a median of $30,000 in 2011.

Most households are in debt.

The average household owed $70,000 in 2011, fully 37 percent more than in 2000 after adjusting for inflation.

Debt peaks among the middle-aged.

Householders aged 35 to 44 are most likely to be in debt (80 percent) and owed the most ($108,000).

Net Worth Has Plunged

Householders aged 35 to 44 experienced the biggest decline in net worth.

Net worth is what remains when a household's debts are subtracted from its assets. The most valuable asset owned by the largest share of households is a house. As housing values climbed during the first half of the 2000s, so did net worth. By 2005, median household net worth exceeded $100,000. Then the housing bubble burst and the Great Recession set in. Median household net worth fell 36 percent between 2005 and 2011, to $68,828 after adjusting for inflation.

The median net worth of householders aged 35 to 44 fell by a steep 58 percent between 2005 and 2011—a larger decline than any other age group. Behind this decline was the fact that many were recent home buyers, purchasing at the price peak and experiencing the biggest decline in home equity as the housing market collapsed. Net worth fell the least among householders aged 75 or older, in large part because most were long-time homeowners who owned their homes free and clear.

■ Householders aged 65 or older have the highest net worth, with more than one in five having a net worth of at least $500,000.

Net worth fell sharply between 2005 and 2011

(median household net worth, 2005 and 2011; in 2011 dollars)

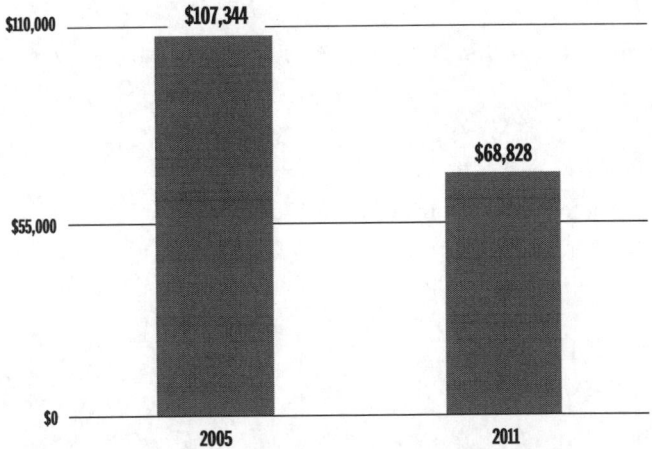

Table 11.1 Median Household Net Worth by Age of Householder, 2005 and 2011

(median net worth of households by age of householder, 2005 and 2011; percent change, 2005–11; in 2011 dollars)

	2011	2005	percent change
Total households	**68,828**	**107,344**	**–35.9%**
Under age 35	6,676	8,901	–25.0
Aged 35 to 44	35,000	84,044	–58.4
Aged 45 to 54	84,542	151,673	–44.3
Aged 55 to 64	143,964	207,778	–30.7
Aged 65 to 69	194,226	225,737	–14.0
Aged 70 to 74	181,078	233,746	–22.5
Aged 75 or older	155,714	184,512	–15.6

Source: Bureau of the Census, Wealth and Asset Ownership, Survey of Income and Program Participation, Internet site http://www.census.gov/people/wealth/; calculations by New Strategist

Table 11.2 Distribution of Net Worth by Age of Householder, 2011

(number of households, median net worth, and percent distribution of net worth, by age of householder, 2011)

	total households	under 35	35 to 44	45 to 54	55 to 64	65 or older
Total households	**118,689,091**	**22,876,706**	**21,741,098**	**25,494,745**	**22,328,534**	**26,248,007**
Median net worth	**$68,828**	**$6,676**	**$35,000**	**$84,542**	**$143,964**	**$170,516**

DISTRIBUTION OF HOUSEHOLDS BY NET WORTH

	total households	under 35	35 to 44	45 to 54	55 to 64	65 or older
Total households	**100.0%**	**100.0%**	**100.0%**	**100.0%**	**100.0%**	**100.0%**
Zero or negative	18.1	32.0	22.0	17.4	12.4	8.3
$1 to $4,999	9.1	15.4	10.2	7.6	6.3	6.6
$5,000 to $9,999	4.8	8.8	5.9	4.0	2.9	2.7
$10,000 to $24,999	6.6	10.9	7.8	5.7	4.8	4.1
$25,000 to $49,999	6.9	7.8	8.5	7.5	6.5	4.7
$50,000 to $99,999	10.4	9.8	10.8	11.1	10.0	10.4
$100,000 to $249,999	17.9	9.7	16.2	18.4	20.7	23.7
$250,000 to $499,999	12.6	3.6	10.2	14.1	15.2	19.0
$500,000 or more	13.5	2.0	8.3	14.2	21.2	20.6

Source: Bureau of the Census, Wealth and Asset Ownership, Survey of Income and Program Participation, Internet site http://www.census.gov/people/wealth/; calculations by New Strategist

Married Couples Have the Greatest Wealth

Female-headed households saw their net worth fall the most between 2005 and 2011.

Married couples had a median net worth (assets minus debts) of $139,024 in 2011, well above the $68,828 median for all households, according to the Census Bureau's Survey of Income and Program Participation. Male-headed households had a net worth of $27,310, and the net worth of female-headed households was $22,184.

Almost every age group by household type saw its median net worth fall sharply between 2005 and 2011, after adjusting for inflation. For the average household, median net worth fell 36 percent during those years. Married couples saw their net worth fall 29 percent, and the decline was an identical 29 percent for male-headed households. Among female-headed households, however, net worth fell by a larger 43 percent. The only exception to across-the-board declines in net worth occurred among male- and female-headed households with a householder under age 35, but their net worth increased by only hundreds of dollars.

Net worth rises with age regardless of household type. It peaks among married couples aged 65 or older at $284,790. Nearly one-third of elderly married couples have a net worth of $500,000 or more. In contrast, more than one-fourth of the youngest married couples have no wealth at all—meaning their debts are greater than their assets. Among male- and female-headed householders under age 35, the percentage with zero or negative net worth was a larger 32 and 40 percent, respectively.

■ Net worth exceeds $100,000 among married couples with a householder aged 35 or older and for male- and female-headed households with a householder aged 65 or older.

The net worth of married couples exceeds $100,000

(median household net worth by type of household, 2011)

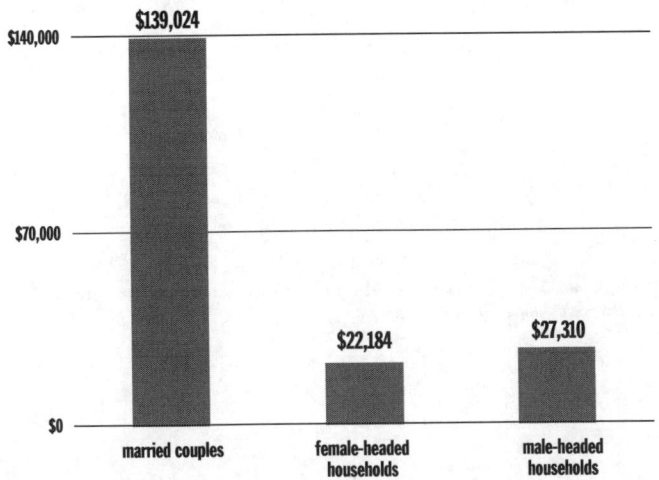

Table 11.3 Median Household Net Worth by Type of Household and Age of Householder, 2005 and 2011

(median household net worth by type of household and age of householder, 2005 and 2011; percent change, 2005–11; in 2011 dollars)

	2011	2005	percent change
TOTAL HOUSEHOLDS	**$68,828**	**$107,344**	**–35.9%**
Married couples	**139,024**	**194,742**	**–28.6**
Under age 35	19,526	36,292	–46.2
Aged 35 to 54	116,170	202,057	–42.5
Aged 55 to 64	239,847	335,825	–28.6
Aged 65 or older	284,790	338,648	–15.9
Female-headed households	**22,184**	**39,073**	**–43.2**
Under age 35	1,392	1,270	9.6
Aged 35 to 54	9,640	25,532	–62.2
Aged 55 to 64	61,879	90,906	–31.9
Aged 65 or older	104,000	143,826	–27.7
Male-headed households	**27,310**	**38,266**	**–28.6**
Under age 35	6,200	5,509	12.5
Aged 35 to 54	24,813	48,596	–48.9
Aged 55 to 64	55,718	85,188	–34.6
Aged 65 or older	130,000	146,577	–11.3

Source: Bureau of the Census, Wealth and Asset Ownership, Survey of Income and Program Participation, Internet site http://www.census.gov/people/wealth/; calculations by New Strategist

Table 11.4 Distribution of Net Worth among Married-Couple Households by Age, 2011

(number of married-couple households, median net worth, and percent distribution of net worth, by age of householder, 2011; number of married couples in thousands)

	total couples	under 35	35 to 54	55 to 64	65 or older
Number of married couples	59,918	9,672	26,519	12,610	11,117
Median net worth	$139,024	$19,526	$116,170	$239,847	$284,790

DISTRIBUTION OF MARRIED-COUPLE HOUSEHOLDS BY NET WORTH

	total couples	under 35	35 to 54	55 to 64	65 or older
Total married couples	100.0%	100.0%	100.0%	100.0%	100.0%
Zero or negative	13.0	25.8	14.3	8.0	4.2
$1 to $4,999	5.3	10.6	5.3	3.3	2.8
$5,000 to $9,999	3.2	6.3	3.3	2.1	1.4
$10,000 to $24,999	5.6	11.0	5.7	3.5	3.0
$25,000 to $49,999	6.6	10.4	7.4	5.0	3.0
$50,000 to $99,999	9.9	12.3	10.8	8.0	7.8
$100,000 to $249,999	20.2	14.3	20.2	21.4	24.0
$250,000 to $499,999	16.5	5.9	16.5	18.7	23.2
$500,000 or more	19.9	3.5	16.5	30.1	30.6

Source: Bureau of the Census, Wealth and Asset Ownership, Survey of Income and Program Participation, Internet site http://www.census.gov/people/wealth/; calculations by New Strategist

Table 11.5 Distribution of Net Worth among Female-Headed Households by Age, 2011

(number of female-headed households, median net worth, and percent distribution of net worth, by age of householder, 2011; number of female-headed households in thousands)

	total female-headed households	under 35	35 to 54	55 to 64	65 or older
Number of female-headed households	35,522	7,132	11,592	5,882	10,915
Median net worth	$22,184	$1,392	$9,640	$61,879	$104,000

DISTRIBUTION OF FEMALE-HEADED HOUSEHOLDS BY NET WORTH

Total female-headed households	100.0%	100.0%	100.0%	100.0%	100.0%
Zero or negative	24.3	40.3	28.9	19.4	11.8
$1 to $4,999	13.4	21.5	14.0	9.5	9.5
$5,000 to $9,999	6.4	11.6	7.4	3.8	3.5
$10,000 to $24,999	6.8	9.8	7.3	5.9	4.8
$25,000 to $49,999	7.0	5.1	8.6	8.0	5.9
$50,000 to $99,999	10.9	5.5	11.4	13.1	12.7
$100,000 to $249,999	15.8	4.5	12.3	20.2	24.6
$250,000 to $499,999	9.0	1.2	6.0	11.1	16.2
$500,000 or more	6.3	0.5	4.1	9.0	11.0

Source: Bureau of the Census, Wealth and Asset Ownership, Survey of Income and Program Participation, Internet site http://www.census.gov/people/wealth/; calculations by New Strategist

Table 11.6 Distribution of Net Worth among Male-Headed Households by Age, 2011

(number of male-headed households, median net worth, and percent distribution of net worth, by age of householder, 2011; number of male-headed households in thousands)

	total male-headed households	under 35	35 to 54	55 to 64	65 or older
Number of male-headed households	23,249	6,073	9,125	3,837	4,215
Median net worth	$27,310	$6,200	$24,813	$55,718	$130,000

DISTRIBUTION OF MALE-HEADED HOUSEHOLDS BY NET WORTH

Total male-headed households	100.0%	100.0%	100.0%	100.0%	100.0%
Zero or negative	21.8	32.1	22.6	15.9	10.3
$1 to $4,999	12.5	15.9	12.5	11.1	8.7
$5,000 to $9,999	6.4	9.7	6.1	4.3	3.9
$10,000 to $24,999	8.7	11.8	8.9	7.6	5.0
$25,000 to $49,999	7.8	7.0	8.8	8.9	6.1
$50,000 to $99,999	11.0	10.9	10.9	11.8	10.9
$100,000 to $249,999	15.4	8.4	15.7	19.5	20.9
$250,000 to $499,999	8.3	2.7	8.3	10.1	14.9
$500,000 or more	8.1	1.4	6.3	10.7	19.2

Source: Bureau of the Census, Wealth and Asset Ownership, Survey of Income and Program Participation, Internet site http://www.census.gov/people/wealth/; calculations by New Strategist

Non-Hispanic Whites Have the Highest Net Worth

Blacks and Hispanics have little wealth.

The median net worth (assets minus debts) of non-Hispanic white households was $110,500 in 2011, well above the $68,828 net worth of the average household. The median net worth of non-Hispanic white households exceeds the $89,339 of Asian households and is more than 10 times that of black or Hispanic households.

Between 2005 and 2011, net worth fell regardless of race or Hispanic origin. Hispanic households experienced the largest decline, their median net worth falling by an enormous 61 percent after adjusting for inflation. Non-Hispanic whites experienced the smallest decline, a 26 percent drop—well below the 36 percent loss recorded by the average household, according to the Census Bureau's Survey of Income and Program Participation.

■ The percentage of households with zero or negative net worth ranges from a low of 13.7 percent among non-Hispanic whites to a high of 33.5 percent among blacks.

Net worth of Asians is well above average

(median net worth of households by race and Hispanic origin of householder, 2011)

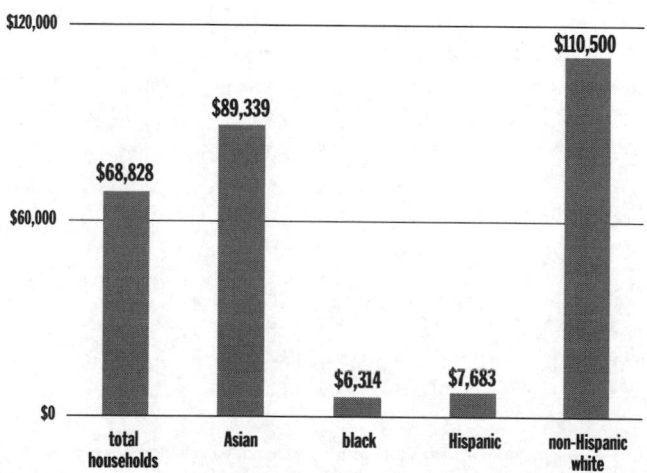

Table 11.7 Median Household Net Worth by Race and Hispanic Origin of Householder, 2005 and 2011

(median net worth of households by race and Hispanic origin of householder, 2005 and 2011; percent change, 2005–11; in 2011 dollars)

	2011	2005	percent change
Total households	**$68,828**	**$107,344**	**–35.9%**
Asian	89,339	175,890	–49.2
Black	6,314	12,684	–50.2
Hispanic	7,683	19,670	–60.9
Non-Hispanic white	110,500	150,132	–26.4

Note: Asians and blacks are those who identify themselves as being of the race alone. Non-Hispanic whites are those who identify themselves as being white alone and not Hispanic. Hispanics may be of any race.
Source: Bureau of the Census, Wealth and Asset Ownership, Survey of Income and Program Participation, Internet site http:// www.census.gov/people/wealth/; calculations by New Strategist

Table 11.8 Distribution of Net Worth by Race and Hispanic Origin of Householder, 2011

(number of households, median net worth, and percent distribution of net worth, by race and Hispanic origin of householder, 2011)

	total households	Asian	black	Hispanic	non-Hispanic white
Total households	**118,689,091**	**3,939,591**	**15,056,795**	**14,099,126**	**83,245,166**
Median net worth	**$68,828**	**$89,339**	**$6,314**	**$7,683**	**$110,500**

DISTRIBUTION OF HOUSEHOLDS BY NET WORTH

	total households	Asian	black	Hispanic	non-Hispanic white
Total households	**100.0%**	**100.0%**	**100.0%**	**100.0%**	**100.0%**
Zero or negative	18.1	15.4	33.5	28.5	13.7
$1 to $4,999	9.1	9.0	14.6	16.5	6.8
$5,000 to $9,999	4.8	5.5	7.0	7.4	3.9
$10,000 to $24,999	6.6	6.6	7.9	8.4	6.0
$25,000 to $49,999	6.9	7.2	6.6	8.0	6.7
$50,000 to $99,999	10.4	8.2	9.0	9.9	10.8
$100,000 to $249,999	17.9	17.0	12.6	11.2	20.1
$250,000 to $499,999	12.6	13.8	5.6	6.1	15.1
$500,000 or more	13.5	17.3	3.3	3.9	16.9

Note: Asians and blacks are those who identify themselves as being of the race alone. Non-Hispanic whites are those who identify themselves as being white alone and not Hispanic. Hispanics may be of any race.
Source: Bureau of the Census, Wealth and Asset Ownership, Survey of Income and Program Participation, Internet site http:// www.census.gov/people/wealth/; calculations by New Strategist

Homes Are the Most Important Asset

Home values plunged between 2005 and 2011, driving down net worth.

The automobile is the most commonly owned asset in the United States. Nearly 85 percent of households own at least one motor vehicle. The second most commonly owned asset is an interest-earning account at a financial institution (70 percent). A home is the third most commonly owned asset, with 65 percent of households owning a house. The nation's homeowners had a median of $80,000 in home equity (home value minus mortgage debt) in 2011. They had a median of $6,824 equity in their motor vehicles, and just $2,450 in their savings accounts.

Behind the higher net worth of older householders is their greater homeownership and home equity. Nearly 80 percent of householders aged 65 or older owned a home in 2011, with a median equity of $130,000. In contrast, only 37 percent of householders under age 35 were homeowners. Those owners had just $20,000 in home equity.

■ The median value of 401(k) retirement accounts peaks at $47,000 among householders aged 55 to 64.

Retirement accounts are modest, even among those approaching retirement age

(median value of 401(k) accounts owned by households, by age of householder, 2011)

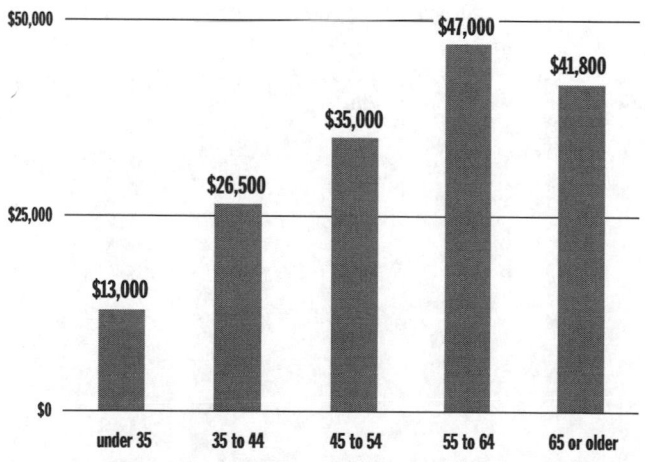

Table 11.9 Asset Ownership of Households by Age of Householder, 2011

(percent of households owning selected assets and median value or equity of assets for owners, by age of householder, 2011)

	total households	under 35	35 to 44	45 to 54	55 to 64	65 or older
PERCENT WITH ASSET						
Interest-earning asset at financial institution	69.8%	63.2%	68.6%	69.7%	73.3%	73.8%
Regular checking account	29.0	29.2	30.8	31.2	29.1	25.0
Stocks and mutal fund shares	19.6	11.3	16.4	19.4	24.3	25.4
Own business	13.8	10.6	15.6	18.3	17.1	8.0
Motor vehicles	84.7	81.5	87.5	86.9	87.8	80.2
Own home	65.3	36.7	61.3	70.4	76.7	78.9
Rental property	5.5	2.1	4.1	5.8	7.8	7.2
IRA or Keogh account	28.9	16.1	26.3	30.3	37.5	33.7
401(k) and thrift savings	42.1	39.2	52.5	52.6	48.7	20.2
MEDIAN VALUE OR EQUITY OF ASSET FOR OWNERS						
Interest-earning asset at financial institution	$2,450	$1,000	$1,500	$2,500	$3,700	$5,000
Regular checking account	600	500	500	528	700	800
Stocks and mutal fund shares	20,000	6,000	12,000	20,000	27,000	50,000
Own business (equity)	8,000	5,000	10,000	7,000	10,000	6,000
Motor vehicles (equity)	6,824	4,698	6,492	7,113	7,113	7,113
Own home (equity)	80,000	20,000	40,000	70,000	97,000	130,000
Rental property (equity)	180,000	70,000	98,000	165,000	200,000	240,000
IRA or Keogh account	34,000	10,000	23,000	34,000	48,000	52,000
401(k) and thrift savings	30,000	13,000	26,500	35,000	47,000	41,800

Source: Bureau of the Census, Wealth and Asset Ownership, Survey of Income and Program Participation, Internet site http:// www.census.gov/people/wealth/; calculations by New Strategist

Motor Vehicles Are the Most Commonly Owned Asset

A home is the second most commonly owned asset among married couples.

Most households, regardless of household type, own a motor vehicle. The figure ranges from a high of 93 percent among married couples to a low of 74 percent among female-headed households. Among married couples, a home is the second most common asset, owned by 79 percent. The median equity couples have in their home rises from a low of $20,000 among the youngest couples to a high of $150,000 among couples aged 65 or older.

Among male- and female-headed households, a savings account is the second most common asset, owned by 62 to 64 percent of female- and male-headed households, respectively. In third place is a home, with 52 percent of female-headed households and 51 percent of male-headed households being homeowners.

The majority of married couples have a 401(k) account, and those accounts have a median value of $40,000. A smaller 29 to 33 percent of female- and male-headed households have 401(k) accounts, respectively, with a median value of $15,000 for female-headed households and $20,000 for male-headed households.

■ Among asset owners, the equity held in rental property exceeds the value of all other assets. But few households own rental property—just 8 percent of couples and 3 to 4 percent of female- and male-headed households.

Homeownership is an important asset for most households

(percent of households that own a home by type of household, 2011)

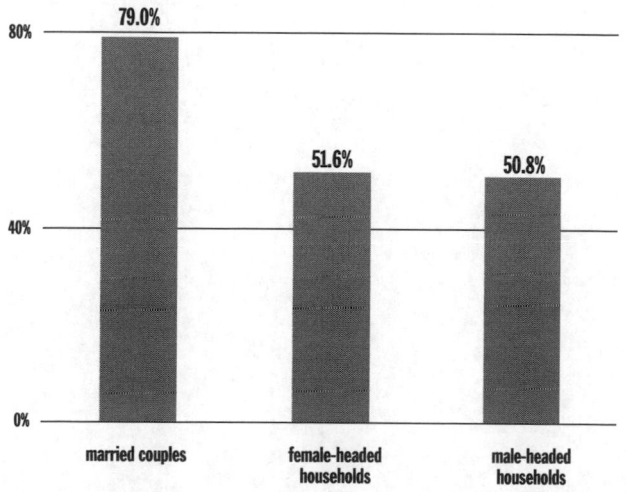

Table 11.10 Asset Ownership of Married-Couple Households by Age, 2011

(percent of total and married-couple households owning selected assets, and median value or equity of asset for owners, by age of married-couple householder, 2011)

	total households	married couples				
		under 35	35 to 44	45 to 54	55 to 64	65 or older
PERCENT WITH ASSET						
Interest-earning asset at financial institution	69.8%	76.9%	70.1%	76.0%	80.1%	81.3%
Regular checking account	29.0	30.8	32.1	32.5	29.4	26.9
Stocks and mutal fund shares	19.6	25.6	14.7	23.3	31.4	33.8
Own business	13.8	18.4	14.6	20.9	21.6	12.3
Motor vehicles	84.7	92.9	91.2	93.1	94.3	92.2
Own home	65.3	79.0	56.4	78.4	87.8	90.4
Rental property	5.5	7.5	3.9	6.6	10.1	10.2
IRA or Keogh account	28.9	36.6	21.3	34.9	44.8	44.8
401(k) and thrift savings	42.1	53.4	51.4	62.0	58.4	29.1
MEDIAN VALUE OR EQUITY OF ASSET FOR OWNERS						
Interest-earning asset at financial institution	$2,450	$4,000	$1,900	$3,320	$6,000	$8,000
Regular checking account	600	900	700	800	1,000	1,200
Stocks and mutal fund shares	20,000	25,000	6,619	19,000	32,000	65,000
Own business (equity)	8,000	10,000	10,000	10,000	10,000	8,000
Motor vehicles (equity)	6,824	8,485	5,986	8,657	10,226	9,445
Own home (equity)	80,000	85,000	20,000	69,000	118,000	150,000
Rental property (equity)	180,000	200,000	90,000	170,000	220,000	330,000
IRA or Keogh account	34,000	42,000	11,000	32,300	60,000	75,000
401(k) and thrift savings	30,000	40,000	17,000	40,000	58,000	50,000

Source: Bureau of the Census, Wealth and Asset Ownership, Survey of Income and Program Participation, Internet site http://www.census.gov/people/wealth/; calculations by New Strategist

Table 11.11 Asset Ownership of Female-Headed Households by Age, 2011

(percent of total households and of female-headed households owning selected assets, and median value or equity of asset for owners, by age of female householder, 2011)

	total households	female-headed households				
		under 35	35 to 44	45 to 54	55 to 64	65 or older
PERCENT WITH ASSET						
Interest-earning asset at financial institution	69.8%	61.8%	51.8%	59.8%	66.2%	68.1%
Regular checking account	29.0	27.6	26.5	30.1	31.2	23.6
Stocks and mutal fund shares	19.6	12.6	5.4	10.2	14.9	18.5
Own business	13.8	6.8	5.9	9.4	9.1	3.3
Motor vehicles	84.7	74.5	71.8	78.8	79.8	68.8
Own home	65.3	51.6	18.9	47.6	64.5	70.4
Rental property	5.5	3.1	0.4	2.2	4.3	5.0
IRA or Keogh account	28.9	20.9	10.2	19.6	29.2	24.8
401(k) and thrift savings	42.1	28.7	27.4	39.3	38.8	12.9
MEDIAN VALUE OR EQUITY OF ASSET FOR OWNERS						
Interest-earning asset at financial institution	$2,450	$1,000	$500	$600	$1,100	$2,500
Regular checking account	600	305	202	280	400	500
Stocks and mutal fund shares	20,000	16,000	7,000	10,000	16,000	25,000
Own business (equity)	8,000	3,000	2,000	4,000	4,000	2,500
Motor vehicles (equity)	6,824	4,113	3,383	4,091	4,825	4,415
Own home (equity)	80,000	75,000	15,000	43,000	72,000	115,000
Rental property (equity)	180,000	139,000	–	90,000	150,000	155,000
IRA or Keogh account	34,000	20,140	6,500	19,000	30,000	30,000
401(k) and thrift savings	30,000	15,000	6,800	15,000	25,000	25,000

Note: "–" means sample is too small to make a reliable estimate.
Source: Bureau of the Census, Wealth and Asset Ownership, Survey of Income and Program Participation, Internet site http://www.census.gov/people/wealth/; calculations by New Strategist

Table 11.12 Asset Ownership of Male-Headed Households by Age, 2011

(percent of total households and of male-headed households owning selected assets, and median value or equity of asset for owners, by age of male-headed householder, 2011)

	total households	male-headed households				
		under 35	35 to 44	45 to 54	55 to 64	65 or older
PERCENT WITH ASSET						
Interest-earning asset at financial institution	69.8%	63.7%	65.3%	61.3%	61.7%	68.6%
Regular checking account	29.0	26.6	27.9	27.9	24.8	23.7
Stocks and mutal fund shares	19.6	14.7	12.9	12.9	15.5	20.8
Own business	13.8	12.8	9.7	15.7	14.6	9.2
Motor vehicles	84.7	79.1	77.5	80.8	78.8	77.8
Own home	65.3	50.8	26.4	54.2	59.2	70.5
Rental property	5.5	3.8	1.1	4.1	5.7	5.2
IRA or Keogh account	28.9	21.5	14.9	21.0	26.5	27.5
401(k) and thrift savings	42.1	33.4	33.7	42.1	31.6	15.7
MEDIAN VALUE OR EQUITY OF ASSET FOR OWNERS						
Interest-earning asset at financial institution	$2,450	$1,255	$800	$1,000	$1,700	$5,000
Regular checking account	600	600	700	500	500	1,000
Stocks and mutal fund shares	20,000	15,000	6,000	10,000	25,000	65,000
Own business (equity)	8,000	7,000	4,000	10,000	8,000	7,000
Motor vehicles (equity)	6,824	4,892	4,178	4,759	5,500	6,338
Own home (equity)	80,000	60,000	25,000	40,000	73,000	110,000
Rental property (equity)	180,000	100,000	–	65,000	100,000	160,000
IRA or Keogh account	34,000	25,000	7,759	20,000	36,427	51,000
401(k) and thrift savings	30,000	20,000	12,000	26,000	33,000	38,000

Note: "–" means sample is too small to make a reliable estimate.
Source: Bureau of the Census, Wealth and Asset Ownership, Survey of Income and Program Participation, Internet site http://www.census.gov/people/wealth/; calculations by New Strategist

Homeownership Boosts the Net Worth of Non-Hispanic Whites

The lower homeownership rate of blacks and Hispanics reduces their net worth.

Although Asians are equally as or more likely than non-Hispanic whites to own a variety of assets, there is one glaring deficit that makes all the difference: a home. Fully 73 percent of non-Hispanic whites own a home compared with a smaller 59 percent of Asians. In large part because of that difference, non-Hispanic whites have a higher net worth than Asians.

Blacks and Hispanics are less likely than the average household to own most assets, including a home. Only 44 percent of black and 47 percent of Hispanic households owned a home in 2011 compared with 65 percent of all households. Because housing equity accounts for the largest share of net worth, the lower homeownership rate of blacks and Hispanics largely explains their below-average net worth.

■ Among race and Hispanic origin groups, Hispanics are least likely to have any retirement assets.

Non-Hispanic whites have the highest rate of homeownership

(percent of households that own their home, by race and Hispanic origin, 2011)

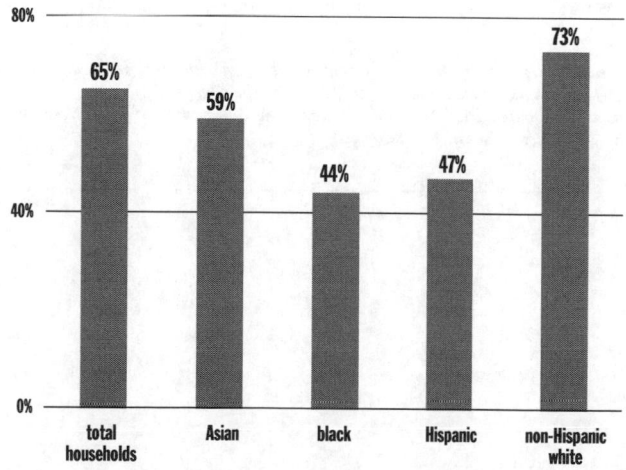

Table 11.13 Asset Ownership of Households by Race and Hispanic Origin of Householder, 2011

(percent of households owning selected assets and median value or equity of assets for owners, by race and Hispanic origin of householder, 2011)

	total households	Asian	black	Hispanic	non-Hispanic white
PERCENT WITH ASSET					
Interest-earning asset at financial institution	69.8%	77.7%	51.9%	53.6%	75.4%
Regular checking account	29.0	35.8	24.6	30.2	29.1
Stocks and mutal fund shares	19.6	22.6	6.4	4.3	24.5
Own business	13.8	15.2	7.4	11.5	15.3
Motor vehicles	84.7	84.2	70.5	77.3	88.3
Own home	65.3	58.7	43.8	47.2	72.6
Rental property	5.5	7.0	2.9	2.6	6.4
IRA or KEOGH account	28.9	31.5	11.2	9.9	35.4
401(k) and thrift savings	42.1	50.0	31.7	25.8	46.4
MEDIAN VALUE OR EQUITY OF ASSET FOR OWNERS					
Interest-earning asset at financial institution	$2,450	$4,500	$500	$700	$3,250
Regular checking account	600	900	242	300	800
Stocks and mutal fund shares	20,000	19,000	4,750	8,000	24,000
Own business (equity)	8,000	6,000	2,000	2,000	10,000
Motor vehicles (equity)	6,824	7,839	3,916	5,267	7,113
Own home (equity)	80,000	120,000	50,000	47,000	85,000
Rental property (equity)	180,000	130,000	155,000	150,000	180,000
IRA or Keogh account	34,000	26,000	15,000	17,000	36,500
401(k) and thrift savings	30,000	38,000	12,000	15,000	35,000

Note: Asians and blacks are those who identify themselves as being of the race alone. Non-Hispanic whites are those who identify themselves as being white alone and not Hispanic. Hispanics may be of any race.
Source: Bureau of the Census, Wealth and Asset Ownership, Survey of Income and Program Participation, Internet site http://www.census.gov/people/wealth/; calculations by New Strategist

Most Households Are in Debt

The percentage of households with debt declined in most age groups between 2000 and 2011.

Sixty-nine percent of households have debt, owing a median of $70,000 in 2011. The median amount of debt owed by the average debtor household increased 37 percent between 2000 and 2011, after adjusting for inflation.

Householders aged 35 to 54 are most likely to be in debt, with 79 to 80 percent owing money. Debt declines with age, falling to a low of 44 percent among householders aged 65 or older.

Four types of debt are most common—home-secured debt such as mortgages (41 percent of households have this type of debt), credit card debt (38 percent), vehicle debt (30 percent), and "other debt"—a category that includes student loans (19 percent). Mortgages are the largest debt for the average household. The median amount owed by the average homeowner for home-secured debt was $117,000 in 2011. For householders under age 45, other debt exceeds vehicle and credit card debt.

■ Behind the 9 percentage point decline in the percentage of householders under age 35 with debt is the reluctance (or inability) of young adults to become homeowners.

Debt declines with advancing age

(median amount of debt owed by households by age of householder, 2011)

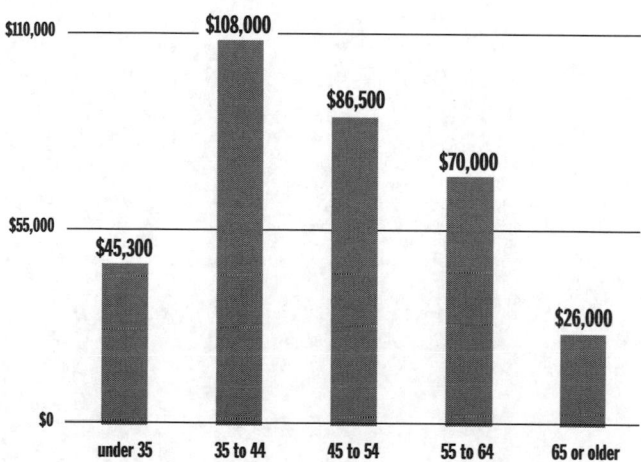

Table 11.14 Debt of Households by Age of Householder, 2000 and 2011

(percent of households with debt and median amount owed by those with debt, by age of householder, 2000 and 2011; percentage point and percent change, 2000–11; in 2011 dollars)

	2011	2000	percentage point change
PERCENT WITH DEBT			
Total households	**69.0%**	**74.2%**	**–5.2**
Under age 35	72.2	81.5	–9.3
Aged 35 to 44	79.6	85.5	–5.9
Aged 45 to 54	78.9	85.9	–7.0
Aged 55 to 64	73.0	76.8	–3.8
Aged 65 or older	44.4	41.0	3.4

	2011	2000	percent change
MEDIAN AMOUNT OWED			
Total households with debt	**$70,000**	**$50,971**	**37.3%**
Under age 35	45,300	40,240	12.6
Aged 35 to 44	108,000	86,650	24.6
Aged 45 to 54	86,500	63,445	36.3
Aged 55 to 64	70,000	42,654	64.1
Aged 65 or older	26,000	12,072	115.4

Source: Bureau of the Census, Wealth and Asset Ownership, Survey of Income and Program Participation, Internet site http://www.census.gov/people/wealth/; calculations by New Strategist

Table 11.15 Debt of Households by Type of Debt and Age of Householder, 2011

(percent of households with debt and median amount of debt for debtors, by age of householder, 2011)

	total households	under 35	35 to 44	45 to 54	55 to 64	65 or older
PERCENT WITH DEBT						
Total debt	**69.0%**	**72.2%**	**79.6%**	**78.9%**	**73.0%**	**44.4%**
Secured debt	55.3	53.4	66.3	67.2	60.9	31.3
Home debt	40.5	31.3	51.9	53.4	46.1	21.8
Business debt	4.1	3.2	4.3	5.8	5.5	2.0
Vehicle debt	30.4	37.7	38.8	35.0	29.4	13.5
Unsecured debt	46.2	52.5	54.2	52.0	47.2	27.8
Credit card debt	38.3	38.3	44.7	44.3	41.4	24.7
Loans	6.8	7.9	8.3	8.1	6.8	3.6
Other debt	18.6	31.3	22.9	20.5	15.0	5.4
MEDIAN AMOUNT OF DEBT FOR DEBTORS						
Total debt	**$70,000**	**$45,300**	**$108,000**	**$86,500**	**$70,000**	**$26,000**
Secured debt	91,000	76,500	128,500	99,000	85,000	50,000
Home debt	117,000	125,000	150,000	110,000	100,000	75,000
Business debt	25,000	20,000	20,000	25,000	30,000	25,000
Vehicle debt	10,000	10,000	10,000	11,000	10,000	9,000
Unsecured debt	7,000	9,700	8,400	8,000	6,000	3,450
Credit card debt	3,500	3,000	4,000	4,000	4,000	2,200
Loans	7,000	6,000	8,000	6,000	7,000	7,000
Other debt	10,000	13,000	12,000	10,000	8,688	4,000

Note: Secured debt is backed by collateral, unsecured debt is not. "Other debt" includes student loans and medical debt.
Source: Bureau of the Census, Wealth and Asset Ownership, Survey of Income and Program Participation, Internet site http:// www.census.gov/people/wealth/; calculations by New Strategist

Married Couples Have the Biggest Debts

Couples aged 35 to 54 owe the most.

Most households, regardless of household type, are in debt. The figure ranges from a high of 80 percent among married couples to a low of 57 percent among female-headed households.

Four types of debt are most common: home-secured (mortgage), credit card, vehicle loans, and "other debt"—a category that includes student loans. Home-secured debt is the most common type among married couples (53 percent). For male- and female-headed households, credit card debt is most common (30 and 33 percent, respectively).

Married couples with debt owe the most money, a median of $99,000 in 2011. Female-headed households with debt owe a median of $30,000, and male-headed households with debt owe $45,900. Home-secured debt is the largest for the three types of households, and business debt ranks second—but few households own businesses. Other debt (much of it student loans) exceeds vehicle debt among male- and female-headed households.

■ Fewer than half of households have outstanding credit card debt, and the median amount owed by those with credit card debt ranges from $2,500 to $4,000.

Most households have debt, including female- and male-headed households

(percent of households with debt by type of household, 2011)

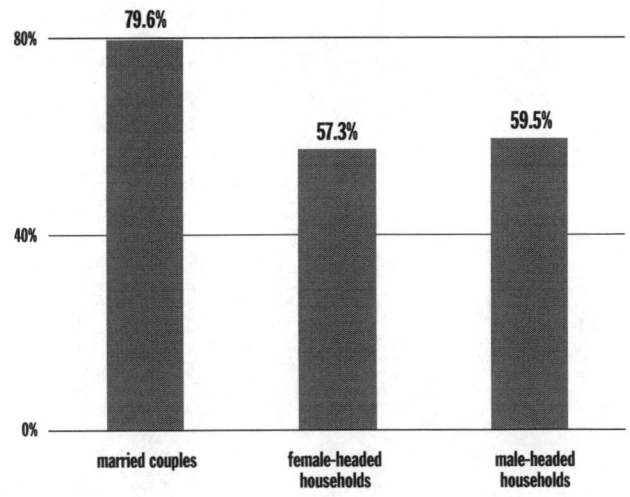

Table 11.16 Debt of Married-Couple Households by Type of Debt and by Age of Householder, 2011

(percent of total and married-couple households with debt, and median amount of debt for debtors, by age of married-couple householder, 2011)

	total households	married couples				
		under 35	35 to 44	45 to 54	55 to 64	65 or older
PERCENT WITH DEBT						
Total debt	**69.0%**	**79.6%**	**83.7%**	**87.4%**	**80.9%**	**55.9%**
Secured debt	55.3	68.6	71.1	77.9	70.4	41.8
Home debt	40.5	53.5	49.6	64.7	54.3	29.0
Business debt	4.1	5.9	4.9	6.8	7.1	3.1
Vehicle debt	30.4	38.9	50.0	44.6	36.0	19.2
Unsecured debt	46.2	53.4	59.2	59.6	52.7	34.4
Credit card debt	38.3	45.1	44.5	50.7	46.2	30.8
Loans	6.8	8.5	10.1	9.6	8.0	4.8
Other debt	18.6	21.4	35.5	24.3	17.2	6.8
MEDIAN AMOUNT OF DEBT FOR DEBTORS						
Total debt	**$70,000**	**$99,000**	**$100,000**	**$121,750**	**$85,500**	**$33,000**
Secured debt	91,000	110,000	111,000	128,500	92,500	57,178
Home debt	117,000	128,000	138,000	140,000	100,000	87,000
Business debt	25,000	25,000	20,500	25,000	26,000	25,000
Vehicle debt	10,000	11,000	11,000	12,000	10,600	10,000
Unsecured debt	7,000	8,000	10,000	9,000	6,900	4,000
Credit card debt	3,500	4,000	3,400	4,600	4,000	3,000
Loans	7,000	8,000	7,000	8,000	9,000	7,800
Other debt	10,000	10,000	13,000	10,900	10,000	2,700

Note: Secured debt is backed by collateral, unsecured debt is not. "Other debt" includes student loans and medical debt.
Source: Bureau of the Census, Wealth and Asset Ownership, Survey of Income and Program Participation, Internet site http://www.census.gov/people/wealth/; calculations by New Strategist

Table 11.17 Debt of Female-Headed Households by Type of Debt and Age of Householder, 2011

(percent of total households and of female-headed households with debt, and median amount of debt for debtors, by age of female householder, 2011)

	total households	female-headed households				
		under 35	35 to 44	45 to 54	55 to 64	65 or older
PERCENT WITH DEBT						
Total debt	**69.0%**	**57.3%**	**61.4%**	**69.4%**	**67.9%**	**36.1%**
Secured debt	55.3	39.8	36.9	50.7	52.2	23.3
Home debt	40.5	26.1	15.3	35.4	38.5	16.6
Business debt	4.1	1.6	1.2	2.1	3.2	0.5
Vehicle debt	30.4	20.7	27.2	26.5	22.6	9.2
Unsecured debt	46.2	39.9	47.6	47.6	45.6	23.7
Credit card debt	38.3	32.5	33.6	38.1	40.7	21.5
Loans	6.8	4.7	5.6	6.2	4.9	2.5
Other debt	18.6	16.5	29.3	21.6	14.1	4.1
MEDIAN AMOUNT OF DEBT FOR DEBTORS						
Total debt	**$70,000**	**$30,000**	**$18,000**	**$43,000**	**$47,500**	**$18,900**
Secured debt	91,000	55,000	16,500	70,000	70,000	40,000
Home debt	117,000	90,000	107,000	100,000	90,000	60,000
Business debt	25,000	14,000	–	7,000	–	–
Vehicle debt	10,000	8,000	8,000	8,500	8,000	7,600
Unsecured debt	7,000	5,400	8,000	6,800	5,000	2,800
Credit card debt	3,500	2,500	2,000	3,000	3,000	2,000
Loans	7,000	5,000	5,000	5,000	5,000	7,000
Other debt	10,000	10,000	12,000	11,000	7,000	6,000

Note: Secured debt is backed by collateral, unsecured debt is not. "Other debt" includes student loans and medical debt. "–" means sample is too small to make a reliable estimate.
Source: Bureau of the Census, Wealth and Asset Ownership, Survey of Income and Program Participation, Internet site http://www.census.gov/people/wealth/; calculations by New Strategist

Table 11.18 Debt of Male-Headed Households by Type of Debt and Age of Householder, 2011

(percent of total households and of male-headed households with debt, and median amount of debt for debtors, by age of male householder, 2011)

	total households	male-headed households				
		under 35	35 to 44	45 to 54	55 to 64	65 or older
PERCENT WITH DEBT						
Total debt	**69.0%**	**59.5%**	**66.5%**	**67.8%**	**54.9%**	**35.6%**
Secured debt	55.3	44.6	44.5	54.8	42.9	24.4
Home debt	40.5	29.2	20.7	40.0	30.7	16.5
Business debt	4.1	3.4	2.9	4.2	3.5	2.5
Vehicle debt	30.4	23.2	30.2	26.8	18.4	9.8
Unsecured debt	46.2	37.5	47.6	40.9	31.9	20.6
Credit card debt	38.3	29.9	33.9	34.4	27.0	17.2
Loans	6.8	5.8	7.0	6.5	5.4	3.2
Other debt	18.6	14.7	26.9	13.6	8.8	5.0
MEDIAN AMOUNT OF DEBT FOR DEBTORS						
Total debt	**$70,000**	**$45,900**	**$27,000**	**$75,000**	**$44,209**	**$25,500**
Secured debt	91,000	75,000	28,000	96,000	68,000	55,000
Home debt	117,000	106,000	107,000	120,000	89,000	70,000
Business debt	25,000	25,000	–	25,000	–	–
Vehicle debt	10,000	9,000	9,200	9,000	8,000	8,000
Unsecured debt	7,000	7,000	9,500	7,500	5,800	4,000
Credit card debt	3,500	3,000	2,500	4,000	3,800	2,000
Loans	7,000	5,000	5,000	6,000	5,000	–
Other debt	10,000	12,000	16,000	10,000	7,477	6,500

Note: Secured debt is backed by collateral, unsecured debt is not. "Other debt" includes student loans and medical debt. "–" means sample is too small to make a reliable estimate.
Source: Bureau of the Census, Wealth and Asset Ownership, Survey of Income and Program Participation, Internet site http://www.census.gov/people/wealth/; calculations by New Strategist

Asians Are Most Likely to Be in Debt

Asian households with debt owe more than other race and Hispanic-origin groups.

Asians are slightly more likely than non-Hispanic whites to be in debt, 72 versus 71 percent in 2011. The median amount of debt owed by Asian households is higher than the median owed by non-Hispanic whites: $108,000 versus $80,000. The reason for their greater debt is housing, with Asians owing a median of $190,000 in home debt compared with $117,000 owed by non-Hispanic whites. Behind the higher housing debt of Asians is their younger age and the fact that many live in California, where housing prices are relatively high.

Black households are less likely than average to be in debt—62 percent of black households versus 69 percent of all households. The same is true for Hispanics, with 63 percent of Hispanic households in debt. Among black and Hispanic households with debt, the median amount owed was $35,000 and $41,000, respectively, compared with $70,000 owed by the average household. The lower homeownership rate of blacks and Hispanics accounts for their smaller debts.

■ A substantial 21 percent of black households have "other debt," a category that includes student loans.

Households headed by blacks are least likely to be in debt

(percent of households with debt by race and Hispanic origin of householder, 2011)

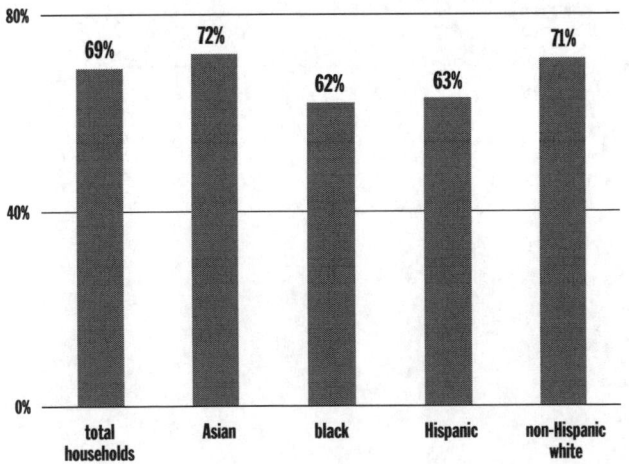

Table 11.19 Debt of Households by Type of Debt, Race, and Hispanic Origin of Householder, 2011

(percent of households with debt and median amount of debt for debtors, by race and Hispanic origin of householder, 2011)

	total households	Asian	black	Hispanic	non-Hispanic white
PERCENT WITH DEBT					
Total debt	**69.0%**	**72.2%**	**62.0%**	**63.3%**	**70.9%**
Secured debt	55.3	57.0	44.1	48.6	58.3
Home debt	40.5	43.8	29.0	31.7	44.0
Business debt	4.1	3.7	2.0	2.4	4.8
Vehicle debt	30.4	27.5	25.3	29.2	31.5
Unsecured debt	46.2	45.2	44.3	41.5	47.2
Credit card debt	38.3	40.4	35.1	34.3	39.4
Loans	6.8	5.0	6.4	5.8	7.1
Other debt	18.6	14.5	21.2	14.8	18.8
MEDIAN AMOUNT OF DEBT FOR DEBTORS					
Total debt	**$70,000**	**$108,000**	**$35,000**	**$41,000**	**$80,000**
Secured debt	91,000	160,000	60,000	77,000	97,500
Home debt	117,000	190,000	97,000	120,000	117,000
Business debt	25,000	–	18,000	12,000	25,000
Vehicle debt	10,000	11,000	9,000	10,000	10,000
Unsecured debt	7,000	7,000	6,800	5,000	7,470
Credit card debt	3,500	4,000	3,000	3,100	3,650
Loans	7,000	–	5,000	5,000	7,200
Other debt	10,000	14,000	10,000	8,000	10,800

Note: Secured debt is backed by collateral, unsecured debt is not. "Other debt" includes student loans and medical debt. Asians and blacks are those who identify themselves as being of the race alone. Non-Hispanic whites are those who identify themselves as being white alone and not Hispanic. Hispanics may be of any race. "–" means sample is too small to make a reliable estimate.
Source: Bureau of the Census, Wealth and Asset Ownership, Survey of Income and Program Participation, Internet site http:// www.census.gov/people/wealth/; calculations by New Strategist

Glossary

adjusted for inflation A dollar value that has been adjusted for the rise in the cost of living by use of the consumer price index.

age Classification by age is based on the age of the person at his/her last birthday.

American Community Survey The ACS is an on-going nationwide survey of 250,000 households per month, providing detailed demographic data at the community level. Designed to replace the census long-form questionnaire, the ACS includes more than 60 questions that formerly appeared on the long form, such as questions about language spoken at home, income, and education. ACS data are available for areas as small as census tracts.

American Housing Survey The AHS collects national and metropolitan-level data on the nation's housing, including apartments, single-family homes, and mobile homes. The nationally representative survey, with a sample of 55,000 homes, is conducted by the Census Bureau for the Department of Housing and Urban Development every other year.

American Indians American Indians include Alaska Natives unless those groups are shown separately.

American Time Use Survey Under contract with the Bureau of Labor Statistics, the Census Bureau collects ATUS information, revealing how people spend their time. The ATUS sample is drawn from U.S. households completing their final month of interviews for the Current Population Survey. One individual from each selected household is chosen to participate in the ATUS. Respondents are interviewed by telephone about their time use during the previous 24 hours.

Asian The term "Asian" includes Native Hawaiians and other Pacific Islanders unless those groups are shown separately.

baby boom Americans born between 1946 and 1964.

baby bust Americans born between 1965 and 1976, also known as Generation X.

Behavioral Risk Factor Surveillance System The BRFSS is a collaborative project of the Centers for Disease Control and Prevention and U.S. states and territories. It is an ongoing data collection program designed to measure behavioral risk factors in the adult population aged 18 or older. All 50 states, three territories, and the District of Columbia take part in the survey, making the BRFSS the primary source of information on the health-related behaviors of Americans.

black The black racial category includes those who identified themselves as "black" or "African American."

Consumer Expenditure Survey The CEX is an ongoing study of the day-to-day spending of American households administered by the Bureau of Labor Statistics. The CEX includes an interview survey and a diary survey. The average spending figures shown are the integrated data from both the diary and interview components of the survey. Two separate, nationally representative samples are used for the interview and diary surveys. For the interview survey, about 7,500 consumer units are interviewed on a rotating panel basis each quarter for five consecutive quarters. For the diary survey, 7,500 consumer units keep weekly diaries of spending for two consecutive weeks.

consumer unit *(on spending tables only)* For convenience, the terms consumer unit and household are used interchangeably in the spending section of this book, although consumer units are somewhat different from the Census Bureau's households. A consumer unit includes all the related members of a household or any financially independent member of a household. A household may include more than one consumer unit.

Current Population Survey The CPS is a nationally representative survey of the civilian noninstitutional population aged 15 or older. It is taken monthly by the Census Bureau for the Bureau of Labor Statistics, collecting information from 60,000 households on employment and unemployment. In March of each year, the survey includes the Annual Social and Economic Supplement, which is the source of most national data on the characteristics of Americans, such as educational attainment, living arrangements, and incomes.

disability The National Health Interview Survey

estimates the number of people aged 18 or older who have difficulty in physical functioning, probing whether respondents could perform nine activities by themselves without using special equipment. The categories are walking a quarter mile; standing for two hours; sitting for two hours; walking up 10 steps without resting; stooping, bending, kneeling; reaching over one's head; grasping or handling small objects; carrying a 10-pound object; and pushing/pulling a large object. Adults who reported that any of these activities was very difficult or they could not do it at all were defined as having physical difficulties.

dual-earner couple A married couple in which both the householder and the householder's spouse are in the labor force.

earnings A type of income, earnings is the amount of money a person receives from his or her job. *See also* Income.

employed All civilians who did any work as a paid employee or farmer/self-employed worker or who worked 15 hours or more as an unpaid farm worker or in a family-owned business during the reference period. All those who have jobs but are temporarily absent from their jobs due to illness, bad weather, vacation, labor management dispute, or personal reasons are considered employed.

expenditure The transaction cost including excise and sales taxes of goods and services acquired during the survey period. The full cost of each purchase is recorded even though full payment may not have been made at the date of purchase. Average expenditure figures may be artificially low for infrequently purchased items such as cars because figures are calculated using all consumer units within a demographic segment rather than just purchasers. Expenditure estimates include money spent on gifts for others.

family A group of two or more people (one of whom is the householder) related by birth, marriage, or adoption and living in the same household.

family household A household maintained by a householder who lives with one or more people related to him or her by blood, marriage, or adoption.

female/male householder A woman or man who maintains a household without a spouse present. May head family or nonfamily household.

foreign-born population People who are not U.S. citizens at birth.

full-time employment Full-time is 35 or more hours of work per week during a majority of the weeks worked.

full-time, year-round Indicates 50 or more weeks of full-time employment during the previous calendar year.

General Social Survey The GSS is a biennial survey of the attitudes of Americans taken by the University of Chicago's National Opinion Research Center. NORC conducts the GSS through face-to-face interviews with an independently drawn, representative sample of 1,500 to 3,000 noninstitutionalized people aged 18 or older who live in the United States.

generation X Americans born between 1965 and 1976. Also known as the baby-bust generation.

Hispanic Because Hispanic is an ethnic origin rather than a race, Hispanics may be of any race. While most Hispanics are white, there are black, Asian, American Indian, and even Native Hawaiian Hispanics.

household All the persons who occupy a housing unit. A household includes the related family members and all the unrelated persons, if any, such as lodgers, foster children, wards, or employees who share the housing unit. A person living alone is counted as a household. A group of unrelated people who share a housing unit as roommates or unmarried partners is also counted as a household. Households do not include group quarters such as college dormitories, prisons, or nursing homes.

household, race/ethnicity of Households are categorized according to the race or ethnicity of the householder only.

householder The householder is the person (or one of the persons) in whose name the housing unit is owned or rented or, if there is no such person, any adult member. With married couples, the householder may be either the husband or wife. The householder is the reference person for the household.

householder, age of The age of the householder is used to categorize households into age groups such as those used in this book. Married couples, for example, are classified according to the age of 'either the husband or wife, depending on which one identified him- or herself as the householder.

housing unit A housing unit is a house, an apartment, a group of rooms, or a single room occupied or intended for occupancy as separate living quarters. Separate living quarters are those in which the occupants do not live and eat with any other persons in the structure and that have direct access from the outside of the building or through a common hall that is used or intended for use by the occupants of another unit or by the general public. The occupants may be a single family, one person living alone, two or more families living together, or any other group of related or unrelated persons who share living arrangements.

Housing Vacancy Survey The HVS is a supplement to the Current Population Survey, providing quarterly and annual data on rental and homeowner vacancy rates, characteristics of units available for occupancy, and homeownership rates by age, household type, region, state, and metropolitan area. The Current Population Survey sample includes 60,000 occupied housing units and about 9,000 vacant units.

housing value The respondent's estimate of how much his or her house and lot would sell for if it were for sale.

iGeneration Americans born between 1995 and 2009.

immigrants Aliens admitted for legal permanent residence in the United States.

income Money received in the preceding calendar year by a person aged 15 or older from any of the following sources: earnings from longest job (or self-employment), earnings from jobs other than longest job, unemployment compensation, workers' compensation, Social Security, Supplemental Security income, public assistance, veterans' payments, survivor benefits, disability benefits, retirement pensions, interest, dividends, rents and royalties or estates and trusts, educational assistance, alimony, child support, financial assistance from outside the household, and other periodic income. Income is reported in several ways in this book. Household income is the combined income of all household members. Income of persons is all income accruing to a person from all sources. Earnings are the money a person receives from his or her job.

industry Refers to the industry in which a person worked longest in the preceding calendar year.

job tenure The length of time a person has been employed continuously by the same employer.

labor force The labor force tables in this book show the civilian labor force only. The labor force includes both the employed and the unemployed (people who are looking for work). People are counted as in the labor force if they were working or looking for work during the reference week in which the Census Bureau fields the Current Population Survey.

labor force participation rate The percent of the civilian noninstitutional population that is in the civilian labor force, which includes both the employed and the unemployed.

male householder *See* Female/Male Householder.

married couples with or without children under age 18 Refers to married couples with or without own children under age 18 living in the same household. Couples without children under age 18 may be parents of grown children who live elsewhere or they could be childless couples.

median The median is the amount that divides the population or households into two equal portions: one below and one above the median. Medians can be calculated for income, age, and many other characteristics.

median income The amount that divides the income distribution into two equal groups, half having incomes above the median, half having incomes below the median. The medians for households or families are based on all households or families. The median for persons are based on all persons aged 15 or older with income.

metropolitan statistical area, or MSA To be defined as an MSA, an area must include a city with 50,000 or more inhabitants, or a Census Bureau–defined urbanized area of at least 50,000 inhabitants and a total metropolitan population of at least 100,000 (75,000 in New England). The county (or counties) that contains the largest city becomes the "central county" (counties), along with any adjacent counties that have at least 50 percent of their population in the urbanized area surrounding the largest city. Additional "outlying counties" are included in the MSA if they meet specified requirements of commuting to the central counties and other selected requirements of metropolitan character (such as population density and percent urban). In New England, MSAs are defined in terms of cities and towns rather than counties. For this reason, the concept of New England County Metropolitan Area is used to define metropolitan areas in the New England division.

millennial generation Americans born between 1977 and 1994.

mobility status People are classified according to their mobility status on the basis of a comparison between their place of residence at the time of the March Current Population Survey and their place of residence in March of the previous year. Nonmovers are people living in the same house at the end of the period as at the beginning of the period. Movers are people living in a different house at the end of the period from that at the beginning of the period. Movers from abroad are either citizens or aliens whose place of residence is outside the United States at the beginning of the period, that is, in an outlying area under the jurisdiction of the United States or in a foreign country. The mobility status for children is fully allocated from the mother if she is in the household; otherwise it is allocated from the householder.

National Health and Nutrition Examination Survey The NHANES is a continuous survey of a representative sample of the U.S. civilian noninstitutionalized population. Respondents are interviewed at home about their health and nutrition, and the interview is followed up by a physical examination that measures such things as height and weight in mobile examination centers.

National Health Interview Survey The NHIS is a continuing nationwide sample survey of the civilian noninstitutional population of the United States conducted by the Census Bureau for the National Center for Health Statistics. In interviews each year, data are collected from more than 100,000 people about their illnesses, injuries, impairments, chronic and acute conditions, activity limitations, and use of health services.

National Household Education Survey Sponsored by the National Center for Education Statistics, the NHES provides descriptive data on the educational activities of the U.S. population, including after-school care and adult education. The NHES is a system of telephone surveys of a representative sample of 45,000 to 60,000 households in the United States.

National Survey of Family Growth Sponsored by the National Center for Health Statistics, the NSFG is a periodic nationally representative survey of the civilian noninstitutionalized population aged 15 to 44. In-person interviews are completed with men and women, collecting data on marriage, divorce,

contraception, and infertility. The 2006–10 survey updates previous NSFG surveys taken in 1973, 1976, 1988, and 1995, and 2002.

National Survey on Drug Use and Health The NSDUH is an annual survey of a nationally representative sample of people aged 12 or older living in households, noninstitutional group quarters (such as college dorms), and military bases in the United States. It is the primary source of information about illegal drug use in the United States and has been conducted since 1971. Interviews are held in person and incorporate procedures (such as anonymity and computer-assisted interviewing) that will increase respondents' cooperation and willingness to report honestly about their illicit drug use behavior.

nonfamily household A household maintained by a householder who lives alone or who lives with people to whom he or she is not related.

nonfamily householder A householder who lives alone or with nonrelatives.

non-Hispanic People who do not identify themselves as Hispanic are classified as non-Hispanic. Non-Hispanics may be of any race.

non-Hispanic white People who identify their race as white and who do not indicate a Hispanic origin.

nonmetropolitan area Counties that are not classified as metropolitan areas.

occupation Occupational classification is based on the kind of work a person did at his or her job during the previous calendar year. If a person changed jobs during the year, the data refer to the occupation of the job held the longest during that year.

occupied housing units A housing unit is classified as occupied if a person or group of people is living in it or if the occupants are only temporarily absent—on vacation, for example. By definition, the count of occupied housing units is the same as the count of households.

outside principal city The portion of a metropolitan county or counties that falls outside of the principal city or cities; generally regarded as the suburbs.

own children Own children are sons and daughters, including stepchildren and adopted children, of the householder. The totals include never-married children living away from home in college dormitories.

owner occupied A housing unit is "owner occupied" if the owner lives in the unit, even if it is mortgaged or not fully paid for. A cooperative or condominium unit is "owner occupied" only if the owner lives in it. All other occupied units are classified as "renter occupied."

part-time employment Part-time is less than 35 hours of work per week in a majority of the weeks worked during the year.

percent change The change (either positive or negative) in a measure that is expressed as a proportion of the starting measure. When median income changes from $20,000 to $25,000, for example, this is a 25 percent increase.

percentage point change The change (either positive or negative) in a value that is already expressed as a percentage. When a labor force participation rate changes from 70 percent to 75 percent, for example, this is a 5 percentage point increase.

poverty level The official income threshold below which families and people are classified as living in poverty. The threshold rises each year with inflation and varies depending on family size and age of householder.

principal city The largest city in a metropolitan area is called the principal or central city. The balance of the metropolitan area outside the principal or central city is regarded as the "suburbs."

proportion or share The value of a part expressed as a percentage of the whole. If there are 4 million people aged 25 and 3 million of them are white, then the white proportion is 75 percent.

race Race is self-reported and can be defined in three ways. The "race alone" population comprises people who identify themselves as being of only one race. The "race in combination" population comprises people who identify themselves as being of more than one race, such as white and black. The "race, alone or in combination" population includes both those who identify themselves as being of one race and those who identify themselves as being of more than one race.

recession generation Americans born from 2010 to the present.

regions The four major regions and nine census divisions of the United States are the state groupings as shown below:
Northeast:
—New England: Connecticut, Maine, Massachusetts, New Hampshire, Rhode Island, and Vermont
—Middle Atlantic: New Jersey, New York, and Pennsylvania
Midwest:
—East North Central: Illinois, Indiana, Michigan, Ohio, and Wisconsin
—West North Central: Iowa, Kansas, Minnesota, Missouri, Nebraska, North Dakota, and South Dakota
South:
—South Atlantic: Delaware, District of Columbia, Florida, Georgia, Maryland, North Carolina, South Carolina, Virginia, and West Virginia
—East South Central: Alabama, Kentucky, Mississippi, and Tennessee
—West South Central: Arkansas, Louisiana, Oklahoma, and Texas
West:
—Mountain: Arizona, Colorado, Idaho, Montana, Nevada, New Mexico, Utah, and Wyoming
—Pacific: Alaska, California, Hawaii, Oregon, and Washington

renter occupied *See* Owner Occupied.

Retirement Confidence Survey The RCS—sponsored by the Employee Benefit Research Institute, the American Savings Education Council, and Mathew Greenwald & Associates—is an annual survey of a nationally representative sample of 1,000 people aged 25 or older. Respondents are asked a core set of questions that have been included in the survey since 1996, measuring attitudes and behavior toward retirement. Additional questions are asked about current retirement issues.

rounding Percentages are rounded to the nearest tenth of a percent; therefore, the percentages in a distribution do not always add exactly to 100.0 percent. The totals, however, are always shown as 100.0. Moreover, individual figures are rounded to the nearest thousand without being adjusted to group totals, which are independently rounded; percentages are based on the unrounded numbers.

self-employment A person is categorized as self-employed if he or she was self-employed in the job held longest during the reference period. Persons who report self-employment from a second job are excluded, but those who report wage and salary income from a second job are included. Unpaid workers in family businesses are excluded. Self-employment statistics include only nonagricultural workers and exclude people who work for themselves in incorporated business.

sex ratio The number of men per 100 women.

Survey of Income and Program Participation
The Survey of Income and Program Participation is a continuous, monthly panel survey of up to 36,700 households conducted by the Census Bureau. It is designed to measure the effectiveness of existing federal, state, and local programs and to measure economic well-being, including wealth, asset ownership, and debt.

unemployed Unemployed people are those who, during the survey period, had no employment but were available and looking for work. Those who were laid off from their jobs and were waiting to be recalled are also classified as unemployed.

white The "white" racial category includes many Hispanics (who may be of any race) unless the term "non-Hispanic white" is used.

Youth Risk Behavior Surveillance System The YRBSS was created by the Centers for Disease Control to monitor health risks being taken by young people at the national, state, and local level. The national survey is taken every two years based on a nationally representative sample of 16,000 students in 9th through 12th grade in public and private schools.

Bibliography

Bureau of Labor Statistics
Internet site http://www.bls.gov/
—American Time Use Survey, unpublished tables, Internet site http://www.bls.gov/tus/
—Characteristics of Minimum Wage Workers, 2012, Internet site http://www.bls.gov/cps/minwage2012.htm
—Consumer Expenditure Survey, Internet site http://www.bls.gov/cex/home.htm
—Current Population Survey, Internet site http://www.bls.gov/cps/tables.htm#empstat
—Employee Tenure, Internet site http://www.bls.gov/news.release/tenure.toc.htm
—Employment Characteristics of Families, Internet site http://www.bls.gov/news.release/famee.toc.htm
—*Monthly Labor Review*, "Labor Force Projections to 2020: A More Slowly Growing Workforce," January 2012, Internet site http://www.bls.gov/opub/mlr/

Bureau of the Census
Internet site http://www.census.gov/
—American Community Survey, American Factfinder, Internet site http://factfinder2.census.gov/faces/nav/jsf/pages/index.xhtml
—American Housing Survey, Internet site http://www.census.gov/housing/ahs/
—Current Population Survey, Annual Social and Economic Supplement, Internet site http://www.census.gov/hhes/www/income/data/
—Educational Attainment, Annual Social and Economic Supplement, Internet site http://www.census.gov/hhes/socdemo/education/
—Families and Living Arrangements, Current Population Survey Annual Social and Economic Supplement, Internet site http://www.census.gov/hhes/families/
—Geographic Mobility/Migration, Current Population Survey Annual Social and Economic Supplement, Internet site http://www.census.gov/hhes/migration/
—Health Insurance, Current Population Survey Annual Social and Economic Supplements, Internet site http://www.census.gov/hhes/www/hlthins/
—Historical Income Data, Current Population Survey Annual Social and Economic Supplements, Internet site http://www.census.gov/hhes/www/income/data/historical/index.html
—Historical Poverty Tables, Current Population Survey Annual Social and Economic Supplements, Internet site http://www.census.gov/hhes/www/poverty/data/historical/index.html
—*Historical Statistics of the United States, Colonial Times to 1970*, Part 1, 1975
—Housing Vacancy Survey, Internet site http://www.census.gov/housing/hvs/
—Income, Current Population Survey Annual Social and Economic Supplements, Internet site http://www.census.gov/hhes/www/income/data/index.html

—Number, Timing, and Duration of Marriages and Divorces: 2009, Detailed Tables, Internet site http://www.census.gov/hhes/socdemo/marriage/data/sipp/2009/tables.html

—Population Estimates, Internet site http://www.census.gov/popest/index.html

—Population Projections, Internet site http://www.census.gov/population/projections/

—Poverty, Current Population Survey Annual Social and Economic Supplements, Internet site http://www.census.gov/hhes/www/poverty/index.html

—School Enrollment, CPS Historical Time Series Tables on School Enrollment, Internet site http://www.census.gov/hhes/school/data/cps/historical/index.html

—School Enrollment, CPS October 2012, Detailed Tables, Internet site http://www.census.gov/hhes/school/data/cps/2012/tables.html

—Voting and Registration, Internet site http://www.census.gov/hhes/www/socdemo/voting/index.html

—Wealth and Asset Ownership, Survey of Income and Program Participation, Internet site http://www.census.gov/people/wealth/

—What's It Worth: Field of Training and Economic Status in 2009, Detailed Tables, Internet site http://www.census.gov/hhes/socdemo/education/data/sipp/2009/tables.html

Centers for Disease Control and Prevention

Internet site http://www.cdc.gov/

—Behavioral Risk Factor Surveillance System, Prevalence and Trends Data, Internet site http://apps.nccd.cdc.gov/brfss/

Department of Homeland Security

Internet site http://www.dhs.gov/

—Estimates of the Unauthorized Immigrant Population Residing in the United States: January 2011, Internet site http://www.dhs.gov/estimates-unauthorized-immigrant-population-residing-united-states-january-2011

—Yearbook of Immigration Statistics, Internet site http://www.dhs.gov/yearbook-immigration-statistics

National Center for Education Statistics

Internet site http://nces.ed.gov/

—Digest of Education Statistics: 2012, Internet site http://nces.ed.gov/programs/digest/2012menu_tables.asp

—Early Childhood Program Participation, From the National Household Education Surveys Program of 2012, Internet site http://nces.ed.gov/pubsearch/pubsinfo.asp?pubid=2013029

—Parent and Family Involvement in Education, from the National Household Education Surveys Program of 2012, Internet site http://nces.ed.gov/pubsearch/pubsinfo.asp?pubid=2013028

—Projections of Education Statistics to 2021, Internet site http://nces.ed.gov/programs/projections/projections2021/

National Center for Health Statistics
   Internet site http://www.cdc.gov/nchs/
   —*Anthropometric Reference Data for Children and Adults: United States, 2007–2010*,
   National Health Statistics Reports, Series 11, No. 252, 2012, Internet site http://www.cdc
   .gov/nchs/nhanes.htm
   —*Births: Preliminary Data for 2012*, National Vital Statistics Reports, Vol. 62, No. 3, 2013,
   Internet site http://www.cdc.gov/nchs/births.htm
   —*Current Contraceptive Use in the United States, 2006–2010, and Changes in Patterns of
   Use since 1995*, National Health Statistics Reports, No. 60, 2012, Internet site http://www
   .cdc.gov/nchs/nsfg.htm
   —*Deaths: Preliminary Data for 2011*, National Vital Statistics Reports, Vol. 61, No. 6, 2012,
   Internet site http://www.cdc.gov/nchs/deaths.htm
   —*Health, United States*, Internet site http://www.cdc.gov/nchs/hus.htm
   —*Summary Health Statistics for the U.S. Population: National Health Interview Survey,
   2011*, Series 10, No. 255, 2012, Internet site http://www.cdc.gov/nchs/nhis/new_nhis.htm
   —*Summary Health Statistics for U.S. Adults: National Health Interview Survey, 2011*, Series
   10, No. 256, 2012, Internet site http://www.cdc.gov/nchs/nhis.htm
   —*Summary Health Statistics for U.S. Children: National Health Interview Survey, 2011*,
   Series 10, No. 254, 2012, Internet site http://www.cdc.gov/nchs/nhis.htm

Substance Abuse and Mental Health Services Administration
   Internet site http://www.samhsa.gov/
   —National Survey on Drug Use and Health, 2012, Internet site http://www.samhsa.gov/data/
   NSDUH.aspx

Survey Documentation and Analysis, Computer-assisted Survey Methods Program, University of
California, Berkeley
   Internet site http://sda.berkeley.edu/
   —General Social Surveys, 1972–2012 Cumulative Data Files, Internet site http://sda
   .berkeley.edu/cgi-bin/hsda?harcsda+gss12

Index

401(k), as household asset, 560–566

abortion, attitude toward, 45
accidents, as a leading cause of death, 146
African Americans. *See* Race and Hispanic origin.
age
  AIDS, diagnosed with by, 138
  alcohol use by, 122
  assets owned by, 560–564
  at first marriage, 372
  attitudes by, 7–33
  births by, 117–119
  cigarette smoking by, 121
  college enrollment by, 91–92, 96
  contraceptive use by, 113
  debt of household by, 569–573
  disabled by, 140
  drug use, illicit, 123–124
  dual-earner couples by, 287
  educational attainment by, 49–51
  employment status by, 275–282, 287, 291–292, 314
  fertility rate by, 115
  health care visits by, 142
  health conditions by, 130–133, 135–137
  health insurance coverage by, 126–128
  health status by, 107
  homeownership by, 153–154
  hospital stays by, 143
  households by, 341, 343–344, 351, 363–366
  income of households by, 198, 206, 210–215, 219–224, 236–237
  income of men and women by, 241–242, 247–248
  job tenure by, 311–312
  life expectancy by, 148–149
  living arrangements by, 368–369
  marital history by, 381
  marital status by, 371, 374–375
  medical care, problems receiving by, 144
  minimum wage workers by, 319
  mobility by, 433–434
  net worth by, 551
  of husbands and wives, 377
  of same-sex couples, 387–388
  physical activity status by, 111
  population by, 391–392, 396–397, 399
  poverty status by, 270
  projections of labor force by, 326
  projections of population by, 399
  same-sex couples by, 387–388

  school enrollment by, 61
  self-employed by, 314
  spending of households by, 455–463
  time use by, 536–541
  union representation by, 316
  unmarried partners by, 387
  weight status by, 109
AIDS, people diagnosed with, 138
air conditioning, 177
alcohol use, 122
alcoholic beverages, spending on, 450–527
alimony, as source of income, 267
allergies, 130–132, 135–137
Alzheimer's disease, as a leading cause of death, 146
American Dream, attitude toward, 19
American Indians. *See* Race and Hispanic origin.
ancestry, 441
apartments, 169
apparel, spending on, 450–527
arthritis, 135–137
Asian language. *See* Language spoken at home.
Asians. *See* Race and Hispanic origin.
  assets owned by households, 560–566
asthma, 130–132, 135–137
attention deficit hyperactivity disorder, 133
automobile as means of travel to work, 324

back pain, 135–137
bathrooms, number of, 170
bedrooms, number of, 170
Bible, belief in, 32
birth control pill use, 113
births
  by age, 117–119
  by birth order, 119
  by race and Hispanic origin of mother, 117–118
  to unmarried women, 118
blacks. *See* Race and Hispanic origin.
blood pressure, high, 135–137
Buddhism, preference for, 29
business
  debt of households, 569–575
  equity as household asset, 560–566
  rooms used for in home, 170

cancer
  as a health condition, 135–137
  as a leading causes of death, 146
capital punishment, attitude toward, 44
carbon monoxide detector in home, 175
caring for household members, time spent, 531–548
caring for nonhousehold members, time spent,
cash contributions, spending on, 450–527
Catholic religion, preference for, 29